A TREASURY OF CATHOLIC DIGEST

Favorite Stories of Fifty Years 1936-1986

A TREASURY OF CATHOLIC DIGEST

Favorite Stories of Fifty Years

1936–1986

Compiled by Henry Lexau
Editor of *Catholic Digest*

IGNATIUS PRESS   SAN FRANCISCO

Where no copyright is given for an article
the copyright is held by *Catholic Digest*
or the College of Saint Thomas.

Dedication

For Father Kenneth Ryan, who showed me how to edit the *Catholic Digest* and introduced me to an editor named Eileen.

Contents

CONTENTS

Through A Child's Eyes

The Documents in the Case

The Editor's Favorites

What Is God's Game?

Growing up

CONTENTS

CONTENTS

Just for Laughs

The Mass

A Natural Explanation

On Being a Parent

CONTENTS

People Observed

Prayer

Some Priests

Nostalgia

CONTENTS

CONTENTS

Sin

Things

Thought Provokers

Second Thoughts

Vatican II, Behind the Scenes

Introduction

It has been a pleasure to pore through the old volumes of the *Catholic Digest* to select these articles.

It brought back memories.

The sound of tennis balls, for example. Every time I hear the *plonk, plonk* from a tennis court, I think of an old, old priest struggling through a Mass he can celebrate only under supervision. Outside the church window, on the tennis court, the world is going on its way in counterpoint, oblivious to the poignance within. I know the association of sound and vision came from a *Digest* article, and I finally found it in a 1961 issue. I've remembered that sound for 25 years.

I remember "Listening for the Children", and how well it described a parent's feelings late on a Friday night. Listening for the cars that stop; the incessant peering at the clock; the worrying over make-believe disasters. It all was happening to me, too, when we published Mary McPhee's article, and I read it so many times that I've never forgotten it.

I remember the heat, and the high summer sky and the feel of the grass whenever I walk across the prairie to find the cottonwood where Noah Jumping Eagle saw God. I can see the tree, too. The leaves are rustling, and it is empty, but I, too, know that Noah saw God. (But I didn't need to look for this article; I'm always pointing it out to new editors as the best thing the *Digest* has ever published.)

Every Christmas I remember a glorious sentence we published in a midsummer issue. The article wasn't about Christmas at all: it was called "Dream Girls, Dream Churches", and it compared marriage, the institutional Church, and the Incarnation. It ended, "When God became man (choosing for his arrival in this world the strangely arbitrary coordinates of 31 degrees 42 minutes North, 35 degrees 12 minutes East) He committed us to concrete particulars."

I remembered that little Ralph Reppert column that forever cured me of drinking my Martini from a jelly glass.

I remembered a cold winter day in the St. Paul Public Library when I saw a bundled up man in rags holding a *Catholic Digest.* He was laughing so hard that tears were flowing down his face. I sneaked up behind him, in the interest of editorial research, and it was "My Skunk Nikki" that he was reading.

I've always liked that un-Digestlike saga of revenge, but my candidate for the funniest article we've ever published is from Father Basset's account of the Second Vatican Council, "The Japanese Bishop and the Italian Photographer".

Whenever I am thirsty or hungry or tired, I often think of a diary we called "52 Years After Columbus". Late in their year-long journey to Chiapas, Mexico, the 36 surviving Dominican friars are climbing "a dreadful mountain—at times on foot, and at times on all fours . . . hanging on to the roots of trees." They have been climbing for days; 13 of them are sick. But there is something else: from casual remarks dropped in passing, you gradually realize that it is Lent, and they are all fasting!

As I leafed through the old *Digests,* I remembered many things: editors in heaven who worked on these articles, Father Paul Bussard and Father Louis Gales, Ed Harrigan, Harold O'Loughlin, Joe Aberwald, Maurice Murray.

I remembered wonderful Catholic magazines that have died, and I wished that I could pore through their bound volumes, too: *Jubilee, Ave Maria, The Sign, Integrity, Today, The Victorian, St. Joseph's, The Friar, The Lamp, Immaculata.*

But there were some articles that I did not remember, stories that were as fresh to me as they must be to most of you readers.

How could I have forgotten that magnificent statement of faith by that magnificent woman Barbara Ward?

And "No Prayer Goes Unanswered": that lovely story completely passed me by. It's astonishing the tricks memory can play.

I hope you readers enjoy my memories of old *Catholic Digests* as much as I enjoyed reading "No Prayer Goes Unanswered".

Henry Lexau

The Amazing Story of "Amazing Grace"

Its author was indeed lost, but finally found, in a way he always considered miraculous

By EVE R. WIRTH
September 1980

AMAZING GRACE, one of the world's most famous hymns, was written by a former slave-ship captain who ended his life as a popular preacher.

John Newton was born in England on July 24, 1725. His mother died when he was seven, and his father, a sea captain and a good Christian, took full responsibility for his upbringing. When John was 10 years old, he joined his father aboard ship.

By his 17th year, tired of his father's religious ways and bored with life on the sea, John left his father to seek pleasure in the fleshpots of England.

Reprinted with permission of the author.

After several months of debauchery, he was found by some English naval officers in a tavern and dragged aboard a British man-of-war. He soon deserted ship, but was rapidly captured, chained in irons, and whipped.

He deserted a second time, however, and made his way to a small island off the coast of West Africa. After living for a short while among the slaves, he was sold to a cruel native woman. She took great joy in making young Newton beg for food from her table. So hungry was he that he scrounged for wild potatoes at night.

After several years of trying to escape, he finally made his way aboard a visiting slave ship. Before long he was the ship's captain, but the crew did not seem to favor his command. They mutinied and left him marooned on a desolate island.

All this time, Newton's father had no idea where his son was, but he prayed for him daily and sent a friend to find him and bring him back. The friend succeeded, but back in England Newton resumed his life of pleasure-seeking and joined once more in the African slave trade.

It took one more near-disaster to make an impression on the rebellious 23-year-old. A storm at sea lashed the slave vessel Newton captained; soon water was rushing into the hold. Newton ordered the crew to cast all the cargo overboard, and along with the others he pumped as much water as he could from the hold, but the ship looked doomed.

Newton finally became so alarmed that he uttered his first prayer to God since his childhood: "Mercy! Mercy!" And, as desperate men have been known to do, he promised that if he came out of the storm alive he would turn his life over to God.

The ship righted itself, the sea grew calm, the ship's hold was water free. "It's a miracle from the Lord!" cried Newton.

If the captain had been a sinner, he seems to have been a man of his word. He immediately left the slave trade. For the next seven years he studied the Bible, and dealt only in legitimate cargo. Eventually he married a London woman and left the sea to become a surveyor.

Newton had begun to feel a "leading from the Lord," a divine call within himself. "There is something I must do that is very special for the Lord," he told his wife.

Impressed with the preaching of the Anglican George Whitefield, and influenced by the Wesley brothers, founders of Methodism, Newton decided to enter the ministry. He studied at Liverpool and was ordained at the age of 39. His first assignment was as pastor in the English village of Olney. So dynamic and impressive were his sermons that the tiny church had to be enlarged to hold the many new parishioners.

He remained at Olney for 15 years, conducting evening meetings in a huge converted manor house presented to him by the Earl of Dartmouth. In the afternoons he gave Bible lessons to youngsters, who also had the good fortune to hear his true stories of the sea.

One night Newton was preparing a sermon about his conversion experience. No matter how hard he tried to find just the right ending for it, nothing came to him. He prayed: "Lord, you know how I was lost and that You, dear Jesus, found me and saved me!" Suddenly the words flowed from his pen:

Amazing grace! How sweet the sound
That saved a wretch like me!
I once was lost, but now am found,
Was blind, but now I see.

'Twas grace that taught my heart to fear,
And grace my fears relieved;
How precious did that grace appear,
The hour I first believed!

Through many dangers, toils, and snares,
I have already come;
'Tis grace hath brought me safe thus far,
And grace will lead me home.

Newton composed most of his 300 hymns at Olney, although he continued to write after his transfer to St. Mary Woolnoth Church, where he preached for the remaining 28 years of his life. He died at age 82.

On his tombstone he had inscribed the words:

"JOHN NEWTON, Clerk. Once an infidel and libertine; A servant of slaves in Africa; Was by the rich mercy of our Lord and Saviour Jesus Christ, Preserved, restored, pardoned, And appointed to preach the Faith He had long laboured to destroy." ❏

IN OUR HOUSE

My father has always had a rather poetic nature, and when engrossed in thought can easily become oblivious to his surroundings. As our family was walking to Mass one Sunday morning, my grandmother noticed that father had forgotten to bring his missal.

"Well, thank goodness, there's plenty of time for you to go back for it," grandmother sniffed. "You'll be finding it on the mantel by the clock," she announced, speaking very distinctly so as to penetrate father's fog of abstraction.

Father turned obediently and retreated to fetch the book. We were just reaching the church when father overtook us, the clock from the mantel tucked securely under his right arm.   S.M.M.

Sister Elena, Pope Leo, and Pentecost Century

A curious foreshadowing of the modern charismatic movement happened in 1900

By VAL GAUDET, O.M.I.
June 1974, condensed from *New Covenant**

MANY PEOPLE assume that the Catholic charismatic movement began with the prayer of Pope John XXIII asking the Holy Spirit to renew the wonders of Pentecost in today's Church. But this prayer has an interesting prehistory.

The first person to be beatified by Pope John was Sister Elena Guerra. The foundress of the Oblate Sisters of the Holy Spirit, Sister Elena was born in Lucca, Italy, on June 23, 1833. She broke away from her sheltered Christian upbringing at the age of 19 to work in the countryside of Lucca among the victims of cholera. She later founded a "Pious Union" that grew to 500 persons.

In 1872, with several close friends from this group, Elena experimented with the contemplative life. She soon realized, however, that she and her companions were better suited for the active life. At that time, a fierce anticlericalism was rampant in Italy, especially in schools. To fight this trend, Elena and her companions dedicated themselves to educating girls from Lucca.

By the age of 50, Elena had matured as an educator and as a writer of devotional books. At this time, she felt inspired to write to Pope Leo XIII to urge him to renew the Church by

*This article © 1973 by Charismatic Renewal Services, Inc. Reprinted with permission.

means of a return to the Holy Spirit. She revealed her secret inspiration to only one "good person."

"Preposterous!" was the answer. "To do that would be pride." Thus, she kept her secret to herself, "waiting for better days and hoping that more light would come to her about this project."

It came eight years later. In 1893, a humble woman from the kitchen staff, Erminia Giorgetti, felt that she heard the Lord tell her to go to Sister Elena to reveal what the Lord wanted her to do. She told Elena that she must write to the Pope urging him to unite all the faithful in a continuous prayer to the Holy Spirit, asking him to bring all hearts back to God. She also predicted that the Pope would soon write an encyclical on the Holy Spirit.

Elena confided all this to her spiritual director, Bishop Giovanni Volpi, and with his help she was able to send 12 confidential letters to the Pope between 1895 and 1903.

In her first letter to Pope Leo, Elena called for renewed preaching on the Holy Spirit, "who is the one who forms the saints." In the last paragraph, she says that Satan's empire will be broken by the Spirit, and that God will "grant us a longawaited renewal of the face of the earth."

Soon after, Pope Leo published *Provida Matris Caritate,* in which he required the whole Church to celebrate a solemn novena to the Holy Spirit during the nine days before the feast of Pentecost. At this time, Elena began to form prayer groups, called "Permanent Cenacles."

In a subsequent letter to the Pope, Elena expressed her desire to see the whole Church united in a continuous union of prayer in the same way that Mary and the Apostles were united in prayer in the Upper Room before Pentecost.

She went on to say that even though she called this union a "Universal Cenacle," she did not care much about the name. The important thing was that the faithful were "being united in unanimous and ceaseless prayer to the Divine Spirit," bringing unbelievers and dissenters back to Christ. She ended with the wish: "Oh, if ever the *Come, Holy Spirit* could become as popular as the Hail Mary!"

In 1897, Bishop Volpi returned from a visit to Rome and told Sister Elena that the Pope had promised that he would do everything so that the Holy Spirit would be honored. Shortly afterwards, the Pope published his encyclical *Divinum illud munus,* the richest doctrinal treatise about the Holy Spirit any Pope has produced. In this document, Pope Leo explicitly recommended to all Christians a devotion to the Spirit. He saw in it the means of renewing society, the family, and individuals: it would bring about Christian unity among churches and the conversion of the universe. Again he prescribed the celebration of the novena for Pentecost in all parish churches.

Later, in a letter dated Oct. 15, 1900, Elena suggested that Pope Leo begin the first new year of the new century by singing *Come Holy Spirit* in the name of the whole Church. He did.

Elena complained that bishops and priests showed little enthusiasm to implement *Divinum illud.* Pope Leo soon sent a private letter to the bishops of the world, along with an extra copy of the encyclical. In his letter he deplored the fact many of the clergy had thought the novena was to be held only for the year 1897.

When Pope Leo died in 1903, Sister Elena was 70 years old. She had written extensively about spreading the good news and had sent her nuns as missionaries to distant countries. Her next ten years were a time of trial. She was deposed from her superiorship by the local bishop at the instigation of three younger Sisters, and after five months of excruciating pain she died on Holy Saturday, April 11, 1914.

The prayer to the Holy Spirit for the success of the Vatican Council that John XXIII issued in September, 1959, ended: "Renew Thy wonders in this our day as by a new Pentecost." Pope John used the same expression speaking to pilgrims from Lucca who came to Rome to attend Elena's beatification on April 26, 1959: "Her (Elena's) message is always relevant. We are all aware, in fact, of the need for a continued effusion of the Holy Spirit, as of a new Pentecost which will renew the face of the earth." Pope John repeated his call for a new Pentecost on many occasions.   ❑

EXPERTS AND AMATEURS

A noted astronomer found a bishop seated next to him on a plane. In the course of conversation, the astronomer said, "I never had much interest in theology. My religion can be summed up in 'Do unto others as you would have them do unto you.'"

The bishop responded, "Well, I've had little time for astronomy. My views are summed up in 'Twinkle, twinkle, little star.'"   Lois Mae Cuhel.

A Death on the Prairie

I was the only priest in all that trackless plain
but a man's faith brought me to him in time

By FRANCIS J. KELLER
September 1957, condensed from *Friar**

O NE WEEK END in June, 1909, I took a 140-mile stagecoach-rail journey to Gillette, Wyo., which had recently been attached to my Buffalo, Wyo., parish. I sent word ahead to the Catholic settlers that Mass would be offered on Sunday. Some of them had not seen a priest for such a long time that they had only a fond memory of the faith.

After Sunday Mass, a man I had seen in church rode up leading a beautiful saddle horse. "Father," he called, "you can't get a train till late tonight. Would you like to take a ride in the hills?"

"Splendid!" I replied. We were soon out on the trackless prairie. Wyoming was green that year;

---

*This article © 1957 by *Friar,* Butler, N.J.
Reprinted with permission.

the tall grass rippled like the sea. We could just barely see the mountains far in the distance. The air was as heady as wine.

We had gone about nine miles, as my guide told me later, when we saw something white moving in the distance. We thought it might be a signal from a cowboy, so we rode hard in that direction, breaking trail through the grass. We came upon a woman, who might have been about 30 years of age, waving a white tablecloth.

"Father," she said without excitement, "I've been looking for a priest." To this day I have not forgotten the impression she made upon me: she was happy, but not at all surprised that in that wilderness a priest had answered her signal. "My brother is dying."

23

Not far from where she stood, a tent was pitched. She led the way to it.

As she held open the flap, the first thing that caught my eye was the light gleaming from two candles on a small table. A crucifix stood between the candles, a prayer book was opened at the Litany of the Dying, and there was a small glass ("That's holy water," she whispered) with a tiny green branch in it.

Her brother was on a cot. He was very thin, and may have been about 35. His eyes were clear and he seemed alert. Quickly I heard his Confession, and then anointed him; in those days every priest in the West carried the holy oils with him at all times, but, of course, I could not give him Viaticum. The man had been able to make his Confession clearly. But as soon as I concluded the prayers for the dying, he died.

Afterwards the woman told her story. "I had no idea where we might find a priest around here; nobody told me you were having Mass at Gillette today. But all his life my brother has been praying every day for a priest at death. This morning he and I prayed together for the last time. We said only three Hail Marys. Then I went outside and started waving the tablecloth." ❏

HEARTS ARE TRUMPS

Since I've been widowed, I've had the good fortune to be a housekeeper for a young, vivacious priest in one of our city's older, more affluent parishes. For several years now, Father has spent all of his free time across town, teaching underprivileged kids how to play sports. I can tell when he's going off to play with them because he always puts on an old, many-times patched sweater. I know he gets presents from his parishioners on his birthday and at Christmastime, and I've often suspected that they contain new sweaters. Yet, he never would change out of that old one, and I never could figure it out.

Then one day on my way home from shopping, I decided to stop by the playground to see if Father might want a lift home. His own car is a notorious clunker that breaks down more often than not. I found him with an assorted group of boys practicing basketball on an outdoor court. The weather was chilly, for the middle of Spring, and Father had on his old, holey sweater, of course. But each boy on the court was wearing a bright new one.   Geri Grondin.

The Blue Lady

A strange story from old New Mexico

By MADGE HARRAH
March 1977

I N THE YEAR 1630 the Franciscan Fray Alonso de Benavides wrote a book called the *Memorial* about his experiences as Religious superior of the New Mexico missions from 1622 to 1629. He included in it a strange story.

Among the priests under his supervision had been Fray Juan de Salas of Isleta Pueblo (this pueblo is still occupied, 20 miles south of Albuquerque, and the church is still in use). Fray Juan traveled from time to time east of the Manzano Mountains to minister to Indians who came to gather salt at some large salt ponds. Among them were the Jumanos, a large nomadic tribe which wandered over the area now represented by northern Mexico, eastern New Mexico, and western Texas, Oklahoma and Kansas.

Delegates from the Plains Jumanos kept begging Fray Juan

Reprinted with permission of the author.

to send them missionaries. They had been told to do this, they said, by a "lady in blue." Fray Juan was amazed by these repeated requests. But he couldn't assign the Jumanos a priest, for there were not enough missionaries available to serve the pueblos along the Rio Grande, let alone so vast an area as the eastern plains.

Then, on July 22, 1629, a group of 50 Jumanos came over the mountains to Isleta Pueblo itself, where Benavides was visiting with de Salas. Again they asked that a missionary be sent with them. They reminded the priests that they had been requesting this favor for six years, and they begged that their petition be honored.

Benavides asked them how they had come to be so concerned over Baptism, and they repeated in greater detail their story of the blue lady. Pointing to a painting of the Mother Luisa de Carrion, a Poor Clare nun,

25

the Indians said that a woman dressed like that had been preaching to them in their own language, and that she had urged them to seek out the Fathers for Baptism and instruction, saying that they must not be slothful about it. They went on to explain that the woman who had visited them had worn clothing exactly like that shown in the painting, but that she had been younger and more beautiful.

As it so happened, the Jumanos were finally petitioning at the right time. Fray Estevan de Perea and 30 new missionaries had just arrived in New Mexico. Fray Estevan took over at Isleta, and Fray Juan de Salas then set off for the eastern plains, guided by the Jumanos, and accompanied by Fray Diego Lopez and three soldiers.

Benavides, reporting on the stories which were told to him later, says that the waiting tribes out on the prairies were getting discouraged. The water holes had dried up and the buffalo had departed.

The Indians' sorcerers announced that the people must change location. After all, they argued, the Jumanos had sent each year for six years for these priests, and they had not yet come. The present Indian delegation had now been gone much longer than usual. Surely something bad had happened. Perhaps the men would never return. There was no longer any excuse to delay moving the camp, not when the people were being threatened with starvation.

The chiefs consulted with the sorcerers and finally ordered that the tents be struck at dawn of the next morning; but that night the blue lady appeared to each of them individually, saying that they must not go, for the delegation was on its way back with the priests.

After another consultation, 12 of the most trusted chiefs were selected to scout for the delegation. After three days, these chiefs met the de Salas group and de Salas showed them the painting. The chiefs examined it closely and agreed with the delegation that, although the clothing was the same, the face in the painting was that of a much older woman.

The chiefs prepared to hurry back to the camp to give word of the padres' approach, but the entire party was then met by a procession of Jumanos from the camp carrying two crosses, as they had been instructed to do by the blue lady.

The Spaniards, amazed by what was happening, took out the crucifixes which they wore about their necks. The Jumanos came forward at once to kiss these replicas of the cross "as if they were very old Christians."

De Salas asked them if they desired Baptism "with all their heart." To this the chiefs responded positively, saying that it was for this purpose that the priests had been summoned. De Salas replied that he understood that the chiefs were supposed to speak for all the people, but that he preferred to hear from each individual. Since there were too many people for him to question one by one, he asked that the word be passed that each Indian desiring Baptism should lift his arm.

The *Memorial* reports: "A marvelous thing! For with one great cry all uplifted their arms, rising to their feet...."

The padres remained with the Jumanos for several days. While they were there, messengers showed up from many neighboring bands requesting that the priests come to them, too, for the blue lady had appeared to them, telling them where the priests were.

De Salas and Lopez felt overwhelmed by the number of supplicants and the vastness of the territory, and they decided to return to Isleta to ask Benavides for more missionaries.

Before leaving, they brought all the people together once more. Fray Juan told the Indians that they should come every day to pray near the cross which he had placed upon a pedestal. The head chief said that his people still did not understand this power of the padres' God, and he asked that the two priests cure the sick before they left. At three o'clock in the afternoon the priests began their healing service. One by one the sick of the various tribes came forward for the padres' prayers, with the procession continuing all through the night until ten o'clock the next morning. Benavides reports that miraculous cures took place, including the healing of the lame and the blind. Not only were the Indians impressed, but so were the Spanish soldiers.

When the de Salas people were on their way back to the Rio Grande, ambassadors from other distant Indian nations caught up with them and continued with them to Benavides headquarters, where they repeated the story of the blue lady. Benavides took notes on all this, meanwhile dispatching more padres.

When Benavides returned to Spain the next year, he talked about this mysterious woman who was teaching the Indians. His superior, Father-General Siena, was excited about the account. He knew of a nun who was claiming to have been carried by St. Michael and St. Francis to the New World while her body remained in a state of prayer in her convent in Spain. She was Maria de Jesus, the abbess of a convent in the small town of Agreda. Siena had already met Maria, having heard eight years previously her story that she was being transported back and forth to the New World. He was convinced of the truth of her claims.

Benavides went to Agreda and interviewed Maria for a period of two weeks. She was now 29 years old. She described New Mexico in detail—the landscape, the Indian's dress and customs, the churches, the padres—and she told Benavides of many events which he felt she would have had to have personally witnessed.

She said that sometimes she had been visible and sometimes invisible, and that, in the invisible state, she had accompanied Benavides at the Baptism of the Piros Indians. This she described.

She also said that she had assisted a certain Fray Cristobal Quiros in several of his Baptisms, and she gave details of his appearance—that he was old but that he did not show any signs of gray hair, and that he was longfaced and ruddy. She described one time in particular, when Father Cristobal had been trying to persuade a group of shy Indians, who had gathered just outside, to enter his church. Suddenly they stumbled and fell over each other through the open doorway. They then laughed and looked around, saying that someone had pushed them from behind. Maria said that she had been that person. (Benavides had already written of this event in his *Memorial,* stating that the Indians had insisted that someone had pushed them, even though no one could be seen.)

Maria also told of Fray Juan de Salas and the Baptism and healing of the Jumano Indians, giving her own version of the many events which Benavides had recorded in his *Memorial.* Her descriptions were so detailed that they recalled to Benavides much which he had seen but forgotten.

On May 15, 1631, Benavides obtained from Maria, in the presence of her confessor, a signed document in her own handwriting attesting to the truth of her assertions. Anyone reading *The Mystical City of God,* a long book which Maria later wrote, becomes convinced that this nun was indeed a God-fearing woman who would not deliberately lie. Whether or not she deceived herself, and in so doing deceived others, is another question. Some people believe that she got hold of a copy of the *Memorial* before

Benavides visited her, and that she used information from that report in her own stories. This may be true. But it is also on record that Father-General Siena did indeed visit her before the *Memorial* was published, and that she told him some of these same stories at that time.

Another argument used by the skeptics to say that Maria did not appear to the Indians is the fact that the Poor Clare habit of that day was black, gray, and white. The Indians all reported that the woman's clothing included a blue mantle—hence their name for her, "the blue lady." Since Maria says that the angels were responsible for her appearance, perhaps they are the ones who furnished her with the blue mantle. Who knows? The whole story is so extravagant, that many people dismiss it all as a fraud.

In 1689, long after Maria's death, a man named Don Damien Manzanet, living in the province of Coahuila in Texas, had an experience which he later described in a letter to Don Carlos de Siguenza y Gongora. Manzanet said that he had come to that area because of the stories which Maria de Jesus had told to Benavides, long ago, about her work there. He then goes on, in his letter, to describe a visit to a nearby Indian village, where the governor asked him one evening for a piece of blue baize from which to make a shroud for his mother.

Manzanet suggested that a different cloth might be more suitable, but the governor replied that he would have no other color but blue. Manzanet asked why the color made any difference. The governor said that his tribe was very fond of that color, particularly for burial clothes, because in times past his people had often been visited by a very beautiful woman who used to come down from the hills dressed in blue. The governor added that this was before his time, but that his aged mother had seen her, as had the other very old people of the tribe. Manzanet then concludes that this woman in blue must have been Maria de Jesus.

Maria's flights ended in 1631. For the next 32 years she continued to serve, with the exception of one three-year period, as the abbess of her convent. During this time she claimed to have experienced many visions of the Virgin Mary. Also during these years Maria became the spiritual, and sometimes the political, advisor of King Philip IV. He wrote her long letters, filling the left side of each page, and she wrote her replies to his questions on the right side. These letters still exist and have been published in Spain. ❏

The Creed in Other Words

A fresh view of our beliefs, from East Africa

By JOHN S. AHEARN, O.F.M.
November 1982, condensed from *The Beacon**

M Y JOB as a mission director requires me to keep up with the Third World. To do that, I need more than a paid-up subscription to *National Geographic.* I need a strong sense of oneness with people, especially Catholics, of other climes and cultures.

The most satisfying interchange with these people comes, in my opinion, from participating in liturgies that draw freely on local speech, gestures, and symbols. Oriental gestures of reverence, for instance, are acutely appealing: they can bring charm, life, and fresh insight into the familiar Mass routines. African hymns chanted to the tribal rhythms of drums, seeded gourds, and tympani also are wonderfully stimulating.

I like the version of the Creed used by the Masai people of East Africa. The sturdy translation given by Holy Ghost Father Vincent Donovan in his book *Christianity Rediscovered* (Orbis Books) is a worthy introduction to these warrior-shepherds of East Africa. Here it is:

W e believe in the one High God, who out of love created the beautiful world and everything good in it.

He created people and wanted them to be happy in the world.

---

*First published April 29, 1982. Reprinted with permission.

God loves the world and every nation and tribe on the earth.

We have known this High God in the darkness, and now we know Him in the light.

God promised in the book of his word, the Bible, that He would save the world and all nations and tribes.

We believe that God made good his promise by sending his Son Jesus Christ:

A man in the flesh,

A Jew by tribe,

Born poor in a little village,

Who left his home and was always on safari doing good,

Curing people by the power of God,

Teaching them about God and humanity,

Showing that the meaning of religion is love.

He was rejected by his people, tortured, and nailed hands and feet to a cross, and died.

He lay buried in the grave, but the hyenas did not touch Him, and on the third day He rose from the grave.

He ascended to the skies.

He is the Lord.

We believe that all our sins are forgiven through Him.

All who have faith in Him must be sorry for their sins, be baptized in the Holy Spirit of God, live the rules of love, and share the Bread together in love, to announce the good news to others until Jesus comes again.

We are waiting for Him.

He is alive. He lives.

This we believe. Amen. ✝

HEARTS ARE TRUMPS

Several years ago, as scoutmaster of a Bakersfield, Calif., troop, I took our then inexperienced boys up into the Sierras for a week of camping and fishing. A friendly game warden stocked our camp-site stream as we unpacked the gear, and the fun began.

It was obvious to other campers that this was our first fishing trip so they came to my rescue and helped instruct the boys in the art of fishing. With their aid, my scouts learned a new outdoor skill.

About a year later, I was fishing a nearby stream with some of my boys when we heard a woman cry for help. Upon reaching the lady in distress, we found that she had fallen and broken her leg. In true Boy Scout fashion we furnished splints and transportation back to her camp.

It was then that her husband recognized us as the Boy Scouts they had taught how to fish the year before.   Michael R. Rector.

Why Is Man Here?

Christianity's answer is both true and exciting

By BARBARA WARD

November 1957, condensed from *The Interplay of East and West**

CURIOSITY IS ONE OF the first marks of the human race. Man knows that his life is transient, he witnesses death and destruction, he is conscious deeply in himself of being not self-sufficient but wholly dependent upon things that he does not understand. Thus, from the beginning, in his most primitive religions, man has attempted to reach out for explanations.

One question lies behind all the others that man proposes: why is he here at all? What is the purpose of this whole vast panorama of human, physical, terrestrial, and planetary events in which he is plunged, yet wakes to self-consciousness with intimations of infinity and the agonizing knowledge of death?

Three kinds of answer to the riddle of man's being have been given.

1. Fatalism, the answer that we do not know, and that the whole thing is meaningless. One of the products of ancient thought was the conviction that man's whole existence is bound to a fixed, revolving system in which all is predetermined and all recurs. Greek thought envisaged a Great Year which brought the cycle of centuries full circle. Buddhism saw man bound to a "melancholy wheel" driven by his own desires. Individual life is no more than a flash of consciousness playing on a vast and meaningless pageant of unending revolving change.

In a sense, communism harks back to that kind of fatalism. Calling fate by any other name does not change its nature. You may call your stern goddess "dialectical materialism"; nevertheless she remains a goddess of inescapable destiny, from whose path you cannot swerve and who controls the whole development of history according to iron law. Man is no more than a product of this process, and has no further significance.

This is the position that the Marxist ought to take, because human freedom can find no room in the strict theory of economic determinism. Nor, unless he adds the quite unprovable belief that private property is the source of all evil, can the Marxist explain why at the end of all the conditioned economic change, a Utopia should put an end to history.

Ancient thinkers introduced no such gimmick; they thought that the revolving universe would go on being "nasty, brutish, and short." They did not expect a happy ending. But the communists have lived too near to the Christian hope of resurrection and of all things made new. And so, at whatever cost to logic, they envisage a happy ending. There may be no logical foundation for it; nevertheless, there it is.

2. Marxism, in spite of its philosophy, really belongs to a quite different approach, not of fatalism but of humanistic materialism. This is a second answer to the riddle of man's being, that man himself is the explanation of it all, is his own answer and justification. Humanity itself is an object for sufficient worship. The development of the human race is enough to give meaning to the vast processions of nature by which it is surrounded.

This is, in many ways, a noble view. It is certainly one that has been fostered with great strength in the West, where man by the use of his reason, imagination, energy, and creativeness, has transformed the face of the earth. Its supporters claim that it embraces all humanity and that it is a possible moral basis for a world-wide order. The service of man transcends all frontiers. Here is the ideal for which we seek.

Yet I think, for all the noble lives and actions that this religion of humanity has inspired, that it is not enough. Nor do I think it gives full rein to the potential creativeness and vision of mankind.

The first limiting factor in choosing man as the meaning and center of the universe is, alas, to consider oneself. Each man, if he stops to consider, is aware of his total dependence upon a million things beyond his control simply for the daily business of living. When they fail, as fail they will, dependence turns to death.

Nor is the question simply one of physical limitations. We are as aware of mental limitations. And heaven knows most of us are painfully aware of moral limitations, of a will so weak and a moral purpose so feeble that we hardly keep troth or faith, or pursue, even over a few weeks, any consistent line of conduct. Not even the wisest and best escape discouragement when they look at themselves.

Few people have made gods of themselves; the result is disaster if they do. When people turn to a religion of mankind, they are nearly always thinking of something beyond themselves, of humanity in its collective aspect. But since humanity is a very big idea, the worship of humanity tends to become something more precise. Lip-service may be paid to a wider ideal. But practical, effective service is rendered to the organized units of humanity: dynasty, empire, nation, class. And these ideals have in them dangerous possibilities of perversion.

To seek the meaning of life in a collective organization is to give it religious significance. Now, history shows that when politics takes on a religious color citizens look for a godlike man to guide them, rather than to committees, assemblies or "collective leadership." The French Revolution begins with the religion of humanity and ends with Napoleon. Stalin twisted world communism into Great Russian dictatorship.

No mortal man can bear the full weight of his fellows' adoration. When all the freight of human questioning, longing, and

despair is shifted onto the shoulders of one man, the more likely consequence is that he will run mad—as we have seen it even in our own day: Hitler in his bunker, Stalin dying among the terrors of his "doctors' plot." Human nature cannot bear the loneliness and the stress.

Horrors of destructiveness and mania have marked the paths of dictators throughout history. And when we blame them, we should perhaps remember the weight with which they have been loaded by the communities they led. They may have started in pride and ambition. They end carrying the burden of the whole community, scapegoats as well as leaders. Men are not born to be their own gods.

There is another sense in which the collective image of man can lead to disaster. Our ideal may be the nation. Or we can express our wider striving in terms of the class to which we belong. But often we find that what we have produced is not a wider vision, but an organization in the name of which we will commit crimes and atrocities which, in our private capacity, we would not even contemplate.

When man makes a religion of his collective self, there is almost no horror that he will not commit in that name. This capacity to behave worse in one's collective capacity can even be observed in religious communities. By giving themselves to the collective whole, some men, instead of using greater vision and wider humanity, have actually fallen to lower, more vicious and more brutal standards than would have been tolerated for a moment in private life. It is not only in the name of liberty that high-minded crime has been committed. Every collective ideal has exacted its martyrs and its blood.

These are not abstract historical reflections. In our own day, communism has both caught the loyalty of sincerely convinced lovers of humanity and committed inhuman cruelties in their name.

3. We are then left with a third possible answer to the riddle of human life. It is that man is a being created by a benevolent and omniscient Power and that the meaning of the universe is to be unraveled in the relationship between God and man.

Many of the institutions under which we live, many of the great visions by which we are still inspired, are derived from the day when the idea of a divine order of reality was still a living truth in the minds of most people. The separation of divine and secular, of Church and state, of the things that are God's and the things that are Caesar's, has helped to create a society in which subordinate groups enjoy their own appropriate rights. The notion of a moral law transcending kings and princes is another strong strand in our constitutional practice of government.

Freedom has its roots in the concept of each human soul enjoying infinite value in the sight of God and bearing the grandeur and servitude of personal choice and responsibility. And if all men are children of a common Father, they are brothers at the roots of their being. Christianity has often betrayed but never denied the brotherhood of man.

And, unique among world religions, Christianity, inheriting the vision from its Jewish roots, has seen the whole of history not as meaningless repetition but as the unfolding of the drama of God's purpose for man—a drama in which man, as free agent, has a creative part to play, transforming himself and his environment into a better, higher reflection of an ideal order. ✝

Why I Remain a Catholic

The Church is the only real vessel of human hope

By CHRISTOPHER DERRICK

July 1974, condensed from the *National Catholic Reporter**

"LORD, to whom shall we go? You have the words of eternal life." So, almost desperately, the disciples replied when Jesus asked them whether they were going to follow the trend of the moment and turn away from Him.

For me, the heart of the matter still lies there. I remain a Catholic because I cannot see a workable alternative.

I could, of course, answer this question in more moralistic terms. I believe that it is still the duty of all men to seek Baptism in Christ, and thereafter to

Mr. Derrick is the author of Too Many People, C.S. Lewis and the Church of Rome, That Strange Divine Sea, Church Authority and Intellectual Freedom, *and other books.*

*This article © 1973 by the *National Catholic Reporter,* P.O. Box 419281, Kansas City, MO 64141. Reprinted with permission.

continue as faithful members of the visible Church which He founded. Whatever the current fashion may be, I believe that I would sin grievously if I ceased to be a Catholic, and perhaps most of all if I started to approach the life and revelation offered by God in the critical picking-and-choosing spirit that we call heresy.

But such an answer might seem self-righteous, as if I were so perfect that any kind of wrongful action was quite out of the question for me. The question therefore needs to be answered also in a more personal, and perhaps a much more ignoble way.

How is it that a man like myself, capable of all the sins in the book, can nevertheless hold fast to membership in the Roman Catholic Church?

Subjectively, my answer is that

of the Apostles: There is the old Church and the old faith, or else there is nothing at all, nothing between us and despair.

Does this sound unacceptable? Many people, after all, seem to lead reasonably happy, hopeful lives without being Catholics, and even without any religion at all. Do I consider myself too grand to join them?

Well, for one thing, their happiness and hope may not be quite what they seem. Thoreau had something when he observed, "The mass of men lead lives of quiet desperation." And where happiness and hope are in fact achieved, this is (in my experience) very commonly by means which are not open to me.

In the first place, men keep themselves busy, and often drugged, in the martini culture or the pot culture, and thus distracted from the despair which underlies the condition of fallen man. In the second place, they find other, subChristian objects for their hope: revolution, or the affluent society, or man's conquest of nature, or evolution, or something of that sort.

Such things don't work for me. I am far too lazy to anesthetize myself with honest toil. I take the drugs willingly enough, or some of them: whiskey and brandy and gin, but not (as it happens) pot or heroin.

So I am stuck with full consciousness. I am 52, well into

what some doctors once called the "cancer and coronary belt," and incurably aware of what, if there is no God or no redemption, must be the total meaninglessness of everything. As for those other hopes, those false gods, well, one burden and benefit of being a Catholic is that it spoils you for such illusions.

Hence, for me, the threefold relevance of Christ and his body, the Church. I am mortal: everything that I now value will be taken from me in the fairly near future. I am a sinner. Some people talk as though "guilt" only existed in the public domain: war, injustice, racial hatred. But I know better. And finally, there is the tormenting riddle of existence: we are lost in a dark wood, and can't work out the meaning and purpose of life, not one little bit.

Mortal, guilty, and perplexed, I need something or somebody to be the way, the truth, and the life. And there is only one serious claimant for the title. The rival claims are made halfheartedly or unclearly, and, for anybody of my aggressively analytic sort of mind, on lines that don't stand up to ten minutes' serious criticism.

So I find myself in the Church: the body of Christ, the thing He works through, His presence on earth until He comes again, the specified (though not exclusive) instrument of that way and truth and life.

The basis upon which we identify the Roman Catholic Church (though not its churchmen) with Christ, seems to me clear and cogent: scripturally, theologically, historically speaking, it seems to me unarguable in principle, and only argued in fact by those who are prepared to dissolve all accurate thought for the sake of a brotherhood that will inevitably be rooted in falsity.

But it may be more to the point to say that it makes sense in experience. The Church turns out to be in fact all that one might expect of an ark of salvation.

The ancient image is extremely useful when we consider possible attitudes to the human reality of the Church. If I were shipwrecked, close to drowning in deep water, I would be extremely glad to be picked up by any seaworthy vessel, and I wouldn't be unduly critical if I then found that the company on board was less than perfect and that old father Noah was captaining the ark on lines open to objection.

There might come a moment when it was my duty to rebuke him. But that would be exceptional, a matter of reluctance. My predominant mood would be continuing gratitude for the fact of rescue. I might also wonder why, if it is so great to be a Catholic, I was chosen for the privilege, when so many people had to go without?

Perhaps this privilege was saved for the hard cases, the weak swimmers who would drown otherwise. At any rate, we have no cause for conceit in our Catholicism; humility and gratitude are much more appropriate.

I have not had much humility to boast about, but gratitude comes fairly easy to me. I find it possible, in fact, to love the Church, at a time when many sensitive people seem nearly frantic over its tiresome ways. I see their point. For people too spiritually minded, imperfectly aware of the depth to which God descends in the humility of his incarnation, it may be hard to see any connection between "the body of Christ" and the human realities immediately perceived: the fat pastor with his whiskey and his bullyings about money, the crabbed legalism of the diocesan chancery, the telephones and filing cabinets of the Vatican.

But my own response to such things can best be indicated by an analogy. Many years ago, I planned to take my children on a holiday abroad. As the great day approached, they naturally became more and more wild with excitement. On the day before departure, I came home from the travel agency and showed them the tickets which I had just bought.

Consider those tickets for a moment. They were plain documents of the financial, legal, and administrative sort, with figures and details, and some mention of possible penalties and cancellations. What could possibly be duller? And yet, my children gazed upon them in ecstasy, seeing right through the dull legalism, real and necessary though it was, and perceiving only the instruments of their wondrous journey over the sunlit sea and into the peacock lands.

You and I are still children, and Christ warns that we must retain or regain that character if we hope to find the one holiday place that will never let us down. And just as a child will see glory in even the dullest details surrounding his approaching holiday, so also a Catholic who really believes will instinctively romanticize the Church, finding glory in even the human and imperfect paraphernalia of its life—even in the priest who asks for money as that travel agent did, even (perhaps) in the telephones and filing cabinets of the Vatican.

This does not mean that he will be wholly uncritical. I want travel tickets to be well-printed and conveniently set out; and those regulations in small type ("Not valid before . . . " "Passengers are warned . . . " "Extra charges will be incurred . . . " "In an emergency, obey the crew") should be as fair and generous to the traveler as is possible in an imperfect world.

But if our minds are set on the glory to come, on what the dull "tickets" are going to do for us, then we children only attend to these other questions with a certain reluctance.

It is on these lines that I hold aloof from the present fuss about the imperfection of the Church's human arrangements. Of course they are imperfect. Popes and bishops are only human, and it has even been whispered that the emerging layman can have his faults.

But it seems a very unChristian thing to make these imperfections the object of our habitual and indignant attention. In view of what it means to call the Church "the Body of Christ" and "the ark of salvation," we should have more interesting things to think about than the bad typography of the ticket or the bad manners of the girl at the check-in desk.

I don't think I have any illusions about our battered and shabby old ark, but it continues to give me a happier voyage than I deserve. In a lifeboat or rescue ship, one can hardly expect to find the amenities of a luxury liner. I must admit that I sometimes feel queasy when the water gets rough, and that there are some passengers and some members of the crew whom I find it better to avoid, just as there are some who find it necessary to avoid me.

But I don't worry. If this ship were sinkable, it would have sunk a long time ago. Unless we are foolish enough to jump overboard, we are going to get there, to a holiday better than we could ever imagine. ✝

DESIGN FOR LIVING

A psychologist was giving an intelligence test to a group of eight-year-olds. He took a map of the world from a picture magazine, tore it into tiny pieces, and handed the pieces to one of the boys. "Let's see you put these together properly," he said.

The lad studied the pieces. Then he quickly assembled the map without a flaw.

"Wonderful!" exclaimed the psychologist. "How did you do it so fast?"

"Well," said the boy, "there was a big picture of a man on the other side. If you get that man straightened out, the world will come out all right."

T. and J. Gootée.

PEOPLE ARE LIKE THAT

I was a young artist in Chicago in 1941, trying to support a widowed mother. After six months of harassing the display director of Charles Stevens Department Store, I landed a mural commission. On the first day of my job, I proudly surveyed the Thermolux glass screen, 12 by 36 feet, which I was to decorate. Enthusiastically I began, only to find the glass wouldn't take oil paint. I didn't know what to do.

Then I thought of Raymond Katz, a well-known Chicago artist, and an authority on mural painting. I consulted him and learned that I would have to draw the design on glass with a litho-pencil, and use lacquer paint smoothed on with medical swabs. But I had evolved a complicated design and was supposed to finish it in two weeks. Lacquer-painting goes much more slowly than oil painting.

I'm sure that I never would have finished the mural on time if Mr. Katz hadn't helped me. The generous man actually came down to paint with me. He helped me especially with the center of the design, which was particularly difficult. "I'll never forget this!" I told him. And I never have.

Margarita Walker Dulac.

Vistas of the Eternities

By ARNOLD LUNN
October 1939, condensed from *America**

MOUNTAINEERING does not consist merely in climbing mountains, but in the solution of the particular problems which mountains provide.

I remember leading down a great face which ended in the labyrinth of an impossible icefall. It was essential to hit off a miniature saddle some ten feet in breadth which interrupted the downward sweep of the rock ridge on our right. All but the immediate foreground was blotted out by driving snow, but I banked on the possibility that the shoulder would correspond to some ill-defined belt of gentler ground across the slope we were descending, and when the slope eased off—a change of gradient more perceptible to the foot than to the eye—and turned sharply to the right, suddenly the clue to our descent loomed up through the grayness. At such

*First published Aug. 19, 1939. Reprinted with permission.

moments one feels not only the intellectual thrill which is the reward of a correct deduction from obscure clues, but also the more primitive joy which follows peril safely past.

Many years ago I spent a New Year's Day with a companion struggling up through storm to the crest of the Eiger. A sudden lull tempted us up to the final ice slope, but just as we started down from the summit a low mutter broke the silence and struck fear into our hearts. We knew what was coming, but were not prepared for the tornado which broke. The mountain quivered beneath the impact. Stone, whipped off the ice, screamed past like shells. A flood of loose snow poured down the ice and blotted out the steps which we had cut with such labor. I had left my climbing irons behind and was hurled out three times at full rope's length before I regained control. I remember a sudden vision of the valley below, but my companion's equipment saved us. Slowly and with infinite care we crept down the ice, in which every step had to be recut. And when, at last, we felt beneath our feet the reassurance of rough and friendly rock, we threw ourselves on the ground, and lay huddled together for many minutes, indifferent to cold, intoxicated with the relief of safety, and far too weary to raise our voices above the storm.

But even that day had its moments of calm beauty. We had been climbing for 13 hours and had seen nothing but the same drab foreground of ice-fretted rock and gray mist, and then suddenly toward evening we paused, for the blanket of gray mist seemed subtly changed, stirred by movements which destroyed its cohesion. The mist was beginning to disintegrate. Soon only a diaphanous veil separated us from the windy spaces of the sky. And then even this dissolved to reveal the dark blue water of Thun and the distant groundswell of the Jura.

The most hackneyed of peaks provides the climber with a problem which he must solve afresh if he climbs it in bad weather. To lead in a storm up a ridge one has never climbed in fair weather is a stimulating test of mental and physical powers. There are moments when it is difficult to believe that one is contending with inanimate matter, for there is a human touch about the bluster of a storm and the peculiar malice of the wind. For the wind will suddenly peter out when the mountaineer reaches good anchorage and make a great parade of having business in a neighboring gully, only to leap upon him with an exultant scream as he leaves a secure ledge for the perils of an exposed slab.

When I was young, I was caught by a storm while skiing alone among the Oberland glaciers. I had been climbing for some days and I had run out of food. Most of those who die of exposure in the Alps first exhaust themselves in the search for shelter. I did not make this mistake and resigned myself to the inevitable while I still had reserves of strength. I divided my time between digging a hole in the snow to keep warm and taking shelter in the hole until I had once again begun to freeze. It was not until the small hours that I was in danger. But toward morning the strain began to tell. I heard siren voices in the little winds which gathered strength in the hollows of the hills. There was a caressing touch in the snow-laden breezes which moved so gently over the surface of the glacier. It would have been easy to die, if only to avoid the recurring strain of forcing myself to my feet just as my frozen limbs relaxed for sleep. While I was contending with the gathering darkness, I had known the fear of night and the misery of solitude.

Fear left me when I gave up hope of shelter and the loneliness of the snows did not oppress me. In those days, I should have resisted the instinctive urge to pray as a collapse more ignoble than the surrender to sleep; but, in some dim fashion, I knew that I was being sustained by a Power not myself and encouraged to continue the struggle by a Companion, nagging and insistent, who forced me to my feet when I fell back half asleep and who would never let me rest. Later, I dismissed this experience as an interesting example of the recrudescence of primitive beliefs under conditions of fear and exhaustion. Perhaps I was right, for primitive man saw clearly many truths which are forgotten in the clamor of great cities, and. among the mountains our intuitions of truth break through the mist of modern falsehood.

Passage after passage in Mr. Irving's anthology, *The Mountain Way,* bears witness to the search for some clue to the mysticism of the hills, but few are the mountaineers who follow up with the same courage the mountain clues which lead to truth as those which lead to mountain crests.

"The solemn dome resting on those marvelous buttresses, fine and firm above all its chasms of ice, its towers and crags; a place where desires point and aspirations end; very, very high and lovely, long-suffering and wise. *Experience,* slowly and wonderfully filtered; at the last a purged remainder. And what is that? What more than the infinite knowledge that it is all worth while—all one strives for? To struggle and to understand— never this last without the other; such is the law."

How much this passage would have gained not only in precision but in beauty had the writer admitted that among the mountains he was conscious of the presence of God. Contrast the vagueness of this Alpine religiosity with the clarity of two other writers, quoted in the same anthology, who had thought out their mountain *credo,* the first a Shintoist, the second a Catholic.

"The mountains themselves," writes Prince Chichibu, "stand as symbols of eternal Life, and serve as the expression of a mighty spiritual Being."

The same conclusion emerges from the famous passage in which Mr. Belloc describes the distant view of the Alps which "link one in some way to one's immortality. From the height of the Weissenstein I saw, as it were, my religion. I mean humility, the fear of death, the terror of height and of distance, the glory of God, and my confidence in the dual destiny."

To the Shintoist and the Catholic the mountains speak the same language and proclaim the same truths, truths which the shy prophets of a vague religiosity dimly perceive but dare not boldly profess.   ✝

SPECIAL DELIVERY

When people fuss about the discourtesy of bus drivers, I always think of the one I knew in Houston in the spring of 1957. I was working in a hospital during a leave from college and carrying on a long-distance romance with a boy in the service. The bus I took to work each morning arrived at my corner promptly at 8:20, while the custodian of my precious daily letter from my boy friend ambled up the street any time from 8:15 to 8:30. Mornings when the postman arrived before the bus, I faced the day with a radiant smile. When the bus was ahead of the mail, I climbed aboard despondently.

One morning when my letter had not arrived, the bus driver stopped his bus two blocks down the street, where he had spotted the postman approaching. "Go get your letter," he ordered me. Then turning to the other passengers he said, "We don't mind waiting, do we?"

The busload waited cheerfully while I leaped down the steps, grabbed my letter from the smiling postman, and hurried back aboard. We kept up the schedule until my boy friend returned from the service and we were married.   Helen LeBeau.

TRAFFIC TICKET IN THE HOLY CITY

When a foreigner in Rome commits a minor violation or is discovered parked in a restricted area, the policeman hands him a blue ticket, signed by the mayor and printed in French, German, Spanish, and English.

It reads, "Dear Sir: Rome, the most cherished goal of international tourism, is happy to welcome you among the visitors to the city. It often happens that even the most careful driver infringes, without meaning to, upon the traffic regulations. In this particular instance you have failed to observe the rule contained in Article _____. The communal authorities are quite convinced that this infringement was unintentional and wish you a very happy stay in Rome. The Mayor."   Quote (21 June '64).

How the Bible Says It

How the Bible Says It

A little language lesson can enrich our reading of the Gospels

By JOHN WIJNGAARDS, M.H.M.
May 1983, condensed from *Handbook to the Gospels**

Our READING of the Gospels will be greatly enriched if we appreciate their characteristic forms of speech. Many forms of Semitic speech cannot be translated into English without losing some of their impact.

Parallel Statements. Semitic poetry tends to express a thought twice in slightly different forms. This parallelism is often used to express completeness.

Give to him who begs from you, and do not refuse him

who would borrow from you (Mt. 5:42).

Lay up for yourselves treasures in heaven, where neither moth nor rust consumes them and where thieves do not break in and steal (Mt. 6:20).

In such cases we should not look for a different meaning in each half of the parallelism. Both really express one truth. The repetition simply embellishes the statement, clarifies it, and further imprints it on the hearer's memory.

Negative and Positive. In one form of parallelism the same truth is put first in the positive and then in the negative form. This is the Semitic way of excluding all other possibilities. Suppose that you want to say, "Only adults may see this film." In a Semitic language this could be expressed, "Adults may see the film; nonadults may not." Jesus employed this form:

If you forgive people's sins, they are forgiven;

If you do not forgive them, they are not forgiven (Jn. 20:23).

Meaning: "You will have universal power to forgive sins."

Do not condemn others, and God will not condemn you;

Forgive others, and God will forgive you (Lk. 6:37).

Meaning: "God will forgive you to the same degree in which you forgive others."

This principle of exclusion can be applied even more extensively. In the parable of the Last Judgment (Mt. 25:31-46), Jesus first praises the blessed "for all that you have done to the least of mine you have done to Me"—the positive statement —then curses the wicked "for what you have not done for the least of mine, you have not done for Me"—the negative statement. The parable thus expresses that all persons without exception will be judged regarding their fraternal charity.

Inclusion, or Ring Construction. The Jews also had the custom of beginning and ending a passage with the same thought. It was a natural way of bringing out the unity of idea in their statement. This form of speech has received the official name *inclusion,* since one particular thought or statement includes, grasps, or embraces the intermediate phrases. It is also known as ring construction. We find numerous examples in the Gospels. Consider this one from Matthew 7:16-20:

You will know them (false prophets) *by what they do.*

Thorn bushes do not bear grapes, and briars do not bear figs. A healthy tree bears good fruit, but a poor tree bears bad fruit. A healthy tree cannot bear bad fruit, and a poor tree cannot bear good fruit. And any tree that does not bear good fruit is cut down and thrown into the fire.

So then, you will know the false prophets by the way they act.

One thought brackets the passage. Notice that this sentence is also the most important one—it accurately summarizes what Christ wants to say by the examples. Other instances of such inclusive phrases abound in the Gospels. Here are a few familiar phrases that are repeated at the beginning and the end of passages:

The Kingdom of heaven belongs to them! (Mt. 5:3 and 10).

Unless you give up all you cannot be my disciple . . . (Lk. 14:26 and 33).

This is my commandment: love one another! (Jn. 15:12 and 17).

The Hebrew Genitive (Possessive). On the whole, Semitic languages do not use many adjectives. This gives rise to some very peculiar constructions. Instead of speaking of a "fat pig," one would say, "a pig of fatness." "Beautiful ring" becomes "ring of beauty." "A courageous hero" would be "hero of courage." In this construction we should particularly notice that it is the second noun which substitutes for the adjective: "the God of mercy" means "the merciful God."

In good translations this noun construction, commonly known as the Hebrew genitive, is simply translated by the appropriate adjective. However, we will meet cases where the noun construction has not been translated.

The Hebrew Superlative. With the exception of Arabic, Semitic languages do not possess a special form for the superlative ("best") or the comparative ("better"). Superlatives and comparatives have therefore to be expressed in other ways. At times we simply find a positive statement which is meant as a superlative.

Blessed are you among women (Lk. 1:42) means "You are the most fortunate woman that ever lived."

Which is the great commandment in the Law? (Mt. 22:36) means "Which is the greatest commandment in the Law?"

At other times a comparison between two things is expressed simply by affirming the one and denying the other:

I desire mercy, and not sacrifice (Mt. 9:13; 12:7) means "I prefer mercy to sacrifice."

He who believes in Me, believes not in Me but in Him who sent Me (Jn. 12:44) means "Faith in me rests more on Him who sent Me than on me."

Notice in these examples that the denial is only partial. Matthew 9:13 does not say that God does not want sacrifice. It only says that God (who wants sacrifice) prefers mercy. In other words, He thinks mercy more important.

These Hebrew constructions may sometimes be badly misunderstood. A typical case of use of denial for the comparative form may be seen in the word *to hate.* This word often means "to love less than." The two passages below are parallel, but seem to say different things in English.

1. *If anyone comes to Me and does not hate his own father and mother and wife and children and brothers and sisters, he cannot be my disciple.*

2. *He who loves father and mother more than Me is not worthy of Me; and he who loves son or daughter more than*

Me is not worthy of Me (Mt. 10:37).

Jesus does not demand that we hate our parents, but that we love them less than God. In this way we also have to understand the phrase "You shall love your neighbor and hate your enemy" (Mt. 5:43) to mean "Love your neighbor more than your enemy." Jesus does not mean that the Old Testament commanded the Jews to hate their enemies; but it allowed them to love their friends more. Jesus taught that we have to love our enemies just as much.

Hyperbole, or Exaggeration. Quite a few Jewish statements are phrased in such strong terms that they cannot be taken literally. We call these statements hyperboles. We meet this form of speech in every language ("It's raining cats and dogs," "So-and-so is snowed under with work"), but for Jews it was not a matter of repeating fixed expressions—they would employ hyperbole whenever the occasion offered itself, even in new situations. Jesus used this form of speech often:

How dare you say to your brother, "Please, let me take that speck out of your eye," when you have a log in your own eye? (Mt. 7:4).

You strain a fly out of your drink, but swallow a camel! (Mt. 23:24).

Such expressions are obviously not to be taken literally. They are very strong statements intended to bring the truth home in a way that we will never forget.

If we understand this hyperbolic aspect of Jewish speaking, we will be able to solve some apparent conflicts in the texts. For example, the apparent conflict between these two passages has troubled many readers:

Anyone who is not for Me is really against Me; anyone who does not help Me gather is really scattering (Mt. 12:30).

Whoever is not against us is for us (Mk. 9:40).

Seen out of context, these would seem to contradict one another. But the first was spoken when Jesus was accused of being helped by the devil. He replied that only those who actually support him by constructive action can be reckoned to be his helpers.

The second was spoken in the story of the man who drove out the devils in Jesus' name. Jesus said that such a person should not be reckoned an enemy. There is no contradiction, but in both cases Jesus expressed one aspect of the same truth very strongly: only really constructive support makes us helpers of Jesus, yet we should allow for certain people who support Him at least to some extent.

Idiomatic Expressions. Many fairly common phrases in the

Gospels have rather specialized meanings. Let us look at several important ones:

Adulterous generation (Mt. 12:39, 16:4; Mk. 8:38). *Generation* stands for the average period between the time a man becomes an adult himself until his son becomes an adult, about 30 years. When Jesus said "this generation," he meant his contemporaries.

In the Old Testament, *adultery* is often the name given to Israel's fall into idolatry. Israel was "married" to God; therefore her turning to other gods was called adultery. Jesus used the term in this Old Testament sense. It has nothing to do with physical adultery. "This adulterous generation" means "the faithless, unreliable people of my time."

Amen, Amen, I say to you (Mt. 5:18, 6:2). This phrase introduces a solemn declaration. The Jews employed *Amen* as a solemn affirmation of one's obligation ("I agree"). However, they never used the expression in the way in which Jesus used it—that is, to emphasize that He pronounced the statement on his own authority (see Mk. 1:22).

Brother and sister. For Jews all relatives were "brothers" and "sisters" (Mt. 5:22 ff). The Gospels speak of Jesus' sisters (Mk. 6:3) and brothers (Mt. 13:55) in this sense (see also Mt. 12:46ff; Jn. 2:12). The early Christians always addressed one another as "brother" and "sister," because all Christians are brothers and sisters of the Lord.

Son of.... this phrase may express any type of relationship in Hebrew. One has to examine the word for its exact meaning in practically each case.

Sons of the bridechamber (Mt. 9:15) means "wedding guests."

Sons of thunder (Mk. 3:17) means "impetuous men."

Son of peace (Lk. 10:6) means "a peaceful person."

Sons of this world (Lk. 16:8) means "worldly people."

Sons of light (Lk. 16:8) means "those who received light."

Sons of God (Lk. 20:36) means "people who live in and through God."

Visiting. According to Semitic mentality one does not visit another person without giving help, advice, consolation, and so on. The word can acquire various meanings of this sort in different contexts.

God has visited his people (Lk. 1:68, 7:16) means "God has helped, redeemed his people."

I was in prison and you visited me (Mt. 25:36, 43) means "I was in prison and you looked after me."   ✝

Editing the
Jerusalem Bible

The man responsible for the new version
describes the problems of translating—and
reading—the Scriptures

By ALEXANDER JONES
April 1967, condensed from *Jubilee**

I GOT INTO this project of translating the Bible because I felt the Bible was being ignored. Scholars were doing some deep research, but it was not getting through to the ordinary people at all. I felt that the general Catholic public was not in touch with the scholars and therefore the time would come when there would be a great explosion and people would say, "Why weren't we told?" and their faith would suffer a shock.

I felt that a new translation of the Bible, with adequate and up-to-date notes, would be an opportunity to filter Biblical scholarship through to the public. And then I found that it had been done in French, namely, the Jerusalem Bible. I remember someone saying that it should be in English, and I said, "Well, let's do it. If we don't, who will? We can do it in no time, in three years, perhaps." That was ten years ago.

My very first idea was this. "Here we have a French translation; now why not get a lot of people who are masters of English and get them to translate the French, because surely most of them can read French, but they can't read Hebrew or Greek." So I wrote to Edith Sitwell, Roy Campbell, J. R. R. Tolkien, and a few others.

I thought Edith Sitwell might do the Psalms, but she sent me a nice letter saying that she was very sorry but she thought she was dying and she felt she had a very important thing to write.

*This article © 1966 by the A.M.D.G. Publishing Co., Inc.

I thought Roy Campbell, who did the poems of St. John of the Cross so beautifully, would be just the man for the Psalm of Psalms, but he was killed in a motor accident. His wife survived the accident and sent me the one page that Roy had done. I wish now that his name had appeared on the list of collaborators. Then in Australia I met a very good poet, James McAuley, so I asked him to do the Psalm of Psalms.

I still feel it possible for the thing to be done from the French first and then corrected from the Hebrew and Greek; in fact we were able to do that in two or three cases and they proved perfectly satisfactory, but for the most part, when the English is free with the French and the French is free with the Hebrew, then you are getting miles away from the original. So the whole of the New Testament has been done from the Greek and all of the Old Testament was done from the Hebrew.

I always had on my desk the Hebrew Masoretic text, that is, the text as established by the Jewish scholars at the end of the 1st century; plus the Septuagint, the Greek translation of the Old Testament. My business was not to establish a text; that had been done by the French scholars, taking into account various arguments, con-

texts, manuscripts, and even the Dead Sea scrolls.

The French scholars had decided whether something was to be changed or not. For example, there is an odd phrase in Job 6:6, which the Revised Standard version translates as "or is there any taste in the slime of the purslane?" I eventually discovered that purslane is an herb, but the phrase still sounded very odd. By a slight change in the Hebrew, however, you get "white of an egg" instead of "slime of the purslane" and that's what the French editors of the Jerusalem Bible had done. In that case I didn't have to decide; the French had done it.

We also had the advice of various critics, notably J. R. R. Tolkien on the use of archaic words or phrases. I fought Tolkien, for instance, on the archaism: "Thy brothers and thy sisters stand without." I said, we can't say that. We simply say: "Your brothers and your sisters are standing outside."

He wrote back that that was a very good example, but that it is also a jingle, and that we had lost a good deal of its beauty because we had damaged the rhythm. Of course, he had a point, but it was not a line embedded in poetry such as you find in the book of Job. So we decided to let the people speak naturally.

The chief archaism we had

to deal with was *thou* and *thee.* It is not *thou* and *thee* I hated so much, but all the awkward verb forms that had to go with them; "thou hatest" and "didst" are very awkward. Although other versions, such as the Revised Standard, have eliminated *thou* and *thee* for human beings, they kept them for God.

That seemed to be removing God farther from us. So I examined myself on this and found that I always address God as "You." For example, I would say, "I hope You help me." I would never say to myself, "I hope Thou willest help me."

The real difficulty is that sometimes *You* sounds rather brusque. And in the Our Father if you say "You who are," well, there is "You who" for the start. This is where the Greek helped, because the Greek doesn't have "who art"; it is simply "Our Father in heaven." So we have, "Our Father in heaven, may your Name be holy and your will be done."

With words like *drachma* or *denarius* you have to let your tact operate. I'd rather have the Good Samaritan give a denarius than a penny to the innkeeper. *Denarius* is a rather pompous word, but the penny seems silly in the context.

I hope our translation will be subject to almost constant revision as the different editions come out. I tried to make it as simple as I could, as far as the original would let me be simple; of course that was difficult in the sections containing poetry or high prose.

On the whole I wanted the Bible to speak through; I wanted to be as unobtrusive as I could. Now, whether publishers will tolerate changes, especially small ones for future editions, remains to be seen. Every letter of criticism that comes in is filed and I would frankly distrust something in our translation if there is considerable objection to it. For instance, just after the Jerusalem Bible came out in England I got a letter from a man who questioned our use of "in meadows He lets me lie" in Psalm 23.

He said: "I'm not a Biblical scholar, but I do keep sheep and I do know that there are no sheep in the meadow. If you can recall the rhyme of *Little Boy Blue,* you know that when the sheep were in the meadow, and the cows were in the corn, it was a disaster." He said that he did not let his sheep in the meadow except in the spring and in the autumn. So I thought, here's where the man knows what he's talking about. I immediately called the publishers to try to make the change, but it was too late. Anyway, I am open to all sorts of suggestions like these.

My biggest headache was in

distinguishing where translation ended and paraphrase began. Take for example the Nicene Creed: "He rose, according to the Scriptures." Now, to my mind, that means "So the Scriptures say, but I don't believe it." It is possible to translate word for word and yet falsify the original. I would certainly translate that: "He rose on the third day, as the Scriptures said He would." The word *said* doesn't occur in the Greek, but that's the meaning of that line.

Literal translations can also make someone sound pompous when he is not. As an example, the Revised Standard version translates a section of one of the Epistles of St. Paul as "Be not eye-servers or men-pleasers." But this is pidgin English, surely. It was simply the result of taking two portmanteau words from the Greek and almost transliterating them. I forget what we have for this, but it is something like "Act always as if your master were watching you, and don't take account of human respect."

I say this is paraphrase. I have worried about such things, but as long as the extension of the word keeps the sense of the thing, I think we are all right. The objection to this is taking dogmatic argument from a translation: if you are going to translate freely, what becomes of a close dogmatic argument?

I say, close dogmatic arguments can never come from any translation; they must always come from the original. All you can hope for in a translation is that it gives you the general sense.

Now, the Catholic dogmatic argument for the perpetual virginity of our Lady cannot be demonstrated from the Bible. On the other hand, it cannot be contradicted from the Bible, either. The Bible is at least a negative norm, of course, and if we say anything against its clear meaning, we must be wrong. But that does not mean we can find out everything from the New Testament; in fact, this is the Catholic position.

The word *virgin* in the Hebrew means a young girl of marriageable age. It comes from the root "to mature" and is feminine. If you want to use the word *maiden* you are free to do so. But in the New Testament the Greek word *parthenos* is a different matter. There Matthew is quoting Isaiah, but through the Greek translation. *Parthenos* is commonly agreed to mean "virgin." *Maiden* is used in Isaiah itself, but when Isaiah is quoted in the New Testament it is not quoted from the Hebrew, but from the Greek, so it is translated "virgin."

I believe in the living word of God. That is, the Spirit is operating here and now, just as it was operating in ancient Israel. I would be inclined to say that the Spirit was so working with the term "young woman of marriageable age," that eventually, in the 2nd century, it became "virgin." Some people have maintained that the Septuagint is inspired. As a translator, I think that is a bit extravagant, but I think the idea behind it quite accurate, that is, that we are in a dynamic situation. And so, I think that the Church has a right to say that the perpetual virginity of Mary is manifested in the growing belief of the faithful.

In the Catholic Church, because we have always believed in the living word, we are not alone with the Book. We refer to the Church as well as to the Bible. I honestly believe that the Biblical revival should be critically scrutinized. There are many stretches of the Bible that are not meant to be read by people of today at all, long lists of genealogies for instance: I would never hand a Bible to anyone and say, "Go away and read it." This to me is undiscriminating. It does the Bible little honor and the people no good at all. We believe it is the word of God, but it doesn't follow that we must read all of it.

Starting at the beginning is the worst way. I remember when I was young doing precisely that. But when I got to a chapter which I thought was a little bit off—like the Noah business—I said to my confessor, "I've come to a certain chapter in Genesis and I think it's rather queer. Should I go on?" He said, "No, don't. You had better stop."

He was wrong, of course, but people do get discouraged. They start with some of the most difficult literature of the lot and they still have before them Leviticus, which I would advise no one on earth to read. In it are all those distinctions among animals— clean, unclean—all those types of leprosy, and all those hygienic rules.

Instead, why not start at the back? And since people know, or think they know, the Gospels, they might well begin with the Epistles of St. Paul. Then, if there is something they don't understand, they can check back. In this edition references are very conveniently in the side margin. So you come across a strange name, and you say, "Who the deuce is he?" and then you check the reference. As you go along you will sample many parts of the Bible.

And, at the back of the Jerusalem Bible there is an index of themes, like "prayer," "suffering," "forgiveness," and so on. One might take one theme for a week, forgiveness, say, and look at all the passages that refer to forgiveness. In that way you can build yourself into a Biblical mentality. You will not be able to do a crossword, perhaps, but I don't think that is the object of Biblical reading.

In the Old Testament, I would start with the prophets. Certainly not the historical books, Joshua or Judges, Samuel, Kings, or the Chronicles, and I wouldn't strongly commend the Pentateuch, the first five books.

Ruth is a nice little literary masterpiece, but I feel it is dangerous to reduce the Bible to a book of history or literature. I hope our translation will respect the literary quality of the Bible, and people can read it for that if they want to, but let them know what they are doing. They are not using the Bible for the purpose for which it is intended. Anyway, I would think the prophets would be the best place to begin, then the neglected wisdom books: Job, the Psalms, the Song of Songs. There is magnificent stuff in some of them.   ✝

OUT OF MY CLASS

Mark Twain once observed that the most interesting information comes from children, because "they tell all they know and then stop." During the 13 years that I have taught elementary-school youngsters, I have found that their remarks on scientific subjects can also be hilarious. Here is what I mean:

"A scientific fact was only a theory as a child."

"The axis is just a make-believe line, but the earth still manages to turn on it somehow."

"Naughtical miles tell how far it is to places we should not go."

"Newton noticed that anything at rest tended to remain at rest. For this he grew famous."

"One way to tell for sure if a sweater is made of wool is to hold it over a flame. If it burnt slowly it was wool."

Often, their youngsterisms come closer to the truth than is apparent at first glance. Take these meteorological comments, for example.

"Every snowflake is made into a different shape. Personally, I think our weathermen should spend their time more usefully."

"Tornadoes are usually accompanied by high winds."

"Climate is with us all the time while weather comes and goes."

"When passing through Missouri, a typhoon is really not a hurricane but a tornado."

"The wind is like the air, only pushier."   Harold Dunn

Working with Biblical Manuscripts

Between you and the ancient scrolls stand the
scholars called textual critics

By RICHARD STONE

July 1980, condensed from *The Bible Today**

TEXTUAL CRITICS of the Bible have two strikes against them. First, no one ever heard of them; and second, we don't like people who go around criticizing our Bible. They remind us of smart alecks who write nasty reviews of movies that we thought were good.

But textual critics don't go to many movies. They're wrapped up in ancient manuscripts. What makes them stay up late is a passage that reads one way in one manuscript and another way in another. These things don't bother us lay people because in our English Bibles such differences have been ironed out— well, most of them. Sometimes people speak of Jesus' 72 disci-

ples when we always thought there were 70. Or someone sends us a Christmas card saying, "Glory to God in the highest and peace to men of good will," when we had been raised on "good will toward men."

One scholar says there are 150,000 copyists' variations, but he adds, "Only 400 or so materially affect the sense, and of these perhaps 50 are of real significance. No essential teaching of the New Testament is greatly affected." But many variations are of interest to historians, map makers, grammarians, and people who get curious about the personalities of ancient scribes.

An astonishing 14,800 variant readings are found in a single manuscript, the Codex Sinaiticus. This great work of the 4th century contains the Old

*This article © 1980 by The Order of Saint Benedict, Collegeville, Minn. Reprinted with permission.

Testament, the New Testament, and several epistles that didn't quite make it into the Bible. Still, 14,800! Practically all of these variations are corrections, and some are corrections of corrections. After all, a manuscript copied in the 4th century would have passed through the hands of many who felt they could improve the text.

In our Matthew 22:9, for example, slaves are told to go into the roads to find wedding guests. The original scribe, however, wrote *waters* instead of *roads.* Perhaps he was thinking of 4 Kings 2:21, where a similar expression is used. Anyway, he immediately saw his error and wrote *roads* above *waters,* and he deleted *waters* by putting dots over the letters. Another scribe evidently thought this was messy, so he erased everything and wrote *roads.* That's two corrections.

This mistake was caught and corrected long before anyone tried to translate the manuscript into English. But if it hadn't been, imagine the learned treatises that would have been written to explain why the slaves were sent to find wedding guests at the city wells.

The responsibility of the translator is awesome. What he thinks is the correct version is the reading that goes into thousands of homes. He must be as sure as he can be that the original text has been approved by the most competent authorities. The textual critic stands between the scribe and the translator.

What did Paul have in mind when he asked some Ephesian converts about their Baptism? The literal translation of Acts 19:3 is "Into what, then, were you baptized?" This seems to imply that Baptism projected one into another, presumably supernatural, state. But perhaps "into what" means "for what purpose," asking what the convert expected to get out of being baptized. *The New Jerusalem, The New American,* and other Bibles ask: "How were you baptized?" which inquires merely about the ceremony. There is no question here of the correct reading. The problem for the translator is what the correct reading means even when he starts from the premise that the textual critic has provided him with the most reliable text.

Even the lay person finds some variations important. "If your brother sins," as some manuscripts have it, is one thing; but if he sins "against you," which is the reading in other manuscripts, is something else.

At the end of Acts 11, we have a textual problem that has nothing to do with doctrine but is intriguing in its own right. The Christians in Antioch have sent Barnabas and Saul to Jerusalem with a gift, but at the end of the very next chapter Barnabas and Saul, having completed their mission, return to Jerusalem. Now why would they be returning to Jerusalem when they hadn't left it?

Two manuscripts, of the 5th and 6th centuries, say they went "out of" Jerusalem, instead of "to." A copy in Oxford is quite specific when it says that Barnabas and Saul went "out of Jerusalem to Antioch." Then why not simply adopt the *out of* reading and forget the *to?* Several modern translations do just that. The *Jerusalem Bible,* for example, says: "Barnabas and Saul completed their task and came back from Jerusalem."

The *New American Bible,* however, sticks with Barnabas and Saul returning "to" Jerusalem. There are three arguments in favor of this. First, *to* is found in the earliest and best manuscripts. Second, if there was a mistake in copying, it is more likely that the scribe would have written *out of* rather than *to,* because *out of* would have seemed to him more reasonable. Textual critics have a rule of thumb which states that "the more difficult reading is the better." The third argument is that the Greek word for *return* is almost always followed by *to.* Only once in twelve times in Acts is *return* followed by *out of* or *from.*

An ingenious solution to this problem was suggested a hundred years ago, but it was not adopted by any of the modern translators. Since the Greek word for *to* also means *in,* put the prepositional phrase with the first clause and let the reading be: "Having completed their mission in Jerusalem, they returned." Or we can simply throw up our hands, as one 4th century scribe did when he started writing *from* and ended up writing *to.*

Copying can be tedious work, and being human the scribes made mistakes. They became tired and bored. One of them wrote in the margin of his manuscript: "How I wish this day would end!" Another hoped: "Oh, for a glass of wine!"

Some scribes wrote one word for another that sounded like it. *Your,* for example, in Greek came to sound very much like *our,* the difference being in the value of one letter (as in French and English). So in Matthew some manuscripts read, "It is not your heavenly Father's will that one of these little ones should perish," while other manuscripts read, "It is not our Father's will . . . " From *our* later scribes wrote *my,* probably thinking of the place nearby where reference is made to "my Father."

A mistake of this kind suggests that the scribe was taking dictation. Several types of scribal error are presumed to have been made because of faulty hearing. When two successive lines began with the same word, one of the lines was overlooked. When two lines ended with the same word, the same thing happened. Words that sounded alike were confused.

Other scribal monks working alone in their cells, perhaps with poor light and with badly preserved manuscripts, might try to improve on the text. One, with a flair for vigorous expression, changed "Your Father knows what you need before you ask Him" to "Your Father knows what you need before you open your mouth." Others, not appreciating the deeper meaning of *fear,* wrote "The crowd was amazed" instead of "The crowd feared."

In a few places the scribe's marginal contributions found their way into the text. Often the scribes supplied names where none were originally given. One Old Latin manuscript tells us the robbers crucified with Christ were Zoatham and Camma. Another scribe tells us that what Jesus wrote in the sand was "the sins of every one of" the people who had accused the adulteress.

The textual critic must determine what readings were due to scribal error, what to excessive zeal, what to stylistic preferences. Over the years textual critics have developed certain criteria for judging suspect passages. One of them has been mentioned: "The more difficult reading is the better." Consider Acts 7:46 "(David) won God's favor and asked permission to have a temple built for the house of Jacob." In place of *house* some manuscripts read *God,* but the critics pick *house* as the correct reading because it is more difficult. It is easy to see why a copyist might write *God* rather than *house,* but not easy to see why he would write the more difficult word. It is more likely, then, that the original word was *house.*

Other rules of thumb include the length of the reading. A shorter reading is to be preferred to a longer one. A scribe might add an explanatory phrase; but why would he delete it?

As for witnesses, those manuscript readings found in many widespread places are more likely to be genuine than those found only in one locality. Also, manuscripts that have been reliable in many cases are to be preferred to manuscripts of which the reverse is true. Finally, as Metzger says, "Earlier manuscripts are more likely to be free from those errors that arise from frequent copying."

The problem of finding the nearest equivalent to the original writing is complicated by the incredible abundance of sources. Thousands of New Testament manuscripts exist, yet rarely are they complete. Only one of the very early manuscripts, *Codex Sinaiticus,* in the British Museum, is complete. Some are mere fragments consisting of a few verses. But each one must be considered. Fortunately, one brave scholar, Kurt Aland of Munster, West Germany, has undertaken to keep track of them all.

In contrast to this treasure stands the sparse manuscript witness of secular writers. Homer and Euripides are fairly well attested, each with several hundred sources. But of the first six books of Tacitus' *Annals,* only one manuscript survives.

Josephus was regarded during the Middle Ages as one of the foremost ancient historians. But, except for a Latin translation of the 4th century, only seven manuscript copies are to be found, and these come to us from the 10th century or later.

Oh yes, why do some say, "Glory to God in the highest and peace to men of good will," while others say, "Glory to God in the highest and peace, good will toward men"? The answer is that the Greek word for "good will" (*eudokia*) is translated the first way when it ends in *s,* and when it ends in *a,* it is translated the second way. Many manuscripts have it one way; many have it the other.   ✠

SIGNS OF THE TIMES

In the Roseland Dance City, a ballroom in New York City: "In case of fire, waltz—do not run—to the nearest exit."   A. T. Quigg.

*

On a Manhattan bridge: "In case of air raid, do not stop—drive off bridge."   James Sherman.

*

In a conference room of a business firm in Bridgeport, Conn.: "When all is said and done, usually more is said than has been done."
          Charles Chick Govin.

*

In an Air Force APO snack bar in Long Island City: "No paper bags to be consumed in this cafeteria."   Mrs. S. Lee.

*

In the offices of the research department of an engineering firm: "This problem, when solved, will be simple."   Dr. L. Binder.

The Fifth Gospel

With conscious artistry, St. Luke repeats the
themes of his first book in the Acts of the
Apostles

By LIONEL SWAIN
December 1966, condensed from the *Clergy Review**

S T. LUKE, the author of both
the third Gospel and Acts
of the Apostles, is more than a
historian. He is also a theologian. In the prologue to his
double work, he clearly expresses his intention to write
history: "It seemed good to me
also, having followed all things
closely for some time past, to
write an orderly account for
you"; and theology: "that you
may know the truth concerning
the things of which you have
been informed."

Luke's history of the growth
of the Church is more than the
recording of events. It is inter-
pretative. Inspiration insures
that his interpretation is a valid
one, though not necessarily the
only valid one.

By comparing the individual
manner in which each Gospel

maneuvers common material,
scholars detect the interests,
preoccupations, intentions—in
a word, the theology, of each
Evangelist. Luke's interpretation
is discernible in his choice of
sources and in the way he
repeats certain favorite ideas.
In the case of Acts, however,
no such comparison is available.
There are, therefore, only two
means of ascertaining Luke's
intention. The first is to look
for a revealing plan in Acts itself.
The second is to observe where
and how he re-employs in Acts
the characteristic notes of his
Gospel.

Acts opens with Christ's commission to the Apostles to be
his witnesses "in Jerusalem and
in all Judea and Samaria and to
the end of the earth" and ends
with Paul in Rome, called "the
end of the earth" in another
1st-century book. Luke wants
his readers to see in Paul's wit-

61

ness in Rome the accomplishment of the mission given in the 1st chapter.

The over-all plan of Acts corresponds exactly to Christ's commission: Jerusalem, Judea, Samaria, the Gentile world. The first seven chapters are centered on the life of the Jerusalem community. St. Stephen's death is followed by a violent persecution which causes the Jerusalem faithful to disperse throughout the region of Judea and Samaria and as far as Phoenicia, Cyprus, and Antioch. It is from Antioch that the first missioners are sent into the Gentile world to accomplish the final stage of Christ's commission. Not until chapter 10 does a person who is unmistakably a Gentile receive Baptism.

The plan of Acts resumes the universal tendency apparent in Luke's Gospel. In his hymn of thanksgiving, Simeon refers to Jesus as "a light for the revelation to the Gentiles," and Luke alone lengthens the quotation from Isaiah to include the phrase "and all flesh shall see the salvation of God."

Nevertheless, in Luke's Gospel Jesus does not leave the limits of Judea-Galilee-Samaria. Luke does not record the incident involving the Syro-Phoenician woman found in both Matthew and Mark.

According to Luke's scheme of things, it is only with the Church that the Gospel stretches beyond Palestine, that Jesus becomes "a light for the revelation of the Gentiles," that all flesh is able to see the salvation of God. Acts, therefore, continues the work of Jesus as it is formulated, but left unfinished, in the 3rd Gospel.

The third Gospel would be incomplete without Acts. This literary continuity reflects the theological continuity which exists between Christ and his Church: the Church, for Luke, is the extension of Christ in time and space. How else can one explain the boldness with which Paul is invested in the same mission as Christ's: "For so the Lord has commanded us (Paul and Barnabas) saying, 'I have set you to be a light for the Gentiles, that you may bring salvation to the uttermost parts of the earth' "?

Acts is not just a continuation of Luke's Gospel, but also a doublet, a replica of it. It has frequently been pointed out that the two books make a diptych, the second panel of which corresponds to the first, but the theological significance of this needs to be grasped.

The age of the Church is preceded by an atmosphere of prayers; this can only be because it is to be a new period in the history of redemption, comparable to the coming of Christ. Mary is expressly associated with the birth of the Church (Acts 1:14), to suggest a parity between the Church and Christ.

The Holy Spirit descends on the praying community at Pentecost as it did on the praying Christ at his Baptism; this community is now "another Christ," baptized in the Holy Spirit. The growth of the early community is described in terms recalling those applied to the growth of the infant Jesus. (Acts 2:47. Luke 2:52). Preaching and miracles arouse the same wonder, fear, and praise of God in Acts as they do in the Gospel. This is a fairly clear indication that, for Luke, the former are in the same class as the latter. A similar remark could be made concerning the theme of joy which figures largely in both Gospel and Acts.

All the evidence converges convincingly. The major forces at work during the earthly ministry of Christ, prayer, the Holy Spirit, the orientation towards the Gentiles, wonder, fear, joy, praise of God, are transferred to the Church.

This is no mere literary artifice. It conveys Luke's understanding of the Church's mystery; the Church is not only the prolongation of Christ in time and space, it is also united to Christ in depth.

The hinge of the diptych Luke-Acts is the Ascension, considered in the Gospel as the finale and in the Acts as the overture to Christ's work. There is no hiatus between Christ's redemptive work and the Church. The one is accomplished in the other.

Luke wishes his readers to appreciate the intimate union between the Church and Christ, the Church considered as the Body of Christ, and of the Apostle considered as an instrument of Christ.   ✠

KID STUFF

At Rochester, Minn., the public primary-school teachers were invited to attend the annual Teachers' Institute, and classes were to be dismissed for the day.

Little Susan came happily home to lunch, bringing the good news that "we don't have to go to school tomorrow."

"Oh? And why is that?" mother asked.

"I don't know, just exactly," Susan confessed. "I think it's because the teachers are going to have an innocent toot."

Minneapolis *Tribune* (21 Nov. '63).

What the Bible Doesn't Say

What the Bible Says about Tradition

Scripture itself shows us that it is only part of the teaching handed down by the Apostles through the bishops to us

By BROTHER DANIEL F. STRAMARA, O.S.B.

April 1986, condensed from the pamphlet of the same title*

D URING THE PAST 20 years the Bible has been exerting its authority in a new and exciting way in the lives of many Christians. As more and more people are trying to live by the Bible, they are asking, "What does the Bible say about . . . ?" In this article we ask a number of questions concerning Tradition and use the Bible itself to find the answers.

Isn't everything necessary

*First published by Dove Publications, Pecos Benedictine Abbey, Pecos, N.M. Reprinted with permission.

for salvation written in the Bible?

Yes, but not everything *helpful* for salvation is written in it. John said he could have written a lot more about Jesus (Jn. 21:25). Surely other accounts about Jesus and his teachings would be helpful and life-giving. In fact, the Apostles did pass on such teachings orally. This is what we call Apostolic Tradition. The oral word of God is just as necessary as the written, for the written sprang from the oral. Paul says, "I became a minister of his Church through the commission God gave me to preach among you his word in its fullness" (Col. 1:25). This fullness of Paul's teachings was never written down, but passed on orally through Tradition.

But didn't Jesus condemn Tradition?

Jesus condemned tradition only when it rendered God's Word void. Jesus said, "The scribes and the Pharisees occupy the chair of Moses. You must therefore do what they tell you and listen to what they say; but do not be guided by what they do; since they do not practice what they preach" (Matt. 23:2-3). He thereby affirmed Tradition. But Jesus rebukes the Pharisees when they neglect God's Word. "You pay your tithe of mint and dill and cummin and have neglected the weightier matters of the Law—justice, mercy, good faith! These you should have practiced, without neglecting the others" (Matt. 23:23). Notice that the other traditions and practices were not to be rejected.

The early Christians also had many traditions, that is, customs and practices, such as fasting on Wednesdays and Fridays and saying the Lord's Prayer three times a day (*The Teaching of the Twelve Apostles,* written about 120 A.D.). These traditions, or practices, can be changed with time, but Apostolic Tradition cannot change.

It is the deposit of Jesus' oral teachings as well as that of the Apostles. It is divine, not human. It is preserved in the Church by the Holy Spirit.

If Oral Tradition is authoritative, is it ever quoted in the Scripture?

Yes. Paul quotes an oral tradition that Jesus said, "There is more happiness in giving than in receiving" (Acts 20:35). This saying, which isn't found in the Gospels, must have been passed on to Paul through Oral Tradition. He likewise quotes early apostolic hymns in Eph. 5:14, Phil. 2:6-11, and 1 Tim. 3:15. The Gospels themselves are Oral Tradition written down (Lk. 1:1-4).

Where does Tradition get its authority?

From the Lord Jesus. Paul commends the faithful for following what was passed on, saying it was given "on the authority of the Lord Jesus" (1 Thess. 4:2).

Is Apostolic Tradition binding at all?

The Bible says, "As they visited one town after another, they passed on the decisions reached by the Apostles and elders in Jerusalem, with instructions to respect them" (Acts 16:4). The Apostles were given authority by Christ and spoke under the Spirit's anointing (see Acts 15:22-29). "These remained faithful to the teachings of the

Apostles, to the brotherhood, to the breaking of bread, and to the prayers" (Acts 2:42).

How do we know what is authentic Apostolic Tradition?

We believe by faith that Jesus preserves the Church in truth by the Holy Spirit. Jesus gave the Apostles authority to teach. The giving of the keys to Peter is a symbol for teaching authority (Matt. 16:18-19 and 28:18-20). A tradition is acknowledged by the Church as valid and apostolic because of its antiquity in the writings of the Church and because it does not contradict Scripture. Nothing in Apostolic Tradition will contradict Scripture.

Then all I need to do is follow the Bible?

Not exactly. The Bible itself tells us, "Stand firm, then, brothers, and keep the *traditions* that we taught you, whether by word of mouth or by letter." (2 Thess 2:15, italics added) Besides the written Word of God, therefore, *Oral Tradition* is also to be followed by Christians. Tradition helps us be "*fully* equipped" because we follow *all* that the Bible exhorts us to observe.

Can't anybody interpret the Bible?

Not exactly. All don't possess the same gift. Through Peter and the Apostles the keys of teaching authority were passed on to the succeeding leaders. Paul writes

to Timothy, "You have heard everything that I teach in public; hand it on to reliable people so that they in turn will be able to teach others" (2 Tim. 2:2). "Each one of us, however, has been given his own share of grace, given as Christ allotted it" (Eph. 4:7). Not everyone has the same gift. A special grace is conferred by Christ upon the bishops. They are the teachers.

Peter says about Paul's writing concerning the Lord's coming, "He always writes like this when he deals with this sort of subject, and this makes some points in his letter hard to understand; these are the points that uneducated and unbalanced people distort, in the same way as they distort the rest of Scripture—a fatal thing for them to do" (2 Pet. 3:16).

So the Bible isn't all that easy to interpret correctly, let alone to teach others what it means. Christians should read the Bible, but seek explanations from those who are trained and educated in the field, especially the bishops who are authoritative interpreters and teachers. Tradition is necessary to understand the Bible, for it allows us to see how the early Christians understood the Word of God.

Can there be new teachings?

No. Teachings might appear as new because they are more clearly and definitively stated, but the truth they present cannot be new in the sense of foreign to the deposit of Apostolic Tradition. Deeper insights can be made than were made in the early Church. As Jesus said, "I still have many things to say to you but they would be too much for you now. But when the Spirit of Truth comes he will lead you to the complete truth since he will not be speaking as from himself but will say only what he had learned; and he will tell you of things to come" (Jn. 16:12–13). The Church continues to grow in the understanding of the revelation made to her in Jesus Christ.

How is Tradition passed on?

Apostolic Tradition is passed on through apostolic succession, that is, the continuous line of bishops from the Apostles. It is expressed especially in the ecumenical councils and the common teaching of the Church Fathers.

Paul lays down this requirement for a bishop: "He must have a firm grasp of the unchanging message of the tradition, so that he can be counted on for both expounding the sound doctrine and refuting those who are against it" (Tit. 1:9)

Then all we need to do is read the early writings of the Church to discover Tradition?

Not exactly. Many documents now lost are mentioned in other documents that have survived.

So not all things believed in by the early Church during the first 300 years are mentioned in books from that period, but are contained in later writings. Also Scripture and Tradition continue to be understood in deeper and clearer ways as they are lived out in the lives of the faithful.

There is also a visible tradition besides the oral. "Do all the things that you learned from me and have been taught by me and have heard or seen that I do" (Phil. 4:9). Things like making the Sign of the Cross or prayerful meditation before ikons fall into this category. This visible tradition greatly influenced liturgy and spiritual practices.

Paul likewise says, "My brothers, be united in following my rule of life. Take as your models everyone who is already doing this and study them as you used to study us" (Phil. 3:17). Besides studying the Bible, Christians should study the Tradition of the Church lived out by the People of God.

But is it necessary that I believe in Tradition?

Jesus Himself teaches that we must follow the Apostles and their teachings when He said, "Anyone who listens to you listens to Me; anyone who rejects you rejects Me, and those who reject Me reject the One who sent Me" (Lk. 10:16). The Christian is "part of a building that has the Apostles and prophets for its foundations, and Christ Jesus Himself for the main cornerstone" (Eph. 2:20). To be founded in Christ one should also be grounded in Apostolic Tradition. Paul goes on to say that the mystery of salvation was revealed primarily to the Apostles and prophets (Eph. 3:5). Authentic faith in Jesus calls one to follow the Apostolic Teaching.

How are we to view those who reject Apostolic Tradition?

"In the name of the Lord Jesus Christ, we urge you, brothers, to keep away from any of the brothers who refuse to work or to live according to the traditions we passed on to you" (2 Thess. 3:6). This does not mean that we should not associate with other Christians who reject Apostolic Tradition, but we should be careful not to accept their biblical interpretations if they contradict Apostolic Tradition.

The Bible itself is the product of the living experience of faith in God. The Gospels are no less than oral teaching written down. The oral word and Tradition preceded the written word, the fruit of that living experience. God continues to dwell in his people and shape them.

The Catholic Church strives to be faithful to this living experience of the Bible and Tradition. She still hears resounding the words of the Apostle, "You have done well in remembering me so constantly and in maintaining the traditions just as we passed them on to you" (1 Cor. 11:2). ✤

SIGNS OF THE TIMES

From a church bulletin: "Easter Sunday will begin with a Yawn Service at 6:00 A.M." Thomas LaMance.

*

In a health food co-op: "You think beef is too high? Cigarettes cost $11.99 per pound." Nancy Carr.

*

From a marble table-top manufacturer: "We're marbelous. Don't take us for granite." Dolly Bliss.

*

In a donut and coffee shop: "No slam-dunking." Frank Tyger.

Jesus Never Said I Told You So

He had lots of opportunities, though

By SISTER M. MELANNIE SVOBODA, S.N.D.
April 1981

THE GOSPELS record many words spoken by Jesus, but there are four words never ascribed to Him. They are "I told you so." I think this gives us an insight into the way Christ dealt with people.

When someone says to us, "I told you so!" they are really telling us three things. First, that they possess superior knowledge and wisdom, which circumstances have just clearly shown. Second, they are reminding us of our own lack of knowledge and wisdom. And third, they are saying that we did not trust them and, obviously, we should have.

That Jesus possessed superior knowledge and wisdom is without question. And people around Him frequently gave evidence of their own stupidity or foolishness. Their repeated lack

_____

Reprinted with permission of the author.

of faith in Him was equally apparent. Yet Jesus never said, "I told you so."

What did He say instead? Four incidents in his life can show us.

One is the raising of the daughter of Jairus. Jairus came to Jesus and asked Him to cure his daughter. Jesus went with him to the house, but when they got there the daughter was already dead. Then Jesus said, "The child is not dead—she is only sleeping." The Gospel tells us that the crowd, upon hearing these words, "started making fun" of Jesus. And we all know what happened next. Jesus raised the girl from the dead, and instead of saying to the crowd, "I told you so," and said simply, "Give her something to eat."

Jesus was similarly derided when He approached the tomb

containing the four-day-old corpse of his friend Lazarus. But dramatically He ordered Lazarus to "come forth," and when Lazarus came staggering out of the tomb still partially bound by the burial cloths, what did Jesus say? Not "I told you so." Rather, "Untie him and let him go."

The occasion when Jesus could have used the four words most effectively was after his own resurrection. The scene is a familiar one: the Apostles were cowering in fear and disillusionment in the upper room. All of a sudden, Jesus appeared in their midst and said, "Peace be with you. As the Father sent Me, so I send you."

Perhaps the one person Jesus would have been most justified in telling "I told you so" was Peter. At the Last Supper, Peter boasted of his love for Jesus when he said, "If all of these betray You, I will not." Shortly after, Peter does betray Jesus, not once, but three times. But when Peter encounters the risen Christ on the shore in those early morning hours, Jesus says only, "Feed my sheep."

There is a common element in all of these responses of Jesus: "Give her something to eat," "Untie him and let him go," "As the Father sent me, so I send you," "Feed my sheep." In each of them, Jesus is giving someone a job to do. If we reflect on the psychology here, we see his profound sensitivity.

In each of these instances, someone demonstrates in an unquestionable way his stupidity, his foolishness, his lack of faith in Jesus' words. As a result, the person's self-esteem is very low. Saying "I told you so" would only add to his feeling of worthlessness. But by giving that person a job to do, Jesus gives him an opportunity to rebuild his self-esteem. By making the person focus on another's need (a little girl's hunger, a flock without a shepherd), Jesus subtly prevents him from dwelling on his own inadequacies.

Furthermore, by giving the scoffer or the braggart a job to do, Jesus demonstrates his own trust in that person, despite his or her lack of trust in Him. Jesus says, "I trust you so much that I am giving you a responsibility, a job to do." And what is that job? It can be as simple as giving a little girl something to eat or as monumental as becoming a chief shepherd of the Church.

As followers of Jesus, we can remove the words "I told you so" from our vocabulary. And we can get rid of the *attitude* behind the words. As Christians, we must be about the work of "building up" people, rather than tearing them down. As imitators of the compassionate Jesus, we must say to others (as Jesus says to us again and again): "I love you so much, I trust you still." ✣

THE PERFECT ASSIST

Getting a wrong number is a minor nuisance for most people. But because I am blind, it can be a big problem for me. One Monday I needed to call a tool rental company to reserve a rotary tiller so that my husband could prepare the garden for fall planting that evening. I would plant on Tuesday; Wednesday we were to leave for vacation.

My husband had read me the rental company's telephone number from a billboard several days earlier when we had been out for a walk with the children. I had stored it neatly and efficiently in my memory—or so I thought.

Confidently I dialed 825-3223. "Hello. Is this the tool rental store?"

A woman's pleasant voice informed me that, though I had dialed correctly, I had not reached the rental company. My heart sank. I didn't want to call directory assistance and say, "Hello. I don't know the name of the place, but there's a tool rental on such-and-such a street and I need its telephone number." I could easily pack up my babies and walk to the billboard, but what good would that do? If I didn't reserve a tiller, my husband couldn't prepare the garden and I couldn't plant before returning from vacation. And that would be too late.

But what was this I was hearing at the other end of the telephone line? "Do you know the name of the place?" the friendly voice was asking. "I could look it up for you."

"Well," I said hesitantly. "I do know what street it's on."

My anonymous friend chatted comfortably as she unhurriedly leafed through the thin pages of the directory. After perhaps ten minutes of light conversation, she cheerfully announced that she had found the number.

"Here it is!" she said, with a note of triumph in her voice that indicated that together we had achieved a major goal. "You were just one digit away."

I reserved the tiller, and my garden was planted on time. A trivial problem—a wrong number—but the simple kindness of one woman transformed an ordinary Monday into a memorable day. Perhaps the nicest thing was that she didn't know I am blind. She helped me in that matter-of-fact fashion in which one of God's children lends aid to another.

Deborah Kendrick.

What the Blind Man Did Not Say

When you want to ask Jesus for help,
remember the faith of Bartimaeus and take the
direct approach

By MARK HILLMER

March 1983

TO MEET JESUS was to know that something was afoot. To see Him pass was to sense, if you had the faith to sense it, that your chance-in-a-lifetime was passing by. The blind Bartimaeus was one who seized his chance (Mark 10:46–52).

Bartimaeus, of course, didn't see Jesus pass. He only heard of his coming. In his darkness he listened well to the reports about this rabbi from Nazareth. As Jesus' arrival was announced— Bartimaeus could hear the bustle, the gathering crowd— his heart leapt within him. He cried out for an audience with the traveling preacher. Overcoming initial timidity and then opposition, he heard himself summoned.

Reprinted with permission of the author.

What plausible responses could Bartimaeus have made?

And Jesus said to him, "What do you want Me to do for you?"

And the blind man said to Him, "Begging your pardon, Sir; You will forgive my audacity. I have heard much about You. They say You do miracles. I myself could use one. But I wonder. I have also heard— indeed have been taught—that the last time there was anything like a significant number of miracles around here was in the time of Elijah and Elisha. That was a long time ago. And people were credulous then. They believed almost anything. We've become wiser since then—and sadder. The official word is that there are no more prophets. Well, it's been nice chatting with You. Good luck, whatever You're doing. You sure do have a reputation."

But Bartimaeus did not say that.

And Jesus said to him, "What do you want Me to do for you?"

And the blind man said to Him: "Nothing! If You are truly the Son of God, You would know what I want without asking me. I don't feel I should have to get specific about my personal needs."

But Bartimaeus did not say that.

And Jesus said to him, "What do you want Me to do for you?"

And the blind man said to Him, "Nothing, really. I thought for a moment that I wanted to ask You for my sight. But on second thought, I feel that would be very selfish of me. I know enough about true religion to realize that I must stop thinking about myself and become more concerned about others. So, never mind. Excuse the interruption."

But Bartimaeus did not say that.

And Jesus said to him, "What do you want Me to do for you?"

And the blind man said to

Him, "Oh, nothing. On reflection I realize that You may not be able to—or may not want to—heal me. Frankly, I'm afraid to risk asking You, for fear of being disappointed. I guess I'd rather not push it. Let's just leave it be."

But Bartimaeus did not say that.

And Jesus said to him, "What do you want Me to do for you?"

And the blind man said to Him, "Oh, nothing, I guess. As I was stumbling up here— (thanks, anyway, for calling to me, that was thoughtful of You)—it occurred to me that I really don't want to see. I've grown accustomed to the dark. I'm afraid the light of sight would frighten me. You see, I've learned to cope. Thanks anyway."

But Bartimaeus did not say that.

And Jesus said to him, "What do you want Me to do for you?"

And the blind man said to Him, "Nothing, Lord. Forget it. What if You heal me and not others? You should have seen— did You?—how angry they got back there when I merely started calling for You. If now I do receive my sight, think of how many more angry people and jealous blind people there will be. Why, they'd be angry with You, too. Some would be upset with You because You did heal me, others would be angry because You didn't heal them. We'd better think of them. We'd better forget the whole thing."

But Bartimaeus did not say that.

A nd Jesus said to him, "What do you want Me to do for you?"

And the blind man said to Him, "Master, I realize that faith is far more important than mere physical sight. So I do not ask for my sight. I ask that my faith be increased."

But Bartimaeus did not say that.

The blind man said, "Master, let me receive my sight."

And Jesus said to him, "Go your way; your faith has made you well."

And immediately he received his sight and followed Him on the way. ❖

THE PERFECT ASSIST

Years ago when we had just moved to Seattle, our shaggy little dog got out one night and was instantly hit by a car on busy Rainier Avenue. A neighbor saw it happen and ran to tell us. The dog was knocked unconscious. We were sure he was dead, but our ten-year-old son picked him up in his arms and carried him to the car. My husband drove him to the nearest vet's office while I called, praying the vet would be there. It was so important that the dog live. Our son had just left all of his friends a thousand miles away. The dog was his only friend in this new town.

The veterinarian did answer the telephone and promised to run right over to his office to meet them. The dog was alive, and stayed in the animal hospital for seven days. The X-rays revealed a broken tail, but internal and head injuries seemed evident when the dog refused either to walk or eat. Daily this kindly vet called my son to report his condition, and finally told me that we should bring him home.

I had dreaded the day when we had to talk money. Seven days in the hospital, X-rays, and all the personal care . . . it would cost far more than we could afford because of our moving expenses.

"Five dollars will cover it," the vet said, smiling at my son holding the dog who was frantically licking his face, and trying to wag his broken tail.

Because of the fine care and generosity of this compassionate man, the dog was eating and running and jumping again within days. And our son made the transition to new friends more easily.   Jessie Bruntsch.

The Kitchen Where Our Parents Taught Us Prayer

A good, warm place to know a loving God

By SISTER MARY TERESE DONZE, A.S.C.
December 1979

I FIRST LEARNED TO PRAY in a kitchen. It was a practical arrangement. The kitchen was the only place in our house that was heated in the winter, and in the kitchen Mama could help with the prayers while she darned our socks and stockings; electricity was too expensive to light up more rooms than were necessary. Besides, the kitchen sights, smells, and sounds were attuned to the heart, and the people gathered there were family.

A big range dominated our

Reprinted with permission of the author.

kitchen, and threw out a welcoming warmth that took in the whole room. The occasional blasts of cold air that rushed in when someone opened an outside door never won out against the heat of the old cookstove. If anything, the chill drafts created an exhilarating freshness that intensified the warmth and made prayers, meals, anything that went on there a delight.

Each evening the mingled odors of supper hung around the kitchen like the memory of a welcomed guest who had come and departed. Smoke from Papa's pipe blended with the smell of food, and at times, when one of us had a cold and was in for a chest rub, the pungent odor of turpentine and goose grease joined in. Incense *domestique.*

The singing of the teakettle on the back of the range, the shifting of the burning coals as they settled deeper into the grate, the soughing of the draft through a long, black stovepipe were like background music, peaceful, reassuring.

Sights, smells, sounds, they all helped. But it was mostly the family presence that made prayer in the kitchen so good a thing. An older sister and my two older brothers sat at the table doing homework. While Mama helped me and my younger brother with our prayers, they whispered, giggled, got into arguments. Occasionally Papa had to "Ahem!" them into silence, but the distractions were a happy part of the total setting.

While we were small, Mama helped us with our prayers. My youngest brother prayed first. Scrubbed pink and smelling fresh from Sweetheart soap, he climbed onto his high chair and folded his small fists against the stiff chairback. All day long he had torn about the house, playing himself out; by prayertime he was groggy with sleep. Mama had to support him with her arm, and even so, as he babbled his half dozen words to God, his soft little body kept sagging.

When he had been put to bed, it was my turn to pray. Dressed in a long gown, I knelt near the range, my toes bared to its heat. Most of my prayers were in rhyme. The rhythm of the words, more than their meaning, was my worship then. It made possible my speaking to God the only bit of German I ever learned, *"Ich bin klein, mein Herz ist rein . . . "* and only vaguely wonder why God should be concerned about "mine hairs."

I was not yet six when I learned to drop the dramatics from my prayer. My sister had taught me a prayer-poem from her reader. Next to the poem in the book was a picture of the holy child Samuel. Clad in a skimpy white night shirt and squatting on his heels, the boy prophet knelt with his arms crossed over his heart and his eyes lifted toward some unseen source of light.

Once at prayertime it occurred to me to be like Samuel. Straightway I unpropped my hands, pressed them over my chest, and swayed back onto my heels. My eyes were raised, not to a source of light, but to the thing directly within my new line of vision, the summer "Ice" card hanging from a large nail above the kitchen sink. I was slowly settling my weight and staring up at the numbers on the card when I heard Mama. "Kneel up straight, Terese."

I was off my heels in a hurry, but I was piqued. Couldn't Mama see I was like Samuel? But then I watched her praying. She never so much as raised her eyes from the stocking she was darning. I got the message. Prayertime was not a time for pretending. You were real with God, and that did not include being anybody but yourself.

When I was several years older and could stay up later, I became part of the family praying together. By then I no longer knelt on a chair. I took my place with Papa and Mama and the others, kneeling on the kitchen floor with the seat of a chair to support my elbows.

At that time I passed through another prayer-learning phase, one in which the kitchen environment became my undoing. As a part of the family, I had been given my turn in leading the prayers. Impressed by the dignity of my appointment, I performed with proportionate propriety—at first. But as evening after evening went by, the relaxing therapy of the cozy kitchen atmosphere became too much for me. I began to punctuate the prayers with yawns, stifled a bit in the beginning, but later fully indulged. Soon I was yawning audibly at regular intervals, ending in a complete fadeout of the prayer for a moment.

I had gone on like this for some time when one evening Papa cut in on the prayers abruptly. "Stop that yawning, Terese. This is a time for prayer."

I was taken aback. Stark silence reigned a moment, then someone giggled softly, and I took up where the yawn had given pause. But Papa had made his point. Now I never hear anyone yawn during prayer without hearing Papa calling me to order.

One Saturday morning when I was 11, a new element entered my prayer life. Mama was wetmopping the linoleum. I was sitting to the side, peeling potatoes for the noon meal and chattering endlessly. Mama seemed to be listening as she pushed the heavy mop back and forth. Suddenly she stopped and looked at me.

"Terese, do you ever think of keeping quiet for just a little while and praying as you work?" Her voice was gentle as always. I looked up. Our eyes met.

"Why . . . no, Mama," I faltered.

Mama went on mopping and I continued with the potatoes. I tried to pick up the easy chatter, but now only to hide my feelings. Something had happened to me as Mama spoke. Until then it had never occurred to me that anyone spoke to God while mopping floors or peeling potatoes.

Over the years I have read many books on prayer. I have yet to find a prayer pattern that differs essentially from my kitchen experience. Today no one is sitting at a nearby table giggling as I pray, but I have corresponding distractions. I am no longer tempted to put the Samuel image into my prayer, but occasionally the torpor of routine threatens, and I need to be jolted into a new awareness of the continuous presence of God.

From time to time, too, as I peel away layers of self-deception, I am given fresh insights that make what went before seem elemental. And over all linger memories of my first conscious prayer, and of the kitchen magic that made God seem warm, loving, and approachable. ✼

PEOPLE ARE LIKE THAT

During the last months of the 2nd World War, our outfit was bivouacked in a small Italian village along the Allied supply route. One day I was standing on the main street watching the truckloads of American GI's rumble through the town. Because of bomb damage, they were forced to slow to a crawl at one intersection, and as each truck passed, the soldiers would throw down C rations, gum, and candy to the village kids.

As I watched, I noticed that one of the kids, a year or two older than the others and quite a bit taller, seemed to grab much more than his share of the stuff raining down from the trucks. He would scramble around greedily for his loot, then cram it into the pockets of his ragged, ill-fitting coat.

"That one knows how to look after himself," I thought cynically. "This sure is a rotten war."

When the trucks passed, I turned down a side street and made for our company headquarters. Suddenly a small bundle of rags came tearing round the corner, passing me in a rush. It was the kid who had been getting more than his share. He turned into an empty lot, shouting something in Italian. Curious, I followed him.

As I peered over a pile of rubble, there he was, surrounded by a dozen children much smaller than he, dividing the food he had picked up in the street. "Maybe," I said to myself as I moved silently away, "this isn't such a bad war after all."   John L. Powers.

My Mother's Rosary, My Father's Belt

Both taught me unforgettable lessons

By THOMAS F. KELLY
May 1977

FOR MANY YEARS, my parents were convinced that there was some mystical connection between the seat of my pants and the memory section of my brain. Books on child psychology were not exactly evident in our household. If my parents had owned one, I am sure they would have used it to give their hands or the hairbrush a rest.

Mom and Dad were not cruel, but they were dealing with someone who was convinced that he was much smarter than they. So they had to be tough as nails and one step ahead of me all the time. There was never any question in my mind but that my mother had eyes in the back of her head, and that she could really hear the grass growing.

I was at least 12 before I realized that she did not actually

Reprinted with permission of author.

sleep in her hat and house coat. For that was the only way I saw her, from the first whiff of fresh bread in the morning until the last Hail Mary of the evening Rosary.

There was no time of the day I liked more than the time after supper when we prayed the Rosary. There was a wonderfully warm closeness about the family then which was special to all of us. The only light in the room came from the turf and logs spluttering in the fireplace, and the flames sent shadows dancing across the walls and ceiling. My introduction to meditation came from watching those shadows and imagining the mysteries of the Rosary on the kitchen walls.

Mother demanded attentiveness. It was not uncommon to hear, "Hail, Mary, full of grace,

79

pay attention now, the Lord is with Thee. . . . "

Saturday night was the longest Rosary of the week. It was then that Mother added her special intentions, or "trimmin's," as we called them; we prayed for everything from Aunt Nellie's lumbago to "may Joe Doyle's goat give more milk." During the week we groaned loudly every time some pious soul asked mother to remember a special intention. She did not shortchange anyone. Very special intentions rated a decade; ordinary requests received at least three Hail Marys. Aching knees did not impress Mother. She knew that none of us had any place to go in a hurry anyway.

After the Rosary we had mugs of hot sweet tea or cocoa, with generous helpings of home baked bread. This was the prelude to an hour of story-telling before bedtime. Ghost stories were the most popular, and although I was often scared going to bed, I never missed a single word of them.

Mother prayed for us as hard as she and Dad worked for us. Dad did so much for me, and he was gone before I was old enough to repay him. He was strict on obedience; he spoke of the fallen angels as if he had witnessed the entire scene. Indeed the virtue of obedience, combined with my love of trains, set me on a collision course with the great leather belt he wore around his waist.

We lived within sight and sound of the most picturesque railroad station in all Ireland. The signal cabin, the station master's house, and the one waiting room were all whitewashed and had green trimmed doors and windows. The platforms were gravelled and caressed by flower beds, and only the trains and passengers betrayed the secret that it was a station at all.

One of the engine drivers, Mr. Gunning, and his fireman, Mr. Flynn, lived in our town. They were always on at least one of the four daily trains that ran through the station, and would wave to me as I stood on the grassy bank near our house.

After waving back I would sprint to the station before the engine was uncoupled from the train, and my friends would lift me up into the cabin with them. The engine had to go to a siding, where, with much huffing and puffing, my heroes would turn it on the massive turntable. We would then steam north of the station before backing up to the front of the train for the trip back to the city.

Most people in our town set their clocks by the arrival of the train. The most important timecheck of the day was at 6 P.M., when the last train from the city steamed under Church Hill bridge to mingle its sounds with the Angelus Bell. What a grand sight it was to see the train pass, driver and fireman bareheaded to honor Mary.

The Angelus Bell had more than devotional significance in my life. It also meant one hour to go before supper and Rosary time. My parents would not have accepted any excuse for lateness.

So I must have acted under the influence of steam, smoke, and oil on the night I planned a way to get a longer ride in the engine cabin.

It was surprisingly simple. All I had to do was ride the train to the city, and then surprise my friends. They would surely allow me to ride home with them on the engine.

They were surprised indeed to see me, but hardly as surprised as I was to discover that there was no train home until the next morning. There was a bus, however, and my friends paid the fare and told the conductor where to let me off.

My parents were strangely calm when I arrived home at 10 P.M. A search had been organized for me on the railroad and beach and in the hills behind our house. One of my uncles had to go to the church and toll the bell three times to call it off.

My father postponed for a day further mention of the episode. His sense of fairness would not permit him to act in the heat of high emotion. Before the assembled household next evening I told my story. I was lectured by my father, and when the punishment was announced I should have had the wisdom to keep my mouth shut.

"You will not go near the station for a whole week," he said.

"I will," I heard myself say. It was too late. The words could not be taken back.

"Go to your room," my father said, and came in five minutes later. The belt was off, and no cleaner could have done a more thorough dusting job on the seat of my pants. I had asked for it, and there was little use crying.

The next time I saw the belt was the next morning. It was partly charred, at the back of the blazing logs in the fireplace where Dad had thrown it. At the Rosary that night, in the firelit room, I saw tears glistening in his eyes. I reached out and took his hand, and he held it for the longest time.

In the remaining years before God called him, we grew very close to each other. I never gave him cause to punish me again. No matter where we were, all it took was a train whistle to set the pair of us laughing.   ✳

The Documents in the Case

Grandpa's '24 Chevy

His accounting ledger tells a tale of frustration leavened possibly by a small romance

By MARGARET H. LOUPY
December 1975, condensed from the *Lackawanna Independent**

A YELLOW SNAPSHOT of a shiny black automobile, square as a box, slid from the brittle pages of my grandfather's ledger, "Accts. 1924, 1907 Washington Blvd." As I studied the picture, a dozen memories crossed my mind. An unsmiling Grandpa, erect in his high-collared shirt and narrow, black suit, held open the rear door of his newly acquired "Chivolette" like St. Peter attending the gates of heaven.

I could hear him speaking, "Come girls, mustn't be late on

*This article © 1974 by the *Lackawanna Independent, Yesterday's Magazette.* Independent Publishing Company. Reprinted with permission.

the first day of school. Grandpa drove all the way from Chicago to take you in his new car. Not every girl gets a ride to school."

"But does Daddy have to take our pictures?" from me, an impatient ten-year-old.

"Of course, honey. Doesn't he always on the first day of school?"

There was the flurry of setting up the camera on its tripod. Dad kept popping out from under the black cloth to adjust the three spindly legs, and to rearrange us, while Grandpa removed a speck from the windshield with saliva and a grimy handkerchief. We froze to the count of five, sighed with relief at having recorded one more moment in family history, and began the lurching, perilous, six-block journey to school.

But why was this particular snapshot in the account book instead of Grandpa's family album? For a clue I leafed through crumbling blue and red-lined pages that were filled with the daily problems of operating his rooming house.

The first few months were a dreary list of expenses: calcimine, wallpaper, bedbug powder, underwear, light bulbs, gas bills, and a constant "ad for housekeeper." Then, during April, alien items appeared.

Reading through the next nine months, I discovered entries which told a tale of frustration and possibly a small romance, a hitherto unknown segment of Grandpa's lonely existence.

It all began innocently:

1924 April

Repair garage roof	$14.00
Cement alley	12.00
New garage doors	70.00
Garage lock	2.89

Since, according to receipts, his rooms rented for $8 and $10 a month, the above represented a tremendous outlay to the frugal man. However, the last item in April explained his extravagance: "Ad for auto—$2.70."

Then, on May 1st: "Chevrolet Sedan—$550."

How Grandpa's blue eyes must have gleamed as he made that entry! And what fun he must have had shopping for the accessories listed during the next weeks: a rubber mat, auto robe, vase-and-flower, auto fringe (whatever that was), chamois, and a new suit, shirt, and tie.

His final expense in May:

Auto license	$3.00
Auto insurance	34.00

And then his troubles began.

June

Repair garage door	$5.00
Auto repairs	6.00
Auto sill	.50
Carfare (4 @ 5¢)	.20

During July "gas and oil—$1.20" appeared four times, indicating increased activity. But more problems soon arose.

July

Repair garage door	$8.50
Black auto paint	.75
Auto from ditch	5.00
New wheels (2)	16.00
Carfare (5 @ 5¢)	.25
Tow line	1.00
Chicago Auto Club	11.00

The last item probably resulted from pressure applied by my father. But it didn't stem the flood of minor annoyances during August.

Repair neighbor's garage	
door	$12.50
Auto repair	20.00
Black auto paint	.75
Tyre and tube	15.00
Wheel rim	2.00

Toward the end of August came a flurry of shopping. Grandpa planned a break from the aggravations of his rooming house.

Auto running board box	$3.15
Auto gas stove	6.00
Fry pan for auto	1.18
Pocket map	1.00
Fishing pole	1.75

September began with four days bracketed together, probably the Labor Day weekend; and for Grandpa, apparently, a very special weekend.

Aug. 30
Gas and oil	$1.20
Food	1.45
Fox Lake camp ground:	
(3 nights @ 50¢)	1.50
Dance	.75

Aug. 31
Dance (2 @ 75¢)	$1.50
Ice cream sodas (2 @ 25¢)	.50

Sept. 1
Rowboat	$1.25
Corsage	.75
Dinner (2 @ $1.50 & tip)	3.25
Dance (2 @ 75¢)	1.50

Sept. 2
Breakfast (2 @ 65¢)	$1.30

Souvenir bracelet	1.32
Souvenir ashtray	.73
Gas and oil to Chicago	1.15

Home once again, Grandpa fell back into his old routine.

Repair neighbor's steps	$22.50
Auto repairs	13.00
New clutch	5.25
Carfare (7 @ 5¢)	.35

October
Repair garage door	$5.00
Auto repairs	3.00
Headlights	1.82
Auto insurance	35.00

November
Repair brick wall	$15.00
Black auto paint	.75
New gas cap	.65
Auto battery	13.60

In December, misfortunes followed one another like a series of blizzards:

Repair garage door	$5.00
Repair brake	5.35
Black auto paint	.75
Tear down busted	
brick wall	5.00
Auto fender	5.50
New rear axle	13.55
Doctor	2.00
Arnica and iodine	.45
Dentist pull 2 teeth	2.00

The old man's feisty spirit collapsed. Two pitiful entries brought the glorious adventure to an abrupt close:

Auto for sale ad $2.65
Garage for rent sign .20

I recalled Mother saying that Christmas: "Grandpa phoned from the Aurora Elgin station. I do hope he wore his rubbers so he won't slip on the ice." And Dad sighed, "Thank goodness he's on foot again. A 70-year-old man has no business driving a car."

My eyes returned to the yellowed photo. Dear, spunky, little close-mouthed Grandpa. Did the lady at Fox Lake blush with pleasure over that 75¢ corsage? Did she smile coquettishly from her seat in the rowboat, trailing her hand in the water like the Gibson Girls? Did she vow to think of you whenever she wore the bracelet?

Now I know why you scolded when I broke the ugly Fox Lake ashtray and why we found it, years later, carefully mended and hidden among your handkerchiefs.

Did that three-day romance compensate for all the sadness of your being too old to drive? I'd like to think so. ∞

THE PERFECT ASSIST

It was Christmas Eve, 1956. Snow was falling outside the three-room farmhouse where our family of nine lived. I was five years old and so excited I couldn't sleep. As I listened quietly for sounds of Santa Claus, I heard instead my mother's sobs.

I crept into mama's bed and asked what was wrong. Mama whispered that she was crying because Daddy wasn't coming home for Christmas. He couldn't leave his job in the city. That meant we wouldn't be getting any presents this year. There would be no tree or Christmas dinner.

We were very poor, and the only black family for at least 100 miles. Some of our neighbors had made it clear that we weren't wanted, but we stayed anyway in hopes of building up a homestead. My father tried to find work nearby, but when nothing turned up, he had to go to the city. This Christmas his foreman had told him to work on Christmas day . . . so that was that.

Mama and I cried ourselves to sleep in each other's arms. We awoke around 7:00 to the incredible sound of Christmas carols. A group of about 25 young people were singing to us in the snow. After a few more songs, they shouted, "Merry Christmas, Harris family," and offered us armloads of presents and food. Mama was crying again, but this time for joy. I later found out that those dear young people had come to us from a local Catholic church. Thank God for Christian goodwill. C. Harris.

December Cards

Christmas is the season for some families to issue their annual report

By RALPH REPPERT

December 1969, condensed from the Baltimore *Sun Magazine**

YESTERDAY the mailman came around with this year's first December card.

No, I don't mean Christmas card. I mean December card. The two are as different as chalk and cheese. The December card comes in as though it were a Christmas card, but basically it is not. It is a chummy, chatty annual report, a sort of there's-Christmas-every-day-at-our-house.

It is aimed at cheering you up the same way one woman might cheer up another by saying, "But let's talk about *you* for a change. What do *you* think of my new mink?"

Some December cards are written on the backs of Christmas cards. Some are scribbled around the margin of a special Christmas picture taken last April in front of a $60-a-day hotel in the Bahamas. Often they are miniature family newspapers.

All have one thing in common: they make the recipient feel as if he had shown up an hour late and a buck short.

Our first December card this year came from Charlie and Polly Wickham, who live somewhere on Long Island. Their little family paper was a mimeograph job, red and green inks, headed *The Wickham Gazette.*

The lead item was a column called *Polly's Ponderings.* "Things so hectic ... an 18-room house is really just too much, what with only two inside servants and a yard man ... and just getting back from Europe (loved that month in Spain) in time to pack up Darlene and get her off to Smith.

"But really shouldn't complain. Charles has had five promotions in three years ... and getting to a point now where he

*This article © 1968 by the *Baltimore Sun Magazine.* Reprinted with permission.

can delegate work to some of the junior vice presidents and spend more time with us on the new boat (48 feet, and a positive dream).

"Charlie-Junior made the dean's list again, and Little Bill got into the National Scholastic society and was offered three scholarships. He's inclined to VPI, although MIT would be so much closer to home.

"Darlene all in a dither since the student body at Exeter voted her their Queen of Charm and Beauty. She's been dating a boy there who, although horribly rich, is such a darling child."

There are columns by the whole family. In *Charlie's Chatter* we learn that Polly (who is 54 and wears a size 22) "is getting prettier every day and as wonderful as ever . . . never would be taken for the grandmother of the most beautiful baby girl in the world."

In *Junior's Jottings* we see that "dad is still wearing the same size suit he wore in college . . . a

real swinger and probably the only executive in town who drives a fire-truck-red Cadillac convertible . . . a touch of gray at the temples, which makes him look like Jim Stewart, but still brimming with enough pizazz to win the squash tournament."

And in *Dashes by Darlene* and *Little Bill's Corner* and in bits and dabs and some handwritten footnotes to give the message a personal touch, we learn that:

Little Bill, who makes $200 a week on his paper route, was named most valuable player by his baseball team.

The Wickhams met some people in London, name of Frick, who think they might know my boss.

"I'd really better finish off now (Polly's handwriting) because the yardman is waiting in the jeep to run this letter down to our mailbox.

"P.S. If you get to the President's ball, be sure to look us up." ∾

FISH STORIES

A fisherman was lugging a fish twice his size along the beach when he met another fisherman with a half-dozen small fish on his stringer.

"Howdy," said the first fisherman, dropping his huge fish and waiting for a comment.

His fellow fisherman stared and stared, then said calmly, "Just caught the one, eh?"   Henry E. Leabo.

My Sister's Diary: 1937-1945

It showed me a witty, romantic young woman
I had barely known

By PAUL SALSINI

June 1983, condensed from *Milwaukee Journal/Insight**

ONE OF THE little books is black and her name is engraved on the cover. The newer one is brown. The bindings are torn, and the locks are broken.

They were found only recently among the jewelry and letters and photo albums, stored in a cedar chest until the time came when others had to sort things out.

When my niece pressed the two little books into my hands on a recent visit, I didn't want to take them. And then I didn't want to read them. And I didn't think I'd be writing about them.

But I don't feel I'm intruding into my sister's privacy in sharing her diaries. Rose obviously was recording history. I have

always said that she should have been the journalist in the family. And I am not including the truly personal parts.

Rose was the eldest, and I the youngest, of the six children. She was 18 when I was born. Our two sisters were in high school, our two brothers in grade school. Our dad was on WPA (Works Project Administration) work, mostly road construction as I recall, and our mother kept house.

We lived in Hubbell, a copper mining town of 1,000 in Upper Michigan where the winters are legendary. One of the earliest entries says: "Because of ice blockade, water must be boiled ... Snow is 6 feet high along roadway."

I suspect that Rose received her first five-year diary for Christmas in 1936, when she was

---

*This article © 1982 by the *Milwaukee Journal*. Reprinted with permission.

*This article © 1982 by the *Milwaukee Journal*. Reprinted with permission.

88

19, for she started keeping the diary on Jan. 1, 1937. The books allowed only four lines each day, and Rose did not miss a day for more than eight years.

Because of our age difference, I don't think I ever got to know my eldest sister. We tend, many of us, to place people at certain age levels, and Rose, to me, was always about 40, a wife and mother. I have discovered in her diaries a person I never knew before, a young person.

It was both amusing and wonderful to find entries like these, written when she was 19: "Went to skating rink. Nobody interesting there."

"Boy, can I tap dance! Whew!"

"Met 3 Tech kids. One real cute."

"Went for a ride with S. & S. The sheriff stopped and wanted to see Sep's license. Whew!! Got a date for Monday?"

And I love this entry: "Went for a ride with a kid from Calumet. Got his comb. Nice & friendly. But he got sick. Sent him home."

This was, of course, in the Depression. Rose had a low-paying clerical job at the high school and took part in federally sponsored National Youth Administration projects. She also did odd jobs: "Typed stencils for Mr. Graham. Lions club. $1. It all helps."

I discovered, from reading her diaries, that we must have been poor. At one point, she reported that our dad was laid off and only one sister was working. I don't remember feeling poor then. Whatever our condition was, it was the same for everyone.

I found a girl growing up. She made fudge and played the piano, went to dances and visited friends.

"Claire, Bernice, Marie, Cecilia, and I went to Irene's. Irene & I did the Shag. It's fun."

She loved to dance and went frequently to the Amphidrome (locally known as the "Drome") in Houghton, Mich. She took books out of the library and read two or three a week. She devoured movie magazines. And the radio was a big part of her life.

"Listened to the 'Hour of Charm.' I like soothing music."

There may have been some family disputes over the programs, however: "Can never hear anything on the radio; Dora (our sister) always has the baseball game on."

Occasionally, Rose longed for a more exciting life: "Gosh this town is dead. Not a thing to do."

I found a sister's perspective of our family's life in a time I can barely remember. Our sisters, Arlene and Dora, graduated from high school and I started kindergarten. One brother, Robert, went into the Civilian Conservation Corps and then into the Navy; the other brother, Louis, went into the Navy, too.

Even our dad had to register for the draft. Mother painted the kitchen white and we got a new rug for the dining room. We acquired two cats, which Rose named Shorthand and Bookkeeping.

Our parents celebrated their 25th anniversary: "About 25 people for dinner. Received some beautiful gifts. I made the hiballs, my my. Jean, Bern, Ar, Dora, and I did the work—more fun."

I had heard that Rose was embarrassed by having a baby brother born when she was in high school. But she certainly was proud of me. OK, I admit I cried when I read this of me, at age 2: "Gee he's cute and smarter than a whip."

And sometimes there were tragedies: "Eddie Dragovich was killed in a mine accident. It's terrible. We had planned to go to a dance and carnival."

I found a young woman, in an isolated region, intrigued by the events, big and small, in the world. After the Duke of Windsor's abdication, she wanted to go to George VI's coronation. She was surprised by Charles Lindbergh's pacifism.

I found a feminist. She was devastated by Amelia Earhart's disappearance at sea: "July 22, 1937: America's first great woman aviatrix perhaps lost in the depth of the sea will not be lost but more deeply imprinted on minds of American youth. Who can say but that if it weren't for women like Amelia, we would be a slow-progressing nation?"

The shadows of war begin to stretch over the diaries early ("Oct. 15, 1937: There is talk of war everywhere.") and finally envelop every part of Rose's life. Through the war years, there is almost a daily report on a battle or a crisis. She commented that Stalin was a "ruthless dictator—he ought to be scolded." Appalled by the persecution of Jews in Germany, she predicted that Hitler "one of these days will go one step too far."

And then I found a young woman in love. The first mention of Clark, from nearby Ripley, is on Sept. 23, 1937, when he came to visit. They saw each other occasionally for another year and then things started to get serious: "Jan. 8, 1939: Clark told me how much he liked me. Like him but ... !"

"Sept. 20, 1939: Was supposed to have a date with Clark but he didn't come down. Am I wild. Wrote him a darn sassy letter. Who in the devil does he think he is?"

"Sept. 21, 1939: Clark came

down today but I couldn't stay angry."

"Jan. 1, 1940: Clark came down. We played cards and games. Wonder if I'm falling!"

"June 13, 1940: Clark & I went for a walk. He's 23 years old today. Bought him a carton of Luckies. He certainly likes to smooch. My, my!"

"June 30, 1940: Clark and I went for a stroll. Told me I was selfish, spoiled, impulsive, sarcastic, and belittling, but he still loves me. Can't understand it."

"Aug. 25, 1940: I'm afraid I like Clark very much. I'm quite sure he loves me."

Two days later, Clark joined the Army Air Corps as a welder and was sent to Belleville, Ill. He came home for the holidays that year; they had Christmas dinner at our house and he gave her an Evening in Paris perfume set. He left on Dec. 28: "I said good-by to him tonight. Am not going to the train 'cause I'd cry too much."

Clark was supposed to return home the following Christmas. He did not: "Dec. 7, 1941: Japan bombs Hawaii without warning at 7 A.M. While their emissaries are in Washington discussing peace terms—vile trick. Two hours later Japan declares war on US. Hundreds killed."

"Dec. 8, 1941: US declares war on Japan. Clark must leave for Calif. Tuesday. Will not come home for Xmas. Terribly dis-

appointed. US must fight for its very life.

"Dec. 10, 1941: Letter from Clark. Tells me to believe in divine guidance and that he's not afraid."

Gradually, I discovered a woman, no longer a girl, suffering the pains of a wartime romance. Through 1942, 1943, and 1944, Rose stayed at home, working as a secretary at what is now Michigan Technological University at Houghton.

She wanted to enlist in the Women's Army Corps "but Mom disapproves very much." She made bandages at the Red Cross center and took rifle lessons.

Rose received her engagement ring in the mail. Clark's letters from the South Pacific sometimes were censored, and she often did not know exactly where he was or what he was doing. Over and over she wrote: "I miss Clark so much."

Finally, in 1944: "June 16— Letter from Clark, says he's leaving in July for US. Oh happy day. Dear God let it be so!!"

"July 7: Two letters from Clark. One very sweet, the other disgusted. I'm getting so mad about this Army red tape."

"Aug. 22: No letter from Clark. It makes me frantic."

"Oct. 24: Letter from Clark. No date. Imagine, still waiting. I was so mad I could have spit."

"Nov. 3: At last, oh happy

day! Clark called from San Francisco. Going to Chicago to meet him."

"Nov. 7: Election day, voted for Roosevelt. Went to see Father Eiling today about necessary details for our wedding."

"Nov. 17: Going to have Arlene and Cecilia and Louis and Lowell stand for us. Dad will give me away. Nuptial High Mass at 8 Thursday.

And then: "Nov. 23: Married today. Beautiful sunny day. Everyone complimented us. Breakfast and dinner at home, also reception. Left for Marquette for honeymoon."

Clark was assigned to a base at Carlsbad, N.M. Rose waited anxiously at home while he found a place for them to live: "No letter. I'm so darn disgusted, restless, and blue I could cry or scream." It turned out Clark "is in a hospital with sweating spells he gets once in a while since returning from S. Pacific."

On Jan. 23, 1945, Rose wrote: "Telegram from Clark. Wants me to leave Thursday. Burma Road opened. Russians 150 miles from Berlin."

T hat is the last entry. Was the diary packed up and left at home? Did she get another, now lost? Or—what I like to believe

—could she now confide in her new husband?

The war ended in August of that year. Rose and Clark moved back to Hubbell and then to Flint, where he was a welder in the auto industry. They raised five wonderful children. The malaria that Clark brought back from the South Pacific developed into other ailments. He died in 1969 at the age of 52.

Rose lived quietly, but as always greatly interested in everything around her and in the world, making witty comments in weekly letters that I wish I had saved.

On March 20, 1980, she died of a heart attack in her sleep. She was 62. We couldn't believe it, but we have discovered something else in her diaries—how so often 40 years ago she wrote that she didn't feel well, though she told no one.

Sometimes in the last few years I have thought of Rose as 60, and sometimes as 40. But now I also think of her at 20, her hair in curls, wearing the yellow dress our mother had made for her and writing this before she crawled into bed: "Went to the Drome with Marg. Danced with loads of Tech kids and Houghton kids. Grand time. Danced every number. Fun!"

Good night, Rose.   ∞

The Vision of Noah Jumping Eagle

"Only those who have already found God can seek Him like that"

By HARRY W. PAIGE
September 1972

I T WAS LATE in the summer of '64. The sky over the Dakota prairie was cloudless and a hurting blue.

Noah Jumping Eagle walked ahead of me leading the way toward the banks of the Little White River, which meanders darkly through the Rosebud Sioux Reservation, adding still another age-line to the face of the land.

Noah was a big man who had started to settle beneath the weight of his years. He had a classic Indian face with sharp, chiseled features and dark, liquid eyes.

Reprinted with permission of the author.

In most places I can think of, Noah would have been considered slightly mad or, at the very least, wildly eccentric. But here, in this mystical land among a mystical people, many considered him a holy man. He was as respected as a priest or surgeon might have been in another community. Mystics go with the territory.

Noah Jumping Eagle was a practicing Catholic, a pillar of his tiny parish in the Spring Creek community, but he was also an Indian and his imagination leaped to where the air was thinner and the more orthodox feared to follow. He tracked his God like a hunter—through the rim-rocked canyons, over eroded, table-top buttes, and even across the star trail.

He hungered after God—not just the *idea* of God, but the living flesh. And finally, in his 67th year, he found Him.

I believed him. I had known he was a man of faith ever since the day we were discussing the drought in the East, one of the worst in years. Water supplies were dangerously low and the governor had declared a state of emergency. When our conversation had trailed off into a solemn shaking of heads, Noah startled me with his simple proposal.

"Why don't you use prayer?"

"Some of us probably do pray," I answered vaguely. "Farmers and people like that."

He shook his head. "I mean *together,*" he said, as though he were speaking to a child who didn't quite understand. "A state day of prayer. When everybody prays together. So God will be sure to hear."

Suddenly I thought I knew how Peter felt when the cock crowed for the third time. How Thomas felt when his finger found the nail holes. I, too, was one of little faith.

As an outsider, an easterner, and an academic doing research on the legends of the Sioux, I was a prisoner of the culture that had shaped me. I saw through St. Paul's glass darkly

and might never come to see face to face.

It was a sad, even a frightening thought. Noah and I shared the same God, yet he was free to run the hounds of heaven while I must wait, sifting the heart's evidence against the head's.

"It is not far now," Noah said, breaking into my thoughts, grinning his gold-toothed grin.

After another five minutes, Noah turned back to me. "The holy tree," he said softly in Lakota, the language of the trans-Missouri Sioux.

I saw it. The holy tree. A huge cottonwood rising like a fountain. This was the tree, according to Noah Jumping Eagle, in which a vision of the Lord had appeared to him—not once, but every Friday throughout the summer.

Noah pointed to a V made by the meeting of the two largest branches on the tree. "There," he said, pointing. "There is where He stands."

A shiver of expectation ran through me. At the same time, I remembered the words of a priest friend when I had told him about Noah's invitation to visit the holy tree.

"You won't see anything," he told me matter-of-factly. And then he added, somewhat sadly I recalled, "Only those who have already found God can seek Him like that." I didn't know what he meant then. I do now.

My friend had been a missionary to the Sioux for 12 years and had never ceased to wonder at their faith. It almost seemed as though he were jealous of their mystical ties with the land and the Great Spirit, who was also the Christ.

But the heightened sense of anticipation would not leave. And so we stood, looking up into the rustling cottonwood. I looked at my friend. In profile, with the sun pouring over his features, he looked like a hawk on fire. A predatory God-seeker.

Suddenly he slumped to his knees, bent his head, and struck his breast three times.

"My Lord and my God!" The words broke from him like a sob and I found myself kneeling beside him in the dust. As I knelt, I raised my eyes to the tree, searching the V of its branches. I saw nothing. Nothing but the upturning of silver leaves. In the back of my mind I kept hearing the echo of my priest friend's sad prediction: "Only those who have already found God can seek Him like that."

Then, without any warning, Noah broke into song, "Great Spirit, have pity on me!"

He sang it four times and then four times four in a tuneless chant that was almost a keening. His body shook. Then his voice faded and there were only the prairie sounds—the wind shaking the tree, the gurgling of the river, and the drone of locusts sawing on the afternoon.

After half an hour or so, Noah rose and without speaking a word, started back toward the tar-paper shack that he called home.

Later that night, in the flickering light of a kerosene lamp, Noah and I drank coffee. He was still visibly shaken from the effects of his visit to the holy tree. His gnarled fingers trembled around the warmth of the tin cup as a novice priest's might have trembled on the chalice. He had not spoken for hours, not since the song had burst from him. Now he was returning to the everyday world, a dream at a time.

"I didn't see anything," I said, my words falling awkwardly. I felt as though I were making my confession to an indifferent priest.

He continued to sip his coffee, holding the cup with both hands. He reminded me of a 2nd World War photograph I had seen. A merchant seaman whose ship had been torpedoed from under him was clutching a mug of coffee. A blanket covered all but the dazed expression on his face.

"I saw nothing," I repeated.

Noah nodded, his face expressionless. Then the tight seam of his mouth moved like the opening and closing of a leather purse. "But He saw you."

That was all he ever said. When I left his cabin later that night, it was for the last time. The following summer when I returned, I learned that my friend had died during the winter. He had frozen to death. Somewhere by the holy tree.

I tried to find out where he was buried, but none of the Indians would talk about Noah. I checked the tribal offices and they had no details. Finally, I went to see my friend at the mission.

"Noah was a good Catholic," he told me. "He's in holy ground."

The next morning I went alone to the holy tree. It was a jewel of a day, very like the one on which Noah and I had made our visit together. As I came within sight of the river the feeling came over me that I had traveled in a giant circle and had returned to my point of departure. Memories drifted like lazy clouds across the span of time.

The tree seemed smaller somehow, as though I were seeing it through the wrong end of a telescope. I felt like a man returned to the scenes of his childhood who finds things dwarfed by absence.

I went to the far side of the tree. There was a mild depression in the earth there, a settling that I recognized. A chunk of rough jade as big as a man's fist and a withered branch from the holy tree were stuck in the ground. A prayer stick, its top painted red and dangling a turkey feather, leaned over at an odd angle.

I looked around, trying to imagine what the tranquil place was like with the winter wind lashing the kneeling tree. I tried to imagine what might happen to a man who fell through the ice and froze his legs. I tried; but the distance was too great. I was only a summer friend.

I felt that I should say something over the place. But there was nothing to say. Noah had said it all when he knelt before the holy tree, borrowing the words of an anguished Thomas. I made the Sign of the Cross, the sign language for what I felt inside.
 ✍

INTERPRETING THE 1040

A taxpayer recently sent the I.R.S. 25¢ with a note saying he understood that he could pay his taxes by the quarter.   Edna Elsaser.

Dream Girls, Dream Churches

The scandal of particularity: a little theology
for those who are always seeking rainbows

By CHRISTOPHER DERRICK
August 1976, condensed from *The Wanderer**

W HEN PEOPLE REJECT the
Faith, they will often tell
you that their reasons are
logical, or historical, or scientific. But I've never found it easy
to believe this. In my experience,
the underlying difficulty is imaginative far more often than it is
intellectual.

One particular imaginative
difficulty which holds many
people back from the Church
has been called "the scandal of
particularity."

You meet some man who is
perfectly prepared to accept the
idea of a universal God; also,
the idea that such a God might
have his message for mankind.
But he has a stubborn feeling
that such a God would only act
generally, on sweeping or abstract lines, never making any-

thing like a particular or arbitrary choice.

There would be no problem
for this man if the Good News
were eternally written across the
firmament in letters of gold and
fire, for everyone to read; that's
how the Absolute might be
expected to do things.

What sticks in this man's
throat is the *particularity* of
God's action as proclaimed by
Christianity—the idea that salvation should come through
one particular man (Jesus of
Nazareth), in one particular
nation (that of the Hebrews),
and at one particular moment
in history, and would then be
promoted by one particular institution (the Catholic Church) and
have its headquarters in one particular place (an agreeable
through somewhat villainous
city on the banks of the Tiber).

*Reprinted with permission of the author.

97

This is certainly an imaginative difficulty, not a logical one. God's mind (if I may put it that way) is so obviously different from ours that we really can't say much about what He would and would not do. And we know Him first through his creation; and from this, it's obvious that He *does* operate in a highly particular manner, making "choices" (that isn't really the right word) which seem highly arbitrary. Whatever made Him decide to create the giraffe but not (as far as we know) the unicorn? Why did He actually create Dickens but not—in the same sense—Mr. Pickwick?

I'm glad He did: that is to say, the particularity of creation is one of the things I like about it. But it does baffle the imagination. The questions that I've just asked are unanswerable. "Who hath known the mind of the Lord, or who hath been his counselor?"

I don't mention this scandal of particularity in order to refute it, but only to point out its importance. Our religion is—quite uniquely—the religion of Incarnation, of particularity. We certainly believe in the Absolute, the Universal, the Timeless: so—in one way or another—do men of every religion.

But we Christians go on to say that the Absolute has "chosen" to work through the particular, to be incarnate. If God was to become man at all, He had to become *this* man in *this* place and at *this* time; He had to start with that particularity.

It is certainly irrational to be held back from the Faith by this scandal of particularity. But it is an understandable irrationality.

You and I have not held back from that Faith and that Church. Even so, our commitment may well be more imperfect than we suppose.

Even here, inside the Church, particularity can still trip us up. We can seek the perfect, the absolute, too impatiently; in our pride, we can then forget the humility of the Incarnation, and the fact that God sees fit to work through secondary and particular things, demanding of us (in this life) much commitment to what is secondary and even imperfect. That's his way of doing things; and if we are impatient with it, the consequences are likely to be disastrous in one way or another.

It is in marriage that this kind of disaster may perhaps become most easily apparent. The better we are, the more we hunger for absolute perfection; and if we're young and in love, we can suppose too easily that we've found it. But in fact great patience will still be needed, great toleration of the imperfect.

How often do we hear of the *breakdown* of some marriage? For my part, I regard that as a rather hypocritical word. *Breakdown* sounds as though it were some kind of disaster striking from outside, like the roof falling on our heads, whereas what the words actually refer to is the culpably bad behavior of one spouse or of both.

But it's very understandable. This young man (let us say) was in love; virtuously so, romantically so. He therefore idealized this girl's very genuine merits into absoluteness, into perfection; she became for him the goddess Venus, and he thought that in marriage to her he would live happily ever after.

He thus forgot the incarnational principle—the fact that perfection is hereafter, and is to be sought here on earth through commitment to concrete particulars, which are never perfect in this world.

In due course he discovered that he hadn't married the great goddess Venus at all, but only this particular young woman, Jane Smith or Elizabeth Brown as the case may be, nice enough but with all the particular faults and failings and follies and tiresome silly little ways that characterize every member of our species. This came as a cruel shock to him; he'd been seeking perfection (shouldn't we all seek that?), and he'd been let down.

Soon some other girl will happen along—one whose charm is apparent to him, but whose faults and failings and follies and tiresome silly little ways are (for the moment) invisible.

And so the oldest of old sad stories will start to tell itself once again; his marriage will (as they say) "break down." (But will he find total bliss with this second girl? Don't you believe it—even though she may in fact be the nicer girl of the two. The rainbow's end is always just beyond your reach. Those who impatiently seek perfection in this world are doomed to seek forever. That's their chosen Hell.)

As a charter member of Persons' Lib, let me point out that this story could have been told the other way round. Its moral is not that it's a mistake to be young and romantically in love. Its moral is the danger of proud, impatient highmindedness. If that young man had gone astray through mere sensuality and the roving eye, he'd have known the sin for what it was; I'm imagining him as a good Catholic. As things are, he is (partly at least) in the much worse condition of feeling innocent and having a grievance; his idealism has been betrayed.

Against such disasters, our

best insurance is a constant remembering of the incarnational principle. Let us never forget that the Perfect, the Absolute, chooses to work and be served and be discovered through particulars—through one particular Galilean first of all, but also through other particulars, and through commitment to them, human and imperfect though they be.

This is some part of what's implied in the idea of a sacrament. It has great practical relevance to Matrimony; it has equal relevance, I think, to Baptism. When we are baptized, we are certainly committed to the Absolute, to God. But we also are committed to a particular method of attaining Him—that is, to membership in his Son's Body, the Church, which is divine on the one side but very human on the other.

If (in our pride) we overlook this and entertain expectations which are impatiently high-minded, we are going to get a cruel shock sooner or later. Then—if we are as foolish as that young man, as unwilling to accept the incarnational principle—we shall go running off in search of a perfect dream Church, just as he went running off in search of a perfect dream girl. Eternal frustration will be our doom, as it was his; perfection is hereafter.

This has happened again and again in history. Some people leave the Church, of course, because they are bored with serving God and don't like moral constraint. But it's important to remember that much heresy and schism, like some adultery, is motivated by a kind of highminded impatient idealism which is really pride.

The analogy between Matrimony and Baptism is (I think) fairly close. This bride, this girl you're in love with, she's made in the image and likeness of God. But she isn't in fact a goddess, or any total perfection: she's another human being like yourself and must be accepted as such.

Matrimony (in other words) is sacred but is not Heaven. It is a way of getting to Heaven through commitment to an imperfect human particular, through obedience, through acceptance of the real but limited goodness thus attained in the meantime. (And when thus regarded, it will have the best chance of being happy in this world's sense, of not "breaking down.")

So with the Church: here also, the good—the only real good, which is God—is to be sought in and through commitment to human particulars. You don't just get baptized into God. Remember the incarnational principle. You also get baptized into the human particularity of his Son's Mystical Body, into the particular particularity which the Church has in *this* parish and *this* diocese, under *this* Pope and at *this* moment in history. And in all these things and people, Pope, bishop, pastor, laity, there will be imperfections certainly and folly and grave sin quite possibly.

The sacred and indefectible and infallible nature of "the Church" itself, theologically considered, will not be affected thereby. But if what chiefly interests you is the mote in your neighbor's eye, you'll find plenty to talk about in this human Church of your Baptism, today, and in any possible century. (A husband takes his sympathetic secretary out to dinner and tells her all about his wife's failings. He won't need to invent, and he won't need to exaggerate very much. A sense of grievance can always claim some justification from the facts. It's always a sin and a folly nonetheless, a mode of pride.)

The moral danger of concentrating upon other people's failings, those of your wife, or those of churchmen, will be obvious enough. What I want to stress is the theological danger. That marriage "broke down" because the foolish proud young man was looking for perfect womanhood and thought he had found it, whereas nobody can find it on this earth.

But we can make a corresponding mistake as Christians, as baptized people; and I want to stress that if we do, it will be a distinctively Protestant mistake. "Private judgment" will lead us to conceive "the Church" too high-mindedly, too idealistically, as an assembly of the perfect. The danger is that we shall then reject the clearly visible Church because of the imperfections of its human side, and perhaps especially the imperfection of its human leaders.

To illustrate this, let me invent a little story. (It will have to be invented rather than factual, since I lead a secluded life and don't know much about what actually goes on.)

Imagine some group of Catholics who feel that they've been horribly let down by their Holy Mother the Church, perhaps by some pastoral decision which (to take one possibility at random) might lie in the liturgical field. This decision seems to their private judgment to be wildly foolish, destructive, even heretical. Their feelings run high. How will they then behave?

Good Catholics, people who, although not saints, have the stuff of the Faith in their bone marrow, will accept this new situation. Maybe Rome has behaved imprudently. It sometimes does. On the other hand, Rome sees things in a wider and longer perspective than is available to most of us. There are human as well as theological reasons for being very cautious about one's own superior righteousness.

Faith can therefore go through a somewhat rough time; obedience, too. But this can be spiritually advantageous. Obedience was easy when the orders given coincided with one's own desires, when the children could perceive their mother's good sense. But when they fail to perceive it but still obey, honoring the particularity of their commitment to this particular mother, obedience becomes a saving virtue.

But the people I'm thinking of, in this wholly fanciful story, respond differently. They behave rather as that young husband did, when he felt so bitterly let down by the discovery that his wife wasn't a perfect dream goddess after all.

Let me tell you what he did. As a Catholic, he knew that divorce wasn't for him. But his sense of betrayal seemed unendurable. He chose not to endure it, anyway.

So by way of an escape route, he cooked up the illusion that the wife who had betrayed him so dreadfully (that's how he saw it) was not really his wife at all. He found a sympathetic priest and a suitably broadminded ecclesiastical tribunal, and told everybody that he was in totally "good faith" about this, and was believed. And soon it was all on paper and signed and sealed and official. His marriage was invalid. That tiresomely human girl wasn't his wife. She never had been his wife. He'd been under a dreadful illusion. (And she had helped that illusion along by *pretending* to be his wife, so adding deception to the long list of her other faults. How terribly the innocent get exploited, in this cruel world!)

So now he was free to find a *real* wife in this other girl, who was, quite certainly, perfect beyond all risk of disappointment.

That's what he did; and it's very much what this group of indignant Catholics (in my wildly improbable story) will do with their corresponding sense of betrayal. They believe that their Holy Mother the Church has let them down, and hideously; so they will cook up a theory that she isn't their *real* mother at all, but only a sham, masquerading as the true Church just as that evil girl masqueraded as a true wife. Off they go, therefore, just as an unfaithful husband goes off; and it will be no trouble at all for them to invent a phantasmal but supposedly genuine Mother of their own, guaranteed never to let them down, guaranteed to give only those orders which they already want to accept.

They have failed to honor the incarnational particularity of their baptismal commitment. They end up in schism, which stands in relation to Baptism very much as adultery stands in relation to marriage.

The pathetic joke is that they'll almost certainly see themselves as the only true defenders of authentic Catholicism. It will be screamingly obvious to everybody else that they're thinking and acting on strictly Protestant lines. They were too highminded for the actual Church.

Now I only tell this little story, both of these little stories, in order to emphasize the importance of particularity in the Christian commitment. Such things could never happen in actual fact.

Or could they? Unfaithful husbands do exist, even husbands who are unfaithful through proud, highminded idealism; and I've heard rumors (lies, perhaps, told by ill-disposed people) that there might exist here or there some ecclesiastical tribunal uncharitable enough to endorse the self-deception of such a husband's "good faith." So one of my stories might be true.

But what about the others? Good Catholics, fiercely loyal to the Catholic Faith and the tradition of the Church, could

such people ever start thinking and acting on lines so closely analogous to schismatic Protestantism and to marital infidelity?

I'd like to think it impossible. The trouble is that things of just that kind have happened so often in the past. It has to be considered a permanent danger. Within one's Catholic life as within one's marriage, feelings of grievance and betrayal ought to be treated as very serious alarm signals, as symptoms that the proud kind of highmindedness may be at work, undermining one's commitment to concrete particulars.

But I understand the temptation; I even feel it myself. Let me confess a strictly private foolishness, probably not shared by anybody else in the world: I sometimes have a wild longing to hear *Introibo ad altare Dei* once again, and all that went with it. If it comes to that, I sometimes see some beautiful girl in the street, and think how glorious it would be to fly off and start a new life with her in Buenos Aires or somewhere.

Beautiful words, beautiful girl, beautiful apple in the Garden of Eden.

But obedience has to be to the *actual* wife; dreams of something better (available in fact, or just imagined, or perhaps remembered from the past) come from the Old Liar down below. When God became man (choosing for his arrival in this world the strangely arbitrary coordinates of 31 degrees 42 minutes North, 35 degrees 12 minutes East) He committed us most redemptively to concrete particulars. &

THE PERFECT ASSIST

My home is in Mexico, but I'd managed to put enough money aside to come to college in the U.S. I had not budgeted money for extras, however, so when I broke a tooth, I postponed going to the dentist. An infection soon set in, and I had no choice. I looked up a dentist in the phone book and made an appointment.

The dentist did a very good job, but he had to take ten X rays before pulling the tooth. He then went on filling a couple of cavities that he claimed could not wait. I expected a bill that would put me in the red for weeks.

When he was through, he handed me my bill with a big smile. It read:

For dental work $53.50
Contribution to further
American–Mexican good will $50.00
Balance due. . . . . $ 3.50   Tina Pruneda.

HEARTS ARE TRUMPS

Even after age and illness dimmed my mother's sight and tangled her talented fingers, her desire to make beautiful gifts for those she loved never waned. Nursing care became necessary, and still she struggled with hook and yarn. She was particularly intent on making a patterned scarf for a beloved friend. She seemed pleased enough with the progress, although I had to shudder as I watched her work row after row of hopelessly uneven stitches.

At Christmas time, she produced the most beautiful white scarf with popcorn stitches for her friend. We were all astonished and overwhelmed. What none of us knew at the time was how the night nurse, after tucking mother in, would pick up the scarf, rip out the jumbled work, and crochet the exact amount accomplished each day. Then she'd put the piece by her patient's chair, ready for mother to pick up in the morning. Truly it was a precious scarf, crafted with double stitches of loving kindness.

Mary Elizabeth Potter.

Lincoln's Catholic Cousins

One of them was named Abraham, and they brought their faith to the southern Illinois frontier

By ALBINA ASPELL
February 1978

I T'S HARD TO get there from here. You park along the blacktop road, then walk back a quarter mile past a wheat field now barren and frozen under light snow. You climb a rail and barbed wire fence, and then search among fallen tree limbs.

Suddenly, there it is: the grave of Abraham Lincoln, Catholic.

Another Abraham Lincoln, 16th president of the U.S., lies entombed in the Illinois state capital of Springfield. But the man here, in this desolate prairie plot, is a close relative.

His marble marker is broken, like the ones around it. But the inscription and design, weathered by many seasons, are still bold. There is a cross,

sign of his membership in the Church, carved into the stone, and beside it, a weeping willow tree. The date on the tombstone: January 22, 1851.

Eerie white in the winter stillness, this now untended spot is the old cemetery of St. Simon the Apostle, located in Fountain Green, just west of the city of Macomb on the west central Illinois plain.

Here, where the ancient markers now tilt at grotesque angles, sleep the Catholic Lincolns — three cousins of the president, some second cousins, and other pioneers related by marriage — who made up this little remembered branch of the Lincoln family.

Where did they come from? And how were they Catholic while the president himself was

105

not? Did they bear any resemblance to the famous man? Though the trail grows dim after a century has passed, history provides some of the answers.

The story begins in Virginia, with a third Abraham Lincoln, the grandfather of both the president and his Catholic first cousin.

This early Abraham lived in the 1770's with his wife, Bathsheba Herring, three sons, and two daughters, in Rockingham County, Va., where he had inherited 210 acres from his father "Virginia John" Lincoln. Hearing rumors of the rich land in Kentucky, Abraham in 1782 sold his holdings and moved his family to Floyd Creek, Jefferson County, where he bought and proceeded to clear several large tracts.

While so engaged in the spring of 1788, Abraham was shot from ambush by an Indian, who was then himself shot by the oldest son Mordecai. Of the two other boys at the scene, one, Josiah, ran across field and wood to seek help at a fort; the youngest, Thomas (who was to become father of the president), was a helpless witness to both murders.

Abraham's death was a tragedy that left the acreage uncleared, and his widow and children with few personal possessions: three cows, three calves, a bull yearling, a sorrel horse, some pewter dishes, three weeding hoes, three feather beds, and some tools.

Leaving the hostile territory, the widow and children went to Washington County, Ky., where Mordecai, who had inherited title to his father's real estate, began to parlay his holdings into a tidy sum. Well thought of and well-to-do, he was soon elected sheriff of his county and became known for his sporting tastes, his great ability as a story teller, and perhaps understandably, for his bitter hatred of the Indians.

As a young man of both means and good reputation, he won the hand of Mary Mudd, daughter of Catholic Luke Mudd. The two were wed in a ceremony performed by Father William de Rohan, who placed the certificate of marriage on record at Bardstown, Ky.

Since the Mudd family was Catholic, it is safe to assume that Mordecai became a Catholic convert at the time of his marriage. The couple had three sons: Abraham, the subject of this story, James, and Mordecai, Jr.; and three daughters, Elizabeth, Mary Rowena, and Martha.

I n the fall of 1830, his children by now grown to adults, Mordecai yielded to the call of the frontier. He sent his son James ahead to blaze the trail, then packed up his family and moved to Hancock County, Ill., and the Military Bounty Land Tract, a section set apart for the veteran survivors of the war of 1812. The central portion of the county consisted then of one grand prairie, bordered on the west by the wooded bluffs of the Mississippi, and on the east and south by the timberlands skirting the margins of Crooked and Bear Creeks. The Lincolns arrived in late 1830 and were followed soon after by other Catholic families: the Cambrons, Yagers, Rileys, Hardies, Brannams, Kellys, Gittings, Fagans, Joneses, and McDonoughs.

The move from Kentucky, made by oxen, horse, and wagon, took months. It was a painful adventure for all, and for Mordecai, Sr., it was fatal. He came to the unsettled frontier during "The Great Snow Winter of 1830–31," a season that caused the worst suffering the county has ever known. It snowed for weeks without end, and drifts 30 feet high obscured what roads there were. Mordecai, away from home in open country, died in the killing cold and blizzard.

His body was found in the spring and he was buried on a farm plot, with prayer but without priestly ceremony, leaving his family and the Catholic community bereft of his leadership.

By 1832 there were enough Catholics in the area to merit the service of Father Irenaeus St. Cyr, a pioneer priest who hunted out his scattered flocks along the Mississippi Valley from St. Louis to Chicago. With his help, the Catholic cemetery where the Lincolns now lie buried was consecrated, and the chapel of St. Simon the Apostle started. The structure had the help of Lincoln hands; James was a carpenter, as was Robert, son of Abraham.

The church was finished in 1837, small, rude, but strong, and it was used for 20 years. Then its congregation moved almost in a body to the neighboring village of Tennessee, Ill., where work could be found on the construction of the Burlington Railroad. The church building was sold and moved to nearby Carthage by its new owners.

Father St. Cyr rode through the territory often to say Mass in Tennessee as well as Fountain Green, and he later recalled, if somewhat hazily in his old age, his experiences with the Lincolns. (He allegedly believed he spoke of President Lincoln's family, but historians attribute his recollections to the Lincolns at Fountain Green.) In 1866, he said that he visited the Lincolns several times. He described them as not well-instructed in their religion, but strong and sincere in their profession of it. "I said Mass repeatedly in their house," he said, and told of being presented with a gift of handmade chairs.

From the cemetery now it is difficult to visualize where the church of St. Simon stood, since no foundation lines remain; but it is reputed to have been only some 250 yards distant. Only parish records at the Immaculate Conception Church in Carthage, and state archives, reveal the existence of this early house of God and its founding families, some of whose members now lie in the cow pasture. Other Catholic Lincolns have found resting places at Calvary Cemetery at Carthage which is still in use and at LaHarpe and Tennessee, the last burial ground also untended and all but forgotten.

Curiously, Mordecai Jr., brother of Abraham and James, who died a bachelor in 1866, is reported buried just outside the cemetery fence. Why outside? Was he out of the Church? A suicide perhaps?

R eading the inscriptions of the headstones, many split and pushed over by the cattle that have grazed here for decades, one feels a kinship with the Lincolns.

The pioneer life seems to have been one of bleak loneliness and austerity, with scarce a hint of romance or beauty. Transportation was hazardous: creeks had to be forded and marshes and ravines avoided lest one get mired. Moving farm goods, and even getting the grain to the mill, was at best a testy adventure. Food was plentiful, but the rough dwellings and barns of the pioneers afforded little protection against severe weather, and cabins and livestock were several times blown away by tornadoes.

The grave markers bear grim evidence of this hard life which was, too often, a short one. So many died young, carried away by cholera, pneumonia, consumption, accidents—even accidental poisoning from herbs taken because they were thought to be beneficial in sickness.

Elizabeth Mudd Lincoln, wife of Abraham, died at the age of 51 just eight months after her husband was laid to rest; she was buried near him. And here is the grave of James, Abraham's brother, who died Sept. 18, 1837, and here lies his wife, Frances Childers Day, who was blessed with a longer life; she died at the age of 85 in November, 1884. But here, too are buried two of their children, a daughter, Martha, who died at the age of 5, and a girl named Amanda who died at 3.

W hat did the Catholic Lincolns look like? John Hay,

President Lincoln's secretary, once recalled a railroad journey he made in 1867, two years after the president was assassinated. He rode to Carthage in the same seat with the Catholic Abraham's son Robert. He described him thus:

"He is 41 years old, looks much older. The same eyes and hair the president had, the same tall stature and shambling gait, less exaggerated; a rather rough farmer-looking man. Drinks hard, chews ravenously. He says the family is about run out. 'We are not a very marrying set.' He is dying of consumption, he said very cooly." (Robert did indeed die not long after at Carthage, but he is buried in Fountain Green.)

"There was something startling in the resemblance of the straight, thick hair and gray, cavernous eyes framed in black brows and lashes," Hay continued. "He was a pioneer of our country, knew my father since long years. . . . told me that in 1860 he had talked with 'Abe' about assassination. Abe said, 'I never injured anybody; no one is going to hurt me.' He says he was invited by Abe to go to Washington at the time of the inauguration, but declined, thinking it dangerous . . . "

William E. Barton, who in 1915 wrote a two-volume life of Abraham Lincoln, often visited Fountain Green township. He,

too, reports that the Lincolns there resembled the president, not only physically, but in their emotional make-up as well. He also found the handwriting of the young Mordecai strikingly like that of the president, and recorded that their mental traits had been arrestingly similar.

"It is little wonder that John Hay was impressed by the startling resemblance of the one of these cousins," he wrote. "These Lincolns resembled Abraham Lincoln not only in stature, color of hair, eyes, gait, and manner of speech, but, what is more striking, they possessed and recognized as a family trait the moods to which the president was all his life subject. They went from boisterous mirth to the depths of despair without visible occasion.

"They had what they called 'the Lincoln horrors.' None of them ever went insane, but all of them, the men even more than the women, were subject to violent transitions from one mood to another." (Might that explain the fate of Mordecai, that plot outside the fence?)

While the president and his cousins could not be described as especially close, Lincoln did visit them on occasion, as they lived in his congressional district. By the time he came to political prominence, however, James and Abraham had already died. Nevertheless their 14 children turned out in number to support his presidential campaign. Fountain Green gained momentary fame for sending the largest delegation to a Keokuk, Ia., Republican political meeting in 1860, and a Lincoln portrait there awarded was later presented to the widow of James. It is now in a Springfield museum.

Political elections were rough and fiery events in that era, and the Fountain Green Lincolns, supporters of Abe, bore the brunt of his opposition. They were slandered as illiterate, a charge untrue, obviously, since handwriting samples exist and since both Abraham and James had served as justice of the peace. Abraham had, in fact, been a member of the first grand jury called to try the murderers of the Mormon leaders, Joseph and Hiram Smith, who were mobbed and shot at the Carthage jail in June, 1844. (He did not serve at the final trial, long postponed, when the accused nine were found not guilty.)

The advent of the Civil War brought increased anxiety to the township as 132 men, Lincoln relatives included, joined the Union forces. And of course the assassination of the president, a national tragedy previously unmatched, made a profound impact on the family. Add to this the ever present memories of the Indian wars and the fate of Grandfather Lincoln, and perhaps the Lincolns could be excused their emotional "horrors."

Requiescat in Pace, IHS, Gloria in Caelo Deo—the markers bear testimony to the faith of the pioneers: this is indeed a Catholic cemetery.

There is a move now by church, township and state authorities to preserve it, to make repairs to the fence, to spruce it up and keep out the cows. But whatever happens, this forgotten plot will still be a prettier place come spring. The ground will grow spongy under the thaw, the prairie grass will green again.

The resting place of the Catholic Lincolns is a hallowed spot, just as it is, and one moves lightly, reverently, with a bow and a prayer to the famous name, as the path is retraced back to the rail and barbed wire fence, back through the wheatfield and onto the road . . . and 1978.

One last look back, and it's gone. Swallowed up by its own century, it ceases to exist; there is only a haunting memory of tall, angular people given to "horrors"—people who proudly carried a famous name, and just as proudly practiced their Catholic religion.   ⌑

What Is God's Game?

What Is God's Game?

A spiritual writer meditates on hide-and-seek

By GEBHARD MARIA BEHLER, O.P.
November 1967, condensed from *Cross and Crown**

IN THE GOSPELS, during the Easter octave, the risen Saviour manifests Himself to his disciples in different places and ways, and then He goes into hiding. Not only does He suddenly appear and just as quickly disappear, but He comes in disguise He joins the young men on their way to Emmaus as if He were a pilgrim leaving Jerusalem after the Passover. He stands on the shore, and the disciples in the fishing boat think He is a stranger. He appears to the weeping Mary Magdalene at the grave and sympathetically inquires why she is so sad. She thinks He is the gardener.

Why this hide-and-seek? Is it meaningless? By no means. The risen Saviour wishes to teach the disciples and us the game which God wishes to play with mankind.

The Jewish philosopher Martin Buber tells a story, entitled *Hide-and-Seek,* that contains such a wealth of meaning that a person could meditate on it all his life.

Rabbi Baruck's grandson Jechiel was playing hide-and-seek with another child. Jechiel hid and waited for his friend to search for him. He waited a long time, and finally left his hiding place. His playmate was no-

*This article © 1967 by B. Herder Book Co. Reprinted with permission.

where to be found. Now Jechiel realized that his friend had not even bothered to look for him. With tears in his eyes he came running to his grandfather. Then Rabbi Baruck also began to weep and said, "That is the way God acts: I hide, but nobody wants to look for me."

The idea of the hidden God is in accord with the Bible. "Truly with you God is hidden," said Isaiah. He conceals Himself, and waits for us to come and seek after Him. Psalm 13 says so expressly, "The Lord looks down from heaven upon the children of men, to see if there be one who is wise and seeks God." And often the prophets and the Psalmist tell us, "Seek the Lord."

God hides well. "Should He come near me, I see Him not; should He pass by, I am not aware of Him" (John 9:11).

The best example of the hidden God is the Incarnation. First the Son of God is hidden in the womb of the Blessed Virgin; then as a child He hides in the crib. For 30 years He remains hidden at Nazareth. And when He departs on his public life, He is in the desert or in the midst of a milling crowd.

His practice of hiding continued up to the bitter end. "He humbled Himself, becoming obedient to death, even to the death on a cross." He concealed the fact that He is God by assuming the form of a man covered with wounds.

His hide-and-seek does not end with his ascension into heaven. The glorified Saviour still treats us as pilgrims, as gardeners, just as He did in the Easter Gospels. We meet Him in everyday life. He is likewise in the Church and the sacraments, especially in the Eucharist. The Cure d'Ars would point to the tabernacle and exclaim, "Our Lord is hidden there."

The 8th chapter of Proverbs describes Wisdom. "When He established the heavens, I was there; when He marked out the vault over the face of the deep, when He fixed the foundations of the earth, when He set for the sea its limits. Then was I beside Him as his craftsman, and I was his delight day by day, playing before Him all the while, playing on the surface of his earth and I found delight in the sons of men."

Picturing Wisdom as God working in the world, the Old Testament prophets paved the way for the new revelation of Christ, Wisdom become man. The description in the Book of Proverbs fittingly depicts Him. He "plays all the while" and "He has found delight in the sons of men." Only faith recognizes the game behind the puzzling events of the world. The playing Lord is seen only by those who believe and love.

God has devised many ways in which He can give us the joy of recognizing Him despite all the trappings. He engages us, not only in the sublime play of the liturgy, but also in his word, in our neighbor, and in the most insignificant duty of the moment.

Jesus himself places his person and his word on the same plane. "If you abide in Me, and if my words abide in you" means quite the same as "Abide in Me, and I in you." So to receive the word of Christ is like receiving his Person. If we would accept his word in sermons, in the liturgy, in Scripture, and let it sink down deeply into our hearts, we would more and more "be given the power of becoming children of God" and so enter into his game of love.

Christ also manifests Himself to us in the disguise of our neighbor. If we do not recognize Him here, we shall have no excuse on the Day of Judgment. "Amen I say to you, as long as you did it for one of these, the least of my brethren, you did it for Me." Those who have not exercised mercy to their fellow men will hear, "Depart from Me, accursed ones, into the everlasting fires, for I was hungry, and you did not give Me to eat; I was thirsty and you gave Me no drink; I was a stranger and you did not take Me in; naked, and you did not clothe Me; sick and

in prison, and you did not visit Me."

God makes known his will by using frail humanity. If He would issue an order directly, expressly state a wish, who would dare to disobey or refuse? God, however, conceals Himself behind mankind to teach us humility and to give us a chance to prove our love.

Everything in life presents new possibilities for a personal engagement with God. Paul in his address to the Areopagus in Athens, speaking of mankind, says that God "determines their appointed times and the boundaries of their lands; that they should seek God, and perhaps grope after Him and find Him, though He is not far from any one of us. For in Him we live and move and have our being."

To seek God is the most important duty given to us in this life. "To seek" God means to follow his footstep, his trace. The word *seek* is an ancient hunter's term, related ultimately to the Latin *sagire* (to scent out keenly) and to the Greek *hegeomai* (to follow the scent). Originally the word referred to the hunter who follows the trace of wild game.

To seek God, then, is to follow *his* footsteps by renouncing our own will and not allowing anything to lure us from the track. "Happy the man who meditates on wisdom, who ponders her ways in his heart, who pursues her like a scout, and lies in wait at her entry way" (Sir. 14:21). A good hunter does not let himself be misled by anything that might throw him off the track of his quarry.

We should seek God simply, humbly. Our attitude should be one of humility and confidence, like that of a child. "Amen I say to you, whoever does not accept the kingdom of God as a little child will not enter into it."

Those who seek God with all their heart will inevitably find Him. Christ Himself assures us most emphatically, "Ask, and it shall be opened to you. For everyone who asks, receives; and he who seeks, finds; and to him who knocks, it shall be opened."   *

PEOPLE ARE LIKE THAT

Paul came from a small town to the city to find employment. After several interviews and some disappointments, he got a job at the Ford plant, working five days a week with Saturdays off. He was also fortunate in securing modest rooming quarters near the plant.

On Saturdays he often went for a walk in the neighborhood, observing the tidy homes which seemed comfortable, neither rich nor poor. Only one stood out for its lack of care. Outside this home he would sometimes see children playing basketball, using a crude net wired against a tree. Often an older boy would be supervising the four or five younger ones. Evidently the family was Indian.

Then one Saturday Paul read in the morning paper: "Local Indian Youth Commits Suicide." Details followed: the teen had been out of work, depressed, etc. Paul couldn't help thinking of his hometown and how the neighbors would pitch in when tragedy hit. His own mother would spend hours baking and cooking for the sorrowing family.

Before noon, Paul was on his way, carrying a casserole to the family a few blocks from his room. As he entered their home, five children surrounded him. Despite their grief and their obvious need, they seemed cheered by the prospect of a hot meal.

Paul went to the funeral the next day and was surprised to see so many neighbors there. One woman greeted him: "Are you the young man we saw carrying food to this family?"

"Yes," he nodded.

"We hesitated about going near them," she said, "but your example set us all thinking. They have plenty of food now."   Albertine Peyton.

The Tent in the Living Room: A Meditation

When Jesus comes to me at the end of my pretending, it will be a familiar experience

By DONALD X. BURT, O.S.A.

July 1984, condensed from *The Inn of the Samaritan**

THE DAY WILL COME when I must leave these familiar places and go home with Jesus. What will it be like? Perhaps it will be like the times when I played in my tent in the living room.

When I was little I sometimes played prudent explorer. My exploring was prudent in that I never left home. I would build my tent out of boxes and blankets in the middle of the living room. I would then crawl inside and let my imagination roam through foreign places. Sometimes I would fall asleep in my cardboard and cotton hermit-

*This article © 1983 by the Order of St. Benedict, Inc. Originally published by The Liturgical Press, Collegeville, Minn. 56321. Reprinted with permission.

age and when wakened by some noise I would cry in fright not knowing where I was. At my cry, a loved one would come and touch the walls of my tent. The tent would fall to the floor and I would discover happily that through all of my imagined travels I had in fact been safe and secure at home.

Perhaps that is how my death shall be. Looking back, I shall see that it was nothing more than crawling from a tent in the living room of my Father. Right now it is not easy to believe that this is so. It seems right now as though I must spend my days passing from room to room, from event to event, until the day comes when I am called to begin the long journey home.

My tent seems so solid that it is hard to believe that anything worthwhile exists beyond its walls. The walls of my life seem so thick that it is hard to believe that any human, any God, can break through to touch me. As I sit here quietly in my life with its cardboard and cotton walls, it seems that there is no one to know me or to hold me or to listen to the story of my great adventures. I cry deep down inside, "Here I am! Poor Sir Donald, searching for the Holy Grail in a foreign land!"

Imagine my happy surprise when the Lord finally comes. There will be this soft thump as the flimsy walls of my life fall to the ground, and I shall discover that I have not been living in a strange and foreign land after all. All the while I have been living in the midst of the mansion that the Father prepared for me.

Perhaps then I shall remember that I have had the same experience before. When I was born my parents brought me home but for many years I did not realize that I was truly at home. It seemed like a fearful foreign place populated by giants. And even after I realized that I was living a life surrounded by love, I would sometimes crawl into my little tent and forget where I was. I would forget in my pretending that my life was in fact being lived in a little tent in the living room.

And thus when Jesus comes for me at the end of my pretending, it will be a familiar experience. He will nudge my life, and my imaginings will fall away, and I will see how silly it was to worry. Why, all the time I had been living out my days in a tent in the living room—in the place prepared for me by the Father's love.   ✳

IN OUR PARISH

In our parish, a boy in my religion class always spoke very softly. Only if you listened carefully could you understand him. At Confirmation the bishop was examining the students, and, as luck would have it, he called on Tommy. "What is the Blessed Trinity?" he asked.

Tommy whispered his reply: "Three divine persons in one God."

The bishop leaned closer and said, "I didn't quite understand."

"Of course you didn't," said Tommy. "Nobody does. It's a mystery."

Sister M. Amata.

In the Dark at the Foot of the Stairs

I found a young man declaring his independence

By BERTHA BECK
June 1979

TRYING TO UNDERSTAND my son Charlie is getting harder. Last night I dreamed Charlie put his new suit in the washing machine and kept washing it until there was nothing left but the label with instructions for dry cleaning.

I woke. It was still dark outside, but getting lighter. I had the feeling that the dream was telling me something. Would Charlie really try to wash his new suit before he had to wear it to the big wedding tomorrow? Surely that wasn't the hum of the washing machine I heard down in the basement? At this hour?

I was in such a hurry I forgot to switch on the light. I tripped on the cellar stairs. I knew right away that someone was down there.

I clutched my bathrobe to my heart and whispered, "Who's there?"

"Ma?" a voice said. "How'd you know I was down here?"

Now I was hearing voices. No, I told myself, not voices—Charlie's voice! He *had* washed his new suit! We couldn't go to the biggest family wedding in history. I wouldn't wear my new dress and my new shoes. My husband wouldn't wear the new tie I bought for him that he liked so much. Charlie wouldn't be

117

getting dressed up—for the first time since his Baptism. I wouldn't get to see him in a real outfit, real clothes—blue pants, not jeans, and a vest to match and a coat and a tie and a white shirt with a collar that had to be buttoned to his neck. Oh, Charlie, I thought, how could you do this to me?

"Charlie," I said, trying to keep my voice calm, "you didn't— did you?"

"I didn't what?" he said.

"If you didn't, then why are you down here?"

A pause.

"I couldn't sleep."

"Why?"

"I was thinking. About the wedding."

"What wedding? What were you thinking? Tell me and make it quick!"

"What about the wedding?" my husband's voice cut through the darkness. He has that kind of voice. I turned and saw him standing at the head of the stairs, silhouetted in the doorway. "What's going on here? Why are you down there, Bertha? Don't tell me you decided to do a wash at this hour?"

"I came down here to talk," I said. "You go back to bed, Dear." I was desperate. He complicates things between me and Charlie. It's hard enough to understand Charlie.

"You came down here to talk?" he said. "Talk to yourself? Has the wedding got to you?"

"I am not going to talk to myself. Charlie's here with me."

"Oh, that's different," he said, and he came down and sat on the steps near me. "But why the dark? Charlie, are you there?"

"I'm here," Charlie said, "but don't put the light on, Dad. Ma and me, we like to talk in the dark, don't we?"

"We do," I said, running my fingers through the setting that only yesterday made me feel glamorous and cost me five dollars. "You talk first, Charlie. Then I'll talk."

"O.K." Charlie said, "I'm not going to the wedding."

"You don't know what you're talking about, Charlie," my husband said in his this-is-all-nonsense-and-I-won't-stand-for-any-nonsense voice. "You are going to the wedding. We bought you a new suit and a new shirt and a new tie and new shoes, and all that cost a pile of money. So forget it, you're going to the wedding."

"Maybe he's got a reason," I whispered to my husband. To Charlie I said, "Is there a reason—anything about the suit?"

"Yes. The pants are too tight. I'll suffocate if I wear them. And the shirt. It chokes me. I hate collars. If you don't want me to die of suffocation at the wedding, you'd better let me wear my jeans and a T-shirt."

"You won't suffocate," my husband said. "You'll suffer maybe—but you won't suffocate. It won't hurt you to suffer a little for such a good cause. A wedding is the best cause in the world. Everybody suffers a little at a family wedding."

"I don't care what everybody does. I won't! Do you think suffering will make me grow up faster so I'll be a man like you? I'd feel like I was dressed up for Halloween. I hate that suit!"

I cut in quickly. Things were getting heavy. "Why didn't you tell them at the store they were making the pants too tight?" I said.

"They never asked me. Anyway, weddings are for grownups. Why do I have to go?"

"It's a good lesson for you," my husband said. "You should see a decent kind of wedding."

"You mean—you want me to get married soon?"

"No!" my husband had almost reached the shouting stage. "If we ever talked about your getting married, we were only joking. I don't want you to get married before you are well established in a career. I want you to go to college and become a doctor. You have all the qualities that will make you a great doctor."

"Suppose I don't feel like being a doctor?" Charlie said.

I could feel the tears in his voice. I cut in again. "If you don't want to be a doctor, Charlie, you can be a lawyer."

"That's right," my husband said. "You will be a lawyer like me. You'll come into my firm."

"I don't want to be a lawyer," Charlie said.

"Charlie, dear," I said, pleading. "Why can't you just say yes once in a while?"

"Sure. That's what you want me to say—yes all the time. But I'm not going to that wedding in that suit. I'll go if you let me wear my jeans and a T-shirt. I'll wear the new shoes, if you want me to, but not that suit."

I lost my wits. "Well," I said, "if you don't come with us wearing that suit, I'll just have to believe you don't love us."

"Ma! Love has nothing to do with this! Why do you always have to put love into everything? I've got other reasons. Can't I have other reasons?"

"There is no other reason," my husband said, standing up.

"There is so! Can't you and Ma just be ordinary people and forget you are my mother and father for once? Haven't you got any other kind of feelings about me? Why do you always have to keep working on me to make me something I'm not?"

"Like what?"

"Like a lawyer. Or a doctor. I don't want to be a lawyer just so I can get into your company, Dad, or because you'd like that. If I ever become a lawyer or a doctor, it will have to be because that's what I want, and not because it's what you want for me. I want to wear jeans and a T-shirt, and I'm going to the wedding in jeans."

"Charlie!" my husband shouted. "What will people think of us? How do you think the bride will feel, seeing you in jeans at her beautiful wedding that cost so much?"

"See?" Charlie said. "See, that's what I was talking about. You don't care about what I feel . . . "

He was so close to tears that I shouted, "Charlie, all we want is what's right for you!"

"How can you know what's right for me if you never ask me what I think? Why don't you ever say to me, 'Charlie, let's talk about this—or that; let's see if you can work this out for yourself.' Why do you always have to work things out *for* me? Is there something the matter with me?"

I finally began to understand how scared he was about telling us, how it had kept him from sleeping, how he'd come down here to the cellar to sit in the dark and think.

For the first time in my life as his mother I saw him as a separate and private person whose feelings and miseries I had to respect. I wanted to take him into my arms, but there was this new feeling that he needed to work things out for himself. He was pleading with me to let him grow up.

I sat on the step in the dark and waited. I had the queerest feeling. Suddenly I was so relieved not to have the responsibility of being a perfect mother raising a perfect son that I said without thinking, "O.K. Charlie, do what you want. You don't have to go to the wedding."

Charlie's squeaky voice, the one that comes out when he's excited, said, "Wow! O.K. I'll go to the wedding! I decided it won't kill me to wear the monkey suit."

And then he said, "I guess I can take my jeans out of the washing machine now and put them in the dryer. Come on, let's all go up and have breakfast."

I didn't think of breakfast. I was thinking of wearing my new dress and my new shoes. I was so happy, I giggled. I guess I'll never grow up.   ✎

SIGNS OF THE TIMES

In a greasy spoon diner: "Twenty Million Flies Can't Be Wrong."

Ralph Foral.

My Father's Easter Gift

The lesson he gave my brother helped all of
us children to find our way after he was gone

By MICHAEL FLYNN
April 1982, condensed from *America**

I T WAS DURING the days
when Lent ended at noon on
Holy Saturday, and people who
had thought about life and death
contending waited for the morrow. I was a little boy of four
playing under the kitchen table.
My father came down to get
breakfast and then drive Judge
Bowen to the cemetery to place
Easter flowers on Mrs. Bowen's
grave. I saw him reach for the
cereal and say to my mother,
"Liz, I have a pain in my chest."

She said, "Why don't you go
upstairs and lie down for awhile?
I'll call you when Judge Bowen
comes." So he walked up to the
bedroom, and I wandered along
with him. In a short time I came
down to the kitchen and said,
"Daddy won't answer me any-

more." The ambulance, the
police, the doctors came, but
daddy was dead.

The wake was in the house
that afternoon. My older brother
and sister and I knelt by the bier,
said a Hail Mary, and went over
to our cousin's apartment in New
York City to stay the weekend.

When we came home after
the funeral, the house seemed
so big and empty, and my
mother said, "Your father will
be with you in a new way now."
It was difficult for Charles and
Mary, but I listened as a little
child and was assured. It was
clear that God would take care
of us. I was too young to
know how sad death was, but
old enough to see it wasn't
frightening.

As I grew older I was aware
that my father must be happy
when we laughed. He would be

121

proud as I learned to read. I knew tales of his gentleness and patience and heard of his quiet humor. There were memories too: his taking us out for a ride in a pony cart, his being a "horse" on the living room floor. I can still picture him lathering up and shaving, see the brown suits and Panama hats.

A few years after ordination I was asked to preach an Easter sermon and was searching all over my mind for a story to bring this great mystery home. I recalled a story about my father and brother.

When Charles was about 9 years old my father said, "I want to take you down to my office and show you what I do." As they stood on the 111th Street El Station, my father pointed out that they were getting on the No. 15 train. When they walked into the car he brought Charlie over to the map, and put his finger on the blue line that described the ride. My father told Charlie that during rush hours the train skipped some of the stations it was stopping at now. On they rode, into New York City, going over the Williamsburg Bridge and down underground into the darkness. At Delancy St. they switched to the F train and got to the office.

The office was a wonderful land of typewriters, Eberhard pencils, and all the paper clips and yellow pads you could ever play with. Everyone said, "Oh, you're Dan's son!" and pointed out how big Charlie was. After a while my father turned to Charlie and said, "Do you remember how we came down here? Now, I'd like to see if you can get home by yourself."

Eyes widened, mouth dropped, and Charlie was scared to death, but he thought he could recall the directions our father had told him. He went to the subway platform and made sure that he was standing on the side that was going away from New York City. As soon as the subway opened its door he walked over to the map, found the station with his finger and traced the route of the train as it headed towards Delancy St. where he would switch to the El. Delancy St. came and Charlie worked his way through the corridors to the platform of the train that would bring him home.

He boarded the El and again went straight for the map and was putting his finger on the route as the train left the station. It traveled upwards through the tunnel, bucked, and entered the light as it crossed over the Williamsburg Bridge. It was good to see all this again and pass over the waters that were such a sure sign of things going right. Suddenly, he was alarmed as the train whizzed by one station after another, but then he remembered our father saying the journey would be different during rush hours. The train pulled into Myrtle Ave., then went onward past other stations until it came to a stop at the East New York station, and then turned out of Brooklyn and into Queens.

There was no need to watch the map for the last few stops; Charlie could look out the windows and see his neighborhood. The station signs read "Woodhaven Blvd.," "102nd St.," and finally "111th St."! The doors opened and Charlie, proud and happy, walked out of that train. He had found his way home.

What he didn't know was that our father was in the next car watching him all along.

Certainly, our father didn't want anything less than for Charlie to have all the confidence and freedom of Dad's own life. When Charlie got fright-

ened on that journey, he relied on the signs and words our father had given him to overcome that fright. In later years, when Mary or I would be asked to go out on our own, it would be all the easier because we knew of our brother's journey and our father's watchfulness. It was Charlie's going first that allowed us to trust our father all the more, because we knew he was seeking ways to bring us into his own life.

Easter arrives each year, and each year I travel that journey with Charlie and our father looking over him and come to know them better. Each year, I see more clearly what our father wanted to give all his children. Through the days of Lent, when I look on Christ's life and see his trust in our Heavenly Father, and I think of life and death contending, I pray more thankfully because my family revealed the victory and the Victor.   ✎

IN OUR PARISH

In our parish, Father Flynn was speaking to the third grade on the importance of love in the home. " 'Honor thy father and thy mother' is a commandment we should all remember," he said.

"Is there a commandment that says how we should treat our brothers and sisters?" one child asked.

Tommy, from a family of ten, piped up from the back of the room, " 'Thou shalt not kill.' "   Mrs. Howard Greer.

33 Basic Skills for Living

Can he sew? Can she replace a fuse?

By BARBARA WEEKS BOLTON
October 1980, condensed from *Sunday Woman**

HERE'S A LIST of basic skills each member of your family should have by age 17 or 18. Don't be surprised if Mom and Dad are missing a few. This list was developed by a group of adult homemakers, and no one present could do everything. They all just wished they could!

Safety

1. Know what to do in case of fire.
2. Know basic first aid.
3. Be certified in cardiopulmonary resuscitation.
4. Be able to administer the Heimlich maneuver to aid a choking victim.
5. Know how to call police, fire department, local physician or clinic, and poison center.

Travel

6. Be able to read and use a map.
7. Be able to read and use a timetable.
8. Know how to drive a car and change a tire.
9. Be able to gather information and plan a realistic budget for a two-day and two-week trip.
10. Know how to pack a suitcase neatly.

Grooming

11. Be able to sew on buttons.
12. Be able to hem slacks or skirts.
13. Know how to press pants, shirts, jackets, and skirts.
14. Be able to remove spots from natural or synthetic fabrics.
15. Know how to shine shoes.
16. Be able to operate a washer and drier.

---

*Reprinted with permission of the author.

Home Maintenance

17. Be able to do general housekeeping, including windows.
18. Master bed-making.
19. Master the art of folding sheets and table cloths . . . alone.
20. Be able to prepare ten simple but complete dinner menus.
21. Be able to repair a screen.
22. Be able to install washers on faucets.
23. Know how to replace a fuse.
24. Know how to change an electric plug on a lamp or appliance.
25. Know the location of main shut-off switches for water and gas.
26. Be able to turn furnace and any auxiliary equipment on and off.
27. Know how to plan and use a household budget.

Business

28. Have experience in two skills that will enable you to earn money on short notice.
29. Be able to write checks and balance a checking account.
30. Be able to read and understand insurance and hospitalization policies.

31. Know how to keep records for income tax.
32. Know how to use a library.
33. Know how to find a good lawyer.

In many cases, family members can instruct one another. If there's something on the list that no one in your home knows how to do, there are plenty of outside sources for help.

High schools and colleges hold "no-credit" evening courses in everything from cooking to driving and auto mechanics. Affiliates of the American Heart Association sponsor cardio-pulmonary resuscitation classes.

Ask your own insurance agent or a business friend to come to dinner and give the family pointers on reading an insurance policy, a contract, or other legal papers. Ask the manager of your bank for tips on keeping good home financial records. Your motor club or travel agent can provide tips on reading maps and planning trips.

And wait until you see the pride on a youngster's face when asked to teach a specialty to the rest of the family!

The Divine Plan for Teen-age Girls

By WILLIAM E. (BUD) DAVIS

January 1972, condensed from *Empire**

M Y GOOD FRIEND, Larry Rice, not only is a professor of English, he also is a philosopher, which seems only right because that is what he is a doctor of. As a philosopher-scholar, I'm not in his league. What we both have in common, though, are 17-year-old daughters, and that would make a philosopher out of almost anyone.

I tried to be sympathetic one night as he reflected on his theory of God's divine plan for teenagers. His carefully modulated tones oozed with self-pity as he reported the events of the day— namely how he had given his daughter, Carlyn, permission to drive his coveted Scout on a picnic for some junior class girls and later that afternoon had received a telephone call. The plaintive, humble tones on the other end of the line were in such contrast with the ac-

customed authoritative, self-righteous outbursts from his daughter that he immediately began to suspect that something was wrong.

His worst fears were confirmed. She had driven his beloved Scout off a small cliff. The girls were all right, the sandwiches were soggy but edible and, while the canned pop had later exploded upon opening, the picnic, by and large, was a success. But the car was totaled.

As I said, he was philosophic about the whole thing and attributed it to a part of God's divine plan. According to Larry, it goes something like this: "If all children were as lovely and delightful as they are at age 4 or 5, parents could never bear to kick them out of the nest. So God invented the teen-ager, and made her behavior so obstreperous and rebellious and, at times, so downright outrageous, that frustratated fathers can hardly wait to send them away

*This article © 1971 by the *Denver Post*. Reprinted with permission.

126

to college or give them away in marriage."

I agreed aloud that this indeed reflected infinite wisdom. But to myself I quietly chuckled.

I wasn't chuckling at 2 A.M. as I sat on the front stairs waiting up for my 17-year-old daughter, Debbie, who had not yet arrived home from a drive-in movie that had let out at 1:30. When her boy friend's car pulled up, I flashed on the front lights, the hall lights, and greeted them at the door. The balmy May night suddenly took on the chill of a February blizzard.

Debbie showed no concern for the fact that we were up past our bedtimes. She stormed by me with a look that would wither Frankenstein's monster, leaving me holding the door open for her startled boy friend. (I think his name was Elmer.) I said the first thing that came to my mind, which was, "Good night."

Had this been but an isolated incident, I might have forgotten the whole thing. But as I lay awake, I recalled other grievances that had accumulated— such affairs as driving the car without permission, fighting with her sister over the hair dryer, grumbling about taking her little brother to Little League practice, arguing about whose turn it was to set and clear the table, refusing to wear her warm coat on cold nights, and now forgetting what time she should be home. It was a long and formidable list. In short, it clearly was high time that she either shape up or ship out. And considering how understanding I was, I had no doubt that when confronted with my reasonable approach, she would choose to shape up.

Debbie, of course, slept through breakfast, but this just gave me additional time to finalize my plan. A direct confrontation with Debbie, I reasoned, was enough to ruin the day for the whole family. Thus, I chose the less noble route of writing her a letter. When she marched into the kitchen, eyes flashing, fire rolling from her nostrils and smoke from her ears, I quickly handed her this missive.

Dear Debbie:

Your mother and I love you very much and want you to grow up and be a bright, strong, happy, healthy girl. We appreciate your being willing to get a job, your making your own clothes, and your getting yourself up in the morning on school days. We also know we should be thankful for those things you are not, such as—a hippie, a drop-out, a pot-head, a boy-chaser, a sitter-inner.

There are, however, one or two things which could be improved. One can, for example, hardly walk through your room without tripping over a bra or yesterday's underwear. We don't care whether you change the diapers on your new baby sisters, just as long as you aren't howling louder or more often than they. Affection or a kind word to your brother or sister understandably can be reserved for Christmas or birthdays, but a friendly smile occasionally would go a long way.

There also seems to be some confusion about who is running this household in terms of what time we get home, whom we ask for the car, when we get permission to stay all night with a girl friend. No doubt I am responsible for this communications gap and have failed to make myself clear. As the chief moneychanger and provider in his household, I am the boss. From time to time I delegate this authority to your mother.

In the past few days I particularly feel I have been had. I interceded to relieve you of baby-sitting duties (while your mother and I attended Commencement) by bribing Becky and a friend. Instead of gratitude you stay up until 2 o'clock this morning, and arrive home as irascible as a hungry barracuda.

Much as I would like to overlook these small deviations from your normal, sweet, loving behavior, I feel that it is my duty as a father to register our protest and dissent—also to invoke a little discipline, painful as it may be for us all.

Thus, you are to be home by 10:30 each evening (providing we let you out in the first place), are to drive the car only by specific permission in each instance, are to spend the night with girl friends only with prior approval, and are to love your brother and sisters and mother and father. Relief from these arbitrary and capricious rules may be granted only by formal petition and unanimous vote of your supervisors.

Your loving father

From the expression on her face I learned a startling fact about my eldest daughter—she had no sense of humor.

"Ten-thirty?" she asked, incredulously.

I nodded firmly.

"Ten-thirty?" she asked her mother. My wife just turned her palms upward and shrugged her shoulders. I suppose I can be thankful that she didn't also tap her forehead and point at me.

"I'm leaving home," Debbie announced.

"Good," I said jovially. "I'll help you pack."

"I mean it. I really mean it."

I decided to play along. "Where do you think you'll live?"

"I'll go live with Cindy."

"Oh, no," I protested. "Cindy's mother works. Her dad works. They have enough family to support without you, too—what with your appetite for clothes and food."

That stopped her for a minute. "Then I'll rent an apartment and live alone."

I guffawed at that. "You can't. You're under-age. It's against the law." I was only guessing, but my tone implied that I was sure of my ground—I thought.

Debbie was getting desperate. "I'll go away to school."

"I'll settle for any good school that requires reasonable hours— like 10:30—and no dates except on weekends."

"I know . . . " she said, changing the subject.

"Know what?"

"I'll get married."

"To whom?"

"Elmer."

"I'll bet that news would gladden his day," I chortled. "Tell me, has he seen you with your hair up in curlers?"

She glared. "He'd marry me. I know he would."

"Oh yeah," I bluffed. "Well, let's get this settled right now. You just call him up and tell him to come over here. In fact, I'll do it for you." I walked toward the telephone.

"I'll do it myself," she said, snatching the phone from my hand.

"She's bluffing," I told my wife as Debbie dialed the number.

"Hello, Elmer," Debbie cooed. I could hardly believe the change in her voice. "Can you come over for a few minutes?" Debbie continued. "I just told my father we want to get married."

There was a long silence on the other end of the line. Debbie clicked the phone, "Elmer, Elmer, are you there?" Evidently he said something, because she hung up and announced, "He'll be here in a few minutes." As that thought sank in, she sprinted up the stairs and into the bathroom.

By the time the doorbell rang, she emerged as her most glamorous going-out-in-the-evening self. I could hardly believe the transition. Elmer was ushered in in an atmosphere of strict formality. We seated ourselves around the family hearth. He practically sat at attention as he blurted, "Mr. Davis, I think Debbie is a nice girl, but we're too young to get married. I'm only 19!"

I had to give Debbie credit. She survived this blow without blinking an eye. "But, Elmer," she purred.

"How come she talks to him like a contented kitten and to me like an unhappy bobcat?" I thought to myself as she continued.

"But, Elmer, you don't understand how miserable things are around here. You've got to take me out of all this."

Good old Elmer—he looked very skeptical.

Debbie was losing her patience—also her composure. Suddenly, the tears popped out, slopping up her mascara. "Here," she said, throwing me a defiant glance as she handed Elmer my letter, "read this!"

Elmer read the letter, then laid it on the coffee table. Without giving him a chance to comment, Debbie launched into a tirade about how intolerable life in our household had become, concluding with the proclamation that she had no choice but to leave home.

At this point Elmer looked me in the eye and shrugged, "Mr. Davis, I know just how you must feel. We had to go through this at my house a couple of years ago with my older sister."

Debbie looked as if she'd been pole-axed by a two-by-four. But I had to give her credit—she rolled with the punch. Within the flash of a second she was smiling sweetly and fluttering her eyelashes demurely as Elmer continued, "I don't think these rules are unreasonable. I'll get Debbie home whenever you say."

At this tender moment, I could not help but think about Larry Rice and his theory on God's divine plan. I put my hand on Elmer's shoulder and said, "Son, I'm going to barbecue some steaks tonight. How'd you like to stay for dinner?" ✎

And They Shall Be Healed

How I Received the Gift of Healing

I shook my head and muttered, "This can't be"

By FATHER RALPH A. DIORIO with DONALD GROPMAN
May 1981, condensed from *The Man Beneath the Gift**

O N FRIDAY, February 20, 1976, God began to move one of the final pieces of my puzzle into place, the piece from which my healing gift would grow. His agents were several young members of my Hispanic congregation in Fitchburg, Mass., who approached me that Friday and asked, "Please, Father Ralph, will you let us go charismatic?"

Charismatic? I thought. I knew that the Charismatic Renewal was a contemporary

*This article © 1980 by Father Ralph A. DiOrio and Donald Gropman. Originally published by William Morrow, and Co., Inc. Reprinted with permission.

restoration of the spiritual atmosphere of the early Church. I also knew the Renewal was dedicated to reaffirming the presence of the Holy Spirit in everyday life. But I had no strong personal feelings about the Renewal because I simply didn't know enough about it.

After I thought about it a minute or two, I said, "Going charismatic is not a fly-by-night emotional adventure. It calls for a commitment. We can only go into it if you feel that you can handle it and be faithful to it."

As soon as they left, I ran up to my room and phoned my Auxiliary Bishop, Timothy Harrington. "Bishop," I said, "they've asked me to go charismatic. I'm not sure it's my cup of tea." He laughed, perhaps as if he'd expected this turn of events, and invited me to attend the Charismatic Renewal prayer meetings held in St. John's Church in Worcester.

Four days later, on Tuesday, February 24, when I went to my first Charismatic Renewal Service, I was relieved because the service didn't look fanatic or farfetched in any way. And I was immediately impressed by the Charismatic Renewal for two substantial reasons.

The first was the way the service completely surrounded the Eucharistic celebration. For a Roman Catholic priest—I had been one 19 years—the Eucharist is the very heart and soul of God's presence among his people.

The second essential element was the Renewal's obvious and direct connection to the most basic values of Christianity, its clear link to Christianity's first days.

Any further proof I needed came at the inner healing session of the service. Suddenly I saw the unity of all the studies I'd made in the supposedly separate disciplines of philosophy, ethics, psychology, sociology, and theology. At that moment, my entire life of priestly studies fused into the eternal truth that

mind, body, and spirit are parts of the whole, and I realized beyond doubt that I could best bring people to their God and God to his people through a holistic approach.

I returned to my young parishioners and told them the answer to their question was yes. We would go charismatic.

My first contact with the Charismatic Renewal occurred in February, but the signs of what was coming began two months earlier, around Christmastime. My body was constantly aflame. When I touched anything, sparks came out of me. Electricity jumped out of my body. I didn't know what was happening. For a while I couldn't touch anything. At first I thought it was a static electric charge from the carpets, but it wasn't, because it happened whether there were carpets or not, and it was stronger than any static charge I had ever felt before.

After the electricity started, my knuckles began to hurt, as if I were getting arthritis. Then pains began to pass through other parts of my body. I was frightened because I still didn't know what was happening to me. Now I can see that the Lord was allowing me to experience the pains of the physical body so I could respond to the pains of others. He was preparing me for my healing ministry.

At the beginning of May, I went home to see my mother in Providence, R.I. She was very sick, but I didn't seem to be able to help her, and I suffered in my own heart. I sat at the table in my mother's kitchen. A rage at my powerlessness to help her came over me. I banged my fist on that table. I said things I had never said before in my life. I said, "Here I am, a Catholic priest, a priest! A minister of God! I am obedient to my bishop. I am submissive to everybody. I am working for the poorest of the poor. Here my own mother is suffering, and I can't even help her, Damn it!" I shouted. I banged the table again.

That kind of behavior was completely out of character for me. I do not use that kind of language. I don't bang furniture. The moment I realized what I had said and done, I asked my mother to forgive me, and she did.

But a little while later, when I was getting ready to leave, my mother asked, "Son, will you do me a favor before you leave?"

"Sure, Ma," I answered.

And she said, "Will you pray for me?"

"Pray for you!" I shouted. Her request made me angry again. "What good is it?" Of all things for a dedicated priest like myself to say, that was about the worst. My dedication to my priesthood was battling with my frustration at not being able to help my own mother. But I cooled down quickly and said OK.

My mother knelt down, and I laid hands on her head. When she got up, I left. I got in my car and drove back to my rectory. When I got there, I phoned my mother. She told me that after I left, she had had a dizzy spell for an hour. And she had felt something go through her body, and she had been healed of her illness. From that moment on, the Spirit was working through me. I still didn't understand or even see what was happening. But I didn't have long to wait.

L ess than three months after my first visit to a charismatic service, my own healing gift broke out. I had begun attending the charismatic services led by Father McDonough in Boston. I was at one of his services on a Saturday in early May when I felt something happening to me.

Some people in the church asked me to pray over them. I felt myself, my body, filled with a new power, and the power flowed out of me and into them. "Could it be?" I asked myself, and I was frightened. I pulled back from it. I didn't even finish the prayer. I pulled away from the people. I shook my head and muttered, "This can't be." I said to my friend, who had driven me to Boston, "Let's go home." But I didn't tell him what had happened.

The next day I conducted my regular Sunday service. When it was over, a few of my parishioners came up and asked if we could go to Father McDonough's again. I said, "Oh, let's not go. I don't think we should go today." I was uncomfortable at what had happened the day before.

But my parishioners were insistent, and they wouldn't take no for an answer. "Let's go, Father Ralph. Come on, we've just got to go today. And it's special, too, because it's Mother's Day." I was still apprehensive, but I finally agreed because it seemed so important to them.

We got into various cars and drove the 50 miles to Boston. What happened to me later made it a day I shall never forget.

When we arrived at the church, I didn't even go behind the sacristy to speak to Father McDonough. I went to the very rear of the church, all by myself, hoping that Father McDonough would not even see me. And as I stood there, a small girl of six or seven came around with papers for petitions. She recognized me from previous services when Father McDonough had introduced me and I had preached. "Hi, Father Ralph," she said, "here's a piece of paper.

Why don't you write a petition to God? Whatever you like."

"And what should I write?" I asked her.

"Oh," she smiled, "what is in your heart."

I looked down at her smiling face and saw a little child was leading me. I smiled back and said all right. I took a piece of paper and wrote a message to God, a personal petition that would be placed on the altar during the charismatic service.

I wrote my petition in three languages: Latin, Italian, and Spanish. I hoped that if Father McDonough did read those petitions, he wouldn't understand them. Though I wrote the petition three different times in three different languages, I had no control over what I wrote. My beseechings just poured right out of me: "God, if it be your will, give me the fulfillment of my life as a priest. Grant me a new, complete, and worldwide ministry in the Charismatic Renewal, specifically in the healing ministry, the thing I have always wanted. Grant me a ministry to heal the bodies and souls of mankind."

The smiling little girl took my petition and placed it on the altar. As soon as she put it down, it seemed, Father McDonough spotted me in the shadows at the back of the church and immediately called me up to preach. I still hung back, even though I had just written that petition asking God to grant me a new ministry, but I couldn't refuse Father McDonough. I walked up to the front of the church. Since it was Mother's Day, I preached a sermon on the Blessed Mother.

The congregation was excited by my sermon. People began clapping. They seemed to want me to say something more, maybe even do something. But I was holding back. I tried to slip off quietly behind the altar and be by myself. Suddenly a woman ran into the small room where I was and shouted, "Father, hurry up, quick! My husband is bleeding inside his stomach!"

"Bleeding?" I asked. "Then you have to get him to a doctor. Let's call an ambulance right away and get him to a hospital."

"No! No!" she insisted. "*Pray* for him."

"Pray for him? Come on," I said. "Call the doctor."

But this woman would not back down. In fact she grew even more insistent. "Father!" she demanded. "Pray!"

So I gave in to it. All right, I said to myself, I'll pray. And I did, and *poom!* The man went down. Just like that. In a minute he looked up at me and said, "I feel great. The pain has gone. My ulcers don't seem to be bleeding anymore."

My natural instinct was to wonder if the man was pulling my leg. It didn't make any sense. He is bleeding, and I pray over him. All of a sudden the bleeding stops and he's OK? I felt certain he was tricking me for some reason of his own. How slow I was to believe what was happening to me!

Then I wondered if the man was crazy. He didn't look crazy, though. He was just an ordinary-looking, well-dressed, middle-aged man. While I was wondering about him, he got up, brushed himself off, and went back to his seat singing, "Hallelujah!"

At that moment a nun, Father McDonough's sister, came up to me, and said, "Father, there's a woman going crazy here. She wants to kill her son and daughter. Will you do a deliverance on her?"

Deliverance? But the nun quickly brought the woman into the hallway where I was. I laid hands on her for about ten minutes. The woman got totally freed. She went back happy. I said to myself, "Holy mackerel! Is this real? Is this happening to me?"

My head was still spinning with wonder when a school teacher came out, a young woman about 25 from Cambridge, and she said, "Father, I have some problems, serious problems. Will you pray with me?"

"All right," I said. "Let's sit down." So I sat with the woman in the stairwell, holding her hand. I held her hand and prayed with her, and she was overpowered. A moment later she told me, "I felt the heat go through my body, a healing through my brain."

When she went back to her seat happy and smiling, I was left alone near the stairs in the hallway. I was in something of a daze. I couldn't understand what was happening to me.

As soon as the service was over, I rushed up the side aisle of the church, trying to flee. But Father McDonough called me back from the pulpit and asked me to pray over a little crippled boy. I couldn't say no in front of all those people. I went up to the little boy and placed my hands on him. He started *moving*, and people saw this.

My fear rose in one last pull. I drew back from what was happening, but a lady cried out to me, "Father, pray over me! Touch me!" And when I did, *poom!* She went right down. "Father, touch me!" the people shouted. And when I did, *poom!* One after the other, they went down. By the time I got to the other end of the church, the whole place was laid out. People on all sides of me had been "slain in the Spirit."

Then I knew I had broken out. I understood that God had granted me my healing ministry.   ✳

WHO'S IN CHARGE HERE?

A small boy, paying a 2¢ fine for an overdue-book, looked thoughtfully at the librarian and asked: "Can you make a living out of this?"

Grand Rapids (Mich.) *Press* (3 Feb. '62).

*

"Just because you have been kept waiting," said the nurse to the impatient expectant father, "doesn't necessarily mean that the baby will be a girl."

A.M.A. *News* (12 Nov. '62).

*

The giant tackle had received his quarterly grade report, and he sadly displayed the card to his friend the head coach. "Well, coach, what am I gonna do now?" he inquired.

With furrowed brow the coach studied the report. "Look, Moose, you got a D and three F's. Seems to me you been putting in too much time on one subject," he opined. *Manhattan Inter-Mountain Press* (2 Nov. '61).

The Doctor Is Sick

I didn't know if I could stand the burden of kidney dialysis any longer. Then God answered my prayers

By C. P. TRANISI, M.D.
June 1979

IN THE PALE PRE-DAWN, I drove toward the hospital where I had served as an intern a long time before. I shuddered when I saw the aging structure, for I approached it now as a patient, not a physician.

A stoplight delayed me. In those few moments, I saw the window of the room where I had watched spring appear as I waged a month-long war against my own death. Ten trips to surgery; twice-weekly runs on the kidney machine: the standard treatment for uremia.

Atop the hospital stood a neon crucifix in garish yellow. I remembered how amused we interns were when an old nun insisted that pilots looked for that crucifix as a guide on their final approach to the airport. We smiled, for we thought that Sister Mary X-ray's mind was

Reprinted with permission of author.

wandering. But after those unending nights as a patient at that hospital, listening to jets screech overhead, I came to think that Sister knew what she was talking about.

The noisy elevator transported me to the floor, where a long and familiar corridor, heavy with tile, led to the dialysis unit. I had often referred to the unit as the "laundry." And each time I entered, I recalled the end-stage of another patient.

Call her Rose, one of eight patients in the ward. She was in the final stages of cancer. Her body had been ravaged, but her mind remained lucid. Too much so; sleep eluded her. It was the intern's duty to bring a sedative to her each night.

Promptly at 10 our little entourage would assemble. The nurse entered the darkened ward first: the beam of her flashlight hopscotched on the tile floor

137

ahead. We went directly to Rose's bed. A few other patients stirred protestingly at the first intrusion of the night.

Rose would be sitting up in bed, broomstick arms clamped around her knees. Her eyes seemed uncommonly large because of the wasting so evident in her face.

"Oh, I'm glad it's you, doctor," Rose would whisper to me. "Because you know how to use the needle." Her veins were studded with scarring from preceding punctures. Finding a likely spot, I injected the sedative that would give Rose what she sought, freedom from reality. In a few moments, Rose sank into her pillow, scarcely indenting it.

I never forgot Rose and what I had failed to do there. I had treated her mechanically, not as a fellow human being. I could have given her more than chemical comfort.

"Over here," Sheila hailed from the corner of the unit. The air was permeated with the smell of disinfectants, alcohol, and Clorox, wafted about by whirring blood pumps. I came to stand by the bed. Was it the same bed where Rose met death? I feared that it might be.

As Sheila unraveled the gauze covering the shunt in my arm, I watched her face for a telltale sign. "Oh, Oh! Something wrong with the shunt. It's clotted and I can't use it. I'll call the doctor."

Shunts are notorious for being temperamental. "I've warned you," the doctor said, "that this day was sure to come. Now we have to use the fistula in your other arm for dialysis. This is as good a time as any to find out if it is mature enough."

I tried to read, but it was difficult to hold a book with one hand. And it was impossible to ignore that initial backache of the dialysis process. A red light flashed on my machine accompanied by a loud, incessant "beep, beep, beep." Sheila checked. Another problem—a "blowout" in the fistula. She put in a page for the doctor.

"What if they can't run me?" I wondered. "Will they send me home? I've still got four hours to run. I'd sure get sick again."

There was no alternative. Another trip to surgery to revise the shunt. It would be my 11th. A scheduled 20-minute procedure stretched into an hour of needles, novocaine, wires, pains, cries of protest squelched, and tears blinked back.

Back on the machine, the run was uneventful. For another hour. Then, it became necessary to revise the opposite side of the shunt which had clotted. During the three-hour wait for the surgeon to return from another hospital, I tried to distract myself by finishing *Les Miserables*. Two passages struck me: "We should love each other dearly and always, for there is no other thing in the world—but that we love one another." And, "It is nothing to die but frightful not to live."

Mercifully, my 12th session in surgery was over in 20 minutes. It was well into the afternoon. The other patients had gone home.

After a long interval, a dreaded swimming sensation developed. Beads of sweat covered my face. An intense nausea. I was in a "blood pressure crash."

Sheila tilted me, ran in the saline, squeezed the blood pressure cuff desperately. Slowly, the symptoms abated and I stabilized. A cool wet cloth seemed a luxury on my forehead.

A figure in black loomed over me. "Heard you are having a tough day," the priest said. Bad news travels fast in a hospital. "How about Communion?" he asked.

I looked to Sheila for her approval. "He's been sick to his stomach," she reported, "but I think it would be safe now."

The priest and Sheila stood apart from me. I was left alone for my Communion: "You know, Lord, I have wondered if You would ever come to this place. I mean, if You did not, well—I would understand.

"About this sickness again, Lord—why me? This sort of trial is really for the making of a saint. Now, we both know that I do not merit such consideration. To be honest, I just cannot live with the thought of this burden for the rest of my life. Please, Lord, give me grace and strength to cope with it. I cannot do it of my own will."

It was just past six o'clock when Sheila took me downstairs. Though shaky, I stood and walked to the scale with resolve, for I sensed that she wanted me to stay at the hospital overnight. When I left the unit for my car, I felt like a flat tire.

By the time I turned onto our driveway, I felt a little better. I paused there to savor the sight of my home.

My wife had heard the car drive up. Now the door flew open; her eyes searched for any sign of my state. My voice betrayed me: "Lazarus has come home!"

After picking at the first food since early that morning, I went to the welcome of my chair. Flames from the fireplace danced across my newspaper, but I was merely staring at it. She must have guessed, for she said, "Why don't you go to bed early tonight?" I welcomed the suggestion.

The comfort of my bed. "If sleep and death are brothers, there is nothing to fear," I thought. And, "It is nothing to die, it is not living that is frightening." At last sleep came.

Fortunately, most of my dialysis sessions were not so severe. Each month, blood specimens were analyzed, the results were referred to as "numbers." Finally, one month, a particle of hope, as my fellow physician uttered, "H-m-m-m." When I asked for his meaning, he merely replied, "We'll see what your 'numbers' are next month."

After that glint of hope, I intensified my assault on heaven and all its saints. Nothing dramatic came of it, but indirect signs developed. On one occasion, I had to be "taken down" after only an hour of dialysis. "Come back next week on your regular turn," I was told.

I was certain that the poison in my blood would be driving me back to my machine before the week passed. But I survived the week with no ill effects.

When I inquired about the feasibility of traveling to Phoenix for a long weekend, I was encouraged to stay for an entire week. After I survived that week as well, the doctor became more optimistic; my own confidence lagged far behind.

My runs on the machine were reduced to once a week, which seemed quite hard on me. But the numbers slowly improved. Then I came to be dialyzed on a "smaller kidney." I tolerated those sessions better. I could almost consent to live by that manner and schedule.

The doctor telephoned me. "We've got your new numbers and they are not bad. Since we are scarcely dialyzing you now, I think you can be managed off the machine!"

Though I had longed to hear those words all those many months, I reacted inappropriately. Instead of euphoria, I felt abandoned. That first week off the machine I was beset with doubts, anxiety, and unpleasant symptoms. My interval off the machine extended and at last I dared to think it: "Off the machine! After 15 months, free to live again!"

Again, I asked, "Why me?" I recalled, with pain, how we interns would rationalize away medical science's ineptness at treating uremia in the old days. "It's not a bad way to go," we would say. What did we know about death?

Why me? Was it modern medical technology? Certainly, the machine saved my life, and for that I am most grateful. But the machine alone couldn't have restored sufficient kidney function to maintain me off the machine.

Was it a miracle then?

During those interminable months I prayed, even as the leper, "Jesus, Master, take pity." And I dared to hope that the words Jesus spoke of Lazarus would come to have meaning for me: "This sickness is not to end in death; rather it is for God's glory."

And I dared to imagine the emotions that prevailed when Jesus stood before the tomb and called loudly: "Lazarus, come out." The dead man came out bound hand and foot. "Untie him," Jesus told them, "and let him go free."

On Thanksgiving Day, my wife guessed, "You have been thinking about the other patients down there today, haven't you?" Yes, they had been in my thoughts, especially since I had spent part of the preceding Thanksgiving day on the machine alongside them.

I stopped by for a visit and met three fellow patients. We shook hands and I sat to visit with them. "Well, how does it feel to be off dialysis?" one asked me.

I hedged. If I said, "Great," it would only emphasize the agony of his plight. If nothing else from my ordeal, I have learned the language of suffering. Never again shall I treat a patient the careless way I treated Rose.

"I think you can imagine how it would be to go off the machine," I replied.

He smiled a wan smile. He understood.   ✳

A QUESTION OF IDENTITY

When I was a newly ordained priest, I went out to help in a certain parish over Holy Week. The pastor was a tough character who seemed never to have a kind word for me during the entire week. He did, however, have a dog on whom he lavished all his affection.

Easter Sunday evening, the pastor offered to drive me home. We three got into his car, with the dog going to sleep on the floor of the back seat, and myself riding next to the pastor up front. We stopped to get gas, and while the attendant filled the tank and wiped the windshield, Father paced restlessly up and down outside.

Then the attendant made a move to wipe the side windows. Father waved him off, shouting, "Don't bother with those. That fool inside will just slobber all over them anyhow!" I tried to get the dog to sit up and take a bow, but he was too smart to move.

Joseph T. McGloin, S.J., in the *Twin Citian* (March '63).

The Holy Man Who Said I Would Be Healed

Father Solanus Casey of Detroit is being
studied as a candidate for sainthood

By TED WARNER
November 1984, condensed from *Liguorian**

B ERNARD (Barney) Casey left
his home in Superior, Wis.,
on Dec. 21, 1896, in the midst
of a blizzard. The tall, frail
young man traveled by train
through St. Paul, Milwaukee,
and Chicago before arriving
at last, three days later, in
Detroit.

He stepped down from the
train in Detroit, grasping a small
valise that held all of his
possessions. After asking directions, he boarded a streetcar,
rode out Jefferson Avenue, and
alighted at the corner of Mt.
Elliott Avenue. The weary
young man trudged the last half
mile through blinding snow,

finally coming to his destination
— St. Bonaventure Monastery.

Bernard Casey hesitated momentarily before he raised his
hand to knock at the heavy door.
From within, voices raised in
joyful song drifted into the night,
reminding the traveler that it
was Christmas Eve.

This was Barney Casey's second attempt to prepare himself
for the priesthood. In 1892 he
had entered St. Francis de Sales
Seminary in Milwaukee. After
nearly four years of frustrating
study, one of the superiors called
him aside. "You obviously have
a calling," the superior explained
with sympathy, "but your inability to grasp the necessary theology and your trouble with Latin
and German are restricting your

*This article © 1984 by Liguori Publi-
cations. Reprinted with permission.

progress." Dejected, Barney accepted the decision and returned to his home in Superior. At home, he consulted with the Franciscan priest who had been his spiritual adviser in the past. The friar, impressed with Barney's strong desire, encouraged him to write the Jesuits, the Franciscans, and the Capuchins, confident that one of the Orders would accept him. Barney wrote the letters immediately and then eagerly awaited an answer, praying constantly.

During this interlude of prayer and indecision, though he neither saw nor heard anything, the young man was conscious of Mary Immaculate urging him to "go to Detroit." And so, on Christmas Eve in 1896, heeding the silent call of our Lady, Barney Casey stood at the threshold of his future.

On Jan. 14, 1897, Barney Casey received the brown habit of the Capuchins, taking the name Francis Solanus.

After the profession of his first vows, his piety and his humble acceptance of the most menial tasks caught the attention of the Provincial. He recognized Solanus's sincere and resolute yearning for the priesthood and had the young novice sent to the Capuchin seminary in Milwaukee.

Unfortunately, the books were again in Latin. Once more, Solanus faced the problem that had haunted his earlier years. But this time the head of the seminary, impressed with the novice's faith and determination, tutored him privately. In 1904 he designated Solanus for Holy Orders.

Not everyone on the faculty was pleased with this decision, however. After much debate, it was decided that Solanus could become a "simple Mass priest." In other words, he could say Mass but would not be able to hear confessions or preach Church dogma.

On July 31, 1904, in Appleton, Wis., Francis Solanus sang his first Mass. Shortly after, he was assigned to Sacred Heart Friary in Yonkers, N.Y.

For the next 20 years, Father Solanus served several churches in the Yonkers area. Stories of cures and miracles obtained through his prayers filtered back to the Provincial. Finally, in 1923, convinced there might be something special about this man, the superior ordered the priest to jot down all requests and note if favors were granted. From then until the time of his death, Father Solanus filled over seven ledgers with requests, intentions, and favors.

In August, 1924, Solanus was transfered back to St. Bonaventure in Detroit and was assigned the lowly duty of porter. His reputation continued to spread, and in 1939 word of his powers reached my mother.

On March 24 of that year, we left Mackinaw City, Mich., and traveled south on our way to the University of Michigan Hospital. We were headed for the first in a series of operations on my legs to help correct the effects of infantile paralysis. As we drove, Mother spoke of the quiet, holy man in Detroit whose prayers could bring about miracles. She was taking me to see him, she explained, in hopes that his prayers would help my recovery.

We drove all night through a raging snowstorm and arrived at St. Bonaventure's about mid-morning the following day. We were greeted by an elderly bearded monk who reminded me of my grandfather. As we each grasped one of his outstretched hands, I felt a warmth pass into my body from his.

"You've had a very long trip," he said softly, releasing our hands as he reached around us to shut the door. "Has the weather been this bad all the way from the Straits?"

My mother and I looked at each other in surprise, impressed that this priest knew how far we had traveled. "Yes, Father," my mother answered, "it hasn't let up since we left. I hope it stops soon. We have to go on to Ann Arbor today."

Father Solanus led us through a short hall into a large, warm room. He stopped in front of a wide window and looked out onto the wintery scene. Spreading his arms wide, he spoke in barely audible words, "The storm will cease." As if in answer to his quiet command, the snow stopped and the sun broke through the clouds. Then, ignoring our amazement, he continued. "Now, how may I help you?"

I squeezed Mother's hand tightly as she told the priest of my forthcoming operations. "The doctors are going to transplant some of the muscles from Teddy's right leg to his left in hopes that it will strengthen the weaker one. It's something they've never tried before, so we're here to ask your prayers."

Father Solanus smiled warmly. "Of course. We will remember him in our daily prayers. We'll also enroll him in our Seraphic Mass Association. He will receive the grace of all our missionaries. First, let us kneel and pray together."

A concerned expression crossed his face as he advised, "Theodore, you don't have to kneel if it's too uncomfortable for you." Without hesitation, I reached down and unfastened the steel brace at my left knee. What had always been an awkward movement for me came with ease and I knelt beside them.

Joining hands in a small circle,

we said the Lord's Prayer and Hail Mary in unison. Then he asked if we could sit and visit a while longer. He sat at a large oak desk and we took our positions across from him.

Reaching into the top right drawer, Father Solanus removed a box of candy. "I have a penchant for chocolates," he explained, "but it is Lent." He looked in my direction and pushed the box toward me. "However, if you'd like one, you're welcome to it." I thanked him and swallowed the sweet morsel.

When he spoke again, his eyes took on a faraway look. "Now then, as for this operation Theodore is to have, I can only tell you this. It will be scheduled three times before he has it. When it finally does take place, it will have a religious significance." A reassuring smile crossed his wrinkled face as he concluded, "The surgeons at Ann Arbor are very competent men. While Theodore will always carry the effects of the paralysis, he will eventually walk without the use of braces."

We thanked Father Solanus for his prayers and words of encouragement and stood to leave. He placed his right hand on my mother's shoulder and patted her gently. "Rest assured, Mother, he will come through it just fine. Now, please kneel and I will give you our blessing." He made a slow Sign of the Cross over us as we knelt before him. We promised to return the following year to let him know the results of the surgery and my progress.

Later that afternoon, I was admitted to the hospital. My operation was scheduled for the following Monday morning. But on Monday, I had a chest cold and the surgery was postponed for a few days. Then an outbreak of an infectious disease elsewhere in the building called for another postponement. This time it was rescheduled for the week between Palm Sunday and Easter.

Good Friday morning, April 7, I lay on a bed outside the surgical amphitheater. I was drowsy from the sedative, but this did not alleviate my fright. My mother touched my hand reassuringly. "Father Solanus promised you would be fine." I relaxed at the memory of the old priest's gentle smile.

The two attendants wheeled me into the sterile white room. As they lifted me onto the surgical table, I looked up into the large, round light suspended above it. Beyond that, the eyes of student spectators sitting behind a glass wall stared down at me. My arms and legs were secured to the table. Without warning, someone placed an ether mask on my nose and mouth. As I drifted into sleep, I noticed a clock on the wall. It was noon.

I woke feeling nauseous. Though I could barely make out the blurred images of my parents sitting beside me, I could hear their voices clearly. "Dad took the day off from work. We've been to *Tre Ore* services at the chapel," Mother announced. "How do you feel?"

"I think I'm going to be sick," I replied. I tried to sit up. As I did, my eyes focused momentarily on a clock hanging over the door. The hands read shortly past three o'clock.

I had been on the operating table during the exact hours of *Tre Ore:* noon until three. In my dazed condition, Father Solanus's words came back to me: "It will be scheduled three times . . . but when it finally does take place, it will have a religious significance."

The following spring, on March 28, 1940, my mother and I returned to Detroit. After visiting Father Solanus and explaining how well the surgery had gone, we stood to leave. He thanked us for coming back and offered his blessing. As we rose from our knees, he took his pen and began to write in a small book.

Many years later, thanks to the kindness of Brother Leo at St. Bonaventure, I had the opportunity to read the entry myself. On page 200 of ledger 8, Father Solanus had written: "Theodore Warner, nine, infantile paralysis since six months old, was prayed for and enrolled in S.M.A., March 25, last year— was on the operating table on Good Friday for three hours while his parents prayed *Tre Ore . . .* quite improved."

I never saw Father Solanus again, but his reputation continued to grow. Though he seldom left the monastery, the world sought him out. When he was with someone, that person became the most important individual in the world. Even after he retired, the crowds and letters continued to come. He finally had to admit, in a letter to a friend, "I am growing old! I used to be able to go on for 22 hours a day. Now I can't stay up more than 18."

Early in July, 1957, Father Solanus was taken to a hospital in Detroit. Fully aware that he was dying, he had one request— that he be conscious when death came so he could surrender his soul to God.

At 11 A.M., July 31, 1957, Father Solanus sat up in his bed. In the presence of the doctors and nurses, he extended his hands and said loudly, "I give my soul to Jesus Christ"—and his body fell back on his bed. Father Francis Solanus Casey was dead.

Although Father Solanus's

canonization cause is still being studied, there is not the slightest doubt in my mind that in 1939 and again in 1940, I had the rare privilege of visiting a saint.

In 1976 the cause for beatification and canonization of Father Francis Solanus Casey was presented to John Cardinal Dearden, then Archbishop of Detroit. In January, 1977, Cardinal Dearden ordered the collection and organization of Father Solanus's writings. In June, 1980, the collected works were taken to Rome for official examination.   ✻

Two Supreme Court Decisions

Slavery
1857

Although he may have a heart and a brain, and he may be a human life biologically, a slave is not a legal person. The Dred Scott decision by the U.S. Supreme Court has made that clear.

A black man only becomes a legal person when he is set free. Before that time, we should not concern ourselves about him. He has no legal rights.

If you think that slavery is wrong, then nobody is forcing you to be a slaveowner. But don't impose your morality on somebody else!

A man has a right to do what he wants with his own property.

Isn't slavery really something merciful? After all, every black man has a right to be protected. Isn't it better never to be set free than to be sent unprepared, and ill-equipped, into a cruel world? (Spoken by someone already free.)

Abortion
1973

Although he may have a heart and a brain, and he may be a human life biologically, an unborn baby is not a legal person. The Roe vs. Wade decision by the U.S. Supreme Court has made that clear.

A baby only becomes a legal person when he is born. Before that time, we should not concern ourselves about him. He has no legal rights.

If you think abortion is wrong, then nobody is forcing you to have one. But don't impose your morality on somebody else!

A woman has a right to do what she wants with her own body.

Isn't abortion really something merciful? After all, every baby has a right to be wanted. Isn't it better never to be born than to be sent alone and unloved into a cruel world? (Spoken by someone already born.)   *Friar.*

Dorothy Day
Comes to Visit

. . . and leaves with a three-day-old peanut butter sandwich

By PATRICIA MCGOWAN
April 1976, condensed from *U.S. Catholic**

S UPPOSE A WOMAN took the Gospel literally and decided to feed the hungry, clothe the naked, harbor the harborless. What would she be like? "She's just like Grandma," said our ten-year-old. That was also the reaction of a young Episcopal clergyman who visited us. "I walked into the living room," he said, "and there was this grandmotherly old lady. Next thing I knew, I was being introduced to Dorothy Day."

Dorothy Day stayed with our family in Fall River during her Massachusetts lecture tour. Our

*This article © 1975 by Claretian Publications. Reprinted with permission.

six children didn't know what to expect. They had heard of her all their lives, but couldn't imagine meeting her face to face. It was a little bit like having St. Francis of Assisi drop in. For over 40 years now Dorothy Day has kept open house for the poor in New York City, offering food, shelter, and clothing to all. The cofounder of the Catholic Worker Movement, now 77, looks like almost anyone's grandmother. But her impact is still like that of a delayed-action bomb.

"She says these things as if she were talking about going to the store," remarked a student at Bridgewater State College in

Massachusetts after Dorothy Day had lectured there.

"People say our work with the poor is utterly useless, like putting a Band-Aid on a cancer," she said placidly. "They say society itself must be changed. But what about the people in need *now?* They can't wait. Scripture says we should do what comes to hand.

"We like direct action—give the man in need your coat or cloak. Scripture goes further than any welfare worker. But we can't ask anyone else to help unless we first do all we can ourselves."

Now painfully arthritic, she gave her Bridgewater lecture sitting down, and the effect of her low-key address was as if she were chatting in someone's living room. She wore a long-skirted blue suit which, like all her clothes, had come from the Catholic Worker supply of donated garments.

Dorothy Day said that as a young girl she had worked on *The New York Call,* a socialist newspaper, and had been so horrified by the conditions under which she saw the poor living that she decided the only way to get over her aversion was to share their misery.

Her father, also a journalist, was conservative. He insisted that his daughters "never saunter in public, but walk briskly and always appear in hats, gloves, and shoes." But when 19-year-old Dorothy left home to share the lot of the poor, he approved. "He was glad to see me go because he thought I was a bad example to my younger sister."

Life in an unheated, dimly lit New York tenement was Dorothy Day's introduction to the life of the poor. "To bathe, I had to walk half a mile to a municipal shower. Some people in New York still have to do that."

During this period she was jailed after participating in a demonstration for women's suffrage. And she joined some Columbia University students in protesting U.S. involvement in the 1st World War. Through the years she has often suffered imprisonment in behalf of causes ranging from civil disobedience during the 2nd World War air raid drills to demonstrating last year in the United Farm Workers' struggle, when she spent two weeks in a California jail.

"My whole life has been one war after another," she said. "In my long lifetime I've never seen conditions worse. Things are harder now than they were in the Depression. There's no living space. The Depression seemed heaven compared to now."

Dorothy Day told her Bridgewater audience that she was

attracted to Communism while she was on *The Call,* but that her friends maintained she "was too religious to make a good Communist." They were proved right in 1927 when she became a Catholic. She was 30 years old, and part of the price of conversion was separation from her husband, by whom she had one daughter.

She continued writing for socialist publications, and her work brought her to the attention of Peter Maurin, a French peasant and former Christian Brother who had come to the U.S. propounding a "green revolution." His plan included development of Christian farming communes, roundtable discussions of workers and scholars, and the establishment of city houses of hospitality operated with the simplicity of the Gospels. On May Day, 1933, Peter Maurin and Dorothy Day published the first issue of *The Catholic Worker,* a tabloid setting forth these ideas.

Thereafter, until Maurin's death in 1949, the two crossed the country, lecturing and aiding in the establishment of green-revolution houses and farms. Dorothy Day's daughter Tamar was always a part of the work, being brought up partly in boarding schools and partly in the succession of tenement buildings which over the years housed the expanding Catholic Worker organization. Now the mother of nine and grandmother of eight children, Tamar lives in Vermont.

After Maurin's death Dorothy Day continued his program, aided by a procession of young idealists, including either as brief visitors or long-term staff workers many notable lay Catholics of the past four decades.

Not long ago, she was fined $250 as a slumlord after the Catholic Worker building was found to be in violation of the New York City building code.

"A rumpled man I thought was from our breadline shambled up to me and put something in my hand. 'For the fine,' he mumbled. I didn't look at what he'd given me until a little later and then I saw it was a check from W.H. Auden. I hadn't recognized him."

The Catholic Worker organization is opposed to war and totalitarianism. "We were about the only Catholic group opposing the Spanish civil war." But not all staff members agreed with its pacifism. In the 2nd World War a split occurred as many of their young men joined the armed forces.

But neither did the *Catholic Worker* subscribe to the actions of the Berrigans. "We did not support their destruction of property because you don't do to others what you wouldn't want them to do to you. We believe in non-violence, following the teaching of Gandhi."

A Gandhian technique used by the Worker organization, said Dorothy Day, is that of openness. "If we're going to march, picket, fast, or whatever, we tell the authorities about it. The peace movement doesn't actively resist evil. It's the whole business of accepting the cross. In houses of hospitality you have many opportunities to do that. There's violence all about—but we've never had anyone hurt. Windows get broken, not heads. At tense moments we pray."

Dorothy Day sums up her life and philosophy. "Don't say No to things," she advises. "And be what you want the other fellow to be."

During her stay with us Dorothy Day shopped at a department store, seeming thoroughly to enjoy selecting an inexpensive woolen hat. She wanted to see the ocean, so we drove to a nearby rock shore, where she insisted that we park well back from its edge. Unafraid of human hostility, she is "terrified of dogs and cliffs."

She spoke of women: "Women's liberation is very necessary because women have always been minimized and underpaid. But a great deal of it is too self-centered. It's not geared to the poor, but to articulate middle-class women with time

on their hands, the ones who have the least to complain about. Among the poor the position of women is dreadful.

"And I think women need the companionship of women. Women are so lonely."

As for women priests: "It's a vocation that doesn't attract me but I wouldn't disapprove of it. If there are women premiers and prime ministers, why not a woman Pope?"

On population control: "I would be afraid to say when I wanted children for fear I wouldn't be able to have them when I was ready. Birth control and abortion are both forms of genocide."

On the U.S. South: "It is now the most peaceful part of the country. The seed fell into the ground in the South and it was fertilized by young people giving their lives. Now there is an atmosphere of peace and loving kindness in Mississippi you don't find up North. Our breadline is three-quarters black, and I feel like telling them to go back to Mississippi."

Whenever possible, Dorothy Day attends daily Mass, and on a Wednesday she went to St. Mary's Cathedral in Fall River, where she melted into the crowd of elderly ladies forming most of the congregation. She responded enthusiastically when a woman in the pew ahead of her shook her hand and wished her a pleasant day at the kiss of peace. The priest kept looking at her as if he couldn't quite place her, doubtless half-remembering a score of magazine and newspaper pictures.

During her stay we had much good talk with Dorothy Day. She is no one-track reformer, but a sophisticated theater and concert-goer, at home with modern American fiction, Russian literature, and the novels of 19th-century England. Herself a writer of grace and distinction, she has written several books—for the most part autobiographical—and she contributes a monthly column, "On Pilgrimage," to *The Catholic Worker.*

The Catholic Worker, usually eight pages, has a circulation of 85,000. The work of mailing it is done by a pick-up crew from the 1st St. house.

"For office equipment we have a stencil machine held together with hairpins, and three typewriters," said Dorothy Day. "Everyone helps put out the paper: men from the breadline, staff members, visitors."

She has frequently appeared on television, and she recalled a recent occasion in Boston. "It took us hours to tape the show. The technicians and cameramen kept putting down their equipment and getting into discus-

sions on abortion, birth control, war, and peace."

Dorothy Day lives poverty. When she left Fall River, she took a Greyhound bus to New York, carrying with her a paper-bag lunch. She insisted on including in it a three-day-old peanut butter sandwich. "It's still edible," she said.

She has not read her recently published biography, *A Harsh and Dreadful Love* by William D. Miller. "People have told me I might not like it."

The title, however, is part of what is probably her favorite quotation, from *The Brothers Karamazov:* "Love in action is a harsh and dreadful thing compared with love in dreams. Love in dreams is greedy for immediate action, rapidly performed in the sight of all. But active love is labor and fortitude."

Through the years the federal government has paid frequent attention to Catholic Worker activities. Often agents have come searching for young draft resisters and pacifists, and treasury officials have sought payment of back taxes. Insisting on the personal nature of works of charity, the Worker has never incorporated as a non-profit organization, and gifts to it are not tax deductible.

But recently, said Dorothy Day, the Internal Revenue Service at last conceded that she and her co-workers were not "making profits out of the poor," and tax claims were dropped.

Possibly Internal Revenue decided it was next to impossible to collect taxes from one whose philosophy is, "We aim to give away everything we have. You always get back what you need."

Also confusing might be the observation that donations to the Catholic Worker movement are apparently obedient to the law stated in Pie-Raymond Regamey's book *Poverty:* "All these things that we cannot get hold of as long as we seek them so avidly come freely as we need them for the service of God and our fellows. It is a fact that God sends us what we need—whether money, interior strength, or good fortune. The law is so certain that the more daring saints have even founded institutions on it."

Catholic Worker institutions, thus founded, include a colony of Staten Island summer cottages where the weary and sick can flee from the torrid city; a Harlem apartment house set on its feet by the Worker organiza- tion and now cooperatively owned by its tenants; and always a farm. The present one is a large former estate in Tivoli, N.Y., where knights of the road are sheltered and where there are facilities for summer workshops and other programs.

There have always been varying numbers of houses of hospitality throughout the country, all autonomous, but taking their inspiration from Dorothy Day and keeping in touch with each other through the pages of *The Catholic Worker.*

The New York house itself will soon move into large quarters where "We will be able to take care of a great many more needy and helpless old women than before."

To the organizational ability needed to manage undertakings of this scope Dorothy Day joins "a supreme disinterestedness which seeks God Himself, not his gifts," to quote Regamey once more. Asked what will happen to the Catholic Worker movement upon her death or disability, she shrugged. "It doesn't matter."   ◥

SIGNS OF THE TIMES

On a plumbing truck in Michigan: "In our business, a flush beats a full house."   Lucille Christensen.

The Church and I

Standing on the corner, proclaiming the faith

By FRANK SHEED
January 1975, condensed from the book*

W HEN THE SHIP arrived in England I saw my future clearly. I would enjoy my year in Europe; then I would go back home to Sydney, Australia, and practice law.

But on my second Sunday in London I was sold a ticket to a concert. The purchase changed my life.

The concert was to raise money for a society I had never heard of, the Catholic Evidence Guild. I discovered that the Guild sent volunteers each day to the parks and street corners of London to defend the faith.

Mr. Sheed, with his wife, Maisie Ward, founded the publishing house of Sheed & Ward (recently sold), a key outlet for the Catholic literary revival of the 1930's, 40's, and 50's. He was also the author of what are now Catholic classics, "A Map of Life" and "Theology and Sanity."

---

*This article © 1974 by Frank Sheed. Originally published by Doubleday & Co., Inc. Reprinted with permission.

I had no thought then of joining them. But out of curiosity I went to one of their training classes. It was conducted by Jack Jonas, one of the best outdoor speakers I have ever heard. The subject was the Marks of the Church, a phrase unknown to me, though I knew of the words, *One, Holy, Catholic,* and *Apostolic* from the Nicene Creed. Jack gave his lecture on how to present the Marks to people at meetings. Then he called on us to answer the questions hecklers had asked him. I volunteered, and he cut me to pieces. It was a superb demonstration of my ignorance of the faith.

I did not mind being taken apart publicly. But the realization of my intellectual barrenness was shattering. Obviously I could not leave it at that. I came back for more. I attended the classes. Since the Guild speakers were not paid, I got a job, and ended up staying in London for four years.

In those years I read practically nothing that did not involve the faith. I lived, breathed, ate, and slept theology. Yes, slept it. I once had a high temperature. When my Catholic secretary came to wake me one morning I told her that I had just seen quite clearly how man's freedom could be reconciled with God's eternal foreknowledge, and I must tell her at once. She insisted that I take my medicine first. By the time I had taken it, I had forgotten the answer. Pity.

After a couple of months of attending classes and reading furiously, I appeared before two priests. They heard my lecture on Confession, heckled me hard, and gave me permission to speak at Highbury Corner the following Sunday night. There were to be two other junior speakers and an experienced speaker would be in charge. I went to Highbury praying that rain might wash out the meeting. (I learned later that the Guild speaker might hope for rain but it was not good form actually to pray for it.)

My prayer was not exactly answered. There was fog, which prevented the other two juniors from arriving. So the senior and I ran the whole three-hour meeting. I, having the stronger voice, did two hours.

The first meeting went well. At the end of my two hours I felt that street speaking was right up my alley.

I was soon cut down to size. It was at Finsbury Park. The senior speaker, a woman, had a vast crowd. She came down. I got up. In five minutes I had lost them all. She got me down, got up herself, and won the crowd back. I was miserable. I balanced things up later by marrying her, but the wound still throbs faintly.

On Good Friday some other speakers and I went on a retreat, my first. It was given by Father Ketterer, a Jesuit. Naturally he talked on the Passion. I had never before heard anyone talk as this Jesuit did. When the retreat ended, the small group of us were so fired with zeal that we went directly up to Highbury Corner, borrowed a fruit box from a stall near by, and ran a meeting.

There I met my first Christadelphian. They teach that everyone, good and bad, dies and stays dead till the end of the world. Then the good rise to eternal happiness, the bad continue dead. This man challenged me to prove that, apart from Christ, there had as yet been any life after death. I fell apart.

I could not even remember Dives and Lazarus. Still less did I remember Our Lord's saying on Calvary to the repentant thief, "I say unto thee, this day thou shalt be with me in Paradise." I was out on my feet.

I told my sad story at the next

Guild class. They referred me to the fifth chapter of 2nd Corinthians, where Paul notes how he would rather die sooner in order to be with Christ sooner: "We would rather be away from the body and at home with the Lord."

On the Hyde Park platform one Sunday I was discussing the Incarnation with a heckler. I was fairly new to the doctrine myself, and the heckler and I were soon out of our only slightly different depths. There was a cleric in the crowd, not looking happy. When I got down I spoke to him.
"Are you a priest?"
"Yes."
"A Catholic priest?"
"Yes."
"A Roman Catholic priest?"
"Yes."
"Didn't I make a mess of it?"
"Yes."
As it happened, he was Cardinal Merry del Val, Papal Secretary of State.

The Cardinal fortunately had listened to other speakers besides me, and was pleased. In due course we were given by Rome the canonical status of catechists, with an indulgence granted each time we spoke outdoors. I remember how pleased we were about the indulgence. Who, apart from me, cares about indulgences now?

Our lectures usually took around 15 minutes. In the rest of the hour the crowd questioned us. Upon the papacy and Church history generally we had as rigorous an examination as has been known in the world. Every charge ever brought against a Pope was leered at us, sneered at us. And from the beginning we were bound to the strictest honesty—there must be no bluffing or sidestepping. If we did not know the facts we must say so. We must find them out and tell them to the questioner at the next meeting.

So the crowd forced us to grow ever more clear-eyed about the distressingly human side of the Church, while we remained wholly determined to teach what the Church taught. We talked theology with one another all the time—at the meal we ate together before the class, on our way to and from the outdoor meetings (some of us spoke at four or five meetings a week).

A powerful theological influence was a speaker who earned her daily bread scrubbing floors. Louisa Cozens had as gifted a theological mind as I have met. She had only a grade-school education, but had read and thought and lived theology. From her I first heard Boethius' definition of *person,* "a complete individual substance of a rational nature." In a Cockney accent, but with complete clarity, she told me what it meant.

In 1928, after Maisie Ward and I were married, she came to our apartment after her day's scrubbing (having no quiet place of her own). Then, without reference books, she wrote *A Handbook of Heresies,* which is still in print. More than anyone she helped me to see the value of precision. The last conversation I had with her was on the problem of how the infinite simplicity of the divine mind could know individuals.

Meetings could be splendid, but they were not all splendid. Talking outdoors in all weathers to a handful of people can be dreary. Once a Catholic questioner told me that we did the work because it gave us a sense of power. I said that the Guildsman's nightmare was of talking through all eternity on the windiest street corner in hell to three devils and a dog.

Small audiences and bad weather were not the worst of it. Our own performance could leave us miserable— answers muddled, Scripture misquoted, tempers lost, crowds antagonized. Coming back from a meeting one of the girl speakers said (in response to my request for criticism), "You have an ugly face and an ugly voice and very bad manners. I don't know why anybody listens to you." The occasional letter to the Catholic papers asking if we were not doing the Church more harm than good we could have taken in our stride. But often we were asking ourselves the same question.

We really did care, especially about the lost tempers. My wife began one meeting by telling a heckler she was sorry she had been rude to him the previous week. The heckler said, "You'll have to confess that to your priest," Maisie said, "I already have."

When, 18 years ago, I fell off a platform in Hyde Park and was carried unconscious into a hospital, the doctor said, "A street corner speaker is he? They're all crackpots." The Guild speakers, most of them anyhow, were not. Their sole eccentricity was that they could not sleep quietly while millions were starved of food Christ meant them to have. They were an unusual combination of dead-seriousness and total light-heartedness. They took the faith seriously but not themselves.

It was always our rule to begin every meeting by saying the Our Father and Hail Mary, and end with the Creed. One of our songs ran:

With a Pater and Ave and Gloria too,
We offer these prayers that some good we may do.

But if by our teaching our crowds we mislead,
At least we are orthodox saying the Creed.

We constantly compared our experiences, analyzed our failures, made rules for ourselves. Talking to audiences who could simply walk away, we learned the art of communication the hard way.

The outdoor speaker needs questioners if he is to gain and hold a crowd. We had them. At almost every meeting we could count on members of certain violent No-Popery groups to heckle us about the bloodstained history of the Church and the sexual misconduct of Popes and priests and nuns.

Before long we were telling our crowds that at the beginning of every Mass the Pope says like the rest of us that he has sinned, in his thoughts and his words, in what he has done and in what he has failed to do. This may strike us as truer of some Popes than others. But, simply looking at what history records, while we may feel that the Popes present a magnificent totality, they have their souls to save.

I am devoted to the papacy—without it there would be hundreds of debates and no adjustor for any of them. I hope that if the test came I should die rather than deny it, as St.

Thomas More and St. John Fisher did—though in their boyhood they had lived under Alexander VI and they went to their deaths under Clement VII. I admire all the Popes I have lived under, but there have been some whom no one could admire.

Outdoor heckling did not make an ideal context for delivering Christ's message. But there was no avoiding it. As one of our ablest speakers, Cecily Hastings, used to say, "We are the ones who work the stony ground." If anyone found the crowds repulsive, he could always stay indoors. The world that needs Christ so urgently would never be there to trouble him.

We got people interested in God by going out to them, and bringing to the surface needs in themselves that only God could meet. It was only a beginning. But a man thus brought into contact with God could come to want God not as a healer or provider, but as Himself. With all the noise and mockery and confusion and lost tempers of the outdoors, we learned to get true dialog.

There were many of them. One man used to stand in front of my platform and tell the crowd of abominable crimes for which I had been imprisoned. Once he told me that he had been challenged by an atheist on the existence of God. He asked me to instruct him in some of the arguments he had heard me use. When I arrived for my next meeting he told me that he had won the debate. Five minutes later he was telling the crowd of my unspeakable past.

Another would tell the crowd that our young women speakers had solicited him the night before in Piccadilly. When he died, a young woman speaker said the *De Profundis* on the Hyde Park platform for his soul's repose.

We learned to handle the hecklers, and use their questions as a basis for the instruction of the crowd. But we occasionally ran into one who could disrupt the meeting. There was an old man in Hornsey, over 80, with a bellowing voice, who would denounce me nonstop. I tried everything—outshouting him, threatening, appealing. Desperate, I said, "It's dangerous for an old man like you to be out on a cold night like this. You should be sitting at home by the fire, meditating on your latter end." "I'd like to put my boot to yours," he said. The crowd could not stop laughing.

One of our Dominicans was on the Hyde Park platform, discussing the commonest sins, helping his listeners to examine their own consciences. He came to "sinful thoughts." He said, "I won't go into detail. You have all had thoughts of lust, for instance. You know how trying they can be." A voice from the crowd: "Ow! I've got one now."

At every religious meeting outdoors there is a religious lunatic. There was a man who believed he was the "whosoever" so frequently referred to in Scripture. He would repeat texts containing the word; after each text smiting his chest and saying, "That's me." There was a woman who spent the whole meeting praying for me—aloud! It was very distracting. I couldn't help listening with half an ear to find out what she was saying to God about me.

The questioners who were out for fun were a relief. They kept the crowd and ourselves happy. There was the man at Hampstead Heath who said to me, one night when I had a bad cough, "Excuse me, sir. I think there's something wrong with your throat. If I were you I'd get it cut." After 40 years I have not been able to think up a snappy retort.

Not all crowds were difficult. American crowds in particular are notably courteous: I have never been called a liar on an American street corner. But the Catholic speaker who goes "out into the highways and by-ways" must be prepared for humanity in the rough.

The man in Hyde Park who asked if there were lavatories in heaven was no profound theo-

160   HEROES IN OUR TIME

logical thinker. Maybe he could
not face the thought of eternity
without a wall to write on, or
maybe he was just being funny.
The speaker answered, "There
will only be lavatories in heaven
if there is waste matter to
eliminate, as to which I have no
information." I doubt if an Ecumenical Council could have
improved on that.

One atheist ended a long catalog of what was wrong with the
universe by saying, "I could
make a better universe than your
God made." The speaker replied, "I won't ask you to make
a universe. But would you make
a rabbit, just to establish confidence as a start?"

Over the years the Guild
helped a number of people
to join the Church, but conversions were not our immediate
concern. Most of our listeners
were too far away from any
active belief in God. When we
did hear of converts from our
meetings we were delighted,
of course. From one lunch
hour meeting on Tower Hill,
a few yards from the spot
where Thomas More was be-
headed, two hecklers joined the
Church and went on to become
Cistercians.

One other story of conversions pleases me by the way it
falls into a pattern. It concerns
two atheist hecklers, one in
London, one in the Midlands.

Atheist No. 1 became a

Catholic, and a Guild speaker.
When his daughter was nine she
was found to be suffering from
a kidney disease. Our ex-atheist
prayed that she might be spared
the pain, that he might have it
instead. She died without much
pain. Then it was found that he
had the disease. I used to visit
him in St. Thomas's Hospital.
He suffered greatly, and died
thanking God that his daughter
had not suffered.

Atheist No. 2 became a
Catholic, a Guild speaker, a
priest; he said a Requiem Mass
for Atheist No. 1.

In our first days on the Catholic outdoor platform we had no
idea of the intellectual labor we
were letting ourselves in for.
Against the Reformation Protestant we felt we had only to prove
that Scripture was not the sole
rule of faith. Against the materialist we would prove the Existence of God, the Immortality
of the Soul, the credibility of
the Gospels, and the Divinity
of Christ.

On all these topics there were
well-tried "proofs." We had only
to make sure we understood
these, then go out and use them
victoriously. But very early we
discovered that, valid as the
arguments might be, they made
little impression on the man in
the street.

There were a few concerned
opponents who would fight
them with considerable skill. But

the ordinary listener did not attach enough meaning to God, or the soul, or the Gospels, or even Christ, to care whether the proofs were valid or not. If our conflict with the hecklers entertained him, he would stay and listen to it; but he himself remained untouched. To contend with that we had to go ever deeper into the reality of God, and the soul, and the Gospels, and Christ. The outdoor crowd turned into a school of theology.

It had none of the calm orderliness of a seminary. But it had an immeasurable vitality. Our listeners were their natural selves, only more so. And they forced us to be ourselves, too, often our worst selves.

In a seminary the examinations are conducted by Christian men who already know the doctrines. On the street corner we offer them to men without such knowledge, to get them to change their lives. Whatever we accomplished by our teaching, we ourselves certainly learned as we never could have learned elsewhere.

One way or another we learned the first rule of ecumenism, that we must not attack other religions. Rather we had to find out what they meant to those who held them and lived by them. That meant that we must never try to make a questioner look foolish. That would only push him further away from the faith.

One occasion I remember on which the rule was broken but the speaker was not criticized. He was speaking on Confession. A rather ghastly woman in the crowd called out, "Your priests send young men from the confessional to make love to me." The speaker said, "I didn't know they gave such severe penances nowadays."

I think the strangest objection to the faith I ever heard was, "Christ on the cross was unnecessarily melodramatic. He made too much fuss." The speaker, stunned by the objection's strangeness, said, "If ever you come to be crucified, I hope you will set us all an example of quiet good taste."

An occasional test of our charity was the Catholic who had had a few drinks, and who insisted on helping. It seems that three martinis will turn the most lukewarm Catholic into a crusader (or at least they used to—crusading is out of fashion now). The non-Catholic drunks were easier to handle. I remember a big man at a New York meeting who wanted a fight. He said to the speaker on the platform, "How much of a man are you?" The speaker said, "I fulfill the definition." The other stared at him for ten minutes, then went away muttering.

Another man said to me, "What's the use of giving us all this religious hogwash? Why don't you give us something to eat? I'm hungry." He was well-dressed and looked well-fed. I offered him a dollar and told him of a hamburger stand 50 yards away. He would not take the dollar; he was only making a debating point. So, I suppose, was I.

Talking of "debating points" reminds me how common is the habit of dismissing an argument one cannot answer as "a mere debating point." At a meeting in Newark, N.J., a rather persistent heckler, unable to counter some statement of mine, said, "That's merely verbal." He felt that as long as he said something, anything, the argument was not lost. Once I was discussing Our Lord's Ascension:

Objector: If he'd gone up into the sky in Australia, he'd have been upside down.

I: I can correct you on that. I have been up in the sky in Australia, and I was not upside down.

Objector: Ah, but you were in an airplane.

Hecklers were a kind of mirror in which occasionally we might catch a glimpse of ourselves. They were bigoted and prejudiced, but what about us? Their one desire was to win the argument at all costs; so too often was ours. Bigotry does not mean believing that people who differ from you are wrong. It means assuming that they are either knaves or fools.

Outdoors we saw enough of it, directed against ourselves, to begin to understand it. But I was shown its very essence by a story told at a Catholic Truth Conference in 1922. A new convert from Ireland, Shane Leslie, told of two old Catholic ladies in Dublin, passing by a lawn on which an elderly cleric was throwing a ball to a dog. Said one lady, "That's the Archbishop of Dublin." Said the other, "Ah, the dear old gentleman, simple and innocent as a child, playing with his little dog."

Said the first lady, "It's the Protestant Archbishop, you know."

Said the second, "Ah, the silly old fool, wasting his time with a pup."

Prejudice means weighing our side and the other side on different scales. The other side kills a lot of people, and it's a bloody massacre. Our side does exactly the same, and it's a regrettable necessity. Our side is accused of evil action and we demand the most rigorous proof. The other side is accused, and we accept the accusation out of hand; it's just the kind of thing those people would do.

Prejudice conditions not only our judgment but our memory. We remember what they did to us—the martyrs Queen Elizabeth hung, drew, and quartered at Tyburn, for instance. They remember what we did to them, the martyrs Queen Mary burnt at Smithfield. They remind us that we burnt Cranmer. We remind them that Cranmer was one of the judges who sent Thomas More to his beheading. And for good measure we throw in the Anabaptist, Joan Bocher, whom Cranmer burnt. And we all feel so reasonable.

Upon the human failings of Popes and bishops, we of the Guild were the best-instructed body of laymen in the Church's history. But none of this dimmed our certainty that from papacy and hierarchy the Holy Spirit would see to it that we got true doctrine and true sacraments. Unworthy pastors were the Holy Spirit's problem, not ours. It took us a while to grow into this knowledge.

I smile when I think of our beginnings. We would plunge to the defense of Christ's vicars with as little actual knowledge of papal history as our objectors had. A questioner would say, for instance, that Pope Alexander VI had four children. At first, our speakers usually reacted in one of two ways. 1. The earnest ones would say, "Oh, no, only three were ever proved"; 2. the combative would say, "What if he had? Henry VIII had six wives" (the odds clearly in our favor six to four). It took us a while to realize that we were missing the point totally.

We were there to introduce people to Christ's Church. We were not prettying the Church for its photograph. Still less were we like lawyers with a shady client, trying to keep his worst crimes from the jury's knowledge. We had to show them the Church Christ founded exactly as it was and is. If they were scandalized by what they saw, they must take it up with Christ, who founded it, or with the Holy Spirit, who vivifies it.

The plan adopted by me and others was to begin our talks on the papacy with some "bad" Popes. And I don't mean only ones who were sexually corrupt, like John XII, but worldly Popes, cruel Popes, frightened Popes, like Clement V and Innocent X—one behaving badly, one madly, before the threats from French monarchs. Our aim was to show why we, knowing the worst, still knew ourselves in union with Christ. However ill He might be served by his representative at any given time, we could still find in his Church, as nowhere else, life and truth and the possibility of union with Him to the limit of our willingness.

The principal fact of life I did not know when I began is that one must never talk for victory—to show oneself right and the other man wrong. If you talk for victory, sooner or later you will cheat. You may not actually lie, but you will be tempted to shade facts that might seem to weaken your case, or divert the discussion away from them.

But if your aim is simply to show how what you hold affects life as it is lived, there is no temptation to cheat. You open your mind, you ask your hearers for their comments. You are not trying for a decision. The questions under discussion are too serious for a quick settlement. Their roots lie too deep in the person.

When ideas call upon a man to change his life, the self of the teacher has to make contact with the deepest self of the hearer. In plain words, each sort of union demands love.

The speaker must labor at his utterance. If he does not spend a good part of his time making sure his hearers know what he means when he says "God," he risks wasting the whole of it. A questioner once asked me what the word *Spirit* meant. I answered, "A spirit has no shape, no size, no dimensions, no color, does not occupy space." His comment, admirably just, was, "That's the best description of nothing I ever heard."

Somehow one must get one's listeners to see that the truth one is uttering makes a difference that matters. Time is wasted talking on the forgiveness of sins to people for whom sin is a dead word. With only

actions that damage others seen as wrong, the notion of sins against God is meaningless. There is no gain in talking about an infallible teaching authority if your hearers attach no importance to certitude in religion. Before discussing the Virgin Birth, find out whether your hearers think there is any value whatever, spiritual or other, in virginity.

Dialog means two people looking at the same reality and comparing what they see. If on some matter—animal suffering perhaps—we see no light, there must be no pretense. Sharing our vision includes sharing our darkness.

With this I am at the high point of what the platform has taught me: there is no stopping short of the Trinity. I have never heard a sermon on the Trinity in my own Church. The books which tell one how to teach religion to the modern man vary in value, but not the best of them mentions the Trinity.

When I began, I assumed that the Trinity would be beyond the minds of all but the highly educated. I was wrong. There is a real difference between highbrows and lowbrows, but intelligence has nothing to do with it. There are stupid highbrows, intelligent lowbrows—intelligence is pretty evenly distributed over the brows.

The real problem for every

teacher of religion, from God down to the street corner speaker, is simply finding the words. The right words are light-giving. They are life-giving, provided the "unpinpointable something" in the hearer responds. And over that the speaker has no control at all, and even the listener not very much.

I have mentioned occasions on which the response surprised the speaker. I end with the one which has surprised me most, namely the fascination that the doctrine of the Trinity has for the man on the street.

We have all had the experience of recognizing a photograph of ourself that we had never seen before. I think the response to the Trinity is rather like that, but in reverse—not the original recognizing the image, but the image stirring toward the original. For in God's image we are made.

HEARTS ARE TRUMPS

Years ago, as a teacher of English, I was looking over some compositions submitted by my class. A city-wide speech contest was to be held, and I had been appointed to select the student who would represent our school. I told each to write a draft of the speech he would give if selected.

I was discouraged to find that nearly all the compositions turned in were either copied from famous speeches or showed signs of parental help.

Finally I came upon one which was youthful and sincere in tone. It was just the kind of thing an intelligent 12-year-old boy might have written. Its author was a lad named Harry; and I selected him for the contest.

Every morning for weeks Harry and I would meet before and after school, and go over his oration. As I coached him, I could see Harry turning almost before my eyes from a harum-scarum boy into a hard-working, well-poised youth.

The night of the contest came, and Harry won first place. He received a great ovation. His parents and he were grateful for my coaching, and said so. But soon Harry was graduated, and I thought no more about him.

Twenty years later, I was invited to attend a Chamber of Commerce luncheon. The guest of honor, a lawyer from another city, turned out to be my former pupil Harry. He made the principal speech of the occasion, and my eyes filled with tears as I heard him pay tribute to me for having had a part in starting him on a successful career in the law. I felt amply repaid for the help I had given him.   F. K. Kelley.

The Last Days of Pope John

"My bags are packed. I'm ready to go."

By LAWRENCE ELLIOTT
October 1973, condensed from *I Will Be Called John**

POPE JOHN'S last illness began about the time of his 80th birthday, November, 1961. Late that month he wrote in his journal, "I notice in my body the beginning of some trouble that must be natural for an old man. I bear it with resignation, even if it is sometimes rather tiresome and also makes me afraid it will get worse. It is not pleasant to think too much about this; but once more I feel prepared for anything."

By summer he felt the first clear symptoms of an intestinal growth. Later it would be said that months passed before he realized the seriousness of his illness. But it is hard to believe that a man who had lost a

*Condensed from *I Will be Called John: A Biography of Pope John XXIII,* by Lawrence Elliott. Copyright © 1973 by Lawrence Elliott. Reprinted by permission of the author.

mother, brother, and four sisters to cancer would be taken completely unaware by the onset of the disease in himself. A sad note crept into his public statements, not yet a goodby, but rueful acknowledgement that the end of his glorious adventure on earth must be fast approaching.

"We are entering our 82nd year," he told a group in St. Peter's that winter. "Shall we finish it? All days are good for being born, all days are good for dying."

To several hundred children gathered in the courtyard of St. Damascus not long after, he spoke of Pope Leo XIII, who lived to be 93. "Still, at last he had to undergo that which happens to all of us, and probably soon to the Pope who stands before you today."

But his homely good humor

never deserted him. Told by the doctors that he had a "gastropathic condition," he laughed aloud and said, "That is because I am Pope. Otherwise you would call it a stomachache." After the early reports of his illness called forth the predictable Roman rumors that he was already at death's door, he said wryly, "Tell them the Pope still lives. And there is no reason to bury him before he dies."

Throughout the summer of 1962, while the council weighed the future course of the Church, Pope John followed their deliberations from his quarters, and though pale and perceptibly weaker, maintained a regular schedule of audiences and conferences. In November he chose his old friend from Bologna, Prof. Antonio Gasbarrini, to be his personal physician, replacing Dr. Filippo Rocchi, who had died. Extensive X rays and tests were undertaken. Some of Italy's leading specialists were called into consultation. The diagnosis was inoperable cancer. Only palliative treatment was possible and, at best, Pope John had perhaps half a year to live.

In the evening of that shattering day, Gasbarrini told him that he was suffering from a tumor. "A tumor," the old man repeated, understanding everything, and at the same time full of concern for his friend. "*Ebbene,* very well, let God's will be done. But don't worry about me, because my bags are packed. I'm ready to go."

A gifted young anesthesiologist, Dr. Piero Mazzoni, moved into the Pope's quarters to provide the close, constant attention he would require over the next months. Only a few days later, during the night of Tuesday, Nov. 27, Dr. Mazzoni was awakened: the Holy Father was in desperate pain. Mazzoni came running, and saw at once that his patient was in the grip of a massive intestinal hemorrhage. He administered coagulants, blood plasma, and morphine, and by daylight the bleeding was under control. His face drawn and gaunt from the struggle, Pope John slept for a few hours, his strong peasant sinews gathering fresh strength for the struggles yet to come.

The public audience scheduled for that Wednesday was canceled, and the Vatican press office began issuing a series of vague and contradictory reports that served only to feed the rumors. The Pope had a bad cold, said the first announcement; was "indisposed," said the second; and, on Nov. 29, that there were "symptoms of a gastropathy which has provoked a fairly intense anemia." This last was just ambiguous enough to touch off the wildest public speculation: the Pope had undergone radical surgery; the Pope would not survive the week; the Pope was already dead.

But on Sunday he appeared at his study window as usual to recite the Angelus with the crowd gathered in the square below.

They cheered, as had the council fathers when they were told that the Holy Father was resuming his usual activity. Moved by their affection, Pope John wept.

Under Dr. Mazzoni's care, and with regular periods of rest, the Pope rallied remarkably. Although he was still not strong enough to attend the regular Wednesday audience at St. Peter's, it was announced that he would offer the papal blessing from his window. The council adjourned their session so the bishops could join the crowd, and by noon that day the piazza was filled. As soon as the study window on the third floor was opened, a great joyous burst of horns and bells and cheering swept up toward it. Finally it was quiet, and Pope John said, "My children, as you see, Providence is with us. From day to day there is progress *piano, piano,* sickness, then convalescence. And your presence gives us joy and strength and vigor."

Indeed that was true. Incredibly he worked on. His bags were packed, he had said, but it was as though, on the eve of his departure, he remembered some urgent matters that required his attention. He would go, and willingly, but in those last months, when he was never really free of pain, and sometimes tortured by it, he would see to the resolution of the council's gravest conflicts, to the writing of *Pacem in Terris,* and to the personal good-byes of a man who had never forgotten, amid the press of highest duty, that he was also a son and a brother and an uncle and a friend.

He wrote a long letter to his family at Sotto il Monte. He considered it his spiritual testament, and though he addressed it to Zaverio, his eldest brother, it was clearly intended for all the Roncallis.

"I think it is three years since I last used a typewriter. I used to enjoy typing so much, and if today I have decided to begin again, using a machine that is new and all my own, it is in order to tell you that I know I am growing old—how can I help knowing it with all the fuss that has been made about my 80th birthday? But I am still fit, and I continue on my way, still in good health, even if some slight disturbance makes me aware that to be 80 is not the same as being 60.

"This letter which I was determined to write to you, my dear Zaverio, contains a message for all the members of our large family, and I want it to be to all of them a message from my loving heart, still warm and youthful. Busied as I am, as you all know, in such an important office, with the eyes of the world upon me, I cannot forget the members of my dear family, to whom my thoughts turn day by day.

"It is pleasant for me to know that, as you cannot keep in personal correspondence with me as you did before, you may confide everything to Msgr. Capovilla, who is very fond of you all, and speak to him just as you would to me.

"My 80 years of life completed tell me, as they tell you, dear Zaverio, and all the members of our family, that what is most important is always to keep ourselves well prepared for a sudden departure, because this is what matters most: to make sure of eternal life, trusting in the goodness of the Lord who sees all and makes provision for all.

"Go on loving one another, all you Roncallis, with the new families growing up among you, and try to understand that I cannot write to all separately. Our Giuseppino was right when he said to his brother the Pope: 'Here you are a prisoner de luxe: you cannot do what you would like to do.'

"I am well aware that you have to bear certain mortifications from people who like to talk nonsense. To have a Pope in the family, a Pope regarded with respect by the whole world, who yet permits his relations to go on living so modestly, in the same social condition as before! But many know that the Pope, the son of humble but respected parents, never forgets anyone; he has, and shows, a great affection for his nearest kin, moreover his own condition is the same as that of most of his recent predecessors; and a Pope does not honor himself by enriching his relations but only by affectionately coming to their aid, according to their needs and the conditions of each one.

"At my death I shall not lack the praise which did so much honor to the saintly Pius X: 'He was born poor and died poor.'

"As I have now completed my 80 years, naturally all the others will be coming along after me. Be of good heart! We are in good company. I always keep by my bedside the photograph that gathers all our dead together with their names inscribed on the marble: grandfather Angelo, 'barba' Zaverio, our revered parents, our brother Giovanni, our sisters Teresa, Ancilla, Maria, and Enrica. Oh what a fine chorus of souls to await us and pray for us! I think of them constantly. To remember them in prayer gives me courage and joy, in the confident hope of joining them all again in the everlasting glory of heaven.

"I bless you all, remembering with you all the brides who have come to rejoice the Roncalli family and those who have left us to increase the happiness of new families, of different names but similar ways of thinking."

Now, with the outcome of his illness apparent to all those around him, he did his best to lift their spirits. He kept urging his secretary, Monsignor Capovilla, to get more rest, "or you will go off before your boss."

Not long after, he told Dr. Mazzoni that he would like to meet his family. They came on a Sunday, the doctor and his wife and two daughters. "He was so kind, so *interested* in them," Dr. Mazzoni recalled. "He talked to them for half an hour and afterward, when I took them home, I asked my younger daughter, who was then eight, what she thought of the Pope. She said that he looked like an ordinary priest, and I could tell she was disappointed. But when she is older and can understand such a thing, I will explain to her that that was Pope John's glory, that he *was* just an ordinary priest—who took Christianity seriously."

Pope John had no interest in the clinical aspects of his illness. At the very beginning, he had told Dr. Mazzoni, "You will do what you must do, and I know you will do it well. But for myself, I ask only one thing: that you tell me honestly when the end is at hand."

Early that spring Pope John received Father Pietro Bosio, the parish priest of Sotto il Monte, who had brought for his blessing the first stone of a seminary for foreign missions, to be built adjacent to the Pope's birthplace. There were many in Sotto il Monte who wanted to come and see him, Father Bosio said, to which Pope John replied, "Well, tell them to come quickly. Are they waiting until I am dead?"

After inspecting a model of the proposed seminary, he made this little address: "Let the people of Sotto il Monte rejoice, not so much because one among them was born one of the successors to St. Peter, but because the Lord has deigned to arrange that among those fields and vineyards, future missionaries will be prepared. Let them rejoice to house in the ample circle of their lovely hills, a lighthouse of missionary light, young hearts vibrating with love for God and souls who, in their eagerness, beat in unison with the heart of the Pope." Then he added, "If you hurry up and build it, maybe I will come personally and dedicate it."

On April 30 he suffered another hemorrhage. This time he required several blood transfusions, further coagulants, and morphine for the pain. For 24 hours Dr. Mazzoni did not leave his side. There was some talk among the doctors of radiation therapy. But they quickly agreed, as each, secretly, had known in his heart from the first, that it would be futile, and might even provoke more severe bleeding.

But again Pope John found the strength to weather the storm. On May 5 he received a special group in audience at St. Peter's, and a week later, over Dr. Mazzoni's objections, went to the Quirinal to be present for the awards of the Balzan prizes for music, mathematics, and chemistry.

It troubled him to hear of the predictions, some from inside the Vatican, that once he was gone everything he brought to the Church would go, too: the spirit of *aggiornamento,* the council, everything. He did not believe it, but of course he could not be sure. "May it be God's will that the council fathers be able still to crown the great work that they have begun," he prayed. "I offer all my suffering *ut unum sint* [that they may be one] that all may be a sole entity in Christ."

On May 20, Cardinal Stefan Wyszynski, primate of Poland, came to see him. Msgr. Capovilla had suggested that he be received in the bedroom, but John flatly refused. "We haven't come to that yet," he said, and walked purposefully down the stairs to his library. When their talk was over, Cardinal Wyszynski, referring to the next session of the council, said, "Until September, Holy Father!"

And Pope John, with a smile, replied, "In September you will either find me here, or another. You know, in one month they can do it all: the funeral of one Pope, the election of another."

That night he had another hemorrhage and more transfusions. Now his stomach would tolerate no food at all; he had to be fed intravenously. On the morning of Wednesday, May 22, while preparing for the audience at St. Peter's, he fainted. But he recovered quickly and went to the window to tell the people that the audience would have to be canceled: "I was expecting to see you at noon, but instead we are advancing our appointment a bit. So here I am. I know that our meeting was to have taken place inside St. Peter's, but what is the difference, inside or out?"

He had yet another massive hemorrhage on the 26th, and

Gasbarrini was hurriedly summoned from Bologna. But it was not the end. By Thursday, May 29, Pope John's astonishing stamina had fought the ravaging disease to a momentary standstill, and he got out of bed and conferred with Vatican aides.

But what Pope John had reverently spoken of as Sister Death was now close at hand. That night, Dr. Mazzoni was dozing in the study when a feeble cry for help wakened him shortly before midnight. The bleeding had begun again, and this time the cancerous mass had flooded the abdominal lining with poison: peritonitis. For four more days Pope John would drift between coma and agonizing consciousness.

In the morning, he lay spent and gaunt. A flight of swallows swept by as he gazed through the window, free and untroubled in the spring sky. Then he turned again to the ivory crucifix on the wall opposite the bed, placed "so I can see it with the first glimpse in the morning and the last one at night."

D r. Mazzoni came in with Msgr. Capovilla. The secretary, torn with anguish, tried to speak and could not. Dr. Mazzoni went to the edge of the bed. "Holy Father," he said, "you have asked me, many times, to tell you when the end was near, so you could prepare."

The wasted face on the pillow fixed itself into a gentle smile. "Yes," Pope John said. "Don't feel bad, doctor. I understand. I am ready."

Msgr. Capovilla fell to his knees by the side of the bed, burying his face in the covers, sobbing. John caressed the dark head. "Courage, courage, my son," he said softly. "I am a bishop and I must die as a bishop, with simplicity but with majesty, and you must help me. Go, get the people together."

"Santo padre, they are waiting."

The smile widened, the smile of a father suddenly and greatly moved by the love of a beloved son. "Send in my confessor," he said.

A fter his Confession and last Communion, he received the holy oil of Extreme Unction. Again and again he whispered the words of Jesus after the Last Supper, "Ut unum sint" (that they may be one). Slowly the small room filled up as cardinals and monsignori gathered to witness the death of the Pope.

In the afternoon his nephew Battista, now a canon in Bergamo, arrived. He could not believe that his uncle was dying. But by evening, when Assunta, Zaverio, Alfredo, and Giuseppe were brought to the bedside by Cardinal Montini, Pope John had slipped back into coma.

Later, Battista described the scene in the bedroom as the Pope's family tried to find a place among the worthies of the Church, "They were told that they must not weep. If it turned out that they could not hold back their tears, they were to leave. Those four poor souls were trembling and still upset from their airplane trip, which was the first for any of them. There was only a dim light in the room. We were all standing back because we were told that the Pope was having great difficulty breathing, that he needed air, and that if we stood too close we would deprive him of it."

He recovered consciousness again and embraced his brothers and sisters. "Do you remember how I never thought of anything else in life but being a priest?" he whispered. "I embrace you and bless you. I am happy because in a little while I shall see our mother and father in heaven. Pray."

On Sunday, June 2, with his temperature at 104°, he told Dr. Mazzoni, "I am suffering with love, but with pain, too, so much pain." He wanted the faithful doctor to have something of the Pope's as a keepsake and, fumbling, he found his fountain pen on the night stand. "Take it," he said to Mazzoni, who was now crying, too. "It is nearly new."

To Capovilla he said, "I am sorry to have kept you from your mother such a long time. Promise me when this is over that you will go to see her."

On Monday he lost consciousness for the last time. He lay back on the pillow gasping for air.

In the evening, Luigi Cardinal Traglia, Pope John's vicar for Rome, offered an outdoor Mass for the thousands drawn to St. Peter's Square. The spring breeze was so soft that the altar candles barely flickered, and the murmur of prayer seemed to hang in the air even after the Mass ended. A little before eight, Cardinal Traglia spoke the traditional words of dismissal, *"Ite, missa est."*

At that same moment, upstairs in the dimly lit bedroom where Sister Death waited, Pope John XXIII took a last breath and died.

Conversion

Students teach teacher

By KNUTE ROCKNE
condensed from the *Notre Dame Bulletin**

I USED TO BE deeply impressed by the sight of my players receiving Communion every morning, and finally I made it a point to go to Mass with them on the morning of a game. I realized that it appeared more or less incongruous, when we arrived in town for a game, for the general public to see my boys rushing off to church as soon as they got off the train, while their coach rode on to the hotel and relaxed. So, for the sake of appearances, if for nothing else, I determined to go to church with the boys on the morning of a game.

One night before a big game in the East, I was nervous and worried about the outcome the next day and was unable to sleep. I pitched and rolled about the bed and finally decided to dress and go downstairs. It must

have been two or three o'clock in the morning when I stepped into the deserted lobby, so I took a chair and tried to get that football game off my mind by engaging some of the bellboys in conversation.

Along about five or six o'clock I started pacing the floor, when suddenly I ran into two of my own players hurrying out. I asked them where they were going at such an hour, although I had a good idea. Then I retired to a chair in the lobby where I couldn't be seen, but where I could see everyone who went in or out the door. Within the next few minutes other players kept hurrying out of the door in pairs and groups. Finally, when most of them had gone, I stood near the door so I could question the next player who came along.

In a minute or two, the last of the squad rushed out of an elevator and made for the door. I stopped them and asked if they,

*Notre Dame, Ind., Oct. 21, 1940. Reprinted with permission.

too, were going to Mass. They replied that they were so I decided to go along with them. Although they probably didn't realize it, these youngsters were making a powerful impression on me with their piety and devotion. And when I saw all of them walking up to receive Communion, and realized the several hours of sleep they had sacrificed in order to do this, I understood for the first time what a powerful ally their religion was to those boys in their work on the football field. It was then that I really began to see the light, to know what was missing in my life.

Some time later I had the great happiness of joining my boys at the Communion rail. ⬤

THE PERFECT ASSIST

In our little church we always made our first Holy Communion in the middle of June, after school was out. One time I went with my older sister Mary to see the procession, and she explained everything to me. I was only nine years old but I'll never forget how thrilled I was at the sight of a veil, and orange blossoms on the heads of the girls. They looked like angels!

I couldn't wait till my time came. Oh, how I hoped that day would fall on my birthday, June 18, three years later when I would be twelve!

Soon after, my sister Mary left home. I wasn't told why, but she and papa didn't get along very well. We all were sad and I often saw mother silently crying. We didn't hear from Mary. Her name was never spoken. As time went on she left my mind and it seemed as if she were dead. I got the impression she was "bad."

We were very poor, and when the time came for me to make my first Holy Communion I had no new white dress, no orange blossoms, no veil. I cried bitterly. Mother said she would have to make over an old dress.

As we were coming home on the last day of school mother said, "A package came for you from a big store, and a letter, too." I couldn't think of anybody writing to me, or sending a package, either. I gave the letter to mother to read. It said, "Dear sister: I have not forgotten that you were supposed to make your first Holy Communion this June. I hope you will be pleased with the dress I am sending you and it arrives on time. May you be very happy. God bless you. Your sister, Mary."

I opened the box. The dress was a dream, and there were veil, orange blossoms, and rosary. My "bad" sister had done this for me. Mother and I cried, then got on our knees and offered a prayer for her.   Adle Lambert.

My Good Angel of Death

Father Lord reflects on his doctor's diagnosis of cancer

By DANIEL A. LORD, S.J.

July 1954

I HAD COME TO St. John's hospital in St. Louis for my quarterly anesthetic and fulguration. I hope I have that word right: it means literally to be struck by lightning. And that is what my surgeon, Dr. Bartels, says he does when he puts his instruments deep into my bladder and with electric current hits the small but annoying growths. That has been going on for almost six years; ask me anything about going under an anesthetic, and I can be very vivid. This time, as often before, I also had X rays taken of my lungs.

I had emerged from the anesthetic, and was relaxing peacefully in bed, when Dr. Bartels entered the room. With him was one of the kindest men

Reprinted with permission of Ligouri Publications.

who ever lived, my physician, Dr. A. P. Munsch. It was clearly a committee, so when they sat down, I grinned, and they smiled wryly. I asked, "News?" And they said, "Yes."

Then I started guessing. "Return of my old TB? Heart condition?" They shook their friendly heads.

"Don't tell me it's cancer," I said, half joking.

"You'd want to know the truth, wouldn't you?" they quickly asked.

Well, all my life, I've wanted to know the truth. I have always thought the truth, pleasant or unpleasant, is something to which people have a right; and in the end, truth is the only kind answer. So I nodded. "It's cancer," said the doctors, "cancer of the lungs."

I suppose my next question

was inevitable. "How long do I live?"

They answered in a sort of quick and eager dialogue. They were good friends as well as great doctors, and they wanted to make it as easy as possible.

"Who knows? There is no predicting with cancer. If you were a young man, your time might be short indeed. The same natural law which makes healthy tissue and cells in a young man grow fast, makes his wild tissues and cells also grow fast. At your age, 65, it may move very slowly. We never can tell. Patients show all the signs, register on the plates, come back six months later, and no cancer. We can build up, as we mean to do with you, a buttress, a containing wall of healthy cells around the wild ones; and they may hold the bad boys in check for a long time."

There was a second question. "Can I go on with my normal life and work?"

Their answer was wonderfully reassuring. "Absolutely. In fact, that is precisely the thing to do. If you come to regard yourself as an invalid, you'll hamper treatment, and speed up the disease. If you keep at your normal work, see your friends, eat well, and put back that weight you've dieted off, keep cheerful and contented, you'll be a perfect patient, and we can have

all possible hope. What's the schedule for the next few months?"

It was a fairly heavy one, and we discussed it. "You mustn't get yourself overtired. You have to get decent sleep and rest and, once more, all the good food you care to eat. We'll watch, and God is good."

I write this little message of hope and confidence three months and a half after the decision. The doctors kept me in the hospital for a bit, and then turned me loose. In a sudden spurt of energy and a determination to use time to the best advantage, I found that I was itching to be at my typewriter and to write some of those books that I had long planned.

Then I hit the road, back at my routine of talks and meetings. I went out to Loretto Heights college, Denver, to keynote their Christian Humanism conference and give the opening and closing talks. Milwaukee offered me a chance to talk to 8,000 CYOers in the big municipal auditorium. In Detroit, we finished up the details of *Light Up the Land,* a film version of our University of Detroit musical on American education. In Toronto, I worked with the local committees on *Joy for the World,* which next October the Catholics will present as their contribution to the Marian year. Back to the University of Notre Dame

for the senior retreat, and on to
Boston for the *Tre Ore*. Easter
at the Carmel in St. Louis, and
I write this as I ride back from
the Kansas State Sodality Union
conference in Dodge City. I am
a little shortwinded, perhaps; a
little quicker to tire, but thus
far I live with cancer and find it
a gentle enough companion.

But the interest of the general public has astounded me.
Cancer is big news, a great
national concern, a preoccupa-
tion of the press and the general public. The St. Louis papers
kindly gave my illness just the
most general notice. But out-of-
town papers and the news agencies wished details. How did I
feel? What happened when I
was told? What did I plan? How
long would it be? Would I still
attempt the Toronto spectacle?
Did I consider myself an invalid?

Then the mail poured in. It
came from kind friends and
complete strangers; from hundreds who had sure cures which
they generously shared with
me; religious sects bent upon
converting me; childhood companions who wrote sympathetically 50 years later; important
people whom I hardly had met
in passing; fellow victims writing in encouragement or for
encouragement. And with the
help of my infallible secretary,
Marian Prendergast, I tried to
answer them all. They had been
kind; cancer interested or fright-

ened them, too; and they wanted
to share with me their sympathy and ask if I had anything to
share with them.

Perhaps I had and have. I cannot quite understand the appall-
ing fear of cancer. I have known
so many who died gracefully
from it: the dear old nun portress across the street from my
office who never missed a day
on phone or door until she went
to bed to die within weeks of a
cancer no one had suspected;
my priest friend who, with cancer of the tongue, went quietly
to his room, spent months
becoming a saint, and died with
a smile; the dean of the women's
college who ran the school from
her bed, held interviews, pushed
forward the college's development, and served almost better
sick from cancer than in the
full bloom of her health.

When the verdict was cancer,
I was relieved. I had expected
to die some day of heart trouble,
or a stroke, and I dreaded that
sudden and perhaps sacrament-
less death. I had been shelved
once before with TB, and a
recurrence would paralyze me.
I doubted if I had the courage
to accept the martyrdom and
passion of arthritis. Cancer
seemed kindly, almost like the
preliminary coming of the Angel
of Death to say, "Not quite
yet, but you've time to do
some thinking and praying and
straightening out life's ledgers."

I liked the gentle warning, for I had always in the Litany of the Saints said with great feeling, "From a sudden and unprovided death, O Lord, deliver me."

Cancer actually seems to incapacitate less than most fatal diseases, and loving my life, my work, and my friends, I was grateful that I could cling normally and affectionately to all.

Perhaps at the moment of the verdict, I appreciated most keenly my Religious priesthood. No one could be more aware of his sins, faults, and bad jobs than I am, and of my failures as a priest. Yet my priestly and Religious vows had prepared me for the calm acceptance of what I heard. Dear as friends have been and are, none of them so essentially depends upon me that my loss will disarrange a life. Much as I have loved my work, laying it down will upset nothing and no one. So often have I taught the faith to others, that of a sudden, I found my new friend, cancer, teaching the faith to me.

There is a God who permits disease as the prelude to death, the deliverer.

Death is not the end but the beginning of the only life which can satisfy the restless, limitless, glorious cravings of a human soul.

If there should be pain, Christ bore pain first and shares it in divine generosity.

And well or sick, we are God's children, deeply loved and providentially guarded.

Almost without thinking, I told a reporter, "God knows His business, and I think He can handle this without too much worry from me." More than a hundred people have written to tell me they are glad that is so. I have felt the warmth and friendship of friends who have been kind without any thought of gratitude from me. I have known the loving and highly skilled service of the Sisters of Mercy. My doctors have given me complete confidence that, if there is a cure or a palliation, they will find it. I lived for a month in St. John's hospital across the street from the great Cancer Clinic of St. Louis and I'd look at it and think, "Over there, patient scientists are working to discover a cure for me." From Canada came an invitation to come up and let them try the new radioactive cobalt. I have met the Toronto doctors and they have set a date for my first bombardment.

Some newspapers have been a bit ghoulish. (One paper headlined an account of our Toronto spectacle thus: "Show Must Go On, Producer Probably Will Not.") Most friends ignore the subject, treat me as a perfectly healthy man, and are as gay as I care to be. And that is peacefully and sincerely gay.

I cannot but feel that the

dread of cancer is vastly exaggerated. People with cancer live often long and sturdily. Cancer does not necessarily withdraw a man from his normal routine. Since we all must die, God seems kindly when He sends a messenger in advance with a gentle but emphatic warning. Surely we can all use a little time to get ready for the Judgment. The realization that one has cancer sharpens one's whole outlook on life; the earth is more beautiful, the sky a little clearer, and every moment of the day precious, a thing to be hoarded.

May I close this inadequate statement with a little joke on myself? It was January, 1954, when I was told I had cancer of the lungs. The other day, I returned to St. John's for a chest plate and the scientific lightning. Sister Mary Johnita took my plate, and said, "I wonder why the sudden interest in your lung cancer. After all, it's a secondary cancer. Why didn't someone get excited over the cancer of the bladder which you have had for probably eight years?"

I gulped in astonishment. Four times a year I had returned for bladder treatment. Since I dislike amateur doctors as much as I admire professionals, I had never asked my physicians what they were treating, and since they could keep the "growths" in control, there was no point in disturbing me. But I confess I laughed. Here I have been living with cancer for eight full years, continuing all my normal work, branching into new fields like our civic spectacles in Midland, Ont., Detroit, and Jamaica, bothering no one, and completely untroubled in mind.

I am glad that the nation is cancer conscious. But when I read that it is man's worst enemy, I am not so sure. I do not think God allows enemies to prevail; rather He seems to use the things we dread to draw us closer to Him. Since we must die, and since death is really the entrance into life, I am personally glad that cancer, the kindly messenger, came quite a bit in advance . . . and that I have been permitted to read what often sounds suspiciously like my own obituaries.

And life seems sweetest when it melts gently into the Life that is our Eternal Promise.

The Nun Who Spent $1,000 A Day

Not content with giving her fortune to the blacks and Indians, Mother Katharine Drexel gave her life, too

By SISTER MARTHA MARY MCGAW
December 1980, condensed from *The Sooner Catholic**

UNTIL LAST YEAR, Mother Katharine Drexel was little more than a name to me. Just a few odds and ends of information about her floated in my memory. Then I interviewed Frank Keah-Tigh, 75, a fine Kiowa Potawatomi. He said, "St. Patrick's in Anadarko (Okla.) was the best thing ever happened to me. That was a wonderful place."

Immediately I thought of Mother Katharine. I knew she

had given the money to start the school in 1892.

A few months later, Michael Sweezy, 29, who is Cheyenne, Arapaho, Oneida, and Oto, also expressed a deep love for St. Patrick's. He said, "I was five years old when I went there. I loved it. Those were good years. Maybe the best in my life. That's when I gave myself to God. I got baptized and made my First Communion."

"Now that's the kind of thing Mother Katharine would like to hear," I thought to myself. "Faith is what she wanted most for her

Indians." And I knew I wanted to know more about her.

When I learned that the extensive correspondence between Mother Katharine and Bishop Theophile Meerschaert and Bishop Francis Clement Kelly had been preserved in the Oklahoma City archdiocesan archives, I asked if I could see her letters.

They were written in beautiful Spencerian, telling the bishop that she would send him $1,000 or $2,000 to pay for the schools or churches, or both, in Anadarko, Guthrie, Langston, Purcell, Vinita, Ardmore, Muskogee, Antlers, Hennessey, Hominy, Boley, Pawhuska, and Chickasha; for the salaries of the Sisters in Guthrie and Langston; for the First Communion boys; for the salary of priests; for a buggy; for furniture; and on and on. According to a letter written by Bishop Kelley, Dec. 30, 1933, the amount she gave "for Oklahoma Indians often went to over $50,000 annually."

I would occasionally pinch myself as I was reading, and say, "Do you know whose letters you are reading? This woman is a saint if there ever was one." Then I would read more. These letters were quite formal, mostly about business matters.

K atie Drexel (that's what she was called for 31 years) was born into a very rich and deeply religious family in Philadelphia. Her mother died when Katie was born. Her father, Francis Anthony Drexel, married again when Katie was one year old, and Emma (Bouvier) Drexel loved Katie and her sister Elizabeth as much as she loved her own daughter, Louise. Louise was the only child of this second marriage.

Katie was privately tutored, traveled in Europe and the U.S., had a stable of horses, and was an accomplished musician and writer. She made a brilliant debut at 21.

But as much as Katie enjoyed parties and theater and travel, she loved God more. When she was 14, she began telling her pastor, Father James O'Connor, what was going on in her heart. When, four years later, he was made Bishop of Nebraska, she continued to stay in touch with him. Sometimes she would tell him about her "convent thoughts," that she might like to be a nun.

He never encouraged her. He thought she had already given herself to God and that her example in society, probably married, would be very great.

His diocese consisted mostly of Indian lands, and he began to tell Katie about the deplorable state of Indian affairs. The story of Custer's last stand did not arouse any admiration for Custer.

Katie already had taken the

Indians to her heart. As a child reading about Columbus, she saw an illustration of him with an Indian standing in the shadows behind him. It came to her then that Columbus had really discovered America so that the Indians could learn about God's love for them. It was simple as that. And somehow this would have to be accomplished.

When Katie's stepmother died of cancer in 1883 and her father died suddenly two years later in 1885, the three Drexel girls came into an inheritance exceeding $15 million.

To keep fortune hunters from seeking his daughters in marriage, Mr. Drexel had designated one-tenth of the inheritance to go to specific charities, and the rest to be put into a trust fund. No future husband could touch any of this. His daughters were to share equally in the income. If one died, the other two should share. If two died, the surviving daughter would have it all. Their children would inherit the principal. If they had no children, the principal would go to the charities originally specified.

So Katie's yearly income was enormous. She was asked almost immediately to give to the Indian Missions. She did, very generously. Oklahoma benefitted from the start. In 1886 she built two schools for the Osage children: a school for 50 boys, St. John's in Gray Horse;

and a school for 50 girls, St. Louis in Pawhuska. Pawhuska was always one of Katie's favorites. Later, in 1942, she sent her own Sisters there. This school was closed in 1949.

But Katie wanted to give herself to God, not just her money. And she had a surprising nudge in this direction. In a private audience with Pope Leo XIII, he asked her pointblank why she did not become a missionary. She had first asked him if he knew of any missionary priests who could go to Nebraska to help with the Indians.

She took the Pope's question very seriously; in fact, she was overwhelmed with the thought that God might be telling her how to order her life. In all her "convent thoughts" she had always thought she would like to be a contemplative. Now a missionary?

Katie decided to start her own Religious Community, which would take as its single goal to help the Indians and the blacks. (Katie always used the term "colored".) She didn't know for sure how to do this, and she wasn't even eager to do it, but she did it because she believed God was asking this of her.

Her friend Bishop O'Connor finally encouraged her.

Without fanfare or dramatics, Katie went to make her notiviate with the Sisters of Mercy in

Pittsburgh. That was on May 7, 1889.

Thirteen young women joined her, and her new Community, which was to be called the Sisters of the Blessed Sacrament for Indians and Colored People, was on its way. As Mother Katharine, she made temporary profession on Feb. 12, 1891 and final profession on Jan. 9, 1895.

There was sorrow along the way. Bishop O'Connor, who had helped her much, and had encouraged her to start this new Community, died in 1890 before it was started. But his friend, Archbishop Patrick Ryan of Philadelphia, offered to assist her in her enormous undertaking. (St. Patrick's in Anadarko is named for him.)

The young women who joined Mother Katharine as the nucleus of the new Community came from the same social stratum she did. None of them knew much of anything about cooking, washing, cleaning, canning fruit, or stuffing mattresses with cornhusks. They learned the hard way. Sometimes Katie's former servants, with pity in their hearts, would casually drop by to give a helping hand.

Mother Katharine continued to give away all her income to help the Indians and blacks. Her Sisters kept only enough to get along. When Mother Katharine was asked why she did not put money aside for them and their future needs, she said she would rather rely on Providence.

She refused elegant travel, preferring to sit up all night in the coach on the train and brown-bag all her meals. And she got used to bumping over the deep ruts of country roads in rickety wagons. In what was probably the understatement of the year, she once commented, "Forty miles in a wagon is guaranteed to give you a thorough shaking up."

Mother Katharine never took herself or her new kind of life too seriously. She withdrew gracefully from praise for what she was doing and said that it was the work of her Sisters. They were all doing it together.

She noticed everything in her travels and recorded it in whimsical, affectionate language in long letters. It meant something to her when she found some of the little Indian girls did not have their own tin wash basin. It made her happy to see that sheets were snowy white. If paint was peeling, she saw it. She went out to the barn to see what the grain crop was like.

She breathed the thick red dust of Oklahoma, used the outdoor plumbing, slipped into the knee-deep mud, and forded swollen rivers with her feet perched on a box placed on the floor of the wagon.

Mother Katharine had a "promise book." Conscious of budgets, she told the bishop in advance how much she could send him the following year and for what purpose. Always she said or implied, "If I live..." for when she died the source of money for the Blessed Sacrament Sisters would be gone. Providence was kind, though. She lived to be 96, and for the last 12 years of her life, when she was the only one of the Drexel sisters living, her income was $1,000 a day.

A tax exemption law was passed, chiefly for her benefit. Her taxes had kept climbing. Through the efforts of Senator George Warren Pepper, the 1932 Revenue Act, Section 120, exempted charitable contributions in full when, for the preceeding 10 years, 90% of the taxpayer's net income had gone to charity. That had been the case with her for more than 40 years.

When the white property owners of Nashville and New Orleans refused to let her buy property for black schools, and followed up their refusals with threats, Mother Katharine calmly went ahead with her projects. She kept looking until she found a suitable piece of property that she could obtain.

Before anyone else had thought of it, she went to a prominent newspaper service to ask better headlines where blacks were concerned. "You don't say 'White man kills two.'" she said. She pointed out how unfair the common practice was. Probably to settle the matter, the director told her to make note of which newspapers did this, and to write directly to the editor about it. And she did.

In the last years of her life, when at times she grew forgetful, Mother Katharine prayed constantly, Rosary after Rosary, for everyone connected with her in any way. She wore out holy cards picturing St. Pius X. The Sisters would silently replace them. She was devoted to the Sacred Heart, but most of all to the Eucharist. In her younger years it had pained her greatly that daily Communion was not allowed.

When she died on March 3, 1955, people came by the hundreds to get one last look at the face of this great woman. Parents held up their children and said, "Mother Katharine is a saint." Her coffin was guarded by four Sisters because some admirers had started to get relics by snipping pieces of her habit.

Newsweek (March 14, 1955) gave Mother Katharine about two inches of obituary and said in the last lines, "She gave her $360,000 annual income to her Order and lived on an allowance of 41¢ a day."

I doubt the 41¢ figure, but it would have been like her. Every- thing for others, nothing for herself.   ✳

Aloysius Randolph Remembers Mother Katharine

Her kindness touched his life

By PAUL J. CULLEN

Although Mother Katharine died in 1955, Aloysius Randolph, a black man in his 70's, remembers her well. In a sense, Randolph's ties to Mother Katharine began before his birth. His Mother was among the first of Mother Katharine's pupils at St. Francis de Sales School in Powhatan, Va. "Mother Katharine founded the school and took a special interest in its students," said Randolph from his Philadelphia home. "They were her first students."

His mother came from a Baptist family in Richmond. The family didn't want her to have contact with Catholics, but she enrolled in St. Francis just the same to learn sewing.

With constant pressure from relatives to leave the school, she decided to leave her family instead. Marriage was her only avenue. She went to Philadelphia at the turn of the century and married "with Mother Katharine's blessing." She also became a Catholic, due to Mother Katharine's influence.

"The bond between my mother and Mother Katharine was intense,"

Randolph says. "Mother Katharine was out to get her soul. But she would never broach the subject of becoming a Catholic for fear of isolating her. She allowed her to finish school and maintain her Baptist religion."

After her conversion, his mother and Reverend Mother grew even closer. "I often heard her say to my mother, 'Lucy, if only I could share your problems, if only I could feel the troubles and suffering. Lucy, please, when things get tough, call me, come to me. I want to help.'"

Randolph himself remembers Mother Katharine from the time he was three or four years old. He and other children used to spend summers at the Blessed Sacrament motherhouse while their parents worked. Mother Katharine would send her buggy around to pick them up and bring all of them to the motherhouse in Cornwells Heights, near Philadelphia.

She took a personal interest in the children. "If Mother Katharine was busy with her work, she would keep everybody else busy, too," Randolph says. "All the kids had chores to do."

When he got older, his duty was to help mow the lawn at the motherhouse.

"One day I was out cutting and the big bell rang. That meant that all the kids should go to get a loaf of bread loaded with molasses as a snack. I got mine and went back to finish the lawn. I was wrestling with the bread trying to eat it and push the mower at the same time."

Little Aloysius was holding the molasses bread in both hands and trying to push the mower with his stomach, when someone shouted, "Hurry up!"

This shout distracted Mother Katharine. "Don't ever do that," she scolded. "You'll rupture yourself as sure as you are two-foot high." She even had a physician examine him. "That was concern," Randolph comments.

Reverend Mother also touched Randolph's little sister with her concern. The 18-month-old child was left unattended for a short time and climbed to a window sill. A radiator released some steam, burned her, and scared her so that she lost her balance and fell out the window. The four-story fall didn't kill the girl, but for three or four years she needed intensive medical care. "Mother Katharine took care of everything," Randolph remembers.

He remembers one more incident, when he was 13 or 14 years old and worked in a Philadelphia bootblack parlor for his father.

At the end of every summer, Mother Katharine took her children to an amusement park for the day. Aloysius Randolph wanted to go but his mother said he had to work instead. "The shock of not being able to go almost knocked me over," he says. "Never in my life had I questioned my mother."

Young Aloysius carried on and complained in the hearing of Mother Katharine. "Do I have to go to work?" he asked her.

"Mother Katharine took my mother by the hand and walked off to talk with her. My mother shook her head 'no.' Mother Katharine came back to me. She put her arm around my shoulder and never said a word. We just walked toward the gate. There wasn't another word spoken. The moment she put her arm around me, I had no resistance. You see the influence she had on me."

He remembers other details about Reverend Mother.

"She was intense. I don't think she was smiling, but it was what they call inner peace.

"She had a fine voice. It sounded like an organ when she was leading the prayers.

"She would listen to anybody, hear any story. If she could help with advice, she would.

"Every time I had contact with her, she was anxious to do something for us."

Many people hated Katharine Drexel for her work, says Randolph, adding almost as an afterthought, "I never for sure could understand how a woman with all the wealth in the world would get caught up in the web of other people's problems."   ✳

Tom Playfair, All-American Catholic Boy

He was the turn of the century creation
of a priest some have called the "Catholic
Horatio Alger"

By JAMES KULP
November 1981

EVERY KID who went to parochial school 50 years ago probably got a dose of Tom Playfair, the all-American Catholic boy. Tom was just one of the heroes in a series of 27 novels about Catholic boys written by Father Francis J. Finn, S.J. Tom Playfair's story, like most of the others, stages a Horatio Alger-type rise from hardship to success in a Catholic boarding-school setting.

Jesuit Father Francis Finn was a college professor of literature and classics, and later a parish school administrator. He wrote Tom Playfair *for the boys in a class he was teaching.*

While Father Finn's books have been out of print for years, a collection has been assembled at St. Stanislaus Jesuit Seminary Historical Museum in Florissant, Mo. — a suburb of St. Louis. Father William B. Faherty, S.J., the museum's curator, is looking for four missing titles to complete the collection: *Mostly Boys, The Story of Jesus, Sunshine and Freckles,* and *Boys' and Girls' Prayerbook.*

Tom Playfair, or Making a Start (1891) is about a boy from St. Louis who is being reared by his widower father and an aunt. Tom tends to lead a reckless life and gets sent to St. Maure's, a Catholic boys' school, in the hope it will straighten him out.

Father Finn describes him this way: " . . . a stout, healthy, dark-complexioned lad of ten . . . His rosy face and jet black hair gave token of a hasty toilet. His shoes were partially buttoned, his sturdy legs were encased in a pair of bright red stockings and rather tight knickerbockers, and his chubby cheeks wore an air of serenity, which, coupled with his naturally handsome features, made him a pleasing sight to all lovers of the genuine American boy."

The adventures begin once Tom hits school. He tames a bully, and organizes the smaller boys against the larger boys to win a baseball game; gets injured in a storm—in which two of his classmates are killed by lightning—while bravely crossing a flooded river to get medical help; visits a cousin in Cincinnati where he gets lost, and befriends a destitute newsboy and his little sister; captures the murderer of a saintly fellow student; becomes ill and nearly dies, and, in the end, makes a "good start" in life through the influence of good old-fashioned Catholic piety.

Percy Wynn (1891): Percy, a new boy at St. Maure's, is befriended by Tom Playfair who says he's too girlish and vows to "make a boy of him." He's taught how to fish, swim, and row a boat, and has encounters with school bullies and a vicious gang from the nearby village. Following the rescue of a drunken man and his little son from the gang, Percy converts both the man and his son to Catholicism. Percy and Tom aid a starving man and influence his death-bed repentance. The novel ends with the school bullies reforming their ways; the town gang also become friends with the two heroes and throw off rowdy habits for good manners and better clothes. Percy comes out of it a real boy, kind, cheerful, and modest.

Harry Dee, or Making It Out (1892): Harry is a sleepwalker who, when he finds his mother dead one morning, comes to love the "night nurse" hired to look after him. A rich uncle disowns a servant from his will to leave everything to Harry; the uncle is soon found stabbed to death, and a large sum of money is missing. Suspicion is thrown on the nurse and on Harry himself. Harry is sent to St. Maure's to shake him out of his depression, and he meets Tom Playfair and Percy Winn.

After such adventures as saving a haughty rich boy and his sister from their swamped yacht, Harry ultimately solves the mystery of the uncle's death: the servant, in trying to steal the money, had killed him. In the end, Harry's problem is "made out," the servant dies a penitent, Tom enters the Jesuit novitiate, a beloved St. Maure's teacher and prefect is ordained a Jesuit priest, and Harry and Percy resolve to start a Catholic magazine for boys and girls with the missing money that has been found in a secret hiding place.

Lucky Bob (1917): Bob is ejected from his father's car in Dubuque, Ia., with $50 to make his way in the world, as his father had before him. He goes on the road with a literate tramp who speaks Latin, writes poetry, and quotes Milton and Shakespeare. In the course of the novel, Bob brings an old man back to the Church, helps the tramp overcome a drinking problem, rescues a girl from a "brute," lives in a cave with a pious Catholic boy, makes his First Confession and Communion, and reduces his weight from a chubby 190 to 155 pounds through robust outdoor living, prayer, and the Mass.

The tramp, meanwhile, begins to sell his poetry and shares the profits with Bob. Bob enters St. Xavier's School where he learns from a teacher that meeting all those people wasn't luck but love, the keynote of life. The novel ends with a hint that, in future adventures, Bob will discover the secret of why his father cast him out into the world.

Cupid of Campion (1916): Clarence, a 14-year-old boy whose parents are missing in a train wreck, is robbed and set adrift on the Mississippi River in a boat. Though he tries to pray, his mother and father were not religious, and he knows only the Our Father and "Now I lay me down to sleep." Plucked from the river by gypsies, he finds they have kidnapped Dora, a girl of 12 who offers to instruct him in Catholicism. One day while swimming in the river, Clarence is swept away and rescued by a student of Campion College. He meets Will, who has lost his little sister in a flood. Both set out on a mission to rescue Dora, whom Will has discovered is his missing sister.

It develops that Clarence's parents weren't killed after all, because they had left the train before the accident. At the end, Clarence is baptized a Catholic, his mother pledges to return to the faith, and his father also plans to join the Church. In gratitude, his father gives $5,000 to Campion College, in which Clarence enrolls.

Throughout the stories, the reader is lectured on such topics as prayer, brother and sister relationships, school life and athletics, and the evils of reading dime novels, cheap detective stories, or Indian tales with false ideas of beauty and heroism.

The novels reflect the times:

automobiles are called "ma-chines," a 10-day stay in the hospital costs $20, board and lodging is $5 a week, and baseball has another name, "rounds." Characters often fall into a "brown study" when they are depressed, and the boys habitually use such quaint Victorian terms as "Pshaw," "You goose," "You sneak," and "Good gracious!"

Tom Playfair was the most popular of Father Finn's novels. It was written during his scholastic year as a Jesuit, 1883-84, but wasn't originally intended for publication. He wrote it for the boys in a class he was teaching, "with nothing else in my mind than to present, once and for all, my ideal of the typical American Catholic boy."

When *Tom Playfair* was published in 1891, the year of Father Finn's ordination, it attained almost immediate popularity. His publisher, Benziger Brothers, called it "the most successful book for Catholic boys and girls ever published in the English language."   ✱

Father Finn

A Biographical Note

Francis Finn was born Oct. 4, 1859, in St. Louis and died Nov. 2, 1928, in Cincinnati. He was the son of John Finn, who served as sheriff of St. Louis, and Mary Whyte, both Irish immigrants.

On March 24, 1879, he entered St. Stanislaus Seminary. His studies were constantly interrupted by teaching assignments at St. Mary's College in St. Mary's, Kansas, St. Xavier College in Cincinnati, and Marquette University in Milwaukee. He was professor of literature and classics at St. Xavier's but was relieved of teaching in 1899 because of his health. He then began a long career at St. Xavier's Church in Cincinnati, where he was in charge of the parish school.

The mythical campus of St. Maure's, on which many of Finn's novels are set, is patterned after St. Mary's College where he taught.

The American Catholic Who's Who for 1911 describes Father Finn as "universally acknowledged the foremost Catholic writer of fiction for young people." After he died, the late Daniel A. Lord, another famed Jesuit writer, said of his work: "He pioneered in Catholic literature at a time when Catholic literature in the U.S. was at a dismally low ebb."   ✱

Because of Father Baker…

Thousands of children have been fed, housed,
and educated
A successful gas well was drilled on faith alone
Uncounted numbers of unborn lives have been
saved, and unwed mothers cared for

By ALICE M. PYTAK
October 1981, condensed from *Courier-Express/Sunday**

H IS FIRST DAY on the job was challenging. Angry creditors pounded on his door, bankers left threatening messages, and not one cent was available to pay the bills. Father Nelson H. Baker might have had second thoughts about accepting the post as director of the St. Joseph's Orphanage. Financial ruin was a new phenomenon to the man who gave up a prosperous business to enter the priesthood. His thoughts flew back

Father Baker made Our Lady of Victory Parish internationally famous for its basilica, and for his remarkably resourceful works of charity.

*This article © 1981 by the *Buffalo Courier-Express*.

momentarily to that day in his old feed store when he told his partner of his decision.

"Won't you reconsider, Nelson?" Joseph Meyer urged. "Surely you don't want to give up all this?" He was not happy to lose a partner with whom he had built up a prosperous enterprise. In 1868, business in their Buffalo, N.Y., establishment was booming. Together they had forged a solid reputation in the expanding city of 120,000 and, after only five years, each had accumulated a comfortable bank account.

Nelson, at 26, was a handsome, dark-haired bachelor for whom life should have been exhilarating. Instead, an increasing unrest filled him. The years since his discharge from the Union Army had been split between his business and his volunteer work for the St. Vincent de Paul Society. As his business prospered, it left him strangely unfulfilled. In contrast, his work with the poor proved satisfying and comforting and helped to shape his decision.

He entered Our Lady of the Angels Seminary in Niagara Falls the following year. Although a severe attack of erysipelas, an infectious skin disease also known as St. Anthony's Fire, almost cost him his life and left him in frail health, he completed his studies and was ordained on March 19, 1876.

His first post was at Limestone Hill, a section south of Buffalo, later renamed Lackawanna. Here the Diocese of Buffalo had established a boys' orphanage and a home for older boys judged delinquent. Both institutions required large sums of money to keep functioning. Funds from government agencies were meager, and although their own farms and cattle supplied some of the necessities, the cost of feeding and housing the hundreds of residents reached astronomical proportions.

When Father Baker was assigned to assist the director, the homes were $27,000 in debt. Soon discouraged, he requested a transfer from what he considered a doomed venture. After a year's absence, he was asked to return to the orphanage as director and, after some deliberation, he accepted. By now the debt of the homes had risen to $56,000.

Armed with the total assets of a personal bank account left from his feed and grain business, Father Baker invited in the unhappy creditors and offered this proposition. "Gentleman, I am ready to settle the accounts, some partially, some in full," he told the surprised group. "But," he added firmly, before handing out any money, "you must realize that from now on your business will never again be sought by these institutions."

An awkward silence filled the room. The new director had been recognized by some of the creditors as the highly respected merchant they had dealt with years before. Success in one area might predicate a turning around of the enterprise he now headed. Should they take a chance of losing such a large account? After some thought, a few took the money and left. Most decided to wait out their payment a bit longer. Father Baker had won the first round, though the victor was now as penniless as the homes under his care.

The burden of administration lay heavily on his shoulders. Father Baker's consolation came in the hours when he knelt in prayer in the adjoining St. Patrick's Church. During his seminary days, he had sailed to Europe on a pilgrimage to religious shrines. In Paris's Notre Dame des Victoires he was deeply impressed by the crutches, canes, and other artifacts that attested to cures by the intercession of Mary. He had promoted a special devotion to Our Lady of Victory since that time and now, kneeling in prayer in the small church, he was struck by a novel idea. He could spread devotion to his favorite saint and raise money for his homes at the same time by forming an Association of Our Lady of Victory and charging a small annual membership fee.

He sat night after night at the huge oak roll-top desk in his room, writing to postmasters all over the country to request names of Catholic women in their communities who were active in social and religious work. Working from lists the officials sent him, he then wrote to the women, explaining his position and asking them to recruit members for his association at an annual dues of 25¢. In return, he promised to pray for them and their intentions in personal prayers as well as parish novenas. He appealed to their sympathy for orphans and succeeded.

Quarters pouring in from all over the U.S. and Canada formed a solid base for the homes. A newsletter and, later, a magazine kept donors informed of the progress of the homes and sparked more contributions. It was the first mailorder solicitation of funds for a charity. Soon there was enough money not only to meet the bills, but to think of expansion.

L ife in the late 1800's was not easy, but for the young it was often unbelievably cruel. Children were frequently orphaned by epidemics. Children of poor parents often were cast out to wander the streets, sleep in fields, and, frequently, starve. Father Baker eagerly accepted all of them. One estimate reports a peak of 1,500 children housed, fed, and educated in the homes at one time.

Since many of the children spent their entire youth, from infancy through adolescence, in the home, Father Baker recognized the need of preparing the older boys for a self-supporting adult life. He added workshops, and training given in carpentry, mechanics, plumbing, and electricity turned out able craftsmen. Some boys opted for the professions, and Father Baker willingly supported their ambitions and their entry into medicine, law, education, and government. For the boys who entered industry, he organized the Working Boys Home in Buffalo to provide them with decent living quarters.

The businessman in him surfaced again when he read of newly discovered Canadian natural gas deposits. He felt that the Limestone Hill property might contain similar pockets. The large buildings consumed enormous amounts of fuel for heating and cooking that ate up a large portion of the budget. Drilling could provide an answer, but it would be very expensive, and there were no extra funds. Fortuitously, Bishop Stephen Ryan had just received a gift to the diocese of $5,000, and Father Baker asked to use it.

"You want $5,000 to drill for gas?" the incredulous bishop asked. "Absolutely not!"

"I prayed long and hard before I came here, Bishop Ryan, and I believe that Our Lady of Victory is telling me there is gas under our land," Father Baker said, standing his ground. The bishop hesitated. This frail but energetic priest, who subsisted on a spartan diet—sometimes only a cracker for a meal—had done amazing things at Limestone Hill for the past 15 years and was certainly a man to be respected. But a gas well?

"I'll give you $500." The bishop was weakening. It must have taken a lot of convincing, but when Father Baker left the chancery that day, he had $2,000 to begin digging. And when that proved insufficient, he talked the bishop into donating the rest of the $5,000.

The gas well, dubbed "Father Baker's Folly," was considered a bad gamble by everyone connected with the drilling. He never viewed it as anything but a sure thing. When the workmen waited for Father Baker to bring in some engineers to plot out the site, he appeared, instead, leading a procession of the faithful reciting prayers and carrying a statue of Our Lady of Victory. Selecting a spot where he daily recited prayers, and which the local residents named "Father Baker's prayer path," the confident priest marked a spot with the statue, and instructed the workers to start digging there. While the drill dug, Father Baker prayed.

Finally, months later and at 1,137 feet—more than twice the depth where gas was usually struck—success came. "Victoria Well" heated the institutions for many years, and Father Baker provided homeowners within a two-mile radius with low-cost fuel until the supply showed signs of thinning. Another well was dug with similar success and still provides fuel for several of the huge buildings. A hunch and a prayer resulted in 90 years' supply of gas and immeasurable financial savings.

A shrewd manager with a keen business sense, Father Baker had a love and compassion for the unfortunate that outweighed all other interests. In 1906, shocked by the news of infant bodies and bones dredged out of the Erie Canal, he built the Infant Home. Understanding the shame of the unwed mothers of that era, he instructed that the Home's doors be left unlocked and an empty crib placed just inside, where unwanted babies could be left. Not many mornings dawned when the Sisters of St. Joseph, who staffed the Home, did not find a baby sleeping peacefully in the crib. To provide support for the Infant Home, he devised a system of solicitation in which patrons were asked to donate $25 to purchase a crib, a plan which is still used.

Thousands of children were raised in the Home, and tens of thousands of youngsters passed through the portals of one or another of the Home's facilities. A few years later, Father Baker built a Maternity Hospital for unwed mothers, where they lived and received medical care. He suffered denunciation by moralists who accused him of condoning sin. He saw only the agony of young girls, shamed and disowned by parents, who had nowhere to turn for help. The Maternity Hospital later became the 275-bed Our Lady of Victory Hospital, which still serves the community.

Throughout Father Baker's busy years, one thought underlined all his work—someday he would build a suitable shrine to Our Lady of Victory, whom he frequently called his business manager. In 1926, at the age of 84, he completed the magnificent basilica which stands today in Lackawanna, N.Y.

During the Depression years Father Baker was a familiar sight each morning handing out money to long lines of people. He fed, clothed, and housed thousands during those difficult years.

Father Baker died on July 29, 1936, at the age of 94. His name had become known all over the world, and over half a million people stood in a mile-long line to view the body of the "Padre of the Poor" whom many, by now, considered a saint. Though his work in 60 years of priesthood left gigantic monuments and involved millions of dollars, he died penniless.

He unwittingly summed up the philosophy which underlined his life of charity one day when he was asked to turn away some unscrupulous alms seekers. He refused, with the comment:

"When I die the good Lord won't ask me if they were worthy— but He might ask me if I gave."   ✳

Our Lady of Victory Today

By SISTER MARY ANN WALSH
Condensed from *Liguorian**

"There's a power from the beyond here," explains Sister Mary Walter Love, S.S.J., executive director of Our Lady of Victory Infant Home. "We've seen programs develop here in the last ten years that can't be found anyplace else in the entire country." She listed programs for pregnant unmarried teenagers, single parents, profoundly retarded and multiple-handicapped children, couples hoping to adopt, emotionally disturbed preschoolers, and homeless teenage girls.

"Money just comes when I need it," adds Sister Veronica Anne Armao, who directs the infant home's program for the retarded. "Sometimes I ask for it, more often I don't."

As if to attest to her words, a telephone call brings an offer of $100, "perhaps for toys for the children," the president of a local organization suggests. With visions of new colorful, educational toys to entice a child to focus his eyes or to reach out to touch, Sister smiles and hangs up the receiver. Most of the donations come in

the form of $1 and $2 contributions from people all around the country. Other gifts are from those wishing to express gratitude to Our Lady of Victory for special blessings.

One time Sister Veronica Anne needed a specialized wheel chair for a child. She was hesitant to spend $700 on something that would benefit only one youngster. While she was thinking about the chair, she received a memorial donation for $350. She bought the chair with faith that the rest of the money would come. It did.

Another program that has received and given many blessings is the program to help unwed mothers, newborn infants, and couples seeking to adopt.

"When abortion was legalized in 1971," recalls Kathieen Kearns, associate director of the Infant Home, "we had 53 girls living here. Almost immediately the number dropped down to 10. The home also went from placing up to 200 infants a year for adoption to placing 30 a year or less.

"We began a mass media campaign," she recalls. "We started a 'Choose Life' hotline. Girls were being rushed into abortions. Without guidance, they would, we felt, become pregnant again. We went public with the promise that if a girl wanted to bring her baby to term, we'd take care of her.

"We were spending $500 a month

on publicity alone, with no idea where the money would come from to pay for it. But we knew that this was the right way to go and it would be successful."

It was. Today the maternity services help more young women than ever before.

"I feel it when I go to our girls' weddings," Kearns says. "On these occasions, we can look back to when they thought their whole world had come to an end. Everything looked bleak. But then they got their lives together. What seemed impossible happened."

Sometimes a girl who has given up a child will come back later to adopt.

"I sense that she's being paid back for her earlier sacrifice. Some come, afraid that they'll be denied the right to adopt because of their past. We point out how different they are now that they have motivation, love, and the security to provide for a child."

Even the crisis of the unwed pregnant teenager can be turned into a miracle.

"Many of your young women suffer from a poor self-image," Kearns says. "Many have been in trouble with schools and with the courts. We can't help an unborn child without helping the child's mother."

Staff members also have developed a speakers' bureau to educate the public. They provide education in sexuality to both teenage boys and teenage girls. Their program builds upon Gospel principles: developing self-esteem, emphasizing values, understanding God's gift of sexuality, and making youths feel so good about themselves that they can say No when pressured into being sexually active.

The programs at the Infant Home have adapted to the times. For example, when the maternity program directors saw that some of their girls had no place to go after they'd given birth, they opened Mack House, a group home where adolescents are prepared to live on their own successfully.

When the rise in the number of unwed mothers choosing single parenthood meant a corresponding rise in child abuse, Our Lady of Victory started a single parenting program. Our Lady of Victory offers single parents medical care for their children and themselves, education in the needs of an infant, and moral support.

"I don't know if it's Our Lady of Victory, God, or Father Baker, but there's something special here," Kate Gallagher, director of the nursing department at the home, says. "For anyone in need, this seems to be the place to be. I've seen kids come here hostile and rejected and then leave with a totally different attitude.

"It's all part of the spirit of Our Lady of Victory," she adds. "The whole mystique here gives me shivers when I think of it."   ✳

Fifty-Two Years After Columbus

Friar Tomas de la Torre's journal of a
missionary journey in 1544

Edited and Translated by FRANS BLOM
October 1974, condensed from *The Sewanee Review**

O N SATURDAY, Jan. 12,
1544, all we priests arose
early in the morning and
said Mass. All those who were
not priests received the Holy
Eucharist, and the prelate who
had said Mass gave general
absolution.

After the meal we began to
take leave of all our good
friends. There was not one
Religious, both of those who
were departing and of those who
remained, who did not shed

*This article © 1973 by the University
of the South. This condensation is freely
adapted from Dr. Blom's 140-page scholarly edition; many transitional passages have
been rewritten, and much material omitted.
Reprinted with permission.

*In January, 1544, 46 Dominican
friars left their monastery in Salamanca, Spain, in order to follow
Bishop Bartolomé de Las Casas to
Chiapas, Mexico. When the friars
set out from the monastery, "it
was ordered that all the most
notable happenings should be written down." To do this Friar
Tomas de la Torre, a professor of
Philosophy, was selected.*

*His record includes the first
detailed account of a trans-Atlantic
crossing, and vividly depicts not
only the difficulties of land and sea
travel 400 years ago, but also the
determination which characterized
the first missionaries to the New
World. The account begins on the
day the friars leave the monastery
on foot for the port of Seville.*

tears. The Headmaster of the Novices, who had raised us all, and the other old people, cried like children.

They asked us to write them about what happened to us in the Indies, and to behave as true sons of St. Dominic; or to say it better, as Apostles of Jesus Christ, so that they would always hear good news from us. Never had such a large group of friars departed from this house who were so much needed, nor had a company going to the Indies been sent with such confidence; wherefore we must do our best.

The friars, because of weather and bureaucratic delays, remained in or near Seville for four and a half months. The famous Friar Bartolomé de Las Casas joined them here, and took charge of the party. During the wait, he was consecrated Bishop of Chiapas.

The bishop, apart from the many difficulties which he had suffered at court, suffered many more in Seville because he had seen to it that all the Indian slaves which they had there were freed; and other things that he did awakened a perpetual hatred for his name among the *Indianos* who lived there. (*Indianos* was the name given to all Spaniards who had been in the New World or who held property there.)

I t pleased Our Lord that on Wednesday morning, the 9th of July, 1544, one-half year after we had left Salamanca, we stepped into the boats and from them onto the ship. The season was not good for sailing, but the fleet was prepared and ready. There were 26 ships, counting the large ships and the caravels and one armed galleon.

Leading our party was the Most Rev. Bishop Friar Bartolomé de Las Casas, Bishop of Chiapas. He was bringing the remedy for the Indies, consisting of many royal laws and provisions, obtained and issued by the Council of the Indies, and cast by him against the unworthy, and for the benefit of the worthy. He carried powers to liberate all the slaves, and to institute Royal Courts of Appeal, many other things; but most of all, he was pleased to have assembled the largest group of Religious that ever had left our Order for the Indies.

Once on board the ship, we stayed all that day roasting in the heat. Next day, with very little wind, we set sail.

We suffered indescribable heat those two days. The pitch on the decks of the ship burned; and we were so crowded that when we were seated or lying on deck, we were often stepped upon, not on our tunics, but on our beards and faces, and with no respect at all, even though we were friars. The passengers and sailors gave us other hardships and annoyances which cannot be described.

The first day we sang Divine Service, but because of the way in which we were molested, we only sang the *Salve* on the second day, and our prayers we said each one when we could.

The next day, July 11, we lost sight of Spain. Shortly, the sea made us understand that it was no place for human habitation, and all of us collapsed as dead with seasickness.

For those who know nothing about the sea, and of what one suffers there, I will tell a few things. First of all, the ship is a narrow prison, very strong, from which nobody can escape even though there are neither bars nor chains. No distinction is made among the prisoners who are all treated and punished alike. The crowded space, the suffocating air, and the heat are unbearable. The deck is usually the bed, though we have some cheap mattresses, filled with dog's hair, and cheap blankets of goat's wool.

People are irritable and rough, and few have any desire to eat. The thirst which one feels is heightened by eating hardtack and salted food. We get 1¾ pints of water every day, and he who has brought wine drinks it when he pleases.

The place is full of lice that eat every living creature, and one cannot wash one's clothes, as they shrink when cleaned in sea water. The air is foul, especially below deck, and intolerable when the pumps are going, which happens at least four or five times a day, in order to drain out the water that leaks into the ship.

In addition, there is no place to study or recuperate. One must be seated all the time as there is no space to walk. Whatever one does must be done seated, or lying down, and very little can be done standing up. Death is before one's eyes constantly, and only the thickness of a few planks separates you from the fish.

Our ship was badly ballasted, and this placed us in grave danger. As the ship was empty in the bottom and loaded on the top, it began to roll in an unusual way. One railing was swamped in water and, at times, the ship was thrown on its belly, so that the water reached to the middle of the deck, and some barrels which we had on board began swimming around.

It was impossible to cook, and half of the ship could not be used. Those who were lying crosswise were practically in a standing position. They hoped to correct this situation somewhat by moving cannon balls and other things below deck, but it did not help in the least.

Accordingly, we were in constant fear of death from the Sunday after we embarked until we reached port. Those who sailed on the other ships prayed for us every day, and many times, especially on two occasions, they blessed us because they thought that our ship was sinking.

Archuleta, the captain general, came alongside twice a day in his galleon to see how our ship was coming, and suggested tying our ship to his with hawsers, but our sailors were haughty and would not consent. There was no talk of transferring us to other ships, because we were so many and all the ships were loaded with people, and we did not realize the true danger.

Those who understood were the pilots of the other ships, who later visited us, and marveled at how we had escaped. When we reached land everybody congratulated us upon being alive. We just went along as one may think best, but truthfully we did not understand the danger, nor could we persuade ourselves that our good Lord intended to drown us.

The Spanish-Indianos who traveled on board our armada said that our sins and the sins of the bishop, who was destroying the Indies, caused all our troubles. But almost immediately afterwards God provided the finest season that ever was seen at that time of the year, which seemed a very marvelous thing. The sailors were surprised and they, as well as everybody else, said that God must have improved on the weather.

Some sailors respected us, but others called at every moment, friar here, friar there, and they made us go below deck like slaves, and stowed us as ballast against which way the ship was listing. With all this, and our ills, and seasickness, we were bruised and fatigued more than can be described. Then it was realized what a great mistake it had been to bring us all together on board one ship, for even those who ship merchandise divide it among different ships, so that if some of it is lost another part is saved.

With great joy on July 19, we discovered land, one of the Canary Islands, called Tenerife. The next morning we woke up close to the Island of Gomera. The father vicar (Tomás de Casillas, who had been the superior of the Salamanca monastery) ordered us to go ashore which we did with great pleasure. Once on shore we could hardly balance ourselves; it seemed as if the ground were rolling under us. We were also very emaciated. We went directly to the church to give our thanks to the Lord for the mercy He had shown us by allowing us to escape.

Under no circumstances did we wish to travel together again. We were frightened of that ship, and we considered it to be murder of all of us if we again were placed on board. Therefore, we begged the father vicar to give new instructions regarding our voyage.

When the sailors heard this they took as ballast six boatloads of stone, and threw out some boxes of merchandise, insisting to the father vicar that no friar was to be taken away from their ship, but that he should pay the passage, as the ship was in good shape to navigate. They went through much arguing, and the captain general did not know which way to turn. Finally it was decided that 19 friars should leave the ship. Before the remaining embarked, the ship was carefully inspected, and three pilots made statements under oath that it was seaworthy.

On July 30, we left the Port of Gomera with favorable winds. Our ship sailed so much faster than the others, that nearly without any sails we traveled faster than those which were under full sail.

Frequently some of the ships came close together and then we saw our brothers and heard from them, and all were well. A man fell overboard from the flagship and they could do nothing about it. On our ship somebody drilled one of our water barrels, but we did not permit the culprit to be punished, and this stopped other robberies which had been committed every day.

With such things happening we traveled along, sometimes shedding tears and at other times praying the Rosary and singing Psalms and hymns. The seculars would play their guitars and sing romantic songs, each in his own way. When there is tranquility and health then love raises the heart greatly towards God.

Usually there was very little food, and I believe that in part the reason was that it was difficult to cook it. They gave us a little bacon in the morning; at noon a little boiled salted meat and a bit of cheese, and the same thing in the evening. Each meal did not amount to as much as a pair of eggs. One's thirst is incredible. Though we were people used to temperance we felt dry. This thirst is caused by the kind of food we eat, and the great heat that one suffers, as well as knowing that there are restrictions.

As we were waiting for the caravels which sailed slowly, the calm caught up with us, and for two or three days we did not advance a step. So the seculars jumped into the sea for a swim and played around the ship while the sailors caught sharks, which we all ate. There is nothing wrong with them except that they taste somewhat strong, as with all large fish.

The sea was like milk and the ship did not move from its place. The planks and the rigging burned to the touch with the great heat. The fish which we had eaten augmented our thirst, and our rations of water were reduced as we did not move. During another four or five days there was little wind, and then again calm, and what little wind there was was against us.

All the pilots of the armada said that we were already near land. One day they made us get up from the table, making believe that they had seen land, and for three days we with the rest of them said that we had seen it, but later we found that it was nothing, and therefore became very sad.

On Aug. 26, at sunset, the ships in the lead signaled with shots. Believing that they had seen land we struck our sails. That night we slept with pleasure, and the next morning we saw an island called Mariagalante, which is the most beautiful land we had ever seen. If I had been the discoverer of this island I would without any doubt have thought that it was paradise on earth.

During the afternoon, we came in sight of more islands which we kept on our right hand—one is called Guadalupe, which is large, and the other is called the Friars, because it is covered with small bushes. I think that it is so beautiful and fresh looking that it is proper to thank the Lord. In general, all the islands are like that, fresh and very green at all times.

On Sept. 3 we lay off the City of San Juan de Puerto Rico, and we passed within sight of our monastery which is located outside of the town. It was very white and beautiful. Here ships which were destined for that port separated from us with several other ships, as many of their people had died, and others because they were leaking a lot of water.

Thus there were only 12 ships and one caravel left in our armada, and some of these were in great need of drinking water. The general decided that we should not take water here, but pass on to the Port of San German, which is on this same island, 87½ miles further on. We continued close to the shore of that beautiful island, blessing Him who had created it, as certainly its beauty is such that not even Spain is like it.

On Sept. 6, Father Vicar, with old Father Rodrigo, and some of the people from the ship, went ashore. They returned in the evening, and said that there was a small settlement of Spaniards, living in houses of boards, and the church is of the same material. There is also a small house of our Order, very poor and likewise built of boards, where they found two Religious, one of whom was sick. There was nothing to eat but casavi, garlic, and some fruits of the country.

They brought us some of the native fruits, among which was pineapple. Although the Spaniards and the Indians praise it highly, and like it, we could not put it in our mouths. Its smell and taste to us was like an over-ripe melon, roasted in the sun.

They also brought us bananas, which are a fruit usually about 8 inches long. They are nearly as thick as a wrist and where they come together they look like sausages tied together, and when they are ripe they also look like that, as if they were smoked. They have hides like goats and it is very easy to undress them, and inside they are yellowish white. It is an excellent fruit, raw, fried, boiled, or roasted, and dry it is much like very fine figs. But to us at first it tasted like a salve, or something similar, prepared by a druggist.

They also brought us guayavas, which are green, somewhat toward yellow, like peaches filled inside with small grains which one swallows without chewing them. They consider it a good fruit on the Spanish islands, but to those who come from Castille they smell like bedbugs, and are abominable to eat.

They also brought sweet potatoes, which are roots that grow underground like turnips. Some are white, and others red, and they are eaten baked or boiled. They taste exactly like baked or boiled chestnuts and therefore they tasted good to us.

What we enjoyed most was the quantity of drinking water. They brought back so much that we drank without restriction, and we washed our faces with it, and gave to those who did not have any.

Tuesday, Sept. 9, 1544, 43 days after we embarked at Gomera, we went ashore in the City of Santo Domingo on Española Island.

The journal describes heated arguments there between the Spaniards and Bishop Las Casas. The Spaniards insisted that to free the enslaved Indians would ruin their estates and mines, while the bishop defended the Indians against the brutality and cruelty of the slaveholders. Meanwhile, the friars were worried about those of their companions who stopped over at Puerto Rico, and also had difficulty in finding transportation to Mexico. The citizens reviled

them when they begged for alms,
and once some of them were
beaten and stoned, but a few
citizens came to their aid.

The reason for this severity
was that the laws for the liberation of the Indian slaves had
already been promulgated, and
therefore the Spaniards could
not stand the sight of the bishop
any better than that of the devil.

Our Lord awakened a lib-
erated Negro slave woman
who lived there and she practically supported us. She never
stopped, either night or day;
now she came loaded down with
casavi, and again with fish and
bananas, and with everything
else she could bring with devotion and charity, so much that
she placed upon us the obligation to pray to God for her.
Some other persons also gave
us alms, with which we lived
modestly, and there we learned
to drink casavi and left off drinking wine, and we learned also
to eat the native fruits and we
stuffed ourselves with them.

In our great need, Our Lord
touched the heart of a rich
widow who had many slaves.
Hearing of our preaching, she
determined to emancipate them
all, saying that she had never
thought that it was a sin, but
that we were better than she.
Having emancipated them she
began to provide us liberally
with bread and wine and,
although it now was expensive,
she sent us 105 gallons of wine.
She also sent us heifers, goats,
sheep, casavi, fish; at times she
sent us cooked food, and then
food ready to cook, now in part
and then all at once; then again
she sent 100 reales ($13.30) with
which to buy food, and she never
stopped this good work as long
as we were there. After she had
gone to Confession and had
freed her slaves, in her house
she prepared salt beef for our
sea voyage, and sent us lemon
peels preserved in sugar, marzi-
pan, and what she could think
of, and the bishop of the Island
of San Juan also gave us alms.

The Negro woman appeared
to conquer all with her faith;
she never stopped, but as a little bird she went and came back
with her burden. She told us
that she had lost a newly married daughter, and as God had
taken the wife He also should
have the dowry, through her giving it to the friars.

I will not speak about all the
great difficulties we had trying
to find a ship which at that time
would be going specially toward
the Bishopric of Chiapas. I will
only say that after some time
we met a pilot who had his own
ship chartered for Peru. He said
he knew of a port (Campeche),
not mentioned to us until then,
which was in the Province of
Yucatan, which lies on the border of the Bishopric of Chiapas.
With the help of our royal

decree his agreement to go to Peru was cancelled with great difficulty, and the bishop chartered the whole ship at the cost of 1,262 castellanos ($3,817.55). (This caused the bishop much trouble, and kept him in debt through many years.) On our behalf, the king gave the 300 pesos ($907.50) which was the cost of our passage. All the remainder ($2,910) was spent by the bishop, one reason being that he wanted us to leave the island and all the trouble we had there, and the other was that he wanted to have us in the presence of his flock which needed us.

The third Sunday of Advent, Dec. 14, 1544, we departed for the high seas with a good wind. Hardly had we left the mouth of the river before all of us collapsed as dead; even many of the sailors became seasick. We all behaved as if we were enchanted. We ate little, or nothing at all, that day and the following day, until the following afternoon when we began to recover.

The night of the Day of Our Lady (Dec. 18), at midnight, a great storm sprang up again, so strong that we all got up and half kneeling, half lying, said our litanies and commended ourselves to God until morning. The tempest was so violent, and the roar of the sea so loud that it seemed as if the waves would smash the ship. The sails were immediately lowered.

The next night was even worse. All night long we prayed in the small cabin. Now we were silent, and then, again, we said litanies and prayers. But in spite of all this the waves increased, and collided so violently with the ship that we thought each blow would be the last.

On Saturday afternoon all the sailors confessed, as well as all the ship's company, and they made many promises. A Portuguese started talking loudly and with devotion, calling on San Telmo, and saying that if God saved him from the tempest because of his prayer, then he would swear never in his life to go to sea again. Somebody laughed when they heard this, although there was more reason to weep than to laugh at that time.

That Saturday night the waves seemed to reach the sky. The wind was so violent that it broke the foremast.

Some of the Religious modestly commended themselves to God. Others loudly called the name of our Lord Jesus Christ. The bishop exorcised the sea, ordering it in the name of our Lord Jesus Christ to abate and be silent. He called to the people to be without fear, for God was with us. This consoled us and we did not fear to die, and I believed that if we should die then God's mercy would save us. Then we sang hymns for a long time, and while we were singing one of the sailors said, "Father, the tempest has ceased." It was as if an angel had said this, and without waiting further, we began to sing a *Te Deum Laudamus,* and then the storm was followed by a great calm.

I am no friend of calling things a miracle when there can be some natural reason, but I have told what happened; ascribe it to whatever cause you will.

It lay heavy on our hearts to realize that we would have to spend Christmas on the sea, and that we could not celebrate the birth of our Redeemer as we wished to do it. But He gave us a wind right aft, so delightful that there was nothing to interfere with what we planned to do. Thus, on the day before Christmas we sang Vespers with great devotion, and in the afternoon the father vicar preached and gave general absolution. We constructed an altar aft, unpacked the Child Jesus which we carried, and wrapped it in hay which we had on board, and kept vigil all night with lighted white candles, prayers, and joyous songs. At midnight we sang Matins and the Mass of the Rooster, and then the morning song.

With the calm of the sea and with our singing the sailors slept, which might have been dangerous if God had not watched over us so marvelously. With the crew asleep, God opened the eyes of Fr. Pedro Calvo, who cried out, "Land, land!" The sailors jumped up at once and saw that it was true, and hurriedly, with much shouting, they turned the ship away. To me, it seemed that we were about two crossbow shots from land, which is a short distance at sea. God marvelously saved us, and that day gave us our lives as a Christmas present.

In the morning of the day of the Kings (Jan. 6, 1545), at daybreak, we landed at Campeche. It is a village with 500 houses and 13 Spanish residents.

We entered the church, which was close to the shore, and there we heard Mass and a *Te Deum Laudamus* and other prayers giving thanks to Our Lord for having ended this long and arduous voyage.

We had not been long in Campeche, however, when the bishop found himself in trouble, as only the cleric recognized and received him as bishop. The Spaniards found excuses not to receive him, for they hated him deeply and would drink his blood if they could. This caused him great sadness, because the Spaniards did not respond with tithes nor with anything to pay for the passage, and he therefore found himself in great distress. He sent to Chiapas to ask for part of the money, and the clergy there sent him a sum. We gave him wine and flour and other things as money of which we had 100 castellanos ($300), and thus he swallowed his misfortune, but still left the place with many debts.

We also were very greatly worried because of the difficulties ahead, as we still had to travel 300 miles to Chiapas. The first 150 miles to the City of Tabasco were the most difficult because we had to travel in large fishing boats which sailed along the coast. We had no desire to go to sea now that God had saved our lives. But we were told that it was not possible to go by land because of the huge swamps and lagoons on the way, and that the mosquitoes would eat us alive. Weighing all these reasons, we decided that it would be best to go by boat.

Ten friars boarded a boat on Feb. 18. The rest remained in Campeche waiting for other vessels.

Many days later while we were in the church praying and reading, a man called the father vicar out of the choir. We did not know what he said, but as we saw that he crossed himself, we judged that something serious had happened. When we had finished with the *Salve,* he told us all to be seated in the choir.

For a while he was so moved that he could not talk. We were all silent and after a moment he spoke, "Padres, our brothers have drowned!" He wanted to say more, but he could not. I, for certain, cannot say what we felt; you can imagine for yourself.

As the father vicar was unable to speak, we threw ourselves on the ground and there, fallen and prostrate in front of the altar, we wept most bitterly. But who would not weep, even if they had a heart of iron? We saw our families and parents whom we had left, our houses and monasteries, our spiritual fathers and brothers whom we had traded for these companions. Now we thought of the anguish which awaited us in this land. With all these worries we did not know whether to go backwards or forwards, and with all this it had now become dark, and from the ship they hurried us to embark. All said that the shipwreck had been accidental, and that it would be unwise not to depart, so we embarked even though it was late.

Immediately seasickness fell upon our sadness, and we did not move from our places until the next afternoon.

The following day, quite late, we got up and with great abundance of tears we sang a responsory.

We desired very much to reach the place where those saintly men had perished, because if we found that the sea had cast a body on the shore then we would bury it, which would be great consolation to us, but the sailors would not take us there.

That day at 8 o'clock a norther started blowing and in a hurry the sailors steered for one of the mouths to seek shelter. God guided us to that entrance that makes the Island of Terminos, which was the place where those servants of the Lord ended their labors. Natives brought us a part of a St. Thomas, which we recognized as having belonged to Fr. Miguel Duarte. Our sorrows were renewed at seeing a book which once had belonged to our brother.

Then we went ashore, the bishop and the rest of us, and walked down along the beach, more running than walking, hoping to find a body. We found many rolls of cotton cloth, the mast, the hatchway of the boat, and other similar things, but of our things and those of our brothers we only found another part of St. Thomas, a companion to the first part, and a bag which had belonged to Father Duarte.

On Feb. 13, they came to the

town of Tabasco on the Grijalva River, whose valley would lead them much of the way to Chiapas. In that town live about 30 Spanish residents. Here we met a friar of our own Order, who in Spain was called Fr. Diego de San Vicente, here called Medinilla, who had his mother and brother in Chiapas. He was on his way to Spain, but when he heard of our coming he decided to remain in this country, and to serve God in our company.

Everybody in this town showed much kindness and gave many presents to the friars, especially three, who gave them canoes. Ash Wednesday (Feb. 18), they embarked in the canoes and started upriver.

Along this river lie some small towns. The natives there are rich in cacao. The cacao bean is money among them. It is a fruit of the size and looks of a large pine cone. It has a thin skin on the outside, and the seeds inside have one hundred parts stuck together. When these are ground and dissolved in water, it makes a drink which is nauseating to those who are not used to it, and cool and tasty and much appreciated by those who know it. Usually, those Spaniards who have no wine drink it, and most of us also drink it, especially when in the hot country we come in from the road.

The friars came to Tlacotalpa,

the head of navigation, on Feb. 22. The next day, we had our first taste of the roads in that country, which are such that one must see them to appreciate them. Fr. Domingo de Medinilla told us that they were as level as the palm of a hand compared to those ahead. We thought he said that in fun, as to us it seemed that the mountainside wanted first to ascend to heaven and then to descend to hell.

But at this time, as it was the first day's march, and as we were not accustomed to this kind of traveling, and were worn down from the country, the rivers, and the sea, we felt it more than I can say, even though we had seen mountains and passes in Spain. There are trees so tall that they seem to reach the sky, with trunks so thick that ten men cannot surround them with their arms. There are lovely mountains, high, slender, and straight, that look like a cypress and these, as well as all the rest of the land, are covered with forests, incredible if you have not seen it. There are an infinite number of charming streams with good and very clear water, in which natural gold is found.

At the end of four leagues (10 miles) on the road which I have just described, the people came out of a village to receive us, with the children in procession carrying a cross. We could not restrain our tears, so we let them flow abundantly, seeing with how much honor they received people whom they did not know. Or was it simply because they knew that we had come to remedy their corporal and spiritual oppressions? This had already been divulged among them, as the bishop said nothing else.

They took us to the church, which they had decorated beautifully, and in the middle of which stood some stretchers covered with long green feathers which are highly valued by the Indians. To the friars these feathers looked very rich and spectacular. Later, they took us to the rest house, which they had built for the bishop, and which was decorated with so many arches of flowers and green branches that God should be praised. All this seemed like things in a dream.

The following day, because we could hardly stand up, as well as because it was raining, it was impossible to leave. Fr. Domingo de Medinilla preached a little in the Mexican language, with the *cacique* translating into the language of the land.

We were surprised to hear how that priest preached and spoke that language. We thought that we would never be able in all our lifetime to do likewise, but there was not one among us who later, in ten days after they began studying a language, did not know more than Medinilla, and we laughed a lot at him, because he knew nothing. Very soon we did not need interpreters, as we learned all the dialects of the country.

Those Indians told us about the intolerable injuries they suffered from the Spaniards, and gave thanks to God that they had been allowed to see the remedy arrive, which they said was us, and they begged us to settle there.

Here, as well as in many other parts of the province, are found some small nocturnal birds which are bats, or like them. They bite people subtly, while they sleep, so deeply that they take away a small bit of flesh, and so gently that it rarely hurts, nor can it be felt, though one bleeds freely. They usually bite the points of the toes and ends of the fingers, or the point of the nose, or the earlobe, and if they cannot reach these they bite where they can. When we got up early in the morning it was fun to watch which one of us had been bitten. Fr. Luis uncovered his feet for them to bite him, as he was fat and full of blood. Now, they rarely bite us as we know how to protect ourselves, even though they do not hurt, and as I said, they are more likely to cause laughter and fun.

Fr. Tomás de San Juan was in bad condition, and it was therefore arranged to send him ahead in a hammock. A hammock is a net made very artfully of strings. Without seeing one it is hard to explain it. They tie ends of the hammock to a strong pole, and with a man at either end of the pole, they carry the seated person. It is very pleasant to ride in one, although some people become seasick.

The Indians, I mean the men, usually sleep in these. They use the hammocks to carry their lords and the sick, and now, the wives of Castilians travel on the roads in these, and even the Spanish men have themselves carried in hammocks when they go to their villages, especially if the road is so bad that horses cannot pass. In one of these hammocks they sent Fr. Tomás, the Indians being willing and pleased. There was no horse, and even if there had been one, he could not have hung onto one on those mountain trails.

I must say these roads cannot be appreciated without having seen them. All I can say is that they are trails which have been made by the rains, which make the streams down the mountain side, and that is how the roads usually are in this country. We climbed up with hands and feet, hanging onto roots of trees, of which there are so many that one can hardly see the sky. There are cool streams in those ravines, but as we were fasting, few of us drank of this water, although we were sweating in rivulets.

We sang Psalms with loud voices, hardly being able to breathe as we went along, but the father vicar encouraged us to sing, as devotion would take away our hunger. His great spirit and devotion made him consider it sacrilege if we failed to fast, since our lives were to be the miracle by which the Indians were to be converted. Keeping the deeds of the saintly fathers in mind, he made us work.

The road is one foot wide, as all of them are, and therefore we walked single file as do all the Indians, even if there are a thousand of them. At times the road follows the hilltop with frightening precipices on the sides. At some downslopes we found handrails, like banisters, which we held on to in order to descend. The forest stopped, and we were hungry and tired to death.

Some of the friars talked about the great Peña de España (Rock of Spain, a mountain), and how, when one reaches its top, it is so pleasant to eat bread and drink water seated in a cool refectory. We thought of the friars who at that hour would be leaving the Vesper service, and go to the refectory to eat good viands and drink cold wine,

and with this we consoled ourselves in our hardships without knowing where we were going nor what to do.

In a deep gorge among those mountains lived a Christian by the name of Pedro Gentile. He was married to an honorable and devoted woman, and the two of them had a letter of brotherhood and were brothers of our Order in Spain. As they knew that we were coming they had prepared what they thought we would be in need of.

After we had said our prayers in the small oratory which stood among the houses this Christian man immediately took us to his house, where we were joyfully received by the wife. Entering the door we saw a table set with covers of German cloth hanging down to the floor, and on the table many drinking vessels and porcelain, with fine bread and many Castilian melons. In that lonely place, they gave us exquisitely clean food and drink—not of cacao, but of excellent wine from Guadalcanal (Spain). Certainly we had found what we needed, and needed very much.

All this luxury, only 20 years after Captain Luis Marin and Bernal Diaz del Castillo, with a small army of Spaniards, retired into the highlands of Chiapas, is noteworthy. The mention of the wine from Guadalcanal reminds us that the Spanish crown, in order to protect its wine industry, had forbidden the growing of grapes in the New World. All the wine which is mentioned in this diary was imported from Spain, as was also the olive oil.

After leaving here, we were to ascend the Tapilula Canyon, which is famous throughout all this country. As the father vicar saw that many were ill, and all of us so tired that we were ready to fall, he gave permission to all the feeble to eat in the morning, and thus each of them had an egg for breakfast.

Leaving our lodgings we began to climb the dreadful mountain, at times on foot, and at times on all fours, from which the sick especially suffered great hardships. The father vicar told us that he who could not climb should not fast, but in spite of this there was not one who failed to fast until then. We reached the top of the climb in such condition that it was impossible to continue without eating, and therefore the father vicar and all of us drank from a clear fountain and ate a little bread and some cheese.

The next day we rested. So many fell sick that I cannot remember their number, except that not one of us was able to serve the other. I believe that 13 of us were stretched out. The supper for the sick, whom the fever had left, was some crumbs. For those who had not eaten they added some wild amaranth, which I know not who had brought.

The next day was the day of our Father St. Thomas (March 7). They gave the sick a little hardtack and cheese for the fever, and to help them to walk. With this we set out, both sick and healthy, on those terrible roads, all on foot.

The father vicar had a particular grace in that he seemed to feel the sufferings of all of us. When a sick person sat down, he made everybody sit, and thus showed that he did not care if we reached our destination that day or next month. This was great consolation to all the feeble.

Afflicted with all these troubles we next met Rodrigo Lopez and another Christian halfway up the climb at a cool stream. They brought us a basket with ringshaped bread of Castille, a box of preserves, and a jug of wine with a fine cup from which to drink. One can imagine the joy which we felt, so great that we blessed it with tears and gave thanks to God.

But we still had the worst of the mountain to climb. This mountain had been an Indian fortification in the war with the Christians, who never were able to get there.

When the Indians heard that we were coming they rushed down those slopes in droves, and in a moment they had all our patients in hammocks carrying them up the mountain. From the top of the climb to the church they had made an avenue of branches with many arches of leaves and flowers, and they received us with a great Indian dance which was meant to be in praise of God. In the church they had a great quantity of very large citrons, the largest we had seen in our lives, and many oranges which they brought from their orchards down in the valley.

From every town they brought us green feathers, eggs, fish, bread, and chickens for the sick. Fruits were in such abundance that it made us weep from pleasure at seeing them, and also, on the other hand, from compassion, as here nearly all were infidels, and those who had been baptized were without any knowledge of God. We told them something through an interpreter, but it was all air, as even we did not know what to say, nor did the interpreter understand our words and therefore we could not translate.

On March 10, we went to the house of a Christian in Nistlan. There were many white lilies and flowers from Castille with which we consoled ourselves.

The chiefs came to ask us to go to their towns.

We were amazed that they kept saying that we had come to set their hearts right, to free them of their sins, and to teach them about God, showing great interest in all the things pertaining to God. Every hour we shed tears remembering our friends who would not come with us, seeing what they were losing, and we wished that we had a messenger to write to them, as they had asked us to do.

At a village called Muztenango, a cacique wanted us to see that an Indian whom he brought with him was instructed in the things of the faith, so that he could in turn teach himself and the villagers. The Christians to whom he paid tribute had not taught him anything. This made us very sad, knowing that in Spain were so many buried desires which could be employed here. This preacher knew the *Credo* in Latin, and the Commandments in Spanish, and this he was going to teach.

He who should have taught the Indians came once or twice a year to see his cattle, and to collect his tribute. The Christians gather the Indians in the church with clubs, to make them say the *Credo* in Latin, and the Ten Commandments in Spanish. I heard them frequently praise themselves at having done this, and calling the Indians obstinate dogs who did not want to know the things of God. And after the friars taught them about God in their own language, it was said that we destroyed the land, and that we were insane because we taught the prayers and articles in the Indians' language, and such like things.

Next morning we went two leagues to the small farm of the mother of Fr. Domingo de Medinilla, where we had been told that preparations had been made for dinner, but when we arrived there we found nobody. Some who were unable to walk ate some of the food which we carried, and others did not eat as they had fever, and some wished to fast and wait until later.

Leaving that place we followed the road to the City of Chiapas (today called San Cristobal de las Casas). The city, as they call it, has about 60 resident Spaniards, although there are better places where they could settle, but this is the center of the government, and of the province. Here come all the Indians from the neighborhood, to pay their tribute, to serve the Spaniards, and to do what else offers itself. Although there are hardly more than 300 houses, there will soon be many more. Here is the seat of the bishop; here is the cathedral, and also the law courts of the land.

From the river which runs close by the city, we all entered in procession, guided by two Spaniards whom we had met. We went to the church and gave thanks to Our Lord for the mercy He had shown us by bringing us to a land of Christians and to the end of our long journey.

We arrived here Thursday, the day of St. George, March 12, in the year 1545, at the end of great hardships and privations. ✐

THEY HAVE MORE THAN EARS

A three-year-old in a hospital was told by his nurse that if he wanted anything he should just push the buzzer. Later the nurse heard the buzzer, and she asked over her intercom, "What can I do for you, Tommy?"

When there was no answer, she repeated the question. There was still no answer. A little worried by now, the nurse asked, "Tommy, do you hear me?"

Over the intercom came a small, frightened voice, "Yes, wall, I hear you." *The Milwaukee Journal.*

Ambrose, Augustine, and the City of Milan

Above its bustling pavements I recalled that great era of Christendom

By H. V. MORTON
June 1965, condensed from *A Traveller in Italy**

FROM Milan's tallest sky-scraper I looked down into the busy streets below and reflected. What a story these streets have to tell!

Here, in 313, Constantine the Great issued the Edict of Milan, which granted freedom of worship to Christians and emptied the prisons and mines of Christ's limping champions. During the first Christian council that followed many of the bishops appeared on crutches, some maimed in the torture chamber and others scarred with the branding iron. Such were the men who drew up the Nicene Creed.

*This article ©1964 by H. V. Morton. Reprinted with permission of Dodd, Mead & Co.

Somewhere in this city, on a site now carrying some massive erection of steel and concrete where the typewriters rattle, St. Ambrose baptized St. Augustine and spoke the funeral orations over four emperors.

Always in Milan, one comes back to St. Ambrose. Even the local communists call themselves Ambrosiani. So much has happened since Ambrose—44 sieges, innumerable burnings, and two complete obliterations—yet the corporate memory of Milan flies over the great gap of time to him on every conceivable occasion. He is Milan's Romulus, Remus, and wolf all in one, and Milan's image of him is one of the oldest loyalties in Europe.

217

During one of my early-morning walks in Milan I came unexpectedly upon the Ambrosian basilica, an old church which stands many centuries below the modern street level. Its Roman gravity, its peace, and, above all, its antiquity, contrasted with the morning bustle in the streets, where trams and buses rumbled along, bearing to work the first wave of clerks and typists.

The church was cold. As I stood shivering, I noticed a glimmer of light under the high altar. I walked towards it and, descending a flight of steps, entered a crypt where old women dressed in black were waiting for early Mass to begin. They looked like a gathering of primitive Christians.

The verger hurried down with a bunch of keys and cranked down some steel panels under the altar. The old women fell upon their knees and blessed themselves. They were in the presence of one of the world's most awesome survivals.

Three clothed skeletons were lying side by side upon a bier within a crystal shrine. The central skeleton was that of St. Ambrose, whose remains have been preserved in the basilica since 397. An antique miter rested upon his skull; upon the finger bones were red episcopal gloves; upon the skeleton feet were golden slippers; and in the crook of the arm bones lay a crosier.

The skeletons on each side are those of the martyrs St. Gervasius and St. Protasius, of whom little is known except that they were Roman soldiers said to have died for their faith. Their skeletons bear plainly the marks of violent death.

The third skeleton has no injury, but the skull shows a peculiarity which long puzzled doctors. The right upper eye-tooth is deeply set in such a way as to suggest a slight facial deformity.

It was left to a young assistant librarian of the Ambrosian library (who later became Pope Pius XI) to point out that the saint's right eye *was* slightly lower than the other. He drew attention to the earliest portrait, a 5th-century mosaic in the Ambrosian basilica, in which this deformity is unmistakable. Until then it had been considered a defect due to the artist. The mosaic may therefore be a true portrait which reflects the recollections of those who knew the saint.

I returned to the basilica morning after morning, the only man among all the old women, until the priest must have thought me the most devout character in Milan. The skeleton of St. Ambrose fascinated me. I never tired of watching what I consider one of the most impressive sights in Europe.

St. Jerome said that when he was a schoolboy in Rome he used to play in the catacombs. The year was about 350, only 37 years after the toleration of Christianity, yet already the younger generation was playing hide-and-seek among the tombs which their grandfathers had approached on bended knee. To a Christian over the age of 40, the times must have seemed incredible. The Bishop of Rome lived in the imperial palace of the Lateran which Constantine had given to the Church. Everywhere in Rome pagan temples and churches stood open side by side. A man could sacrifice to Jupiter Capitolinus or, if he wished, go to the new Basilica of St. Peter and lower his handkerchief on a string to the grating above the tomb of the Apostle.

Elderly Christians who remembered the torture chambers must have regarded their changed world with mixed feelings. It probably seemed to them that something noble had departed. Christianity had become popular, and rich women were relaxing upon silk cushions as they read costly Gospels.

Another Roman schoolboy at this time, said to have been born in the same year as Jerome, was Ambrose. He came of good family, and his mother, a widow, had brought her children from the provinces to be educated in Rome. They evidently moved in the highest Christian circles, for his sister Marcellina is said to have taken the veil from the hands of Pope Liberius himself. There is no record that Ambrose ever met Jerome, though they must surely have sat under the same roof at times: both were law students and attended the courts.

Ambrose was officially a pagan when at the age of 30 he reached the top of the legal profession. Many ambitious men found promotion faster if they remained nominal pagans, and were thus linked to the vested interests of the state religion. Life was much simpler if a man were willing to cast a pinch of incense before a statue of Jupiter, or if he did not make a fuss should his steak come from an altar. Yet for such little things a former generation had gone hamstrung to the mines.

There is no hint that Ambrose had any interest in the Church when he was appointed consular magistrate, or governor, of Emilia and Liguria, with headquarters in Milan. He was immensely important, for Milan was now capital of the Roman West. When he appeared in public with his lictors it was the custom for all to uncover their heads; in the streets the crowds would make way for him; if he attended the circus, theater, or a public meeting, the audience would rise and remain standing until he was seated.

One of the troubles in his region was the Arians. The Arian heresy, which had been one of the chief items on the agenda of the Council of Nicaea, was, to put it simply, that the Son of God was junior to God, and that God created Christ, who had not existed until that moment.

In the year 375, Ambrose anticipated a riot between orthodox and Arians during the election of a new bishop of Milan. With the idea that his presence, accompanied by lictors and guards, might calm the situation, he decided to attend the noisy meeting in the cathedral. At the height of the tumult Ambrose was dismayed to hear the words, "Let Ambrose be our bishop!" taking shape until it became a demand.

Election by acclamation was not exceptional at that time, and others like Ambrose, not even baptized, had been elected in that way to high positions in the Church. Ambrose protested that he did not wish to be made bishop and had never even been baptized. He left Milan and went into hiding, but his admirers found him and brought him back in triumph. Eventually he gave in, and ten days after his Baptism he was consecrated bishop. So the state lost a distinguished governor and the Church gained its first statesman.

During Ambrose's episcopate of 22 years the official end of paganism was effected. That skeleton hand in the scarlet gauntlet was the hand behind the imperial decrees which finally closed the temples, disbanded the vestal virgins, and made worship of the old gods illegal. Alas, during that victory the triumphant Christians began to persecute the pagans as in the old days they themselves had been persecuted.

In 383, a young man of 29 arrived in Milan with an illegitimate son called Adeodatus and a friend named Alypius. The young man wished to become a teacher of rhetoric. His name was Augustine.

Augustine was still sampling the rich variety of faiths in the hope of finding something he could believe. He established himself with his child and his friend in a small rented house, and in the evenings he would go out on his spiritual search. In that way he first heard St. Ambrose, but "not with so good a frame of mind as I ought," he confessed. Gradually he was drawn towards Ambrose, who was always surrounded by people and always accessible. Yet Augustine at first hesitated to approach him, finding him either occupied with others or else reading to himself so intently that he did not care to interrupt him.

It was during this period that a conflict between the Empress Justina and Ambrose broke out. Under Ambrose all Arian churches had been either closed or had become orthodox. The empress asked for the use of two churches for the Arians. Ambrose refused. One day, while he was officiating in church, he was told that lictors from the palace were outside fixing up the imperial draperies which indicated that the building had been taken over by the treasury.

Palace officials begged Ambrose to give way to the empress. Troops surrounded the basilica, but hearing that the bishop intended to excommunicate them, they crowded into the church and said they had come to pray and not to fight.

Fearing that the building might be seized during the night, Ambrose organized several all-night services. To relieve the tedium of these night watches he taught the congregation to sing hymns that he had composed, the first time that hymns had been heard in a Western church.

Among those who sang was St. Augustine. He copied down the words of *Deus, Creator*

Omnium for the first time. Other hymns sung at this time are believed to have been *Eterne Rerum Conditor, Veni Redemptor Gentium, O Lux Beata Trinitas,* and *Jam Surgit Hora Tertia.* It is sometimes claimed that others, including the *Te Deum,* were composed by St. Ambrose, but the five I have mentioned are considered authentic. In the course of the 4th century, they spread from Milan to every corner of Christendom.

In his *Confessions* St. Augustine gives many details of his four years in Milan. He was joined there by one of the most appealing female saints of the period, his mother, St. Monica. She fussed over her son's spiritual search, and had only one desire, to see him baptized into the Church. One feels there were moments when St. Augustine must have found her solicitude rather overpowering.

Monica had come from a simple country parish where it was still the custom for earnest church workers to take baskets of food for the agape, or love feast, to share with the poor after Communion. She did not know that in large cities like Milan, with the flocks of converts who were then entering the Church, the custom had led to what we would call bottle parties, and was being sternly put down by the bishops.

Upon her arrival in Milan, St. Monica packed a basket of cheesecakes, food, and wine, and went off to church. At the church door, the sexton looked sternly at her and told her she could not take drink into the building. St. Augustine thought his mother's dilemma amusing. But he was surprised that she, usually an argumentative character, should have given way without a protest because of her respect for St. Ambrose.

Augustine, his son, and Alypius were baptized together by St. Ambrose on Easter, in 387. Augustine was 33 years old. Soon afterwards he and his little household decided to return to Tagaste, now the town of Souk Ahras, on the border between Algeria and Tunisia. While they were waiting for a ship at Ostia, St. Monica caught a fever and died.

St. Ambrose lived for ten years after the Baptism of St. Augustine. During this time the fourth emperor whom he served, advised, and disciplined was Theodosius the Great. Perhaps the best-known story of Ambrose is that of the public penance he imposed upon the emperor for his massacre at Thessalonica. The bishop denied the Church to Theodosius for eight months until he had humbly repented and promised to pass a law that no criminal should be executed within 30 days of his sentence.

Hardly had he spoken the funeral oration over the body of Theodosius than Ambrose's health began to fail. He died on Good Friday, April 4, 397, and he was buried on Easter morning in the Ambrosian basilica.

A HIGHER APPEAL

My little nephew's tall stories had begun to worry his mother. She thought it was about time he outgrew such fantasies. One morning Timmie was looking out the kitchen window, when their neighbor's huge collie ran into the yard. "Look, Mama, there's a lion in our yard," he called out.

"That's just the neighbor's dog," my sister replied angrily. "Timmie, go to your room and tell God you're sorry for making up such a story." In less than a minute he was back at the window. "Did you tell God you were sorry?" his mother asked.

"Yes," Timmie answered, "but He said it fooled Him, too."

Mary Kachelmeier.

A Letter From St. Ignatius

One of the first Fathers of the Church wrote
this on his way to martyrdom in the arena of
wild beasts

October 1960, condensed from *Readings in Church History**

*L*egend says that St. Ignatius of Antioch was the child our Lord took in his arms when He said, "Whoever receives one such little child for my sake, receives me." This incident is in the 9th chapter of St. Mark's Gospel. It is much more likely, however, that St. Ignatius was not born until about 13 years after our Lord ascended into heaven.

Ignatius was the third bishop of Antioch. St. Peter was the first, Evodius the second. Eusebius, an historian of the 4th century, says that St. Peter himself appointed Ignatius to the See of Antioch. St. John Chrysostom says only that he was consecrated a bishop by the Apostles.

Ignatius was arrested in Antioch, taken under guard to

*Edited by Colman J. Barry, O.S.B.
© 1960 by The Newman Press.

Rome. On the way he wrote seven letters. The one to the Romans has the famous statement, "God's wheat I am, and by teeth of wild beasts I am to be ground that I may prove Christ's pure bread."

He was martyred by the beasts in the Flavian amphitheater in about the year 110.

Here is the letter he wrote to the Ephesians on his way to martyrdom. Every pastor has repeated the exhortation in paragraph 13: come to Mass and receive Holy Communion often. The translation is by James A. Klein, S.J., for the Ancient Christian Writers *series.*

IGNATIUS, also called Theophorus sends heartiest good wishes for unalloyed joy in Jesus Christ to the Church at Ephesus

223

in Asia; a church deserving of felicitation, blessed, as she is, with greatness through the fullness of God the Father; predestined, before time was, to be—to her abiding and unchanging glory for ever united and chosen, through real suffering, by the will of the Father and Jesus Christ our God.

1. With joy in God I welcomed your community, which possesses his dearly beloved name because of a right disposition, enhanced by faith and love through Christ Jesus our Saviour. Being imitators of God, you have, once restored to new life in the Blood of God, perfectly accomplished the task so natural to you. Indeed, as soon as you heard that I was coming from Syria in chains for our common Name and hope—hoping I might, thanks to your prayer, obtain the favor of fighting wild beasts at Rome and through this favor be able to prove myself a disciple—you hastened to see me. In the name of God, then, I have received your numerous community in the person of Onesimus, a man of indescribable charity and your bishop here on earth. I pray you in the spirit of Jesus Christ to love him, and wish all of you to resemble him. Blessed, indeed, is He whose grace made you worthy to possess such a bishop. . . .

3. I give you no orders as though I were somebody. For,

even though I am in chains for the sake of the Name, I am not yet perfected in Jesus Christ. Indeed, I am now but being initiated into discipleship, and I address you as my fellow disciples. Yes, I ought to be anointed by you with faith, encouragement, patient endurance, and steadfastness. However, since affection does not permit me to be silent when you are concerned, I am at once taking this opportunity to exhort you to live in harmony with the mind of God. Surely, Jesus Christ, our inseparable life, for his part is the mind of the Father, just as the bishops, though appointed throughout the vast, wide earth, represent for their part the mind of Jesus Christ.

4. Hence it is proper for you to act in agreement with the mind of the bishop; and this you do. Certain it is that your presbytery, which is a credit to its name, is a credit to God; for it harmonizes with the bishop as completely as the strings with a harp. This is why in the symphony of your concord and love the praises of Jesus Christ are sung. But you, the rank and file, should also form a choir, so that, joining the symphony by your concord and by your unity taking your key note from God, you may with one voice through Jesus Christ sing a song to the Father. Thus He will both listen to you and by reason of your

good life recognize in you the melodies of his Son. It profits you, therefore, to continue in your flawless unity, that you may at all times have a share in God.

5. For a fact, if I in a short time became so warmly attached to your bishop—an attachment not on human grounds but on spiritual—how much more do I count you happy who are as closely knit to him as the Church is to Jesus Christ and as Jesus Christ is to the Father! As a result, the symphony of unity is perfect. Let no one deceive himself: unless a man is within the sanctuary, he has to go without the Bread of God. Assuredly, if the prayer of one or two has such efficacy, how much more that of the bishop of the entire Church? It follows, then: he who absents himself from the common meeting, by that very fact shows pride and becomes a sectarian; for the Scripture says: *God resists the proud.* Let us take care, therefore, not to oppose the bishop, that we may be submissive to God.

6. Furthermore: the more anyone observes that a bishop is discreetly silent, the more he should stand in fear of him. Obviously, anyone whom the Master of the household puts in charge of his domestic affairs, ought to be received by us in the same spirit as He who has charged him with this duty. Plainly, then, one should look upon the bishop as upon the Lord Himself. Now, Onesimus for his part overflows with praise of the good order that, thanks to God, exists in your midst. Truth is the rule of life for all of you, and heresy has no foothold among you. The fact is, you have nothing more to learn from anyone, since you listen to Jesus Christ who speaks truthfully.

7. Some there are, you know, accustomed with vicious guile to go about with the Name on their lips, while they indulge in certain practices at variance with it and an insult to God. These you must shun as you would wild beasts: they are rabid dogs that bite in secret; you must beware of them, for they are hard to cure. There is only one Physician, both carnal and spiritual, born and unborn, God become man, true life in death; sprung both from Mary and from God, first subject to suffering and then incapable of it—Jesus Christ Our Lord. . . .

13. Make an effort, then, to come more frequently to celebrate God's Eucharist and to offer praise. For, when you meet frequently in the same place, the forces of Satan are overthrown, and his baneful influence is neutralized by the unanimity of your faith. Peace is a precious thing: it puts an end to every war waged by heavenly or earthly enemies.

14. Nothing of this escapes you; only persevere to the end in your faith in, and your love for, Jesus Christ. Here is the beginning and the end of life: faith is the beginning, *the end is love;* and when the two blend perfectly with each other, they are God. Everything else that makes for right living is consequent upon these. No one who professes faith sins; no one who professes love hates. *The tree is known by its fruit.* In like manner those who profess to belong to Christ will be known as such by their conduct. Certainly, what matters now is not mere profession of faith, but whether one is found to be actuated by it to the end.

15. It is better to keep silence and be something than to talk and be nothing. Teaching is an excellent thing, provided the speaker practices what he teaches. Now, there is one Teacher who *spoke and it was done.* But even what He did silently is worthy of the Father. He who has made the words of Jesus really his own is able also to hear his silence. Thus he will be perfect: He will act through his speech and be understood through his silence. Nothing is hidden from the Lord; no, even our secrets reach Him. Let us, then, do all things in the conviction that He dwells in us. Thus we shall be his temples and He will be our God within us. And

this is the truth, and it will be made manifest before our eyes. Let us, then, love Him as He deserves. . . .

20. If Jesus Christ, yielding to your prayer, grants me the favor and it is his will, I shall, in the subsequent letter which I intend to write to you, still further explain the dispensation which I have here only touched upon, regarding the New Man Jesus Christ—a dispensation founded on faith in Him and love for Him, on his Passion and Resurrection. I will do so especially if the Lord should reveal to me that you—the entire community of you!—are in the habit, through grace derived from the Name, of meeting in common, animated by one faith and in union with Jesus Christ—who *in the flesh was of the line of David,* the Son of Man and the Son of God—of meeting, I say, to show obedience with undivided mind to the bishop and the presbytery, and to break the same Bread, which is the medicine of immortality, the antidote against death, and everlasting life in Jesus Christ.

21. I offer my life as a ransom for you and for those whom for the Glory of God you sent to Smyrna, where, too, I am writing to you with thanks to the Lord and with love for Polycarp and you. Remember me, as may Jesus Christ remember you! Pray for the Church in Syria, whence

I am being led away in chains to Rome, though I am the least of the faithful there. But then, I was granted the favor of contributing to the honor of God. Farewell! May God the Father and Jesus Christ, *our common hope,* bless you!

ATTENTION, CLASS OF 1970!

Your parents and grandparents, within just five decades, 1919–1969, have by their work increased your life expectancy by approximately 50%; while cutting the working day by a third, they have more than doubled per-capita output. These are the people who have given you a healthier world than they found. And because of this you no longer have to fear the epidemics of flu, typhus, diptheria, smallpox, scarlet fever, measles, or mumps that they knew in their youth. The dreaded polio is no longer dreaded, and TB is almost unheard of.

These remarkable people lived through our greatest depression. Many of them know what it is to be poor, hungry, and cold. They determined that it would not happen to you; that you would have a better life; you would have food to eat, milk to drink, vitamins to nourish you, a warm home, better schools, and greater opportunities to succeed than they had.

Because they gave you the best, you are the tallest, healthiest, brightest, and probably best-looking generation to inhabit the land. And because they were "materialistic," you will work fewer hours, learn more, have more leisure, travel to more distant places, and have more of a chance to follow your life's ambition.

These two generations, through the highest court of the land, fought racial discrimination to begin a new era in civil rights. They built thousands of high schools, trained and hired tens of thousands of better teachers, and made higher education possible for millions of youngsters, where once it was only the dream of a wealthy few.

They made a start, although a late one, in healing the scars of the earth and in fighting pollution and the destruction of our natural environment. They set into motion conservation laws and set aside land for you and your children.

They have had some failures, too. They have not yet found an alternative for war, nor for racial hatred. Perhaps you members of this graduating class will perfect the social mechanisms by which all men may follow their ambitions without the threat of force. But those generations made more progress by the sweat of their brows than was made in any previous time, and don't you forget it! If your generation can make as much progress, you should be able to solve a good many of the world's remaining ills.

Eric A. Walker, president, Pennsylvania State university, in a speech to the graduating class.

Home to My Russian Village

An American returns to the land of her birth

By ELENA WHITESIDE
February 1972, condensed from the *Chicago Tribune Magazine**

W E HAVE ARRIVED! A day by train from Leningrad and 100 years into the heart of Russia, we have reached the village where my mother grew up and where my grandmother, at 93, still forms the sun of our little family universe. After years of city life in New York, I have brought two of my children with me, eight-year-old Nicholas and four-year-old Sylvia. I want them to experience their roots for themselves.

In the honey-colored light of evening there is a grand reunion with aunts and cousins by the red, wooden railroad station. Then we walk the short way to my grandmother's house, everyone vying to carry our rucksacks. They come every summer to vacation with Babushka

(grandmother), but we are the foreign guests. It is hard to answer their questions all at once. My children speak no Russian and are regarding me with dazed expressions.

The railroad tracks are the heart of this village of about 5,000. Although the two main streets are tarred, that is it. All the other streets are grassy meadow with a few deep ruts. Their mud is deeply imbedded with old torn galoshes, boots, shoes, and wires. My children keep exclaiming, "Look, there's a red shoe, look, there's an old sneaker!" but soon get used to it. It is a wonder to me that cars can get through these streets. But they do, occasionally.

Dirt walks are lined on one side with trees, on the other by the tall wood fences which surround every house. Public water pumps stand imposingly on

*This article © 1971 by the *Chicago Tribune.*

every other corner, though some houses have their own wells.

Geese gurgle and chickens cluck in the ruts. They are dyed with spots of red, blue, green, and yellow to identify them for they wander around unfettered. Cats and kittens stalk us. As we walk, the village day is ending. People pass us carrying buckets of water, coming home from work or fishing. Cows and goats meander along the streets, finding their own way home after a day at pasture.

Here is the house. Like the others, it is made of logs chinked with dried moss, but part is covered with boards. It is surrounded by a large garden with a fence. Sunflowers lean over currant bushes. Apple trees stand over neat rows of vegetables.

We pause at the gate. Vaguely, I remember this. Aunt Shura swings it open and we surge into the house.

Who could have expected a warmer welcome? The table is already set with dishes of cucumbers, cheese, sausage, fish, and sweets.

Babushka herself sits in her blue wheelchair beside the window. A year ago a stroke had paralyzed one side, and although she is much better now, able to talk and gesture, she can only sit and lie down. Babushka is like a root: gnarled, wrinkled, dark, ancient, spreading, reaching out. She is the root herself, and we are the branches, boughs, limbs. Our children are twigs and the new-born babes, the blossoms.

"Dochenka, Dochenka (daughter)," she sobs, covers us with kisses, blesses the Lord for our safe arrival.

"She sent a prayer to church yesterday, and money, for the priest to pray for your safe arrival," Aunt Shura whispers. "And see, you've come safely." Although a party member, she is not scornful of her mother's religious beliefs. ("They don't hurt anyone. Let her believe.")

The children are restless to eat. We pull ourselves out of our emotions and turn to the practical. During the eating, chatter, and toasts, I look over the interior of the home.

The living room is dominated by three huge green plants: a Christmas cactus, a tropical palm, and a good-sized lemon tree. Off the big room are two small ones, separated only by the large clay oven-stove, the heating heart of the house.

What catches my eye is the ikon corner. In a brown wooden frame covered with glass, a trinity of saints bless the house. On the wall around it are a dozen smaller ikons: saints, Christ, the Virgin Mary. I recognize, decorated with dried buds and leaves of spring flowers, the Blessed Mary and Child that I had sent her from New York when my grandfather died three years ago. Birch branches add a hint of life to the holy images encrusted with gold and silver.

The walls are hung with maps of the USSR, a small wavy mirror, and rugs along each bed (you can get a chill from the naked wall). There are nails for coats, nails for towels and wash cloths, nails for little bags. One bag contains sewing, another scraps of material. The room breathes a functional simplicity. The atmosphere is pleasant and sincere. I feel at home.

There is one more room, my favorite, the storage room at the back of the house. All along the walls hang sacks, some whimsically embroidered, with dried peas and beans preserved from last summer's harvest. Along the floor stand huge jars of pickled cucumbers, peppers, and green tomatoes. There are containers of coleslaw and sauerkraut, and jar after jar of deep, rich red jams: cherry, red and black currant, strawberry, wild strawberry, wild cranberry, and raspberry. In various corners are other jars of yellow fruit compote, mostly apples. When I open the door to this room I am overwhelmed by the aromas from all these foods deliciously mingling together.

Outside the house is a shed for Aunt Tanya's three goats and an outhouse, attached to the house so that you don't have to get wet on a rainy day. There is no plumbing.

Roosters begin crowing between four and five, competing with long blasts from the whistle on the early morning freight train. The geese join in, gabbling, honking, squeaking, then dogs bark in the distance, and the Russian village shakes the sleep out of its eyes.

By six, Aunt Shura is knocking on my window. Catching up my laundry I slip on my clothes, leaving the children asleep under their heavy feather beds. We walk through the waking streets. Villagers are sending their cows and goats to the meeting place from which they are taken to pasture. People who own the 70 cattle take turns herding them. Occasionally we meet someone with an empty basket, off to the woods for berries, or with a yoke balanced over his shoulder, a pail of water on either end.

The walk to the lake takes us by the *Klub,* where we check the daily movie schedule. We have already seen a variety this week: one from Iran, others from Hungary, Latvia, and Uzbekistan. We cross the railroad tracks to the hills which surround the lake. Some days an early morning reaper-mower is there already, a little old man with an embroidered shirt and wispy gray beard. He is sharpening his scythe in broad, rasping strokes.

We swim some mornings, scrubbing ourselves with soap on rough rope washcloths. Then we wade back in, a bar of heavy brown soap in hand, to do the laundry. Having scrubbed, rinsed, and squeezed, we spread it on the dewy grass to dry in the sun a little. And then we sit down and talk together, sunbathing and resting before the mile walk home for breakfast.

By now, the town is humming with activity. Trucks wait by the *Klub* to take workers to the collective-farm fields. Most of them are women, the men holding technical jobs or jobs in the local factories. "Are you going to mow?" I ask one woman. "No, we've begun to tie the flax now. It's a very dry summer," she calls over her shoulder, and sprints into the back of the truck. From the loudspeaker, strains of a Schubert symphony reach our ears.

Today I am lucky. Babushka talks about her life. "I've lived a long life, a hard life," she reminisces. "It all flew by me like a dream. I can't believe it." She wags her head, clucks her tongue against her last few stubs of teeth. "He was so handsome, Dedushka, so handsome, all the girls in our village, rich and poor, followed him like a tail. Then came his time to marry, but no

one would have him because he was so poor. He had five sisters to marry off. He was an only son.

"I was an only child. My father had died, and my mother and his parents made the match. There was no choice. That's why we had such a hard life together, hard and long. We didn't choose each other. We had no choice in those days, but we lived together for 70 years.

"The biggest one—oh, what's her name? *Foo*—Tanya, yes, Tanya. She was just 12 and she wanted to go to school. Her father was always out enjoying himself. He loved the company of people. So it was my responsibility. I harnessed the horse and wagon to take her 40 miles away to catch the train to the city where the school was. She's a bright one, the oldest. She took one exam, and then another. And then at 17 she was already a teacher. Ay, ay, ay. A teacher, and I, her mother, couldn't even read and write 'til I was over 50."

Just then the door opens and Aunt Tanya shuffles heavily in, swaying from side to side on her bad legs. She is well into her 70's. She wears a loosely fitting coatdress and a plaid scarf. A turned-up nose, which runs all through our family, dominates her wrinkled face. Her speech is sprinkled with little prayers: "God have mercy on us," "Praise be to God," or "If the Lord only wills it."

In my mind's eye, I see Babushka talking to the 12-year-old girl. Do parents ever see their offspring as anything but the little children they raised?

Aunt Tanya sits down on the bed and joins the reminiscences. "Yes, nine children the mother had. Nine. Although only eight grew up."

Later in the evening Aunt Shura tells me how hard it is taking care of an invalid.

"We get so angry and annoyed at Babushka. Paralyzed as she is and still trying to run the household. She has pride. She can't accept her passive role. Listen to her all the time: 'Is there water in the garden barrel?' 'Did we get vodka for the new guests?' 'Have you mowed the grass?' 'Did you pick the currants from the great mother currant bush?' 'Get out the pickles and mushrooms for the guests.' 'Have the onions been tied?' A finger in every enterprise. Always interfering.

"But when I get angry, I stop myself. She is the center now, the matriarch, and we all orbit around her like planets around the sun. When she dies, no one will take her place. The whole system will fall apart. We all have our families, our homes away from here, our cares. She keeps us all together. No one can replace her. And I tell myself fervently: let her live. Even though she can't move and bosses everyone. Let her live as long as possible."

Misha, my eight-year-old cousin from Moscow, came panting back from town today. "Word has it there will be meat and eggs at three at the *Kommission* store," he informed us breathlessly. A stir of excitement. "Run and tell Aunt Tanya," Aunt Shura tells him. Turning to me she says, "Let's go."

We take a clean plastic jar for sour cream, a tin can for milk, and a cloth sack for sugar. At first this struck me as strange, but now I automatically take a few containers whenever I go to the store.

At 1:30 the *Kommission* is still closed, but a line has formed outside. From the conversation, I gather certain foods come sporadically and then are sold out. Although there is plenty to eat, if one wants variety he has to be ready to snap it up when the opportunity breaks.

We take our place in line. In front of the store several gypsies are also waiting. They had come from a town ten miles away when they heard about the meat. We wait awhile longer, chewing on sunflower seeds that Aunt Shura was thoughtful enough to bring (they are the national equivalent of chewing gum).

"Go get some ice cream for the children," my aunt suggests. "I'll keep our place in line." We walk to the small booth across the main square. There is only one flavor: vanilla. The salesgirl spoons it out into an anemic cone, then sets it on her little scale, adding a little, looking, subtracting a little 'til it weighs exactly 100 grams. Sixteen kopeks. Thanking her, we stroll on, eating.

Back at the *Kommission,* a truck is unloading huge slabs of meat clumsily wrapped in heavy brown paper. The line by now numbers about 30. My aunt has already bought what she wants, several kilos of meat and 100 eggs.

"That will last awhile. We have many guests. We'll freeze the meat in Aunt Anya's icebox." And we continue on our round of errands. Our first stop is the discount store, which handles items that are not selling well and on which the government has lowered official prices. The place is quite bare. Several bolts of cloth, shoes, either very large or in old-fashioned styles, a few broken toys, some off-color skeins of yarn, and folded ends of material sparsely line the shelves. On one side on the floor stands a broken motorcycle. No tire. We glance about and leave.

"It's worth stopping. You never know what they'll have," Aunt Shura tells me. "I walked in at the right time recently. They were selling pale pink yarn at a kopek a skein. It must have been an unpopular color, but you can always dye it. I bought ten right away, took them home and decided it was too good a deal not to take more advantage of. I dashed back for more, but word had already gotten round, and out of 100 or more, there wasn't a single one left. If you yawn at the wrong time, you can miss an opportunity."

We stop at the bread store— just black bread today. "Any white bread coming?" someone asks the cashier. "I can't tell you— maybe," she responds, not hiding her annoyance. I guess everyone has been asking her that today. Some days they have it, other days they don't, but no one will tell you anything.

We go over to the bookstore. Seryozha's birthday is the day after tomorrow and we would like to get him a little something. There is a large children's book section, a good collection of posters, and a handful of German, French, and English grammars. There is another section for paper, notebooks, cards, and pencils. No crayons, only pale, colored pencils. They have never heard of crayons. "The Magic Markers you brought were fabulous," my aunt tells me. "We don't have anything like that here."

Our packages are adding up and we haven't covered all the stores yet. There is the hardware store, the clothing and material store, the shoe store, the other general store, the rug store, the toy shop, and several others, but we can hardly manage all our packages. Our last stop is the post office.

As we walk in, we pass the postman: a 20-year-old girl in a gray jumper, red blouse, and a long brown braid down her back. Slung over one shoulder she carries a heavy leather bag. Lots of surprises.

S unday is different from other days. The house will be heavy with the delicious odor of dough rising.

I have decided to go to church with my Aunt Tanya. Aunt Tanya goes every Sunday and on holy days, as old as she is. She goes alone, except when she gathers strength and takes her grandchildren for blessing. She has baptized them all.

Through heavy sleep Aunt Tanya shakes my shoulder. The window is gray, the air fresh, even cold. The hands of the clock point to 3:30. We have to leave so early because it takes two hours to walk the five miles, and the service begins at six. I hop up, slip on my dress. Aunt Tanya shuffles in, holding out a white scarf to me. "Here, child, wear this. In church before God you must cover your head." In a very few moments we are on our way along the dusty road. The village, bathed in early morning haze, is silent. Unexpectedly, several other figures emerge from the shadows before us, other voices murmur behind us.

"They are all churchgoers," my aunt volunteers, walking with difficulty although she leans heavily on my arm. Several motorbikes whiz past us, young men taking their mothers or grandmothers to church. We form a long, scattered procession trudging along the road. Most of the churchgoers are older women, clean scarves tied under their chins.

"This is how you make the cross," my aunt tells me, pressing her thumb and two fingers together. "These two are down. One for good and one for evil. And these three fingers are for the Holy Trinity, the Father, the Son, and the Holy Ghost. You see, in the church everything has meaning." Suddenly the sun hangs low in the sky. The day is born.

It is after six when we reach the small white church. Two painted gaunt saints gesture us to the door, which creaks loudly as I pull it open. Voices singing soft prayers in a minor key come from within.

The entrance is dark, lighted only by candles in front of some ikons. "This Blessed Virgin is for the sick," my aunt whispers, crossing herself. "And this saint is for the journey. And here is our Mother of Sorrows. No matter how we suffer, no one has borne the suffering she has. She understands us. Lord have mercy on me. Lord have mercy." Kneeling with difficulty, she bows her head to the floor three times, and then goes off to buy candles. "They cost 20 or 30 kopeks. This is how the church manages to live."

"Get me one, please," I ask. Many people are around us doing just what we are doing.

The altar is behind a gilded door. The priest in black robes goes in and out the door singing in a deep bass. Everyone stands. Almost imperceptibly, the people form a line before the priest. A white-coated attendant hands him a thin brush and a little pot of holy oil. One by one, he paints the sign of the cross on their foreheads. They bow and kiss his hand.

Most participants are older women, but there are a few men, and I see three young women with their small children neatly dressed. I feel they must be very brave to risk disapproval by coming here. They certainly must be strong believers.

Without ceremony, people begin filing out. The *Utroniye* is over. Now there is a break and then the Liturgy follows.

We return home to find the oven glowing and warm. (A wood fire is built right in the oven, then the coals are spread about and the pans laid over them to bake. I marvel at how time and temperature are gauged. Soft-boiled eggs come out to the minute.) Everyone is gathered for Sunday brunch.

The table looks especially sumptuous. Today there is a steaming hot *pirog* stuffed with cottage cheese, one with chopped onions and groats, another with poppy seeds, sugar, and butter, and a big one with currant and apple jam. There are also sliced cucumbers, homemade pickles, and tomatoes.

Because Uncle Tolya is leaving soon, there is a whole bottle of vodka. The kids eat and run out to play, leaving the glutted grown-ups around the table recounting jokes and gossip. We discuss family.

"I'll tell you about in-laws," says Uncle Tolya. "I met a friend who had just seen his mother-in-law off on the train south for vacation. His face is all black, filthy. 'Hi,' I say, 'did you see her off? Is she gone? What've you been doing? How'd your face get so dirty?' 'Sure, I saw her off,' he says. 'My face, it's black from kissing the engine!' "

We all break into gales of laughter.

"They say the husband is the head of the family and the wife is the neck," Gera proposes. "Whichever way the neck turns, there the head follows!" Everyone cracks up.

I go to the other house to look in at Babushka. Antoshka and two-year-old Lenochka are wrestling with the kitten by her wheelchair. Babushka watches them, absorbed. Suddenly, they all fall over and she is overcome with gutsy laughter.

Later Aunt Shura tells me, "She wept today. I was watering the green plants, the rubber tree, the lemon tree in the corner, and she was looking out the window. She talked about the beauty of the sunflowers outside, the apple trees, and she tells me, 'I am surrounded by so many beautiful plants. I should be happy. But I know I shall never walk out into the garden again.'"

Tuesday, Aunt Shura and I took a long walk through some deserted and dying villages. She talked about the old days. "These used to house families like ours—large, strong, closely knit, tied together by necessity to produce enough bread for the winter. We all worked hard. No one thought or wondered about his lot. We were always too busy. Even the youngest had his job to do.

"I recall autumn. Our father woke us at two at night to help separate the grain from the chaff. He hoarded every seed. Marka, my younger sister—your mother—and I would stagger sleepily through the cold darkness trying to avoid the puddles.

"Our job was to lay each stalk of dried grain side-by-side so that the heads were in an exact row. Then with wooden sticks we had to beat the heads in rhythm. If one of us got out of line, he'd stop us all. We had to get together.

"After we had beaten the stalks sufficiently, my father would throw pitchforksful into the air to blow off the light chaff. Marka and I would crawl around on our hands and knees, gathering up each grain into a sack. Our father would check our work and praise us if he could not find a single kernel.

"Then on our way home he would figure out how many bushels of grain he was getting. And the big question: Would there be enough bread to feed his family of ten for the winter? We lived on the edge. It took so much work, so much planning. But it was our life. And my parents were tied to it forever.

"We who grew up on the land appreciate it, but our children—your generation—they come from their jobs in the cities for

HOME TO MY RUSSIAN VILLAGE   237

their vacations one month a year. For them, the village is a resort. They come, dabble in berries, take a few buckets home to preserve. But they don't have the memories that we do of working the earth. Many have left their country roots altogether. The war did its part, too. Our family, I notice, is one of the few still going strong, still vital. When the matriarch goes, an era will have passed.

"The village was the soul of Russia. And now, the ones like these"—she waved her hand over another ghost town of log cottages—"are dying out, while the ones like ours, situated on the railroad, are expanding. They are collective farm and transportation centers. They are shopping centers. But they no longer have the roots."

As I listen to her talk, I silently compare the transformation she describes with a similar one in the U.S. Was it during the depression and war years? The sudden influence of the car, the mass movements away from the greater family on the land to the nuclear family in the cities.

I relate my thoughts to her. "Do you think the next generation here will become your equivalent of our flower children in America? Will they rebel against their parents' rootless existence in crowded city flats full of material comforts?"

She laughs at the thought.

"No, never here. We don't allow the choice of dropping out. Here, someone swears and the militia will get him. It's against the law."

"But what about morality?" I persist. "How is it changing?"

"The young don't respect their elders, don't help them. Family ties are weaker. They do not have an economic base. When I grew up, family cooperation was based on economic necessity. I am taking care of my mother now because when I was growing up my sisters took care of me.

"But now, husband and wife both work, both bring home a salary. The young try to show they are fiercely independent. At the same time, they realize something is missing, and they are actually very dependent for encouragement and support but very unwilling to be obedient or to help out their parents. The young people today are very demanding. They are too big for their breeches. They want everything but want to give nothing."

Autumn chill in the air. Mid-August has barely gone by but in this cold latitude harvest has already begun. Yesterday we mowed. I tried the scythe. Work in the earth has rhythm which finds attraction for the body.

The harvest work is strenuous because it is continuous,

followed and preceded by numerous equally heavy chores: the chopping of wood and carrying of water before you can cook. The swing of mowing took me over, the frequent stopping to sharpen the scythe, a built-in rest. Then there is the raking, stacking, drying, and restacking of the hay, which all must be done before it is put away.

Another day we cut down the peas, pulled off the shells, and lay them to dry all over the storeroom floor. The apples are ripening. Already the little yellow ones that Uncle Vasya calls "instant apples" are sweet to eat.

On Monday, Aunt Anya took her turn pasturing the cattle, about 70 cows and goats, and an equal number of offspring.

This week I had another mindblowing experience. We all flocked to see *The Apartment*. Jack Lemmon opened his mouth and out came Russian!

The discussions it excited among my relatives lasted a long time. They could hardly believe how horrible, how exploitative life was under capitalism. Women are so manipulated, mere decorations, depending on the whims of men of power. Why do the women allow themselves to be treated that way? And what it shows of work in the U.S.—people are automated. They work like machines. "I guess we can never catch up to you at this rate," Raya exclaims. "Our people could never work like machines. They're too human."

They marveled at the apartment Lemmon lives in, the kitchen especially. They were amazed at the TV dinner he warms up in one scene. They loved the love story and had deepest sympathy for the simpleton hero who drops out of the giant, dehumanizing corporation. They all agreed it was very well filmed.

Besides occasional movies, our evenings are quiet. I usually sew or embroider. Tonight Aunt Shura has put green tomatoes on the barely warm *pechka* to ripen. She has already set Edik and Nicholas to work trimming onions and slicing apples to dry. "We'll give you a big bag to take back to New York," she smiles. "A big bag of fruits of the earth." I am also drying tea: clover, mint, daisies. We listen to the radio often. The evening program is varied: songs, lectures, poets reading from their works, classical music, and at 11 the late evening news.

This week we tied up the onions in batches of ten. Slung over poles, they dry and are used all winter. There is no mistake about autumn signs. Darkness drops suddenly just after eight. The late summer flies are treacherous, their bite stings. The sunflowers, heavy with seed, nod over the garden in bright splashes of yellow.

Tired of sewing, I go to dig potatoes. What a pleasure to work in the earth. For me, a city dweller, labor is not only restful but engrossing. Work with the earth has rhythm. You start, then you are swinging with it, and then the job is done, and you sleep very deeply.

After digging the potatoes, I come in to Babushka. Aunt Tanya pulls out a black velvet bag. "These are treasures," she says. "Here is Babushka's Order of Motherhood. For a whole year she could travel anywhere in the USSR for free on any mode of transportation. And she traveled all over." The medal was silver, heavy, and finely carved. "Our mother has surpassed us all. An order is higher than a medal."

"And here are my treasures," Babushka says, putting aside some savings-bank books and government bonds. "It is a blessing from my father and a letter written in his own hand." She reverently unwraps a piece of newspaper, revealing a folded, yellowed letter, an old coin, and several chunks of dried black bread. "He blessed me with this." She unfolds the letter and reads it to us, then breaks off a small edge of bread, makes the Sign of the Cross and gives it to me and Babushka. "Eat it," she says. The coin was a 20-kopek piece.

"He gave it to me so that I would always have money. And I always have had all that I need." Then she wraps up her treasures and slips them away.

From mid-August, departures begin to creep up on us. At first there are so many guests. The table is always crowded. Then this one leaves, that one. Trips to see people off to the station are more frequent, and suddenly, summer is done.

Amid the departures, like a spring wind in late November, my youngest cousin, Lenochka, arrives unexpectedly. She has just passed all her exams and is accepted at the university.

Lenochka is 17. Her dark hair is tied up in a classic sweep out of *War and Peace*. She is straight as a birch tree. She is soft with modesty in a neat blue and white print suit which she sewed for herself. Everyone is open-mouthed: her youth, her beauty, her modesty, her poise. Lenochka has blossomed, the youngest of 16 grandchildren.

Babushka sobs as she welcomes her. Later, when we are alone, Babushka says, "If only Ded were here to welcome her about to start her life. Eh, eh, eh. But he is buried these three years. If he were alive, he'd burst with happiness over this moment. The last of our grandchildren. The youngest child of our children!"

"But you have great-grand-children," I cut in. "They'll have children, an endless row."

She shakes her head. "It's not the same. They are not my own. They are Tanya's, Vasya's, Anya's. He would have had such joy. And to think I have been granted this privilege." She wags her head from side to side, deep in wonder.

My own departure is creeping up on me. I have a month's interpreting job in Moscow for an American company at the International Chemistry Exhibition.

The day of leaving comes. It goes by in slow motion, like pulling against gravity, trying to stay in the air. The day is heavy, gray, and cold. Rain intermittently.

I wish the day would never end.

We eat a simple meal, Babushka, Aunt Shura, Lenochka, Aunt Tanya, Aunt Anya, Edik, Igor: bouillon, salad, fish, and tea. We finish hurriedly. It is time to go now. Aunt Tanya turns to me. "Take these apples. Three is God's favorite number. So I give you three times seven apples. Seven is also his favorite number."

Babushka blesses me, three times with her right hand, the bad hand, which she has to lift with her left one. "Help me, Lord, guide my hand. Bless you, child, on your journey."

We walk to the station in silence. There is nothing more to say.　　　⬛

WHO'S IN CHARGE HERE?

When I was an army doctor on duty in the South Pacific, I saw a patient whose condition, I thought, could be much better treated back at the base hospital. So I had a medical corpsman send a radio message there: "I have a case of beri beri. Please advise."

The medical corpsman on the other end evidently had never heard of the condition, for he immediately radioed back: "Give it to the military police. They'll drink anything." *Modern Medicine* (2 Nov. '63.)

*

A long hitch of army service has a tendency to blot out everything that has preceded it. An old soldier who at 50 had finally attained the rank of captain was filling out a routine biographical information sheet for the Public Information officer. He came upon the question: "Civilian occupation?"

The captain put down his pencil, pondered a moment. Then he filled in the blank: "Child." C. Kennedy.

We Had
A Depression

By a WOMAN
May 1937, condensed from the *St. Anthony Messenger**

I HAVE BEEN down and out. Terribly so. Here is my story—plain, blunt, ungarnished, the straight truth.

I deposited five hundred dollars in a South Side bank Saturday night, June 6, 1932, bringing my savings up to six thousand dollars, the price of the farm I would buy. I was going to raise chickens, and teach a term now and then. This was to be security for my old age.

I had been principal of a private school in Chicago for eight years, and in summer directed the camp maintained by the school. My work was not actual teaching. I ran the school, hired and fired, ordered supplies, did some field work, met parents, arranged plays and meets, did the bookkeeping and banking, worked sixteen hours a day, seven days a week, and began my days with Mass in St.

Ambrose Church, a block away.

I had come to this school to teach night classes in English and Spanish, but the old man who owned the school told me I had a flair for management and inducted me into the managerial chair.

On Saturday, June 6, I deposited five hundred dollars. On Monday, June 8, the bank closed.

The tuitions fell off 75% after the banks closed; the teaching staff was curtailed from 17 to 1, and I turned the grades over to her—twelve pupils. The high school of sixteen pupils I taught.

Times were troublous. Money did not come in. We had no fuel. The cook, who formerly drew $75.00 a month, stayed with us for $10, and the janitor, who had been receiving $100, also stayed for $10. Miss Hanna Cooley, the grade teacher, whose salary had been $140 and maintainance, stayed for $25.00.

*Originally published in *St. Anthony Messenger*. Reprinted with permission.

241

I had no salary, hadn't had for some time, but felt I could not desert a sinking ship.

One by one our pupils withdrew until we had seven, and they were orphans I had taken in through the years.

We could well afford (in times past) to do a little charity as we charged sixty dollars a month and the extras amounted to forty. The old man who built the school named it for himself, prefixing Saint before his name, and at our board and business meetings he held the floor, embellishing his charity. He had no religion (he said) and believed in nothing but kindness to children.

By February, 1933, we were desperate—seven children, the cook, and myself. We had had no heat all winter, and our food had been insufficient. The owner of the school had gone to Florida, and the day he left he said: "Have my school on a paying basis when I come back." Nice old man!

For thirteen months I had received no wages and my clothes were getting shiny. So, seeing I could not carry on, I set about establishing the seven orphans in institutions. When this was done I notified the owner, and I stayed alone in the school until he returned.

Then, penniless, I came back to my childhood home. I have not paid the taxes on it for four years. They average $150.00 a year, as the street was paved on three sides.

I tried to get work in my home town. I had been an industrial welfare worker there, and a teacher. There was nothing for me. I followed every clue. Tried to get housework, and was classed as inexperienced as I had never worked for a mistress in a kitchen.

I sold Grandma's pictures, chest of drawers, arm chairs, four-poster beds. I had to eat. Tried to sell my car and was offered $30.00 for it, so I locked it in the garage.

I had tried and tried to get work, prayed and prayed, made novena after novena, and the morning I set out for the relief office, in despair I prayed: "Oh, God, are you really listening?"

I waited three hours for an investigator to question me. Six thousand dollars in a closed bank? Four thousand dollars in bonds on the Eastgate Hotel?

"And you are applying for relief?"

The bank was closed, the bonds were not paying. She was insulting—but maybe she had to be to hold her job.

I wrote to Madison for work, stormed the office here at home, but was told, "We have no jobs for an educated woman."

I asked for housework.

"No one wants you, for you are inexperienced."

I asked for office work. "They want younger women in offices."

I went home asking inwardly: "Oh, God, are you listening?" The Government was playing with me, giving me forms to fill out—I must have filled fifty. How old are you? How much did you earn last year, the year before, and the year before that? What did you do with it? (Oh, God, are You listening?) What do you feel you are fitted for? Have you a college degree? (A college degree to sort half-decayed onions out at Turtle Valley Farms ... Oh, God, are You listening?)

I went to Turtle Valley Farms to sort half-rotten onions. We rode to the farm in a truck, packed in like sardines, and the day was cold. The onions (being half gone) were wet. Chapped hands, red noses, intense cold.

Turtle Valley Farm was six miles from my home. I worked two days. The third day we had no transportation.

"Walk," said my case worker.

I knew that evening as I looked into my mail box that God was listening, for there was a check for $50.00 for a story.

I went off relief and started a Hospitality House where I am yet. A few moments ago a young man came in to say, "I am a transient. The relief agencies do not include us in their budget, nor do they pay our fare back to the country from which we came..."

An educated boy ... a cultured voice ... "Come into the kitchen, sonny, and have a plate of stew. Tomorrow you are going to work."

"To work, lady?"

"Yes, elevator boy in the Monterey Hotel. The manager telephoned me half an hour ago."

After he had eaten he talked. The product of a Catholic boarding school. Seven years there, four years high and three years college.

"I began to think God wasn't listening to me, lady," he said, "but I kept pestering Him with my prayers."

Yes, God is listening.

SIGNS OF THE TIMES

Sign on an old car: "For sale: $4000—Rebate: $3850."   *Keene Shopper.*

*

On a Golden Gate Park bench: "Wet Paint. Watch it or wear it!"
Gloria Garamon.

My Skunk Nikki

He and his family avenged the murder of my pet rabbits

By DANIEL P. MANNIX

February 1964, condensed from *All Creatures Great and Small**

M Y FATHER WAS a navy captain on active service so I was brought up in my grandparents' home on the Philadelphia Main Line. I didn't have many playmates; the estates seemed inhabited mainly by regal dowagers and grim old gentlemen who lived in savage seclusion among their horses, formal gardens, and shooting preserves.

In these days when parents are pals to their children, it is hard to understand that era. I was brought up by a nurse until I was six, and seldom saw my grandparents except in the evening, when I was taken to the "grownups' part of the house" to say good night.

When I entered school, I saw my grandparents only at supper. After answering politely some formal inquiries about how things had gone at school that day, I ate my meal in silence. After supper, I did my homework and went to bed. It never occurred to either my grandparents or to me that any other relationship was possible.

My refuge was my pets. When I was eight, I dared to ask my grandparents for a gorilla. They were mildly amused but promised me great things if I did well in school. I slaved over my books and spent my spare time hang-

---

ing string from one chair to another so the gorilla would have something to swing on.

No gorilla arrived. Instead, I was given two Angora rabbits covered with long, white fur. But they were alive, and that was enough to fascinate me. Every morning I went out to their pen to watch them eat their lettuce, carrots, and rolled oats. I would call when I left the house, and by the time I rounded the hedge they would be standing with their forepaws against the wire, waiting for breakfast.

Then one morning I called and there was no answering flurry. Apprehensively I burst into a run.

The pen had been torn apart. On the grass were the dead rabbits. Footprints of dogs were everywhere in the soft earth, and I knew what dogs they were. One of our neighbors allowed a pair of German shepherds to run loose at night.

In a trance, I got a spade, and buried my first pets. Then I sat down to my breakfast. The maid brought me the usual two soft-boiled eggs in a cup. I thanked her, and put my spoon in the cup. Suddenly I was taken violently ill. I began to cry.

I remember our housekeeper Mary Clark putting me to bed and hearing grandmother call, "What has happened, Mary? Has he been hurt?" For a while I must have been delirious. Later the doctor came. By that time I was able to gasp out what had happened. Grandmother exclaimed, "Really now, Danny, I thought it was something serious."

I heard grandmother telling our chauffeur, "But Thomas, if he behaves like this over rabbits, what will he ever do when he has to go out into the world?"

Kennedy cleared his throat, a trick he had before answering an embarrassing question, and gently replied, "He's like the old gentleman, ma'am." Kennedy always referred to grandfather by that term. "Very sensitive. Real gentlemen, both of them. Thank God, neither will ever have to work for a living."

I begged grandfather not to get me any more rabbits. "I'll never have another pet as long as I live," I told him. "I couldn't go through anything like this again." Grandfather said he understood.

True to the traditions of the Main Line, my grandparents never thought of asking the dogs' owners to keep their pets under control. That would have been interfering with their personal affairs. Instead, after several private conferences, they decided that I needed some playmates my own age.

The nearest suitable children were the Willcoxes, who lived in Wawa some 20 miles away.

Although Wawa was not, strictly speaking, on the Main Line some fairly respectable people had been living there since the early 18th century. It was decided to make the supreme sacrifice and use the Pierce Arrow to take me there two or three times a month.

Dressed in a costume suitable for an afternoon of fun, starched linen collar, blue serge suit, and patent-leather pumps, I arrived at the Willcoxes. The children, lined up on the front porch to greet me, had been clearly ordered to Be Nice to Your Little Guest—or Else.

The two boys were younger than I, but the girl was my own age. "Do you like animals?" she inquired.

"I used to, but not any more," I said. I told of the tragedy of the rabbits.

She listened to me sympathetically. "Well, dogs don't come around here," she said. "They're afraid of the skunks. These woods are full of skunks."

"Could I see them?" I asked eagerly.

"You can this evening. They come out only after dark. Say!" the older boy said, his face lighting up. "Why don't you catch a couple of skunks and take them home with you? You can get them tame and then the dogs will be afraid to come around."

We looked at each other with wild surmise and then started an impromptu war dance. "We'll need sacks—and flashlights— and we'll borrow aunty's Cairn terriers. They can always find skunks."

A sudden doubt struck me. "You don't think my grandparents will mind? Don't skunks smell bad?"

"They don't smell at all!" I was assured. "You smell after running into a skunk, but the skunk doesn't smell a bit!"

That made it all right. The girl was the only one who seemed a little doubtful, but all she said was, "I wouldn't introduce them to your grandparents right away. Some people don't like the smell very much, at least not until they get used to it."

The younger Willcoxes explained to me the technique of skunk catching. "One person gets the skunk's attention while somebody else sneaks up behind him and picks him up by the tail. A skunk can't squirt while you're holding him by the tail."

"How do you know?"

"Oh, we've done it often. On Halloween we catch skunks and put them in people's bathtubs. The people can't get them out without being squirted."

I was more convinced than ever that the Willcoxes were an outstanding family.

"Maybe you'd better do the picking-up part," I suggested.

"No, we can pick up skunks

anytime, but you're company, and mother said we had to be nice to you," said the oldest boy firmly.

The Willcoxes explained that it would save an awful lot of unnecessary explaining if we didn't mention our plans, so we had supper in polite silence. As soon as the meal was over, we started out.

I led the excited rush when the dogs began to bark. They were on the side of a railroad embankment; between them, a white V seemed to be floating a few inches above the ground. As I came closer with the flashlight I saw it was, indeed, a skunk.

At the sight of me the skunk fled, humping along like an overgrown inchworm.

The terriers quickly cut him off from cover, and the skunk stopped again, obviously determined to make a stand. When a skunk decides to stand, nothing will move him. Indians on the warpath wrapped skunkskins around their ankles to show they would never run away.

The skunk had raised his tail straight up, with only the white tip on the end hanging down. As I approached, he stamped with his forefeet.

One of the Willcoxes whispered, "That's the second signal that he means business. The first is when he raises his tail.

The last is when the white tip stands up. After that he lets you have it."

I took another step forward. The white tip rose and spread out like a tiny fan. "Stop!" shouted the Willcoxes in chorus.

I stopped. "What do I do next?"

"Give me the flashlight and I'll stay here and hold his attention," said one of the boys. "You sneak around behind him and pick him up by the tail."

I handed over the flashlight and quietly stole up from behind. Then I made a rush and grabbed.

The skunk was quicker. He spun about and let me have it with both barrels. I felt something wet strike my cheek. Then I had the skunk by the tail.

Almost instantly my cheek began to burn as though scalding water had been thrown against it, and I fought for breath as if against tear gas. I managed to lift the skunk clear of the ground; he swung back and forth like a pendulum, trying to reach me with his teeth and claws. I tried to shout to the Willcoxes to bring the sack, but I couldn't speak. The skunk was getting heavy (a full-grown skunk will weigh about ten pounds) and holding him at arm's length was getting trying. And the pain in my cheek, nose, lungs, and eyes was rapidly becoming unbearable. Luckily the skunk hadn't gotten me full in the face, or I'd have been seriously sick.

After what seemed to me an eternity, the Willcoxes finally got the mouth of the sack spread open and the flashlight turned on the opening, and I was able to drop my captive inside.

"My, he really did get you, didn't he?" said one of my hosts, sniffing. "One good thing about it, from now on you can just walk up to any skunk and pick him up. You've got nothing to lose."

I was conducted to a stream nearby. I washed my face and, as the Willcoxes suggested, put some wet mud on my cheek. It helped some. After rinsing out my mouth and eyes time after time, I was ready to go on.

We got four more skunks that evening. By the time we were finished, everyone was thoroughly skunked. I'm inclined to think that the Willcoxes were right in their theory that a skunk can't use his ammunition while suspended by the tail, but we never really had a chance to find out.

Mrs. Willcox was standing on the porch calling for us when we got back. "What have you been doing?" she called indignantly. "Kennedy's here with the car and—oh *no!*" We had gotten in range.

We agreed that I could keep two skunks. The Willcoxes kept the other two as a surprise for some of their friends. I explained to Kennedy that since the skunks had already exhausted their ammunition, carrying them home in the car would present no problems. "Perhaps so, Master Dan, but I can only say the Pierce Arrow will never be the same again," said Kennedy grimly.

My grandparents had already gone to bed when I returned. Following the Willcoxes' suggestions, I put the skunks in my bathtub overnight. My clothes I threw down the back stairs. For weeks afterward on damp days there was a strong odor of skunk about those stairs. After several washings with a good grade of strong carbolic soap I was as good as new, except for my hair. That had to be clipped.

I was so proud of my new acquisitions that my grandparents hadn't the heart to object. I think they judged that to deprive me of the skunks after the rabbit tragedy would be too cruel. Grandmother did throw out a few hints about supplanting the skunks with another pair of rabbits, but when I pointed out that the dogs would surely kill them she said no more. Even Kennedy, who had been forced to spend long hours washing out the car with benzine, realized how much the pair meant to me, and helped build a pen.

Getting the skunks out of the tub without rendering the house unsuitable for human habitation presented certain difficulties, but I solved the problem by popping a box suddenly over the couple, slipping a thin board under it, and carrying them off without giving them a target. Then I happily sat down to watch my first wild-animal pets parade around their new quarters.

Skunks are really extremely handsome animals. Their fur is rich and soft (commercially it goes under the proud title "Alaskan sable"). Although they are a little too low-slung to be called graceful, they march around in an impressively determined manner and bear a strong resemblance to Sir Winston Churchill without the cigar.

After eating from my hands for a few days the pair became tame. The male, always the more friendly, would run out of his house when he heard me coming, and stand up with his feet against the wire, grunting to be let out.

He soon discovered that people were afraid of him; whenever he saw a stranger he would dash at him and do a handstand on his forefeet with his tail bent forward, prepared to fire over his own head (he could do this very skillfully). If the stranger ran—and most people did—he would give chase as long as his short legs could keep up with them. If, on the other hand, they stood still, he'd stop his war dance and waddle up to make friends. He never actually threw his musk on these occasions, but it was pretty hard to persuade visitors that he was only playing. I called him Nikki, after a clown who was famous for walking on his hands.

Skunks aren't generally considered intelligent; Nikki was exceptional. He quickly learned which of the maids were afraid of him and which were not. One maid had no time for Nikki and would shoo him away with a broom as though he were a cat, but Nikki never sprayed her. On the other hand, the parlor maid was terrified of him and Nikki would lie in wait for her behind the garbage cans, rushing out and doing his handstand whenever she appeared.

One day in April Mrs. Nikki made a beautiful nest with a pair of my trousers which a maid had thoughtlessly left hanging on the clothesline. Since I had several trousers, I saw no reason why I should take them back. Miss Mary Clark thought my grandparents would probably share this point of view, as Mrs. Nikki had been housekeeping in them for some time before the loss was discovered.

A few weeks later I found Nikki sitting unhappily outside the trousers. He kept trying to crawl down a leg, his usual entrance, only to be met by violent chattering. He hastily backed out and I lifted up the trouser leg and peered down it. There lay Mrs. Nikki with six squirming newborn babies beside her in an orderly row. Although they were hairless, the white stripes already showed clearly on their bare backs.

I had by now developed a certain amount of caution and said nothing about this to my grandparents.

One evening I met the whole skunk family out walking among the flower beds. They were all parading in single file after their mother, trying to keep their huge tails curled over their backs. Every now and then a baby's tail would droop down and he would step on it and fall on his stumpy nose. Then he would give a twist of his hindquarters and hoist it up again with the gesture of a dowager switching her train into place. They were intensely solemn and obviously on their dignity.

When the babies found that their parents accepted me, they took to following me around just as they did their mother. Our gardener had a small mongrel named Rags; he was about the size of a mop and spent most of his time hunting field mice. The baby skunks obviously considered this great sport and took to following Rags. Poor Rags began to behave like a small boy trying to get rid of a set of determined younger brothers while six devoted baby skunks tagged determinedly after him whenever he set out for the pasture.

Rags soon discovered that it was easy to ditch the babies because they were very nearsighted. He had only to make a quick jump to one side, and the little flock would go marching past. When they came to the end of the trail, they would be completely lost and run around crying miserably until their mother or I came out and collected them.

My grandparents seldom went into the lower garden where the skunks lived, so the babies were half grown before their existence was discovered. It was the parlor maid who betrayed me. She saw the Nikki family marching in procession across the clothes-drying yard one evening, and went to grandmother. Her position was that having Nikki harry her was bad enough but if she was to be pursued by a posse, she would have to give notice.

I was summoned before the family tribunal. Only after a long argument and a solemn oath never to allow any of the Nikki family near the maids' part of the establishment was I suffered to keep the babies.

As the skunks wandered about pretty much at their own sweet will, I had no idea how I was to maintain my part of the contract, but fortune favored me. One afternoon I found the parlor maid having a tea party for the local chapter of the Daughters of the Sinn Fein. The *pièce de résistance* was a large layer cake which I knew grandmother had intended to last the entire household for several days. I said nothing, merely stopped and looked eloquently at the cake before going on.

Before I could get out the back door, the parlor maid had hurried after me to express her passionate love for skunks of all ages, sizes, and descriptions, and to assure me that she would never trouble grandmother again over such a minor matter. I accepted her assurance.

Rags and I used to take the babies for walks in the evenings. The walks were leisurely; the skunks stopped every few feet to dig up grubs, which seemed to be their main diet. Occasionally in a burst of speed they'd run down a snail, and once the biggest baby actually caught a field mouse. They were death on Japanese beetles. The whole flock would collect under the apple trees and I would shake the beetles down to them. The crunching of the beetles' hard carapaces sounded like the crackling of tiny firecrackers.

We hadn't been troubled much by the German shepherds that summer because their owner had gone to Maine and had put the dogs in a kennel. So it was not until autumn, when the skunks were going to the orchard in search of fallen apples, that the two met. I was some distance away when I noticed the shepherds streaking through the trees, evidently thinking they had discovered a perfect bonanza of cats. I started running and shouting, but the Nikki family didn't need me.

The skunks were so used to playing with Rags that they showed absolutely no fear of the oncoming dogs, but as the leading shepherd came closer, Nikki, Jr., turned toward him with a weary expression as though to say he didn't want to be rude but was too busy to play. He made a polite handstand and then prepared to turn away, but the dog would have none of it. He charged, and somehow the adolescent skunk suddenly seemed to realize that this was the real thing.

Instantly he stiffened and gave his warning stamps, but the dogs were almost on him. The next two signals were given almost simultaneously. I saw Nikki, Jr., twist himself into a perfect U and as the leading dog opened his mouth to grab his quarry, the skunk fired.

The dog leaped into the air as though he'd been shot. He fell over on his back, got up, fell down again, and then went around the garden in a series of great circles at full speed. The second shepherd, undeterred by his friend's fate, rushed in to be met by a broadside from all six youngsters. The dog turned a complete somersault and went into convulsions. Then he staggered off, stopping occasionally to rub his eyes against his forelegs. I subsequently had the satisfaction of hearing that he made straight for his owner's sofa.   ❖

THE INSIDE STORY ON THE OUTSIDE

We were fresh from Ireland, and our first job was in the kitchen of a large institution, assisting the chef. He was Irish, too. A very little fellow, this chef, short-tempered, quick, a master cook and an impatient man with our floundering efforts to adjust to his dashing efficiency. His majesty assigned us to the preparing of the vegetables. We soon became quite professional at our task.

We peeled potatoes, shelled peas, husked corn, scraped carrots, and then one day we found ourselves staring at a bushel basket of strange looking things. Whatever they were, we had never seen them before, even if they were as green as we were. But our Irish pride wasn't for letting our friend know that we did not know. So pretending self-assurance, we pertly picked up the basket between us and carried it out to the old back porch, the peeling headquarters.

As we went we whispered one to other. "What are they?"

"Don't know—never saw them before."

"Which part do you save, the inside or the outside?"

Once out of sight and hearing of the chef, we discussed the matter and reasoned that in every other case—potatoes, peas, corn, carrots—we always kept the inside and threw away the outside. No doubt these things required the same procedure. So we saved the inside and threw away the outside. When we were but barely finished, his majesty appeared.

"Where are the green peppers?" he demanded.

"There," said I. "Where?" said he. I pointed to a creamy white substance in the kettle. "You mean . . . ?" He stopped short. "What did you do with the green part?"

"Oh, the peelings? Why I threw them out, of course."

His majesty became a raging little leprechaun. Next day it was eggs. "Keep the *inside!*" he barked. Ever after we were always informed as to the inside or the outside.   Mary Mel Healy.

The Note on the Refrigerator Door

How Harriet carried the bad news from the bank to Ralph

By RALPH REPPERT
November 1973, condensed from the Baltimore Sunday *Sun**

D EAR RALPH: I'm taping this note to the refrigerator door for one important reason. I want you to open the door right now and have yourself a cold beer before you read any further. Please do it this minute. It wouldn't be fair to me for you to learn what I have to tell you on an empty stomach.

Don't be alarmed. The doctor says it is a nice clean break. And, after all, it could have been my right arm instead of the left. But let me give you the facts in order.

The bad news first. Guess what the termite man found? Yep. Three major concentrations along the foundation below the house.

And now the good news. The termite man—he was the *nicest* person—isn't charging us one penny for his inspection. He also says he can kill every termite in the place for only $80, which works out to something less than $.0004 per termite. Certainly a lot cheaper than the $1,200 it will cost to pull out the honey-combed sills and studs (whatever *they* are) and replace them with sound lumber.

And more good news, Ralph. The $1,200 is payable in easy monthly installments over a period of three years. Now before the blue smoke starts curling out of your ears, the way it does every time I handle any of the business, let me tell you that I didn't spend any money. I didn't have to. The only thing required was that I sign the work order, which I had to decide on in a hurry in order to take advantage of a special.

The trouble with the car wasn't so much a result of the termite business as it was the letter we got from your sister.

Once again, the bad news first. Your sister, the four kids, and dog will have to do without husband and father for a month. John's company is sending him to another one of those training seminars.

And now, all sorts of good news. John will surely get a promotion out of it. Also, the seminar is in New York. Because that is within weekend distance of Baltimore, Jean and the kids and the dog will be moving in with us.

I was thinking so hard about where we're going to sleep everybody that I wasn't too alert at the shopping center. I overshot my parking slot and hit the car in front of me. If that stupid bumper of ours (it's in the back seat now) had done its job it wouldn't have let our radiator grill get all tangled up with that other car.

When I backed out in a hurry my foot slipped off the brake and hit the accelerator, and I hit the radiator of the car behind me. The man came limping out of it, waving his arms, and from the way he carried on you'd think his was the only Cadillac in town.

Stupid man! What in the world does his son-in-law being a lawyer have to do with me nudging him a little? He insisted on calling the police because he said he wanted the accident on record. The policeman was a nice man on the way to the hospital, but a positive *ogre* afterwards. Answer me this, Ralph. When a woman scoots over to the supermarket with nothing but a change purse, how is she expected to take along her registration and driver's license?

And now Ralph, I want you to stop reading and have yourself another cold beer.

Back again? Once again, there is good news and bad news.

The good news is that I haven't got a broken arm at all. There wasn't any termite man, no termites, no $1,200 worth of repairs. There wasn't any letter from your sister. There wasn't any accident at the shopping center. I made it all up.

Now the bad news. The man at the bank called me and told me we were overdrawn by $11.34.

I hope you don't mind me telling you about it in this way, but it's the best way I know of making you see our one real problem in its true perspective. Harriet. ❖

It's Just What I've Always Wanted

(What is it?)

By T.E. COSTER
January 1981, condensed from *Atlanta Journal and Constitution Magazine**

I T'S NOT HOW MUCH you pay for a Christmas present that counts, and it's not the thought either. It's the amount of gratitude you express when your loved one shyly hands it to you.

Marriages that have survived poverty, infidelity, and Super-Bowl Sundays can burst like soap bubbles in those few crucial moments after the present has been unwrapped and an unwary spouse, faced with a gift so incredibly unsuitable to his or her needs that it must have been chosen by committee, is shocked into a truthful comment.

I had thought that I was beyond error in this matter. It seemed reasonable to assume that a man who makes the effort

to lock himself in his room for at least half an hour a night during the week prior to Christmas, for the sole purpose of unwrapping gifts in front of the mirror and saying, "WOW! Socks!" with the perfect amount of enthusiasm, could handle any situation. It was the confidence of a fool, of course.

Last Christmas morning, I felt my way gingerly down the stairs, carefully avoiding the living room, where I knew my two tiny offspring were busily destroying a mountain of toys. My sainted wife, Gloria, and I had spent all the previous night wrapping and arranging gifts. In seven hours we had prepared a fairy wonderland that would have made the window dresser of any department store weak with envy, but now the way to the kitchen was littered with broken drums, crashed spaceships,

*This article © 1979 by Atlanta Newspapers. Reprinted with permission.

mangled toy soldiers, and half-eaten sugar plums.

I slumped into the only chair in the kitchen not buried under shredded wrapping paper and stared at the remains of Bongo the Bear. When I last clapped eyes on him only hours ago, Bongo was in perfect health. When you flipped a switch in his back, he switched his little tail from side to side, lights flashed in his eyes, and he walked around on his four sturdy legs, growling realistically.

At least he used to. Bongo's tail had disappeared along with two of his legs and his head. A flick of the switch now sent Bongo's mutilated torso crawling over the cold toast towards his own severed head, still growling gamely from some unknown source. As the high point in a horror movie, the scene would have had no equal.

Gloria, perched behind me on a high kitchen stool, smiled fondly at the sound of a muffled crash from the living room. "The kids are having a marvelous time," she said.

I muttered something that I hoped she would interpret as warm-hearted delight, and reached with trembling hand for what I presumed to be fresh-brewed coffee.

The cup was full of rubber spiders. I did not, when I first raised it to my lips, realize that they were rubber. In fact the echoes of my scream were barely dying before recognition sank in. Gloria was unperturbed. Screams on Christmas morning usually meant delight. Besides, she had other things on her mind.

"This one's yours," she said, pushing a gaily wrapped package along the floor to me. "Why don't you open it now while the kids are still playing?"

Why not indeed? It was a large box and heavy. And I knew what it was.

For weeks, months actually, I had been hinting about a new Select-O-Touch typewriter, with interchangeable ribbons and instant erasure cassette. I had dropped little hints and big hints. I had never missed an opportunity to drag Gloria into a store and admire it. I had done everything except come right out and order her to buy it, and now I was filled with eagerness to feast my eyes on it and heap gratitude on Gloria's head.

I unwrapped the package and looked at the massive red metal box inside. There was a sturdy leather handle on top, and the lid was fastened with two metal catches that I snapped back; I took a long horrified look at the contents before quietly closing it again.

"Gloria," I said faintly, "you've bought me a set of socket wrenches."

"Oh, it's much more than that," she cried happily, flinging her arms around my neck, subtle perfume tickling my nostrils. "There are ring spanners and a complete manual on stripping down a car engine. You didn't guess, did you?"

I assured her I hadn't guessed. I would have guessed two tickets to the moon before I guessed socket wrenches.

"But, Gloria," I began gently, wondering if it was all a joke and any minute now she would bring out my real present and we'd have a good laugh over it, "what am I going to do with a set of socket wrenches?"

In an instant it was all gone. The arms, the perfume, the laugh vanished in a flash, replaced by a stricken-mother-harp-seal look and a voice as chill as an arctic wind.

"You don't like them," she accused.

"Yes. Yes, I do," I lied.

"Well, you were saying how high the car-repair bills are, and you're always going on about getting a hobby and needing more exercise, and I thought that would be just perfect for everything."

"But darling," I replied, "it's almost time to trade the car, and I'm going to take up jogging any time now, and groveling in the bowels of a Buick every Saturday is not the kind of hobby I had in mind."

"I see."

With a flourish of velour she was gone. I tried to head her off, but the bathroom door was securely locked by the time I rattled it.

"Gloria," I cooed through the varnished pine, "I really love the socket wrenches. In fact, I think I'll just nip out to the garage right now and try them out."

My answer was a furious flushing, a favorite tactic of Gloria's to drown out my hated voice and discourage conversation. I struggled into my jeans, sneakers, and a heavy sweater, picked up the wrenches and stopped outside the bathroom, listening for sounds of breathing. Nothing.

"Well," I bawled casually through the wood, "guess I'll just go out and test my new socket wrenches. Yep, that's what I'll do, just tinker around the old Buick before dinner."

More flushing. I walked out to the garage, thinking our utility bill was going to be hellish this month, and raised the hood on the Buick. Actually, the garage man on the corner had said it did need the tappets adjusted, whatever they are. Didn't sound too serious, and theoretically the manual could lay out every step necessary in getting to grips with the mysteries of a car motor.

I opened the manual to the first illustration, located the

appropriate area in the engine, selected a likely looking wrench, and gave it a quick professional twist. The wrench skidded off unyielding metal and dropped out of sight into a writhing mass of cables. Searing pain shot through me as the skin peeled off the back of my knuckles and the grazes began to turn red. As I lifted my head to damn every tool manufacturer in the world to eternal perdition, I noticed two large blue eyes staring at me from above the window ledge in the bathroom.

In a last gallant effort to save a not-bad marriage, I choked back the anguish and gaily waved the hand that wasn't gushing blood. The eyes promptly disappeared. I bent back to my task, knowing that now at least there was a slight chance of reconciliation.

The man from Al's Garage and Towing repeated his price and offered to let me check his arithmetic after he heard my startled, "How much?"

"It's not just the cost of putting it back together, you know," he said severely. "At least half the nuts and bolts have stripped threads. They'll all have to be replaced. All the same, I know how you feel. It must be pretty tough to wake up on Christmas morning and find out a gang of vandals has done your car over.

This used to be a pretty decent neighborhood."

I watched him tow the Buick out of the yard and went back inside the house. In the kitchen Gloria was stuffing the family turkey in wary silence.

"Well, that was a bit of luck," I said casually. "Had the head off the motor and discovered the oil seals were about gone." I'd also done a lot of manual reading while I was waiting for the two truck to arrive. "Could have been a very expensive engine job coming up if I hadn't noticed it. Too tricky to handle myself, of course. Yet."

I looked Gloria straight in the eyes as I made my next statement. "I got old Charlie to come from Al's on the corner. He's going to do it for me. And he said, said it himself, that if I hadn't done the preparatory work on it, there would have been a big difference in the cost."

"Oh, really?"

She was feigning indifference, but I knew I had her. I stashed the tool box as far back in the hall closet as possible and went to run some hot bathwater. Staring at my haggard countenance in the mirror, I began to figure out the best way of sneaking $700 out of the joint checking account to pay Al's. Then I heard it. Singing! Gloria was singing in the kitchen. At

$700 that sound was a bargain. I hummed a few bars myself as I began to scrub off the grease. ❖

SMALL WORRIES

Usually when kindergarten begins in September there are some tears, but they are soon dried. This year was different. Day after day, small Billy wept. Nothing Sister Martha could do would check the flood.

Finally, in exasperation, Sister exclaimed, "All right, Billy. Just keep on crying. Soon we'll have a lake and we can all go swimming."

Suddenly more sobbing was heard, this time from a little girl. Sister demanded, "For goodness' sake, Betty, what's the matter with you?"

"Oh, Sister," she wailed, "I can't swim."   Sr. Eugenia.

*

Little Kenny had just been vaccinated, and the doctor started to put a bandage over the vaccination spot. Kenny objected. He wanted the bandage on the other arm instead.

"But Kenny," said the doctor, "the bandage should be put on the sore arm so that the boys at school won't hit it."

"Put it on the other arm, Doc," Kenny answered. "You don't know those guys!"   *The Catholic Herald Citizen.*

THE PERFECT ASSIST

My mother had a warm sympathy for teachers of young children which she sometimes demonstrated in practical ways. Once when September rolled around she found herself at the end of a long line of mothers waiting to interview the 1st grade teacher before entrusting their darlings to her care. As she waited her turn, mother heard snatches of orders being delivered to the poor teacher:

"Be sure to give Johnnie his medicine every hour!"

"*Never* let Kathy sit near an open window!"

"If Mike starts to cry call me right away!"

"Never scold Molly. She's *so* sensitive!"

And so on and on for many minutes.

When mother's turn came at last, she took one glance at the worn look on the teacher's face. She smiled gently and said, "If I can help, be sure to let me know."

A look of relief passed over the teacher's face. Two friends were made that day.   Sister M. Andrienne Downey, O.P.

Tips of the Slongue

They come mostly from putting the hart
before the course

By FRANK L. REMINGTON
September 1973, condensed from the *V.F.W. Magazine**

THE YOUNG PRIEST sat beside a visiting archbishop at a banquet. Wishing to demonstrate to other diners his perfect poise, the priest clutched the gravy boat and passed it to the archbishop. "Will you have some grace, Your Gravy?" he asked.

In making a TV pitch for a hay fever remedy, a Los Angeles announcer said, "Sufferers, there is hell on the way for you." Attempting to correct himself, he bumbled, "There is help, now that the snark of hay fever season is here." He meant *start.* He finally quit trying and apologized.

A newscaster declared, "A parade will follow the governor's conference. At 2 P.M. the cars will leave their headquarters just as soon as the governors are loaded!" Another newsman reported that a policeman in arresting a motorist had found the suspect "under the affluence of incohol."

Thomas Fuller declared, "Birds are entangled by their feet and men by their tongues." His observation has probably been verified in your own life. But you needn't feel bad about it, for almost everyone occasionally trips over his tongue. It might be highly embarrassing for you, but it is fun for everyone else. Recollecting some of the boo-boos of others may help relieve your mortification the next time your own tongue slips.

A TV spieler blundered, "So ladies, we urge you to shave at Cook's . . . I mean shake at Cook's. What I really mean is that you can shave at Cook's . . . I mean save at Cook's!" Another TV pitchman declared, "Summer is here, and with it those lazy days at the beach; and don't forget your . . . sun lotion . . . is the lotion that lets you burn but never lets you tan."

A radio announcer asked the listeners to stay tuned for the "most apprehensive coverage of the news." A newscaster bumbled into the microphone, "This is your 11 o'clock news with an on-the-spot retort . . . I mean on-the-tot-resort . . . oh well, let's just skip it." An equally mixed-up newsman reported, "In the head-on collision of the two passenger cars, five people were killed in the crash, two quite seriously."

Weather reporters are notorious for their gaffes. One predicted "shattered tunder sours." Another calmly forecast, "Rowdy followed by clain." Still another weather man said the following day's weather would be smoggy with light "ear eyeatation."

Instances of getting the "hart before the course" result in such commercials as, "Come in at the sign of the clock, where it only takes six months to open a three-minute charge account." Another announcer: "We will have to discuss this proposition with Bill Dale, who is brilliant when it comes to transactions like these. Why, he has more brains in his little finger than he has in his whole head!"

Not long ago an actor reach-ing for a bell pull announced that he would "give the bull a pill." Anyone pulling such a fluff should continue on as though nothing had happened. Trying to correct a slip frequently seems to compound it. Another actor, for instance, was giving a butler directions on how to set the table. "Place the sporks and foons," he bumbled. Pausing, he tried again, "The porks and sfoons . . ." The next attempt brought, "I mean, of course, the sforks and poons . . . He never did make it.

At a basketball game in Los Angeles, the sportscaster flubbed, "We will return to the Sports Arena as soon as technical difficulties are resumed." Another sportscaster at a baseball game in Philadelphia watched a long fly ball soar toward the outfield. "Bob Johnson is backing up for the ball," he told the listeners. "Back . . . way back . . . he hits his head against the wall, drops it, picks it up and pegs it home!" The player was flooded with letters asking how he was getting along without his head.

One sportscaster was giving a blow-by-blow description of a boxing match. About the middle of the bout his station cut him off suddenly to announce the death of the local mayor, then cut him back in. Knowing nothing of the interruption, he continued with the blow-by-blow account. "That sounded like quite a blow, but it doesn't mean a thing, really. No damage done at all."

A while back Johnny Logan, former shortstop of the Pittsburgh Pirates and the Milwaukee Braves, attended a testimonial dinner to pay tribute to one of the game's best loved stars, Stan Musial. When Johnny got up to deliver his speech, he cleared his throat and began, "Stan Musical is the greatest immoral in the history of baseball."

In the presidential campaign of 1948, candidate Thomas E. Dewey gave himself a political hotfoot. At Greeley, Colo., he was talking to a crowd gathered around an outside platform. Every few minutes, a low-flying plane buzzed the crowd and a voice boomed over a loudspeaker, "Vote for Hamil." Disturbed by this continuing interruption, Dewey irascibly declared, "That fellow Hamil is no friend of mine." David Hamil, the Republican candidate for governor of Colorado, was sitting behind him on the speaker's platform.

At a party shortly after George Romney's first election as governor of Michigan, the hostess introduced Mrs. Romney to a guest. "I want you to meet the governor's new wife," she said. In embarrassment, she hastily corrected herself, "I mean the new governor's old wife." Another woman told Mrs. Romney, "You always look different; last time I saw you, you looked so nice."

The late Sen. Estes Kefauver was hard put not to choke on a statement which the press picked up during one of his primary campaigns for the Democratic presidential nomination. Campaigning through the Midwest, Kefauver came to be known for his homespun approach. In one town he patted a small boy on the head and asked about his father. "He's dead," the boy replied.

A few hours later, on the other side of town, Kefauver greeted the same youngster again. Obviously he didn't remember the lad, for he once again asked, "How is your father?"

"My father is still dead," came the devastating reply.

Prince Charles, now the Prince of Wales, once remarked that one of the problems a person in his position has is that others sometimes become flustered in his presence. He recalled one occasion when "the wife of a dignitary in Australia greeted me and said she hadn't seen me since my parents' wedding."

At a formal reception in Washington, the harried host cordially greeted the secretary of the treasury, "Good evening,

Mr. Sandwich, won't you please have a secretary?"

Attending his first reception at the White House, a newly-elected congressman grew more nervous by the moment. Finally he found himself obliged to chat with the First Lady. In a hopeless effort to appear poised, he blurted, "I've always admired the White House. Do you know who was the artichoke who designed it?"

There is no protection against making such gaffes, and it is just as well. Everyone gets a chuckle out of tips of the slongue. ♣

KID STUFF

The children were invited to participate in the ground-breaking for a new convent. Each child turned over a small shovelful of dirt. Later in the day the mother of one little girl asked what happened at church that morning.

"Well," she replied dejectedly, "we dug for a new convent, but we didn't find it." Henry E. Leabo.

*

A visitor had left a quarter for my seven-year-old Joey, and there was a bit of a discussion as to what he should do with it. "Why don't you give it to the Red Cross?" suggested his older sister.

"I've thought of that," said Joey carefully. "But I think I'll let the ice-cream man give it to the Red Cross." Mrs. Joseph Felice.

*

Describing his baby sister to a buddy, our son said, "She's got some teeth but her words haven't come in yet." Chicago *Tribune* (9 Feb. '72).

*

Six-year-old Kevin was unhappy after being teased about losing two front teeth. He looked enviously at his 12-year-old cousin who wore braces on his teeth and said, "Well, you'll never lose any of your teeth. They're chained on!" *The Progressive Farmer* (March '72).

*

A teacher showed the class a print of *Whistler's Mother* and asked them to jot down their impressions. One child wrote: "A nice old lady waiting for the repairman to bring back her TV set." *Smiles* (March '72).

*

Worried over what to give his girl for her birthday, a teen-ager asked his mother for help. "Mom," he said, "if you were going to be 16 years old tomorrow, what would you want?"

Her heartfelt reply was: "Not another thing!" H. E. L.

What the Dog Did at the Diplomatic Dinner

The Swiss ambassador, rampant with good
manners, nearly made my private
embarrassment public

By ELIZABETH SHANNON
September 1983, condensed from *Up in the Park**

I KNEW THERE WOULD be pitfalls on this job as wife of
the American ambassador to
Ireland, but the night of March
14th shouldn't have happened
to anyone. There will never be
a social situation now that I can't
handle, no matter how knotty,
no matter how thorny, because
nothing can ever be so ghastly
as what happened to me that
evening.

We gave a black-tie dinner for
24 to honor the newly arrived

*The author is the wife of William
V. Shannon, American ambassador
to Ireland from 1977 to 1981.*

French ambassadorial couple
and to say good-by to the retiring Swiss ambassador and his
wife. I wore a new dress, finished by a Dublin designer only
hours before the party, and
thought I looked terrific. The
house was filled with pots
of spring daffodils and tulips.
The dining room gleamed with
silver, candlelight, and white
linen. Huge Simon Pearce glass
bowls filled with flowers shone
under the sparkling Waterford
chandelier.

The chief butler, Dennis
Buckley, and I made our last-
minute spot check with my faithful Labrador, Molly. Everything
was perfect, no detail forgotten.
At the appointed hour we

floated into dinner, I smiling graciously around a table lined with Dublin's diplomatic, literary, and theater elite. I nodded to the Swiss ambassador on my right, a tall, handsome dignified man with a military-style mustache and a very straight back. I smiled at the French ambassador on my left, small and dapper, dark-eyed and charming. As we all sat down, I thought to myself, "Now, isn't this just perfect, just the way an ambassador's dinner should proceed, everyone looking happy and animated, with lively conversations already springing up around the table."

As I put my feet under the table, I felt something soft and spongy under the chair. Puzzled, I discreetly reached down to see what was there, and to my horror I put my hand into a very large, still warm, newly laid pile of Molly's droppings. Her full amount for the day, lovingly deposited under her mistress's chair, her contribution to my dinner party.

I straightened up, with my soiled hand dangling at the side of the chair. The French ambassador was talking to me, telling me about living in New York in the 1950s. I stared at him wildly. What was he saying? New York. Oh, yes, I used to live there, too. Very changed since 1950, I believe.

My hand was reeking, and both feet were firmly embedded in the pile. I couldn't move.

The Swiss ambassador was asking me about my son Liam's fishing trip. "Did he have any luck?" he inquired solicitously. Did Liam go on a fishing trip? I couldn't remember. I tried to smile. "Do you fish, ambassador?" I asked. My voice sounded weak. The ambassador looked puzzled. "But you remember, I taught Liam how to flycast last week," he said.

I think I'm hysterical. What am I going to do? Should I simply stand up and say, "I'm ill. You will have to go home?"

Or, "Our cook just had a heart attack. There will be no dinner tonight?"

Or, "Will you all please go out and come back in again. That's an old American custom?"

Maybe I could start crying loudly and they would all be so embarrassed they would get up and leave, and I could clean up the mess and then go in to them and say, piteously, "I'm all right now."

But the waitresses were already moving into the room with the food. It was too late now to do anything. I would have to brazen it out.

Kitty came around with the first course, a beautiful, molded salmon mousse. I tried to dish it out just using my right hand, but it kept slithering off the spoon.

"Use both hands," Kitty whispered.

"I can't," I whispered back, nudging Kitty with my elbow and rolling my eyes toward the floor. Kitty looked perplexed and moved on with the mousse. When Dennis came to pour the wine, I whispered for him to bring me some Kleenex. I dropped them on the floor, over my feet, and tried to wipe off my hand.

The dinner progressed: soup, entree, salad, dessert. Talk about France, talk about skiing and Switzerland, about the current play at the Abbey. The French ambassador seemed to have a head cold, thanks be to God. He probably couldn't smell anything.

Finally, champagne was poured and Bill got up to make a beautiful toast to our departing Swiss ambassador. We all had to stand up and toast Switzerland. I managed to look as if I were standing, without moving my feet from where they were now glued. Another toast to France . . . *Vive la France!* Once again, with the rung of the chair digging into my calves, I stood without moving my feet.

At last it was over! I said, very loudly, "Let's go into the drawing room to have coffee." I pushed my chair back, but remained seated. I planned to wait until everyone else was leaving the room, then make a mad dash for the kitchen, where I could get myself and my ruined shoes cleaned up.

But no, my evil genie had one more trick in store for me before the evening was over. My gallant Swiss dinner partner had not been an ambassador for two decades for nothing. He stood, rigid and unmoving behind my chair, waiting for me to stand. As I pushed my chair back, he saw the wad of white Kleenex on the floor. Mistaking it for my white linen napkin, he bent down to pick it up.

"No!" I screamed, grabbing his arm. "Leave it! It's all right."

"Aha," said his Excellency, flushed with wine and champagne, rampant with good manners, "I may be retiring, but I will never be too old to bend down and pick up a lady's napkin."

He tried to wrest his arm out of my grasp as he leaned slowly downward, but I expanded my grip to a half nelson and tugged him away from the table, hissing in his face, "Go have your coffee." He looked quite startled this time, and meekly left the room without another word.

I fled into the pantry, took off my shoes, and threw them into the wastepaper basket. All the tension of the evening broke, and as the maids and butlers were hurrying back and forth between the pantry and the dining room, I sat down on a kitchen table and laughed and laughed until the tears came. "You're very lucky, madam, that it was under your chair, and not one of your guest's," Flanagan, one of our butlers, said.

"Oh, don't say that, Flanagan," I gasped. "Don't even think it!"   ❖

THE HUMAN TOUCH

When Mrs. John F. Kennedy first came to visit Pope John XXIII, the Pope wanted to memorize at least enough English for his opening remarks to the President's wife. Pope John's Secretary of State, Cardinal Cicognani, drawing on the experience he gained during his service as Apostolic Delegate in Washington, explained to the Pope that he should address her either as "Mrs. Kennedy," or just "Madame."

Pope John utilized the few minutes before his audience with Mrs. Kennedy in his private library to practice a few times: "Mrs. Kennedy, Madame; Madame, Mrs. Kennedy." But the minute she crossed his threshold, he forgot everything. He went toward her with his arms outstretched, his face beaming with joy, and cried out, "Jacqueline!"

From A Pope Laughs.

PEOPLE ARE LIKE THAT

Bangladesh is a country where many people beg. They have to. This is a true story told to me by a missionary who witnessed it.

A man was returning home after a hard day of labor. He stopped to rest in the shade of a tree and soon fell asleep. His appearance was much the same as most of the people in the country—poor. His clothes were old and probably torn or threadbare. He had the look of a beggar about him. While he slept some passersby took pity on him and left a coin or two in the arc formed by his sleeping body.

When he awoke he was surprised to find the results of unsolicited generosity. More than a few small coins had collected there. It was a joy to see his surprise and the smile that came across his face. Hard work had not dulled his sense of humor, though, nor had it dulled his heart to justice. He had not begged. He had a job. This money was not his to keep. Sitting there for a moment, passing the coins through his fingers, he saw some blind beggars not far away. Immediately on his feet, he went to these men who were poorer than he was. He divided the coins among them and turned to continue his long walk home.   Patricia Burke.

Five Nuns at a Bullfight

The bulls won, and so did the Mysterious
Lady in Black

By SISTER MARY CORDE LORANG

July 1966, condensed from *Footloose Scientist in Mayan America**

HUEHUETENANGO, in Guate-
mala, goes by the nick-
name of Huehue, pronounced
way-way. It is a likable small
pueblo, the capital of a sparsely
inhabited mountain state.

Sister Albert showed me
around town. She had been a
teacher in Clarence county,
N.Y., then a missioner in up-
country China for 19 years until
the communists took over.
Since then, she has spent 14
years in Bolivia, Panama, and
Guatemala.

The Maryknoll Fathers have
spiritual care of this state. One
of the big difficulties is the

inaccessibility of the towns.
To go to Jacaltenango, for instance, takes four hours by Jeep
and then five hours on horseback. The Maryknoll center at
Huehue keeps in touch with
many missions only by ham
radio.

Brother Carl drove up in a
Jeep. He was elated that he had
won second prize at the agricul-
tural fair just then going on in the
city. Brother has been introducing new crops; his experimental
farm has raised the nourishment
level of the area to a new high.

We continued down Main St.,
past the long, gray city hospital,
now under the direction of the
Incarnate Word Sisters. A vision
out of a 1st World War poster
strode toward us. A tall, good-
looking Indian in red striped
pants and short blue jacket. "We
call them Uncle Sam boys," Sis-

---

*Sister Mary is a science teacher
with a special interest in Mayan
archaeology.*

---

*This article © 1966 by the Maryknoll
Sisters of St. Dominic, Inc.

268

ter Albert laughed. "They are the Indians from Todos Santos, miles away from Huehue, but they bring their products here to be sold."

Many Indians passed us. Sister identified each from his costume. "He's from San Rafael. That one's from San Sebastian. There's an Indian from La Democracia."

A hullabaloo across the street made me turn as red-headed James Reed, a Peace corps worker, came toward me. Stopping short just before he ran me down, he waited to catch his breath and then introduced a short, dark man, muscular and quick.

"My friend, Alfonso Paez from Colombia," Jim said. "He's a matador, here for the bullfights next Sunday."

I raised my eyes to an ad posted on the wall. Yes, it said, "BULLFIGHT, Saturday, 2 P.M."

"Sunday?" I questioned.

"Sunday," Alfonso said.

"The ad says Saturday," I objected.

"No. I will fight on Sunday, ad or no ad."

"Why?" asked matter-of-fact Sister Albert.

Alfonso shrugged his shoulders. "Why? Well, it just is." And that was that.

Once he had been a seminarian, Alfonso said, but "I am much better at fighting bulls than at praying."

Well, there was once a novice in England, I remembered, who had left the convent to go lion taming.

"Have you a piece of paper?" he continued. "I will write you something with my name." We did not look too hard to find one. I am not an autograph collector, not even of matadors' autographs.

That evening two of the muddiest Sisters I ever saw came into the convent. Sister Rose Cordis and Sister Bernice Marie, doctor and nurse, had been riding horseback for 12 hours down the muddy trail from their hospital in Jacaltenango.

They had come to pick up native woolen blankets at the fair. Also medical supplies and pans. The two of them sat around our table, chatting, figuring out how much they could buy, and how they would stow it on their horses or on pack animals.

I marveled at what they have done out there in their small mountain hospital. They are the doctor and nurse who worked all through a night to rejoin a child's foot to her leg. It was hanging by three eighths of an inch of skin when the mother brought them her 18-month-old baby from a nearby village. A similar case, involving a boy's arm, had occurred in Boston not long before. But there, a team of doctors and nurses had worked with all the modern facilities of a large hospital. In Jacaltenango, the lone doctor and nurse worked with a kerosene lamp and few instruments. The child runs now like any other youngster.

Saturday we plunged into the past. A 20-minute drive through peaceful grazing land surrounded by rugged peaks took us back 1,500 years.

"Look at that," Sister Maria Esperanza said. We stood on a mountain curve with a wide, verdant plateau spread below us. Lifting their heads above the large trees were snow-white temples.

"Zaculeu, isn't it?" I asked. This was the Mayan city the United Fruit Co. restored, hiring the famous archaeologist, John M. Dimick, to direct the work.

The road dipped down to the plateau. As we entered the ancient city, not a soul was in sight. It seemed strange to be alone here, almost as if we had wandered out of the fretful present into the calm of the past. The Mayas, we thought, might come back at any moment to welcome us to their empty stronghold. The restoration is complete; each stone is in place. Even the original workmen could not have done more perfect work.

"According to the investiga-

tions carried on by the United Fruit Co.," Sister said, "Zaculeu was flourishing in the 4th century A.D., and, of course, it must have been founded earlier."

A pyramid temple dominates the plaza. It is made up of nine receding layers and crowned by a severely plain temple, almost early Grecian in proportions. A flight of some 40 to 50 steep, narrow steps climbed up one side.

A large ball court is at the left, two long, sloping walls with ample space on top for spectators. Stairways at the ends make it easy to climb up to the viewing stands.

Beyond this is a dainty building something like a low pyramid. Again, the summit is crowned by a temple which relied on its proportion for beauty, rather than on ornamentation. Slender, plain columns form doorways.

"I always call that the Greek temple," said Sister Maria Esperanza. "Last month I brought the Girl Scouts here on an outing, and when the rain burst upon us we took refuge up there in the shelter. It was a thrill to look out at the cloudburst through those lovely openings."

Back at the convent, Sister Albert met us with news. We would go to the fair that afternoon, even though it was raining. Also, she held a large white envelope. In it was a nice bevel-edged card with fancy lettering to the effect that the two of us and three other Sisters were invited to attend the bullfight, as guests of Alfonso Paez, matador from Colombia. Sunday, at 2 P.M., at the football stadium.

"It's the chance of a lifetime!" Sister Maria Esperanza exulted. She is a native of Ecuador; it had been a long time since she had seen a bullfight. The other Sisters had their reservations.

"Must be terribly bloody." "My parents saw one in Mexico City. They were jittery for days afterwards." "Sisters don't go to bullfights. Just as they don't go to prize fights in the States."

The Ecuadorian had some good arguments. "In the big cities, no, we do not go. But this is part of the background of our people. Besides, this is the first bullfight Huehue ever had. It will be very tame."

"Let the idea simmer until tomorrow," said the wisest among us. "We'll see how the fair goes, first." Two o'clock, and pouring rain. But thousands of people were milling around the booths.

Father William Woods stood proudly beside his collection of native woods. He had arranged small pieces in an attractive design which had won first prize. The whole collection of beautiful woods seemed to shout,

"This is one of your resources. Let's use it!"

Brother Carl's exhibit of maize, vegetables, coffee, was not only a winner, but also an education to the Indians passing by. Many people from other areas of Huehuetenango state remarked, "Do you suppose we could get Brother to help us a bit?"

To get background for the bullfight decision, we went around to the football stadium. Looking in, I envisioned a brave matador and ferocious bull. "Where could he hide? It is a long way to the fence."

Sister Esperanza pooh-poohed the idea. "These bulls are the dinnertable kind. They won't get really mad."

Sunday morning we made up our collective mind. We would go, and try to absorb a little more of Guatemala's culture.

Sister Maria Esperanza was calculating. "Let's see. It's advertised to start at 2. It won't, of course. But this is Huehue's first bullfight, so a lot of people will be going. To get good seats we ought to be very early. We should get there by 2:15."

We did, and we were first in line by a long, long shot. Through the wire fence, we could see a few men inside, leisurely nailing boards together to make a sort of chicken coop.

"Probably an enclosure for the bulls," Sister Maria Esperanza said, "although that thing is too flimsy even for dogs."

We walked around the corner and found the bulls in a pen, packed like sardines, but very patient about it all. There were seven, two for each of the three matadors and one extra. It gave me the creeps to look at these inoffensive animals who, in a few hours, would all be dead. Ah! Little did I know.

2:45. Back we went to the ticket office. No claimers for first place yet. We settled down to wait it out. Soon others came and formed a line.

"Where are the tickets?" I asked.

"Probably in the matadors' pockets," our Ecuadorian Sister said. "Usually neither the city officials nor the matadors trust one another."

Enter a mystery woman. A tall brunette, dressed in black, escorted by two male editions of the same, came by. The three of them walked here and there, passing back and forth, eyeing us, and yet trying desperately to ignore us.

"Who's she?" I asked.

"Not local," said Sister Albert.

The crowd behind us was growing fast. They were always pushing, so one more shove did not matter much. Then we saw Alfonso Paez beside us. He greeted us warmly; we thanked him for the passes.

Sister Albert, with the carnage of the bullfight drawing closer, murmured, "And we'll pray for your safety."

"Thank you, Sister," he replied with a far-off look. "I will need it today."

He introduced his friend, a tall, lean matador known as El Seville, directly from Spain. Both wore rose-colored outfits, lavishly embroidered in gold, tight as their skins, and far too gorgeous to wear to a bloody old bullfight.

A lfonso pounded on the door beside the ticket booth. Eventually, a man with a key wobbled over the field to open it. Plainly he had fortified himself for the afternoon's ordeal. As the two matadors entered the arena Alfonso turned to let me take a picture of him.

"I hope that won't be the last picture he ever has taken," Sister Albert moaned.

The two matadors did have the tickets with them. They went to the ticket windows to instruct the sellers. But still no one would sell tickets.

3:30. The crowd surged forward again. The cause was the third matador. A short, thin fellow from Guatemala, he was dressed in blue satin bedecked with gold. He strode up to the gate before us and pounded

again and again. No result. He
threw his arms out, struck his
breast and shouted, "I am a
matador! I am here to fight the
bulls. Let me at those bulls!"

Sister Maria Esperanza looked
through the crowd behind us,
saw one of her Boy Scouts, and
motioned to him to squeeze his
way to us. We locked our hands
together and hoisted him over
the eight-foot fence.

"Find the gatekeeper. Tell him
to open the door and let the
matador in," she said.

The lad scrambled down the
other side of the fence and ran
for the gatekeeper. In ten
minutes he was back.

"He's out cold," he reported.

"Then go tell Alfonso and the
other matador," Sister said. "Tell
them to put the gatekeeper on
his feet and propel him to the
door. They can hold his hand
until the gate is opened." Which
is just what they did.

4:00. Blueboy slipped through
the gate and so did the woman
in black and her two guards.
They all went straight to the
ticket booth.

"Now the tickets will be sold."
The man at my left breathed
out his relief.

"Why, now?" I asked.

"Ah, you do not know. The
matadors brought the tickets.
The town officials do not trust
the matadors. The matadors do
not trust the town officials. All
want their share of the money.

And that lady in black, nobody trusts her. Now they
are all together. Business will
begin."

He was right. The ticket windows flew up. The gates
opened, and we entered. In the
mad stampede for the roofed-
over stands on either side of the
center field, we managed to use
elbows to good advantage and
secured places on the fourth
bench up.

5:00. The crowds overflowed
the seats and stood in a solid
mass behind the wire which
separated the arena from the
bleachers. Every tree, window,
and wall overlooking the stadium was jammed with free-
loaders. The woman in black
and the two men crossed the
field from one side to the other,
bent on some inscrutable purpose. No one greeted them; they
spoke to no one.

5:15. By now, the crowd was
so jammed up against the doors
that it was impossible to bring
the bulls into the stadium. So
the management decided to
open a large boarded-up double
door in the center. With hammer and machete they pried off
the boards. Even then the door,
large enough to admit a house
trailer, would not swing. Ah, a
crowbar! Pushing mightily on
the door and using the crowbar
as a lever, they strained and
panted. At last! The rusted

hinges broke and the whole half-door fell with a crash.

This posed a problem. The bull could now get in, but how to keep him in? It was solved easily. Seven men on horseback had gone out with a flourish and brought in one bewildered bull. After he wandered in, two men stood at either side of the gaping hole and held a plank across it. This would keep the ferocious bull inside the arena.

The inoffensive animal patiently permitted himself to be tied to a slat in the enclosure they had batted together that afternoon. The matadors started practicing passes at the tied-up bull. El Seville got a little close. The bull lunged and El Seville sprinted up a fence.

Then Blueboy made a few passes with his *capa*. The bull twisted his head and captured the *capa* on one horn. Blueboy took to his heels.

Sister Albert put her hands over her eyes. "I'm not going to look. Don't tell me what's happening, either. I only want to know when it's all over."

Alfonso was waiting for the bull to be free. For what seemed an age, probably five minutes, they eyed each other. The spectators eyed them. The guards at the broken door eyed the situation and noted means of exit. It was a scene of frozen waiting.

There came a mighty roar, a violent lunge. The bull yanked off the plank he was tied to and trotted into the arena with a blue *capa* draped roguishly on one horn and a plank tied round his neck. All three matadors pushed back as far as they could go. The men at the broken door stood on one foot ready to sprint elsewhere. The horsemen edged away with their horses. The audience held its collective breath.

The bull strolled to the center of the field, looked over the spectators, and leisurely walked toward the door, flipping the *capa* jauntily and dragging his plank.

The men at the door dropped their plank and ran in opposite directions. The horsemen fidgeted. The matadors ran to intercept their adversary, but he had a head start. As he neared the exit, he tossed the *capa* off and the plank slid out of the rope, so he picked up speed. After him a furious parade poured out the broken door, horsemen, matadors, guards, and spectators. In the commotion a woman and her four offspring slipped through the gate free!

6:30. We started for home. The bullfight would fizzle out into a lynching perhaps? Muttered threats boded ill for the matadors.

Just outside the gate, we found a pretty situation. A horseman had lassoed the bull and was pulling him up to a tree. Suddenly violent protests came down from the leafy branches. Five men had scrambled up there. Their safety spot turned out to be a hot spot.

Amid yells from below and yells from above, the bull's head was tied tightly to one side of the trunk while the five refugees slid nervously down the other side of it. Laughing and clapping, we spectators found it the best part of the show.

The three matadors now walked around to the pen to choose another bull. El Seville would fight this one. Which one did he want? That one away back in the rear. The attendants looked annoyed. How to get one bull out of a pen crowded with six, however, was their problem, not his.

They solved it brilliantly. How about letting the first five out and then catching the last one? A first-rate idea. The only flaw was that, once the gate was open, all six made a prison break at high speed. In a matter of seconds, only the horsemen and the three matadors were left in the bull pen.

A howl went up from the spectators. The howl re-echoed round the field; it went from bleachers to bleachers; it grew to an angry roar. The crowd surged onto the field.

"What's the idea?" "Beat them up!" "The gyps!" "Hanging's too good."

The police surrounded the matadors and they crawled off to the local jail until the crowd dispersed. Then they went to the local hotel for the night.

By that time, the crowd had something else to ponder. All the ticket money was stolen. The finger of suspicion rested on the lady in black and her two escorts. The town officials thought she was employed by the matadors; and the matadors thought she was working for the officials. In the end, both came to the conclusion that she was a city slicker working for herself. ✤

IN OUR PARISH

In our parish, I am the organist. During the summer, I am faced with a peculiar problem. The motor of the church's air conditioner, which is quite old, hums very audibly in the key of B-flat.

If I play quiet music in any other key, it sounds terrible. I now have a complete "summer repertoire," however; every piece is in the same key as the air conditioner.   Robert M. Beuerlein.

The Mass

The Other Miracle of the Mass

By MAURICE FITZGERALD, C.S.P.
November 1975, condensed from *Eucharist**

M IRACLES, many people think, happen in far-off places and remote times. They believe a person has to travel to Palestine, or Lourdes, or Guadalupe, just for the privilege of breathing the air where miracles have happened. Fortunately, they are mistaken. We can see a miracle each day right in our home town.

That miracle is the Mass. Of course, the central miracle of the Mass is invisible. It is the changing of the bread and wine into the Body and Blood of Christ. But there is another miracle in the Mass, one that can be seen and felt.

The Mass has three parts: it is a sacrifice, a sacrament, and

*Reprinted with permission.

276

a memorial. The sacrifice and sacrament are a matter of faith. The miracle I am talking about is the Mass as a memorial. And it is as wonderful as the miracles of Lourdes.

A miracle is an event that is sensible (something you can see), supernatural (beyond human power to accomplish), and divine (explicable only by an appeal to the power of God). The Mass, considered only as a memorial, fulfills all these conditions. It is not as sensational an event as the stilling of the storm at sea, nor as eye-catching as the multiplication of the loaves and fishes. But what are the chances of an obscure supper in a remote land being remembered and repeated thousands of times, every day, all over the world, 2000 years after its initial occurrence? Considering the odds against it, the Mass could only have been accomplished through divine power.

Man is far more inclined to forget than he is to remember. In life, new events quickly crowd out the old. Politicians learn from experience how soon the favor of yesterday is forgotten. Last year's unforgettable ball game is now recalled only with difficulty. We show the same forgetfulness toward the dead. It is a lesson in humility to realize that after death each person probably will be remembered by only a few relatives and friends for a few years.

But what about the more powerful people of the earth? Are they remembered for long? Ask yourself: Who was the King of Portugal in 1297? Or who was the King of France in the same year? Even the more recent mighty men of America, men like Cleveland, Taft, McKinley, and Coolidge, now are fortunate to be remembered in the little marble statues erected to their honor in their native towns. In Statuary Hall in the rotunda of the national Capitol are exhibited 100 bronze and marble statues of famous Americans. The statues represent the greatest men the U.S. has produced in 200 years of history. Yet most of their names are not even familiar to the Capitol's average visitor.

Indeed, among the billions of people who have lived since the beginning of history, only a handful of names are instantly recognized. Christ, Mary, Alexander the Great, Caesar, Demosthenes, Abraham, Moses, Socrates, Confucius, Mohammed, Buddha, Napoleon, and a few others have survived the oblivion of time. But only one of those names is remembered with a living memorial all over the world every day. That is Jesus. In the midst of all the forgetfulness of men, He has established an unforgettable name and memorial.

Yet it did not seem at the hour of his death that He would be remembered beyond the sunset. He was expiring upon a cross. The disciples whom He had carefully trained had deserted Him. His planned spiritual empire had collapsed in a catastrophe of suffering and death. All human experience dictated that He should have been quickly forgotten after the crucifixion. By what accident or miracle did it happen that his name and life are now perpetuated in a living memorial?

By no stretch of the imagination can the memorial of Christ be called an accident. He planned it, confidently and carefully. Not only was his name to be remembered, but the very purpose of his life and death was to be part of a living memorial that would be meaningful and beneficial to his followers.

What is a living memorial? Unlike a statue, it continues a living presence among men after death. It takes only a moment to recall how Jesus accomplished it. At the Last Supper, He took bread into his hands and said: "This is my body, which is given for you." Then He took a chalice of wine and said: "This is the chalice, the new testament of my blood, which shall be shed for you." At the same meal He said: "Do this in commemoration of Me."

That was all; a few mysterious words and Christ's living memorial was instituted.

After the Last Supper came the difficult and amazing part, the perpetuation of the ritual. The words, "Do this" were the only activating power for the miracle of perpetuation. But because of the divine, sustaining power of grace contained in those words, the living memorial rite of the Last Supper has been extended to billions of celebrations over the centuries, in every nook and corner of the world.

The memorial defies imitation by any other world figure. There is no similar memorial to Buddha or Confucius or Moses or Caesar or Lincoln. There are no groups of people who assemble frequently all over the world to memorialize their names. Only Jesus was powerful enough to say: "Do this in commemoration of Me," and have his command carried out through the centuries among all races and nations of otherwise forgetful men.

The achievement speaks for itself. Miracles described in the New Testament showed the wide difference in power between Jesus and his contemporaries. So the miraculous living memorial today demonstrates the difference in power between Jesus and the most famous names of secular and religious history.

Why doesn't everyone recognize this memorial as a miracle? The answer is demonstrated by history. There were people in New Testament times who witnessed the miracles of Christ, yet refused to accept them as miracles. It should not be surprising, therefore, that in these days of skepticism people can look upon this unique and universal memorial to Christ and not be impressed by its miraculous character. True faith is a gift of God. But disbelievers should recognize simply with their natural faculties that memorials like Christ's could never be established by human power alone. When unbelievers appreciate this miracle then logic will have brought them to the very door of faith. ✠

Once When I Served Mass

The "doting" celebrant could no longer be
exact about rubrics; but at the Consecration
he was still one with the great High Priest

By BRYAN MACMAHON
June 1961, condensed from the *Voice of St. Jude**

THE PLACE was a quiet, almost Victorian resort, catering to a cross section of rural Irish life. One sunny morning I was strolling about, my mind in a state of revolt. I tried to keep away from the church. But as it was the single place alive in the quiet village, I was drawn towards it. On an impulse I blessed myself and entered. I knelt at a pew just inside the door.

A tap on my shoulder. The sacristan's face was pressed close to mine. "Can you serve Mass?"

I gagged the temptation to tell a lie. "Yes!" I mumbled.

"Come with me!" In a narrow passageway the sacristan turned. I noticed the white bris-

---
*This article © 1961 by the Claretian Fathers.

tles on his thin face. "This priest is as old as a bush," he said. "In his day, he was a great man. After he leaves here, likely he'll say Mass no more. Watch him!" he said. The sacristan went away.

For a time I stood in the corner of the sacristy looking at the mountainous curved back of the old priest.

"Son!" he said in a faint croak.

I came forward.

The old man turned his face to where I could see it in profile. I sensed the sagged dentures. I saw the drip of moisture at the end of his nose.

"I'm doting, son. Watch me at the Mass!"

As slowly as I could, I moved before him down the passage and into the church. He came tottering behind me, his bog

279

boots dragging, the chalice weighing down his hands. At the side altar, it cost the old man a great effort to raise his legs over the single step. The Mass began.

Young and brash as I was, my mind in a state of revolt against authority, my body straining at the leash of morality, blasphemy as close to my lips as blessing, it was gradually borne in on me that I was partner in the immeasurable. By the simple act of helping a priest who needed help, I was made to realize that the use of the first person plural in the Latin verbs of the Ordinary was not a mere formality. A strange exaltation took possession of me.

After mumbling the opening psalms and the Confiteor, the old man said *"Oremus,"* again surmounted the obstacle of the step, kissed the sacred stone, touched the missal with unsure fingers, paused, turned and came towards me intoning the *De Profundis,* the psalm recited for the dead after low Mass in Ireland.

After making a few responses, I stopped. "Father!" I said, and tugged at his sleeve.

A pause. There was a sense of groping in the great head above me. "That's right, son!" he said.

I led him up to the altar. I led him to the missal. The soiled leaves and the curled markers riffled under his hands. Together we tried to find the Introit of the day. After a long struggle, we found it. The Introit read, he moved with a deceptive fluency into the Kyrie and Gloria. Again he bent slowly to kiss the altar, turned for the Dominus vobiscum, lost himself in the Collects and the Epistle and again murmuring the *De Profundis,* came towards me.

I did my best to set him to rights. Thus the Mass proceeded.

As we approached the Canon I grew uneasy. The old priest and myself had now been on the altar for the greater part of an hour. I glanced around me. Although the altar was almost hidden behind a large pillar, I could sense that the church was empty. Not even the old sacristan was to be seen. The noise of children playing seeped in from the village. I heard the bark of a sheep dog from the hill above and the *lock-lock* of a creamery cart from the roadway below.

"Te igitur, clementissime Pater...." We were now approaching the very core of sacrifice. I left my place and stood at the side of the altar, narrowly watching the priest.

After the Commemoration of the Living, the priest called hoarsely upon the saints, then paused as if lost. I moved a step nearer.

Almost imperceptibly his head turned in my direction.

I yielded the step.

Now the old hands moved over the oblation. The hands trembled, then steadied. I saw the priest gather himself until he was taut as a mountain is taut. His whispering voice, previously blurred, was now rock steady.

It was as if an army retreating had rallied to a bugle call. Inexplicably one with the old priest, I went to my knees.

"Hoc est enim Corpus meum" — the words of Consecration of the bread came clear, firm.

A moment of relaxation, and again the old priest gathered his forces. Certainty was fiercely concentrated in his voice as he said, *"Hic est enim Calix Sanguinis mei . . ."*

The Consecration over, he idled out again into vagueness and unsureness. I was beside him, guiding, leading, collecting, scolding almost. At last we reached the end. We had been at the altar for an hour and a half.

After the old priest had muttered the *De Profundis,* step after agonizing step he dragged his way back to the sacristy. The sacristan was suddenly at hand to help him doff his vestments. Neither priest nor sacristan looked at me. For this I was thankful. I slipped away. I remember that as I emerged into the village, the sound of tennis balls pocked the morning. ✛

RUSES OF ADVERSITY

There was a good turnout at a rural auction of household goods I attended. One woman was especially interested in the many lamps, vases, and knickknacks. She offered a bid on every item. It wasn't long before she had a large accumulation of smaller articles. When a hideous looking vase was put up, she was the only person to make a bid. "Sold!" shouted the auctioneer. "Sold to the lady with her husband's hand over her mouth."
                                                                Clarence Roeser.

*

A man in North Carolina became fed up with the constant stream of junk mail that was clogging his mailbox every month. Finally he hit upon the idea of scrawling "deceased" on each envelope, and returning it to the post office.

Now his wife is being deluged each day with offers from lonely-hearts clubs.
                                                                W. R. Sutherland.

Ceremonies of the Roman Rite Discarded

We bid a fond farewell to the old liturgical manuals

By ARCHBISHOP ROBERT J. DWYER

August 1972, condensed from *Twin Circle**

T HE PROBLEM confronts every lover of books. One has only so many linear feet of shelving. We contemplated our vanishing space the other day, and our eye fell upon a shelf where the dust had been gathering. We read titles off in a kind of chant, as though we were singing their requiem, as indeed in a sense we were. For the first in line was the *Liber Usualis,* relic of our seminary days, when we sang Gregorian Chant. How we had prized that book when first we acquired it.

We looked forward to converting the heathen tribes of our future parishes to an equal love

of the chant, and for a while, actually, we tried. But today the chant is a casualty of the 2nd Vatican Council. Too many prefer jolly folk tunes and the strumming of the steel guitar.

Next in line was the *Ceremonies of the Roman Rite Described,* by the late Father Adrian Fortescue. It is a handsome book, for Fortescue prided himself on his elegant calligraphy. His illustrations of where the archpriest should (nay, must) stand after the Pater Noster at a Solemn Mass in the presence of a major prelate are works of art, only surpassed in fascination by his graphic demonstration of how the purple cushions should be arranged to fit a corpulent bishop's protuber-

*This article © 1972 by *Catholic Twin Circle.* Reprinted with permission.

ance during the Good Friday prostrations.

We much preferred the English Fortescue to his most prominent American competitor, Father Innocent Wapelhorst, O.F.M., whose book, *Compendium Sacrae Liturgiae,* ranked next. There was division in the seminary; Wapelhorst had his advocates, and was recommended by the learned professor of liturgy as "a safe guide." But the young Turks were all for Fortescue.

Three volumes bound in faded linen proclaimed the *Liturgiae Sacrae Praxis* of P.J. B. De Herdt, "A good sound book," says Fortescue, "rather old-fashioned now, but reliable as far as it goes." Somewhat faint praise.

Next came five volumes, *Sacra Liturgia,* the massive and erudite work of Bishop J.F. Van der Stappen. He knows all and tells it in exhausting detail, omitting no gesture, no modulation of voice.

Then the climax, four stout volumes of the *Manuale Sacrarum Ceremoniarum,* the magisterial opus of Pio Martinucci, Papal Master of Ceremonies under St. Pius X. Here is Roman lucidity at its best, limpid prose, amiable concessions to human weakness (Martinucci looked askance at ceremonies lasting more than five hours, six at the outside).

It was painful to part with these old friends of our youth. Not that they had ever charmed our dozy hours. But we had considered that they always looked well on our shelves and cherished the hope that some day a visitor might pause and exclaim, "Ah, Martinucci!" But no one ever did.

What kind of liturgical manuals will take their place in the Brave New Church? Suppose some liturgical fanatic starts raising questions: Should the balloons released at the Sanctus conform to the color of the day's liturgy? Is there any proper order to be observed in arranging a procession of dancing girls up the aisle on Palm Sunday (pardon, 2nd Sunday of Passiontide), and should they be vested in red or purple? Who is there to say?

Perhaps it was too tight a liturgical world we grew up in. Perhaps it was too minutely regulated. Yet, as we look back, there were few more impressive sights in all the world than a Pontifical Mass well rehearsed and carried out as perfectly as it is given human beings to perform.

Nor did it ever seem that we were puppets worked by strings. We were men united in the reverent and orderly worship of God. There had to be rules, otherwise there would be no dignity. It was the holiest thing we could possibly do; we had to know how to do it, not as sheep, but as men.

We wonder when we see the sloppy, casual Masses offered today with so little grace or dignity or reverence, whether we are not the losers. Could it be that Martinucci will have the last laugh?   ✠

AUNT GERTRUDE'S ROSARY

I was a soldier about to go overseas in the early days of the 2nd World War when I received a rosary from my Aunt Gertrude. This was not unusual. Many men carried rosaries that were gifts. But mine was different. My Aunt Gertrude had made it for me out of cotton cord, dyed a dark blue. She had tied small knots for the Hail Marys, larger ones for the Our Fathers, and an even larger one for the Hail Holy Queen. To it she attached a plastic crucifix.

Her rosary was very handy because I could wear it around my neck and it did not rattle against my dog tags. I could cram it into the smallest pocket and it didn't tangle like a bead rosary would. While I did not exactly monopolize the Blessed Virgin's attention through constant use of it, I had many moments of fear and loneliness, while traveling on troop transports or serving in Europe and Africa, when I sought the comfort of Aunt Gertrude's rosary. I will have to admit, though, that its full value was only revealed to me with time.

I carried the rosary for a long time after the war. Finally the loop that attached the crucifix broke, and the rosary was put away.

Time passed, and then in 1969 my son Tim, who was preparing to go to Vietnam with the Marines, showed me a rosary that the chaplain had given him. I was reminded of Aunt Gertrude's rosary and thought how nice it would be if he could use it. I had a crucifix that had been given to me by a Cursillo director. It meant a lot to me and was just the right size for Aunt Gertrude's rosary. I joined the two and gave it to Tim in exchange for the one he had received from the Chaplain. We agreed to trade back when he returned from Vietnam. That wasn't to happen. Tim came home but the rosary didn't.

One night Tim was on watch while his unit was bivouacked in a hostile area. He was relieved by another Catholic boy and lent him the rosary for comfort. An incoming mortar hit the area where Tim had been, killing the other boy. The rosary was never found.

Aunt Gertrude's gift of love had been a great source of comfort to both Tim and me. Only God knows what it meant to the boy who was killed.

Jim Donahoe.

Since the Last Supper

A Pocket History of the Mass

"Changes" have been going on since the beginning

By THOMAS MCMAHON
October 1978, condensed from *The Mass Explained**

O UR CATHOLIC MASS is as old as Christianity itself. The first Mass was, of course, on Holy Thursday.

1. The Last Supper

Our knowledge of what the first Mass was like comes from two sources: the accounts we have in the Gospels of the Last Supper, and what we know of the Jewish Passover meal. Essentially it is the Paschal meal with the Last Supper words of Our Lord at the time of eating the bread and drinking the wine.

The Paschal meal had quite a lot of ritual surrounding it. Before the meal proper, bitter

herbs and unleavened bread were served with a cup of wine. This frugal diet recalled the hunger of the people during their journey out of Egypt. Then the son or youngest member of the family would ask what this meant. The father of the house, with a prayer of thanksgiving to God, then told of their liberation from bondage in Egypt. This ended with the singing of Psalms 112 and 113, during which the people answered "Alleluia."

After this the meal proper began. The father of the house took some of the unleavened bread, broke it, said a blessing over it and passed it around. This was a sign of their brotherly communion in the one bread and it marked the beginning of the meal. It was over

*This article © 1977 by Mayhew-McCrimmon. Reprinted by permission of Carillon Books.

285

this bread that Our Lord said, "This is my body, which is given up for you." Then the Paschal lamb was eaten.

When the meal was over, again the father of the house took the cup filled with wine, raised it up slightly while he said the grace after the meal, and then all drank from it, and recited Psalms 113 and 135. It was at this point that Our Lord said, "This is my blood of the new and everlasting Covenant."

We can see clearly the pattern of the Last Supper. The consecration of the bread is connected with the blessing before the eating of the lamb, signifying "common-union" or "Communion," and the consecration of the chalice is connected with the grace after the meal.

2. Mass of the Apostles

Our Lord ended the Last Supper by saying, "Do this in memory of me." How was this to be carried out? Before the year 150 we have only glimpses and hints. We do have various references in the Gospels and three references in the Acts of the Apostles.

First of all we know that the celebration was separated from the Jewish rite of Passover, partly because of all the ceremonial surrounding it, but also because the Paschal celebration was restricted by law to once a year.

At an early date Christians brought together the two consecrations. In the Paschal meal there was a gap between the two: "When supper was ended He took the cup...." But, in the account by Matthew and Mark the two consecrations are already together. One clue is the name by which this new event was known: "The breaking of bread." Christians still joined in worship at the Temple in order to pray and listen to the Scriptures, but then followed it by something new which only Christians did, "continuing daily with one accord in the Temple, and breaking bread in their homes." (Acts 2:46).

There is a delightful account in a later chapter when Christians came together one Sunday evening at Troas, "for the breaking of bread" (Acts 20:7), and St. Paul preached a very long sermon which went on until midnight. During the sermon a young man sitting on the window sill fell asleep and so fell out the window from the third floor to the ground, and died. Happily St. Paul brought him back to life again.

Although one cannot be certain, it would appear that this early Mass was usually in the context of a meal, which would be combined with the memorial meal and the essential sacramental rite which Christ had conferred upon it. For early Christians a meal was always a religious occasion and this would make it especially so. The Corinthians certainly combined it with a meal. When on one occasion they had eaten and drunk too much, St. Paul admonished them that they were not in a fit state for the sacramental part of the meal: "He is eating and drinking damnation to himself if he eats and drinks unworthily, not recognizing the Lord's Body for what it is." (I Cor. 11:29).

Therefore, the elements that that composed this early Mass would include: (a) a meal setting; (b) the grace and prayer of Thanksgiving, introduced by the invitation which we still have before the Preface, "Lift up your hearts . . . let us give thanks to the Lord our God"; (c) the two consecrations.

Gradually the meal setting was abandoned, for two reasons. First, the prayer of thanksgiving in this new Christian assembly was no longer just one of thanksgiving for the gifts of food and drink, but one which recalled the goodness of God in all his gifts and especially in redeeming us. Second, the gathering had grown too large for an intimate meal in the home. Thus the meal stopped, and the Eucharistic celebration remained alone. Only one table

was required for the celebrant, leaving room for all the people. There would be only one Eucharistic celebration in each congregation.

Up to this time it had been the Jewish custom to hold these meals in the evening, but now that the meal had been separated from the holy Eucharist the people could meet at any time. Later the custom grew of meeting early in the morning on Sunday. As the people greeted the rising sun they thought of the risen Christ. An early hour also helped them to avoid notice. Gradually the tie with the Temple was broken, and after the break with the Synagogue and the persecutions in the year 44, Scripture readings were added before the Eucharist.

3. The Year 150

St. Justin, philosopher and martyr, wrote the first full account of the Mass which followed Christian Baptism. He was living in Rome.

"After we have baptized him who professes our belief and associates with us, we lead him into the assembly of those called the brethren and there say prayers in common for ourselves, for the newly-baptized, and for all others all over the world. After the prayers we greet one another with a holy kiss.

Then bread and a cup of water and wine mixed are brought to the one presiding over the brethren. He takes it, gives praise and glory to the Father of all in the name of the Son and of the Holy Ghost and gives thanks at length for the gifts that we were worthy to receive from Him. When he has finished the prayers and thanksgiving the whole crowd standing by cries out in agreement, 'Amen.' *Amen* is a Hebrew word meaning, 'So may it be.'

"After the presiding official has said thanks and the people have joined with him, the deacons, as they are styled by us, distribute as food for all those present the bread and the wine mixed with water over which thanks had been offered. These also are carried to those not present. This food is known among us as the Eucharist. No one may partake of it unless he is convinced of the truth of our teaching and is cleansed in the bath of Baptism.

"And on that day which is called after the sun, all who are in the town and in the country gather together for a communal celebration, and the memoirs of the Apostles or the writings of the prophets are read as long as time permits. After the reader has finished his task, the presiding official gives an address, urgently admonishing his hearers to practice these beautiful teachings in their lives. Then all stand up together and recite prayers.

"Following the prayers, as has been shown above, the bread and wine are brought and the one presiding offers up prayers and thanks, as much as in him lies. The people chime in with 'Amen.' Then takes place the distribution to all attending of the things over which the thanksgiving has been spoken. The deacons bring a portion to the absent. Besides, those who are well-to-do give whatever they will. All that is gathered is deposited with the one presiding, who therewith helps orphans and widows."

In this account there is great emphasis on "giving thanks," and hence the name *Eucharist* from the Greek, which means "to give thanks." There is a sense of oneness between priest and people, and their loud cry "Amen" at the end of the Eucharistic prayer puts their seal on all the priest does. Together with the prayer of thanksgiving there is present at this time, though not so clearly expressed, the idea of sacrifice for the purpose of rendering thanks.

The Mass of the first three centuries was still very flexible. There was a unified order and a set framework, but for many of the prayer-texts the priest was allowed to use his own words.

However, the design of the great Eucharistic prayer of thanksgiving was always the same, beginning with the short dialogue, as we have before the Preface, and ending with the great Amen. And so emerges a liturgy with a certain unity and structure, and yet with flexibility. We already find these elements:

1. Lessons taken from the Apostles. 2. Sermon following on the readings. 3. Prayers of intercession. 4. The kiss of peace. 5. The Eucháristic prayer, a prayer of thanksgiving and praise. 6. Communion under both kinds for all. 7. A collection of money for the poor.

The priest used the language of the people and wore no special clothes when celebrating. The vestments he wears now were the ordinary clothes of those days.

4. Mass in the 4th century

In the East. Within the Greek territory of the Eastern end of the Mediterranean, certain areas, such as Alexandria and Antioch, began to dominate. Particular liturgies spread from these centers, together with stricter control of worship. More and more of the text was set down in writing.

We do have a Mass from this period, and it begins with readings from Scripture, a homily, prayers of intercession, and a benediction. Then follows the Eucharistic prayer, beginning with: "Fit it is and proper to praise, to glorify, and to exalt thee, the everlasting Father of the only-begotten, Jesus Christ." The end of the prayer mentions the angels of God and ends with the familiar "Holy, holy, holy Lord of Sabaoth, heaven and earth are full of his glory."

There was also a greater emphasis upon sacrificial worship. At the time of St. Basil, in the late 4th century, there was a growing consciousness of sin and increasing reverence which led to fewer people receiving Holy Communion. This was probably the result of Arianism (Arius denied the divinity of Christ and his views were condemned at the Council of Nicea), which led to a renewed emphasis by the Church on Christ's divinity.

Awe is discernible right through to the Middle Ages. A greater gulf grew between priest and people and between sanctuary and nave. The proceedings at the altar were considered not so much as something in which to take part, but as a miracle to be regarded with wonder. The ceremonial rites which had surrounded the Emperor Constantine at Court were now transferred to the Mass. Hence the use of incense and torches (marks of honor), prostration and bowing, processions, and elaborate vestments. The altar rail between priest and people became more elaborate until it finally developed into the *ikonostasis,* the screen which set aside the sanctuary as a "holy place."

In the West. For the Greek period of the Roman Mass we have guides like St. Justin, but in the West we have very little to go on. Once the language of the Mass had changed from Greek into Latin, it remained in the Latin language alone. The texts were many and varied according to the season of the Church. These gradually developed into our present Roman Canon of the Mass (Eucharistic Prayer I), which is quoted by St. Ambrose as far back as the 4th century. The terms themselves, "Roman Mass" or "Roman Canon," mean "as done in the city and diocese of Rome."

It is from this time also that we have the three prayers: Collect, Prayer over the Offerings, and Post-Communion prayer. The Kyrie was substituted for the prayers of intercession, since many of these prayers were contained in the Canon itself. There were processional chants at the beginning, at the Offertory, and at the Communion, and shorter chants between the lessons. The framework of the Roman Mass had been determined by the turn of the 5th century.

5. The Papal Mass (6th–7th Centuries)

This is so-called because Pope Gregory the Great reformed the Roman liturgy. The papacy of those days was a great political as well as spiritual power, and it was easy to have the rights and honors of a king conferred upon the Pope. Ceremonials which really came from the Byzantine-Roman court crept into the Mass: genuflecting, kissing, bowing, and such marks of distinction as incense, candles, and the ring. Pope Gregory introduced the Gregorian chant which would accompany the entry, Offertory, and Communion. It was too difficult for the people to sing, so that was left to the clergy.

6. The 8th–11th Centuries

In the time of Charlemagne, Church and State almost became one. Charlemagne imposed Catholicism and the Latin liturgy on all his empire. There was great reverence for the Eucharist. About this time pure white wafers were introduced, as they could be broken easily without the worry of crumbs from the consecrated bread falling to the ground.

The Offertory procession became rare, and instead of the breaking of bread for the people's Communion within the Mass, this was done beforehand, or, alternatively, small hosts such as we have now were provided. Receiving Holy Communion on the tongue instead of in the hand became normal practice, and people received kneeling down. Thus the altar rail was introduced.

But priests and people found the kind of Mass imposed by Charlemagne rather too classical and arid. They began to add their own prayers, such as Psalm 42 and a number of Offertory prayers. Genuflections and Signs of the Cross were added, and the Gospel of St. John at the end of the Mass. So what began as private devotions slowly became part of the official liturgy.

7. The 12th–15th Centuries

More and more the people at Mass had been reduced to spectators. The priest had taken over the roles of reader and chanter, and silent prayers said by the priest to himself had appeared. Unable to understand or enter into the liturgical meaning of all the priest was doing, the people began to see meaning in his external actions as he moved from one part of the altar to another, and in the gestures of the Mass.

They applied a pious imagination to interpreting all these things. The five Signs of the Cross during the Canon came to represent the five wounds of Christ; the priest turning round to the people five times during Mass became the five appearances of Christ. The back of the chasuble was embroidered with pictures.

To correct a contemporary heresy denying the real presence of Christ, emphasis was laid upon the Consecration, and the bread and wine were elevated. People became obsessed with seeing the host and would rush from church to church as the outdoor bell signaled the Consecration; they would adore the host and then leave. There were prayers to be said while looking upon the host.

It was from this that other forms of devotion such as Benediction, processions, and expositions of the Blessed Sacrament arose. There was a multiplication of guild chapels and chantry chapels (where Mass was "chanted" for the dead). In early Rome the people had broken bread in their homes; in the early centuries there were domestic chapels dedicated to the memory of certain martyrs. In later centuries house chapels were common among the rich.

From the house Mass is but a short step to the private Mass. In large monasteries, there would be a series of side altars where each monk would celebrate, while in the town churches there were guild chapels for the various guilds. Also there were votive Masses to be said, Masses for the earnest concerns (*vota*) of the faithful, and especially for the dead. Since these were not the concern of the whole congregation they were said privately.

8. The Tridentine Mass

The Council of Trent in 1545 set itself to define true Catholic doctrine, as a defense against abuse and heresy, and to restore true Christian life within the Church.

For the first time in the history of the Mass, ceremonies were prescribed down to the smallest detail. Rubrics told the priest how he was to keep thumb and finger joined after the Consecration. Everything was to be in complete uniformity throughout the whole Church.

Pius V published an edition of the breviary and missal to be used in the Roman liturgy, and his successor created the Sacred Congregation of Rites to ensure uniformity throughout.

These measures rendered great service in safeguarding the Mass from personal innovations and individual exaggerations. The people, however, unable to take an active part in this great mystery, began to express their own personal devotion in extra-liturgical ways such as novenas, devotions to the Sacred Heart, 40 hours' devotions.

These appealed to the people, because hymns were sung and the prayers were in the local language. But there was an absolute prohibition even to translate the Mass books until just before 1900. It was only in our own century that the people were allowed to read the prayers of the Mass in a missal along with the priest.

9. From Pius X to Vatican II

From 1903 on, changes began to appear which led to the major liturgical reforms of the Vatican Council. One of the greatest of these was a decree in 1905 encouraging a return to the practice of the ancient Church regarding Communion. Once again Holy Communion was seen as an integral part of the Mass, and people were encouraged to receive Communion each time they attended Mass. It was at this time also that children over the age of discretion were permitted to receive Communion.

When the people had a text with which to follow the Mass, they wanted to recite together the parts which really belonged to them. The first uniform text of all the prayers to be read in common was published in 1929, although it was very slow to be adopted by the whole Church. It led to what became known as the "dialogue Mass." Gradually various parts which had been taken over by the choir went back to the people.

Until the Vatican Council, changes were very gradual. In 1955 the ceremonies of Holy Week were restored, and in 1957 permission was given for evening Mass, and new regulations for the fast before Communion were introduced.

10. Vatican II

The word *aggiornamento*, as used by Pope John, means renewal or adaptation, not innovation. It means going back to liturgical principles and being guided solely by them in making any changes.

Christian worship in the very beginning presupposed full participation by the congregation.

The priest led the service, but readers, choir, and servers all took their full part in it. The people were involved in the Offertory and Communion processions, and many of the prayers were in the form of a dialogue between priest and people. But during the Middle Ages the people came to take a less active part.

First of all, they no longer knew the language of the liturgy. By then, the Introit was no longer an entrance procession but a verse of a Psalm recited by the priest at the altar. The readings were no longer intelligible, and were recited by the priest with his back to the people. The Offertory contained a great many prayers and no procession. The Canon was prayed in silence. A Gospel reading was added at the very end of the Mass, and additional prayers (the three Hail Mary's and other prayers) by Leo XIII. People came along now not so much to take part as "to hear" Mass.

So in the Constitution on the Liturgy, the 2nd Vatican Council stated: "The rite of the Mass is to be revised in such a way that the intrinsic nature and purpose of its several parts, as also the connection between them, can be more clearly manifested, and so that devout and active participation by the faithful can be more easily accomplished. For this purpose the rites are to be simplified, while due care is taken to preserve their substance. Elements which, with the passage of time, came to be duplicated or were added with little advantage are now to be discarded. When opportunity allows or necessity demands other elements which have suffered injury through accidents of history are now to be restored."

The prayers at the foot of the altar (Psalm 42), which originally the priest was supposed to say on the way from the sacristy to the altar, and which had grown into the Mass, were to be removed. The Introit was to be once again the hymn to accompany the entrance procession. There was to be one act of penance for both priest and people, instead of the priest saying the Confiteor by himself, followed by the people saying it and even repeating it again just before Communion.

The lessons were once again to be read by the reader, in the vernacular and with both an Old Testament and a New Testament lesson. The prayers of intercession, which were there as far back as the year 150 in the account of the Mass by St. Justin, were to be restored.

For the litany of the Eucharist the priest was to face the people as he did in the early Church, so that they could see and respond. Once again there was to be a real Offertory procession and hymn; and, instead of five long Offertory prayers, two simple prayers inspired by those Christ would have said at the Jewish Passover meal. There were to be three additional Eucharistic prayers, all of them drawing heavily upon similar prayers in the very early Church.

The whole rite was to be simpler, with fewer genuflections, fewer Signs of the Cross, and kissing the altar only at the beginning and end. The ancient custom of acclaiming the Risen Christ after the Consecration was to be revived, as was the kiss of peace. The dismissal was to come in its rightful place at the very end of the Mass instead of before the blessing.

The Gospel of St. John was removed from the end of the Mass, since it was originally part of the priests' private thanksgiving and had grown into the Mass, and was rather incongruous outside the liturgy of the Word. The prayers which followed (three Hail Mary's, Hail Holy Queen) had all been added successively by Leo XIII, Pius IX, and Pius X and were dropped, since the Mass had ended with the dismissal, and the appropriate place to pray for any special intention was during the prayers of intercession. Four years after the Council, all these recommendations were implemented by the Apostolic Constitution *Missale Romanum* (April, 1969) which set the form of the Mass that we now have.   ✚

SENTIMENTAL JOURNEY

Then there's the story of the boy born on the lower East Side of New York to poverty-stricken immigrant parents. He grew up and married a neighborhood girl, and they had several children. For years he struggled; then all of a sudden his luck changed.

He became enormously successful in business. He became tremendously wealthy. He owned steel mills, oil refineries, railroads. He had a home in Miami, penthouse in New York City, a villa on the Riviera, an estate in Rome. But he never forgot.

Every year he goes back to the East Side, just to visit his wife and children.   Steve Allen in *Parade* (29 Nov. '59).

THE EDITED VERSION

A father explained to his seven-year-old daughter that her mother had found a lovely baby sister early that morning among the cabbages. "Now," he said, "you write your brother Jack (away in the Army) and tell him about it."

The child wrote the letter and gave it to her father to mail. He couldn't resist peeking to read her childish explanation. "Dear Jack," the letter read. "It's a girl. You owe me a buck."   *National Enquirer.*

*

An obstetrician and a surgeon had just delivered a baby by Caesarian section. It was an especially difficult case. When the danger was past, the anesthetist asked, "Was it a boy or a girl?" Neither of the weary doctors knew.

A young student nurse standing nearby spoke up shyly. "Let me see the baby. I can tell."   Roberta Rich.

*

In a beauty shop window: "We curl up and dye for you."
                                            Mrs. Carolyn Moore.

*

The cheapest way to have your family tree traced is to run for office.
                                                        Quote.

When Mrs. Kerrigan Saw an Angel

"A miracle, Father!" she shouted. "Big and
white and beautiful!"

By MARTY KELLY
January 1978

I T WAS A bright Sunday morning, many years ago, and the young priest at St. Ann's Cathedral in Great Falls, Mont., made an unusual announcement at Mass. The subject was pigeons. They had to go, he said. They had become so numerous that their droppings covered the statue of Our Lord on the front of the church like a shroud. Also, all the stained glass windows around the building had pigeon droppings crusted on their broad sills like dried kelp after high tide.

When folks went out to look and examine for themselves, they were aghast. Apparently

nobody had even looked up that high in years. The priest was right. Still, no one wanted the beautiful, gentle birds destroyed. But what to do?

The problem came up in city council meetings, and at the school board. Some elected officials suggested poisoning the soft, gray pets, but they were met with cries of outrage. Others considered trapping them to feed the animals at the dog pound, but the dog pound was despised by every decent member of society to begin with.

One bold member of the parish council personally arranged to have the fire department bring up their equipment one bright day to blast the church with water, full force, front and back and across the spires. Monsignor Callahan came running out wildly just in time to save the stained glass windows.

After weeks of searching, a daredevil but nonprofessional cleaning crew was located, and began a complete scrubdown of the cathedral and the attached rectory. But after Mike Rafferty fell off the ladder and broke two legs, and Johnny Rearden tumbled into the church through an open window while scraping down a lumpy ledge, the parish council decided to wait until spring and hire a real steeplejack from Butte to take charge of the job.

We turned our eyes from the defacement of our dear St. Ann's and attended to the details of the fall festival.

With the arrival of winter we had to concentrate on practical things like keeping warm. Not many houses were heated by gas, and the winters were stiff. Icicles hung in huge threatening stalactites, and occasionally, during a sudden Chinook, somebody got crowned by a tent pole of solid ice. That year the editor of the daily paper predicted we were in for an especially hard winter, and urged everybody to lay in a substantial supply of San Cou-

lee nugget coal if they hadn't already done so.

Christmas came and went. January began with an old-fashioned blizzard. Then the thermometer "dropped out at the bottom." Kids went to school, bundled to the teeth, but finally the janitors despaired of the heating and closed the schools for a spell.

Windows froze over in thick coats of ice. Mothers pasted brown paper across the bottom panes, then drew heavy drapes or hung sheets to hold back the chill. The sun shone bleakly during the middle of the day, then sank into a smother of dusk about three o'clock in the afternoon.

Children played outside until their noses ran and their cheeks were as red as their chapped hands. Many a hapless juvenile touched his tongue to the garden gate or metal door knob and learned of the searing fire that accompanies the loss of taste buds on a frosty surface.

It was one particularly frigid afternoon during Confession, when old Mrs. Kerrigan ran screaming into the church, practically falling down in her frenzy.

"Father!" she shouted. "I seen an angel flying down from the belfry just now! I seen it myself this very minute! Big and white and beautiful! A miracle, Father, a miracle! Heaven be praised!" And she fell on her knees at the altar rail and tried to say the Rosary.

But the church was in an uproar. Other penitents had risen from their knees, atonement temporarily suspended, and headed outside; and Monsignor Callahan, muttering, hastily departed the confessional and strode for the big front doors.

Outside in the freezing night, there was nothing. People stood silently, listening and waiting until the cold began to ossify them. Finally, deeply disappointed, they returned to the church vestibule where they lingered in little groups to discuss the miracle.

Confessions resumed, the sinners came and went, and old Mrs. Kerrigan knelt as long as she could, until somebody kindly offered her a ride home and assisted her out. The poor old lady was beside herself, but she wouldn't retract her words. She had seen an angel!

L ater that night, all should have been at peace at the rectory. Monsignor Callahan and Fathers Dunn and O'Brien were quietly reading their breviaries in their rooms.

Then suddenly came a sound of the whapping and flapping of big wings outside, close by. The resident pigeons cuddled closer among the chimneys and burbled distractedly. Their frosty cries pierced the night air.

Peering through the heavy curtains at his window, Monsignor saw something large and white loom on the other side of the glass. He couldn't distinguish anything through the thick ice on the pane, but what he had seen stunned him. He dropped the curtain and stood there, dumbfounded. When he peeked again, it was gone.

He considered hurrying outside to have a look-around, but he was in his robe and comfortable old carpet slippers, and this was no time to test their efficiency. Anyway, it was gone, whatever it was.

He spent a troubled hour while trying to get to sleep, meditating and wondering. Was he frightened? Not really. He was more perplexed than anything.

D ownstairs for early Mass, then to breakfast. He hadn't told the others. In the cold, gray dawn, the anxiety of the previous evening took on a foolish aspect, and Monsignor was not eager to become the sport of the two younger priests.

Mrs. Kerrigan received Communion that morning. Monsignor felt sorry for her when he saw her worn and pious face. He wondered briefly if those two young rogues Dunn and O'Brien could be running a little spoof on him. They were everlastingly up to something, which made them a joy to be around, but this was such a silly situation. Angel, indeed! He tried to dismiss the thought, but it pestered him all during the day.

While he was lining up the memorial Masses for the coming week, Mrs. Woods, the dumpy little English woman who kept house at the rectory, came into the study with an apologetic curtsey and murmered hesitantly, "Monsignor, the pigeons are either all gone or struck dumb today. Have you noticed? I usually hear them fretting and fussing at the upstairs windows, but there hasn't been a sign of them this morning. What would you make of it, do you think?"

Monsignor listened to her and smiled gently. "Maybe Mrs. Kerrigan's angel took them all to glory. Heaven knows the poor things are having a hard time of it this winter. No, I hadn't noticed, Mrs. Woods, but they will be out and around when the sun comes up a bit. Aren't they always?" And he returned to his calculations. The cold got colder. The mercury went down to 42 below. A couple of large boulevard trees split open with resounding cracks one night, and they had to be hauled out of the street until the city could get rid of them. But by the time the street crew got there, the trees had been sawed by eager residents and stowed in cellars.

Kids all over town were pulling sleds behind them, heading for terraced lawns and sunken vacant lots for belly whopping. Mailmen frosted their faces while making their appointed rounds. Grocery boys cussed like pirates to each other as they delivered orders, for driving was hazardous and most of the stuff froze in the trucks. Chimneys smoked in tall, straight spirals, and at evening, it was beautiful to see.

Then one afternoon some little girls on their way home from school thought they saw something big and white and "holy looking" spread its wings and settle on a window sill at St. Ann's. They ran home and regaled their parents with contradictory stories. There were numerous telephone calls and questions at the rectory.

In his study, Monsignor pondered. At suppertime, the priests talked about the unusual silence of the pigeons. "Just too cold for them, I guess," Father Dunn observed.

But after he had gone to bed, it was but a short while before he knocked hastily on Monsignor's door.

"There's something outside, Monsignor," he explained. "I heard this scratching at my window and when I looked out through the ice, I could barely see a white shape standing there. I tried to open the window but it was frozen tight.

"Just now I slipped out to see

if I could see anything. It's bright moonlight, and believe it or not, there really was a big shadow of something swooping around to the back of the church. It gave me the willies. I wonder if we oughta call the police, or the bishop?"

Monsignor, watching Dunn's face, knew there was no trickery there. He tapped his fingers gently, then replied in a comforting fashion, "Well, I think tomorrow will be soon enough." Then he told him about Mrs. Kerrigan's angel, and the young priest, who hadn't been informed, stared at him in delight.

"An angel! Really? Well, why not?" And he returned to his room, chuckling, but Monsignor sat quietly tapping and pondering. Of course Father Dunn told Father O'Brien and they looked out through the iced-over windows from every angle, but saw nothing more. It was an intriguing thought—an angel in the window at St. Ann's. What for? They laughed and said good night again.

Morning brought the answer. In those days, news was spread mostly by telephone and word of mouth. Newspaper writers traveled on foot to interview and photograph objects of interest, and although the public was informed of anything unusual, it sometimes took a few

days before the news went to press.

And so, it took a lot of chasing back and forth before the townspeople discovered that Great Falls had unexpectedly become host to a stranded flight of great snowy owls. Betrayed by their instinct and the intense cold, they had been swept from their own natural habitat in the Arctic, and had landed exhausted and battered in our city beside the frozen Missouri River.

They settled on lawns and among the trees, perched on porches and, of course, on rooftops. Because they were unaccustomed to humankind, they knew no fear. They began hunting for food, and owing to the lack of lemmings and other choice owlfare, they gorged themselves on the most plentiful prey in the area. Overpopulated and complacent, the pigeons were almost wiped out, as well as a few careless alley cats and one small dog that noisily goaded a mother owl from her territorial perch on a frozen snow drift.

The men at St. Ann's organized a search of the grounds with the enthusiastic assistance of at least a dozen kids from the parochial school. Sure enough, roosting high and dry, like celestial guardians, stood three large, white owls. They were almost three feet tall, looking more like seven. And when their wings were spread for business, it was no wonder the children believed they had witnessed an apparition.

When the first warming breath of Chinook wind swept over the frozen prairies, the feathered freeloaders took their bearings, and headed back to the north country. They had been stranded here almost a month. In two days, they were gone.

It was years before the pigeon colony recovered from the slaughter. Young boys hunted for, and coveted, the little hard knots of feathers and grit and bones which the owls discarded after meals each day.

In time, St. Ann's clean-up crew scoured the outside of the building and a steeplejack from Butte put up a nice, wide-mesh screen around the statue of Our Blessed Lord. It would be protected forever.

And Mrs. Kerrigan? To this day, she staunchly maintains that she saw an angel in the window at St. Ann's.   ✳

PEOPLE ARE LIKE THAT

When I was nine my family was desperately poor. Many of our meals were bowls of oatmeal. To distract myself while I ate, I'd stare at the beautiful doll pictured on the cereal box. There was little hope of getting it since my mother used all the coupons to redeem household necessities.

One evening before Christmas, my Mom and I were window-shopping when I saw *the doll* — an exact replica of the one on the oatmeal box. Pulling Mom closer to the window, I pointed to the beautiful doll with outstretched arms. Mother shook her head, and I turned away, my heart heavy.

On Christmas morning, I walked down the stairs thinking of the awful oatmeal we'd have for breakfast. But I entered a kitchen that had been transformed. The table was covered with lace and adorned with a little potted evergreen centerpiece. Propped against the tree was my doll.

Since then there have been many Christmases that money has made more festive, but that Depression Christmas means the most to me. It's memory lingers bittersweet, for my mother died shortly afterward. Years later my aunt told me that my mother begged the premium store manager to let her work to earn the display model. The doll now has a place of honor in my home — a cherished symbol of a mother's love for her child.

S. E. McDonald.

The Drunk Who Didn't Drink

The doctors wouldn't believe me

By CHARLES SWAART
January 1978, condensed from *The Arizona Republic**

I HAVE COME off what might be the world's record binge: I was under the influence of alcohol three times a day, every day, for almost 30 years. Yet I do not drink.

For more than 20 years, teams of specialists in leading medical centers from coast to coast put me through tests ranging from the routine to the most exotic. Somewhere along the line, each doctor made his joke: "We don't know what you have, but if we can bottle it, we'll make a million."

Friends envied me: "Look what you save on liquor bills." It was all very funny to everyone, except to me and my family. Even when I felt normal, we lived in dread. Always, there was that fear of

unexpected and unpredictable drunkenness.

Spells of intoxication jeopardized my professional life. My speech slurred. In business conferences I became opinionated, even rude. At times I talked and wrote total nonsense. In a letter of reference, one former employer gave a glowing account of my abilities and achievements, concluding with, "He is a genius—if you can keep him sober." I did not get the job.

We dreaded social engagements. I argued and became insulting at the drop of a remark. Following one dinner-theater party, the police picked me up and threw me in the drunk tank overnight. Although our attorney convinced the court my symptoms were caused by an illness, such performances did not endear me as a guest.

Even our family life was disrupted. Attacks brought a sudden change in personality. "I never knew what to expect," my wife Betty recalls. "Before my eyes, my dignified, considerate, and loving husband would turn sloppy, overbearing, and hostile — sometimes even violent."

I do not know how she stuck by me all those years. She endured the misplaced sympathy of friends who assured her they knew what she was going through. She battled doctors who labeled me "a sneaky drinker."

Although I had attacks as far back as 1945, it was in the spring of 1954 that I first realized I could get drunk without so much as a short beer. I had suffered severe liver damage from a prolonged attack of viral hepatitis. My internist warned me not to touch anything alcoholic for at least two years. I followed his advice to the letter. And got drunk.

My doctor put me back in the hospital for a total check. When he found no explanation, he called in other specialists. They found nothing wrong except that lab tests showed alcohol in my blood and on my breath. I swore I did not drink. Most of the doctors had a handy explanation for this seeming contradiction: the patient is lying. Likely, he is an alcoholic.

But not all of them ruled me alcoholic. A neurologist concluded I had myasthenia gravis, a then little publicized and mysterious disease of the nerves and muscles.

A pair of internists gave me six months to live with cancer of the liver. I quit my job so Betty and I could tour the country visiting family and friends. When, a year later, I was still alive, and another team of specialists found no sign of cancer anywhere, I went back to work.

A urologist discovered I had an enlarged kidney, a result of stones accumulated over a lifetime, and wanted to remove it. Since he admitted removing my kidney would not solve the problem of my mysterious drunkenness, and because I had never had a single symptom of kidney stones, I refused.

Only one physician believed I did not drink. She is Dr. Frances Sierakowski, a general practitioner who has been our family doctor for years. On her own, she researched medical literature and developed theories to explain the attacks. She referred me to specialists who checked out her theories and generated some of their own. None could be verified.

One of her theories did bring some relief. She decided my weight had to be cut from 240 pounds to a normal 170, and put me on a high protein diet. My attacks became less frequent and less severe. Nobody knew why.

Then, from an unexpected and unlikely source, came the first real clue. In the autumn of 1968, after a business conference, one of my associates noticed I did not join in the round of highballs. I explained I could get drunk on an Italian dinner. "I've read about a case like that in one of the medical journals," he said. I told him dozens of specialists had searched medical literature for years without finding a similar case and that he must be mistaken.

The next afternoon he telephoned me. "You were right and the doctors were right," he said. "There is no record of a case like yours in the scientific medical literature. The case like yours was reported in *Time Magazine* in its medical section, July 20, 1959."

I rushed to the library, dug out the issue of *Time*, and, under the heading "The Secret Still," read the article.

"Kozo Ohishi, 46, went home to Pippu in northern Japan last week, celebrating with proud sobriety the end of a 25-year binge during which he 'never touched a drop,'" the article began.

It told how Ohishi felt flushed and giddy, and his head got heavy, "like a sake hangover," soon after he ate bread or potatoes. Friends reproached him for secret drinking. During the war "his officers abused him for drunkenness, while enlisted buddies searched in vain for his source of booze."

Six doctors in a row refused to believe him when he said he did not drink, and they would not treat him. Even his family wrote him off as a sly, solitary drinker. Finally, doctors put him on a series of test diets. When he ate meats, poultry, and fish, he was normal. When he ate rice, pastas, and bread, he got drunk.

Then, in samples of Ohishi's digestive juices, microbiologists found the culprit: a flourishing growth of a yeastlike fungus, *Candida albicans*. The yeast hid in Ohishi's bowel, multiplied, "and busily fermented carbohydrates to form alcohol."

Of all the specialists who had examined and treated me over the years, none had ever tested for the existence of Candida. I had traveled all over Japan and Korea for a year after the war, serving on General Douglas MacArthur's headquarters news staff. Could I have picked up some of Ohishi's yeast?

I took the article to Dr. Sierakowski. The lab tests she ordered showed massive colonies of yeast in my intestines. A course of treatment with the drug Mycostatin seemed to wipe out my Candida. For the first time in years, I went months without feeling intoxicated.

I was exultant, but my wife was troubled. "There have been thousands of Americans stationed in Japan since the end of the war," she said. "I just can't believe you are the only one who picked up the Candida. If there are others going through all we had to go through to find a diagnosis and cure, you simply have to write your story so their doctors will know what to look for."

So I began researching in highly scientific medical books and articles. The authorities agreed that Candida exist all over the world. They estimate that from 40 to 60% of the population have colonies in their intestines. Most often, even when found in patients with other ailments, Candida are viewed as harmless free-loaders. But under certain circumstances, they can become lethal.

Debilitating chronic diseases — cancer, diabetes, tuberculosis — can so weaken a patient's resistance that the Candida take over and cause death. Widespread use of broad-spectrum antibiotics may clear the way for increased Candida infestation, and radiation diminishes the body's resistance to the yeast. According to one expert, if left untreated, "systemic

Candidosis has a mortality rate approaching 100%."

These findings left me shaken. For years my doctors had been loading me with broad-spectrum antibiotics in an attempt to wipe out the mysterious cause of my illness. Not only had I been in Japan shortly after the A-bombs fell, I had been put through the whole gamut of X-rays, brain scans, and other diagnostic radiology every time I had been hospitalized during the long search for a diagnosis. In the last ten years, I must have had ten times the exposure to X-rays the average patient experiences in a lifetime.

Worse yet, my research had been inconclusive, for nowhere did I find an explanation of the drunkenness I had experienced.

But this time my secret still was going again. Now the attacks were more frequent and more severe. The Mycostatin seemed to have lost its punch. I couldn't ignore the dire warnings that neglected Candida can cause death.

I had written to doctors in London and Tokyo who were reputed to know of cases similar to mine. Upon receiving a letter from London, Betty and I flew there. But three weeks in a London hospital for exhaustive tests, replete with another full round of X-ray exposure, provided no new insights.

We returned home to find a

letter from Dr. Kazuo Iwata, professor of microbiology in the University of Tokyo School of Medicine. He enclosed a sheaf of medical journal reprints that reported on some 30 cases of meitei, or "Japanese drunken disease." One article suggested that the Candida found in meitei patients in Japan is more virulent in producing alcohol than the Candida strains found in other parts of the world.

Meanwhile, my condition worsened so that I required almost constant hospitalization. I had shown the articles about meitei to my doctors. At that time they were unable to secure the drugs used by the Japanese to treat meitei and suggested that I go to Japan.

Before leaving the country again, I decided to try one last shot. I had been told that the Veterans Administration could get drugs not available to civilian doctors. I supplied the VA with all my past medical records and with translations of the meitei articles, and spent the next year in and out of the VA hospital, all for nothing. Although the doctors found Candida colonies in my intestines, they refused to believe this was the source of the alcohol in my system. I was back where I'd started; the VA doctor branded me a sneaky drinker.

So, in 1975 Betty and I flew to Japan. Dr. Iwata arranged for specialists to examine me at Tokyo's Juntendo University Hospital. Familiar with the disease, they diagnosed meitei in just four days.

After three weeks of therapy, we returned home. Dr. Sierakowski took over where the Japanese doctors left off, administering Ancobon, a new antifungal chemotherapeutic, in carefully controlled doses. She relied on first daily, then weekly, and finally monthly lab reports to regulate the dosage.

In mid-July, 1975, the lab reported 6,740 Candida colonies per gram, a total of more than 900,000 in a single bowel movement. That must have marked the grand exodus of the Candida tribe. From that day to this, no Candida have been found, although medication was discontinued in September, 1975.

And I have not had one symptom of intoxication. ✳

A Doctor's Most Unforgettable Case

I still have cards from Eleanor; to me they're like monuments to a miracle

By J.A. MACDOUGALL, M.D.
As told to DOUGLAS HOW
November 1985

That December, I finally had to tell her. Medically, we were beaten. The decision lay with God. She took it quietly, lying there, wasting away, only 23, and the mother of a year-old child. I will call her Eleanor Munro. She was a devout and courageous woman. She had red hair and had probably been rather pretty, but it was hard to tell anymore; she was that near to death from tuberculosis. Now that she knew it, she asked just one thing.

"If I'm still alive on Christmas Eve," she said slowly, "I would like your promise that I can go home for Christmas."

It disturbed me. I knew she shouldn't go. The lower lobe of her right lung had a growing tubercular cavity in it, roughly one inch in diameter. She had what we doctors call open TB, and could spread the germs by coughing. But I made the promise and, frankly, I did so because I was sure she'd be dead before Christmas Eve. Under the circumstances, it seemed little enough to do. And if I hadn't made the promise, I wouldn't be telling this story now.

Eleanor's husband had the disease when he returned to Nova Scotia from overseas service in the 2nd World War. It was a mild case and he didn't know he had it. Before it was detected and checked, they married. She caught the disease and had little immunity against it. It came on so fast and lodged in such a difficult place that it

307

confounded every doctor who tried to help her.

To have a tubercular cavity in the lower lobe is rare. When they took Eleanor to the provincial sanitarium in Kentville, it quickly became obvious that the main problem was how to get at it. If it had been in the upper lobe, they could have performed an operation called thoracoplasty, which involves taking out some of the upper ribs to collapse the lobe and put that area of the lung at rest. Unfortunately, this operation couldn't be used for the lower lobe because it would have meant removing some of the lower ribs, which her body needed for support.

With thoracoplasty ruled out, the doctors tried a process called artificial pneumothorax: air was pumped in through needles to force collapse of the lung through pressure. Although several attempts were made, this process didn't work either; previous bouts of pleurisy had stuck the lung to the chest wall, and the air couldn't circulate.

Finally they considered a then-rare surgical procedure called pneumonectomy—taking out the entire lung—but rejected it because Eleanor was too sick to withstand surgery, and steadily getting worse. The alternatives exhausted, Eleanor's doctors reluctantly listed her as a hopeless case and sent her back to her home hospital in Antigonish.

I was 31 when she arrived. I had graduated from Dalhousie University's medical school in 1942, gone into the Royal Canadian Air Force, and then completed my training as an anesthetist in Montreal once the war was over. A native of Sydney, N.S., I accepted a position with St. Martha's Hospital in Antigonish. I was to provide an anesthesia service and take care of the medical needs of the students at two local colleges. I was also asked to look after a small TB annex at the hospital, a place for about 40 patients, most of them chronics with little or no hope of being cured. That's how Eleanor Munro came to be my patient in 1947.

She had weighed 125 pounds. She was down to 87 the first time I saw her. Her fever was high, fluctuating between 101 and 103 degrees. She was very ill, and looked it. But she could still smile. I'll always remember that. If you did her the slightest kindness, she'd smile.

Maybe that encouraged me. I don't know. But I did know that I had to try to help her.

I first called Dr. I. Rabinovitch in Montreal because he was a top expert on the use of the then-new drug streptomycin. Early information was that, in certain circumstances, it might help cure TB. Dr. Rabinovitch told me the drug wasn't available. When I described the case, he said he would advise against its use anyway. I then phoned a doctor in New York who was experimenting with a procedure called pneumoperitoneum.

Pneumoperitoneum consists of injecting air into the peritoneal cavity to push the diaphragm up against the lung. If we could get pressure against that lower lobe, we could hope to force the TB cavity shut. If we could do that, nature would have a chance to close and heal the cavity by letting the sides grow together.

At the hospital, we considered the risks and decided we had to face them. The operation took place the day after my phone call. We pumped air into the peritoneal cavity, but it nearly killed her. It was obvious that the amount of air she could tolerate would not help.

Every doctor in the room agreed we shouldn't try a second time. We were licked.

It was then that I told her medical science had gone as far as it could go. I told her that her Creator now had the final verdict and that it would not necessarily be what either of us wanted, but would be the best for her under the circumstances. She nodded, and then exacted from me that promise.

Amazingly, she was still alive on Christmas Eve, but just barely. The cavity was still growing; she was so far gone that she had already had the last rites of the Church. But she held me to my promise.

With renewed doubts, I kept it. I told her not to hold her child and to wear a surgical mask if she was talking to anyone but her husband. His own case had given him immunity.

She came back to St. Martha's late Christmas Day, and she kept ebbing. No one could have watched her struggle without being deeply moved. Every day her condition grew just a bit worse, yet every day she clung to life. It went on, to our continued amazement, for weeks.

Toward the end of February she was down to or below 80 pounds; she couldn't eat, and new complications developed. She became nauseous—even without food in her stomach. I was stumped. I called in a senior medical consultant; he was stumped too. But with a grin, almost facetiously, he asked me if I thought she could be pregnant.

I can still remember exactly how I felt: the suggestion was utterly ridiculous. Everything I knew about medicine added up to one conclusion: she was so ill, so weak that she couldn't possibly have conceived. Her body just wasn't up to it. Nevertheless, I ordered a pregnancy test. To my astonishment, it was positive. On the very outer frontier of life itself, she now bore a second life within her. It was virtually impossible, but it was true.

Legally, medically, we could have taken the child through abortion; it imperiled a life that was already in jeopardy. But we didn't do it. Eleanor and her husband were against it. We doctors at St. Martha's were against it, not only as Catholics, but because we were certain the operation would kill her. Besides, she was so far gone we were sure her body would reject the child anyway.

The struggle went on for weeks, and never once did we doubt that she was dying. But she kept living. And she kept her child. And in late June, 1948, an incredible thing happened. Her temperature began to go down. For the first time we noted some improvement in her condition, and the improvement continued. She began to eat, and to gain weight. A chest X ray showed that the growth of the TB cavity had stopped. Not long after, another X ray showed why: the diaphragm was pushing up against the lower lobe of her diseased lung to make room for the child she was bearing. Nature was doing exactly what we'd failed to do: it was pressing the sides of that deadly hole

together. The child was saving the mother.

The child did save her. By the time it was born, a normal, healthy baby, the TB cavity was closed. The mother was markedly better, so much better that we let her go home for good within a few months. Her smile had never been brighter.

I still find it hard to believe, and I've never heard of a comparable case since. I never discussed it with the young woman, even when she came in for checkups which confirmed the full return of good health. And never, until recently, have I cited the case publicly.

But I do now and I do so for a reason. I'm concerned about the liberalization of abortion laws and the growing clamor for even greater liberalization.

I'm against it. I'm against it on medical grounds: a doctor doesn't exist to take life, but to save it. I'm against it on religious grounds: I believe that human life is sacred, that only He who creates life has the right to take it away.

I'm against it, finally, because of the case I've described. The child didn't destroy its mother. It saved her. Call it the will of God; call it human love; call it the mystical quality of motherhood, the turning in upon herself to fight still more because she had still more to fight for; call it what you will: It happened. And I still wonder at what she did and at the unfathomable force it signifies.

I remember too, with delight, the Christmas cards Eleanor sent me for years afterwards. They were just ordinary cards, with the usual printed greetings and her name. But to me they were like monuments to a miracle. ✳

GLASS OF FASHION

The elderly priest picked his suitcase off the baggage conveyor at the airport, took it to a nearby bench and, opening it, started to resettle the contents. As he refolded his clerical black rabat he suddenly realized he had an interested observer, a small boy of about six.

For a moment there was silence. Then came the question, "Why do you wear a black shirt?"

The priest took a quick look round in a conspiratorial manner, and in a loud whisper said, "So that it won't show the dirt."

The small boy nodded in comprehension, "That's what mom says I should have," he said. C. G. A. Storey.

THE REASON WHY

When little Linda's friend came over and found her playing with a new housekeeping set, she asked, "Are you washing dishes?

"Yes," replied Linda, "and I'm drying them too, because I'm not married yet." Mrs. F. Majewski.

*

Mother and daughter were in the kitchen washing dishes while father and seven-year-old Johnny were in the living room. Suddenly father and son heard a crash of falling dishes. They listened expectantly,

"It was mom," said Johnny.

"How do you know?" asked his father.

"Because," answered Johnny, "she isn't saying anything." Helen Bender.

*

Several men in line at the phone booth groaned in dismay when they saw a teen-age girl step in for her turn.

"Don't worry," she confided cheerily. "I'll just be a minute. I only want to hang up on him." Dorothea Kent.

The Thing from Underground
(Like Grandma Used to Bake)

How an old monster recipe returned to
terrify a neighborhood

By THELMA LACY

March 1976, condensed from *Marriage**

W HEN I GOT married I was
a pretty good cook. My
sister-in-law had told me that
Bill liked old-fashioned cooking,
so I'd been practicing. I could
boil coffee with egg shells until
it looked like ambrosia. I could
make crackling cornbread that
almost floated to your mouth.

Bill complimented my cooking often, but one thing bothered
me. We never sat down to the
table that he didn't remark with
a far-off gleam in his eye. "Gee, I
sure wish I had some of that good
old homemade light-bread like
Grandma Long used to make."

Well, I was a new bride, and
I'd always been trained to
believe that a woman should try

to please her husband. Not only
that. If I heard Bill make that
statement one more time over
a meal I'd slaved to make just
right, I was going to scream.

So I called Bill's mother.
"Clara," I asked, "do you have
your mother's recipe for light-
bread?"

"Am I hearing right?" she said.
"You're hearing right, all right,"
I told her grimly. "I want your
mother's recipe for homemade
light-bread."

"What for?" she said. "There's
a day-old bakery just around the
corner."

"Don't give me any of that
Hoover stuff," I answered. "It's
a matter of life and death."

"It may well be," she said, "if
you don't have any better luck
with it than I did. Besides, it

*This article © 1975 St. Meinrad Arch-
abbey. Reprinted with permission from
Marriage magazine, St. Meinrad, IN 47577.

takes a lot of pounding and mauling."

"If I don't get that recipe," I said desperately, "dough is not the only thing that's going to be pounded and mauled."

"All right," she told me. "But Bill's father left me because of Grandmother Long's cooking."

"It made him sick?" I stammered.

"I hit him in the head with one of her biscuits," she said.

As soon as Clara brought the recipe, I started out with my big mixing bowl—and ended up in the sink. My arms ached, my legs felt like soda straws about to collapse, and perspiration trickled down into my shoes. But eventually I put the big ball of dough in my dishpan and set it on top of the hot water heater in the closet (for some strange reason it had to spend a lonely night, unmolested).

As usual, that evening, Bill sighed wistfully, as he bit into my tortillas, "I wish I had some of that good homemade light-bread like Grandmother Long used to make!"

I smiled sweetly. Tomorrow night he would have a crusty loaf of it in front of him—or maybe several, depending on how many a sack of flour would turn out.

The next morning as Bill gulped his coffee, he started

sniffing. "Somebody's making home brew." he said. "It smells awful!"

"Maybe they'll have better luck next time," I told him. Then my gaze focused on the closet— and my eyes popped. Something gray was oozing out from under the door. I jumped up and stood spread-eagled in front of Bill. "The clock," I stuttered. "It's slow. I tried to fix it, but—you're going to be late to work if you don't rush!"

"I wish you'd quit fixing things," he grumbled as I shoved him out the door.

I sprang across the room and opened the closet. Our hot water heater looked like a giant octopus, complicated by a terminal case of the gray sickness. Slimy tentacles oozed toward my feet.

Something more than my reputation as a cook was at stake now. I had to subdue this monster and get it out of the house before Bill came home.

I couldn't put it in the garbage. Even the can in the alley wasn't big enough.

I went out to the back yard and started digging. Then I scraped the monster off the water heater, picked up the tentacles with Bill's trowel, and took it all out to the hole in a washtub and laid it to rest.

After the funeral I went in to the house and had a good cry and a bath—and took off window-shopping to forget my troubles.

On my way home I felt almost like my old self again. Then fire trucks and police cars started screaming past me. My hair stood on end. They were stopping at my apartment house!

I made a mad dash for home and burst into the building. The halls were deserted. So were all the downstairs apartments. I had a terrible sinking feeling. Maybe the gray monster had risen up from its grave and devoured all the tenants.

Then I heard voices. I peeped out from under the shade. Everybody was in the back yard—the firemen, the police, the tenants—including Bill.

I stumbled down the steps and reached for him.

He gave me a shove that sent me reeling. "Oh, gosh, honey!" he exclaimed, "I'm sorry. But I didn't want you to get any on you." He pointed.

I stared in fascinated horror at the ground. It was bubbling and heaving.

"Only this morning," my neighbor was saying, as he pointed at me, "that poor little woman was spading there to make a garden. God knows what she's contaminated with!"

Bill put his arm around me. "They're taking samples," he comforted me. "They're going to have the stuff analyzed at the lab!"

A deep and terrible sickness hit the pit of my stomach. I jerked away from him, ran bawling into the house, and started slinging my clothes into a suitcase.

Bill grabbed me. "Can't you wait until the lab report?" he pleaded. "It's probably just some sort of natural phenomenon."

"It's the most unnatural phenomenon that human hands ever created," I said bitterly. Suddenly Clara was there, standing in our bedroom door.

"Grandmother Long's lightbread?"Clara asked, when Bill stepped out.

I nodded miserably.

"Don't worry about bread for supper," Clara said. "I brought you a loaf from the day-old. It's on the kitchen table."

Bill came back in. "They'll call us as soon as they get a report," he said.

"Thelma has decided to be brave," Clara told him. "She's going to stay. Neither sleet nor snow nor. . . . "

"That's postmen," Bill interrupted with disgust. Then he caught me in a big bear hug. "If we go," he said dramatically, "we go together!"

Things didn't settle down until it was time to begin dinner. I sprinkled Clara's scroungy loaf of bread and popped it in a brown paper bag to heat it in the oven.

At supper time I hacked off a chunk and passed it across to Bill. (As if it hadn't been bad enough to start with, I'd burnt it.)

Bill's eyes bulged out. He dashed around the table and jerked me out of my chair. "Honey!" he roared. "You did it! You made Grandmother Long's bread. How did you do it?"

I started to blurt the truth. Then I thought: One day-old loaf of sourdough french bread, sprinkled with water, and burnt in a brown paper bag. I'd be a fool to reveal the secret formula for a perfect marriage.

"I guess I have the knack," I murmured modestly against his lips.   ✹

HEARTS ARE TRUMPS

Three summers ago I worked in a branch bank in Grand Rapids, Mich. Every morning a gnarled old man would come in and deposit money which he took from an old pouch. He always wore dirty coveralls. I found out that he worked at a coal company down the road. Many of the tellers did not want to be bothered with him, but I would always smile at him. One day he came over to my window and I handled his business. He liked to talk and trade jokes. I found myself looking forward each morning to his visit.

That fall I decided to go back to college. On my last day at work, the old man came as usual, handed me the same tattered pouch. When he left the window I noticed that he had forgotten a manila envelope. By the time I got to the door, he was gone.

I asked the manager if it was all right to return the envelope on my lunch hour, and he agreed. Since I did not know the old man's name, I asked to see the boss. One of the men working in the yard went to find him.

"Yes, miss," a familiar voice said, "what can I do for you?" I turned around; it was the old man. He was the boss! I tried to cover my shock by explaining the lost envelope. He only smiled and told me that he had left it for me. He said I was always nice to him and that not too many people were.

When I got home I opened it. Inside there were two objects: a crisp $50 bill and a short note thanking me for my kindness. He had heard that I was going back to college and wanted to help me in some way. I just sat there and cried.   Barbara Jean Atkins.

On Being A Parent

Listening for the Children

Friday nights are long when you're the mother of teenagers

By MARY MCPHEE
May 1975

T HE FEELING the children have, that because they've been stuck all week in "this old prison" (school/home), they must go out. The phone that begins to ring as soon as everyone sits down to dinner. The different children who keep popping up to answer it. The daughter who gets three calls to see if she knows where any parties are. The son who gets four calls to see if he knows of any rides. The next to youngest who accepts a baby-sitting job with people you've never heard of before. The nine-year-old who

stays home with you and Daddy and the new kitten.

The new kitten. A drowsy angel, a ball of fluff who curls in a chair all day. The Mr. Hyde demon who comes to life at night, rips through the house, over the footstool, up the draperies. The dog next door who barks insanely whenever anyone enters or leaves your house.

The children who come by for your children. The pale boy with long black hair who asks for your daughter. His reluctance to come in and your husband's stare as he passes by in the hall. Your daughter's embarrassment that you ask the boy's name after she says, with a secret smile at him, "This is da lug." Your "have a good time and don't be too late." The long-haired one's smirk, your daughter's embarrassment because you were there, and spoke.

Your son who goes out. His hair. The car that honks for him. Your trying to see who are all those people in it. Your wondering what the neighbors will think. The doorbell that rings for the 12-year-old who is being picked up for her baby-sitting just when you've learned from her that they have five children under the age of eight. Your son's jacket left on the newel post.

The peace that descends upon the house. The dishwasher you discover the girls got away from without emptying. The table you discover your son got away from without clearing. The nine-year-old who set it. Your cajolement of her. Her sunny nature which does not include doing extra chores. Your appreciation of the fact that just because she's the only one left at home she shouldn't be a "Martha." Your finally getting everything cleaned up.

Your going to bed. Her going to bed, but not before she's brought you the kitten to kiss. Your sigh as you slip between the covers. Your setting the clock on your night table so you can see its lighted dial.

Your going right off blissfully until the dog next door starts barking. Your wondering which one it is. Your telling by the tread on the steps that it's the 12-year-old. Your relief she's survived the five children under eight. Her soft whisper in your ear, "Mom, I'm home." Your pretending to have been sound asleep. The noise she makes stealing the kitty from the nine-year-old's pillow and going to bed.

The silence during which you hear the electric clock whirring and the kitten chasing its tail around the 12-year-old's bed. The sudden soft footfalls on the floor. The kitten in bed with you. Your amused decision to let it stay awhile. Your trying to go to sleep again. Your wishing the front door didn't have to remain unlocked because the children keep losing their keys. Your wondering who may have the keys now. The kitten biting your toes through the blanket. Your putting it gently down. Its leaping up on the table and spilling a cup of water. Your putting it down.

The whirring clock. The lighted dial. The cars that go by. The cars that stop. The dog barking. People down the street.

Your dropping off. Your just as sudden waking up. Your looking at the lighted dial of the clock. Your recalling a wise friend's advice, "If they're lying in a ditch someplace, worrying isn't going to change things." Your indecision on whether to take an old sleeping pill you have, or will you need all your wits later? Your making sure the phone, also by your bed, *is* on the hook.

Your being awakened by a figure silhouetted in the hall light. Your wondering, with the long hair, the trousers, the smell of cold night air if it's your son or your daughter. Your son's voice saying, "I'm home, Mom."

Your son stealing the kitten from the 12-year-old's bed. His turning on his radio. Your yelling softly to him, "Close your door!" Your husband flopping over in his bed like a beached whale.

The whirring clock. The lighted dial. Your wishing the neighbor's dog *would* bark. Your agreeing that the wise friend's advice about lying in ditches and not worrying is correct but not necessarily right. The blissful barking of the neighbor's dog. Your not breathing so you can hear if the door is opening downstairs. The heavenly relief when you hear it does. Your anger which is weaker than the relief. Your daughter coming into your room smelling of night air and cigarettes.

Your scolding of her while the muscles in your stomach slide into warm Jello. Your admonition to "lock the door and make sure all the lights are out." Her going back downstairs, opening the door and slamming it, and going into the kitchen. The smell of something cooking. Your wondering but not caring what it is. Her coming upstairs. Her stealing the kitten from her brother's room. Her going to bed. The peace that surpasses all understanding settling upon the house.

Your waking up with a start, staring wildly at the lighted dial which reads 4:30. Your bounding out of bed and rushing into the hall. The kitten who leaps at your ankle.

Your going into the dark rooms. Your peering into faces. Your touching bodies. Your returning to your own bed. The room being much lighter. The kitten on your pillow. Your decision to take a nap right after lunch tomorrow. Your hope no one will go out Saturday night. Your knowing they will. ♡

The Son
I Didn't Want

He brought me more joy than I could have imagined

By MARJORIE KUNICE
April 1982, condensed from *The Lookout**

T HE LIGHT from the hallway filters through the half-open door, its beam outlining my "baby's" leg as it dangles over the side of the bed. My baby is a 16-year-old, 185-pound linebacker, but in sleep his face is as sweet and innocent as it was when he was nine years old and sharing his bed with a floppy-eared Snoopy.

I straighten his covers and lean over to kiss his sleeping face, just as I've been privileged to do for many years. As I stand up I think to myself, *this is my unwanted child.*

I remember well how stunned I was when I first suspected that I was to have another child. We had four children already and

had just purchased our first home, so money was very scarce. Our third child, after a prolonged and heartbreaking illness, was left severely brain-damaged. And our youngest was only six months old.

I didn't expect this pregnancy. I didn't want it, and even though I knew many childless women were longing for babies, I didn't understand or feel grateful for my own fertility. I felt trapped and helpless, that awful, lonely feeling of resentment that only a woman carrying an unwanted child can know.

I don't remember when resentment became acceptance or acceptance became love. Certainly by the time he was born, I both loved and wanted him. But throughout his early years, I was too tired and overworked to realize what a gift of love he was.

Just an ordinary little boy in many ways. He yelled, he sulked, he broke things. His giggling could "drive us up a wall" in less than five minutes, and he could make a complete shambles of a neat, orderly room in ten. He couldn't sit still, he talked too loud, and he was accident-prone. I was continually having little conferences with his teachers because he was bright enough to finish his work quickly and then spend the balance of his time acting the class clown.

But, oh what love and sunshine he brought into our home. He gave his hugs and kisses freely and was lavish with his compliments. When he told me that I was prettier than Farah Fawcett, for a few seconds, I *felt* prettier than Farah.

Yet only now do I realize what a blessed gift he is. At an age when many young people rebel against parental authority and question parental values, he shares his hopes and dreams with us. He even listens to us talk about our own dreams and encourages us when we think we've failed.

His enthusiasm and zest for living are contagious, his interest in anything and everything unlimited. Best of all he can make us laugh when everything falls apart at once.

I like happy endings. I am grateful that my story turned out so well. But standing beside his bed, rearranging his blankets and my own private thoughts, I shed a few tears and say a prayer for people everywhere that no one, except Almighty God, will ever want.   ♡

IN OUR PARISH

In our parish, the stewardess on the jet in which Sister Theresa was traveling was passing out sample packages of cigarettes to all the passengers.
"No thank you," Sister said. "One habit is enough."   Mrs. Jack Dublin.

*

In our parish I drained the last drop of holy water from its container in the back of the church and turned to apologize to a man waiting behind me.
"That's all right," he said. "I'll make my own."
"Make your own?" I asked, wondering whether this was some new Church reform.
"Yes," he answered, his eyes twinkling. "Just put a pot of water on the stove and boil hell out of it."   Mrs. Mary Ann Popick.

How Children Learn to Love

They watch their parents

By JOHN DRESCHER
November 1976, condensed from *Seven Things Children Need**

WHEN A PARENT is asked if he loves his child, we expect him to answer "Of course." Yet a more important question is, "Do your children know they are loved?

A study of maladjusted teenagers in a large Oklahoma high school shows how important it is to tell the child that he is loved.

First the counselors worked a long time to gain the confidence of ten students whom the faculty felt were the most neglected and maladjusted in the school. Then the team asked each of them, "How long has it been since your parents told you they loved you?" Only one of the students remembered hearing it at all, and he couldn't remember when.

*This article © 1976 by Herald Press. Reprinted with permission.

In contrast, the counselors used the same procedure with ten persons the faculty felt were the best-adjusted students in the school. Without exception all of them answered that they had been assured verbally of their parents' love within the past 24 hours.

The parents of the poorly adjusted teenagers may have loved their children a great deal. But clearly they were not communicating that love. Here are some facts about expressing love that might have helped them.

1. *Love is a learned response.* A child is born without knowing how to love but with great capacity to love. Some babies actually die when denied love. Other children develop twisted personalities.

A child needs warm, outgoing affection daily, and especially when he is feeling unlovely or in trouble.

As a baby receives love, he responds and learns to give love in return. This response keeps growing. Some people, particularly men, are victims of the "taboo of tenderness." But to be strong is to be tender. The weak are cruel, unconcerned, and loveless.

2. *Love between parents affects a child's ability to love.* Knowing his parents love each other provides a child with a security, stability, and a sense of the sacredness of life which he can gain in no other way. A child who knows his parents love each other, who hears them speaking their love for each other, needs little explanation of the character of God's love or the beauty of sex.

Love between parents should be visible. It means faithfulness in performing little acts of love. It means thoughtfulness; writing love letters when away from home. It means whispering loving words about a wife or husband into the ears of a child. It means praising each other in the presence of a child.

A child wants to know about love more than anything else. If he does not see it at home, he can pick up false ideas about love from movies, television, and magazines. A highschool student wrote, "The thing that adds to my happiness and that of my family is the way my father and mother love each other."

3. *Love must be spoken.* Parents can "speak" love in many nonverbal ways. Holding, embracing, smiling, patting on the shoulder, and looking deeply into a loved one's eyes are examples.

In my family we use a simple code to convey our love. When walking along hand-in-hand, seated at the table, or whenever the time seems right, three short squeezes of the hand signal "I love you." Many times before going to sleep the children will come for a good-night kiss and reach out with three short squeezes.

Some parents feel words of love to their children are too personal to be worn on the sleeve. Usually such persons will not hesitate to wear words of disapproval. But to be consistent, they should let their children guess about feelings of disapproval also.

One of the common expressions in every home, particularly from children, is the question, "Do you know what?" One family I know always responds immediately with, "Yes, I know what. I love you." A small son in this family was seriously ill in the hospital, unable to speak. When his parents came to his bedside they whispered quietly to him, "Do you know what?" Even though he was weak and speechless, his eyes flashed back the answer clearly.

4. *Love calls for action.* To speak words of love, yet not to do what love would dictate, is futile. A little boy said sadly, "Daddy says he loves me. But he doesn't have any time for me."

Another small son kept asking his dad to help him build a club-house in the back yard. The father said he would. But each weekend he had a business appointment, a golf date, some pressing homework, or a social engagement.

One day the boy was hit by a car, and was taken to the hospital in critical condition. As the father stood by the bedside of his dying son, the last thing his son said was, "Well, Dad, I guess we'll never get to build that clubhouse."

A father told of a compliment he received from his son who had graduated from high school and was preparing to leave for college. The boy invited his dad to go on a boat trip with him.

The father wasn't anxious to shoot the rapids, carry the boat around falls, and rough it in the wilds. "Well," he explained to me, "I'm not a good swimmer. It looked like a rather exhausting trip. So I said to my son, 'Get one of your buddies to go with you and I'll pay the bill for both of you.'" But his son replied, "Dad, I don't want a buddy. I want you to go with me."

5. *Love involves trust.* Rufus Mosely tells how he was reared in the backwoods of the Southern mountains. Life was rugged. Nobody had much of anything. But, inspired by his parents, he won a college scholarship. On the day he left for college his father summed up his anxieties and expectations: "Son, I don't know much about the world into which you are going, but I trust you."

6. *Love requires a willingness to listen.* Most parents find it hard to listen. They are busy with the burdens of work and are often tired. A child's chatter seems unimportant. Yet we learn much more by listening than by talking, especially from a child.

Listening carefully to the little hurts and joys of a child communicates love. Giving the child our complete attention and looking into his eyes when speaking conveys love. Have you seen a child take his parent's face in his hands and turn it toward his own? Yet how often parents look in every other direction when the child is speaking.

Certainly there is a close relationship between the parent's listening to a small child's concerns and the extent to which that child will share concerns when he is in his teens. The parent who takes time to understand what his child says early in life will be able to understand his child later in life. And parents who listen to their child when he is small will have a child who listens to the parent when he is older.

7. *Love means sharing our experiences.* Sharing work and play tells the child his parents love and accept him.

One mother tells how her adolescent daughter became resentful and defiant and burst into tears at the slightest reprimand. "Instead of punishing Betty and constantly reminding her of her age, I determined to give her large helpings of love and approval," she says. "I stopped ordering her to do certain things and asked her instead to work with me and share my duties. She had had to do the evening dishes alone; now we did them together, chattering as we worked.

"I made it a point to give her an affectionate hug now and then, and to praise her warmly when she deserved it. Both my husband and I laid aside our hobbies in the evenings to play games with her. We gradually found our child again."

When parents show their child how to do things, when the work and play together create a pleasant atmosphere by sharing enjoyable times, the child learns how love acts.

A sense of unity and understanding depends upon a feeling of sharing. When sharing is absent, loneliness takes its place.

I've often asked adults, "What good times do you recall from your childhood?" Invariably the good times most remembered are those shared as a family. Often an experience, small and seemingly insignificant at the time, was special because it was shared. And each time such an experience is retold it is shared again.

8. *Love builds open, comfortable relationships.* A child's most important reason for wanting to be good is the love of his parents for him. When that is lost he has little motivation to be good. Love needs to be present all the time, not conditional. Dr. David Goodman advises, "Never say to a child, "I will love you, if . . . !' Nor say, 'I will love you, but . . . !' Just say, 'I love you' and mean it."

Love always looks beyond childhood pranks to the real person. It seeks to understand the child's search for identity. Love listens even when it hurts.

9. *Love recognizes persons as more important than things.* It is difficult for many parents to learn that there is more security in love than in things. Children may receive wonderful gifts and still feel hated. They need parents, not presents.

One family left their small son with some friends while they took a trip. Upon their return they gave him a beautiful and expensive toy. He burst into tears, threw the toy to the floor, jumped on it, and broke it to pieces.

These parents had often left their son with friends for several days. Each time they returned, rather than throwing their arms around their son to greet him, they profferd a gift. He sensed that he was being bought off.

Parents sometimes say, "I've struggled hard all my life. I'm going to make it easier for my child." Such parents usually produce the very opposite of what they desire. They want to let the child know they love him deeply. But they rob the child of their time while they work hard to provide the things they think will make him happy. The child feels that things have become more important than persons.

Love is taking time for each other. It is chatting around the table. It is a family walking in the woods. It is happiness that comes from doing favors for each other. Love is joining hands in some project. It is playing a game all can join.

Love is laughing at ourselves and giving another a sense of belonging. It is talking about a common concern, or praying together. Love is listening. It is any word or act which creates the feeling that I love and am loved. ♡

PEOPLE ARE LIKE THAT

The last of the Oct., 1935, earthquakes that rocked Helena, Mont., struck on Halloween at 11:37 A.M. Our home was wrecked, and my husband told me to take our boys, aged one and three, to my parents' home in Iowa. That evening the children and I joined a crowd of panic-stricken, ticketless refugees bound for Havre, Mont., St. Paul, Minn., and points east. The conductor on the overcrowded train took fares, but insisted that Pullman reservations would have to be made at Havre.

At Havre there was a scramble for the ticket office. Carrying my sleeping baby and dragging my tired toddler, I was the last in line. By the time I got to the window, all sleeping space was taken. Just then an old gentleman approached me with a lower berth reservation to St. Paul in his hand. "Take this," he said. "You and those little towheads need a place to sleep tonight. I'll phone my missus that I've decided to lay over in this town till tomorrow. I'll say I just gave berth to a woman and two boys."

Alice E. Feldman.

Dr. Ice and
the Christmas Angel

"That man isn't human," the nurse said. "He doesn't have the warmth of a clam!"

By J. J. MCNALLY
January 1985, condensed from the *Milwaukee Journal/Insight**

IT WAS CHRISTMAS EVE and the little girl lay dying of leukemia. When I came on duty at 11 P.M. the evening nurse reported that Karen's condition was deteriorating rapidly and that her parents had been notified.

I checked Karen's pulse and blood pressure, then looked in on her two roommates, Susie and Pauleen. Both were asleep. They, too, were in the hospital with leukemia, but both were in the earlier stages of the disease. The three had been together for quite a while. Karen's death would hit them hard.

When I returned to the nurses'

station to telephone the house physician, Carol, the nurse working with me, said, "You know who's on tonight, don't you? Dr. Ice."

I groaned. To have Dr. Ice on duty tonight was something I hadn't counted on.

Dr. Ice was given his name a year ago when he joined the hospital staff. From the start he was cold and aloof, refusing to join in the good-natured banter that goes on between nurse and doctor. We didn't even know whether he was married or single. No one knew anything about him other than his medical qualifications, which were impeccable.

When Dr. Ice came on the line, I described Karen's worsen-

---

*This article © 1983 by the *Milwaukee Journal.* Reprinted with permission.

ing condition and asked him to see her. He agreed, adding that he would call the girl's own physician after the examination to appraise him of her status.

Just as I was about to hang up, he asked me if a private room was available.

"Yes, room 312, right next to the nurses' station, if you feel it's necessary, but I don't think . . . "

"Move her right away," he ordered, and hung up.

"How do you like that?" I said to Carol. "Dr. Ice wants us to move her to 312. That's the only private we have, and if we get any admissions tonight who need isolation, then we'll have to play musical beds again and shift people around. And Karen's been with Susie and Pauleen for so long. They'll be devastated."

"It might be worse if she dies in there with them."

"I don't know. Kids are funny. Sometimes they're able to handle death better than adults."

But there was no time to waste talking, not with Dr. Ice the Terrible due to arrive at any minute. He didn't take lightly any delay in executing his orders.

Lori, the nurse's aide who was to help me with the transfer, and I walked down the hall to the ward. She asked who the doctor was.

"Dr. Ice," I told her. "I wish anyone else were here tonight but him."

"He can surprise you," Lori said. "Once I saw him just sit-ting with the wife of a dying patient. He was holding her hand and talking to her, and he was very gentle and patient. Of course, when he saw me watching him, he got up and left right away, but it happened. I don't think he likes to be seen in his gentler moods."

"He doesn't have to worry," I said. "I've never seen him in one."

Lori and I rolled the bed out of 336 and down the hall into 312. We didn't talk while we were in the room with the sleeping girls. I thought about Lori's words. Was there a hidden gentleness in Dr. Ice? Maybe I had misjudged him.

When Dr. Ice came about 20 minutes later, all was ready. The intravenous pump was plugged in and running, the chart was on the bedside table. The doctor examined the child, then announced, "Not good at all. She won't last the night. You'd better notify her parents."

"We already did," I told him. "They're on their way."

He looked at me as if I were some new species of microorganism he had just discovered.

"We do have that prerogative, Doctor," I reminded him. He didn't comment, but went next door to call Karen's own doctor.

I remained with Karen, checking her vital signs and making sure the room was neat for her parents' arrival. Later, when I entered the nurses' station, Dr. Ice had gone, but he had told Carol to call him when Karen died.

"Specifically, he said, 'When the patient expires'—he couldn't even use her name," Carol said. "That man isn't human. He doesn't have the warmth of a clam!"

"A real spirit of Christmas," I agreed.

Karen's parents soon arrived, in tears, even though they had been expecting this for days. I spent as much time with them as I could, leaving occasionally to give medications and check on other patients.

Shortly before dawn, it was over. Little Karen didn't go out with memorable last words, or even a dying gasp. She merely stopped breathing.

I cried along with her parents; I always do when one of my patients dies. We work so long with some of our patients that we become very close. It seems to help the families, too, to know that someone else grieves with them.

Dr. Ice returned to the floor and talked with the parents, then he left, telling me he would return in an hour or so. Karen's parents also left, their arms around each other, looking confused and lost. I walked with them to the elevator.

"I hope Karen's roommates will be all right," the father said as the elevator doors opened. "The three of them were so close."

His voice broke and he turned away. His wife was quietly weeping. I hugged them both and said, again, how sorry I was. They thanked me and the other nurses for our care of their daughter.

When I got back to my desk, I was drained. I looked up at the clock over the door. Only two more hours left on my shift and I could go home.

Soon I would have to begin the "A.M. cares": giving pills, taking temperatures, and washing faces, in preparation for the day staff's arrival.

I was so busy when 6:30 arrived that I almost didn't notice Dr. Ice emerge from the stairwell and head for 336. When I did, I nearly dropped the basin of wash water I was holding in my hurry to follow him.

What the devil was he doing in there? Susie and Pauleen weren't his patients.

If he says anything snide to them or breaks the news of Karen's death to them too harshly, I'll really have things to say to him! I stopped outside the door to their room and listened.

The girls had awakened and were anxiously awaiting the day's activities, which included a visit from Santa Claus. They were holding their stockings, which their parents had brought the night before and Lori had placed at the feet of their beds.

I heard Susie say, "Good morning, Doctor."

He replied softly, then Pauleen

asked him, "Where is Karen?"

I held my breath. Lori and Carol walked past me and I waved at them to stop. We all listened, not moving a muscle.

"What day is today, girls?" Dr. Ice was saying.

"Christmas Day," the girls replied together.

"And what does Christmas mean?"

"Presents," Susie chirped.

"Santa Claus," Pauleen added.

"Oh, it's more than that," the terrible Dr. Ice said. "What do we really celebrate on Christmas?"

A short silence, then 7-year-old Pauleen said, "Baby Jesus was born today."

"That's right. Today is his birthday. When you girls celebrate your birthdays, your parents always get your presents ready for you and make sure you have the gifts you want, isn't that right?"

The little girls said yes, and he continued. "Well, last night, Jesus' Father, God, looked over the presents for his baby Son's birthday and He realized that He was short one thing. He needed an angel to put on top of the birthday cake."

"Why didn't he use a candle?" Susie wanted to know.

"They don't use candles in heaven," Dr. Ice replied. "The stars are heaven's candles. So God looked down here on earth, wondering who He should call to come up to heaven and be the angel on the baby's birthday cake. And He saw Karen.

"Girls, Karen had been sick for so long. She was in pain and very, very tired. When God asked her if she would do this for Him, would go with Him to heaven and be the birthday angel, she said she would. She would miss her mother and her father, and you girls, too, but she was tired of being sick, tired of hurting.

"So last night, Karen went to heaven with God. Right now she's happy, well again, and the brightest angel any birthday cake ever had. Karen is Baby Jesus' birthday angel."

I didn't stay to hear any more. I retreated to the safety of the nurses' station and began to cry.

A little while later Dr. Ice passed the station. I had calmed down, and I stopped him.

"Doctor?"

He paused. "Yes, Judy?"

"Thank you for telling the girls about Karen. And . . . Merry Christmas."

"Merry Christmas."

Without another word, he left.

It has been years since that Christmas Eve, but I still think of Dr. Ice and wonder where he is. I hope he has let his gentler self show a little more often. His story of the birthday angel made a sad and terrible thing into something very beautiful. He taught me not to judge people so hastily.

Merry Christmas, Dr. Ice. And bless you.　　　　◊

On a Beach in Cornwall

A tough French priest explains the
essence of sin

By BERNARD BASSET, S.J.
March 1964, condensed from *We Neurotics* *

I was sitting on a beach in Cornwall when I met the Abbé Delpierre. First, ten laughing, pushing boys came into sight. They looked slightly French with their bedraggled uniforms and berets.

They were followed by a most unusual looking man. He was dressed in a dirty suit two sizes too big. His trousers were stuffed into thick white bedsocks which, in turn, had been squeezed into thin, black, pointed boots. He wore a beret but no collar. A hand-rolled cigarette, yellow and crooked, was dangling from his lips.

I overdid my greeting, and he bounded across some seaweed. With his boys giggling behind him, we solemnly shook hands.

In studied English he announced himself as the Abbé Delpierre. He explained that he had taught English in Cairo, had served in the Middle East with British forces, and so spoke English reasonably well. "It is because of this," he said, "that I must bring these pupils to England for the summer to practice your excellent tongue. You forgive my speech; I am a little rusty; and" (placing his hand across his collar) "forgive me also my dress." He sat down on the grass by my side.

He was an astonishing little man, alert, sensitive, kindly but, like so many Frenchmen, unemotional and as hard as nails.

For a while we spoke about ourselves. He told me about his mother, about his Citroën parked in Calais. He came from a farm in the Vosges, was now part-time chaplain to the Young Christian Workers. Politely he inquired after Sir Winston Churchill and the queen.

"And now what?" he asked, rolling a cigarette.

"What about God?"

"A good subject," he remarked, wagging his head. "But, perhaps, a little too big. Judging by the British officers I knew in Cairo, I formed the impression that God was rather like the headmaster of one of your public schools; you could count on him to behave like an Englishman in a crisis and for the rest, well, he was harmless if not disturbed."

I asked him about his boys, but he dismissed them with an irritable flick of the fingers. "With any luck," he said, "they'll all drown."

Next, we spoke a little about nerves. He agreed that tension was a problem even in his own country and that people talked about neurosis too easily. "It is our generation which has given a label to a state of uncertainty which all other ages took in their stride."

I pressed him further on this.

"Neurosis," he said, "is always the beginning, never the end. Do you ever read the French journal *Cahiers Mystiques de Limoges?* No! So much the better; I am able to borrow the thoughts of the learned author and pass them on to you as my own."

He paused and moved his head sideways, like a woman arranging flowers in a vase. "A great many saints," he said, "showed what we would call neurotic symptoms at the start of their quest for God. St. Teresa of Avila suffered many pains, disturbances, and imaginings when she started praying during the time which she called her 'double' life. St. Thérèse of Lisieux was not much better, full of self-pity and easily reduced to tears. Her piety was worried and artificial for some years.

"St. Francis de Sales had what we would call a breakdown while he was an undergraduate at Padua. He thought after reading Calvinist doctrines that he was damned. St. Margaret Mary was very neurotic in her convent; her trouble, she often claimed, was that she could not swallow cheese.

"Even St. Ignatius of Loyola, a middle-aged soldier, passed through a worrying time; he saw a hole in the cloister of the Dominican convent in which he was staying and was tempted to jump in and kill himself.

"St. John of God actually pretended to be mad, and was locked up in an asylum—a most curious symptom this. Two prelates wanted to put Don Bosco away in an institution; he must have given some grounds for such a step."

"Neurosis is only the beginning?" I asked.

"Yes, if you recognize it for what it is and master it. It is what one might call suppressed ambition, a state of worry because we are so anxious to succeed. Did you read last April's issue of *Letters Psychologiques et Mystiques de Lyon?* No! Good, I am able to continue as a learned man."

It was a glorious afternoon with the sun playing on the water; the deep, luminous blue of the Cornish coast was ravishing to the eye. "Almost all the great psychologists would agree, he went on, "that neurosis is a certain symptom of self-centeredness. The more neurotic, the more self-centered, though perhaps I should put it the other way round."

He turned the phrases round with his hands. "The more self-centered, the more neurotic. The will for power is so very great. Ambition to succeed, deep down in your heart, will produce neurosis when it is blocked by outside impediments. Some persons are so ambitious that they work their minds and bodies too hard.

"Others feel that they are not going to succeed because health, environment, money, social prejudice is against them

and then, unconsciously, they must look around to find an excuse. They know their own excellence and they lack the humility just to sit down and admit failure. So much do they esteem the opinion of others that they must be able to explain their failures to their friends.

" 'I, too, would have done as well,' they like to say, 'only I had poor health, a cruel father, class prejudice against me or— and this is far more dangerous— I was so holy that I did not want to succeed in this world.' "

He bowed to me, "So, it is easy to be neurotic, it is very much harder to become a saint. You may lie on the floor *comme çi;* you may even induce the stigmata by auto-suggestion; but you cannot so easily become a little child *comme ça,* " and he gestured gracefully to the boys shrieking by the waves.

"Have you read the current issue of *La Revue Ascétique de Chartres?* No! The author there makes the point that all words prefixed by *dis-*, meaning two-, apart-, separate, are almost always unhappy words. I do not know if I am familiar enough with your language but I can think of *disappointment, disillusion, disagreeable, dissatisfaction,* and perhaps *distress.* There may be many more.

"All these words suggest duplicity. Duplicity means conflict, indecision, unhappiness.

There is always unhappiness where men lead double lives. Our Lord Jesus Christ said that we cannot serve two masters at once, yet so many attempt it. Neurosis is the result. The center of our hearts is double and the conflict is painful.

"And this," I asked, "this is the root of sin?"

"Precisely," he returned, nodding in agreement. "Sin is always a self-centered choice for my own immediate gain. There is much humbug in speaking about sin. We like to make lists and to say that this is a big sin and that is a little sin, but we forget the essential: nothing is a sin unless it is due to this self-centeredness."

He leaned back, plainly annoyed with most Christians and especially with himself. He made those funny hissing noises heard in Paris during a heated argument. I could sense his genuine anger against such bourgeois pettiness.

When he resumed, he had changed his manner and was most precise. "Why," he asked, "do we look further than the Passion of Christ for a picture of ourselves? We see no impatience, no impure thoughts, no using of swear words, but only self-centeredness.

"All those who played a key part in the crucifixion were, on the surface, good men. Pilate had a sense of justice, Peter was devoted, Judas had enough virtue to be picked out of hundreds to be one of the twelve. Even the Pharisees were churchgoers on a big scale.

"Next, they all loved Christ, they knew that his cause was a noble one and they admitted that He was innocent. But they were double through self-centeredness. They wanted two things at once: they wanted Christ to be successful but, in their hearts, they wanted their own interests more.

"Pilate wanted his job, Peter wanted his skin, Judas wanted his money, Herod wanted to show off before his friends. Even the Pharisees only wanted to be top men.

"None of them would have minded going to Confession to accuse themselves: 'a little impatience . . . a little greedy . . . my mind wandered during my prayers.' What they should have said was 'Dear Lord, I am very devoted to You but I love myself far more.'

"They could not say that except poor Peter—when he wept. Judas threw the money back, Pilate washed his hands in public, Herod made friends with Pilate, the Pharisees scrupled to enter the governor's house on the feast day. But they could not face their real guilt.

"They reproduced the sin of Adam and Eve and all that nonsense of hiding in the bushes and blaming each other for their fault. I have often wondered what would have happened to our world if Adam and Eve had behaved as little children, rushed out naked from the bushes to admit how self-centered they were.

"They were afraid of God; Judas killed himself from fear, the Pharisees were afraid and put a guard by the tomb, Pilate's wife had nightmares. Why? Because they were all double, they served two masters, they could not admit their self-centeredness even to themselves. True contrition wipes away all fear."

He paused to consult his watch. "I must be going," he said. "I have ruined your relaxation and I have happily almost forgotten my boys. I feel very strongly on this self-centeredness. I feel that the symptoms of this cancer, sulking, deceit, flattery, jealousy, spite, which were all present in the Passion, do not worry us enough. That is why we are afraid of God."   ◊

OLD-TIME RELIGION

A very religious man owned a store in a small Louisiana town. Every time he made a sale, he would quote something from the Bible.

On this particular day there weren't many customers. A little boy selected a nickel's worth of candy, and as the owner rang up the sale he said, "Suffer the little children to come unto me."

Later a poor man came in with just enough money for a loaf of bread. In ringing up this sale the owner said, "Blessed are the poor, for they shall inherit the earth."

About an hour before closing, a brand-new Cadillac pulling a horse trailer stopped at the store. A Texan came in to buy a blanket for his horse.

Now the store owner had only one kind of blanket, but it came in four colors. He brought a green one out first and told the Texan he could have it for $10. That was too cheap for his horse. So the owner brought out the black blanket and offered it for sale for $25. Still too cheap. Next he brought out the blue one for $50. Finally the Texan settled on the red one for $100. He paid with a crisp new $100 bill and drove off.

As the store owner rang up this sale he said, "He was a stranger, and I took him in."   *Cappers Weekly.*

Prayer

"Cardinal Bernardin, How Do You Pray?"

The Archbishop of Chicago talks about his personal spirituality

An Interview with CARDINAL JOSEPH BERNARDIN
By the editors of U.S. CATHOLIC
January 1986, condensed from *U.S. Catholic**

*M*OST PEOPLE *think a cardinal must spend a lot of time talking to God. How did you get started?*
First, I think you have to know that I grew up in a situation that was totally unlike the one I'm in now. My mother and father had emigrated from northern Italy, and they moved to South Carolina because my father and his brothers were stonecutters. Columbia, the capital of the state, is near some very fine granite quarries. Other

*This article © 1985 by Claretian Publications. Reprinted with permission.

than two cousins who lived in the same house as we, my sister and I were the only Catholic kids on our block; we were also the only Italians—and probably the only ethnic family—in the neighborhood. Because the Catholic school was far away, I went to the public grammar school until fifth grade.

I hardly remember my father because I was only six years old when he died. But my mother was a good, strong woman. She always saw to it that we went to church, that we said our prayers. We weren't an overly religious family, but we went

335

to Mass on Sundays and said our prayers.

When did you decide that you wanted to be a priest?

During my high-school years I wanted to be a doctor, and I got a scholarship to the University of South Carolina. After one year there, I changed my mind and decided to become a priest. Nobody believed it at first because I had never really talked about it.

So what influenced you to make that decision?

I think it was basically a couple of parish priests whom I got to know very well. I was oriented toward some kind of service to people, but I was thinking of medicine. But through the influence of these priests, I decided to go to the seminary.

When I was ordained I had the same ideals as any young person, and I worked hard at them. But I have to admit that I kept so busy I really didn't take time to develop a deep spirituality. I remember thinking, even then, "One of these days you're going to have to root all of this activity in a much deeper spirituality."

What finally made you do something about it?

It didn't happen until a number of years later when I had become Archbishop of Cincinnati. One evening I was in a restaurant with three young priests, two of whom I had ordained. We were talking about this, and

I realized that all three were further advanced than I in spirituality. They told me, "If you really feel this way, you should do something about it." I thought at the time it was kind of strange that these three younger men were telling me, the bishop and the older person, what I should be doing!

In any case, I made a decision then that I would make the development of my spirituality a priority in my life, and that that would be the foundation for my ministry to people. Without it, I knew that I would just begin to dry up after a while. That was really a turning point in my life— it was about eight years ago.

What changed after that?

I found that my most precious commodity was time—the thing I had the least of. Nonetheless, I decided that I'd give the first hour of my day to God, no matter what my schedule might be. And I've tried to do that ever since. Starting out the day that way has made a big change in my life. It changes my whole perspective. I find that throughout the day I'm praying more than I did previously.

One of the best things about this experience is that I've been able to share it with people. So many who are spiritually hungry come to me; they want to enter into a close relationship with the Lord, but they don't know exactly how to do it.

Somehow when people come to me, they just take it for granted that I've got everything put together, that I've never experienced the problems they're experiencing. And when I can tell them that I've gone through the same thing, that we're all pilgrims together, it gives them a great deal of encouragement, a big boost.

What about specific forms of prayer? It seems that some people feel very cut adrift because the family Rosary of their childhood may not comfort them any longer, but they're not comfortable with the newer forms of prayer either.

I always tell people to pray in the way they feel most comfortable. What works for one person may not work for another. My understanding of the Rosary, for example, has changed over the past few years.

When I prayed the Rosary in earlier days, it was highly mechanical; it was almost an end in itself. That's obviously not the way it should have been, but that's often how it was for me.

In the last few years, however, I found that I often became distracted during prayer. I discovered that it was helpful to have the beads and a set prayer, that these things helped bring what I was doing into focus. The purpose of the Rosary for me now is not so much to say the set prayers over and over again, but to give me an opportunity to reflect on the Lord and the specific events in his life which have so much importance for the Church and for my own personal life. It was almost a matter of looking for help, for a crutch. And then I found out that the Rosary is a very good help. I saw it in a different light, as a means to an end, as a way of helping me to pray.

Is the Rosary for everyone?

Again, I feel that everyone needs to find the ways to pray that best suit him or her. But we should never be ashamed to admit that some of the old forms of prayer really work; we don't have to be committed just to the newer forms of prayer — shared prayer and all the other forms which I enjoy very much. I personally use the newer forms together with some of the older forms.

How do you achieve a deeper prayer life? I'm sure that so many people have made a decision to "do it right," to really spend time in prayer. And all of a sudden they find themselves sitting there saying, "Okay, now what?"

I went through life doing that very thing. I'd go on a retreat or Lent would come along, and I'd make all kinds of promises. Then a few weeks later I'd realize I wasn't doing anything about it. Real change comes about only when you make a serious commitment. Unless you make that commitment, you're going to forget about the promises. But with God's grace and the help of other people, you can keep your commitment to change.

What's the minimum daily prayer requirement for the average Catholic?

There's no "right" amount. I spend the first hour of my day in prayer, but if I were a married man with a family I'm not at all sure I'd be able to do that. The demands on my life are very different from those of other people. In the final analysis, what's really important is to spend time with God. Maybe that can be done in a few seconds, or maybe it takes longer.

What about listening to God? Where do you hear God best?

That's hard to say. God talks to us in so many ways. He talks through the Scriptures, for example. But God speaks in many other ways as well—in the events that occur from day to day. Part of prayer is simply reflecting on what has been happening to us, the ways in which God is talking to us through our life experiences, through things that other people have done or said. So prayer is not just talking; it's listening, too.

I also have to say that sometimes prayer is better than at other times. Sometimes, when you try too hard, you realize that you're daydreaming or problem-solving. That's okay. The important thing is the continued desire to spend time with the Lord, even though nothing much seems to be accomplished. The desire will keep you going.

But if part of prayer is listening, what is it that you listen for? Isn't it solutions to problems?

Maybe I overstated it. I find, though, that when I'm sitting there in the quiet of my room, I start thinking about all the things that are going to happen during the day. Should I write a letter to so-and-so? If so, what should I say? And I think about all kinds of other problems. That kind of problem-solving doesn't really touch at the heart of prayer.

Prayer obviously can be a great help in discerning the direction you should take with your problems, in dealing with the challenges of your life. Maybe that is a kind of problem-solving, but it's very different from mentally dictating a letter or deciding how you're going to tell someone off. You're always going to worry about those things to a certain extent, especially if you're a worrywart as I am. But as you develop spiritually, you probably become less concerned about those details, and you focus more on what's happening in your life and the direction you're heading. *What does it mean to pray about God's will? If I pray for someone with cancer to be healed, should I instead be praying for God's will to happen, whatever it might be?*

I tend not to pray for specific outcomes; rather, I try to pray that there will be a good outcome, whatever it might be. For example, I have my litany of things that I pray for in the morning. Most of them have to do with problems in the archdiocese, and frankly, I don't know how these problems should be resolved. But I pray that I will have the strength, the integrity, and the patience to deal with them in the best way possible. That's what I pray for. *Where do you get that attitude? Is it a gift from God, or do you supply it yourself with a "positive mental attitude" approach?*

It comes both ways. There is a personal dimension, but I also think it's a grace. One difficulty is that sometimes we place too much of a burden on God. We have to do our share. I see prayer as helping in that collaboration between me and God. We pray for strength, as Paul did in his epistles. But then we have to do our part. We can't shift the burden totally onto someone else, whether that be God or the saints or whomever.

At the same time, we are not gods ourselves; and we have to have enough faith and trust to believe that somehow, in God's providence, things will work out. Let me get more specific. Chicago is a huge archdiocese, and it's very diverse and complex. There are many wonderful things happening here, but there are also many problems. The biggest mistake I could make would be to think that somehow the resolution of all those problems depends totally on me, that I have to be responsible for everything that happens. If I were to do that, first of all it wouldn't work. Second, I would end up unable to function effectively.

Therefore I have to trust. I have to trust at the human level—trust other men and women in the archdiocese, in the parishes. But I also have to trust in God. To be perfectly honest, if I didn't have that kind of faith and that kind of trust, I wouldn't be doing what I'm doing. I wouldn't be in this job. *How can someone try to "imitate Christ" when our lives are so different from his?*

For me, imitating Christ means living out in our lives the values that He witnessed to. But I don't think that happens only by learning about those values. More than knowledge is needed. People will accept the teaching of Christ only if they have first accepted Christ. There has to be a conversion; when that happens, the person is more disposed to live out in his or her life the values that Christ taught.

When does that kind of conversion happen? During dramatic encounters with the Lord? During something as tried-and-true as the sacraments?

All the sacraments are encounters with the Lord. While I don't deny that God can work independently of the sacraments, they are his gift to us; they were given for our benefit. I think God gave them to us because we're all looking for tangible signs. We need to hear and see and feel things. The sacraments have a human dimension that's extremely important.

Some people say they can deal directly with God, and that they don't need the sacraments to intervene. We hear this often about Confession, for example.

Sure, people can deal directly with God. But we also believe that the Lord did establish a Church, and that the sacraments were part of his gift to his Church. Why not use the gifts we were given?

If you could tell every Catholic in the country just one thing, what would it be?

I do have a message that I try to stress in my homilies, in my personal contacts with people. I don't know how successful I am, but the general thrust of what I try to say, whatever the form, is that God really loves you. You are very important— no matter how mixed up you might be or think you are, no matter what difficulties you may be facing, no matter how hopeless the situation might seem to be. You are very, very important, and the Lord loves you. If you really believe that, then a lot of the other problems will be worked out without too much conflict or worry.

I think what people are looking for from their ministers today—both ordained and unordained—is the assurance that God is present and that somebody loves them and cares for them. People don't expect to have priests or ministers answer all their questions or solve all their problems. Rather, people are looking for the kind of presence that assures them that they're not alone, that they're not going to be abandoned. They're looking for someone to pray with them and hold their hand, both literally and figuratively.

Even when I don't have a chance to talk to people, I try to communicate that message. I stand in those receiving lines until I'm blue in the face. What

I try to convey to people is that somebody does care. You know, you can do that even if you don't have time to use many words. Sometimes I think the words get in the way. ❧

SIGNS OF THE TIMES

On a real estate office: "The Greatest Earth On Show."
Margaret Krupicka.

*

On a subway wall: "Shakespeare Married An Avon Lady."
The New York *Sunday News.*

*

At a service station: "Have Wrench, Will Monkey." Peter Bach.

*

On an out-of-order cigarette machine: "Sorry, I Quit—Why Don't You?"
Tom McKievick.

*

On the door of a karate school: "Please Do Not Knock Before Entering."
Family Weekly.

*

In an automobile showroom: "Free Yourself from Foreign Clutches."
Thomas LaMance.

A CRY FROM THE HEART

I had the pleasure of caring for my daughter's two small sons while she and her husband took their first real vacation in six years. Along with the children's clothes she left a note with a few suggertions on their schedules and behavior. At the bottom was this blessing:

"And when Brian has devastated all your cupboards and is walking around with a box of cereal upside down, and David has thrown up on your new brocade couch or is fighting Brian for the cereal, think of me lying on the beach and you will know the joy of being the recipient of eternal gratitude. You will be guaranteed at least four extra stars in your heavenly crown; St. Peter will welcome you among the true martyrs, and you will have accomplished your Lenten sacrifices for eight years in advance. Keep in mind I *shall* return; and, in the meantime, I'll ask the children's guardian angels to keep an eye on them, St. Anthony to keep them from wandering off, and for you—I'll pray to St. Jude. Thanks, Mom." Susan Klingbeil.

The Prayer of General Patton

Answered on schedule

By CHAPLAIN JAMES H. O'NEILL
January 1949, condensed from the Military Chaplain*

I RECEIVED a telephone call the morning of Dec. 8, 1944, when the 3rd Army headquarters were located in the Caserne Molifor, in Nancy, France. "This is General Patton; do you have a good prayer for weather? We must do something about these rains if we are to win the war."

My reply was that I knew where to look for such a prayer, and that I would report within the hour. As I hung up the telephone receiver, about 11 in the morning, I looked out on the steadily falling rain, "immoderate" I would call it, the same rain that had plagued General Patton's army throughout the Moselle and Saar campaigns from September until now.

The few prayer books at hand contained no formal prayer on

*Reprinted with permission of the *Military Chaplain.*

weather that might prove acceptable to the Army commander. Keeping his immediate objective in mind, I typed on a 5″ x 3″ filing card, "Almighty and most merciful Father, we humbly beseech Thee, of Thy great goodness, to restrain the immoderate rains with which we have had to contend. Grant us fair weather for battle. Graciously hearken to us as soldiers who call upon Thee that, armed with Thy power, we may advance from victory to victory, and crush the oppression and wickedness of our enemies, and establish Thy justice among men and nations. Amen."

This done, I donned my heavy trench coat, crossed the quadrangle of the old French military barracks, and reported to General Patton. He read the prayer copy, returned it to me with a very casual directive, "Have 250,000 copies printed and see to it that every man in the 3rd Army gets one." The size of the order amazed me: this was certainly doing something about the weather in a big way. But I said nothing about it but, "Very well, sir! If the general would sign the Christmas greeting on the other side of the card the men would like it." He signed the card, returned it to me, then said, "Chaplain, sit down for a moment; I want to talk to you about this business of prayer." He rubbed his face in his hands, then rose and walked over to the high window, and stood there with his back toward me as he looked out on the falling rain. As usual, he was dressed stunningly, and his six-foot two, powerfully built physique made an unforgettable silhouette against the great window. The General Patton I saw there was the commander to whom the welfare of the men under him was a matter of personal responsibility. Even in the heat of combat he could take time out to direct new methods to prevent trench feet, to see to it that dry socks went forward daily with the rations to troops on the line, to kneel in the mud administering morphine and caring for a wounded soldier until the ambulance came. What was coming now?

"Chaplain, how much praying is being done in the 3rd Army?" was his question. I parried, "Does the general mean by chaplains, or by the men?" "By everybody," he replied. To this I countered, "I am afraid to admit it, but I do not believe that much praying is going on. When there is fighting, everyone prays; but now with this constant rain—when things are dangerously quiet, men just sit and wait for things to happen. Prayer out here is difficult. Both chaplains and men are removed from a special building with a steeple. Prayer to most of the soldiers is a formal ritualized affair, involving special posture and a liturgical setting. I do not believe that much praying is being done."

The general left the window, and again seated himself at his desk. "Chaplain, I am a strong believer in prayer. There are three ways that men get what they want; by planning, by working, and by praying. Any great military operation takes careful planning, or thinking. Then you must have well-trained troops to carry it out. But between the plan and the operation there is always an unknown. That unknown spells success or failure. Some people call that getting the breaks; I call it God. God has His part, or margin in everything. That's where prayer comes in. Up to now, in the 3rd Army, God has been very good to us. We have never retreated; we have suffered no defeats, no famine, no epidemics. This is because a lot of people back home are praying for us. We were lucky in Africa, in Sicily, and in Italy, simply because people prayed. But we have to pray for ourselves, too. A good soldier is not merely a thinker and worker. A man has to have intake as well. I don't know what you call it, but I call it religion, prayer, or God."

He talked about Gideon, said that men should pray no matter where they were, in church or out of it; that if they did not pray, sooner or later they would "crack up." To this I commented that one of the major training objectives of my office was to help soldiers recover and make their lives effective in this third realm, prayer. It would do no harm to reimpress this training on chaplains. We had about 486 chaplains in the 3rd Army at that time, representing 32 denominations. Once the 3rd had become operational, my mode of contact with the chaplains had been chiefly through Training Letters issued from time to time. Each treated of a variety of subjects of corrective or training value to a chaplain working with troops in the field.

"I wish you would put out a Training Letter on this subject of prayer to all the chaplains. Write about nothing else, just

the importance of prayer. Let me see it before you send it. We've got to get not only the chaplains but every man in the 3rd Army to pray."

With that the general arose from his chair, a sign that the interview was ended. I returned to my field desk, typed Training Letter No. 5, touching on the general's reverie on prayer, and after staff processing, presented it to Patton on the next day. He read it, and without change directed that it be circulated not alone to the 486 chaplains but to every organization commander down to and including the regimental level. Every unit in the 3rd Army received 3,200 copies. Because the order came directly from General Patton, distribution was completed on Dec. 11 and 12, in advance of its date line, Dec. 14, 1944. It read, "At this stage of the operations I would call upon the chaplains and the men of the 3rd U.S. Army to focus their attention on the importance of prayer.

"Our glorious march from the Normandy beach across France to where we stand, before and beyond the Siegfried line, with the wreckage of the German army behind us, should convince the most skeptical soldier that God has ridden with our banner. Pestilence and famine have not touched us. We have continued in unity of purpose. We have had no quitters, and our leadership has been masterful. The 3rd Army has no roster of retreats, none of defeats. We have no memory of a lost battle to hand on to our children from this great campaign. But we are not stopping at the Siegfried line. Tough days may be ahead of us before we eat our rations in the Chancellory of the *Deutsches Reich.*

"As chaplains it is our business to pray. We preach its importance. We urge its practice. But now is the time to intensify our faith in prayer, not alone with ourselves, but with every believing man, Protestant or Catholic, Jew or Christian, in the ranks of the 3rd U.S. Army.

"Those who pray do more for the world than those who fight; and if the world goes from bad to worse, it is because there are more battles than prayers. 'Hands lifted up,' said Bossuet, 'smash more battalions than hands that strike.' Gideon of Bible fame was least in his father's house. He came from Israel's smallest tribe. But he was a mighty man of valor. His strength lay not in his military might, but in his recognition of God's proper claims upon his life. He reduced his army from 32,000 to 300 men lest the people of Israel would think that their valor had saved them. We have no intention to reduce our vast striking force. But we must

urge, instruct, and indoctrinate every fighting man to pray as well as fight. In Gideon's day, and in our own, spiritually alert minorities carry the burdens and bring the victories.

"Urge all of your men to pray, not alone in church, but everywhere. Pray when driving. Pray when fighting. Pray alone. Pray with others. Pray by night and pray by day. Pray for the cessation of immoderate rains, for good weather for battle. Pray for the defeat of our wicked enemy, whose banner is injustice and whose god is oppression. Pray for victory. Pray for our army, and pray for peace.

"We must march together, all out for God. The soldier who 'cracks up' does not need sympathy or comfort as much as he needs strength. We are not trying to make the best of these days. It is our job to make the most of them. Now is not the time to follow God from 'afar off.' This army needs the assurance and the faith that God is with us. With prayer, we cannot fail.

"Be assured that this message on prayer has the approval, the encouragement, and the enthusiastic support of the 3rd U. S. Army commander."

The timing of the prayer story is important. My "prayer conference" with General Patton was Dec. 8; the 664th Engineer Topographical company, at the order of Col. David H. Tulley,

C. E., assistant to the 3rd Army engineer, working night and day, reproduced 250,000 copies of the prayer card; the adjutant general, Col. Robert S. Cummings, supervised the distribution of both the prayer cards and Training Letter No. 5 to reach the troops by Dec. 12-14; the breakthrough was on Dec. 16 in the 1st Army zone when the Germans crept out of the Schnee Eifel forest in the midst of heavy rains, thick fogs, and swirling ground mists that muffled sound, blotted out the sun, and reduced visibility to a few yards. The few divisions on the Luxembourg frontier were surprised and brushed aside. They found it hard to fight an enemy they could neither see nor hear. For three days it looked to the jubilant nazis as though their desperate gamble would succeed. They had achieved complete surprise. Their 6th Panzer army, rejuvenated in secret after its debacle in France, seared through the Ardennes like a hot knife through butter.

The 1st Army's VIII Corps was then holding this area with three infantry divisions (one of them new, and in the line only a few days) thinly disposed over an 88-mile front and with one armored division far to the rear, in reserve. The VIII Corps had been in the sector for months. It was considered a semirest area and outside of a little patrolling was wholly an inactive position.

When the blow struck, the VIII Corps fought with imperishable heroism. The Germans were slowed down but the corps was too shattered to stop them with its remnants. Meanwhile, to the north, the 5th Panzer army was slugging through another powerful prong along the vulnerable boundary between the VIII and VI Corps. Had the bad weather continued there is no telling how far the Germans might have advanced. Dec. 19, the 3rd Army turned from east to north to meet the attack. As Patton rushed his divisions north from the Saar valley to the relief of the beleaguered Bastogne, the prayer was answered. On Dec. 20—to the consternation of the Germans and the delight of the American forecasters, who were equally surprised at the turnabout—the rain and fog ceased. Bright clear skies brought perfect flying weather. Our planes came over by tens, hundreds, and thousands. The 101st Airborne, with the 4th, 9th, and 10th Armored divisions, which saved Bastogne, and other divisions which assisted so valiantly in driving the Germans back, will testify to the great support rendered by our air forces. General Patton prayed for fair battle weather. He got it.

It was late in January of 1945

when I saw General Patton again. This was in the city of Luxembourg. He stood directly in front of me, smiled, "Well, padre, our prayers worked. I knew they would."   ❋

SCHOOL DAZE

When Jimmy came home after his first day in kindergarten, his mother asked, "Did you learn anything today, dear?"

"No," he said disgustedly. "I gotta go back again tomorrow."

Agatha Brungardt.

*

From the composition of a sixth-grader: "My father's life was hard, as he had to get up early in the morning and shave. Then he would drive to the market with a load of vegetables. A girl used to ask him for several pounds of string beans which later proved to be my mother."

Catholic Herald Citizen.

*

Fourth-grade Tommy forgot to bring to class the unusual flower he had promised to bring. "I'm sorry," he apologized, "but I keep forgetting things."

"How long has it been like this?" I wanted to know.

Puzzled, he replied, "How long has it been like what?"   Edna Elsaser.

HEARTS ARE TRUMPS

When I was young, I was harassed by periodic outbreaks of pimples on my face. I think only adolescents can know how tortured I was.

Finally my mother took me to see Dr. Edward Beecher Finck, a direct descendant of Harriet Beecher Stowe, of *Uncle Tom's Cabin* fame. The doctor said that I should eat yeast cakes, but my mother, thinking this was very unorthodox, refused. When my pimples went uncured, the 80-year-old doctor took pity on me. He bought me the yeast himself, charged no fees, and let the matter remain a secret between the two of us. The pimples vanished, and I knew the wildest joy.

Years later, I was driving home in a blizzard. As I passed the hospital a white-coated figure dashed out and waved me to a stop.

"We need blood in a hurry," he said. "Will you volunteer?"

I did. As I prepared to leave, the interne asked, "Would you like to see who will get your blood?" He led me down a corridor, opened a door, and there on a bed lay a dying man. It was my old benefactor, Dr. Finck.

Harry J. Miller.

Fulton Sheen's Secret

Each day I fulfill a promise I made God on my ordination day

By FULTON J. SHEEN

January 1981, condensed from *Treasure in Clay**

O N THE DAY of my Ordination, I made two resolutions:

1. I would offer the Holy Eucharist every Saturday in honor of the Blessed Mother to solicit her protection of my priesthood. The Epistle to the Hebrews bids the priest offer sacrifices not only for others, but also for himself, since his sins are greater because of the dignity of the office.

2. I would spend a continuous Holy Hour every day in the presence of Our Lord in the Blessed Sacrament.

I have kept both of these resolutions. The Holy Hour had its origin in a practice I devel-

*Excerpt from "The Hour That Makes My Day" from *Treasure in Clay.* © 1980 by the Society for the Propagation of the Faith. Reprinted by permission of Doubleday & Co., Inc.

oped a year before I was ordained. The big chapel in St. Paul's Seminary would be locked at six o'clock; there were still private chapels available for private devotions and evening prayers. This particular evening during recreation, I walked up and down outside the closed major chapel for almost an hour. The thought struck me—why not make a Holy Hour of adoration in the presence of the Blessed Sacrament? The next day I began, and the practice is now well over 60 years old.

Here are some reasons why I have kept up this practice, and encouraged it in others.

First, the Holy Hour is not just a devotion; it is a sharing in the work of redemption. Our Blessed Lord used the words *hour* and *day* in two totally different connotations in the Gospel of John. *Day* belongs to God; the *hour* belongs to evil. Seven times in the Gospel of John, the word *hour* is used, and in each instance it refers to the demonic, and to the moments when Christ is no longer in the Father's hands, but in the hands of men. In the Garden, our Lord contrasted two *hours*— one was the evil hour, "this is your hour"—with which Judas would turn out the lights of the world. In contrast, Our Lord asked, "Could you not watch one hour with me?" He was asking for an hour of reparation to combat the hour of evil; an hour of union with the Cross to overcome the anti-love of sin.

Second, the only time Our Lord asked the Apostles for anything was the night He went into his agony. Then He did not ask all of them, perhaps because He knew He could not count on their fidelity. But at least He expected three to be faithful to him: Peter, James, and John. As often in the history of the Church since that time, evil was awake, but the disciples were asleep. That is why there came out of his anguished and lonely heart the sigh: "Could you not watch one hour with me?" Not for an hour of activity did He plead, but for an hour of companionship.

The third reason I keep up the Holy Hour is to grow more and more into his likeness. As St. Paul puts it: "We are transformed into his likeness, from splendor to splendor." We become like that which we gaze upon. Looking into a sunset, a face takes on a golden glow. Looking at the Eucharistic Lord for an hour transforms a heart in a mysterious way, as the face of Moses was transformed after his companionship with God on the mountain. Something happens to us like that which happened to the disciples at Emmaus.

On Easter Sunday afternoon when the Lord met them, He asked why they were so gloomy. After spending some time in his presence, and hearing again the secret of spirituality—"The Son of Man must suffer to enter into his Glory"—their time with Him ended, and their "hearts were on fire."

The Holy Hour. Is it difficult? Sometimes it has seemed hard; it might mean having to forgo a social engagement, or rising an hour earlier, but on the whole it has never really been a burden, only a joy. I do not mean to say that all the Holy Hours have been edifying. Once at the Church of St. Roch in Paris, I entered about three o'clock in the afternoon, knowing that I had to catch a train for Lourdes two hours later. There are only about ten days a year in which I can sleep in the daytime; this was one. I knelt down and said a prayer of adoration, and then sat down to meditate and immediately went to sleep. I woke up at exactly the end of one hour.

When I was ill in Chicago, I asked permission from a pastor to go into his church to make a Holy Hour about seven o'clock one evening, for the church was locked. He then forgot that he had let me in, and I was there for about two hours trying to find a way to escape. Finally I jumped out of a small window and landed in the coal bin. This frightened the housekeeper, who finally came to my aid.

At the beginning of my priesthood I would make the Holy Hour during the day or evening. As years passed and I became busier, I made the Hour early in the morning, generally before Mass. Priests, like everybody else, come in two classes: roosters and owls. Some work better in the morning, others at night. An Anglican bishop who was chided by a companion for his short night prayers explained, "I keep prayed up."

The purpose of the Holy Hour is to encourage deep personal encounter with Christ. God is constantly inviting us to come to Him, to hold converse with Him, to ask for such things as we need, to experience what a blessing there is in fellowship with Him. When we are first ordained it is easy to give self entirely to Christ, for the Lord fills us then with sweetness, just as the mother gives candy to a baby to encourage her child to take the first step. The exhilaration, however, does not last long; we quickly learn the cost of discipleship; the honeymoon soon ends, and so does our self-importance.

Sensitive love or human love may decline with time, but divine love does not. The first is concerned with the body, which becomes less and less responsive to stimulation, but in the order of grace the responsiveness of the divine to tiny, human acts of love intensifies.

Neither theological knowledge nor social action alone is enough to keep us in love with Christ unless both are preceded by a personal encounter with Him. When Moses saw the burning bush in the desert, it did not feed on any fuel. The flame, unfed by anything visible, continued to exist without destroying the wood. So personal dedication to Christ does not deform any of our natural gifts, disposition, or character; it just renews without killing. As the wood becomes fire and the fire endures, so we become Christ and Christ endures.

It takes some time to catch fire in prayer. This has been

one of the advantages of the daily Hour. It is not so brief as to prevent the soul from collecting itself and shaking off the multitudinous distractions of the world. Sitting before the Presence is like exposing one's body before the sun to absorb its rays. Silence in the Hour is a tete-a-tete with the Lord. In those moments, one does not so much pour out prayers, but listening takes its place. We do not say: "Listen, Lord, for Thy servant speaks," but, "Speak, Lord, for thy servant heareth."

We priests are meant to know Christ, not just to know *about* Christ. Many translations of the Bible use the word *know* to indicate the unity of two in one flesh. For example, "Solomon knew her not," which means that he had no carnal relations with her. The Blessed Mother said to the Angel at the Annunciation: "I know not man."

The closeness of that identity is drawn from the closeness of the mind with any object that it knows. No knife could ever separate my mind from the idea that it has of an apple. The ecstatic union of husband and wife described as "knowing" is to be the foundation of that love by which we priests love Christ.

Intimacy is openness which keeps back no secret, and which reveals a heart open to Christ. Too often friends are just that, and nothing more. Carnal love,

despite its seeming intimacy, often can become an exchange of egotisms. The ego is projected into the other person and what is loved is not the other person, but the pleasure the other person gives. I have noticed that whenever I shrank from demands that the encounter made on me, I would become busier and more concerned with activities. This gave me an excuse for saying, "I do not have time," as a husband can become so absorbed in business as to forget the love of his wife.

The Eucharist is so essential to our oneness with Christ that as soon as Our Lord announced it in the Gospel, it began to be the test of the fidelity of his followers. First, He lost the masses, for it was too hard for them to understand and they "walked with Him no more." Second, He lost some of his disciples, for Judas is here announced as the betrayer.

So the Holy Hour, quite apart from all its positive spiritual benefits, has kept my feet from wandering too far. When one is tethered to a tabernacle, one's rope for finding other pastures is not so long. That dim tabernacle lamp, however pale and faint, had some mysterious luminosity to darken the brightness of "bright lights." Even when it seemed so unprofitable and lacking in spiritual intimacy, I still had the sensation of being at least like a dog at the master's door, ready in case He called me.

Finally, making a Holy Hour every day constituted for me one area of life in which I could preach what I practiced. I very seldom in my life preached fasting in a rigorous way, for I always found fasting extremely difficult; but I could ask others to make that Hour, because I made it.

Many of the laity who have read my books or heard my tapes are also making the Holy Hour.

A state trooper wrote me that he had my tapes attached to his motorcycle and would listen to them as he was cruising the highways. "Imagine," he wrote, "the bewilderment of a speeder being stopped by me while from the tape recorder was coming one of your sermons about the Eucharist."

Most remarkable of all was the effect my preaching of the Holy Hour has had on non-Catholic ministers. I preached three retreats to Protestant ministers—on two occasions to over 300 in South Carolina and in Florida, and to a smaller group at Princeton University. I asked them to make a continuous Holy Hour of prayer to combat the forces of evil in the world, because that is what Our Lord asked for on the night of

his Agony. Many came to me later to inquire about the Eucharist, some even asked to join with me in a Holy Hour before the Eucharist.

One of the by-products of the Holy Hour was a sensitiveness to the Eucharistic Presence of Our Divine Lord. I remember once reading in Lacordaire, the famous orator of Notre Dame Cathedral in Paris: "Give me the young man who can treasure for days, weeks, and years the gift of a rose or the touch of a hand of a friend."

Seeing early in my priesthood that marriages break and friends depart when sensitiveness and delicacy are lost, I took various means to preserve that responsiveness. When first ordained and a student at the Catholic University in Washington, I would never go to class without climbing the few stairs to the chapel in Caldwell Hall to make a tiny act of love to Our Lord in the Blessed Sacrament. Later, at the University of Louvain in Belgium, I would make a visit to Our Blessed Lord in every single church I passed.

When I continued graduate work in Rome and attended the Angelicum and Gregorian, I would visit every church en route from the Trastevere section where I lived. This is not so easy in Rome, for there are churches on almost every corner. Fred Allen once said that

Rome has a church on one corner so that you may pray to get across the street; the church on the other corner to thank God you made it.

Later as a teacher at the Catholic University in Washington, I arranged to put a chapel immediately at the entrance of the front door of my home. This was in order that I might never come in or go out without seeing the sanctuary lamp as a summons to adore the Heart of Christ at least for a few seconds. I tried to be faithful to this practice all during my life, and even now in the apartment in New York where I live, the chapel is between my study and my bedroom.

I can never move from one area of my small apartment to another without at least a genuflection to Our Lord in the Blessed Sacrament. Even at night, when I am awakened and arise, I always make it a point to drop into the chapel for a few seconds, recalling the Passion, Death, and Resurrection of Our Lord, offering a prayer for the priests and Religious of the world, and for all who are in spiritual need. Even this autobiography is written in his presence, that He might inspire others when I am gone to make the Hour that makes life. ❈

THE PERFECT ASSIST

Just before Christmas my husband was transferred to another state. I felt very lonesome, especially since he was tied to his job, "learning the ropes." Although a welcoming hostess had paid me an official visit bringing me gifts from local merchants, and asking me general questions, none of the neighbors dropped in. This was vastly different from my home town where the mover was always followed by a parade of covered dishes.

One day when I was feeling particularly blue, I heard pounding on my back door, and a chorus of off-key singing. About a dozen rosy-cheeked youngsters were caroling. When they finished, the littlest one handed me an envelope. Inside was a welcome from a small neighborhood Catholic church. Puzzled, I suddenly remembered that I had told the welcoming hostess that I was a Catholic. The truth was that I had drifted away from my religion. As I was looking at the beaming faces of the children again, a lump rose in my throat, tears blurred my eyes. I felt the warmth of a sincere welcome and realized that Christmas bells ring in the heart no matter where one makes her home.   Sue Bullock.

Family Prayer: We Tried it Ten Different Ways

Sometimes the seeds planted bear fruit years later

By RONDA CHERVIN

January 1978, condensed from *Our Family**

W HEN I ASKED my children about our family prayers, I found that they could remember lots of them they really enjoyed.

"If you liked them so much why did we drop them?" I grumbled.

The reply: "Well, we liked them for a while but not *forever!*"

When I pondered this I decided that perhaps our sense of failure about family prayer wasn't completely justified. The more I thought of our attempts at prayer as seeds, or as introductions to meeting Jesus, the

*This article © 1977 by the Oblate Fathers of St. Mary's Province. Reprinted with permission from *Our Family,* Battleford, SK Canada.

more I could see all the good results they finally did produce.

Here are ten family prayers which my children remember with pleasure:

1. Very little children like songs. I used to have my twins march to bed to the strains of *When the Saints Go Marching In.* It was hilarious. I got sick of it after a few years, but they enjoyed it immensely. And now they are in the Sunday choir.

When my son was born, I had just learned the folk hymn *Day is Done,* with the refrain "And if you take my hand, my son, all will be well when the day is done." I crooned it to him while feeding him and now, five years later, he still falls asleep to this melody with God knows what good feelings about Providence.

2. When they are a little older, children like stories. "Then why do they so often reject books about Jesus?" you may ask. Many books *we* like fail because they are not at the child's level of understanding. But what *all* my children like is having a Gospel story told by us with lots of extra descriptions of secondary characters thrown in. As a result of many Gospel stories told and retold, my twin girls, now in junior high school, write beautiful spiritual stories of their own.

3. You can develop a habit of praise and thanksgiving in children by pointing out beautiful things to them. As you walk down the street you can tell them, "Praise God for beautiful roses," for instance.

Timing is important. When they reach the age where anything unusual a parent does in public is mortifying, they will walk to the other side of the street rather than have the neighbors hear mom chanting praise to the flowers on the block.

But even though I have only my five-year-old son now for my praise-and-thanksgiving walks, my older children have a true sense of beauty. They will grab me and insist that I leave my typewriter and come see a sunset. I'm sure they will never forget God's connection with beauty.

4. When the twins were about six, we started making up feast-day plays. We celebrated each one's saint's day by having the child plan a skit about the life of his or her saint, and involving all the family in the play. Each year the drama would become more intricate. For example, St. Helena advanced from finding the true cross under the dining room table to digging it out in the back yard in the dark by candlelight.

What killed this custom for my twins was that proud, foolish mommy started inviting her friends to watch the darling children celebrate their feast-days. This led to embarrassment, shyness, and the refusal to do any more skits.

5. One of the prayer experiences I treasure most involved the Rosary. The girls had to search through all the reproductions I had on holy cards or in art books to find their own favorite depictions of the mysteries. They were put into an album and for a few months we said the Rosary while gazing at the pictures.

I was disappointed when they did not want to join me forever in my vow of praying the Rosary daily. But they did get a strong sense of the mysteries, so Mary may not be half as disappointed as I was.

6. When my twins were about 11, I tried having the family chant the psalms of Vespers. The old breviary had Latin on one side and English on the other. Can you imagine my delight and utter amazement when my children opted for the Latin! Without understanding a word, they chanted it because they loved the way it sounded.

For a while it was beautiful; but then they started competing for precocity in Latin diction before admiring guests. Soon our elevated traditional prayer session became the nightly fight.

Another failure? I thought so, until this year when one of the twins found the old breviary and chanted in Latin by herself.

7. We also tried family Scripture reading with shared prayer. It was a complete failure until the children came up with the idea of doing it their own way. One drew pictures to illustrate the Gospels and another wrote poems.

Alas, after a month, boredom set in and their little Bibles began to collect dust on their bed tables. But the seed was planted. They still love the parables when they hear them at Sunday Mass and they enjoy Bible study best in school.

8. Another idea was to get each child to take turns planning a nightly prayer session for the family. The most successful of these involved each member telling the others everything they loved about each other. Another winner was having each one's Lenten resolutions decided upon by the others. "Mommy, you've got to give up yelling at us about things even before we've done them," was one of their suggestions.

9. About this time I got deeply involved in charismatic prayer. I was eager to lay hands on the children's heads and pray over them in season and out of season, on the way out the door, during difficult conversations, in the middle of fights, and even while they slept. At first they enjoyed the warmth, and I saw remarkable results, but after a bit they found it annoying. One finally said, "You know, Mommy, it gives me a headache when you press on my head that way."

Failure again? Not really. I have found it invaluable in times of acute misery in children, when they are so vulnerable they will accept anything. When my children were unable to control their fears, holding them tight and praying aloud certainly helped much more than my previous insensitive method, which consisted of yelling at them to calm down and shut up.

10. Now my eldest are teenagers. They long for independence and seem reluctant to participate in any prayers I devise except on formal occasions.

A final proof of failure? I thought so, until I found that when questioned they claim they have a very deep inner prayer life. They really love God, they just don't like having to adjust their own spiritual lives to fit mine.

Maybe the best family prayer for teenagers is the parents' prayer for the grace to let them alone. After all, our own favorite prayers are rarely those that were forced on us, but the ones which opened to us the most satisfying way of meeting Christ personally in times of need. ✿

OH, NO!

A Russian named Rudolph looked out his window one morning and announced, "It's raining."

His wife looked out, too, then said, "No, it's sleeting."

"It's raining," corrected her husband. "After all, Rudolph the Red knows rain, dear." *Children's Digest.*

TIME MARCHES ON

Agatha Christie, the well-known detective story writer, was married to an archeologist. Someone once asked her how she liked the match.

"An archeologist is the best husband any woman can get," she replied. "Just consider—the older she gets, the more he is interested in her." *Capper's Weekly.*

CARD ATTACK

The Christmas card we found on the front seat of our car was from the boys at the garage where we park nightly. We were pleased that they should remember us with a greeting. A week later we found another card from them. It read: "Merry Christmas. Second notice."

Mrs. Christina Tyler.

*

This note was attached to a computer card renewal notice that an indignant subscriber returned:

"Dear Machine: You have again misspelled my name. If not corrected by next month, I shall severely bend your card." *Liguorian.*

Married Prayer

"Prayer for a couple is more intimate than
sex . . . You can no longer say, 'I am going to
hold back' "

An Interview with GENE and MARY LOU OTT
November 1985, condensed from *Stories of Prayer**

G ENE AND MARY LOU Ott
have been active for ten
years at the national level in developing marital spirituality and
fostering prayer between married couples. The Otts helped
form the Retorno program "to
help people get in touch with
their own married spirituality
and enter into a life of couple
prayer." Giving workshops and
retreats for the program has
taken them to 40 states and to
Ireland. Gene was a family physician for 22 years and now
teaches at the University of Minnesota Medical School. The Otts
have ten children.

What is couple prayer?

Gene: To start, it's Mary Lou
and I sitting down and inviting
the Lord to enter our presence,
then being attentive to whatever
occurs. We usually pray with
the Scriptures. Sometimes we
use other readings or reflect on
what is going on with us as individuals or as a couple. I look at
this prayer as a listening rather
than doing.

Mary Lou: It's also a way of
life. The time we spend together
in prayer is not the most important aspect of it. Living out the
prayer is. Looking at it this way,
couple prayer is more of a
response in faith. As such, it
colors everything you do and
reflect on. Because the term
"couple prayer" is relatively new,
people often ask what it means,
what we do. It's not complicated. Just begin. Each couple
develops its own style.

Prayer is the most intimate
area a married couple shares.
Yet over and over again, couples will say to us they just can't

*This article © 1985. Reprinted with per-
mission of Sheed and Ward, 115 E. Armour
Blvd., Kansas City, MO 64141.

358

pray together. They say they'll try a few times and quit. Prayer for a couple is more intimate than sex. When we are talking, even about something important, there are parts of ourselves we can hold back. But praying together is like taking a step into a mystery in which you can no longer say, 'I am going to hold back, or give myself only in bits and pieces.' When a couple enters into a commitment to grow together in prayer, the process becomes pretty serious. The outcome is going to be a certain kind of continuing nakedness in front of each other.

Gene: Couple prayer has helped us to become aware of something we didn't understand early in our marriage: that when Mary Lou and I married, something new was created, our married relationship. Couple prayer comes out of this new creation. The uniqueness of this new creation in relationship to God is a reality, even though we do not fully understand it.

Mary Lou: It's like a third self, different from the two of us alone. We like to speak about it in images. One image is that when Gene and Mary Lou got married, we gave birth to a third self, and this becomes like a child. It needs to be nurtured. You have to spend time with it, just like a new child.

What do you do in couple prayer? How do you do it?

Gene: We have gone through a lot of trial and error. In our basic format we use Scripture. For us, the best time to pray is in the morning. We'll sit down together. We'll invite the Lord into that moment. Then we will talk. In the process of talking we will usually identify what is going on with each of us. I'm tired, I'm angry, I'm joyful, whatever. Then we will usually read Scripture. We might take a Gospel and read it in segments, or we might follow the daily readings.

After we have read Scripture, we sit. In this period of reflection, we concentrate on the Scripture. That isn't always easy. Sometimes I am focusing on work or problems I am trying to process. After a time, we share whatever occurred during those moments of quiet. Our whole day will be conditioned by what we shared.

Do you try to do this daily?

Gene: Yes, our usual routine is to take prayer time between six and seven in the morning.

Mary Lou: I know that sounds to people like a terribly long time, but it's our time. We are parents of a big family and we don't have much time when we go off by ourselves. The children have always known this is our time, a sacred part of the day for us. Never again in the entire day are we able to have moments like this. I'd get up at 2 o'clock in the morning if that was the only time we had for prayer, because it is so vital to my entire life.

I feel like I am going to a well to get a drink of nourishment that gets me through the day. We have gone through periods when we didn't pray. For example, we recently went almost a year without praying on a daily basis. There was a big difference in our relationship. It was so obvious that we finally started again. There was a wonderful difference after we started again. I'd describe it as vitality.

Do you pray in the same place?

Mary Lou: Yes, we think that is important. There has to be a kind of sacred spot. We learned many elements of prayer from the Ignatian method, and one is the place of prayer.

Do you use the place you pray in for prayer only?

Mary Lou: No. We always pray in the same room, but it's not like a shrine. We also use the room as an office.

Gene: There are trees right outside the windows and a large open area beyond. As the seasons change, you can sometimes relate what is going on outside to what is going on inside in your prayer.

Mary Lou: We feel safe there. It feels comfortable. But I don't want to give the impression that we are some kind of levitating couple in an upper room. We

pray because raising a big family is a lot of work, and we can't do it any other way. We have as many problems with children as anybody has. We pray out of a need to pray.

Prayer has made a big difference in our family. It has made a big difference in how we respond to the kids. That has been an important part of our prayer. We spend a lot of time praying for our children. A married couple has considerable power to pray for their children. It is awesome. According to Scripture, we as couples are the living image of the relationship God has with us. As a married person, I am going to know the love of God in the way Gene loves me and in the way I love him. That's holy.

Couples have a tremendous power, but we don't realize it. We are too busy living and surviving. But we don't have to live that way. The power and the gifts and the reconciliation are all there in marriage. All we have to do is ask for them.

Gene: The Church commonly uses the Scripture passage "two shall become one" for marriages. But I don't think we understand the depth of that passage. We relate to it only in the physical sense and forget the spiritual dimension. This spiritual oneness is a resource. Mary Lou speaks of it as money in the bank that we can go and draw from as long as we keep making deposits. When a crisis comes, that's the strength we draw from.

Developing our relationship must be a priority. We build such a relationship by becoming vulnerable, intimate, and by making a commitment. If we do that, the relationship will be filled and strong.

Can you take a crisis you have dealt with and show how you have worked with it in prayer and tapped the power you say exists in your relationship?

Gene: Let's begin with a relatively safe one. About three years ago, I was going to a meeting in Boston. Now, Mary Lou loves Boston. If she were going to move anywhere else, that would be the place. Because I had a heavy schedule, I planned to go to Boston by myself, concentrate on this meeting, then meet Mary Lou in New York, where we had a couples' meeting to attend.

Mary Lou wanted to go to Boston with me. I can't recall all the details, but it became a major conflict. A barrier went up between us. I soon realized that although all my reasons might be right, and made sense to me, the right thing was not happening to me and Mary Lou.

Our focus had to be on what was going to give life and strength to our relationship. When we started looking at it from that point of view, we negotiated. Mary Lou came to Boston midway through the meeting and we made certain we spent some time together, and it was good time together. When we went to the couples' meeting, we were revitalized.

How has couple prayer helped you with raising your children?

Mary Lou: I'm sure that if you listed any major crises parents have with children, we have had them. We have to live through these crises the same as anybody else. But they didn't split us apart. I think the fact that we spend time together in prayer is a major reason for that. With prayer, the two of us are together. Somehow, when we go to the Lord and say, "We need some help," it always comes. I can't tell you how it happens. I just know it does, because it has.

Gene: In any marriage when a crisis occurs, especially one relating to children, there is a certain amount of blame and guilt. I know sometimes that is expressed in anger at the other person. I may feel guilty, but that is uncomfortable, so I unconsciously blame Mary Lou, which then makes her feel guilty. But if we acknowledge our negative feelings, and share them, a positive result occurs. We are being open and being vulnerable to one another. The relationship grows in the process.

This is how you experience the power of the relationship?

Gene: Yes, and that doesn't necessarily just come while we are praying. We may sit down to pray and find we can't, because we haven't talked over problems. That comes out loud and clear when you are sitting there and trying to reflect. One of us may have to say to the other, "Look, I can't pray, because I'm angry at you right now. So, let's talk about it."

Mary Lou: I suppose the bottom line is that praying together makes you honest. I don't think anybody could fake going to prayer and pretending, when there is a whole pile of unresolved feelings. In that respect, it keeps our relationship up-to-date.

Gene: It keeps us from building up a lot of garbage. We get the junk out quickly if we are honoring our time together.

When you get the junk out on the table, what happens to it?

Gene: It depends. Sometimes the situation may call for outside help. That was the case when one of our boys had a problem with drug abuse. We wound up going to family counseling. We couldn't deny the problem.

Mary Lou, how did prayer help you with situations like this?

Mary Lou: Through prayer, Gene and I have become more

open to looking at our family systems. This involves looking at all components of a family, including its history—the individual members and the interactions between them. So we ask: Where did we come from? What did we bring into our marriage? How are our children growing up? What are they inheriting from us? What rules exist in our family?

As a result, a few years ago we approached the kids with the notion of some family therapy. Nobody needed it. We didn't wait until someone had a problem. The approach was more like this: Hey kids, you are growing into young adults. A deeper understanding of where you come from can be valuable to you. It can, for example, help you make a good choice when you marry. We were in this kind of counseling for about a year and a half.

And that grew out of your prayer?

Mary Lou: Absolutely. Change is a key element in prayer. If the family isn't getting healthier and holier—and to me the two are the same— prayer is an escape from reality. People must know that. Prayer is serious business. If you are going to face reality, it isn't always fun.

My ears perked up when you said prayer is the most intimate activity a couple can share.

Could you explain what you mean?

Mary Lou: Generally, people who live a Religious life, say in a rectory or in a Community of some sort, rarely pray together. I think that's because it is too intimate, too scary. Oh, they will gather for liturgical kinds of communal prayer, but those are safe. In the same way, families will pray together at mealtime, or they will read the Scriptures. Those are wonderful things to do, but they, too, are safe. Serious prayer on a personal level is different. It's awesome and revealing.

Gene: It was scary for me, because it meant being vulnerable and acknowledging parts of myself I did not like. In my own case it was acknowledging a temper and anger. Praying together called for sharing that. I wasn't proud of it, and I didn't really want to talk about it. But I shared it with Mary Lou. It meant sharing some of the shame. I asked her to help, to tell me if she saw it was building up, and if I wasn't acknowledging it.

This was risky, because I often saw her as the cause of my anger. It was risky for Mary Lou, too, because we had dealt with anger in a very eggshell way, saying, in effect, don't tread on that area. She was able to say, "Look, Gene, what's going on? Are things piling up? I think I

see some unresolved anger and frustration." Not uncommonly, that would come as we sat in prayer. I would probably sit boxed in, very tight, very heady, but I had to respond to that. That's healing.

How would the Scripture help with a situation like that?

Gene: The reading that comes to mind is the one in which the crippled man was lowered through the roof on a pallet. Once, when we were praying with that, I became aware of my anger at the way people were responding to my handicap. I have a birth injury called Erb's palsy or paralysis. During birth, the nerves and muscles in both my arms were damaged. I don't have full motion with them. I can't do anything above shoulder height. Putting on a hat, for example, is a very difficult task for me. I became aware that I had negative feelings toward people when they reacted to my handicap in ways I was not comfortable with.

As I reflected on the reading, I saw myself as the person lying on the pallet. We had learned to put ourselves into the Scriptures and identify with the characters through the Ignatian method of prayer and, as I did that, I felt anger and frustration, and I was thinking, "What are you doing to me? Why are you lowering me to this guy down below who is supposed to heal me? I didn't ask you for that."

The first step in dealing with this anger was to identify it. A lot of the anger was coming from not being able to do certain things, especially common tasks around the house. Dad was supposed to be able to do everything. I had to be honest and say some jobs required more energy and resulted in too much frustration. It also required me to ask, "What are you going to do about it?" Eventually, I went to Mary Lou and said, "Look, I need help with this. Will you help me?"

And Mary Lou became, in a manner of speaking, Christ for you? She became the one you were being lowered to for healing?

Gene: Yes. It was a moment of change for me. I experienced acceptance, acknowledgement, being heard. I received what I needed from Mary Lou. It is another case of couple prayer being an example of living out the marriage relationship differently, because of my being naked and sharing something difficult.

Mary Lou, what would be an example of your experiencing healing as the result of couple prayer?

Mary Lou: Being able to face alcoholism in my family. I come from a chemically dependent family, one that has a history of

it. Through being able to be more open to each other in prayer, we have been able to view my family history in a way we wouldn't have been able to do otherwise.

What keeps couples from experiencing prayer together?

Gene: Fear. Uncertainty. Lack of understanding or of awareness. Couples seem unsure it is for them. To such couples I say, "Try it, you'll like it."

Mary Lou: I think time is a major problem. It is hard to form a new habit, and prayer is a habit.

Gene: It requires commitment. It requires making prayer a priority. Married couples haven't been told they should make it a priority.

Mary Lou: Nor have they been told that if they pray together, life will change. They must be told it is worth sticking to. They also need support. We have several support groups we pray with.

What do you say to couples who say they don't have time for prayer?

Mary Lou: I tell them to begin and to be easy on themselves. They don't have to take a great deal of time. But they need to be faithful to it. I say to couples, "Pick a time period, say, ten minutes a day, and start with that." As it becomes more important to them, they will make some time for it.

Gene: There is another reason, too, that couples have trouble praying. When we first entered into prayer together as a couple, we argued about minutiae, like whether we would read verses nine to eleven or nine to twelve of a Scripture passage. We argued about whether we would sit left to right or right to left. I think this was the result of the evil spirit trying to keep us from prayer. The same thing may happen to other couples who undertake couple prayer. As a result, they experience turmoil, and, because they don't understand why, they'll say, "We can't do it. It isn't for us."

Mary Lou: There's also the fear of change. As I said, prayer produces change if you are open to it. For example, in our prayer, we began asking the Lord to show us how to live a simpler life-style in a Christian way. Out of that, Gene left a good job with a good income and took a position that reduced his income. Life changed around this house. Yet we did that out of our prayer, and it was the right thing to do.

What is the key thing you have learned from couple prayer?

Mary Lou: That the purpose of marriage is reconciliation. Those of us who marry do so to be healed, and to be reconciled with the Lord.

Gene: That marriage as a sacrament truly is a mystery. Couple prayer has been a way to discover that aspects of all the sacraments are present within the Sacrament of Marriage. Couple prayer has enabled us to experience the healing and reconciliation Mary Lou mentioned, and we have also found union, community, and ministry. And there is always more. When I rely on this "more," I know there really is a God. ✿

TIME MARCHES ON

A visitor to the hills of Tennessee saw an old man rocking in a chair on his porch. "Tell me, have you lived here all your life?" the visitor asked.

"Not yet," the old boy replied.   Herm Albright.

*

My five-year-old granddaughter leaned over the arm of my chair and studied my face. Her small fingers gently traced the wrinkles in my cheeks.

"Grandma," she said solemnly, "you must have left your face in the water too long."   *Parents'.*

No Prayer
Goes Unanswered

It took me almost a lifetime to realize that No
is as valid an answer as Yes

By MARGERY FINN BROWN
May 1961, condensed from *Redbook* *

MISS MARTIN brings to my sickroom an exquisite tray every morning. While I sip my coffee and pretend to nibble at the soft, buttery toast, I admire the symmetrical arrangements of silver, blue Meissen, and one yellow rose. My back is massaged. Freshly gowned and bandaged, the sheet taut as a sail, I can feel the death fears of night fade as the morning sun slivers through the window.

"You were walking in your sleep last night," Miss Martin says brightly. "Babbling about chocolates and shoes, and asking someone named Mary Suppler to help you."

I hadn't thought about Mère Supplice in ages. You think you've forgotten something but

it's there, buried deep, waiting for a phrase or a gesture to bring it back. "That was a long time ago," I say. "I was only seven when I went to a French convent."

"You speak *French?*" Miss Martin smiles as if I were a child exhibiting a precocious talent for nuclear physics.

I close my eyes. The enthusiasms of the young can be exhausting, and Miss Martin is but 21. She closes the door with a soft click, leaving me an expanse of room and sunlight. The pain seems to diminish. Always I feel the need to label its myriad guises. At night it grinds across my chest like tire chains, but now it's a small, furry animal, sleeping.

Without conscious effort the scene comes back entire: ten girls in bulky, navy-blue

*This article © 1960 by Margery Finn Brown. Reprinted with permission of Russell & Volkening, Inc. as agents for the author.

serge uniforms sitting around a linoleum-covered table. We are just finishing our two-o'clock glass of hops, a detested ritual during the month of May. "Hops are an excellent tonic that cleanses the blood and subdues *non-recherché* elements in the body," says the Mother Superior.

She holds the catechism aloft. "Do not dawdle, girls. We must commence our final review before First Communion tomorrow. We'll begin with the first question: 'Who made you?' "

" 'God made me,' " we answer in chorus.

" 'Why did God make you?' "

" 'God made me to know Him and love Him and serve Him in this world and to be happy with Him forever in the next.' "

"Mary Dee." Mary Dee was a pale, elongated day student with chilblains and a two-story pencil box. " 'What does Confession do to the soul?' "

While Mary Dee intoned the answer I thought about my soul, a strange entity the catechism did not explain. My soul was shaped like a dog bone—rounded on either end and slender in the middle. Off-white in color, it hung by a string from my brain down my throat to the spot where my chest stopped and my stomach began, swinging to and fro at will.

I did not confide my notions about the nature of my soul to anyone. Already there were too many things that made me different from the other girls. Unlike Flora, the class beauty, I never received packets of mail and candy from my family. My father wrote about twice a semester—short, scrawling letters signed "Yours without a struggle," interspersed with witticisms the nuns enjoyed far more than I. And yet I always carried his letters in my uniform pocket with my rosary and my red pencil sharpener, written proof that I, too, had a family, a connection outside the convent.

Unlike Ursula, I had neither curly hair nor five older brothers. Ursula said her brothers could lick the Ku Klux Klan without half trying. Ursula snored at night while I, an unprotected only child, screamed with terror as the white dormitory curtains billowed into ghostly Klan shapes. Mother Gabrielle, the dormitory mistress, would hold me in her arms, singing a French lullaby off key and indistinctly, for she had her teeth out.

The next morning at breakfast, Ursula or one of the other girls would say, "Crybaby, don't you want your milk in a bottle?" and I'd wish that the refectory floor would open up like the Red sea and swallow me whole.

What a fearful, deadly earnest child I was at seven! Hair cut in a bang, plump, gauche, I was constantly torn between a desire to be liked and to be like the others. But I had a passion for accuracy that endeared me to no one. Although I believed what was written in the catechism (for one thing, it was in print) the anecdotes with which Mother Superior interlarded the text made me bristle with doubt.

"When Napoleon was on his deathbed," she was saying now, "the doctor asked him what the greatest day of his life was. Do you know what the great Napoleon answered?"

"His First Communion day!" answered a chorus of ten minus one. Mother Superior, I thought, wasn't old enough to have been a personal witness.

Our class was finished. Father Duchesne was waiting now to hear our first Confessions in the chapel. "Don't be frightened," Mother Superior said. "And if you are, show countenance; put a good face on it! Don't forget, girls, to say a prayer for Mère Supplice and for the Propagation of the Faith, for parents, the Pope, and the souls in purgatory."

Two by two, heads covered with black veils, we filed into the chapel—a small jewel of a chapel, incensed and polished, with a precariously hanging choir loft where every morning the nuns sang magnificent Gregorian. We knelt in the pews, heads buried in our arms, medi-

tating deeply. The contest was to see who could get the largest penance. Mary Dee was positive she'd get at least 20 Our Fathers. In a voice that bespoke utter confidence, Flora said she'd be lucky to get off with a whole Rosary.

I dredged my conscience without conspicuous success. True, I'd called Denise Roehampton a big fat slob when she hit me with a hockey stick. Distractions at prayer time—how many times? this very moment I was worrying that my father would forget to feed my dog Prince, that he wouldn't send the new patent-leather shoes I'd requested a month ago. I needed them for First Communion tomorrow; they *had* to come in this afternoon's mail!

In the rack before me was a prayer book that listed sins according to one's "vocation in life." I brooded over the pages while Mary Dee made her Confession in a stage whisper that embarrassed us severely, although we couldn't hear a word. Ursula swished in and out of the box, curls bouncing. "Thirty Hail Marys," she hissed joyfully.

I could feel my heart beating in my throat when I entered the small dark box. "Bless me, Father, for I have sinned. This is my first Confession and these are my sins"—the approved format. When I had finished with Denise, disobedience, and distractions, he said, "Is that all, child?" and yawned.

"Oh, no," I whispered. "I neglected the duties of my diocese."

"You what?"

Perhaps the *c* in diocese should be pronounced like a *k*. "I neglected the duties of my diokese."

There was a thud on the other side of the screen and a chuckle quickly strangled. The priest pointed out that bishops had dioceses, not First Communicants. He said be a good girl and don't make up sins. I was bitterly disappointed when he gave me only three Our Fathers.

I couldn't lie when the girls asked about my penance. I sat at afternoon tea, removing the raisins from the buns. The four-o'clock mail brought Flora three packages, none for me. I asked for permission to walk by myself in the garden, saying I didn't feel well, which was true.

The garden was planted with grapevines and flowers I didn't know the names of. Kicking a pebble with my toe, I walked back and forth while three nuns sat on a bench practicing Gregorian, their hands rising and falling like white, stricken doves. Half hidden by a row of pines was the hockey field where every day we gave battle, and beyond it, a small gray cottage where Mère Supplice lived. We were strictly forbidden to go near the cottage. When we traipsed back from the hockey field, the nuns always said, "Quiet, girls. Curb the tongue. Mère Supplice is very sick today."

Although none of us had seen Mère Supplice, we knew all about her. She was an old, sick saint. As a young girl of noble blood she had spurned a host of suitors to become a bride of Christ. She spoke seven languages and made wonderful things happen. Mère Supplice also had a private chapel with a beautiful statue of our Blessed Mother wearing a crown of diamonds.

Wouldn't the girls be shocked and envious when I said, "Oh, by the way, I happened to see Mère Supplice's chapel today. The crown isn't diamonds, it's rubies"! Not even Flora would undertake an adventure like this! My reputation as a dyed-in-the-wool coward would cease; they'd forget my babyish cries at night.

I waited until the five-o'clock bell summoned the nuns to chapel. The hedge around Mère Supplice's cottage was alive with little bugs that stung my eyes. My blue serge uniform stuck to a spot between my shoulders, but I persisted. Through the first window, I could see a waxed hallway and a picture of the Sacred Heart with incandescent flaming chest. I could see a white bed and a white coverlet through the next window.

"Come in, come in," someone called.

I tried to creep away.

"Whoever is in the bushes, *entrez.*"

"I don't know where the door is."

"Use the window."

My elbows were shaking as I pulled myself up and swung my legs over the window sill. The woman in the bed wore the same kind of white ruffled bed cap as Mother Gabrielle. Her face was yellow and cracked in a hundred places. She was the oldest person I'd ever seen.

"Come closer—I cannot see you clearly." Her mouth caved in and her nose jutted out like the wolfy grandmother's in Red Riding Hood. On all occasions show *countenance,* Mother Superior had said, *countenance!*

"G-good afternoon, Mère Supplice," I managed to say.

"You are frightened?"

I nodded my head.

"Then why have you come?"

"To see your private chapel," I blurted out.

"There's my chapel," she said, pointing to a small statue of our Blessed Mother on a table. One candle flickered in a soiled red glass. There was no crown of diamonds. Our Blessed Mother had a chip off her nose.

"You are disappointed, eh? Few realities in life measure up to our expectations." I thought it was nice of her to talk grown up. "If you go to the dresser and open the top left drawer— *lentement, lentement* —you'll find a chocolate. Help yourself; take one."

The chocolate in its ruffled cup was old and runny, and for some unaccountable reason tasted of gasoline. I felt a little sick eating it. The chocolate and the gasoline seemed to lodge in my throat. But she was watching me intently and I showed my appreciation with a loud, smacking sound.

"*C'est bon.* Now we shall converse. You are making your First Communion tomorrow?"

Nervousness unhinged my tongue and I raveled on about Prince, my canary; the shoes that hadn't arrived; the "diocese" disaster; how I'd given up the thought of being a nun because I was extremely warm-blooded.

"I, too, am warm-blooded. I was born in the Midi."

"I don't see how you stand it. Don't you itch when you wear woolen drawers in May? I saw 40 pairs hanging on the nuns' clothesline this morning."

Mère Supplice laughed. Instead of being hurt or surprised, my usual reaction when I had unintentionally made a grownup laugh, I felt a little proud of this particular accomplishment.

"It is tiring to laugh, *non?* Come closer." She put her hand on mind and the coldness seemed to slip under my skin. "My missal is on the table. Look there until you find a small blue card, a poem I learned when I was your age. Can you read?" "I've been reading since I was four, almost." "Read, then," she said in a bossy, get-on-with-it tone.

My soul, there is a country
Afar beyond the stars,
Where stands a winged sentry
All skillful in the wars . . .

Her eyes were beginning to close.

If thou canst get but thither,
There grows the flower of Peace,
The Rose that cannot wither,
Thy fortress, and thy ease.
Leave then thy foolish rages—

" 'Ranges,' " she corrected me.

—foolish ranges;
For none can thee secure
But One who never changes—
Thy God, thy life, thy cure.

The room was very quiet and I wanted to leave. "Don't worry about your shoes," she said softly. "They will come tomorrow. Did you understand the poem?" "Not all; it says being dead's not so terrible." She started to smile but something hurt her, making the cor-

ners of her mouth stretch wide. When she spoke again she reminded me of Prince the weekend my father went off and forgot to feed him. "Will you do something for me, child?" "Oh, yes, Mère Supplice!" The sooner the better; I wanted to leave with all my heart. "Tomorrow when you go to the altar for the first time, give Him a message for me. Tell Him to please call me soon. I'm tired. I've waited so long." Her head flopped back on the pillow. I tiptoed to the window and swung my legs over the sill. A crow flew over the bushes, his ugly caw-caw mocking me as I ran for the convent and through the oaken door into the arms of Mother Gabrielle, who was matching socks in the laundry room. I made no mention of meeting Mère Supplice, or of learning Henry Vaughan's poem. But I didn't forget Mère Supplice's message—not that night, which I spent in the infirmary ("Sick with excitement," Mother Moira said, and was quite wrong. It was chocolate and gasoline.) Nor did I forget it the next morning, when my new shoes arrived special delivery. Beautiful, oh, beautiful shoes, cunningly made with patent-leather tips and velvety suede backs! Dressed in our smocked dresses and wreaths of myrtle and wheat, we walked to the altar that morning. I said, "Thank you, Lord, for the shoes. Please take care of Prince and Mother Gabrielle. Mère Supplice says please let her die— she's tired of waiting."

My dog bone of a soul did not, alas, turn dazzling white. It was oscillating at the usual placid pace as I walked back from the altar. Our breakfast was festive: *brioches* and wild strawberries and Mother Dolores playing the piano so vivaciously that the picture of *The Last Supper* shivered on the wall. Speeches were made, and even Mother Gabrielle was in a gay mood.

Then the portress, a little gnome of a woman with a mustache, came and whispered to Mother Superior. Mother Superior put down the cup of coffee with which she was toasting the health and spiritual welfare of the first communicants.

"My dear sisters in Christ, my dear children, Mère Supplice has gone from this life into eternity."

Chairs scraping, we rose and sang that hymn of rejoicing, "*Te Deum Laudamus.*"

As I lie here now in the sunlight, years later, I wonder why Mère Supplice's death did not produce some fearful emotional trauma, some lifelong scar. The fact that she died on my First Communion day seemed, at the time, a natural answer to the prayer I had transmitted. No prayer goes unanswered, the nuns used to say. It is only in full maturity that we realize that No is as valid an answer to prayer as Yes.   ❖

LONG-RANGE FORECAST

The hopeful forecast came from an old Filipino farmer, perched cross-legged on the back of a water buffalo.

According to Columban Father Ed DePersio, a long and destructive drought had parched the southern Philippines in recent months. The missionary priest was hiking down a country lane when he came upon the immobile farmer and stopped to chat about the unusual dry spell.

The old man raised his head, twitched his nostrils and said, "It's going to rain soon." Curious about the Filipino's secret method of forecasting, Father DePersio asked anxiously how he knew.

"I heard it on my transistor radio," the wrinkled old man answered.

Columban Fathers Foreign Mission Society Release (6 May '69).

First Day at the Rectory

It was a busy, tragic time and I was awed by every minute of it

By G. SIMON HARAK, S.J.
September 1980, condensed from *The Jesuit**

DEAR SIS: You asked me to reflect upon my first priestly ministry, now that the excitement has passed. But there was so much to it I'm limiting myself to my grace-filled "baptism by fire" as a priest—two days after my first Mass.

Do you remember dinner after that Mass? Our parish priest invited me to "cover" for him during the middle of the week. I jumped at the chance to begin.

It meant that I was on call for 24 hours at the rectory, Tuesday into Wednesday. Parish

*Reprinted with permission.

Mass, hospital, confessions, telephone, doorbell, all belonged to me. I just plain wanted to get up and dance (like Snoopy). Everything had prepared me for this, the work, the study, the frustration, and the uprootedness of Jesuit life, the Community support (and criticism), prayer and insight, and the call that enables one to touch people's lives at their most intimate point, their relationship to God.

Little could I realize that Tuesday morning as I woke, how widely and deeply his ministry could show itself in one day on call.

373

After the 8:30 morning Eucharist, people approached me for Confession. I was a bit surprised. I'd heard of this and I was certainly *trained,* God knows. Still I didn't expect it so quickly. Maybe God decided to touch their hearts that day. I got out of church late and had to rustle up some brunch.

While I was doing that, a call came from the hospital: I was to anoint two people. I pushed the bread into my mouth, jumped into the brown bomber John had lent me, and dashed off.

The receptionist directed me to Mary Jones' room. I went in the door, sort of hiding behind the little sheet of paper and said, "I'm looking for Mary Jones, please." The woman in the far bed smiled and waved. Good! A cheerful looking first anointing! Besides, the other woman was comatose.

I employed my best tried and true bedside manner. Father Congeniality. This lasted about 40 seconds as I tried to offer the service of the Church: Confession, Eucharist, Sacrament of the Sick. At this presentation she smiled politely and replied, "Oh, no, Father, I'm a Methodist!"

Well, fortunately for me I had all those Methodist ministers pray over me at my Thanksgiving Mass. I mentioned this event to her and she seemed mollified.

So I prayed over her and blessed her. I am God's minister and was glad of the chance to be ecumenical. I anointed the other lady and left, trying not to show my embarrassment.

The second anointing went fairly uneventfully. I began to feel like a pro.

In the corridor I met Dr. Haddad, who had delivered us kids and was our godfather. What a jumble of past and present he must have felt as I stood there in my collar and black!

Back to the rectory about 2:30. And when I closed the door, the front bell rang. Two blond kids, a very small boy and a smaller girl. "Well . . . Father . . . my sister and I have been getting blueberries (Were the pauses shyness or guilt of some sort?) and the bag is breaking! Do you have another one for us to bring the berries home to our mother?"

A half hour later, the phone rang. The hospital again, someone on the danger list. Could the priest come? Into the church for the oils and the Eucharist. Into the brown bomber and off! This one closer to death than the last two. I realized how this last year I had avoided wakes and funerals. And me a priest.

Back to the rectory for supper. Some good-natured ribbing from the curates: How does a Jesuit like being a parish priest?

What would I do if all my days were as wild as this one? The doorbell rang and the on-call priest had to answer. The charismatics wanted the keys to the church. I gave them a right one and a wrong one. So they had to return to ring the doorbell again (much to the glee of the off-duty men at supper). Later they went for a walk, and then came back separately to ring the bell and ask for "that wonderful new priest, Father Harak." They were getting silly and I loved it. More door calls for Mass cards. And the day wound down.

I took some time for prayer and reflection over my first day, what I'd done and left undone. I'd offered Mass, heard confessions, anointed the sick. I decided that I had room for improvement, but much time to learn. For a first day, I'd not done badly.

About eleven o'clock, as I pulled off my shoes, the phone rang again. Father Bob answered it right away. When I went outside he was getting dressed. "Emergency room at the hospital." I have to admit that for a second I toyed with the idea of letting him go. But I mustered my strongest voice, "Where are *you* going? I'm on call."

Into the church for the oils and the Eucharist. Into the bomber and off. Fast this time, fixing the white tab collar as I went. At the emergency room, an officer greeted me: "Aren't you Father Harak, just ordained? Father, I was at your first Mass, really moved. Thank you so much! Father, the body is in the next room."

An elderly attendant, whom we knew as "Pop" from the time we were kids in town (never knew he worked at the hospital), took me into the room and showed me the body.

A little girl. "I'll make it easier for you, Father . . . here," pulling back a sheet slightly. "An accident, Father, she was killed." Twelve years old. Still. Quiet. As though she were holding her breath. I, too, held my breath, as though waiting for her to breathe. My duty. The last rites: absolution. Representative of the Church. Pop had left. It was just the body of the little girl and me. And God.

I begged for mercy because she was one of those I had been chosen to pray for. Absolution for her faults because I am a priest. I prayed the Our Father with new conviction and commended her body to rest in peace. I walked outside, stumbled around dazed for a few minutes.

First time I'd ever seen anyone who had so recently died, let alone been killed. I turned back into the room. Because I wanted to make sure I left no prayer unsaid. She was my first death as a priest. And I wanted to remember. I felt a special bond between her and me. Does that sound funny? Her death had changed both of us in the same moment. This small girl; whose death God chose to share with me, the new priest. She was at grace, lying there. And I believed that now, with God, she has a special spot in her heart for me—with that wisdom and sadness that kids sometimes have. Because I was her priest, and she is my sister, in death.

Again outside the room. After midnight. A new day. They began wheeling stretchers. Two, four, five of them—the same accident. All kids. Must have been two cars, I thought. They were groaning, cut by glass, heads split, arms and hands at obtuse angles. Teams of people in white kept coming. White stretchers, white sheets, white blankets, white doctors and nurses, and the priest in black—going from stretcher to stretcher, room to room. (I found out later they called me "the phantom Priest"—apparently always in the right place that night, but I think it was really because of my being the one dark figure in all that white.)

I went from room to room, talking to the kids, praying with them—the most serious ones first, checking on the others constantly. Over and over, "Hi, Andy, it's Father Simon again, feeling any better? Okay, I want you to know that I'm with you. And more important, Jesus is with you. You want either of us, just call." Just call Father Simon. (A little thing; give them a name to hang onto, among all the flurry of healers: something that makes sense.) "Hi, Bob, Father Simon again. You a little scared? (Wide-eyed nod.) I'll bet. What happened?"

It was the youngest, eight years old, who finally told the story, point for point, like a boy reporting to his grade school class. One car, seven kids. Seven kids. "Me and my brother... after the movie... took a ride home from another kid... then bang! And I was squinched up in the seat... crawled out the window... just lay there." ("It looked like a war," an ambulance driver said to me later. "Bodies all over the damn place," making successive tossing gestures with his hands!)

To the next room. I heard one of the nurses say, "Is that all of them?" Seven kids, six stretchers? I said "No" to myself. There had to be another.

Parents began arriving. Numb, shocked, faint, mute, relieved? (One kid was actually discharged that night.) One thing I remembered. Don't say, "Everything will be all right" when you don't know. I wished I could have said it. But deprived of certainty, you fall into silence. You stand by them, try to calm the distraught ones. Strange. One couple was uncomfortable at the sight of the priest. Perhaps on the outs with the Church for some reason. As though it mattered at a time like this.

They were working on Charlie in the next room; broken arm and leg, scalp open; an anesthesiologist, a nurse, one doctor for the scalp, one for the bones. And the priest holding Charlie's good arm. "Now, Charlie, they're putting you back together again all at once so it will be over quicker. O.K. I'm holding this hand. Feel it?" (A squeeze.) He had a greenish cloth over his face. They cleansed the wounds, preparing for the local. I described each step to him.

"Remember the dentist, how he puts in novocaine, so that it won't hurt? Well, that's what they are doing now. It'll hurt at first, then it won't hurt anymore." Injection. A hard squeeze of the hand. Then another and another.

"I'm praying for you, too, doctor."

One pulled the corner of his mouth mask back, "Thanks, Father I could use 'em." But the other said, "They don't work, prayers. I've tried them."

"You watch how fast you get that arm back together, Doctor," I said smiling. We really didn't have time for petty antagonism. But he decided to push his point at the priest. He picked up the kid's arm and I could see it angled near the wrist. He would have to set it, put it straight. He looked me right in the eye and with a powerful motion set the bone. It must have been pretty well anesthetized; the kid barely squeezed. The doctor kept looking in my eyes, to see if I'd flinch. Well, even though I'd never seen a bone set, I was ministering to that doctor as much as to that kid. And right now he needed someone as tough and professional as he was. I didn't bat an eye.

As I was going out of the room, a nurse took my arm. "Father, the other body is in there." For a flash, I was angry. "What other body? Don't we have enough already? There can't be any more," I thought. They had put him in an office. No room left in the emergency room.

Then she left me with the dead. Awed before young death, I completed my task, committing him into the hands of the One who had cast the lot of His life with us. He could have done anything. But He chose to be with us, for us. Forgiveness, Lord, and mercy, and peace. I covered the boy's face, zipped up the bag, replaced the tag with his name on the chest, said another prayer, and left.

The parents of the girl who died and the boy with the broken leg were in the emergency room. The girl had been taken. The boy had his broken leg set in a cast. I just stood with the parents until they were called into the kid's room. He was O.K., not in pain, some lacerations. The boy began asking about the others in the accident. Pop was there, hand on the boy's head. He turned to us and mouthed, "He should be told. He should be told now."

He was right. Tell him now, fast and clean. Otherwise upstairs he might overhear it, read it in the news. The mother tried, but she couldn't. The father tried but faltered, understandably. The boy looked over at me and questioned me with his eyes. A euphemism floated into my mind, and I said, "She received the blessing of the Church." The boy kept looking at me. "You have to understand. (The hardest words I ever had to say, though I'd rehearsed and rehearsed them.) Your sister didn't make it through the accident."

His eyes got wide, wider, and wider and he wept into his dad's arm. And Pop was stroking his hair, saying, "It's better this way. Let it out, let it out. It's better you should know now." But how do you tell a kid?

I left the room and a nurse said, "You have a phone call." At 1:30 A.M.? Who could be calling? It was Father Bob from the rectory.

"Look, I'm not running after you or anything, but is everything O.K.? What's going on? Do you want some help?"

I explained, saying the worst appeared to be over (thinking of that kid crying, 15 feet away). "But I sure would like somebody to talk to when I get back home."

"You've got it. I'll be here when you come back."

It was another hour. Time with the parents, who were torturing themselves in the jumble of their thoughts and misery. We torture ourselves because the alternative is to admit that life is so far beyond us, so incomprehensible, so much greater than our little meanings can order it to be. The Cross. The absolute mystery of God.

I walked into the rectory at 2:30 and this 65-year-old priest came out and put his arm around my shoulder. We talked and talked, sharing the burden. He offered to take my morning assignments but I declined. My goodness, this generous man! To me, he was the real hero. He wasn't there with all the action, all the visibility, all the recognition. He stayed home, and worried about the new curate, was there to patch him up and offer respite. It made me proud to be in the brotherhood of priests. He was up for the early Mass, as usual. I was up for the 8:30 liturgy, with a not altogether coherent homily, I'm afraid. I wonder what my homiletics teachers back at the seminary would have thought. All I know is, I'll never criticize in my heart the homily of a parish priest again. God knows how he might have spent the day before. ✠

CONFUSION OF TONGUES

The news editor of a large daily was doubtful about a report sent in by one of his local correspondents. It said that a farmer had lost 2,032 cows in a sudden thunderstorm. The editor picked up his phone and put in a long-distance call to the farmer. "I have a report here that says you lost 2,032 cows in the storm this morning," he said. "Is that figure correct?"

"Yeth," replied the farmer.

"Thank you," replied the editor crisply, and hung up. Then he picked up the correspondent's report and amended it to read, "John Jones, a local farmer, lost two sows and 32 cows in a sudden thunderstorm this morning." *Lucille Goodyear.*

*

Late home from work, red-nosed and bleary-eyed, the drunk staggered into the living room waving his empty pay envelope.

"Where's your check?" demanded the wife.

"Bought something for the housh," he replied.

"Like what?" she inquired.

"Ten rounds of drinks," he replied. *Pageant* (May '60).

BRING 'EM BACK ALIVE

The greenhorn was bragging to his buddy about his hunting skills. When they arrived at their cabin he said: "You start a fire. I'll go shoot us some supper."

Two minutes later he met a bear. Terrified, he dropped his gun and sprinted for the cabin, the bear right behind him. Just as he reached the cabin, he slipped and fell. The bear was going too fast and skidded right in through the cabin door.

The greenhorn got up and closed the door. Then he shouted in to his buddy, "Skin that one now and I'll go get us another." *Woodmen of the World.*

"Call Father Kern. He'll Come"

For 30 years he has been a friend to the needy
in the oldest neighborhood in Detroit

By ARTHUR P. HAGAN
September 1977, condensed from *The Michigan Catholic**

THE OLD MAN writhed on the dirty bed. He was struggling for breath, his face an eerie yellow in the dim light. The other men in the flophouse stared dully at his torment.

He needed help, but who would respond at four in the morning? The answer was automatic: "Call Father Kern. He'll come."

He did, within minutes, accompanied by a young seminarian. They carried the man to the car which Monsignor Clement Kern had double-parked in the street, and rushed him to the hospital.

Two days later he died, but in a clean gown, between white sheets, with a priest kneeling at

his bedside. He did not die alone.

• "It was three years ago, December 28, a bitterly cold day," recalls Father Sam Campbell. "I remember because I lost my temper.

"I knew the woman sitting outside my office; she had ten children. Her gas had been turned off. No heat in the house and it was zero outside. So she came to tell Father Kern her plight. After she left, he came into my office with the gas bill. He showed it to me: $745!

"I told Father Kern, 'You're not paying this. You can't afford it.' His response was 'Well, the money for it will come from somewhere.' I was really angry."

Four hours later an elderly couple came to the rectory. They told Father Kern that they wanted to make a donation for the poor. Then the man sat down and wrote out a check for $750.

"Father Kern went over immediately and paid the gas bill," Father Sam says. "That's the way things happen at Holy Trinity. Father Kern goes completely on faith."

• On the day before Christmas, the Church of the Most Holy Trinity glowed with a holiday radiance; the altar was banked with flowers, and flanked by tall green trees. The church was almost half-full for eight o'clock Mass. The faithful were freshly scrubbed, neatly dressed, an adornment to the old edifice.

The assembly of the unwashed derelicts at the back of the church, however, provided a jarring contrast. They reeked of accumulated filth and cheap whiskey. The gamy aroma pervaded the church, sweeping back even into the sacristy where Father Kern was robing for Mass.

The usher did not try to hide his annoyance. "Father," he complained, "you must do something about those drunks in the vestibule. Decent people don't like to walk past them. They make the church smell like a stable."

"Isn't that precious?" Father Kern smiled. "On the day before Christmas. The first church on earth was a stable. You remember? Mary and Joseph were outcasts, too. Like those boys in the back of the church. Decent people didn't want them around."

Father Kern—nobody calls him Monsignor—is 70 years old. For the past 30 years he has been the pastor of Holy Trinity in the oldest section of Detroit.

The church is the port of last resort for the men and women who can't cut it, the physical and spiritual casualties of an urban jungle.

Benches line the rectory hallway outside the cluttered offices of Father Kern and Father Sam Campbell, the associate pastor. On an average day earlier this year, from morning to night, 108 men and women come to sit on those benches and wait for a chance to tell their tales of woe to the priests. No matter how long it takes, the priests will see each person privately, listen to their problems, and try to help.

Some lack clothing. The parish clothes bureau can take care of that. Others need furniture. They are referred to the Corktown Cooperative, started by the parish but now operating independently. Others have unpaid bills for rent, food, utilities. Father Kern will somehow find the money.

So many alcoholics. When these trembling, flushed, unkempt supplicants walk into the priests' offices, twisting their hats in their hands, they will get the price of a cheap bottle of wine. Short of a stay in a hospital, nothing else will steady their hands, soothe their raw nerves, and dissipate the debilitation for a little while. Sooner or later, most of them agree to go to a detoxification center where they are dried out, shot full of vitamins, and restored to sober health. Some will never drink again. Others may stay on the wagon for weeks, months, even years. Some head for the nearest bar. Perhaps 15% will drink themselves to death.

Father Kern never gives up on any of them. If they are living on Social Security and fear they may blow their month's check in one night, they can bank at the rectory, withdrawing money as they need it. Many use Holy Trinity as a mail drop. File cards are kept on every person who applies for help. The information is usually taken from their Social Security cards.

"Father Kern loves the losers," says a cop on the beat. "He will take those poor old men in, bathe them himself, let them sleep in the rectory, and give them fresh clothes. On cold nights, I've known him to open the church and let the bums come in where it's warm. He has to send somebody over to stay with them or they'd burn the church down.

"He used to run a 24-hour reading room. Reading room! Sure, there were some magazines and books there if anybody wanted to read them, but nobody ever did. It was just a respectable place for the whiskey heads to sleep it off. Volunteers were in charge at all times. Sometimes Father Kern would take the midnight to six shift."

Father Sam, who has become the pastor's partner in their special ministry, is one of Father Kern's success stories. He was a chronic alcoholic, dismissed from his diocese, with nowhere to turn until Father Kern took him in, encouraged him to quit drinking, and gave him another chance.

Although he has elected to serve skid row bums and alcoholic prostitutes, Father Kern does not deny his compassion to the affluent. They too have fled to him for help in retrieving their careers, their marriages, and their health.

"Father Kern has taken in so many men and women who were down on their knees, beaten, hopeless," says an observer. "He has picked them up and straightened them out. Now some of them are driving big cars and living in fancy homes. He could call one of them and say I want $1,000 in cash on my desk in an hour, and it would be there."

The old pastor, however,

never calls in his I.O.U.'s. "I have never heard him mention money in his sermons," says a parishioner. "Yet he has been a beggar all his life."

A very successful beggar, too. The daily mail brings to Holy Trinity about $500 a week in unsolicited donations "for the poor," most of it in ones and twos and fives. The "Sharing of the Green" on St. Patricks' Day always fills the church to overflowing for a noon Mass. The service includes Irish pipers playing *Amazing Grace* and a dark-eyed colleen singing *Danny Boy*. This year the observance raised almost $20,000. Holy Trinity had a budget of about $120,000 last year. Ninety percent of that amount was raised from sources outside the parish.

"We are absolutely dependent on the goodness of the Lord, and the good will of so many wonderful people," Father Kern declares. "We have certain needs, and the money comes in. We always have enough."

In the late '50's, Father Kern needed almost $25,000 to modernize and expand the parish school. He was confident something would turn up, and it did.

"Elmer Ryan was a wonderful man," Father Kern relates. "He was a professional gambler, you know. Ran the old Chesterfield Club. He told me 20th Century Fox was looking for a church to sponsor the Detroit premiere of *The Story of Ruth*, a benefit performance. I said, 'If it's a bale of hay, we'll take it if it's free.' "

The premiere was set for the 6,000-seat Fox Theater with tickets priced at $25, $15, and $10. Father Kern had no idea how he'd sell such expensive tickets, but Ryan knew. He introduced Father Kern to Bert Brennan, Jimmy Hoffa's No. 1 lieutenant in the Teamsters.

Brennan, an agnostic, was tough as they come. He could spot a phony a mile away, but he had no defense against Father Kern's innocent trust. He scooped up all the $25 and $15 tickets. "I'll take these," he offered. "My boys will sell them." Brennan later turned over to Father Kern a check for $23,000.

"I don't mess with finances," Father Kern concedes. "We have excellent laymen who keep our books, gratis. Sometimes they tell me I can't keep on going this way and I say, 'Well, we'll try it and see what happens.' It always works out."

He says he has no personal financial needs. "I receive an adequate salary," he explains. A carton of cigarettes a week may be his greatest extravagance. He can't remember the last time he bought a suit of clothes. Among his admirers is a clothier who keeps an eye on him. When he thinks Father's suit is getting tacky, he gives the clergyman a new one. "It's last year's style," the clothier always says. "I can't sell it."

A 1977 automobile is his most expensive possession, but this is really community property. Says Father Kern: "Everybody drives it. We have a lot of runs to be made every day."

The parish stays solvent, but not without some wear and tear on his economic advisers. Says Father Sam: "Father Kern despises sitting on money. If he has any money, he'll find a way to spend it. He does not spend irresponsibly. He puts the money where the need is. At the end of the last fiscal year, we had about $600 in the bank."

Father Kern's charity magnetizes support. Doctors, nurses, and pharmacists donate their skills to keep the Cabrini Medical Clinic in operation. Lawyers and social workers offer free legal aid to the needy. Volunteers take care of much of the administrative detail of the parish.

Women run the clothes bureau. Other volunteers prepare and deliver hot meals daily to more than 60 frightened old folks who are prisoners in their rented homes. Now parishioners are operating a soup kitchen in cooperation with two other churches. Members of the parish also train retarded youths as dishwashers and offer adult education programs. All without pay.

"Father Kern is a politician," a volunteer laughs. "He could give Tom Sawyer pointers on how to get a fence whitewashed."

A poet in the city room dubbed Father Kern "The Saint of the Slums," but Holy Trinity parish is no slum. It is a very old, poor, polygot community. The 400 families registered in the parish are mostly Mexican and Maltese with a sprinkling of blacks, Appalachian, Irish, and other minorities. It is said that 16 languages are spoken within its precincts. The crime rate is not high.

Holy Trinity, however, is on the edge of downtown Detroit, where few care to venture after dark. The murder rate in the city is among the highest in the nation. But Father Kern will go anywhere, any time, at any hour of the day or night. So will Father Sam.

"It is not dangerous at all," Father Kern answers firmly. "There is so much talk of fear that now, it seems, everybody is afraid. Well, I don't have any fear.

"I love the city. I get around a lot at night and it's wonderful. We make a lot of runs to hospitals to visit the lonely. Often on the way home, I'll stop in at an all-night downtown drugstore for cigarettes or a cigar or something. It's always crowded. So many people. I love to be with people."

If somebody comes to the rectory door at four in the morning, Father Kern will be down to see if he can be of service. He has never been robbed or assaulted. On Christmas Eve a few years ago, around midnight, a visitor robbed Father Sam at knifepoint. That was the only time a guest has abused the rectory's hospitality.

The pastor of a neighboring inner-city parish was murdered last year. He admitted a man who came begging for help. Although the priest offered no resistance, the intruder shot him in the face and then took what little money he had, about five dollars.

Father Kern grieved for the loss of a dear friend but he never considered shutting people out from his rectory. He saw in the priest's martyrdom a special mark of God's favor. What better thing could a priest do than lose his life in the line of Christian service?

The old pastor stands five-foot-five and weighs 137 pounds. He is apparently inexhaustible. He usually arises at 7:30 and gets to bed somewhere between midnight and three in the morning.

"I'm almost 25 years younger than he," says Father Sam, "but he has three times my energy."

A one-time caddy, Father Kern loves golf. He plays on one of the city's most crowded municipal courses but he can't get out nearly as often as he'd like. He says he doesn't have enough time to read, either. He is a relatively heavy smoker, burning up a pack and a half a day, but he swears off for Lent and Advent.

"By two o'clock Ash Wednesday, I'm dying," he smiles. "I don't really know if I should give up smoking. It makes me so mean."

To some, Father Kern comes across like an aging Pollyanna. Mention the diabetic who has just had his leg amputated; Father Kern will speak enthusiastically about the great care he is getting. Talk about the deprivation and loneliness of the old folks; he will say how he admires their beautiful resolution and faith.

Yet Father Sam remembers one particularly bad day: "It had been terrible. I had been on the go all day long, driving people to hospitals, visiting the sick and the dying, going to families where there was trouble, one terrible thing after another, without a letup. I felt so depressed. All the human misery just overwhelmed me.

"When I went up to my room, after midnight, I saw that Father Kern's door was open and his light was on. He was reading. I had to talk to him. So I went in and poured out my woes. I really felt sorry for myself. He heard me out in his quiet way, never saying a word.

"After I was finished he said, in the saddest voice I have ever heard: 'Father, how do you think I feel?'

"I was ashamed that I had bothered him. For at that moment, for the first time, I realized the heavy burden that this man has carried so lightly, day after day, for 30 years."   ✤

Beautiful Ceremony

In the late '40's, Father Kern instituted a "printer's Mass" at 2:30 Sunday morning for the people who worked on the city's three daily newspapers, for the bartenders, waiters, and waitresses, night club chorines, all the night people, including the boys from the street who found themselves dispossessed when the bars closed.

One night a swarm of college kids came from their prom to attend the printer's Mass: The girls shimmering in their gorgeous gowns, the young men shining in their rented tuxedoes. One of the boys from the street, who dropped in at Holy Trinity because he had just been turned out of his favorite pub, told Father Kern after Mass that he had never seen a more beautiful sight.

"One thing I kinda wondered about, though," he mused. "Who would want to get married at 2:30 in the morning?"   ✤

HO HO, OH OH

Earlier this year, my older son received Confirmation. While the rest of my family sat patiently in the church for the two-hour service, my two-year-old nephew, John, grew increasingly fidgety. Not wanting to disturb anyone seated around us, my sister took her young child to the vestibule of the church where he could enjoy greater freedom of movement.

At the end of the service, the cardinal archbishop began a procession down the main aisle. John, not realizing what was happening, found himself being scooped up into the arms of his mother.

After scanning his surroundings for a minute, he caught a glimpse of His Eminence. Never having seen a cardinal before, John shouted with delight. Enthusiasm was written all over his face. He reached out for the older man who was garbed in vivid red, and with pure excitement squealed, "Santa Claus!"   Michele Bari.

How Monsignors Win at Golf

An ex-caddy tells all

By MICHAEL MADDEN
October 1981

M ONSIGNOR TOOLE studied the putt, about a four-footer. After surveying the green, he decided how much roll to play and how hard to hit the golf ball. Standing a yard away from the ball, he began his practice strokes. Each was short, abrupt, like a boxer's jab. He was muttering something, but his tone was less one of self-encouragement than of supplication.

He continued the practice putts while his partner and two opponents waited impatiently. It was the 18th hole. This shot would decide the match.

The monsignor stepped up to the ball, addressed it, and finally struck it. The dimpled sphere

This story is true, but the names have been changed to protect a bishop.

rolled smoothly, following an arc as it neared the cup. No one was breathing as the ball traversed those long feet, then ducked towards the right lip of the hole. But it was struck a touch too firmly. It rimmed the cup and stayed out.

There were distinct sighs from the opponents, along with murmurs of "Nice try" and "Gee, too bad." Monsignor Toole grumbled something and tapped the ball into the cup. "I thought I had that!"

"Just as well, Tom," said one of the opponents, Msgr. Daniel Ryan. "No fair praying on the golf course. The Lord can't be expected to answer all our prayers."

The other adversary was Monsignor Garry: "That's right, Dan. Not *all* our prayers." He chuckled, adding with a wink, "Maybe one a hole."

387

Supposedly a golf course is the best place to be if you need medical attention on a Wednesday. When I was a caddie, this was certainly true. A bag-toting colleague was once hit by a ball, and the ensuing gathering looked like a hastily called meeting of the Rhode Island Medical Society. But on Tuesdays, Metacomet Country Club in East Providence was the best place for one seeking ecclesiastical succor.

The place was teeming with priests for various reasons. The club had special dues for clerics. The State of Rhode Island and Providence Plantations has not only the highest percentage of Catholics in the country, it has the largest proportion of acreage devoted to golf courses. Thousands of youngsters had become caddies, and enough of them had become priests to result in a flock of frocked golfers.

The competition among the clerics ranged from the mildly fierce to the single-mindedly ferocious. When the Roman collars came off, so did the kid gloves. In particular, there were Msgr. Thomas J. Toole ("T.J. Toole, a man to be reckoned with," he was wont to say) and his archrival, Msgr. Joseph Garry. These otherwise gentle men played bareknuckles golf.

Monsignor Toole was a slight, wiry, animated man several years older than Monsignor Garry, who looked like every other policeman in the St. Patrick's Day Parade. While the former struggled to play in the 80s, the latter was on a first-name basis with par, so the older man received a handicap—a stroke on this hole, a stroke on that hole. They relished the competition, and thereby hangs a tale or two.

In golf, concentration is paramount. No mountain of talent means a whit if the player does not pay attention to what he is doing. Monsignor Garry knew this.

"Why don't you ask Monsignor Toole to hear your confession?" he asked me one pristine day.

"Right now?" I was incredulous.

"Sure. He hit his tee shot into the trees. You'll have plenty of privacy in there. No one will hear you except Tom, God, and the birds."

"But, Monsignor, I doubt the Monsignor is in any mood—"

"Go ahead, go ahead. I hear he gives the easiest penances." I begged off. There were visions of sackcloth, ashes, and Sundays on the church steps. Thankfully, Monsignor Garry relented, but for none of those reasons.

Instead, he pointed out that Monsignor Toole's partner oversaw the Diocesan Office of Cemeteries and, "If he ever thought I had something to do with distracting his partner, I might never get a grave with a view."

Gamesmanship was important. These men would never resort to such tomfoolery as jingling coins when a player was hitting, or moving during someone's backswing. Those were sins punishable by banishment to the tennis court. There were ways, however.

One day they were playing the tenth hole, a long, testing par three requiring a wood shot. But Monsignor Garry stepped to the tee with an iron.

"You're going to use an iron?" Monsignor Toole asked dubiously.

"Sure."

"You can't get there with an iron. Never!"

"How much do you think I can't get there with an iron?"

"I think *dinner* you can't get there with an iron."

"Dinner it is." Monsignor Garry took a couple of confident, whipping practice swings. Then he stepped up to the ball, planted his feet, firmly gripped the club and smartly smacked the shot. It left the tee like a rifle shot, soared towards

Narragansett Bay and eventually settled softly on the putting surface 218 yards away. It was a splendid shot.

Everyone—except Monsignor Garry and his caddie—was stunned. But Monsignor Toole hustled over for a look at that club. "It's a *one*-iron! I didn't know you carried a one-iron. No one hits one-irons anymore!" It was basically true. Precious few players in the world would routinely reach for that club and expect to hit with any proficiency. It has almost no loft.

"I don't usually carry it," Monsignor Garry said oh-so-casually after determining where they would dine, "but this morning I went to the practice tee and hit it for an hour." That's gamesmanship.

It was another Tuesday, and there were three: Monsignors Toole, Garry, and Daniel Ryan. They were scouting about trying to scare up a fourth. Finally they located a man unknown to them, a new member of the club, and a foursome was made.

Introductions were made— "I'm Tom Toole, this is Joe Garry, and that's Danny Ryan." The stranger had no difficulty assimilating this—"Tom, Dan, and Joe." Handicaps were compared and the lines of combat were drawn: Toole-Ryan *vs* Garry-stranger.

The new fellow hit his tee shot, and he hit it badly. This was followed by a remark one would not hear in a convent garden (or most any garden, for that matter).

Nothing was said. It was not earsearing blasphemy, and the subject at hand was golf.

It might be noted that, save physicians, people in the same profession do not usually talk shop on the course. They talk about golf, or maybe—with the three monsignors—the beloved Boston Red Sox or boxing. Furthermore, the caddies would not constantly use titles, because saying "Monsignor" would mean three heads turning and saying, "Yes?" It was decidedly informal. So the stranger had no way of knowing these three were priests.

The round continued with sporadic bursts of verbal effluence. When we finished the 13th hole, Toole-Ryan were one-up. Because Monsignor Garry was the best player, he would have to give handicap strokes on the 14th and 17th. An unenviable situation. He would have to hunker down and play well.

As I gave Monsignor Toole his driver, he spoke to me *sotto voce.* "On the next hole," he said, "call one of us 'Monsignor' or 'Father', doesn't matter which or to whom. Just say it clearly."

After the tee shots, as we walked down the fairway, I said something to "*Monsignor* Toole."

The blood drained from the stranger's face. "Are you a *priest?*"

"A monsignor," he replied, pointing to his red socks. "So is your partner. And my partner. Not the caddies, though," he added.

While Monsignor Toole and Ryan settled down to hit their shots, Monsignor Garry was being pestered by a partner who was "*so* sorry—I didn't *know!*"

Toole-Ryan took the 14th hole; they were two holes ahead with four to play. They would be benefiting from handicap strokes on the 17th. And the way their brother of the cloth was being distracted, the rest was academic.

Walking down the last fairway, Monsignor Toole was pleased. He was not being smug, and he surely was not gloating. But he was pleased.

I pointed out that Monsignor Garry's partner was determinedly contrite. Monsignor Toole replied with a small smile and a cavalier wave. "He keeps asking," I mentioned, "if there's some way he can make it up."

The monsignor glanced at the man's obviously expensive equipment and clothing. "Well . . . a new boiler in the school would hasten forgiveness," he chuckled.

"What?"

"Just joking, just joking. I'm happy that we won the match."

I recalled to Monsignor Toole that in *The Bells of St. Mary's* the nuns managed to get themselves a new school. "And what about in *Lilies of the* Field," I asked, "and *Come to the Stable?*"

"That's Hollywood," said T.J. Toole. "Which is not to say the nuns can't pray up a storm. Me, I try to run a church and school, take care of my parish and, once in a while, beat Joe Garry at this silly game." ❖

SIGNS OF THE TIMES

On a college's catalog of evening courses: "Add a little class to your night life." Mrs. Jean Couch.

*

Highway sign in Nebraska: "Main highway open for traffic while detour is being prepared." Dorothy Hofbauer.

*

On a beautiful lawn in Corpus Christi, Tex.: "Great Dane-ger!" Marjorie A. Farley.

*

In the window of a drama school: "We cure hams." Christina Tyler.

*

In a Washington, D.C., telegraph office: "Telegrams other than government business must be in plain English." Thomas LaMance.

*

In North Dakota: "Pray for a good harvest, but keep hoeing." Mary Farmer.

*

In a hotel room shower in Augusta, Ga.: "Keep that song in your heart. These walls are thin." Dolly Bliss.

*

Bumper sticker: "A toast to the weapons of war: may they rust in peace." K.D. Macisaac.

*

In a watch repair shop: "Come in and see us when you don't have the time." Morris Bender.

I'll Never Forget Father Caruana

His friendship meant everything to our Jewish family

By ESTHER UEBERALL

July 1974, condensed from *Guideposts**

I T WAS A Friday morning in December, 1902, our first day of business. I was a 17-year-old newlywed standing by my husband in our little notion shop on Myrtle Ave. in Brooklyn. We had put all our money and hopes into Ueberall's 3¢-9¢-19¢ Store.

And here was our first customer, a young priest, Father Caruana, of a little storefront Catholic church. As he paid my husband, his face seemed as somber as his suit.

"Why so sad, Father?" Solomon asked.

"Oh," he answered absentmindedly, "the little store we use as a church is about to be closed."

"But why?" pressed my husband. To him religion was an

every-hour devotion. Touching the mezuzah at the door of our rooms above the store was not just a habit but an opportunity to acknowledge the Lord.

Father Caruana explained that unless he could raise $500 by Monday morning, the mortgage on his building would be foreclosed. His was a poor parish, and he saw no likelihood of raising the money.

As my husband listened, his hand gripped my arm. I sensed what he was feeling. Both of us were Jewish immigrants, my husband from Austria, I from Russia. Each of our families had sought sanctuary here from persecution in Europe. We remembered the pogroms in which men broke into homes at night to carry loved ones away.

"No, no," Solomon was saying.

"That cannot be." The thought that a church must be closed for lack of money seemed terrible to him. Here in America, of all places, a house of worship must be safe.

My husband put his hand on the priest's shoulder. "Don't worry, Father," he said. "We will get the money for you somehow." I was astounded; we didn't have even $5 cash.

Father Caruana stared at my husband. Then, unable to believe what he had heard, he shook his head and walked out.

Solomon turned to me. "Esther, you know all those wedding presents we got? I am going to pawn them. Someday we will get them back, but right now we have to raise that $500."

Already he was unfastening the watch and chain my father had given him. He looked down at my engagement ring. I slowly worked it off and handed it to him.

But that afternoon when Solomon returned from the pawnbroker, he reported that he could get only $250 for the gifts. Later, as we ate supper, he exclaimed, "I know! We have a big family. We can borrow from them."

All day Sunday Solomon went from uncle to brother-in-law, from cousin to nephew, many of whom he had helped before. Some were sympathetic, some reluctant. Solomon argued. He pleaded. Finally, in bits here and pieces there, he got another $250.

Each Monday from then on Father Caruana was the first visitor to our store. With him he brought a leather pouch full of change collected from his parishioners. Our friendship deepened. And finally the day arrived when the last cent was paid off.

Meanwhile I was again wearing my ring and we had our gifts back. Our shop prospered, and it became Ueberall's Department Store. As it grew, so did Father Caruana's storefront congregation, until one day the diocese decided to build a large church, St. Lucy's. Solomon watched its construction with fascination.

"Look, Esther," he would exclaim, coming back into the store, "now they are putting the door lintels on."

Through the years the department store was like another parish house. We would provide things for church bazaars, booths, and other functions. Then, in 1919, Father Caruana was called to Rome. He and Solomon parted like brothers.

The next year Solomon died suddenly of a heart attack. So terrible was my shock that I lost my eyesight for almost two years. When it returned, I went back to running the store and raising my two children, Bernard and Stella.

Years passed. I became busy in civic affairs and Red Cross. Now Bernie managed the store. Gradually the memory of Father Caruana faded from my mind. Then Hitler marched into Austria. And again there were pogroms there. Soon we began to get letters from Solomon's relatives and former townsmen in Austria, begging me to help them reach America and escape the death camps. I helped as many as I could, getting them visas to enter America. But soon the immigration quotas were filled.

The letters kept coming. I would lean on the pile and cry, "Oh, Solomon, I know if you were here you could help me."

I went to the Labor Department in Washington, D.C. They told me that refugees could still find sanctuary in Cuba if some prominent person there would sign affidavits vouching for them. What to do? I knew no one in Cuba. Then I remembered that Cuba was a Catholic country, so I went to St. Lucy's. A young priest there gave me a letter of introduction to the papal nuncio in Cuba. He also cabled that I was coming.

Two days later my plane landed at the Havana airport. As I came down the ramp, a boy handed me a bouquet of roses. Looking up, I saw a red-robed man waiting behind him, smiling at me. There was something about his gentle brown eyes that I seemed to remember.

He held his arms out to me. "Esther Ueberall," he called, "don't you know me?"

It was Father Caruana! I collapsed in tears. After we got into his car, he explained that since his assignment in Rome, he had become an archbishop and papal nuncio to Cuba.

With his help, more than two dozen of our family members escaped Hitler and reached Cuba. While they waited for U.S. immigration quotas to reopen, they were not permitted to work. But Archbishop Caruana not only sheltered them but supplied them with clothing and food, including vegetables from his own garden and meats from a kosher market. Within six months they were making new lives in America.

From then on Archbishop Caruana and I kept in touch. Some years later he became ill and was sent to Misericordia Hospital in Philadelphia. I did not know this until I opened a letter from the Mother Superior. "His condition prevents him from seeing anyone, but he calls for you."

In three hours I was at his bedside. He looked thin and pitiful against the background of white hospital sheets.

"Esther," he said, reaching for my hand. We sat there, saying little. I knew he was preparing for a long journey.

After a while he said, "Esther, keep well. I pray for you and your dear family every day."

Then he reached for something under his pillow, something which he evidently treasured. He pressed it into my hand. It was a tiny silver case containing a relic of St. Francis de Sales.

"Keep this, Esther. It will remind you of a great saint."

Tears stung my eyes and I clung to his hand. I couldn't speak. But in my heart I cried, "Dear Father Caruana, you have already done this for me. For in your life I have known God; and that will sustain me all the rest of my years."   ❖

CHILD OF NATURE

Four-year-old Danny was fascinated by the many different colors in the patch of oil standing on our wet driveway. "Mother!" he called, "Come out here and see the dead rainbow lying near the garage."

Amy Trinity March.

DEAR MILKMAN

The milkman whose round was in a very exclusive residential area asked to be transferred. He said the houses were too far back from the road, and he had to walk down a long path to make every delivery. On top of that, the people were very unfriendly. They wouldn't so much as wish him good day.

Eventually he was transferred to an area which, he was told, was not so exclusive. The houses were all right along the streets. And the people were the friendliest in the world.

The milkman was pleased with himself as he started off on his new round. At the first house, he saw an empty milk bottle with a note in it. The note said:

"Dear Milkman—I have a cold today. The key is under the mat. Would you let yourself in and bring the garbage can from the back yard and leave it at the door? Then feed the cat. And please leave the front window open a little bit, and tell the butcher down the street to send up two chops. The boy can put them in the window. When you are at No. 27, tell Mrs. Brown I won't be going to bingo tonight.

"P.S. I don't want any milk."   *Ireland's Own.*

Nostalgia

Bishop Sheen's
TV Show

"Life Is Worth Living" uses only two cameras
to get the biggest stack of mail in the industry

By JAMES C. G. CONNIFF
November 1953, condensed from *The Bishop Sheen Story**

T HE MOST INFLUENTIAL
voice in Christendom next
to that of Pius XII is being raised
inside a TV tube by a 58-year-old
former farm boy from Peoria,
Ill.

Once on a visit to an old folks'
home Bishop Fulton J. Sheen
told the residents that they were
not really old at all. They were
children, he said, children of
God. He tied this thought in
with the fact that their time of
life was, indeed, often known
as second childhood. His own
enthusiasm mounting, he devel-

oped the idea at length. The
audience grew more and more
excited. Finally a bishop in the
front row was heard to murmur,
"If he doesn't stop this pretty
soon, we'll be changing their
diapers!"

The 4,724,410 Catholics in the
world's largest archdiocese feel
that their auxiliary bishop's interest in them is keenly personal,
and Sheen goes out of his way
to prove it. An elderly Irish door-
man at a hotel once held out a
rosary palmed in his left hand
as he opened the door for the
fast-moving bishop. Sheen spotted it instantly, turned his back
on the dignitaries he was with,

and solemnly blessed the beads. He spoke quietly to the man, smiled, and passed on. Whatever Sheen said, Mike isn't telling, but there's at least one rosary in Manhattan that you could never separate from its owner.

This kind of thing is infectious and, of course, typical Sheen. He took the big town to his heart, and it took him. New York itself always seems to have held a strange fascination for him. He used to come up from Washington every week to deliver his Catholic Hour radio talks there. For this, besides the modest $25 stipend Sheen and every other speaker on the program received, there was an additional $25 check for travel expenses. People who talk lightly of how Sheen must have gotten rich all those years broadcasting for NBC will perhaps be jolted to learn the facts.

Humor is one of the bishop's strong points. Comedians old at the game lick their chops in envy of Sheen's sense of timing and his flair for getting laughs when he wants them. Staffers of the DuMont TV network, from Frank Bunetta, who directs the bishop's program, on down to the stagehands and lighting men, swear they've never known anything like it. And in his time, Bunetta has handled pros like Jackie Gleason, Larry Storch, Jerry Lester, and others.

But with Sheen it's different. He may drop a cornball like "Long time no Sheen," the way he did to start off his show last season, but that's just to prove he's no sourpuss. The needs of an audience, including comic relief, are well known to the bishop. He has them at his fingertips. Hollywood friends say he has more true acting genius in one of those fingertips than most professionals. Certain it is that there's no honorable stage device that Sheen does not employ to the hilt to get his points across.

He relishes a joke, on or off stage. Once he was at a friend's ranch out West for a short visit and a rest between speeches in near-by cities. As usual, he fitted right in, dressed like a cowhand—and suffered the usual consequences of too much time in the saddle the first day out.

His last morning at the ranch he drove with the owner down to the entrance gate, where they found a police car waiting. They think nothing of this in the West, so the rancher pulled up and poked his head out. The chief of police came over and said that his fellow chief in the city where Sheen would speak that evening had wired that he would have an escort waiting at the airport. Would the rancher convey the message to his guest?

"Well, he's right here beside

me," said Sheen's friend. "Tell him yourself."

The cop gawked at the skinny cowpoke, and shook his head. "That ain't him," he said.

Sheen was delighted. "'Course it ain't," snarled the man with 12 college degrees. "Any fool can see I'm Two-Gun Sheen."

Idolatry is a good word for the type of reaction Sheen gets even from strangers. They don't have to be in the studio, either, though there's where you see it best. One proof of this is the more than 8,000 ecstatic fan letters his video program draws each week. His is far and away the strongest mail-pull in television. DuMont gets more than 5,000 requests a week for tickets to his half-hour show and can give out only 1,100. That's the total firelaw capacity of the Adelphi theater just off Broadway on 44th St., from which the show is beamed.

When the long black Cadillac bearing Sheen and the two assistants who live with him, Msgr. Charles J. McBride and Father Joseph J. Tennant, rolls up to the Adelphi at 7:25 on a Tuesday evening, excitement reaches fever pitch among the audience, mostly already seated and waiting. It can be felt also among the sidewalk devotees out front.

The bishop started on TV on a sustaining basis in February, 1952, with three stations, and ended up the following May with 35. Nothing like it had ever happened in television. That summer the Admiral Corp. moved in on him with a two-year contract at an annual $1 million for each 26-week series. He takes none of that money for himself. It all goes to his favorite charities, which are numerous, especially throughout the South; and probably it goes in at least some measure to the world-wide missionary work of his Society for the Propagation of the Faith, which supplies funds for 603 missionary districts.

From November, 1952, to May, 1953, his stations increased to 75. When he went off the air for the summer he had a near-perfect Nielsen national listener-viewer rating of 19.0. The Videodex report shows his audience pushing the 10 million mark, while DuMont officials privately guess it to be even higher.

Experienced listener-survey men are stunned. NBC, which could have had him, is still pounding its head against the nearest TV camera. It had handled his Catholic Hour talks since their start on March 2, 1930. From the response to that project alone, it should have known better than to say No. Thousands wrote in weekly for each Sheen talk to the National Council of Catholic Men in Washington, D.C., the show's sponsor. One little prayer book that Sheen offered over the air brought 640,000 requests for copies. There were cash offerings in enough of the envelopes to pay the entire printing bill.

Yet when Sheen's sense of fair play prompted him to offer NBC first crack at the TV show idea, the network politely turned him down. Their theory was that nobody would listen to a bishop yakking for half an hour about St. Thomas Aquinas and Aristotle in enlightened, hydrogen-bomb-minded 1952. CBS, approached next, felt the same way. After all, what could a bishop do for all that time to make people watch? For him to fling pies was out of the question, and it would be even poorer taste to have His Excellency clobbered with one. Thus, with surgical aplomb, two of TV's Big Three slit their own throats.

The hydrogen bomb reminded a DuMont video technician at the Adelphi of an opinion that's fairly widely held. "Maybe that's the very reason they go for him," he said, probing the reason for the Sheen impact on audiences. "When nuclear vapor's the next stop, people get God-minded, I guess."

As it happened, even Du-Mont, third on his list, was not very Sheen-minded at the start. It went for the idea half-heartedly, showing the flabbi-ness of its enthusiasm by spotting the bishop opposite two established supernova of TV stardom, Frank Sinatra and Milton Berle. From the viewpoint of the man who was to become its shooting star overnight, the network couldn't have shown better astronomical judgment.

Compared with the agonies of apprehension, rehearsal, rewriting, and worry about arriving late that veterans like Sid Caesar are said to go through getting ready for their weekly stint on television, Sheen's outlook is almost blasé.

When he arrives at the theater, he'll pause for a word here and there with people on the stairs and along the hall to dressing room B, the only one with a star on its door. Jackie Gleason, Jerry Lester, and other TV greats used the same room when they were on for *Cavalcade of Stars*. Once inside, he does a quick change from street clothes to full bishop's regalia: purple-piped black cassock; gold modern-design pectoral cross given him by Pope Pius XII at his consecration as a bishop on June 11, 1951; purple *zuchetto* or skullcap; and, over all, the swirling *feriola*, the watered-silk purple cape of his rank. Saul Abraham, "the Irishman who runs the Adelphi," can hardly wait for color TV to catch up with his favorite Cock Robin.

"Most Tuesday nights I just stand backstage and let the guy hypnotize me," says Abraham. "He's got everything. In more than 50 years of show business I've never seen such respectful, intelligent audiences as this man draws."

Part of the reason for this is that DuMont carefully screens any group requests for tickets that look as though they might be from girl groups. It wants no bansheeing bobby-soxers on hand to mar the beauty of Sheen's dramatic delivery. Even so, house manager Abraham's assessment of the Sheen drawing power carries considerable weight. The Adelphi's boss is in a position to measure the bishop's performance by the standards of such successes as *Greenwich Village Follies, Rain or Shine, Fine and Dandy,* and other hits of yesteryear he's had a hand in staging.

Sheen's make-up man, Bob Obradovich, now moves in on the bishop with a V5 base and enough light tan powder to tone down the beard. Though he always has a gleaming fresh shave, His Excellency is the dark type of Irishman. Those Irish trace back to Spaniards who intermarried after being shipwrecked on the southern coast by the storm that smashed up the Armada in 1588.

Next comes a fast run-through with 33-year-old Frank Bunetta.

Together they figure out how much time the bishop's talk will take, where any lengthy quotes from poets will require musical background, and so on. Then Sheen, chatting and smiling, will again be surrounded by visitors, as if a fantastically demanding half hour television program— 100% his responsibility and to all outward appearances as extemporaneous as lightning— were years instead of minutes away.

About five minutes before show time, Sheen bows quietly away from the gay, laughing groups and moves to the wings of the set Jo Mielziner created for him on the lines of a comfortable, well-appointed study. There, head bowed, he prays till he catches Bunetta's signal.

Up comes the noble head. The eyes gleam deep in their sockets. The man's whole figure seems to get larger as he steps before the cameras and *Life Is Worth Living* pulses forth to a nation. For millions, it is the TV event of the week. For Sheen, though you'd never guess it from the perfection of his performance, it is another half-hour incident in his 19-hour day.

The bishop is the easiest man in TV to work with, the DuMont staff has found. Frank Bunetta can't do too much for him. It is clear that he regards Sheen as his directorial masterpiece, the best that's come his way, and Bunetta has handled the best in the business. He practically stands on his head to get those cameras in there where they'll do the most good, the stage-lights and floodlights coordinated so that they'll illuminate the bishop's deep-set blue eyes and not leave him looking like a face with two black holes in it. Bunetta feels a personal responsibility not to let anybody miss the dramatic wallop Sheen can deliver with those eyes alone.

The director has developed a sixth sense to tell him when Sheen is about to let go with a graceful, calculated but some-how spontaneous gesture of those marvelous hands, "easily the most eloquent west of Naples!" When he feels one coming, he has his cameraman pull back for a long shot to get it all. He is almost never caught napping.

Any director in the industry will give birth to a new ulcer at the mere thought of a performer whose location dur-ing the course of a program can-not be calculated in advance. Pre-positioning makes it easier to handle the cameras. With Bunetta, Sheen comes first.

He has arranged everything to accommodate the bishop and leave him free to think of practi-cally nothing but what he has to say. Sheen, who must have to devote a tremendous amount of disciplined concentration to his minutely detailed, carefully orga-nized discourses, cannot help but be grateful. For instance, where the majority of network telecasts use three or four cameras, Bunetta cuts his quota to two. That way there is less distraction for Sheen, when he has to switch his gaze from the one camera to the other as the director's little signal light gleams above it.

When Sheen talks like a prophet out of the Old Testa-ment, the camera takes him full and majestic. When he whispers, Bunetta brings his face up large, as though he were telling you secrets. And when the bishop smiles, Bunetta's cameras treat it like the sunrise that it is.

"You couldn't hold a man like that down," Bunetta says with conviction. "If he thinks of something and with it gets the impulse to move about, what he has to say is more important than any acrobatics I may have to do from the control room. That man is completely himself. He believes every word you hear him utter. When he winds up the show with that 'God love you!' of his, we all know he's playing for keeps." ❦

When Six Days Made One Weak

The years before electricity were harder, but I
wonder if maybe they were happier

By COLLEEN L. REECE
December 1983, condensed from *Wyoming Rural Electric News**

SEVEN DAYS make one week. But the schedule my mother and grandmothers used to keep reminds me of the old adage: "Six days like this make one weak!"

I grew up B.E. (before electricity), and the week never varied:
Wash on Monday.
Iron Tuesday.
Clean on Wednesday.
Mend on Thursday.
Hoe on Friday.
Bake on Saturday.
Rest on Sunday.

Monday. When I got up for school on Monday, signs of the washing to follow were already evident. The wood cookstove was blazing. Twin galvanized boilers were steaming.

Work clothes were soaking. Bleach and bluing assailed my nostrils as I ate breakfast, eyeing the big bar of hard yellow scrub soap and the wringer it took two of us to turn when overalls went through.

Later I helped hang clothes on the steel wires strung between two young trees. I also could count on having at least two fingers bitten by those spring-loaded clothespins. None of the slip-on type that could also slip off and drop clothes to the ground.

We propped the lines in the middle with a sapling when we did blankets and heavy clothes. In winter, they freeze-dried until the long underwear stood by itself in the kitchen until we got it hung on hangers up by the ceiling where dad had fitted a

*Reprinted with permission of the author.

steel bar. Of course, summer snapped them so dry they had to be rolled and sprinkled for hours.

Tuesday. Another raging fire, this time with three sadirons heating. A wooden clamp-on handle, a wet finger sizzling against the bottom, and they were ready. Everything was starched and the number of shirts and blouses I scorched before learning the fine art of ironing equalled the national debt.

Wednesday was cleaning day. We were either the dirtiest or cleanest family in town. Ceilings, floors, walls, windows. More boilers of hot water. Suds, wax, aching backs, and pride of work well done. Wednesday suppers were usually stews, racy with onions, or a pot of beans cooked on the back of the stove and filling the house with a potpourri of odors. There wasn't time for "fancies" on Wednesdays.

Thursday we mended. No lumpy darns in our socks. I still see mom with her overflowing basket of socks that were interwoven with soft yarn. The overalls had patches on the patches. A world without Bondex permitted no throwing away of worn clothes. Our grimy feet playing in the dust proudly wore those mended stockings.

Friday released us to the garden. Little fingers learned early to differentiate between weeds and vegetables—at least most of the time. Working together as a family, it didn't seem hard, especially when we knew fruit punch and cookies awaited us as a reward.

Saturday was a fun day. Our world was one that took seriously the admonition, "Thou shalt rest on Sunday, and keep it holy." Saturday was the preparation day. Pies, cakes, set salads. The pantry was filled. A Sunday without company was like rain without water. From 10 to 25—who knew? The more people who conveniently dropped in for dinner, the more jars of pickles, jams, and home-canned vegetables came out of our root house to supplement our Saturday baking.

Saturday night was also bath night. Daily sponge baths kept us neat, but Saturday night we "soaked." Ground-in elbow and heel dirt was attacked. The biggest washtub was filled with water and provided comfort even on the coldest winter nights. We dried in huge towels, wrapped ourselves in flannel pajamas and robes, and sat in front of the living room wood heater, turning like roasts on spits before racing for bed and mounds of heavy, homemade quilts.

Sunday was church and rest. Yet there also were other people around, with everyone helping prepare meals and do dishes afterwards. The best dishes. Linen tablecloth instead of oilcloth. Years later Mom and Dad used Sunday afternoons for drives and dinner out. It must have been a welcome change from the busy Sundays at home after hectic weeks.

Now in the middle of brownouts and blackouts, "We need nuclear power," and "No nukes are good nukes," I mentally run through the same work schedule my mother and grandmothers followed—but with what a difference!

Washday is any day. Toss 'em in a washer, change to a dryer.

Ironing? Who irons?

Cleaning. It still exists, and yet there are electric vacuum cleaners for the floors with rugs, and damp mops for no-wax floors without rugs. Windows, walls, furniture? New and convenient attachments for them all.

Mending? A lost art.

Hoeing and weeding seem a little ridiculous when vegetables can be purchased from a brightly lit supermarket for less than it takes to grow them—and with a lot fewer potato bugs to screech over! Cans on shelves have replaced battalions of glass jars in the root cellar.

Even Sundays aren't the same. I remember being bone-tired but content on Saturday nights as I snuggled deep in my bed, glad Dad would be home the next day. Six-day work weeks did make people weak—ready to rest on Sundays.

How ironic now on Saturday night to look back and still wonder how I got so tired! With all my labor-saving devices, where's all that free time I should have? Those hours of emptiness to dream and scheme?

A few days ago our house was filled with company—and at just before nine that night, the lights went off—for two hours. It was great! No TV. No stereo. We talked, laughed, told stories—to the delight of all from 4-year-old David to 83-year-old Mom. And I wondered.

It is predicted that the time may come when we will have to return to some of the old ways, doing and making do. I shudder at the thought. Yet in my more honest moments I have to admit—six days living in this world of pressure, jets, and detente, politics and rising prices, fulfills the old saying even better than in my grandmothers' days. It is enough to make anyone weak! ❧

Farmer at Forty Hours

Tapers through tears

By ALBERT EISELE
February 1944, condensed from the *Ave Maria*

PETER GREBNER rose at dawn and went to bring in the cows. He felt too tired to tie his shoes; and so he walked with unlaced footgear across the dewy pasture. He felt a sort of disinterested pleasure in the clear November morning. He brought the cows home and milked them, hurried through breakfast, and soon, with his wife and their daughter Mary, was on the way to Mass.

It was Monday, and very unusual for them to be going to Mass on this first of the weekdays, but the Forty Hours was beginning, and the Grebners always made the Forty Hours. Mass was at 6:30, and they were not late. As the sun burst over the clouds, the interior of the church lit up as from a sudden flame. The rays shining through the windows projected patches of color on the opposite wall.

A railingful of people received Holy Communion. These were the ones who had received yesterday. The main body of the parish would go to confession tonight, following the evening services, and they would receive on Tuesday and Wednesday.

The priest in charge entered the pulpit. It was not good old Father Finnegan, the pastor, but a strange priest, slight of build, and mild-mannered. He made some announcements, and followed these with a short discourse on Catholic doctrine. The main sermon of the day would be tonight. Soon church was out and the Grebners went home.

Peter Grebner had finished husking his corn, but there was still much other work to be done before winter came. All afternoon he hauled fodder.

In the evening the Grebners went to church again. First there was the Rosary, and then the sermon by the visiting priest. The sermon was scholarly and kindly, but Peter Grebner from where he sat could see four parishioners in familiar sleep. The sermon progressed. Old Grandfather Kissner arose in his pew; Grandmother Kissner, who was sitting beside him, pulled hastily at his coat and he sat down again. Grandfather Kissner was childish, but grandmother always brought him to church with her, and for some reason he was always getting it into his head that Mass was over. He always wanted to go, go, go.

The sermon drew gracefully to a close and Peter Grebner felt grateful, for his feet were beginning to hurt. His Sunday shoes were not exactly new, but they hurt his feet if he wore them too often.

The penitents lined up for confession. There was a long line before both confessionals. In one sat Father Finnegan, in the other the visiting priest. Peter Grebner, for a change, chose the latter.

The confessions went on, with the strange priest hearing them almost as fast as Father Finnegan. That was unusual, for whenever there was a strange confessor, he usually drew the more sorely afflicted. And to shrive the sorely afflicted took somewhat more time, which seemed natural enough. But tonight the strange priest was turning out the goats almost as fast as Father Finnegan was turning out the sheep. And Peter felt grateful for that. For it seemed that the strange priest had a deep understanding of country people who, worn by the day's toil and often with many miles to go, were wont to become physically wearied with standing in line.

At last it was Peter's turn. He found the visiting priest gentle and understanding and pastorly. Peter said his penance, found his wife and daughter waiting, and they went home.

It was a relief to get out of his Sunday shoes. He fell asleep. But it seemed he had been asleep only a minute when his wife woke him, saying, "Peter! Mass is at 6:30; it's time to get up!"

He went out. The tree by the henhouse was white with roosting Leghorns. The birds caught the gleam of the moon, low in the west and still bright, and they shone like silver. Why did Leghorns always roost in trees? It was November, and time for all chickens to be housed.

He set out for the cows. One of his old shoes had lost its string, and he paused by the strawstack for a sheaf twine. Around the strawstack the frost was heavy and sparkled in the moonlight. Peter selected a twine that had its knot in the exact middle, because no twine knot could be run through the eyelets.

They went to Mass, and received. The visiting priest gave a short homily on Catholic doctrine, but Peter's mind wandered. Catholic doctrine did not bother Peter, what bothered him was getting his pew rent paid and his fall work done. In the afternoon, Peter and his wife worshiped before the Blessed Sacrament from 3:00 to 3:15.

They reached home late in the afternoon, did their chores, and then set out again. "The gas and oil and everything cost us a dollar every time we go to church," Peter complained. His feet hurt, too. Sore feet from Sunday shoes was a sign of a lot of church.

The sermon was like the one on the evening previous, polished and kindly. Chronic sleepers dropped off almost immediately. Grandfather Kissner got up to go; his wife grabbed him by the coat and yanked him down again.

The collection was for the visiting priest. One had to be as generous as possible. But Peter Grebner was pinched for money. He didn't have his pew rent for the year paid yet. He knew that he ought to put in a dollar at

least. But he had only a nickel handy, so he put that in. The spiritual riches which one obtained from the Forty Hours couldn't be paid for in silver anyway.

They drove home. The sky clouded over and it was turning colder.

Wednesday was the final day of the Forty Hours, so the Grebners got up early again. It had snowed in the night, a wet snow, one that striped the trunks of the farmstead trees; and the striped trunks leaped into the air as Peter approached with his lantern. In his dilapidated shoes his feet became wet.

They attended Mass. There was the usual short talk, and a brief appearance by Father Finnegan, who said, "Those who have not yet made their contribution for the officiating priest may do so tonight."

"Peter, you made your contribution last night, didn't you?" asked Mrs. Grebner, as they drove home.

"Yes," said Peter. But he did not tell her that he had given only a miserable nickel. "Where is he from, I wonder?"

"From a little place up north, in the drought district," said Mrs. Grebner. "I forget the name of the town, but it is just a small parish, and a poor one, and somebody said that Father Finnegan felt sorry for this priest and had him come here so he could add a dollar or two to his scanty income."

When he had changed clothes, Peter hunted up his four-buckle overshoes. He needed new work shoes, but could not afford them until he sold his hogs. If the sun came out, the light snow would go, and then perhaps the old shoes would do for another week or so.

Peter had a two-wheel trailer. He pumped its tires and ran it to the granary, where he shoveled it full of oats. He hauled the oats to town. It was a small load, but it brought over $7. Now he had a little money. One had to have money to work with.

In the evening the little church was crowded. Everyone had turned out for the closing services of the Forty Hours. Peter was just able to squeeze into his own pew. He left his hat in the aisle, but on second thought brought it inside—one time an awkward boy had squashed it with a genuflection.

Grandfather Kissner was in his pew. During the sermon he arose to go, but his watchful wife jerked him back by his worn coattails.

The sermon ended; the priest left the sanctuary, and the altar boys came out to light the additional candles for Benediction. The collectors appeared. Grandfather Kissner arose once more: his wife yanked him back; and there were those who maintained (those who sat behind him) that Grandfather Kissner was acting entirely normal.

Sometimes Peter had thought that the business of money should not be mixed up with the business of religion. Tonight, however, as he saw the thin visiting priest, he found himself wondering if he got enough to eat. That would be bad, not enough to eat!

Peter took out a dollar bill, folded it a little, and put it in the collection box. That was for the visiting priest. The visiting priest was his own brother in Christ and his brother in poverty.

The Forty Hours came to a close with the hymn *Holy God, We Praise Thy Name.* Peter joined with the singing, though he was never much for singing. But that was such a wonderful song. His eyes misted until all the Benediction tapers had golden lines running up and down from them. ❦

Remember Your Hit Parade?

It captured much of the golden age of American popular music

By OWEN LEE
April 1973, condensed from *High Fidelity**

I WAS A devoted listener to *Your Hit Parade.* I waited on Saturday nights at nine for the first strains of Mark Warnow's orchestra and *Happy Days Are Here Again.* And no week seemed to have come to a certified end until *This Is My Lucky Day* had signed it off. I sat through the cries of tobacco auctioneers to hear the harp glissandos that would introduce the next three songs in their official weekly positions, for "the song in seventh spot" which was to bring good luck in the coming week, for "the newcomer making its first appearance on the survey." I knew the commercials by heart, from "I've smoked Luckies for nigh onto 45 years" to "Lucky Strike green has gone

to war," from "LS/MFT" to *Be Happy—Go Lucky* chirped by pert Dorothy Collins. I waited through them all as worshipers do through some familiar sermon, till that tense, uninterrupted last segment of the broadcast: the "three top songs of the week, clear across the nation."

Singers came and went: Lanny Ross and Bea Wain. Barry Wood and Beryl Davis. Frank Sinatra and Joan Edwards. Andy Russell and Dinah Shore. Even Lawrence Tibbett, retired from the Met, had a brief fling at *Don't Fence Me In* and *Accentuate the Positive,* after duly explaining that he believed in folk music, "the music of the people."

There was a lot of talent. Buddy Clark, Johnny Mercer, Dick Haymes, the Andrews Sis-

ters, Margaret Whiting, Ginny
Sims, Martha Tilton, Georgia
Gibbs, Doris Day. But it was
kept under tight rein by the
conductors, from Lenny Hayton,
who started it all in 1935,
through all those names familiar to radio listeners—B.A.
Rolfe, Harry Sosnick, Leo Reis-
man, Harry Salter, Carl Hoff—
to the indefatigable Mark Warnow, nervously conducting almost everything as if it were
Runnin' Wild. He did some 496
shows, interrupted only for a
time in 1947 when Frank Sinatra
brought Axel Stordahl and his
more listenable arrangements
with him.

Warnow's baton passed at his
death to his brother, Raymond
Scott (a name chosen from a
telephone book), and Scott took
the show from radio to television in 1950, starring Dorothy
Collins, Eileen Wilson, and
Snooky Lanson. The shenani-
gans they went through attempting visual presentations of things
like *Sh-Boom* is another story.
Radio versions of *Your Hit
Parade* continued sporadically
through the TV years, but it
wasn't the same. *Your Hit Parade*
really died the day it moved.

And now, apparently, it is not
only dead but forgotten, all the
breathless rankings and ratings
from 1935 to 1953 stored on one
roll of microfilm in a single
library. Anyone interested in
American popular music of the

1935
1. In a Little Gypsy
   Tea Room
2. Red Sails in the Sunset
3. Cheek to Cheek
4. On Treasure Island
5. I'm in the Mood for Love
6. Chasing Shadows
7. In the Middle of a Kiss
8. Lullaby of Broadway
9. East of the Sun
10. You Are My Lucky Star

1936
1. Did I Remember?
2. The Way You Look Tonight
3. In the Chapel in the Moonlight
4. Is it True What They
   Say About Dixie?
5. These Foolish Things
6. Lost
7. Alone
8. Goody Goody
9. When Did You Leave Heaven?
10. Lights Out

1937
1. September in the Rain
2. It Looks Like Rain in
   Cherry Blossom Lane
3. That Old Feeling
4. Pennies from Heaven
5. Sailboat in the Moonlight
6. Once in a While
7. Whispers in the Dark
8. It's De-lovely
9. Vieni, Vieni

1938
1. My Reverie
2. I've Got a Pocketful
   of Dreams
3. Music, Maestro, Please
4. A-Tisket A-Tasket
5. Says My Heart
6. Ti-Pi-Tin
7. Please Be Kind
8. Love Walked in
9. I Let a Song Go Out of
   my Heart
10. Thanks for the Memory

1939
1. South of the Border
2. Deep Purple
3. Scatterbrain
4. Over the Rainbow
5. Wishing
6. And the Angels Sing
7. Moon Love
8. Stairway to the Stars
9. The Beer Barrel Polka
10. Jeepers Creepers

1940
1. The Woodpecker Song
2. I'll Never Smile Again
3. There I Go
4. Careless
5. When You Wish Upon a Star
6. Imagination
7. Only Forever
8. Practice Makes Perfect
9. All the Things You Are
10. Indian Summer

1941
1. I Hear a Rhapsody
2. Intermezzo
3. Frenesi
4. Amapola
5. Maria Elena
6. Tonight We Love
7. I Don't Want to Set
the World on Fire
8. My Sister and I
9. You and I
10. Yours

1942
1. White Christmas
2. The White Cliffs of Dover
3. Sleepy Lagoon
4. Elmer's Tune
5. My Devotion
6. He Wears a Pair of
Silver Wings
7. Jingle, Jangle, Jingle
8. One Dozen Roses
9. Don't Sit Under the
Apple Tree
10. Blues in the Night

'30's and '40's can read Sigmund Spaeth's articles in the *Encyclopedia Brittanica* annuals, or Abe Green's *Variety Music Cavalcade,* or back issues of *Billboard.* And maybe these are better, for *Your Hit Parade* was not always the best index of popularity.

In 1935 we believed the survey authentic. But by 1945, when *Billboard* began to run its "Honor Roll of Hits," with pages of charts and calculations, our faith was shaken. *Variety* never ceased to scorn the findings of *Hit Parade:* "The sponsor's mother-in-law sends over a list of her favorites, and they play those." By the mid-Forties, publishers were demanding to know why their tunes, so duly noted on other surveys, were being ignored. The publishers of *Don't Sweetheart Me* even went to the New York Supreme Court.

The survey was always a closely kept secret. Even President Roosevelt, at a White House reception in 1944, couldn't find out from Frank Sinatra what song would be number one the following Saturday.

The secret probably went to the grave with George Washington Hill, long-time president of the American Tobacco Co. He not only sold countless cigarettes with his obsessive slogans, but also may have affected popular music profoundly. The "song sweepstakes" was his brainstorm, an idea taken for granted now.

Hill had to fight his own production men to get his idea across. They thought the same songs most played on every other program had no chance. But *Your Hit Parade* caught on instantly, becoming the most popular show on the air, drawing millions of loyal listeners.

The period from 1935 to 1950 may well be the golden age of American popular music, and *Your Hit Parade* is the most nostalgic bit of that period.

Take this broadcast of Oct. 24, 1942. We were almost a year into the 2nd World War, and it wasn't going to be over soon, as the titles indicate: 1. *My Devotion.* 2. *White Christmas.* 3. *I've Got A Gal in Kalamazoo.* 4. *Serenade in Blue.* 5. *Be Careful, It's My Heart.* 6. *Dearly Beloved.* 7. *Wonder When My Baby's Coming Home.* 8. *I Left My Heart at the Stage Door Canteen.* 9. *Praise the Lord and Pass the Ammunition.* 10. *At Last.*

The essential thing about this list, compared with today's top ten, is not that the songs are better. You might easily find ten better songs around today, though they would not necessarily be at the top. But in 1942 everyone was singing, listening, and dancing to the *same* tunes. They played on all radio stations and juke boxes, and were selling both sheet music and sin-

1943
1. People Will Say We're in Love
2. You'll Never Know
3. Paper Doll
4. As Time Goes By
5. There Are Such Things
6. Sunday, Monday or Always
7. Comin' In on a Wing and a Prayer
8. In the Blue of Evening
9. I've Heard That Song Before
10. Don't Get Around Much Any More

1944
1. I'll Be Seeing You
2. My Heart Tells Me
3. Long Ago and Far Away
4. I'll Get By
5. I'll Walk Alone
6. Amor
7. Swinging on a Star
8. I Love You
9. Shoo-Shoo Baby
10. The Trolley Song

1945
1. Till the End of Time
2. Dream
3. If I Loved You
4. Don't Fence Me in
5. Sentimental Journey
6. It's Been a Long, Long Time
7. My Dreams Are Getting Better All the Time
8. On the Atchison, Topeka, and the Santa Fe
9. Laura
10. Accentuate the Positive

1946
1. They Say It's Wonderful
2. The Gypsy
3. Symphony
4. To Each His Own
5. Oh, What it Seemed to Be
6. Ole Buttermilk Sky
7. Five Minutes More
8. All Through the Day
9. I Can't Begin to Tell You
10. It Might As Well Be Spring

1947
1. Peg o' My Heart
2. The Anniversary Song
3. Near You
4. Linda
5. For Sentimental Reasons
6. I Wish I Didn't Love You So
7. Mam'selle
8. That's My Desire
9. Heartaches
10. How Soon

1948
1. A Tree in the Meadow
2. Now is the Hour
3. Buttons and Bows
4. It's Magic
5. Ballerina
6. On a Slow Boat to China
7. You Can't Be True, Dear
8. Serenade of the Bells
9. My Happiness
10. I'm Looking Over a Four Leaf Clover

1949
1. Some Enchanted Evening
2. Again
3. Far Away Places
4. Cruising Down the River
5. You're Breaking My Heart
6. I Can Dream, Can't I?
7. Bali H'ai
8. Forever and Ever
9. Riders in the Sky
10. Don't Cry, Joe

1950
1. My Foolish Heart
2. Mona Lisa
3. Bewitched, Bothered and Bewildered
4. Goodnight, Irene
5. Dear Hearts and Gentle People
6. All My Love
7. Harbor Lights
8. The Third Man Theme
9. La Vie en Rose
10. If I Knew You Were Comin' I'd've Baked a Cake

gle records. There was no "youth market," no "good music programming" for the over-thirties, no "acid rock" station. Today there is a distinct audience for the Osmonds, for Elton John, for Johnny Cash, and for Barbra Streisand. In 1942 everybody liked *Dearly Beloved*.

Seven of the '42 ten are from films. And three of those, *White Christmas, Be Careful, It's My Heart,* and *Stage Door Canteen,* were the work of one composer, Irving Berlin. Three others, *Kalamazoo, Serenade in Blue,* and *At Last,* were produced for the Glenn Miller film *Orchestra Wives* by Mack Gordon and Harry Warren.

Such accomplishments are rare today. But in *Hit Parade* days it was not uncommon for a composer to have three songs on the top ten at once. Indeed, Gordon and Warren once had four songs on the *Hit Parade*. Irving Berlin scored three songs out of ten in '35, '36, '38, '42, and '46.

Even those comparative unknowns, Joan Whitney and Alex Kramer, got three songs on the top ten in 1941. But that was while the networks were quarreling over royalties with the American Society of Composers, Authors, and Publishers, so no new popular music was broadcast except for a few tunes by Latin-American composers or non-ASCAP songwriters like

Whitney and Kramer. The networks not only brought ASCAP to its knees, but founded the rival Broadcast Music Incorporated, generally credited with the crossbreeding of country and folk and popular styles. That was eventually to change the entire picture.

BMI introduced things like *Pistol Packin' Mama,* then a more authentic folksong craze (*Goodnight, Irene*), and eventually rock and roll. It opened up a range of new songwriting talent and found an eager public. A new middle class had moved up to urban prosperity. In the 50's there was an even larger and less critical adolescent public, prosperous and ready to establish its own identity. The new public rejected subtlety in its music and lyrics, and BMI tunes filled seven, eight, and nine positions on the top ten, even as Oscar Hammerstein and other ASCAP songwriters were in the courts pleading that they couldn't get their kind of music played on the air.

So *Your Hit Parade* died, on both radio and television, in the '50's. Tin Pan Alley, Broadway, and Hollywood lost out to Record Row, its proliferation of novelty, folk, and country tunes, and its gimmick-mad disc jockeys. People spoke no more of a top ten. It had to be a "top 40" or a "hot 100." And those ratings were of individual recordings, not songs. In 1956 only one song from the immensely popular *My Fair Lady* appeared on *Billboard's* weekly ten; later the songs from *West Side Story, The Sound of Music, Camelot,* and *Fiddler on the Roof,* for want of singles of mass appeal, did not figure in the ratings at all, though they won a wide public through recordings in long-playing albums.

Through the '60's, as popular music continued to diversify, there was nothing like *Your Hit Parade* to chart popularity of the songs themselves. The emphasis on single records at the expense of quality brought a decline in the musical product.

One may be appalled today by the exuberant ugliness of many of the single recordings on the *Billboard* "Hot 100," and apprehensive about the cultural values the songs convey to young people. But this is only part of the picture.

There is reason to be optimistic for the '70's. The 15-year cross-fertilization of indigenous American music seems to have produced some interesting styles, and songwriters like Paul Simon, Jim Webb, and Burt Bacharach know how to use them. Fresh modes of expression appear from abroad, from composers like Paul McCartney, Michel Legrand, and Jacques Brel.

Popular song has been freed

from its 32-bar format and its inevitable succession of diminished sevenths. It has learned to sing openly about experiences other than deep purples, moon mists, and falling stars. Music today is concerned with social, moral, ecological, and other human problems.

Yet the new folk-rock-pop music needs time to reach the level of the best music of the '30's and '40's. That, too, was a synthesis. The musical traditions of immigrant groups (largely Jewish, with elements of Viennese operetta and middle-European café music) were blended with the marvelous jazz heritage of American blacks.

The lyrics reflected the urbanity, exhilaration, and occasional loneliness of life in the big New Yorks of the New World. Romantic love was the theme of nine songs out of ten: sentimental, slightly melancholic, often unfulfilled, and wishfully expressed in neat rhymes and witty turns of phrase. It was a music for a slightly sophisticated, urban middle class. Yet, as *Your Hit Parade* indicates, it spoke to and for millions of people for decades.

The longest-running song, and so perhaps the most popular, was Irving Berlin's *White Christmas,* with 15 appearances in 1942–43 (ten of them in first place), and 18 places and shows in subsequent Decembers. But for sustained popularity, no song matches the Rodgers-Hammerstein *People Will Say We're In Love.* Its appeal was immediate, its fresh and inventive words and music never palled through 30 weeks of repetition in 1943–44. Its closest rivals were ballads of war-time sentiment: Irving Kahal and Sammy Fain's *I'll Be Seeing You* (24 appearances in '44–45) and Mack Gordon and Harry Warren's *You'll Never Know* (24 appearances in '43).

Gordon and Warren are the lyricist and composer most often represented on the survey. Each collaborated with other songwriters, but they were most successful in the movie songs they wrote together, like the still popular *Chattanooga Choo Choo* and *The More I See You.* Thirty-nine of Gordon's lyrics made the top ten, and 42 of Warren's tunes.

Other lyricists are, in order of popularity, Irving Berlin (33) Johnny Mercer (32), Johnny Burke (28), Leo Robin (26), Sammy Cahn (23), Al Dubin (23), and Frank Loesser (23). They wrote about slumming on Fifth Ave., dreams, pennies from heaven, moonlight and shadows, lonely Saturday nights, and Indian summers.

And the composers are, again, Irving Berlin (33), Jimmy Van Heusen (25), Jimmy McHugh (20), Harry Revel (20), Richard

Rodgers (19), Ralph Rainger (17), Jule Styne (17), and Cole Porter (16). They wrote about top hats, swinging on stars, the mood for love, a date with a dream, a small hotel by a wishing well, blossoms on Broadway, walking alone, and getting out of town.

Yes, the horizon was limited in the radio days of *Your Hit Parade*. There were no songs of social protest, no ecstasies of gospel and soul, no explorations of nonwestern musical traditions, no affirmations of the essential humanity of all races. But neither were there the bathos, crassness, and sensation-seeking one hears at such ear-splitting intensity today. Silliness, yes. Sentimentality in abundance. But often, too, subtlety, genial understatement, formal discipline, and, above all, melodiousness. ♥

The Ten Best of the Ten Best

One cannot cast an eye over many lists of ten without making one of his own. Some great songs, like *Summertime, Begin the Beguine, September Song,* never made the top ten. And much of the best work of Gershwin and Kern antedates 1935. But for the *Hit Parade* period, these are, I think, the finest, in chronological order:

Where or When, Richard Rodgers and Lorenz Hart. No songwriter can wrest more music from a simple scale than Rodgers, nor any lyricist distill in words such feelings of *déja vu* as Hart has done here.

Love Walked In, George and Ira Gershwin. Kenny Baker sang it in the film *The Goldwyn Follies,* when Andrea Leeds walked into the coffee shop where he was serving up hamburgers and waiting for his big break in show business. Its simple lyric and artfully arranged melodic climaxes indicates the course George Gershwin's popular music might have taken had he not died so suddenly after its completion, age 39.

Over The Rainbow, Harold Arlen and E. Y. Harburg. Arlen touched his arching melody with traces of blues. Harburg regarded the octave skips as too much "for a little girl from Kansas," but penned a lyric about lullabies, bluebirds, and chimney tops that matched the tune all the way. The front office at MGM had doubts about the song, and three times ordered it cut while *The Wizard of Oz* was being made.

All the Things You Are, Jerome Kern and Oscar Hammerstein II. Kern's melody passes through several ingenious and beautiful key changes, and Hammerstein's words pass from sublimated metaphor to unabashed confession. It has been often cited as the favorite song of songwriters.

Blues in the Night, Harold Arlen and Johnny Mercer. Here black

American blues idiom was only slightly commercialized by two white songwriters. The result— three-part jazz construction, 12-bar pattern, immense vocal range, earthy sentiment—won favor with millions.

Skylark, Hoagy Carmichael and Johnny Mercer, was another successful crossing of swing and blues idioms. Mercer's words are as good as those he wrote for *Blues in the Night,* and Carmichael's melancholy tune casts a spell that long outlasts the 32 bars.

It Had to Be You, Isham Jones and Gus Kahn. This torch song, written and popularized in the 20's, was revived in several movies in 1944. As a piano player, I find that this seems to hold the most memories for couples who ask me to "play it again."

Always, Irving Berlin. This is the master's simplest song, and perhaps the best of his 50 years. There is hardly a year since 1925 when it wasn't popular.

If I Loved You, Richard Rodgers and Oscar Hammerstein II. Words and melody conspired to take *Carousel's* stage characters a little further into their emotions than they cared to go, and at the close they were slightly different people than when they started to sing.

So in Love, Cole Porter. This, from *Kiss Me Kate,* is typical of Porter's sophisticated best: a sultry melody rising to a climax over an insistent, beguine rhythm, a sensuous lyric that pleads for the listener to haunt, hurt, deceive, desert. Even after a decade of rock music, where it's easy to get a kick from cocaine or something else under the skin, Porter remains the unchallenged celebrant of the exotic in popular song. ❦

KID STUFF

Nine-year-old Stanley struck upon the idea of hiring his little brother as his servant. "I'll give you 10¢ a week," he said.

"OK," little Larry agreed.

Stanley then felt he'd offered too much money. "I can only pay 5¢ a week, after all" he said.

"OK," said Larry, just as cheerfully.

Thinking he could get the child for even less, Stanley said, "All I can pay is a penny a week."

"Well, OK," said Larry, "but don't raise it any lower."   G. D. Kent.

*

Our three-year-old niece, explaining the dresses she was pretending to make for her doll: "This is her First Communion dress, and this is her second Communion dress."   S. S. Biddle.

What Mother Told Me about Ladies

Remember the Safety Pin rule?

By ZIBBY ONEAL
September 1980, condensed from *Ford Times* *

T HE DAY AFTER my daughter left for college I realized that I'd never mentioned the White Shoe Rule. White Shoes and what else? I wondered wildly. Did she know what to do with a finger bowl? Would she recognize a calling card? Probably not. Somehow I had neglected to mention *all* those things during her longish residence under my wing. In that moment the enormity of the generation gap was borne in on me. What I knew by heart, she'd never heard of.

As anyone my age will remember, a Lady never wore white shoes before the 31st of May. It didn't matter about the weather.

It might have been 90° for three weeks. Before Memorial Day, a Lady didn't. And I'd never told my daughter.

That wasn't all I hadn't told her, not by half.

For instance, there was the Safety Pin Rule. A Lady *never,* whatever the circumstances, secured any part of her underwear with a safety pin. The reason was perfectly clear: She never knew when she might be in an accident.

I spent a lot of time in my childhood imagining scenes in which I was refused admission to an emergency room because of the safety pin holding my undershirt strap. In these scenes, nurses turned aside in disgust and our family's good name never recovered.

My worries were unfounded, though. My underwear was always mended, my mother being a Lady herself.

The operative word here, of course, is *Lady*. That was what we were brought up to be.

Training began at a very young age, so early, in fact, that it is hard for me to remember a time without rules. By the time I had reached the age of reason I could have rattled off a list of "Ladies Do" and "Ladies Don't" for hours.

A Lady never said, "Shut up." She always said, "Please." She used her napkin and ate with one hand in her lap. She did not click her teeth against the edge of her glass in order to make "a cool sound," or say "Yuck!" when spinach was served. She did not kick her sister under the table, no matter how many times her sister looked at her cross-eyed during dinner. She ate fried chicken with a knife and fork.

Some of the rules I could understand. They made sense. Kicking my sister, I could see, risked an escalation into all-out war before dessert. That, of course, meant no dessert. Unless we happened to be having stewed fruit, the pleasure of kicking her wasn't worth the price.

But there were other rules I don't understand to this day. For example, a Lady had a clean handkerchief with her at all times. Period. Not because she had a cold. Not because she might feel like bursting into tears. She just had one.

For years I went around with a fresh white handkerchief tucked into my sleeve or, humiliatingly, pinned into my pocket. Paper tissues, those hygienic and eminently sensible substitutes, were unacceptable. The handkerchief had to be cloth and it had to be freshly ironed. Every Christmas and birthday, several tell-tale flat boxes appeared containing another boring half-dozen or so. And what for? In case I happened upon a passing motorcade and felt like waving? We were never told.

We were told the reasons for some of the rules. The Safety Pin Rule was fully explained, of course, as was the one covering how much a Lady left on her plate at a dinner party. The rule there was one bite: if you left more than one bite you were insulting the food; if you cleaned your plate you were suggesting it had been insufficient.

This rule came in for some dispute during the War. There was a faction that claimed leaving anything at all on your plate was unpatriotic. They were opposed by traditionalists who felt that, War or no War, rules were rules, and that altering them threatened the very foundation of our country. Each household settled the question according to its own lights, but, even within the same household, there was much disagreement.

Long before I needed to know, I was aware that a Lady did not wear black before she was 20. She did not kiss a boy until he had taken her out three times, thereby demonstrating the sincerity of his interest. And, if she found she must turn down a proposal of marriage, she prefaced her refusal with the words, "You have done me a great honor today."

Clearly these latter rules were not intended for immediate use. They were simply mentioned from time to time in a prefatory way. The rules in childhood dealt mainly with such things as using your spoon as a catapult for peas (a Lady didn't) and thanking your hostess for a nice time (a Lady never failed). There were literally hundreds more.

A Lady did not scratch. She did not chew gum on the street or ask personal questions. She did not shove in line or try to get the biggest piece. She didn't say "sweat." She never stared in buses.

In short, there was scarcely a minute of life that wasn't covered by the rules. Being a Lady was all-encompassing.

When I was about ten my uncle married. We didn't know the bride. In fact, *no* one in the family had met her. Speculation was intense. Sunday dinners for a month were devoted to the subject, the usual roast beef and lemon sponge being punctuated by conjecture. My sister and I listened. Slowly we gathered that possibly the new bride was not a Lady! (Ladies always finished and mailed their thank-you notes before the ceremony.) Naturally we were enthralled.

When we finally met her, she seemed disappointingly polite. She shook hands and smiled and looked us in the eye in the approved fashion. It didn't seem promising. By dinnertime we were bored. My sister looked at me cross-eyed. I was about to venture a kick when we noticed, simultaneously and with delight, that the new bride had both elbows on the table.

We watched. She didn't move them. They stayed there throughout the meal in a comfortable sort of way. After dinner she asked me several personal questions and laughed louder than a Lady is supposed to laugh. Evidently nobody had ever told her to "simmer down."

Personally, I thought she was terrific, but I kept glancing at my mother trying to read signs. Oddly, Mother seemed to think she was terrific, too.

"But is she a Lady?" I asked Mother later.

"Of course," said Mother. "Why do you ask?"

"She had her elbows on the table."

"Oh well," Mother shrugged, thereby jettisoning ten years of training in a moment. I was utterly confused.

Gradually my sister and I pieced out that a Lady was more than the sum of her manners. Translated, that meant to us that if you were nice it was somehow okay to put your elbows on the table in spite of the rules. We thought it was worth a try.

So, one night, we sat down to dinner and propped up our elbows. With an inevitability that took our breath away, Mother immediately said, "Please. Ladies don't sit that way."

I'm afraid that with my children I just said, "Elbows off the table" and looked the other way. You can't hope to accomplish anything that way. Bringing up Ladies takes vigilance and, even then, you can barely get all the rules covered before they're grown.

I have to hand it to my mother. To this day when I lean on the table or stare in a bus I know I am breaking a hallowed rule. But I have decided that I am old enough to break them, or at least to break some of them some of the time. I may ask an occasional personal question, pick up a chicken leg, or wear white shoes out of season. I'm flexible. But I would never, absolutely never, wear a safety pin in my slip.   🍒

ODDS AND ENDS

Shortly after we moved into a new neighborhood, our six-year-old was invited to join a "Cookie Club." The only requirement was that she furnish cookies at the first meeting. When I asked our daughter's friend how often the club met, she replied, "Oh, whenever we have a new member."   Mrs. Henry Leabo.

*

Then there was the little lad who was asked what he had learned from the story of Jonah and the whale. He responded knowingly, "People make whales sick."   *Smiles.*

*

Two small boys were waiting to cross a street in heavy traffic. "Come on, let's go," said one. The other hesitated. "Let's wait for an empty space to come along," he said.   *The Daily Mining Gazette.*

"Without Memories We Are As the Wind"

The old Indian woman dropped stones, like
solid tears, on her son's grave

By HARRY W. PAIGE

May 1982

I T HAPPENED almost 20 years ago, on a hot July day, but I still remember it clearly. The old Indian woman was wearing tennis shoes, an ankle-length dress, and a black shawl. She was carrying an open umbrella for protection against the fierce Dakota sun.

I stopped the car and asked her where she was going.

To a small cemetery five miles west, she told me, on the edge of the Badlands. It was a long walk for a woman I guessed to be in her 80s, especially with the noonday sun beating down on the treeless prairie.

It turned out to be a half hour's drive. The gravel road

Reprinted with permission of the author.

stopped suddenly, continuing as two tracks across the open prairie. There were washouts, ruts, and bumps that slowed us to a crawl. But time is not so important on the plains. And the minutes were filled by an old woman's remembering.

She was going to visit her son's grave—to sing a song of remembrance and put a few sacred stones in the dust. He had been killed in the war, on some lonely Pacific island back in 1944, only 18 when he died. She remembered the boy but had never known the man, and so her stories were seen through the eyes of her heart.

She told of his birth in the Moon of Falling Leaves, the white man's November. She told of the time he had wandered off at the Sun Dance at Pine Ridge and was lost for two hours; his first day at school after he had run from the school bus and hidden in the grass; his encounter with a rattlesnake near the wood pile; his First Communion.

I told her it was a long time to remember, to "throw the mind back," as the Sioux expressed it. I had lost friends in that war, had even seen them die, but now the sorrow had passed and there was only an absence, a kind of negative pain.

"We *must* throw the mind back," she insisted patiently. "Without memories we are as wind in the buffalo grass."

The cemetery was four dusty graves facing west. Two were unmarked, but my companion told me who was buried in them. One had died in the 1st World War, a soldier. The other was a child who had died of the measles in the early '30s. Another gray, weathered stone carried the name of Elijah Jumping Elk and the dates 1900–1954. The fourth grave was her son's.

I stood awkwardly nearby as she reached in a pocket and withdrew two stones, kneeling to place them on the grave. I noticed there was a pile of them now, dropped over the years like solid tears. I knew that flowers would have wilted in an hour, and plastic substitutes weren't a part of her world.

Then she sang in Lakota a simple, trembling chant repeated over and over again:

I remember Billy Two Hawk.
He was a warrior
With a strong heart.
A son,
I remember him.

That was all. That was all that needed to be said. The Great Spirit would know the rest. She made the Sign of the Cross and rose to her feet. I took her home.

By the time I returned to the reservation two years later she lay beside her son. I put a few stones on her grave—belated payment for some words she had given me one day, words that have become a part of my own silent requiems for nearly 20 years now.

On two occasions I have spoken her words aloud, once in anger and once in reverence.

The angry words were spoken to an overzealous salesman trying to sell me a word processor. I agreed with him that, in a certain sense, machines have a memory, that data can be stored and recalled later at the touch of a button. But in talking about what he called Random Access Memory, he concluded his pitch, "It has a memory like a mother's."

Instantly my own memory system was activated: an old Indian woman was dropping stones and prayers on a lonely grave near the Dakota Badlands. She was stooped and her leathery face was webbed with the lines of living. She didn't look much like the young woman operating the machine in the salesman's brochure. And the old woman's memory wasn't "Random Access." It was painfully selective. A memory like a mother's?

"Not hardly," I told him. "More like wind in the buffalo grass."

I never bought the word processor, perhaps because memory is more sacred to me than it was 20 years ago. Perhaps because I feel memory should be accompanied by laughter or tears or some human feeling. It wasn't the salesman's fault. He was just doing his job. But in boasting of a machine's memory he had unknowingly tread on mine.

The other time I said her words aloud was at an All Souls' Day Mass.

During the homily my mind wandered. I was thinking of this holy day that the Church has set aside for remembrance. And then in my mind the long parade of the dead began filing past, the faces that matched the list of names on the envelope I had put in the collection basket a week earlier. The parade started with a classmate in first grade and came up through the recent death of a good friend. Maybe 50 years of remembering.

And then it came to me that the Church had elevated memory to a sacramental rite. The Mass itself was the celebration of a living memory. And there was the calendar: almost every day of the year was devoted to the memory of some saint. The collective memory of the Catholic Church stretches back 2,000 years.

And it was then that I said it: "Without memories we are as wind in the buffalo grass." A few heads turned, but it was worth it to me—hearing her words spoken aloud again.

Growing older means living more intimately with memories. The eternal present may be good enough for youth, but maturity demands more of us. Memories give a continuity, a sense of purpose to our lives. They echo back across the years those voices and images from the past telling us what we are and, if we are very lucky, what we should become. 🍏

Growing up Mexican, American, and Catholic

And going to school with the *gringos*

By RICHARD RODRIGUEZ
June 1982, condensed from *Hunger of Memory**

B OTH MY PARENTS grew up Catholic in small Mexican towns. They remember towns where everyone was a Catholic. But with their move to America, to Sacramento, Calif., my mother and father found themselves (she praying in whispered Spanish) in an Irish-American parish.

In a way, they were at ease in such a church. They had much in common with the Irish-born priests and nuns. Like my parents, the priests remembered what it was like to have been Catholic in villages and cities where everyone else was a Catholic. In their American classrooms, the nuns worked

very hard to approximate the other place, that earlier kind of religious experience. For a time they succeeded. For a time I too enjoyed a Catholicism something like that enjoyed a generation before me by my parents.

I grew up a Catholic at home and at school, in private and in public. My mother and father were deeply pious *catolicos;* all my relatives were Catholics. At home, there were holy pictures on a wall of nearly every room and a crucifix hung over my bed. My first 12 years as a student were spent in Catholic schools where I could look up to the front of the room and see a crucifix hanging over the clock.

When I was a boy, anyone not a Catholic was defined by that fact and the term *non-*

*1981 by Richard Rodriguez. Originally published by David R. Godine, Publisher, Inc. Reprinted with permission.

Catholic. In those years I could have told you the names of persons in public life who were Catholics. I knew that Ed Sullivan was a Catholic. And Mrs. Bob Hope. And Senator John F. Kennedy. As the neighborhood newspaper boy, I knew all the names on my route. As a Catholic, I noted which open doors, which front room windows disclosed a crucifix. At quarter to eight Sunday mornings, I saw the O'Briens and the Van Hoyts walking down the empty sidewalk past our house and I knew.

Catholics were mysteriously lucky, chosen by God to be nurtured a special way. Non-Catholics had souls too, of course, and somehow could get to heaven. But in 12 years of Catholic schooling, I learned very little about their beliefs. The little I did learn was conveyed by my teachers without hostility and with fair accuracy. I knew that Protestants differed from Catholics. But what precisely distinguished a Baptist from a Methodist from an Episcopalian I could not have said.

Judaism was different. Before the Christian era Judaism was *my* religion, the nuns said. ("We are all Jews because of Christ.") But what happened to Judaism after Christ's death to the time the modern state of Israel was founded, I could not have said.

Nor did I know a thing about Hinduism or Buddhism or Islam.

While the nuns reminded me of my spiritual separateness from non-Catholics, they provided excellent *public* schooling. A school day began with a prayer—the Morning Offering. Then there was the Pledge of Allegiance to the American flag. Religion class followed immediately. But afterward, for the rest of the day, I was taught well those skills of numbers and words crucial to my Americanization. Soon I became as Americanized as my classmates, most of whom were two or three generations removed from their immigrant ancestors, and all of whom were children of middle-class parents.

When I remember my early Catholic schooling, I recall an experience of religion very different from anything I have known since. Never since have I felt so much at home in the Church, so easy at Mass. My grammar school years especially were the years when the great Church doors opened to enclose me, filling my days as I was certain the Church filled all time. Living in a community of shared faith, I enjoyed much more than mere social re-enforcement of religious belief. Experienced continuously in public and private, Catholicism shaped my whole day. It framed my experience of eating and sleeping and washing. It named the season and the hour.

The sky was full then and the coming of spring was a religious event. I would awaken to the sound of garage doors creaking open and know without thinking that it was Friday and that my father was on his way to 6:30 Mass. I saw, without bothering to notice, statues at home and at school of the Virgin and of Christ. I would write at the top of my arithmetic or history homework the initials of Jesus, Mary, and Joseph. (All my homework was thus dedicated.) I felt the air was different, somehow still and more silent on Sundays and high feastdays. I felt lightened, transparent as sky, after confessing my sins to a priest. Schooldays were routinely divided by prayers said with classmates. I would not have forgotten to say Grace before eating. And I would not have turned off the light next to my bed or fallen asleep without praying to God.

The institution of the Church stood, an extraordinary physical presence in my world. One block from the house was Sacred Heart Church. In the opposite direction, another block away, was Sacred Heart Grammar School, run by the Sisters of Mercy. And from our backyard, I could see Mercy Hospital, Sacramento's only Catholic hospital. All day I would hear the sirens of death.

Well before I was a student myself, I would watch the Catholic school kids walk by the front of the house, dressed in gray and red uniforms. From the front lawn I could see people on the steps of the church, coming out, dressed in black after funerals, or standing, the ladies in bright-colored dresses in front of the church after a wedding. When I first went to stores on errands for my mother, I could be seen by the golden-red statue of Christ, where it hovered over the main door of the church.

I was *un catolico* before I was a Catholic. It was in Spanish that I first learned to pray. I recited family prayers—not from any book. And in those years when we felt alienated from *los gringos,* my family went across town every week to the wooden Church of Our Lady of Guadalupe, which was decorated with yellow Christmas tree lights all year long.

Very early, however, the *gringo* church in our neighborhood began to superimpose itself on our family life. The first English-speaking dinner guest at our house was a priest from Sacred Heart Church. I was about four years old at the time, so I remember only random details. But the visit was too important an event for me to forget. I remember how my mother dressed her four children in outfits it had taken her weeks to sew. I wore a white shirt and blue woolen shorts. (It was the first time I had been dressed up for a stranger.) I remember hearing the priest's English laughter. (It was the first time I had heard such sounds in the house.) I remember that my mother served a *gringo* meat loaf and that I was too nervous or shy to look up more than two or three times to study the priest's jiggling layers of face. (Smoothly, he made believe that there was conversation.)

After dinner we all went to the front room, where the priest took a small book from his jacket to recite some prayers, consecrating our house and our family. He left a large picture of a sad-eyed Christ, exposing his punctured heart. (A caption below records the date of his visit and the imprimatur of Francis Cardinal Spellman.) That picture survives. Hanging prominently over the radio or, later, the television set in the front room, it has retained a position of prominence in all the houses my parents have lived in since. It has been one of the few permanent fixtures in the environment of my life.

I saw a picture of the Sacred Heart in the grammar-school classroom I entered two years after the priest's visit. The picture drew an important continuity between home and the classroom. When all else was different for me (as a scholarship boy) between the two worlds of my life, the church provided an essential link. During my first months in school, I remember being struck by the fact that—although they worshipped in English—the nuns and my classmates shared my family's religion. The *gringos* were, in some way, like me, *catolicos.*

Only now do I trouble to notice what intricate differences separated home Catholicism from classroom Catholicism. In school, religious instruction stressed that man was a sinner. Influenced, I suspect, by a melancholic strain in Irish Catholicism, the nuns portrayed God as a judge. I was carefully taught the demands He placed upon me. In the third grade I could distinguish between venial and mortal sin. I knew—and was terrified to know—that there was one unforgivable sin (against the Holy Ghost): the sin of despair. I knew the crucial distinction between perfect and imperfect contrition. I could distinguish sins of commission from sins of omission. And I learned how important it was to be in a state of grace at the moment of death.

Among the assortment of possible sins to commit, sexual sins were certainly mentioned. With the first years of puberty, the last years of grammar school, we began hearing about "sins of the flesh." There were those special mornings when the priest would come over from church to take the boys to the cafeteria, while the nun remained with the girls—"the young ladies"—in the classroom.

Unlike others who have described their Catholic schooling, I do not remember the nuns or the priests to have been obsessed with sexual sins. The Church in fact excited more sexual wonderment than it repressed. I regarded with awe the "wedding ring" on a nun's finger, her black "wedding veil"—symbols of marriage to God. I would study pictures of martyrs—white-robed virgins fallen in death and the young, almost smiling, St. Sebastian transfigured in pain. At Easter high Mass I was dizzied by the perfume of white flowers at the celebration of rebirth. At such moments, the Church touched alive some very private sexual excitement. It pronounced my sexuality important.

Sin remained, nevertheless. Confession was a regular part of my grammar school years. ("I have disobeyed my parents 14 times . . . I have lied 8 times . . . I am heartily sorry for having offended Thee . . .") God the Father judged. But Christ the Son had interceded. I was forgiven each time I sought forgiveness.

The Mexican Catholicism of home was less concerned with man the sinner than with man the supplicant. God the Father was not so much a stern judge as One with the power to change our lives. My family turned to God not in guilt so much as in need. We prayed for favors and at desperate times. I prayed for help in finding a quarter I had lost on my way home. I prayed with my family at times of illness and when my father was temporarily out of a job. And when there was death in the family, we prayed.

I remember my family's religion, and I hear the whispering voices of women. For although men in my family went to church, women prayed most audibly. Whether by man or woman, however, God the Father was rarely addressed directly. There were intermediaries to carry one's petition to Him. My mother had her group of Mexican and South American saints and near-saints. She favored a black Brazilian priest who, she claimed, was especially efficacious.

Above all mediators there was Mary, Santa Maria, the Mother. Whereas at school the primary mediator was Christ, at home that role was assumed by the Mexican Virgin, *Nuestra Senora de Guadalupe,* the focus of devotion and pride for Mexican Catholics. The Mexican Mary "honored our people," my mother would say. "She could have appeared to anyone in the whole world, but she appeared to a Mexican." Someone like us. And she appeared, I could see from her picture, as a young Indian maiden—dark just like me.

Around the time I was in fourth grade, I was introduced to that text familiar to generations of Catholic students, *The Baltimore Catechism.* The catechism taught me to trust the authority of the Church. That was the central lesson conveyed through the experience of memorizing hundreds of questions and answers. Each answer was memorized *along with the question.* Beyond what the answer literally stated, two things were thus communicated. First, the existence of a question implies the existence of an answer. (There are no stray questions.) And second, that my questions about religion had answers. (The Church knows.)

Not only in religion class was memory exercised. During those years I was also impressing on my memory the spelling of hundreds of words, grammar rules, division and multiplication tables. The nuns deeply trusted the role of memorization in learning. They were in front of the room for hours, drilling us over and over and over (5 times 5 ... 5 times 9; i before e except after c; God made us to know, love, and serve Him in this world ...). Stressing memorization, my teachers implied that education is largely a matter of acquiring knowledge already discovered. And they were right. For contrary to more progressive notions of learning, much that is learned in a classroom must be the already known; and much that is already known must be learned before a student can achieve truly independent thought.

Stressing memorization, the nuns assumed an important Catholic bias. Stated positively, they believed that learning is a social activity, a rite of passage into the group. (Remembrance is itself an activity that establishes a student's dependence upon and union with others.) Less defensibly, the nuns distrusted intellectual challenges to authority. In religion class especially, they would grow impatient with the relentlessly questioning student. When one nun told my parents that their youngest daughter had a 'mind of her own,' she meant the remark to be a negative criticism. And even though I was urged to read all that I could, several teachers were dismayed to learn that I had read the novels of Victor Hugo and

Flaubert. ("Those writers are on the Index, Richard.")

I never read the Bible alone. In fifth grade, when I told a teacher that I intended to read the New Testament over the summer, I did not get the praise I expected. Instead, the nun looked worried and said I should delay my plan for a while. ("Wait until we read it in class.") In the seventh and eighth grades, my class finally did read portions of the Bible. We read together. And our readings were guided by the teachings of Tradition—the continuous interpretation of the Word passing through generations of Catholics. Thus, as a reader I never forgot the ancient Catholic faith—that the Church serves to help solitary man comprehend God's Word.

Of all the institutions in their lives, only the Catholic Church has seemed aware of the fact that my mother and father are thinkers—persons aware of the experience of their lives. Other institutions—the nation's political parties, the industries of mass entertainment and communications, the companies that employed them—have all treated my parents with condescension. The Church too has treated them badly when it attempted formal instruction. The homily at Sunday Mass, intended to give parishioners basic religious instruction, has often been poorly prepared and aimed at a childish listener. But the liturgical Church has excited my parents. In ceremonies of public worship, they have been moved, assured that their lives—all aspects of their lives, from waking to eating, from birth until death, all moments—possess great significance. The liturgy has encouraged them to dwell on the meaning of their lives. To think.

What the Church gave to my mother and father, it gave to me. During those years when the nuns warned me about the dangers of intellectual pride and referred to Christ as Baby Jesus, they were enabling me to participate fully in the liturgical life of the Church. The nuns were not interested in constructing a temple of religious abstractions. God was more than an idea. He was a person, white-bearded, with big arms. (Pictures could not show what He really was like, the nuns said, but one could be sure that He was Our Father.) He loved us and we were to respond, like children, in love.

The Church of my childhood rocked through time—a cradle, an ark—to rhythms of sorrow and joy, marking the passage of man.

The Catholic calendar in my bedroom was printed by W.E. Gormley and Sons, Morticians. Every month there was a different Bible picture in beautiful colors. Every day was something. The calendar noted ferial and ember days, fish days and the feastdays of saints. (My birthday honored St. Ignatius Loyola.) There was another, a "regular" calendar in the kitchen (Capitol Savings and Loan). It noted full moons and crescents and the official change of the seasons. My mother used the regular calendar to write down our doctors' appointments (shots; teeth).

It was the religious calendar that governed my school year. In early September there was a nine o'clock Mass on the Friday of the first week of school to pray for academic success. (Students were grouped according to class. Behind my class would be my new teacher's face, a face I still wasn't used to.) In June, there was a Mass of graduation for the eighth-graders.

Between those events, school often stopped or flowered as routine bowed to the sacred. In the middle of a geography or an arithmetic lesson, the nuns would lead us out of our classrooms and we would walk—400 students in double lines—down a block to church, stopping traffic (We were Catholics!) to attend a First Friday Mass or a Rosary to Mary. In Lent there were Friday Stations of the Cross. (Fourteen meditations on the passion of Christ—He stumbled, He fell—14 times the priest

intoning, "We adore Thee, O Christ . . . ") Benediction, the adoration of the Host, followed. The lovely hymn, the *Tantum Ergo,* sounded as smoke of incense rose like vine. Upon the high altar stood a golden monstrance in the shape of a sunburst, at the center of which—exposed through a tiny window—was the round Host.

We returned to the classroom, came back to the same paragraph in a still-opened book. Routine resumed. Sacred dramas of Church thus fitted into a day, never became the routine. Rather they redeemed the routine.

On Halloween night, all over Sacramento, children dressed up as ghosts or Frankensteins or dimestore skeletons with phosphorescent bones. But only Catholic school kids went to Mass the next morning to honor the white-robed saints on the Feast of All Hallows. For the rest of the day, though, I was free—no school. I could ride my bicycle around Sacramento and watch public school kids walk to school. And people downtown were passing just another day. (They seemed not to know.)

In the secular calendar there was no day like Ash Wednesday. All day I could see on the heedless foreheads of classmates the Hindu-like smudge of dark ash, the reminder of death. (" . . .

Unto dust thou shalt return.")
One year a girl at school was
killed in a car crash shortly after
Ash Wednesday. I took the
lesson.

In our house on Good Friday
we behaved as if a member of
our family had died. There
was no radio or television. In
Sacramento, the blue Easter
morning seemed always to
rhyme with the account of the
three Marys wending their way
through a garden to discover
an empty tomb. At church, at
the altar, there were vestments
of gold and the climbing voices
of a Mozart Mass, tossing rings
sempiternal.

The wheels turned. Two
wheels of time. The secular calendar made plain note of the
hot first day of summer. Fall.
Then winter. Ordinary time:
Labor Day. The first day of
school. Arithmetic class. An
hour for spelling (a test every
Friday). Recess. Church time:
Benediction with classmates.
Candles on St. Blaise's day. Ash.
Palms in April. The red-eyed
white dove descending, descending on Pentecost Sunday. Mary
crowned with dying sweet
flowers on the first day of May.
The wheels turned. Second
grade. Third grade. Fifth grade.
Christmas. Epiphany. The secular calendar announced the ver-
nal equinox. The low valley fog
of late winter would slowly yield
to the coming of Easter.

I went to the nine o'clock Mass
every Sunday with my family.
At that time in my life, when I
was so struck by diminished family closeness and the necessity
of public life, church was a place
unlike any other. It mediated
between my public and private
lives. I would kneel beside my
brother and sisters. On one side
of us would be my mother. (I
could hear her whispered Spanish Hail Mary.) On the other
side, my father. In the pew
directly in front of us were the
Van Hoyts. And in front of them
were the druggist and his family.
Over to the side was a lady who
wore fancy dresses, a widow who
prayed a crystal rosary. She was
alone, as was the old man in
front who cupped his face in his
hands while he prayed. It was
this same gesture of privacy the
nuns would teach me to use,
especially after Communion
when I thanked God for coming into my soul.

The Mass mystified me for
being both a public and a private event. We prayed here, each
of us, much as we prayed on
our pillows—most privately—all
alone before God. And yet the
great public prayer of the Mass
would go on. No one ever forgot where he was. People stood
up together or they knelt at the
right time in response to the
progression of the liturgy. Every
Sunday in summer someone
fainted from heat, had to be

carried out, but the Mass went on.

Never once did I hear a classmate or teacher make an exclamation of religious joy. Religious feelings and faith were channeled through ritual. Thus it was that my classmates and I prayed easily throughout the school day. We recited sublime prayers and childish ones ("Angel of God, my guardian dear... "). And nobody snickered. Because the prayers were always the same and because they were said by the group, we had a way of praying together without being self-conscious.

Children of ceremony: My classmates and I would rehearse our roles before major liturgical celebrations. Several days before a feastday we would learn the movements for a procession. In the half-darkened church one nun stood aside with a wooden clapper which she knocked to tell us when to rise, when to kneel, when to leave the pew, when to genuflect ("All together!"). We'd rehearse marching (the tallest last) up the aisle in straight, careful lines. Worship was managed as ceremony.

My sense of belonging in this ceremonial Church was dearest when I turned 12 and became an altar boy. During the last three years of grammar school, I was regularly asked to serve, and in my busiest year, eighth grade, I served at over 200 Masses, plus about 30 Baptisms and the same number of weddings and funerals.

During the school year I was excused from class for an hour or two to serve at a funeral Mass. In summertime I would abandon adolescence to put the black cassock of mourning over a light summer shirt. A spectator at so many funerals, I grew acquainted with the rhythms of grief. I knew at which moments, at which prayers in church and at gravesides, survivors were most likely to weep. I studied faces. I learned to trust the grief of persons who showed no emotion. With the finesse of a mortician, I would lead mourners to the grave. I helped carry coffins (their mysterious weight—neither heavy nor light) to burial sites when there were not mourners enough. And then I would return. To class or to summer. Resume my life as a boy of 13.

There are people who tell me today that they are not religious because they consider religion to be an evasion of life. I hear them, their assurance, and do not bother to challenge the arrogance of a secular world which hasn't courage enough to accept the fact of old age. And death. I know people who speak of death with timorous euphemisms. I have friends who wouldn't think of allowing their children to attend a funeral for fear of inflicting traumatic scars. For my part, I will always be grateful to the Church that took me so seriously and exposed me so early, through the liturgy, to the experience of life. I will always be grateful to the parish priest who forced a mortician to remove an elaborate arrangement of flowers from a coffin: "Don't hide it!"

I celebrate now a childhood lived through the forms of the liturgical Church. As the Church filled my life, I grew to the assurance that my life, my every action and thought, was important for good or for bad. Bread and wine, water, oil, salt and ash—through ceremonies of guilt and redemption, sorrow and rebirth, through the passing liturgical year, my boyhood assumed all significance.

I marvel most at having so easily prayed with others—not simply alone. I recall standing at the altar at Easter, amid candles and gold vestments, hearing the Mozart high Mass. These were impossible riches. I remember wanting to cry out with joy, to shout. I wanted to shout. But I didn't, of course. I worshipped in a ceremonial Church, one in a group. I remained silent and remembered to genuflect exactly on cue. After the Mass, I pulled off the surplice and cassock and rushed to meet my parents, waiting for me in front of the church.

"It was very nice today," my mother said. Something like that. "It makes you feel good, the beautiful music and everything." That was all that she said. It was enough.   🍎

A CASE OF MISTAKEN IDENTITY

The Seminoles Band had finally made it to the state music contest in Gainsville, Florida. My best friend was nervously waiting to play her clarinet solo. Her anxiety doubled when we realized we couldn't find Sarah Priest who was to accompany her on the piano.

I ran down the halls calling for Sarah at each room. Then I opened the door to the ladies restroom, which was packed with majorettes changing into their uniforms. "Is Sarah Priest in here?" I called breathlessly.

A crowd of faces looked up, jaws dropped, and the noise turned to silence. One of the majorettes rephrased my question in disbelief: "Is there a WHAT in here?"   Marianne Kwiecinski.

Resurrection

Faith and the Empty Tricycle

Two-year-old Clare is only superficially
an angel, but her innocent remark prompted
an Easter insight

By CLAUDIA MCDONNELL
March 1984, condensed from *America* *

I T IS A fundamental truth
of life, long proclaimed by
scholars and saints, that the
really important things are often
the very things we do not see. I
heard this stated recently, in different words, by a young lady
of abundant natural wisdom.
She is not yet a scholar, and she
resembles an angel more than
she behaves like one, but I
excuse her for that on the
premise that few individuals
achieve sanctity by the age
of two.

The lady's name is Clare, and
in addition to being quick-witted
and observant, she is feisty and
strong willed. One day she was
looking at a family photograph
album with her Aunt Betty.
Typically, there were more pictures of the first child, Clare's
older sister, than there were of
Clare.

"That's me," Clare would
say as she pointed to a
picture.

"No, that's Mary Beth," Aunt
Betty would correct.

"No, *me!*" Clare would
insist.

Finally they came to a picture of both girls, Mary Beth on her bicycle and Clare on her tricycle.

"That's me," said Clare.

"Yes, that's you," Aunt Betty agreed.

The next picture showed only Mary Beth, with Clare's riderless tricycle beside her. Clare turned to Aunt Betty.

"That's me," she said matter-of-factly, "after I got off my bike."

Aunt Betty struggled with herself and managed not to laugh until later, when she told the family. Leave it to Clare, we said, to put herself back into the picture she had already stepped out of.

Or had she? She had disappeared from the camera's eye, with its narrow range of vision, but anyone could see that she had only stepped away for a moment, perhaps to explore a corner of the backyard or to retrieve a forgotten toy. She would be back. She belonged there, with Mary Beth and the tricycle. You could feel her presence. You did not need to see her.

Someday when Clare is grown she will be wise as well as clever, and recognize the truth that lies behind the words she spoke as a baby. She will look at a picture of a house, and recall the people she loved who lived inside. She will wear a necklace or a ring, and feel the presence of the one who gave it to her. She will look into the eyes of her children and see her parents. She will pray, and know that those who left her to go to God are living still.

Clare will know with a certainty she cannot yet possess that reality is much more than the visible world. But so many who are older than she is would deny it. Perhaps it is not a lesson one learns with age. Perhaps it is truth one is born with and needs to cherish.

The 20th century takes a lot of blame for enshrining skepticism and producing materialist people, who believe only on the evidence of their senses. But there are precedents. The world's most famous skeptic lived 2,000 years ago. Sometimes the word "doubting" is still attached to his name. "I won't believe it," he said, "unless I put my hand into the place where the nails were." He got his proof, and a gentle observation: Blessed are they who believe without seeing. Blessed, too, are those like Clare, who know that what you do not see may tell you more than what you do see.

That is why her words make me think of Easter. I remember what she said, and then, in my mind's eye, I see a tomb, open and empty and filled with light. I hear another voice, wonderful as Clare's, but stronger, rich with delight and promise and even a secret humor.

"That's Me," says the voice, "after I died." ❊

IN A MANNER OF SPEAKING

Two Irishmen were talking on the bus. "And so your name is Riley?" said one. "Are you any relation to Tim Riley?"

"Very distantly," replied the other. "I was my mother's first child and Tim was her 12th." Delia Wood.

*

A businessman was dashing to catch a plane for Paris when he realized he had no small change in French currency, so he phoned his secretary, "Get me $20 worth of francs and meet me at the airport."

She showed up with quite a large package. You can buy a lot of hot dogs for $20. Vera Farris.

SIGNS OF THE TIMES

In a church nursery: "Noisery—five years of age and under." H. Lancaster.

*

On a downtown window: "We are a non-profit organization. (Not that we intended to have it that way.)" Katia Rudnytzky.

*

From a bumper sticker: "Warning! I brake for no apparent reason." M. Holmes.

*

In a school corridor: "Smoking is prohibited! No whiffs and no butts." Sister Cesira.

*

At a roadside diner: "Bus drivers must have correct change." Josie Butera.

*

In the window of a pro shop: "Out to lunch. Don't get teed off. Back before fore." Dolly Bliss.

*

In a department store: "Men's Suits—Ready to Wear. Boys' Suits—Ready to Wear Out." Philip Lazarus.

*

From a Las Vegas marriage chapel: "A girl friend is delectable, but a wife is deductible." Bea Machi.

The Resurrection and the Ring of Truth

"This thing was not done in a corner," said St. Paul

By J. B. PHILLIPS
April 1968, condensed from *Ring of Truth**

I T IS NOW 25 years since I began translating the Epistles. I undertook the task chiefly for the sake of the young people at that time under my care in wartime London. Like many other clergymen I had never realized what a barrier beautiful but antique words had imposed.

The first effect of my work was astonishing. The people for whom I had made this translation began to see the relevance of the Letters of St. Paul to life. The removal of the old varnish allowed the truth to reach them in a way it never had before.

The second effect was upon me, the translator. Although I

did my utmost to preserve emotional detachment, I found again and again that the material under my hands was strangely alive. I found myself provoked, challenged, stimulated, comforted, and generally convicted of my previous shallow knowledge of the Holy Scriptures. The centuries seemed to melt away, and here was I confronted by eternal truths which my soul, however reluctantly, felt bound to accept.

To me it is the more remarkable because I had no fundamentalist upbringing—and, although as a priest of the Anglican church I had a great respect for Holy Scripture, this very close contact of several years of translation produced an effect

*This article © 1967 by J. B. Phillips. Reprinted by permission.

of inspiration which I had never experienced before, even in the remotest degree.

The letter which really struck me a blow from which I have never recovered was 1st Corinthians. I have come to regard the 15th chapter as in some ways the most important chapter in the New Testament. It is the earliest evidence for the Resurrection of Christ. It was written some 20 years after the Crucifixion and before it there were no written Gospels.

Many persons could still remember Jesus, and Paul lists some of those who saw Christ alive after his public death. I was struck again by the "over 500 Christians" who saw Jesus simultaneously, "of whom," Paul comments, "the majority are still alive." The evidence for the Resurrection does not rest on hysterical visions in the half-light of early dawn but on actual appearances. I noticed the flat, matter-of-fact recital of known events. There is no attempt to persuade or prove, and certainly there is no artistic embellishment. Paul is, in effect, saying: these are the historic facts which we know.

Then, at verse 12, he does allow himself to be moved. Since the risen Christ is the author of the faith which has grown up in the unlikely soil of Corinth, how can anyone, even for the sake of argument, deny that Christ really rose?

Paul is concerned to defend the Christian belief in man's resurrection after the pattern of Christ's Resurrection. The old Greek belief, and its Roman counterpart, held that once the body was dead the disembodied soul lived a miserable twilight existence in Hades. It was the place of shadows, dark and joyless. The Hebrew idea of Sheol was little different. Sadness, silence, and hopelessness brooded over life after death, and death was to men of those days the ultimate disaster.

Paul is determined to correct this negative thinking. The Resurrection of Christ was always to him the key to the human dilemma. Christ had become man, Christ had died for man, and Christ had risen to open the door to the glories that human vocabulary has no words to describe. Paul knew that man's last enemy, death, was now defeated, and men could look forward, not to a shadowy half-life, but to a life fuller and more glorious than human imagination can conceive. No more nonsense, he urges, about what sort of body we shall possess when our mortal bodies perish. That we can safely leave to God, who has demonstrated the defeat of death by the raising up of Christ.

For me, the translator, this

15th chapter seemed alive and vibrant, not with pious hope, but with inspired certainty. Quite suddenly I realized that no man had ever written such words before. As I pressed on with my translation I came to feel utterly convinced of the truth of the Resurrection. Something of literally life-and-death importance had happened in history, and I was reading the actual words of people who had seen Christ after his Resurrection and had seen men deeply changed by his living power.

Previously, I must have been insulated from the reality of these words simply because they were known as "Scripture." Now I was compelled to come to the closest possible terms with them, and I was enormously impressed, and still am. It was borne in upon me with irresistible force that these letters could never have been written if there had been no Jesus Christ, no Crucifixion, and no Resurrection.

The more I thought about it, the more unthinkable it became that any of this new, courageous, joyful life could have originated in any kind of concocted story. There had been a stupendous Event, and from that was flowing strength and utter conviction.

Some years ago I was invited by the BBC to discuss the problems of translation with Dr. E. V. Rieu, who had trans-lated the Gospels for Penguin Classics. I asked him, "Did you get the feeling that the whole material is extraordinarily alive?"

Dr. Rieu said to me, "I got the deepest feeling that I could have expected. It changed me; my work changed me. And I came to the conclusion that these words bear the seal of the Son of Man and God. They are the Magna Charta of the human spirit."

I found it particularly thrilling to hear a man who is a scholar of the first rank admitting that these words bore to him, as to me, the ring of truth.

Suppose that you have spent many hundred hours in putting these four widely differing accounts of some of the sayings and doings of Jesus into today's English. Do you find yourself so confused that you conclude that there was no such person at all? I doubt it. It is, in my experience, the people who have never troubled seriously to study the four Gospels who are loudest in their protests that there was no such person.

I have read, in Greek and Latin, scores of myths, but I did not find the slightest flavor of myth here. There is no hysteria, no careful working for effect, and no attempt at collusion. These are not embroidered tales: the material is cut to the bone. I sensed again and again that understatement which we have been taught to think is more British than Oriental. There is an almost childlike candor and simplicity, and the total effect is tremendous. No man could ever have invented such a character as Jesus. No man could have set down such artless accounts as these unless some real event lay behind them.

While I was translating the Acts of the Apostles, which I renamed the "Young Church in Action," the full weight of the evidence of the Resurrection fell upon me with renewed force. I found Luke's account of the beginning of the young Church strangely moving. This mere handful of early believers, who had deserted their Master in the first moment of danger, and who had, apparently, taken so long to realize that He had demonstrably conquered death, are bidden to wait. They are convinced; they are full of joy. But they lack the power to breach the defenses of an unbelieving world.

The story is told with extraordinary simplicity. There had to be some God-given power given to that tiny band charged with the alarming (and seemingly impossible) task of "preaching the Gospel to every creature." And there was, for the living Spirit of God came upon them in a way no one could have anticipated.

Luke is describing, perhaps 30 years later, something of what men told him had happened at Pentecost. I cannot believe that Luke, or anybody else, concocted such a story. It is superhuman but not magical, and I find it wholly credible. There is this curious mixture of the earthly and the heavenly, typical of most of the New Testament.

As I continued to read Luke's fascinating story, I slowly realized that the message proclaimed was basically that of Jesus and the Resurrection. This was almost farcically true when Paul preached to the sermon tasters on Mars Hill. Some of them thought he was proclaiming two "foreign deities," Jesus and *Anastasis* — resurrection.

The great point to the young Church was that God had become a human being, had been publicly executed, and then had conquered death. He had shown Himself to them alive "by many infallible proofs" and had even eaten and drunk with them. Naturally they could never forget this, and, as the Gospel was preached to the then known world, "Jesus, the risen Lord" was the core of the message.

The Resurrection of Jesus is historic fact. I suppose I have studied the attempts to disprove the story as fully as most men, and I am utterly convinced that this thing really happened. I am deeply grateful to Luke for showing me that it was the

Resurrection which gave the early Church its enormous drive, vitality, courage, and hope.

This emphasis sent me back to restudy the Gospel records. Let us freely admit that the stories of the Resurrection are not arranged as evidence for any court of law. I should be suspicious of them if they were. People who are frightened and despairing, suddenly confronted with evidence which contradicts all their previous experience of life, can hardly be considered as ideal witnesses. Wouldn't you be shaken to the marrow if a young man whom you had seen die publicly on Friday greeted you cheerfully on Sunday?

I am therefore not in the least worried by the story of the walk to Emmaus (recorded only by Luke). I see no difficulty in believing that the minds of Cleopas and his companion were so utterly preoccupied with the collapse of their hopes that they did not recognize Jesus. Obviously, all the time that they had been walking with Him, their despair was melting and their faith in Jesus was coming back to life. But the psychological moment came when they all were relaxed at a friendly table, and a familiar gesture brought instant recognition. It all clicked into place, or, as Luke records, "their eyes were opened and they knew Him." Now, no one makes up a story like this. No

one ever has, or ever will. This rings true; this certainly happened.

There is an almost haphazard recording of the appearances of Jesus after his Resurrection which I find extraordinarily convincing. I think my favorite again occurs in Luke's work. When the two who walked to Emmaus had rushed back to Jerusalem to report their astounding experience to the eleven, they found that they already knew that "the Lord is risen indeed and hath appeared to Simon."

Again, according to Luke, while they are still talking excitedly, Jesus himself appears among them. They were scared out of their wits; they thought they were seeing a ghost.

Then follows this extraordinary, and in a way amusing, test of whether Jesus was really there in person. He asks them, "Have you anything here to eat?" We can imagine the frantic dash to a shelf or cupboard where they kept their food, and we can imagine that they saw no incongruity in offering Him a piece of broiled fish and part of a honeycomb. I myself cannot imagine that our Lord ate this rather strange meal before their eyes without a smile. But this in a way clinched it; whoever heard of a ghost eating? Again I find this is the kind of story which no man would invent, but which any man who was present would remember until his dying day. And Luke, bless him, records it.

John, writing considerably later, contents himself with remarking, "Many other signs truly did Jesus in the presence of his disciples which are not written in this book." We cannot help wishing he had written more.

It was not to a band of expectant hero-worshipers that Jesus appeared, but to men and women stunned by grief and shattering disappointment. We can only guess at the black cloud of disillusionment which must have swept over them. After this terrible, final, and public disaster they had apparently forgotten that He Himself had forewarned them of what would happen.

It was against a background of broken hope and utter despair that the great miracle occurred. All four Evangelists spend quite a lot of their short narratives in recounting the betrayal, the mock trial, the final humiliations, and the criminal execution. I do not think this was done merely for dramatic effect. It was written to show that Jesus was not God pretending to be a man, but God who had become a man.

Thus the resounding triumph of the Resurrection was all the more splendid. Armed with no supernatural equipment, Jesus had conquered man's last enemy, death. He had shown beyond any possible doubt that the victory was complete. To live again was no longer a pious hope or a wishful thought; it was a certainty. No conspiracy, no trick, no hysterical vision was responsible for this new certainty. As Paul remarked crisply some years later to King Agrippa, "This thing was not done in a corner."   ✻

DOMESTIC BLISS

For a special treat at a fancy restaurant, the whole family had lobster tails, served quite elegantly in their shells. After eating all that he could, little Richard asked plaintively, "Do I have to eat the rest of my dinosaur?"

Mrs. H. Priday.

*

An eight-year-old girl came home from school to announce to her mother that she planned to marry a schoolmate. "That's fine. Does he have a job?" asked her indulgent mother. The girl replied, "Yes, he erases the blackboards in school."

Mrs. L. Binder.

The Rosary

Why We Call It the Rosary

The story in Christian art

By EITHNE WILKINS
May 1970, condensed from *The Rose-Garden Game**

T HE BLESSED Virgin Mary is invoked in the Litany of Loreto as Queen of the Holy Rosary, a title inserted at the end of the last century by Pope Leo XIII. In this litany she has also been invoked from medieval times as Mystical Rose. In Christian art, since the rose is queen of flowers, she is the Queen of the Rose Garden.

Why a string of beads should be called a rosary, or thought of in connection with a garden of any kind is not self-evident. It is puzzling to find artists identify-

*This article © 1969 by Eithne Wilkins. An Azimuth book, originally published by Herder & Herder.

ing the beads with a wreath of roses and a garden of roses.

The story of how the term *rose garden* (*rosarium*) came to be applied to the beads goes back through the Middle Ages to classical times and even pre-Christian cults.

Since classical antiquity collections of poetry by various authors have been called anthologies. *Anthos* is Greek for flower. In the Middle Ages there was a taste for calling books "flower gardens" even when the content was not an anthology of poems. The canonical Hours were often made up for some great personage such as Catherine, Duchess of

445

Cleves, into books glitteringly illuminated with little pictures to guide those of the nobility who could not read. These, and similar collections of prayers and hymns, were often prettily entitled "flower gardens." One might be called *The Soul's Little Garden,* another *The Lily Garden.* But *Rose Garden* was a favorite. One of the earliest was *The Rose-Garden of the Wise,* by Arnold of Villanova (c. 1235–1311).

In the 14th century a Benedictine abbess composed a *Rosarium Jesu* of 50 rhymed prayers, from which the hymn *Jesu dulcis memoria* comes. But soon *Rosarium* as a title was reserved for hymns of praise of the Virgin Mary. Henrich Egher, a Carthusian who died in 1408, specified that 50 *Aves* constituted a *rosarium.* During the 14th and 15th centuries the rose, rosebush, rose garden, and rose garland were used with almost monotonous persistence in Marian symbolism, and then gradually with ever more explicit reference to the beads. By the middle of the 15th century the concept "rose garden," as also "wreath of roses," was well established as symbolizing devotion to the Mystic Rose, Mother of the divine Child, and the beads were becoming an accepted element in the whole complex.

During the next few decades the exercise on the beads

became officially known as the Rosary, the Rose Garden, or the Chaplet of Roses; and by extension the beads themselves acquired these names.

Since the rose was already a preChristian symbol of beauty, love, wisdom, and mystery, it was from a very early time used as a symbol of the beautiful, wise, and mysterious Virgin, Bride, and Mother, Mary. In about the year 430 the poet Sedulius, in his *Carmen Paschale,* wrote of her in what was to become a standard conceit about 1,000 years later:

As blooms among the thorns
the lovely rose, herself without a thorn,
The glory of the bush whose crown she is,
So, springing from the root of Eve, Mary the new Maiden
Atoned for the sin of that first Maiden long ago.

Mary is the Rose without a Thorn, the Peerless Rose, the Rose of Sharon, the Rose of Jericho. That is why in paintings there are often roses even at the birth of the Virgin—a glimpse of a rose garden beyond the arches of a Gothic room—roses at the Annunciation, and roses growing in her marble tomb as she floats up to heaven to be crowned. In a carved altarpiece of about 1500 at Vato, Uppland, in Sweden, the tree of

Jesse almost merges with an arch of roses that are arranged in decades, proving that they represent the Rosary. In poetry the best-known example is the German carol *Lo, How a Rose E'er Blooming*, in which Mary is both the rosebush sprung from the root of Jesse and the rose itself, which in turn bears the rose Christ.

The figure by which Christ is the rose born of the rosebush, or of the rose itself, occurs even before the Middle Ages. The learned Benedictine Rabanus Maurus (776–856) compared the birth of Christ not only to the growth of a rose on a bush, but to a blazing rose growing from a bush that is on fire, yet green and unconsumed. The Burning Bush, out of which God uttered the promise of salvation to Moses, was one of the innumerable prefigurations of the Virgin, and hence also a prototype of the Annunciation, in which poets, painters, mystics, and theologians delighted for centuries: the Virgin conceiving by the Holy Ghost without being consumed by the flames of concupiscence and then bringing forth the promise of salvation.

In hymns from the 10th to the 16th century this symbol is always recurring. In a very literary painting, Nicolas Froment's triptych of 1476, all these motives are worked together: Jesse's tree frames the scene in which the burning rosebush contains the Virgin and Child. By 1500 it is often the rosary that is represented as a rose tree, bearing in its branches medallions, like fruit or Christmas-tree decorations, that contain not Christ's royal ancestors but scenes depicting the 15 mysteries.

An engraving of 1615 shows this rosary tree being tended by Dominican gardeners with spade and watering cans; it stands in a walled garden, for the *Garden Enclosed* is one of the Virgin Mary's titles. From this concept, the Virgin as Garden Enclosed, the illustrators of devotional Rosary books took their inspiration at the beginning of the 16th century. The image of the enclosed garden is taken from the Song of Solomon, "A garden enclosed is my sister, my bride: a spring shut up, a fountain sealed."

For the illustrators a garden is a secret place, at once closed, alive with a concentration of natural forces, and open to the sky. Its secrecy may result from its being a small place between high walls, or from its being surrounded by forest, or simply from its being difficult to find.

The secret garden where the roses never die is the place of immortality. The medieval European sacred rose gardens to be seen in paintings are full of ornamental birds; they are chiefly singing birds, but among them the Eastern peacock also appears, as a symbol not of pride but of immortality. Birds are, of course, symbolic of the spirit; and it is amusing in connection with the Ave Maria garden that the Latin for *birds* is *aves*. In the rose garden not only the singing birds, the robin and the death-and-resurrection bird, the goldfinch, make music; so do angels, sometimes with peacock-feather wings, as in Stephan Lochner's *Madonna of the Rose Arbor* on their harps and lutes (see page 74).

The metaphor of the rose was so rich that by the end of the 15th century the transformation of prayers, like laughter, into roses, and of the roses into a chaplet, offered many possibilities. What is not easy to see is precisely how the chaplet of rose prayers turned into the string of beads that is generally called a chaplet or corona and which the Germans and the Dutch specifically call a rose chaplet, *Rosenkranz.*

There is no point in the Rosary's history where one sees the process actually taking place in art, merely a series of implications. There are a few pictures of the Virgin stringing the rose prayers together, but they are not shown as a string of beads. Besides, though the word *Kranz,* like *wreath,* derives from a root with the meaning "twisting and twining," the medieval rose chaplet that came to lend its name to the Ave beads was usually of flowers bound on a hoop. In a 12th-century German poem in which Mary came to a monk for rose prayers to make a chaplet for herself, she carried a gold hoop over her arm, and she bound the roses onto that. Since this is a vision, a dream, or a fairy tale, one need not ask how she did it. But some rosary pictures actually show the chaplets in the process of being made on a light hoop such as one sees in Dürer's *Rosenkranzfest* (see page 68). But there are no pictures that would explain how these hoops for wearing on the head developed into strung beads.

Before 1400, in pictorial art the *rosarium* may be a garden, or an arbor, or only a hedge of roses; very often the roses grow in a high medieval flower bed that resembles a rectangular tub. The Virgin is usually seated, with the Child on her lap, beside her, or playing near by. Sometimes they are attended by saints, usually female (St. Catherine and St. Dorothy are favorites), or angels. The angels may be holding a crown over the Virgin's head or playing musical instruments or offering the Child apples or roses, or merely gazing, timeless and round-eyed; or they may be elongated robed forms that flit about like bright-feathered birds. The idea of the Enclosed Garden is always suggested.

An unnamed Upper Rhenish master, the Master of the Little Paradise-Garden, has a raised rose bed in his painting *The Madonna of the Rose Bed,* where the Virgin is seated by a rose hedge and hands the Child a white rose. There is another such raised bed in his *Little Paradise-Garden* (see page 70), painted about 1410. A low wall surrounds a shaggy carpet of flowers including the traditional lilies of the valley and, at the Virgin's feet, the violets of humility. Pretty little birds, like winged flowers, include the goldfinch, bullfinch, and yellowhammer.

The Lady, a fairy-tale queen with long golden hair and blue mantle, sits abstracted, reading what must be the Psalter. Among the courtiers is a golden-haired girl supervising the Child's playing, with two quill plectra, on a stringed instrument nearly as big as himself. Since the Child (a learned infant, with his writing case at his belt) is a descendant of King David, the harpist and traditional composer of the Psalms, it is logical that this instrument is the kind of harp called a psaltery.

The picture (which includes a great deal more symbolism besides) is a rebus, the sort of pictorial pun of which medieval artists were so fond: the Garden Enclosed is identified with the Marian Psalter. Nearest to the well, "like a rose planted beside the waters," is a rose tree.

Well before this time, indeed, by the beginning of the 14th century, the Paradise-Garden, with its roses, is often clearly and intimately associated with the Marian Psalter. Paintings reveal most beguilingly that at least 50 years before the term *rosary* was established officially as meaning both the devotion and the beads, the connection was recognized in Flanders, the Upper Rhenish district, and Italy. By the end of the century the Madonna of the Rose Garden is a very frequent subject in Florence.

Jan van Eyck's lovely *Virgin of the Fountain* (see page 72) was painted in 1439. In a garden closed off by a hedge of dark pink roses the Virgin stands on a strip of tapestry, the free end of which is held up behind her, like the back of a throne, by two flying angels. The lawn is dense with lilies of the valley and violets. The ornamental fountain that so often constitutes an allusion to her title of Fountain Sealed is here playing, the four jets doubtless symbolizing "the water of life." The Child in her arms dangles from one hand a tasseled pair of coral beads, the same color as the roses.

Probably the most famous *Madonna of the Rose Arbor* is that by Stephan Lochner (c. 1410–51). Here (see page 74) the arbor is a jewellike frail construction lightly wreathed in red roses, and framed in it is a childlike Virgin in a blue robe and mantle, with a jeweled crown including a pattern of roses, ruby red and deep sapphire blue. She is almost completely ringed in by eager and absorbed little angels, most of them making music, one offering the Child an apple, one picking a rose for Him.

In Madonna-and-Child paintings the beads may lie about at the edge of the painting, casually, spilling out of a bowl, as in Grünewald's *Madonna of the Snow* at Stuppach. They may be worn by the Virgin. They may be worn by the Child. Or they may be something that the Child plays with.

Rarely, the Virgin wears the beads as they might have been worn by a lady of the painter's time, either as a necklace or twined over her arm. In the Fröndenberg altarpiece of about 1400 (see page 69) the very long string of about 103 loose-strung beads is worn around the Madonna's neck, twisted to make a second loop held on one side by her and on the other by the Child, and then, passing over his left wrist, forming a third loop. The beads are here both

her jewelry and his toy, and this finespun, almost unearthly looking Mother and Child are together tranquilly playing something like cat's cradle.

The association of the beads with the Child goes through phases. First one sees Him wearing the sort of coral necklace that was worn in the 14th and 15th centuries, and sometimes in our own time, by infants and toddlers, or it may be simply a twig of coral hung from a string. In Jan van Eyck's *Virgin of the Fountain* (see page 72) the matching color of the coral Ave beads and the roses clearly establishes the connection between the beads and the *rosarium*. An actual prayer chaplet is also held by the Child in *The Madonna of the Convolvulus* (Cologne, Wallraf-Richarz-Museum), by a Cologne master; attached to the string is, furthermore, a little alms bag like that on the contemporary beads of the Duchess of Cleves (see page 66).

A painted wood sculpture of the Infant Christ learning to walk, by an Upper Swabian master (Munich, Bayerisches Nationalmuseum), about 1480, has a little rosary of coral beads, with a terminal cross, worn as a necklace, and the beads are disposed in threes. By the end of the 15th century the association between the Child's coral beads and the prayer beads and the rose chaplet becomes explicit.

From 1500 onward it is common to see the Child playing with the beads. In the painting by Gérard David (d. 1523) in the National gallery, London, in which St. Catherine receives the mystic marriage ring, the ethereally beautiful, almost ghostly Child wears, bandolier style, a loosely strung rosary of glass beads, which He lightly touches with his free hand. In Il Borgognone's *Madonna and Child* (Amsterdam, Riijksmuseum) the holy Child, seated demurely on a little stool, is holding a chaplet between both hands and pointing at a book—altogether the most well-behaved, nicely brought up divine Child with the rosary, excepting an Infant by Quentin Matsys who has the beads round his neck and who is also looking into a book.

In many of these works the beads, whether identifiable as Ave beads or not, are as much a domestic detail as a sacred symbol. The way the Child plays with the beads may be so natural that, if his figure were detached from the rest of the painting, there would be little or no reason to suppose there was any religious meaning: one would simply see an infant or a toddler playing with a string of beads. The human aspect of the Child, as also of the Madonna, becomes more marked later, of course, when religious painting degenerates into sentimental naturalism. The Madonnas of the Rosary by such painters as Murillo (1617–82), and Carlo Cignani (1628–1719) are mother-and-baby paintings passed off as sacred art. But this is not true of the *Madonna on the Cloud of Angels* (Munich, Alte Pinakothek) done by Albrecht Altdorfer (c. 1480–1538), even though both the Madonna and the Child are rather countrified, commonplace types: the Child holds the large rosary, casually in one hand, while the rest goes over his Mother's arm, but He holds up his free hand in a gesture of preaching or blessing that proves He is no ordinary child. Here is a transition between the older type of rosary picture, with the often very natural-looking Madonna and Child and one or more of the motifs *Ave gratia plena,* roses, beads, and Garden Enclosed, and a new type, allegorical and increasingly stereotyped, which also uses these motifs and which comes into existence about 1500, that is, after the founding of the Cologne Confraternity of the Most Holy Rosary in 1475.

A catalogue of rosary altarpieces would be very long, indeed, and largely unrewarding; the official cult began too late in the history of Christian art. But not all is pious dullness. Lubeck has two very pretty polychrome wood altarpieces. One of the most delightful, even if far from perfect, is that carved (in either 1631 or 1645) by Michael and Martin Zirn for the minster at Überlingen, on Lake Constance (see page 76). It is all tremendously gilded, the free-standing Madonna poised in an oval of mystery medallions that are linked by circlets of beads, and with her free hand (the other holds the Child) lightly wafting a scepter as though it were a fairy godmother's wand. The lean, sharp-nosed figures of St. Dominic and St. Francis— drolly caricaturing asceticism, and involuntarily elegant—are 18th-century additions.

After the institution of the Rosary feast by Pope Gregory XIII in 1573 altarpieces showing the Madonna of the Rosary very frequently include St. Dominic, usually receiving the rosary from her hand. Works representing this (late) legendary subject tend towards monotony. The legend of St. Dominic's rosary degenerated into an anecdote. It almost seems as though a similar degeneration may soon happen to the beads, when one reads in a newspaper that for business-men suffering from tension there are now "office toys"

that are "simple, sophisticated things, like china eggs, sea-smoothed stones, geometrical crystal shapes, and amber Muslim rosaries."

But maybe not. Recently I went, just before lighting-up time, into a Roman church. There was no one about except for the two or three little old women in black sitting on benches. As the church darkened, more old women came padding in and away up to the benches, where they settled down; and before long they all began quietly, very swiftly, reciting the Rosary. I went nearer to listen. It was a blend of Latin with Italian that such old Roman women make their own, and it went as fast as if in that vast gloom they had set an invisible prayer wheel spinning. *Santa Maria, madre Dio,* it went, and: *Et in ora morte nostra.* All that muttering seemed very old. It seemed to come not only from a dozen or so small, hunched, intent figures amorphous in black, but from everywhere, and to extend everywhere, through Tibet, through Africa, widening ripples, circles interlocking with circles, and opening further and further like an endless shadowy rose.   ✿

Saying the Rosary in Tongues

A new way to deal with interruptions—and to make the prayer even more meaningful

By ROBERT ANDERSON
October 1982

FINDING 10 uninterrupted minutes to pray the Rosary is nearly impossible on some hectic days. So many of us, counting mentally or on our fingers, pray parts of the Rosary at odd times—while walking to work, riding the bus, waiting in the dentist's office, and so on.

After a long interruption, we might forget where we've stopped. So we repeated the preceding decade just to be sure. If two or three interruptions put us back at the beginning, we may never finish.

I finally devised a system that makes it easier to remember where to resume. I pray the first decade in Latin, the second in Spanish, the third in Italian, the fourth in French, and the fifth in German. After an interrup-

Reprinted with permission of the author.

tion, the memory of the particular language and the particular Mystery both help me to resume the Rosary on the correct decade. I still say the Creed and the Mysteries in English.

Of course I had to memorize the Our Father, the Hail Mary, and the Glory Be to the Father in the other languages. Like many Catholics, I already knew the prayers in Latin. Then, by praying only in Spanish for one week, then in Italian for one week, and so forth, by the end of four weeks I was quite proficient in all five languages.

There are other advantages to praying each decade in a different language. When reciting the prayers in English, I sometimes rush through them without thinking what the words mean. Concentrating more on

453

the words in each language keeps my mind on the real meaning of the prayers. The change of language at each decade also diminishes the possibility of boredom.

Other languages, certainly, may be used for the five decades. You may prefer to use Russian, Hungarian, Polish, Norwegian, Swahili, Gaelic, Japanese, or Chinese.

Prayers in other languages can be obtained from Father Benjamin Kuhn, O.F.M., Siena College, Loudonville, New York 12211. He publishes a Family Prayer Card in many languages and has advised me that "anyone who sends a stamp will receive free five copies of the Family Prayer Card. We supply the envelope, and the name will be used for no other purpose." Tell him the languages you want and feel free to include an offering to cover his time and expenses.

Here are the prayers in the five languages I use.

Latin

Pater noster, qui es in coelis, sanctificetur nomen tuum; adveniat regnum tuum; fiat voluntas tua, sicut in coelo et in terra; panem nostrum quotidianum da nobis hodie; et dimitte nobis debita nostra, sicut et nos dimittimus debitoribus nostris; et ne nos inducas in tentationem. Sed libera nos a malo. Amen.

Ave Maria, gratia plena; Dominus tecum; benedicta tu in mulieribus, et benedictus fructus ventris tui, Jesus. Sancta Maria, Mater Dei, ora pro nobis peccatoribus nunc et in hora mortis nostrae. Amen.

Gloria Patri et Filio et Spiritui Sancto, sicut erat in principio, et nunc, et semper, et in saecula saeculorum. Amen.

Spanish

Padre Nuestro que estas en el cielo. Santificado sea tu nombre. Venga tu reino. Hagase tu voluntad en la tierra como en el cielo. Danas hoy nuestro pan de cada dia. Perdona nuestras ofensas, como tambien nosotros perdonamos a los que nos ofenden. No nos dejes caer en tentacion, y libranos del mal. Amen.

Dios te salve, María, llena eres de gracia, el Señor es contigo, bendita tú eres entre todas las mujeres, y bendito es el fruto de tu vientre, Jesús. Santa María, Madre de Dios, ruega por nosotros pecadores, ahora y en la hora de nuestra muerte. Amen.

Gloria al Padre y al Hijo y al Espiritu Santo. Como era en el principio, ahora y siempre, y por los siglos de los siglos. Amen.

Italian

Padre nostro che sei nei cieli, sia santificato il tuo nome, venga il tuo regno, sia fatta la tua volontà come in cielo così in terra. Dacci oggi il nostro pane quotidiano, rimetti a noi i nostri debiti come noi li rimettiamo ai nostri debitori; e non c'indurre in tentazione ma liberaci dal male. Così sia.

Ave o Maria, piena di grazia, il Signore è con te, tu sei benedetta fra le donne e benedetto è il frutto del tuo seno, Gesù. Santa Maria, Madre di Dio, prega per noi peccatori, adesso e nell'ora della nostra morte. Così sia.

Gloria al Padre e al Figlio e allo Spirito Santo, come era in principio, ora, e sempre, e nei secoli dei secoli. Così sia.

French

Notre Père qui es aux cieux, que ton nom soit sanctifié, que ton regne vienne, que ta volonté soit faite sur la terre comme au ciel. Donne-nous aujourd'hui notre pain de ce jour. Pardonne-nous nos offenses, comme nous pardonnons aussi à ceux qui nous ont offensés. Et ne nous soumets pas a la tentation, mais délivre nous du mal. Ainsi soit-il.

Je vous salue, Marie, pleine de grâce; le Seigneur est avec vous; vous êtes bénie entre toutes les femmes; et Jésus, le fruit de vos entrailles, est béni. Sainte Marie, Mère de Dieu, priez pour nous, pécheurs, maintenant et a l' heure de notre mort. Ainsi soit-il.

Gloire au Père et au Fils et au Saint-Esprit. Comme il etait au commencement, et maintenant et toujours, et dans les siècles des siècles. Ainsi soit-il.

German

Vater unser, der du bist im Himmel, geheiligt werde dein Name; zu uns komme dein Reich; dein Wille geschehe, wie im Himmel, also auch auf Erden. Unser tägliches Brot gib uns heute; und vergib uns unsere Schuld, wie auch wir vergeben unseren Schuldigern; und führe uns nicht in Versuchung, sondern erlöse uns von allem übel. Amen.

Gegrüsset seist du, Maria, voll der Gnade. Der Herr ist mit dir. Du bist gebenedeit unter den Weibern, und gebenedeit ist die Frucht deines Leibes, Jesus. Heilige Maria, Mutter Gottes, bitte für uns Sünder; jetzt und in der Stunde unseres Todes. Amen.

Ehre sei dem Vater und dem Sohn und dem Heiligen Geist, wie im Anfang, so auch jetzt und allezeit, und in Ewigkeit. Amen. ✿

A Feud with
St. Joseph Cupertino

Up in the apple tree

By ELISABETH COBB

February 1949, condensed from *From The Housetops**

THE FEUD between St. Joseph of Cupertino, patron saint of the American Air Forces, and me, is over at last. It was initiated, by me, several years ago; maintained, by me, in a state of smoldering animosity for several years, broke out at last into open hostilities, and was concluded, after several months of protracted negotiations, with a formal Declaration of Peace, ratified on March 27, 1948, which happened to be Holy Saturday.

It is strange enough that St. Joseph and I should have ever tangled in the first place. We really had little in common. He was a saint from a small village called Cupertino in southern Italy, way down in the foot of the boot, and born in the year 1603. In 1663 he died, as he had lived from early youth, a Franciscan. He was a lay Brother, later a priest. I was born in Savannah, Georgia, U.S.A., in a year that is strictly my own business, but is yet well within the memory of many living men, of a Methodist-*cum*-Episcopalian mother, and a father raised a Presbyterian, who fled from the doctrines of predestination and infant damnation into the sad refuge of

---

*Printed in *Housetops*, St. Benedict's Center.

agnosticism, and took me with him.

I first read something about St. Joseph in Norman Douglas' extraordinarily erudite and witty travel book, *In Old Calabria.* Anyone who knows Mr. Douglas' work (and there was a time when *South Wind* was practically a missal for the would-be wit) will at once guess, even without reading *Calabria,* that his version of the history of a 17th-century Calabrian monk is at once hilarious and bitterly prejudiced, for Mr. Douglas is a fearsomely intelligent mixture of scholar and scoffer, Renaissance scholar and Calvinist scoffer.

However, even after subtracting a great deal on account of obvious bias, Mr. Douglas does make out quite a case against St. Joseph, the times in which he lived, and the people who believed in him, for St. Joseph was born, never left, and, as the pious books say, "flourished" in that sad and disastrous country south of Naples, the prey of every pirate since the days of Hannibal.

Once upon a time Calabria had known a brief flowering, during the time of the Crusaders and the Norman Kingdom of the Two Sicilies and when Charles Barbarossa and Conrad, his unlucky son, had fallen in love with the South and lived there as much as they could. In those days abbeys, convents, and cathedrals had crowned the fertile hills, richly loved and richly endowed by emperors, popes and people. In St. Joseph's time the hills were not fertile any more and (as the Protestant accounts *always* say) "the land swarmed with idle monks." The question, never put by such authors, is: Where else could a man or a woman swarm to, except a convent or monastery? For anyone with a longing for a life of any peace, dignity or beauty, it had to be the Church; the only other existence offered was in some fever-ridden village where after suffering a few years a man could shake himself to death with mingled malaria and hopelessness.

St. Joseph, to be sure, did not flee this world because it was horrible. His was one of those genuine vocations which turn a man from a palace as easily as from a hovel. He became a monk when he was only a boy, and his holiness, simplicity, and ardor were recognized at once by his superiors. Nevertheless he seemed, even to them, a singularly unlikely candidate for any save heavenly honors.

He was so stupid that the best his superiors could do for him, with all the good will in the world, was to let him remain on in his convent as a lay Brother after his successive failures at learning those things which a priest must know. Indeed, he was finally raised to that honor only because of his many miracles, not because he was ever capable of passing an exam.

And those miracles? In this ravished country of his did he heal the sick or feed the poor? Did he teach the ignorant, rebuke the tyrant? Well, no. St. Joseph flew.

He did not levitate—many saints in ecstasy have been seen to rise in the air to varying heights—he *flew*. Often he had to be called down from the ceiling of the chapel because he was distracting the congregation. Once he flew into an apple tree, where he perched, rejoicing and praising God. Once when some workmen were having a hard time raising a stone figure of a saint to the roof of the church, St. Joseph, taking the statue in his arms, wafted it upwards and set it in place. It is true that he did not cross the Atlantic on a nonstop flight, nor drop a bomb on a city 1,000 miles from his base, but don't let's quibble: St. Joseph flew.

Norman Douglas found the accounts of these and other wonders in an ancient pamphlet in a bookshop in Naples and reprints parts of this work with enormous and quite undisguised delight in what he considers a unique record of human credulity. Implicit in his recounting are the questions which every reader of a like mind to

mine must ask himself: Granting all the people who testified to having seen St. Joseph fly were neither lying nor self-deceived, still, was this the sort of saint required at the time? Surely, what was wanted then was bread and medicine, not the spectacle of an illiterate monk tangled in an apple tree!

From that time on St. Joseph became for me a symbol of all that was basely superstitious, useless and absurd. The time came when I said at the top of my voice and in a passion of distaste to Clare Boothe Luce, when I read that the British and American flyers had adopted St. Joseph of Cupertino as their patron saint, "Have you *and* the Church gone stark mad? Do you know that you are giving, as patron saint, to as gallant men as ever lived, a flea-bitten, illiterate, mangy, parasitical, village idiot? Do you know anything about him? Do you know anything about Calabria? (I told her heaps.) Have you honestly got the nerve to land birdmen in a B-29 with this bird-brain on a flying trapeze?"

At this she murmured something in defense of saints as such, adding with deceptive gentleness (such being her way), that after all it was a moot question whether anybody who flew in any airplane, which had been especially designed to be shot at, wasn't an idiot himself, even though a brave one—and so maybe St. Joseph was a pretty good choice, and on two counts at that.

There was a thoughtful gleam in her eye, fixed on me, as she said this. She was, it was evident, up to something. It's my guess that this was the moment that St. Joseph, invoked by her, entered into the battle.

Mind you, this is only a guess. He may have been in there pitching all the time. For instance, it may have been his idea, not hers, to enlist the aid of a whole convent of nuns (bless their hearts!) and to set them to praying for my conversion from that day on. Yes, St. Joseph was on my trail, he was wheeling up the long-range guns of prayer and marshaling faith's big battalions; and it is well known that God is on the side of the big battalions.

Just the same two long years passed and all the while those devoted women, who had never seen me in their lives, and my dear Clare, and St. Joseph, were forced to maintain the siege. And to all appearances they never made a dent.

Then there came a hot night in an old Long Island house when my friend Marienne and I were drying the dinner dishes together. Usually she and I together made quick and merry of such a task. Tonight there was something very wrong, for Marienne, gayest and most val-iant of women, was obviously as near the breaking point as one can get and still keep functioning at all.

"What's the matter?"

"Nothing."

"Nonsense! Tell me."

"Tell you? Why you know I never could tell anybody what's the matter with me. Sometimes I want to. But I can't. It's a physical impossibility."

I searched my heart and head for something that might help her. A Catholic would not have had to search, of course, but it's different for agnostics. An agnostic can earn a living, love a child, even die without a whimper, but he is no doubt limited when it comes to comforting another's troubled spirit. Still I tried.

"What you need," I said, "is a good psychoanalyst. You need to talk, to someone who's trained to listen, and to draw conclusions, and then to set you straight. I wish I could help you, but I can't, I don't know enough. You need a pro."

"I know," she said. "But I can't afford one. Not at $35 an hour for goodness knows how many years."

"Then the only other solution is to turn Catholic and to tell it to a priest." I said it lightly and she answered laughing, "Me! Why, I'm a hard-shell Baptist! I learned all about those Catholics when I was a girl down in Texas."

Some six weeks later, on Sept. 18, my phone rang. It was Marienne wanting to know if I would get her a letter of introduction to Msgr. Fulton J. Sheen from Clare, I assured her, and, of course, I was perfectly right, that to ask help of Monsignor Sheen was introduction enough; but she was shy, suffering from that sort of social self-consciousness which affects us who have never encountered a priest. It's as though one who had never been to a big dinner party were suddenly plumped down before a great spread of silver, none of whose uses one knew. The food is on the plate all right, but how does one get at it? In a word, does one approach monsignors with a soup spoon or an oyster fork?

Of course, Clare promised to write Monsignor Sheen, but there was a curious note in her voice.

"What's the matter? Do you think it's funny for me to be doing a little proselytizing?"

"I'll tell you some day," she said, "maybe."

What was wrong? Had I violated some strange Catholic etiquette? Well, so what? Thus I dismissed the whole affair.

It was less than an hour before she called me back.

"A little miracle has just happened," she said. "Monsignor Sheen has just walked in my door. There has been a mix-up about an engagement. He has two free hours on his hands, and that is something that never happens. Now, give me Marienne's address and he'll go straight up and see her now."

And I said, "Well, for one who isn't working there, I sure do get quick service from Rome."

Marienne called me after monsignor had gone. Her voice was like a singing bird's in the spring; a bird bursting with glad tidings, fairly pouring forth with joy. It was incredible! She had been so troubled, hard-driven, sad. If two hours with a stranger could do this. . . .

Again Clare called me.

"I've decided to tell you why I was so strange this morning. Actually I was a bit overwhelmed. I went to Mass today, and said a prayer for you. It's St. Joseph of Cupertino's day. And remembering how obnoxious you are about him, I asked him to do something nice for you, just to show you! I was hardly in the house before you called about your friend. And then monsignor came strolling in. Don't you really think it's rather amazing?"

"Well," I said, "Joseph does seem to be a hardworking little saint. But he's still a dope! You ask him to do something for me. He does it for my friend. He got us mixed up. Next time you pray to him, dear, pray in words of one syllable."

And for the last time that day I hung up, in the full and final conviction that St. Joseph and I were quits.

Monsignor Sheen gave his first instruction to his New York class only a short time after that, and Marienne asked me if I would not like to go with her. I hesitated, but then as I was intensely interested in his personality, and had heard that he was one of the great speakers of the day, I said that I should be delighted, on condition that it was understood that I was under no obligation, that I was coming once, from a purely intellectual interest, and that I could leave when I liked.

And they said that I could. But now it seems unlikely that I ever shall, for I was baptized at St. Patrick's cathedral on Holy Saturday morning. Easter morning, in the Lady chapel, I knelt at the altar rail with Marienne and 40 others who were receiving First Communion. It seemed then that for all the rest of my life the only words fitting for me to say were "Thank you. Thank you, my dear Lord. Thank you."

And then, with a kind of snap, as though a great hand had eased and moved a displaced ligament so that the blood might flow freely into a paralyzed limb, realization flowed into me, and I knew why God had sent to His afflicted children someone who felt so strongly the joy of loving Him that the earth had no hold on Joseph's feet.

Up, up, to the top of the apple tree, to the roof of the chapel, to heaven, higher than bird, airplane, or rocket ever went, jet-propelled by joy, thanksgiving, and faith. My little saint, in his charity, had clasped me, sad, weary, heartsick, and troubled, as he did the big stone statue, and for that moment I too flew, rejoicing in Cupertino. ❖

THE ELECTION EXPLAINED

On the Presidential election night last November, a large mob gathered around a big political headquarters in Minneapolis. Fearing trouble, an ingenious policeman dashed into a nearby Catholic church and borrowed a long-handled collection basket. He tossed in some coins and proceeded to pass the basket among the crowd. The mob quickly dispersed.

The policeman turned to me and said, "I've often wondered how being a church usher could help me, and now I know."   Ramona Ziegler.

St. Thérèse of Lisieux

by those who knew her

Testimonies from the process of beatification

Translated By CHRISTOPHER O'MAHONY, O.C.D.

November 1976, condensed from the book*

SISTER THÉRÈSE of the Child Jesus died Sept. 30, 1897. The movement to canonize her grew gradually, as her autobiography *Story of a Soul* and accounts of her intercession spread her fame. By 1908 the initial reluctance of some important people had been overcome, and officials were appointed in Rome and in France to investigate.

A diocesan tribunal was set up by the bishop of Bayeux and Lisieux in 1910. For a full year it interviewed a total of 48 witnesses. What follows are portions of their testimony.

*This article © 1975 by Christopher O'Mahony. Originally published by Our Sunday Visitor Inc. Reprinted with permission.

Mother Agnes of Jesus

No one knew Thérèse better than Mother Agnes of Jesus, her elder sister who was a mother to her in her childhood, and again as prioress of the Lisieux Carmel. It was to Mother Agnes she once said: "You and you alone know me through and through."

Mother Agnes was Marie-Pauline Martin, the second of the nine Martin children. She entered the Carmelite convent in Lisieux in 1882, and made her profession on May 8, 1884, the day of Thérèse's First Holy Communion.

The future saint followed in her footsteps four years later, and had her as prioress from 1893-96. During this time

Mother Agnes ordered her to commit her childhood memories to writing. These memoirs were the first of the three manuscripts that make up her autobiography.

I am happy to testify; it is for God's glory. Naturally, I am glad that it is a sister of mine who is involved; but I found her life so edifying that even had she not been my sister, I would still be very happy to testify in exactly the same way.

My knowledge of the Servant of God stems from having lived with her at home from 1877-82, and here in Carmel from 1888 till her death (1897). During the first five years of her life I was away at boarding school. We were separated too from 1882, when I entered Carmel, till 1888, when she entered herself. But we kept in touch.

She was born on Jan. 2, 1873, in Alencon. Our father's name was Louis Joseph Stanislas Martin, and our mother was Marie-Zelie Guerin. Our father was a jeweler and mother made and sold *Alençon* lace. At the time of the Servant of God's birth, father had retired from business, and we were comfortable.

Our parents were looked upon as religious, even very devout, people. In spite of her hard-working life, mother attended half-past five Mass every morn-

ing with father, and they both went to Holy Communion four or five times a week. Towards the end of his life father became a daily communicant. He observed Sunday rest strictly, even though closing his shop on that day was damaging to his business.

One might say that our spiritual welfare was our parents' only concern. Mother would have like liked all her daughters to be nuns, though she did not try to influence us.

She made us raise our hearts to God often during the day, and brought us on visits to the Blessed Sacrament. She brought us up rather strictly, and let nothing pass, especially anything that savored of vanity. Father was gentler, and was particularly fond of his little Thérèse. Mother used to say: "You'll ruin her!" But I never knew her to take pride in her position at the expense of her sisters.

After her mother's death she regarded her elder sisters, especially me, as her mother. I cannot remember her disobeying me even once; she asked permission for everything. When Father asked her to go for a walk with him, for instance, she would say: "I'll go and ask Pauline."

After Mother's death, in 1877, Father moved to Liseux. His brother-in-law, Isidore Guerin, lived there. Mme. Guerin was a particularly kind and devout woman, and Father thought she would be a great help to him in bringing up his daughters. Thérèse was reared and taught at home by Father, Marie, and myself until she was 8. She then attended the boarding school of the Benedictine nuns in Lisieux as a day pupil.

During the years previous to her going to the Abbey, it was mainly I who taught her. She was very diligent, and profited a great deal from the lessons I gave her. She strove, too, to gain self-control; she trained herself from that time never to complain or to make excuses.

She made her first Holy Communion at the Benedictine Abbey on May 8, 1884. I was already in Carmel at the time, and it was chiefly Marie who prepared her for this. Three months before her First Communion, I gave her a little notebook in which she was to write down every evening her sacrifices and little acts of love for Jesus. Her total for the three months was: 818 sacrifices and 2,773 acts of love or aspirations. She was confirmed at the same Abbey on June 14, 1884.

From a very early age the Servant of God used to say that she wanted to live in a desert so as to be able to pray to God more freely. When out walking in the country with her father she used to ramble off by herself, while he was fishing, and think of eternity, as she put it.

When I became a Carmelite her thoughts then turned towards that form of religious life, and from the time she was nine she was determined to be a Carmelite herself. This determination became clearer as the years passed, and she took the first steps towards realizing her ambition when she was 14.

I was afraid Thérèse might have been thinking of Carmel because of me, so one day I asked her if this was so. This suggestion pained her, and she exclaimed: "Oh, no! It's for God alone." Anyway, she has amply proved that since.

I was the only one who encouraged her when she tried to become a Carmelite; whenever she mentioned the subject to her sister Marie she met with opposition, for Marie thought her too young, and did her best to prevent her from entering. Just to test her I, too, sometimes tried to dampen her enthusiasm; if she had not had a true vocation, then the obstacles she met with in her efforts to respond to God's call would have made her give up the idea immediately.

Eventually Marie joined me in Carmel and Leonie became a

Poor Clare in Alençon. Thérèse did not know how to break the news of her decision to my father, who had already sacrificed his three elder daughters. She was then 14 years old. She chose Whit Sunday for the revealing of her great secret, and spent the whole day praying to the saints to help her find the right words. Father told her she was too young, but her arguments finally won him over and he announced that he considered it a great honor to have God ask him for his children. But there were still some painful trials in store for her.

When her uncle, M. Guerin, was consulted on the matter, he said that as far as he was concerned she must never mention the subject again until she was 17. It was most imprudent, he said, to let a child of 15 enter Carmel: it would take a miracle to change his mind.

Thérèse sought comfort in prayer, and asked Jesus for this miracle. Shortly afterwards she suffered a severe interior trial: for three days she felt totally abandoned. On the fourth day my uncle unexpectedly gave his consent. A few days later she came to the convent to tell me her joy, only to suffer another bitter disappointment when I told her that the ecclesiastical Superior Father Delatroette, parish priest of St. Jacques in Lisieux, would not hear of

her entering before she was 21.

Nobody had expected opposition from this quarter; Mother Prioress was quite favorable. Thérèse asked Father to take her to see Father Delatroette, and Celine went along as well. Thérèse did her best to convince the priest that she had a Carmelite vocation, but he remained cold and unmoved. He told her that waiting would not do her any harm, that she could lead a Carmelite life at home, that not being able to take the discipline would not be much of a loss. He added, however, that of course he was only the bishop's delegate, and that if the bishop did not have any objections, then he would have nothing further to say.

At her request, Father promised to take her to see the bishop. "If the bishop does not give me permission," she said, "I will go and ask the Holy Father."

She told me the whole story of this journey, and afterwards wrote of it in her autobiography. The bishop asked her when it was she had first thought of becoming a nun. "A long time ago," was the reply.

"Still, it can't be as long as 15 years," interposed Father Reverony, the vicar-general, with a smile.

"You don't have to subtract many years from that," she

replied, "because I've wanted to be a nun since I was three, and a Carmelite for as long as I've known this Order."

The bishops said he would have to discuss the matter with Father Delatroette, Superior of the Carmel, and that he would give his answer later. The Servant of God, knowing Father Delatroette's attitude, was broken-hearted, and the tears flowed. In the course of the conversation our father mentioned that he was thinking of paying a visit to Rome; the bishop approved.

When she returned from Bayeux, she came to visit me. I was struck by the fact that in spite of her real disappointment she nevertheless displayed a great peace of soul, founded on her complete surrender to God's will.

In her audience with the supreme Pontiff she overcame great timidity and asked him for his permission to enter Carmel at 15 years of age. Father Reverony was present at the audience and told the Pontiff that the matter was being studied by the superiors; Pope Leo's answer to the Servant of God was: "Do what the superiors tell you to."

She insisted: "But, Holy Father, if you were to say yes, they would all agree."

"Come, come," replied the Pope, "you will enter if God wills it." She wanted to insist further, but the vicar-general and the guards cut short the audience by dragging her away from the Holy Father's feet.

After her return to France she confined herself, with perfect obedience, to acting on the advice I gave her after consultation with Mother Prioress; to obey, she assured me, was the only way to be certain of not making a mistake. Accordingly, she wrote again to the bishop of Bayeux just before Christmas, 1887. This time he granted the longed-for authorization. She did not enter, however, until the following April.

Father Delatroette was displeased at the steps that had been taken behind his back. This is how he introduced her to the Community: "Reverend Mother, you can sing the *Te Deum* now. As the bishop's delegate, I present this 15-year-old child to you. It was you who wanted her here, and I hope that she will not disappoint your expectations. I am reminding you that if she does, the responsibility will be entirely yours."

Father Thomas Taylor

Thomas Nimino Taylor, born the same year as St. Thérèse, was ordained the year she died (1897). Father Taylor read the "Story of a Soul" soon after it appeared, and immediately became an apostle of its spirit-

ual message, and a frequent pilgrim to Lisieux. In 1908 he published a series of articles on Sister Thérèse's life, and he is reputed to be the first person to suggest that the cause for her beatification be introduced. He also translated her autobiography into English.

I did not know the Servant of God personally. I learned what I know about her life first of all from the *Story of a Soul,* which I read about 1901. I was so deeply moved and edified by this book that I then began to correspond with the principal nuns who had known Sister Thérèse.

I talked with Mother Gonzague in 1903, and I remember thinking at the time how different she was from the Servant of God's sisters. She was colder, less enthusiastic; her language was entirely devoid of exclamations, and she seemed less feminine than they were. I knew from the *Story of a Soul* that she had been severe on the Servant of God during her novitiate. But, in spite of that, her judgment about Sister Thérèse's virtue and character was basically the same: she regarded the Servant of God as quite extraordinary in the matter of holiness.

Asked whether he knew of people who disagreed with Thérèse's reputation for holiness, he said:

I remember two incidents that are relevant to the question. The first concerns the Carmel of Blackrock in Dublin. When I spoke to the prioress of this convent about Sister Thérèse's life, she laughed heartily, and told me we might just as well canonize all the nuns in her convent. This was back about 1904, certainly prior to the great movement of devotion that developed later. The prioress is dead now, but I know for a fact that she changed her opinion before she died.

The second occasion on which I heard some unfavorable remarks was on a visit to Lourdes Carmel. I was talking to an Irish nun there a few days ago. She told me that after reading *Story of a Soul* she still had some misgivings. The chief reason for this was that when this nun was novice-mistress, she had a Spanish novice who used to speak and write beautifully about the most sublime things. She was so impressive that the novice-mistress began to feel unworthy and incapable of directing her. The novice afterwards lost her fervor, and left the convent, so that this Irish Carmelite has been a bit suspicious of poetic nuns ever since.

Marie of the Sacred Heart

Marie Martin, Thérèse's eldest sister, was born at Alençon in

1860, and was the future saint's godmother.

Few perceived God's design on Therese as clearly as Marie did. It was she who at the end of 1894 insisted that Mother Agnes order Thérèse to write the memories of her childhood, and it was at her request that Thérèse wrote the magnificent letter which constitutes the second part of her autobiography.

It was she, too, who in May, 1897, asked Thérèse to put her thoughts on the Blessed Virgin in writing. This was the origin of the poem "Why I Love You, Mary," of which the saint wrote shortly before her death: "My little song expresses all I think about the Blessed Virgin, all that I would preach about her if I were a priest."

At a reception in Carmel, she always showed a preference for the company of those who seemed most forlorn. As a novice, she had as her companion a young lay-Sister with a very difficult temperament, but she did not stand aloof from her because of that. Rather, she went to sit by her as often as possible and treated her so gently and kindly that she won her companion's affection and had a very great influence on her.

She wanted to help a Sister in the linen room whose temperament was such that no one wanted to be in her company. This Sister was subject to the blackest moods, and did scarcely any work. I saw her, when Sister Thérèse was already an invalid, come to her to call for the week's linen, which she had given her to repair. Because Sister Thérèse had not been able to complete her task, this Sister reproached her severely instead of thanking her for what she had done in spite of being so ill. Sister Thérèse took the reproaches as if they were so much praise.

This unfortunate Sister became the object of Sister Thérèse's tenderest compassion. One day, when I had confided to her how much trouble that Sister gave me, the Servant of God said: "Ah! If you only knew how necessary it is to forgive her, how much she is to be pitied!"

There was a Sister in the infirmary who tried everyone's patience with her various manias. When we showed a certain reluctance to keep her company, Sister Thérèse said: "How happy I would be to have been asked to do that! Perhaps it would have cost my nature very much, but I think I would have done it very lovingly, because I remember our Lord's words: 'I was sick and you comforted Me.'"

Teresa of St. Augustine

Teresa of St. Augustine was a nun whom St. Thérèse disliked intensely. But Thérèse was so well able to hide her dislike that the nun thought she was very fond of her.

Shortly after the Servant of God's death she wrote a little work entitled "Memoirs of a Holy Friendship," in which she speaks of Thérèse's joy every time she went to see her in the infirmary.

You could say that Sister Thérèse lived mostly in heaven. She spoke to me so many times about her desire to die, and her eyes shone with happiness every time the subject was brought up. The thought of her approaching death was something that brought her only joy and hope. In April, 1895, she confided to me: "I am going to die soon. I'm not saying that it will be in the next few months, but in two or three years. What I experience in my soul makes me feel my exile is nearly over." She was still perfectly healthy when she said this.

She soared above earthly things. Nothing seemed to be able to captivate her soul even for an instant; nothing worried her. "I cannot understand," she used to say, "why people get so upset when they see their Sisters die; we are all going to heaven and we will meet one another there again." If she desired heaven it was only because of the love she could thus give to God; her own interest was entirely set aside. She was not anxious about her crown; she used to tell me to "let God take care of that."

In Sister Thérèse, the love of God dominated everything else; her dream was to die of love. But then she would add: "To die of love we must live by love." So she strove to develop this love day by day, because she wanted it to be of the highest quality.

Virtue seemed to come so naturally to her that people thought she was inundated with consolations. I heard one Sister say: "Sister Thérèse gets no merit for practicing virtue; she has never had to struggle for it." I wanted to know from herself if there was any truth in this, so I asked her if she had had to struggle during her religious life. This was two months before she died.

"Oh," she replied, "but didn't I though! I didn't have an easy temperament. It might not have looked like that, but I felt it. I can assure you that not a day passed without its quota of suffering." Fearing that her pain would get even worse, I told her that I would ask God to give her some relief. "No, no," she exclaimed, "He must be allowed to do as He pleases."

Marie of the Angels

Marie of the Angels and the Sacred Heart was St. Thérèse's novice-mistress. St. Thérèse describes her as "a real saint, cast in the mold of the first Carmelite nuns," and the community as a whole concurred in this judgment. In her testimony Mother Marie underlines, among other things, the discretion with which Thérèse handled the inevitable sufferings of Community living, and her firm detachment from her three sisters.

No sooner had the Servant of God entered Carmel than she seemed to us to be full of kindness to all the Sisters. In the novitiate she showed her charity towards one of her charity towards one of her companions of whose faults she was well aware. She gave her little pieces of advice, tried to lead her to virtue by giving her good example, and, in spite of the other girl's frequent opposition, she was kindness itself to her, and she did eventually succeed in exercising a very touching influence over her. I cannot remember her ever saying a word against anybody, nor ever complaining of Mother Prioress's severity towards her.

In the 1896 elections, Mother Gonzague was elected prioress by only a very slender majority. The Servant of God realized what a disappointment this was to her, and she did her best to comfort her with the most delightful tenderness and tact. She wrote her a marvelous letter, and the poor prioress took it very well.

The later election of her sister Pauline as prioress created a very delicate situation for her with the ex-prioress: Mother Gonzague. But the Servant of God showed astonishing discretion when it came to avoiding friction. I was often in the parlor with the three Martin sisters when their uncle M. Guerin visited them. Whenever a misunderstanding arose about family affairs, her influence quickly dispersed the little clouds. If someone needed advice, it was to her, the youngest, that her sisters turned, and her word was Gospel.

The Servant of God found the cult of God, of the Blessed Virgin and the saints very attractive. Her favorite saints, after our Lady and St. Joseph, were our mother St. Teresa, St. John of the Cross, St. Cecilia, St. Agnes, Blessed Theophane Venard, and Blessed Joan of Arc. She had an intense love of Holy Communion; the inability to receive it daily pained her deeply.

A feature of her piety that

struck me particularly, because I had never heard it spoken of in Carmel or in the lives of the saints, was the role she attributed to flowers. For her, every flower spoke a language of its own, in which it revealed God's infinite love and perfection to her. She also used them to tell God of her own love and other sentiments. Late on a summer's evening, in the time of silence, and often on a feastday at recreation, she would stew petals round the base of the Calvary in the cloister garth.

Her plucking of petals from flowers was only a symbol of what she was doing for our Lord by means of the thousand and one sacrifices she made for him in every area of her life. Even near the end she was still plucking rose petals to perfume her crucifix with. That is what happened to the roses people brought to cheer her up.

One day, when someone gathered up the petals that had fallen to the floor to throw them out, Sister Thérèse whispered: "Oh, no; don't throw them out; they will be precious yet." On another occasion, when the Community was gathered round her bed, Mother Agnes said: "What about throwing some flowers to the Community!"

"Oh, Mother dear," she answered, "don't ask me to do that, please; I don't want to throw flowers to creatures. I would do it for our Lady or St. Joseph, but not for anybody else."

Sister Genevieve of St. Teresa

Celine Martin was born in Alencon in 1869. After Thérèse entered Carmel in April, 1888, Celine remained at home alone, taking care of her father. In 1889 she made a vow of chastity, and renewed it every year in the hope of being able to enter Carmel herself one day. She eventually did so in 1894, less than two months after her father's death.

She took the habit as Sister Genevieve of St. Teresa, and did her novitiate under the firm guidance of her sister Thérèse. When Sister Thérèse was laid low by the illness that was to take her life, Mother Marie de Gonzague appointed Sister Genevieve to help nurse her. She thus became a privileged witness to the Saint's last months on earth.

Fortunately, Celine took her camera with her when she entered Carmel; thanks to her, we possess more authentic photos of St. Thérèse than of any other saint.

I love my little sister very much, but I testify freely. My sole intention in coming to give evidence is to obey the Church, which asked me to do so.

I was separated from her for only six years, from the time

she entered Carmel until I did so myself. The Servant of God was brought up by our mother until she was four-and-a-half years old. Then mother died, and our eldest sisters, Marie, who was 17, and Pauline, who was 16, had the duty of bringing us up. Father left Alençon at this time, and brought the family to Lisieux, where my mother's brother, M. Guerin, lived.

Her attraction to the religious life was something that went back to early childhood. Not only did she often say that she would like to be a nun, she also had a longing for the heremitic life. She would sometimes isolate herself in a corner of her room, behind the curtains of her bed, and talk with God there. She was then seven or eight years old.

Later, at 14, after her "conversion," she thought of religious life chiefly as a means of saving souls. For that reason she toyed with the idea of joining a congregation of missionary Sisters. But the hope of saving more souls through mortification and self-sacrifice made her decide to shut herself up in Carmel.

Finally, when she entered Carmel, she had as her very special purpose to pray for priests and to offer herself for the needs of the Church. She called this kind of apostolate "bulk buying," because if she got the head,

she would get the members too.

Among her duties to God, the Servant of God attached particular importance to gratitude for favors received. She said to me: "Gratitude is the thing that brings us the most grace ... I am content with whatever God gives me, and I show Him this in a thousand little ways."

When I entered Carmel I thought God ought to be grateful to me for the big sacrifice I had made for Him, and I asked Therese to compose a poem for my encouragement, a poem which would list all I had left for God and which would end with the word "remember." She composed it all right, but gave it a completely different meaning from what I had requested: in it, the soul reminds Jesus of all He has done for her; Jesus is the benefactor now, and it is the soul that is indebted.

In June of 1897, before she was really ill, Sister Thérèse told me she expected to die that year. She realized that she had pulmonary tuberculosis, and she said: "You see, God is going to take me at an age when I would not have had the time to become a priest ... If I could have been a priest, I would have been ordained at these June Ordinations.

"So that I would not be disappointed, God let me be

sick: in that way I couldn't have been there, and I would die before I could exercise my ministry."

The sacrifice of not being able to be a priest was something she always felt deeply. The thought that St. Barbara had brought Communion to St. Stanislas Kostka thrilled her. "Why was it a virgin, and not an angel or a priest?" she said. "Oh! What wonders we shall see in heaven! I have a feeling that those who desired to be priests on earth will be able to share in the honor of the priesthood in heaven."

Even during her last illness she preserved those childlike and playful ways of hers which made her so likable. She was delighted to be dying, and enjoyed the preparations, which we tried to hide from her. Once she asked to see the box of lilies which had just arrived to adorn the bed on which she was to be laid out. She looked at them with pleasure and said: "That's for me!"

One evening we were afraid that she would not last the night, so a blessed candle and holy water were brought to the next room in readiness. She suspected this, and asked that they be placed where she could see them. She cheerfully described all the details of her burial in a way that made us laugh when we would have preferred to cry.

She was encouraging us instead of we her.

One day she suddenly exclaimed: "To think that I am going to die in a bed! I would have liked to die in an arena!" When she hemorrhaged, she rejoiced in the thought that she was shedding her blood for God. "It could not have been otherwise," she said. "I knew that I would have the consolation of seeing my blood spilt, for I am a martyr of love."

One day after a very painful attack we saw her face suddenly soften and look angelic. We wanted to know what had caused this, and we asked her about it, but she was too overcome to answer. That evening she passed me the following note: "O my God, how kind you are to the little victim of your merciful Love!"

She asked us to pray that God would give her the strength to persevere to the end. One morning in September, she implored me in these words: "Dear Sister Genevieve, pray to the Blessed Virgin, I would pray so much if you were ill, but I dare not ask for myself." On Aug. 21 she was groaning and breathing painfully, and with each breath she repeated almost mechanically, "I'm suffering, I'm suffering." It seemed to help her breathe. Then she told us: "Each time I say, 'I'm suffering' you answer, 'So much the better!' That is what I want to say to complete my thought, but I haven't got the strength to say it."

In the midst of all her sufferings the Servant of God preserved her serenity. One day I saw her smile and when I asked her why, she said: "It is because I feel a very sharp pain in my side, and I have made it a habit to give pain a good welcome." No matter how inopportune some visits were, she never showed the slightest annoyance.

She never asked for relief, and took whatever she was given. Only in extreme necessity would she call me at night; she would wait until I came of my own accord. The last night she spent on earth Sister Marie of the Sacred Heart and I stayed up with her, in spite of her insistence that we rest as usual in the room next door. But at one stage we dozed off after giving her something to drink, she remained there, glass in hand, until one of us woke up.

The Blessed Virgin was her kindly beacon. One day, while looking at her statue, she said: "I can no longer look at the Blessed Virgin without crying." Later she asked to see her little picture of Our Lady of Victories, to which she had stuck the little flower her father gave her when he allowed her to enter Carmel. In a shaky hand she wrote on the back of it: "Mary, if I were queen of heaven, and you were Thérèse, I would want to be Thérèse so that you could be queen of heaven." Those were the last lines she ever wrote.

She often caressed her crucifix with flowers, and when she was not holding it she used to attach a flower to it, which she would replace at the first signs of withering; she could not bear to see flowers that were at all faded on it.

On one of the last nights I found her gazing heavenwards with her hands joined. "What are you doing like that when you should be trying to get some sleep?" I said to her.

"I can't sleep, so I'm praying," she answered.

"And what are you saying to Jesus?"

"Nothing; I'm just loving Him."

About mid-afternoon on the day she died she was seized with strange pains all over her body. So she placed one arm on Mother Agnes' shoulder and the other on mine, and we supported her like that for a few minutes. Just then the clock struck three, and we could not help being deeply moved. What was she thinking then? For us she was a striking image of Jesus on the Cross; I regarded this coincidence as full of mysterious significance.

Her agony began immediately after this, a long and terrible

agony. She could be heard repeating: "Oh! This is sheer suffering, because there is no consolation, not even one. O my God! If this is the agony, what will death be like?... Mother, I assure you the chalice is full to the brim... Yes, God, as much as you wish... But have pity on me! No, I would never have thought it was possible to suffer so much... never, never! Tomorrow it will be still worse. Ah, well, so much the better!" The poor little martyr's words were broken and heart-rending, but they always bore the stamp of perfect resignation.

Mother Prioress now summoned the Community, and Sister Thérèse welcomed them with a pretty smile. Then she clasped her crucifix to her and seemed to hand herself over entirely to suffering, so to speak. Her breathing was labored; a cold sweat bathed her face, and soaked her clothes, her pillow and the sheets; she was shaking all over.

Sometimes in the course of her illness, Sister Thérèse had said to us (her own sisters): "My dear sisters, you must not be upset if, when I'm dying, my last look is for one of you rather than another; I don't know what I will do; it will be whatever God wants. If he leaves me free, however, my last good-by will be for Mother Marie de Gonzague, because she is my prioress." She repeated these words to us a few days before she died.

Just a few moments before she died, she gave me a beautiful smile, and a long penetrating look. A kind of shiver ran through the Community. Then Thérèse's eyes sought Mother Prioress and rested on her, but with their habitual expression. Mother Prioress, thinking the agony was going to be prolonged, dismissed the Community a few moments later.

The angelic patient then turned to her and said: "Mother, is this not the agony, am I not going to die?" And, when Mother replied that it could take a while longer, she said, in a low, plaintive voice: "All right, then! Let it go on... Oh! I would not want to suffer less!" Then, looking at her crucifix: "Oh!... I love Him... My God. I... love... You!"

These were her last words. The words were hardly out of her mouth when, to our great surprise, she collapsed, her head a little to the right. Then, suddenly, she sat up, as if a mysterious voice had called her. She opened her eyes and fixed them radiantly on a spot a little above the statue of Our Lady. She stayed that way for a few minutes, about as long as it would take to recite the Creed slowly.

I have often tried to analyze

this ecstasy since then, and tried to understand that look of hers. It was not just an expression of beatitude. There was an element of great astonishment in it, and her attitude expressed a very dignified assurance. I thought we had been present at her judgment, and that she had seen that the gifts about to be showered on her were infinitely beyond her immense desires. For there was another expression joined with that of astonishment: she seemed unable to cope with the sight of so much love; she was like someone who is assaulted several times, tries to fight back, but because of his weakness he is happily vanquished. It was too much for her; she closed her eyes and breathed her last. It was 7 P.M. on Thursday, Sept. 30, 1897. ❖

SHORT TAKES

Actor Raymond Burr recalls that at his first meeting with Pope John XXIII, a U.S. congressman brusquely introduced himself saying, "I am a Baptist." The Pope replied, "And I'm John." New York *Times.*

*

A husband asked his wife what the garage mechanic had said about the car's low tire. "He said the air was beginning to show through," she replied. Lucille Goodyear.

*

Wrinkles should merely indicate where smiles have been. Mark Twain.

*

A local man refused to reveal his age at his recent birthday party, but he did admit to living through three revivals of the wide tie. Belleville (Wisc.) *Recorder.*

*

A woman on crutches at a ski resort was talking about her accident: "I just didn't realize that the laws of gravity were so strict." *Capper's Weekly.*

*

Old Miss Smith, the spinster, insisted on having six women pallbearers for her funeral. She said the boys never took her out when she was alive, and they sure wouldn't when she was dead. Mrs. W.P. Kneupper.

*

Salesman, demonstrating sofa to a couple: "And another good feature is that when unexpected visitors arrive, it simply cannot be turned into a bed." Mrs. Nancy Tyler.

They Remember St. Maximilian

Personal testimony of seven Auschwitz prisoners—priests and artists, Protestants and Jews—whose lives were touched by a saint

By PATRICIA TREECE
April 1983, condensed from *A Man for Others**

S T. *MAXIMILIAN KOLBE (1894-1941) was a Polish Franciscan priest, scholar, editor, founder of the Knights of the Immaculata, and missionary to Japan. He organized a large monastic complex and Catholic publishing center outside Warsaw in 1927 and named it Niepokalanow, City of the Immaculate.*

On May 28, 1941, the Nazis arrested Father Kolbe and sent him to Auschwitz. In August, when a prisoner escaped, an SS officer selected ten prisoners to be starved to death. Father Kolbe volunteered to take the place of one of them. On Aug. 14, 1941, still alive after two weeks

in the starvation bunker, Father Kolbe was given a lethal injection of carbolic acid. On Oct. 10, 1982, his countryman Pope John Paul II canonized him.

Many of St. Maximilian's fellow inmates were interviewed in the Beatification Process. One was Joseph Stemler, director of the Polish Education Department, who had been sent to Auschwitz in April, 1941. He said:

I had known Kolbe briefly before, in 1938 at the conference of newspaper editors. He was one of those who have absolutely nothing artificial about them. Far from taking pride in his expertise in the editorial field, he seemed somewhat embarrassed that it was he who knew the answers to so many questions.

Our next meeting was under far different circumstances. It happened in Auschwitz around the end of June or the beginning of July, 1941. It was after the evening roll call. Exhausted and dying of hunger, I was on my way back to Block 8 when unexpectedly in front of me a guard appeared. Yelling and menacing me with his cudgel, he rushed me off to one side of the assembly ground where two lines of other prisoners stood waiting. The SS then chased us all the way to the hospital block, where we were ordered to carry corpses to the crematorium.

I wasn't a young man—had even fought in World War I—but I had never touched a corpse. Now before me was my first. I couldn't move even one step toward him. The guard began to scream at me, but then a calm voice said, "Let's pick him up, my brother."

For a fraction of a second I thought I knew that voice. Filled with repugnance, somehow I took hold of a bloody leg while my companion took the corpse by the shoulder and we deposited it, as directed, with a second body in a kind of trough-like receptacle. This we were to carry to the crematorium.

I was too upset to function. My arms seemed to be failing me, my wooden shoes would no longer stay on my feet. I thought it would be better if it were I being carried out so gruesomely. Suddenly at my shoulder I heard the calm but moving voice of my companion: "Holy Mary . . . pray for us."

Something like an electric current passed through my failing limbs and suddenly I felt strong. Now with vigor I carried the strange casket.

We reached the crematorium, a low building with a flat roof and a tall chimney from which the wind swept away a pestilential smoke. There we had to stack up the two corpses with others after having given the guards the number written with a certain type of pencil on the chests of the dead. One was obliged to witness the macabre catafalque made of a great movable grate over the flames where the poor corpses of the dead prisoners were burning.

In my horror I was at that moment prey for delirium, unconscious. . . . Turning away with my companion, I was trembling all over. My legs were becoming rigid; then my companion very gently pushed the container that had held the corpses and with it pushed me.

As soon as we crossed the threshold of the crematorium I heard his clear, low voice say, "Rest in peace." Moments later he whispered, "And the Word was made flesh."

Only then did I recognize that my companion was the Franciscan from Niepokalanow, Father Kolbe.

A *nother of Father Kolbe's friends was a tailor, 36-year-old Alexander Dziuba, who had been in Auschwitz since September 1940. He remembers:*

I owe to him that I am still alive, that I was able to hold out and lived to be liberated. In that period the capos (criminal prisoners assigned to oversee inmates) and guards often beat me during my work hours. I began to feel, why not end it all by throwing myself on the wires (the electric fences) the way other prisoners did. So one day, in a fit of despair, I rushed for the fence. But I was seized, made to turn back, and given 50 blows in punishment.

Father Kolbe heard about it. He talked to me and calmed me down again. The things he said had such an effect on me that I never thought of committing suicide again. Not only brave himself, he communicated that bravery to me and to others I could name.

During our free periods—that is, after the day's work and on Sunday afternoons—he used to gather a number of trustworthy men around him, not always the same ones, and talk to us on spiritual topics. I recall his saying, "I don't fear death; I fear sin." He kept encouraging us not to be afraid of dying, but to have at heart the salvation of our souls. He said that if we feared nothing but sin, prayed to Christ, and sought the intercession of Mary, we would know peace. He pointed Christ out to us as the one sure support and help we could count on.

We prayed with him and he heard our confessions. Thanks to what he taught me in those conferences and to the three confessions I made to him, I changed my life for the better. I can say that after each confession I was not only relieved in soul but I saw the world differently.

In Father Maximilian we prisoners could sense a hidden superior strength. He was ready to do anything for God. I saw him myself before eating make the Sign of the Cross over his bread with grave devotion without the slightest concern that he might be seen by the capo and beaten for it. And this was not because he was foolish. He never otherwise exposed himself recklessly to beatings. He was a man of deep reflection who acted after meditating on what was to be done. But in everything he did or said we could see the supernatural. It was not a matter of cleverness, foresight, or human interests, but love of God.

For his neighbor, too, he

would do anything and give everything he had. For instance, I recall how in front of the block Father Maximilian once gave his entire serving of soup to one of the prisoners who was young, from the block where the young men were kept. I recall he told him, "Take it. Eat it. You are younger. You, at least, must live." Another time he wanted to do the same thing, but we wouldn't let him. We forced him to have his share.

The prisoners who served as doctors and nurses also were impressed by Father Kolbe. Here is the testimony of one of those doctors, Rudolph Diem:

At Auschwitz, two-thirds of the time between 1940 and 1945, I served as doctor-prisoner. I was uncrowned king among the prisoners because the hospital was the asylum for which every prisoner yearned. Hundreds of thousands of prisoners applied to me for such relief in my five years in the camp. Not because there was more or better food, but because prisoners were removed from forced labor and the merciless beatings of the capos and guards. I examined those who reported sick and determined who got hospital care. Daily I observed the poor creatures crowding into the hospital, each shoving and straining to save his life.

In this formidable throng my attention was drawn to a prisoner about my age who never pushed. His whole conduct was so modest and humble that he seemed almost to apologize for living. He invariably tried to wait until the 200 to 500—and one day 1,000—others crowded in. When I called him out to be examined (he was suffering and fevered from his lungs), I said to him, "You know you're so weak it would be best to admit you to the hospital; therefore, I'll assign you..." He interrupted me to plead, "I think I'll be all right a little longer—why not take the one over there," pointing to some other half-starved soul.

Amazed, I shrugged, "Well, if you don't want to, at least take this," and I gave him some medicine.

After his refusal to let me admit him to the hospital had happened on several occasions, I finally said to him as he was arguing for my taking someone else, "Listen, if you don't go to bed, you'll die."

"I think I'll hold out," he answered.

"What kind of role are you playing, that of a saint?" I snapped. "Are you perhaps a Religious?"

"Well, yes, I'm a Catholic priest," he admitted. So I said, "Well, if you want to be a saint, that's too bad. There's really no sense in that...."

But I admired him. Spiritually, in spite of his physical suffering, he was completely healthy, serene and balanced in disposition, and extraordinary in character. I never saw another like him in Auschwitz—or outside Auschwitz, for that matter.

I asked him once if he still believed that God looks out for us. He tried fervently to show me this is the case and proposed that we meet in the Birkenalei (Birch Alley) to walk and talk sometime. I decided to accept. There one day he said, "Doctor, you've done so much for me, I'd like to repay you in some way."

Though I was very impressed by his sense of gratitude, still I had to smile. "How could you reciprocate?" I asked him. "I have enough to eat. I'm comfortable. What could you give me?"

"Now that it's Easter time," he answered, "maybe you would like a little spiritual comfort?"

Since I didn't understand what he meant, he continued, "Maybe go to confession?"

"How could I," I replied, "since I no longer have any belief? Besides, I'm a Protestant by background, not a Catholic."

After I thanked him for his offer that I could not accept, we discussed religion, he trying to show me I did believe in God, and this discussion, like each

one that I had with him, gave me great satisfaction because of his integrity. To this day I feel great gratitude and admiration toward Father Kolbe.

Sigmund Gorson today is the host of a television program in Wilmington, Del. Although he has written and spoken on life in Auschwitz, he regards his memories of Father Kolbe as "so personal, so precious" that he has never included anything on the priest he calls "a prince among men." He breaks this silence now because he appears to be the only one of the Polish Jews who knew Father Kolbe well in Auschwitz.

I was from a beautiful home where love was the key word. My parents were well-off and well-educated. But my three beautiful sisters, my mother—an attorney educated at the University of Paris—my father, grandparents—all perished. I am the sole survivor. To be a child from such a wonderful home and then suddenly find oneself utterly alone, as I did at age 13, in this hell, Auschwitz, has an effect on one that others can hardly comprehend. Many of us youngsters lost hope, especially when the Nazis showed us pictures of what they said was the bombing of New York City. Without hope, there was no chance to survive, and many boys my age ran onto the electric fences. I was always looking for some link with my murdered parents, trying to find a friend of my father's, a neighbor—someone in that mass of humanity who had known them so I would not feel so alone.

And that is how Kolbe found me wandering around, so to speak, looking for someone to connect with. He was like an angel to me. Like a mother hen, he took me in his arms. He used to wipe away my tears. I believe in God more since that time. Because of the deaths of my parents I had been asking, "Where is God?" and had lost faith. Kolbe gave me that faith back.

He knew I was a Jewish boy. That made no difference. His heart was bigger than persons—that is, whether they were Jewish, Catholic, or whatever. He loved everyone. He dispensed love and nothing but love. For one thing, he gave away so much of his meager rations that to me it was a miracle that he could live. Now it is easy to be nice, to be charitable, to be humble, when times are good and peace prevails. For someone to be as Father Kolbe was in that time and place—I can only say the way he was is beyond words.

I am a Jew by my heritage as the son of a Jewish mother, and I am of the Jewish faith and very proud of it. And not only did I love Maximilian Kolbe very, very much in Auschwitz, where he befriended me, but I will love him until the last moments of my life.

Mieczyslaus Koscielniak, an artist with a degree in philosophy and letters, arrived May 3, 1941, in a transport of 300 political prisoners, only six of whom survived. He has done many pictures portraying concentration camp life. Koscielniak was introduced to Father Kolbe on the Feast of Corpus Christi, June 12.

I looked at him carefully out of curiosity. Although his hair was cut very short, I could see he was turning gray. He was not tall, very skinny, and slightly round-shouldered. What impressed me especially were his calm and his smile. He was a good companion as well as an exemplary Religious and extraordinary man.

Cautiously, in order not to attract attention to ourselves, we sat on some beams and bricks ready for construction. Kolbe began to speak in a subdued voice about the feast day, about God's greatness, and the suffering that we were being permitted to endure. We hung on every word that reminded us we might survive this horrible camp.

He urged us to persevere courageously. "Do not break down morally," he pleaded, promising that God's justice exists and would eventually defeat the Nazis. Listening to him intently, we forgot for the time our hunger and degradation. He made us see that our souls were not dead, our dignity as Catholics and Poles not destroyed. Uplifted in spirit, we returned to our blocks repeating his words, "We will not break down, we will survive for sure, they will not kill the Polish spirit in us."

It is hard to believe now that I was on a first-name basis with such a great spirit, that he actually came to me for a favor. "Our life is very uncertain," he said. "One by one we are taken to the crematorium—maybe I'll be going, too; but meanwhile, would you draw me a couple of little pictures?" He wanted one of Jesus and one of Our Lady to whom, he said, "I have such great devotion." I drew these pictures for him on paper the size of postage stamps. He wanted them that size because he had a hidden pocket sewed inside his rather wide belt and he tucked them in there. Later when he lost these pictures, I made a second set.

Henry Sienkiewicz slept next to Father Kolbe when the priest first arrived in Auschwitz. Sienkiewicz, even after Father Kolbe was in other blocks and work squads, never let a day go by without seeing his friend. He remembers visiting him in the hospital and noting without surprise that, "Father had won all hearts." Henry says:

Once I was going to do heavy labor. That morning before I left, Father Maximilian handed me what was about a quarter of his daily bread ration. I knew that he had been badly beaten and was exhausted, so I was astonished and didn't want to take it. Father Maximilian literally held me and insisted, "You must take it. You're going to do hard labor and you're hungry." I took it reluctantly, with sorrow, for I knew he would get nothing more until evening.

If I was able to hold out and emerge alive, if I kept my faith and didn't fall into despair, I owe it all to Father Maximilian. When I was close to despair and ready to throw myself on the wires, he was the one who gave me new courage and told me I would be victorious and get out alive. "Only keep relying on the intercession of the Mother of God," he urged. Somehow he infused in me a strong faith and lively hope, especially in her motherly protection. Twice he heard my confession. I go to confession frequently, but I often tell my wife that I have never in all my life found another confessor so kind as Father Maximilian.

At this time I was transferred

to a squad that worked outside the camp with some nonprisoners. I won the trust of some of these people and they began giving me things for us prisoners. I smuggled in 400 marks and 30 religious medals they gave me, and brought them to Father Maximilian. He blessed the medals and distributed them. Truly a Religious who never forgot his vow of poverty, he divided the money among the others, keeping not a single mark for himself.

Another time a woman got some hosts for me, which I brought in by hiding them in a can. I gave them to Father and he celebrated Mass twice with great secrecy in between the blocks. About 30 of us attended and received communion from his hands. He could have been punished with death for this.

In February, 1941, Father Sigismund Ruszczak, a younger priest, was shipped to Auschwitz. As a seminarian, he had met Father Kolbe. Except for one other, his is the only priest's portrait of Father Kolbe in Auschwitz:

One day I was supporting Father Maximilian under the arm as we walked and talked, when I felt that he stuck of piece of bread in my coat.

"But then you won't have any, Father?" I argued insincerely,

for I desperately wanted to eat that bread at once.

"Have it!" he urged, "You're young. You need it more than I!"

"But surely you're hungry, Father?" I protested weakly.

"I'm not hungry," he assured me. "Here, take it."

So I ate greedily. It was really the bread of life for me. Once I remember he also gave me some soup.

In a certain sense the concentration camp was beneficial to me. There was certainly nothing routine about my prayers, intense, anguished, filled with the deepest faith, and salted with tears—that's how I prayed at Auschwitz. When I came in contact with Father Kolbe, I was still reproaching God rebelliously: "Why? Why? How can You permit all this?" At that time Father still bore bruises and signs of beating, but he never complained. It was he who helped me penetrate the meaning of suffering.

I remember a day I met him on the assembly square. I asked him to hear my confession. It was a great thing to me to confide my sins and difficulties to a saint and to receive absolution and comfort from his lips.

My confession ended, he said, "Now I want to go to confession to you." And I heard him. Today I thank God for such graces and that he bequeathed to me an iota of his great spirit.

It can be said there is no Father Kolbe without his love for the Blessed Mother of Christ. But this love of his was sublime, theological, universal. One had to be a kindred spirit, an identical soul to understand him. In this veritable hell of the greatest suffering and cruelty, of satanic degradation, of cursing, and the misery of sin, to me he was like the flash of a brilliant light of God and beauty.

We were talking one Sunday. I asked, "Will we ever leave this place? Be free?"

"You will be free," he said emphatically. "You will live to see freedom." Then he added, "We all have a mission to fulfill—all of us here suffering in this camp. You will get out. I will not because I have a mission—the Immaculata has a mission to fulfill...." ❖

HEARTS ARE TRUMPS

On the first day of school we enrolled our children in kindergarten and first grade. We had just moved into the district, and I was a little uncertain about transportation arrangements, but we were assured that the children would return that afternoon on the bus that passed our rural home. Dismissal time was 2:15, and we were only a ten-minute ride away.

By 3:30 they had not returned. Our phone had not been installed, and the neighbors were too distant to seek on foot. When my husband arrived at four I was frantic. I had visions of my little ones boarding the wrong bus and being lost in the confusion.

We decided I should keep watching at home while he drove to school to look for them. He found the children and their teachers still awaiting buses. Our corner of the consolidated district always had to wait, they said. No one seemed to know why.

He came for me and we went to the main office to see the transportation man. But the only person available was the Superintendent of Schools. We expected little help from such a busy man, especially on a matter not strictly among his duties, but he listened kindly, and promised to look into it personally.

At 2:25 the next afternoon his station wagon pulled into our drive with both children. "You were right," said this man who was responsible for over 2700 students. "And beginning tomorrow the bus will bring them home on time. But I wanted to spare you another afternoon like yesterday."

I have since learned that this kindness was only one of many performed by this considerate man. I shall never forget him.   Mary Connell.

I Interviewed St. Frances Cabrini

But in 1916 I did not know I was talking to a saint

By ADELA ROGERS ST. JOHNS

February 1975, condensed from *Some Are Born Great**

I N 1916, I was a cub reporter on the *Los Angeles Evening Herald.*

"I hear the top woman of the Cabrini High School is in town," my editor said one day. "That's the one out in Burbank. She's the big shot for all of them. They tell me she's usually traveling but she's here for a visit and she's quite a character—might be a feature of some kind in it, why don't you go out and take a look?"

The most important thing in an interview is to know the subject's background beforehand. I did a little research. Our newspaper's file under "Cabrini, F." listed more than 60 Houses in the U.S. belonging to her Order, the Missionary Sisters of the Sacred Heart of Jesus. The group also had important hospitals and schools in most of the big cities: New York, Chicago, Denver, New Orleans, and Seattle among them. Frances Cabrini had become an important educator, and the Pope was a great friend and admirer of hers. She was by now an American citizen.

When I met Mother General Cabrini there in the charming California-Spanish high school and convent, she wasn't at all what I expected.

I have tried to find a copy of my interview with her. But Mother Cabrini, growing old and long absent from California, wasn't of much interest except to those who sent their children to her school. Probably my editor put my story on the back

*This article © 1974 by Adela Rogers St. Johns. Originally published by Doubleday Co., Inc. Reprinted with permission.

page of the second section, and in the merging of papers since, the files were weeded out to save space.

So I must rely on memory.

But the memory of my walk up the steep little hill to her chapel back of the Villa Cabrini High School in Burbank in December, 1916, is clearer than most things.

The high school was on a knoll just below the foothills of Burbank. It stood in the most beautiful olive grove I have ever seen. As we walked among those silver-gray-green flowing trees, bending in a desert wind, I thought of another Mount of Olives, and wondered if a young man from Galilee saw them much as they looked to me now. I have no idea how many acres surrounded the fine adobe-and-brick buildings that made up the school and convent, but it seemed to me spacious. The gardens were beautiful with roses and fragrant heliotrope against the walls and gay beds of nasturtiums and marigolds. There were high walls and fences all around it, as there are today, and the convent itself, badly shaken in the 1971 California earthquake and now condemned, was near the gate as I entered.

Mother Cabrini came to me in one of those parlors common to all convents, and a most difficult and deadly feeling of stiffness came over me.

My initial reaction was the size of her! Four feet, eleven inches and not a hundred pounds.

And the second, her eyes. What does she see that makes them look so joyous?

Her eyes were filled with a golden light. Should I have known by that light that she was a saint?

I did not. Instead I felt awkward and stupid. I felt that we had no common tongue, though I'd been told her English by now was perfect.

I felt sure that she sensed my discomfort. So I was glad when, a few moments after we sat down, Mother Cabrini suggested we get up again and go look at her new chapel. We set out across the grounds, past girls in uniform and Sisters in the familiar black habits that had always symbolized both authority and sanctity.

As Mother Cabrini and I and two other nuns began the perpendicular climb to the small building, she turned. I saw the exquisite bone structure of her face, the tender mouth, and the startling bright rose flush under the thin, aging skin. I didn't recognize it as a fever. But she held out a hand to guide me, and as I took it in mine I knew that she was burning up with it. Indeed she was and within a year she did. I realized she must be quite old.

As we took the first few steps, she glanced back and said, "Always have a special place in which to pray if you can, my daughter, however small it may be. Of course when Our Lord told us to go into our closet and shut the door when you pray He did not mean only a physical place. He meant the closet of your heart and soul, to shut out fear above all, to put your trust and faith in God. But I have found it a joy to have a little prayer closet if I can. That is why I wanted this chapel where any of us can go at any time to ask the Sacred Heart for courage and faith as we follow his footsteps."

The chapel was of thick cement, covered over with white plaster. At the end opposite the door was a small altar with candles and some olive branches, and above it a reproduction of the Sacred Heart of Jesus. I do not know how big the chapel was—is—but it was filled with light, though outside it was a gray day. I knelt, though I could not kneel as Mother Cabrini did. Even at her age, she melted down with the grace of a dancer. I do not know how long we stayed there, but my heart was racing. Whether with joy or terror or protest at all this I could not say.

It was near Christmas. And as we went down the rocky, dusty path back to the school grounds we admired the Southern California flowers. She spoke quietly of the fact that she had been here some time for prayer and retreat and meditation. And perhaps a little comfort? She had had so little of that in her life.

Born on a farm in northern Italy, Maria Francesca was the youngest of 13 children. Her parents died when she was only two years old, so she was brought up entirely by her sister Rosa. When Francesca, whose pet name was Cecchina, was eight years old, she informed Rosa that she intended to become a missionary to China. "To convert those poor heathen who do not know our Lord," she said.

"You a missionary!" cried Rosa. "You are too small and sickly and weak even to be a nun. And who ever heard of a woman missionary?" Nobody ever had.

There was money enough left by Cecchina's father to send her away to school with the nuns at Arluno. At the end of her education, she wanted to enter the Order, but she was refused. "She is spitting blood again," the nuns wrote to Rosa. "Her health will never permit her to become a nun." And none of the other Orders to whom she applied would have her either.

After teaching for two or three years in public schools, Cecchina practically backed into a failing teaching Order called the Home of Providence. Monsignor Serrati asked the 24-year-old to see if she could do anything about reforming the group. Here at last Cecchina put on a habit, and took vows, and was soon made superior.

For six years, she did her best to reform and reorganize the Home of Providence. She gathered about her six or seven nuns as dedicated as she herself. But in 1880, when Francesca was 30, the Bishop of Lodi decided that the Home of Providence was a hopeless task, and dissolved it as a Church institution.

He received the superior and her little band of devoted Sisters at his residence. Casually he spoke the words that were to send the undaunted Mother Cabrini on her true career.

"I've heard you tell people you wish to be a missionary," he said with a twinkle in his eye, looking at the tiny frail figure, "But you see there is no such thing as an Order of women missionaries." Then—I somehow feel sure, I saw her do it myself—Mother Cabrini raised those incredibly bright blue eyes to him, filled with fire and pleading, and spirit, and the bishop said slowly, "It appears to me, Mother Cabrini, that if you wish to belong to an Order of missionary Sisters you will have to start one yourself."

And the always practical Mother Cabrini said what she would say so many times. "I will begin looking for a house."

She always found one. The first was in Codogno.

In 1887, she went to Rome to plead with the Pope to send her to convert the heathen Chinese. But the Pope decided that New York was heathener and many of those who became heathens had started as Italians.

There should be something unbearably heartbreaking about the arrival of Mother Frances Cabrini in the vast city of New York on a chill and stormy night in March, 1889. Not only the weather, which was as foul as March can get on Ellis Island, and the late landing, and the fact that she herself could not speak a word of English.

But a letter telling the Pope not to send her at all had crossed her ship in mid-ocean. Thus no one on the American shore expected her or was in any way prepared for her arrival.

When on the following day, the nuns did find the archbishop, he greeted them with cold amazement. And with an uncompromising order. "You are to go back to Italy at once," he said. "We sent many letters to say you were not to come. There is no place for you. Return to Italy."

Whether Mother Cabrini, who had been studying English at every opportunity, understood his words is not certain. But there could be no mistaking his gestures, expression, and the tone of his voice. The other nuns began to take small steps backward in the direction of the docks and the return ship to Rome. But Mother Cabrini, her face very white within the frame of its veil, moved instantly forward.

"No, no," she said. "No, no." And began drawing letters from the voluminous folds of her habit and waving them at the indignant prelate. Letters from the Vatican, from Propaganda, and from the powers that had arranged her voyage to the new world where so many hundreds of thousands of her people had preceded her. It was not the letters, nor the whispered words in broken English, that brought light breaking through the dark clouds on the Archbishop's fine old Irish face. He knew he was dealing with a woman of courage and strength and dedicated faith. In a few moments he had changed his attitude completely. Perhaps he even drew a deep sigh of relief, for he badly needed help.

The condition of the Italians in New York, in the U.S. actually, at that time was deplorable. With unemployment and hunger at an all-time high in their own country, Italians of every class and kind, but especially the uneducated, had flooded into the U.S. They dreamed of a country where gold lay in the streets, hunger was unknown, and work was to be had by all. Of course this wasn't true then any more than it is now. The Italians either worked in the mines under labor conditions we would no longer permit, or were desperate and idle in the cities.

Soon after the arrival of Mother Cabrini and her nuns a New York newspaper published: "We have been seeing some dark-skinned women in our midst, Sisters of some Italian Order. They climb narrow staircases, descend into filthy basements and enter some dives where a policeman would be afraid to go alone. They are slender, delicate women and their mode of dress is a bit different from what we are accustomed to seeing. They belong to an institution that looks after orphans and all the poor Italians. Mother Frances Cabrini is their leader, a woman with big blue eyes and an attractive smile. She can't speak English but her spirit makes itself understood."

And not many years later the same newspaper said: "The sudden appearance of this small, blackclad, blue-eyed figure, Mother Cabrini, often dismays bankers, bishops, politicians, and philanthropists."

There was the man on whose valuable property she inadvertently (?) built a much-needed hospital. She got permits and labor crews, and ignored all the red tape that drives most of us up the wall. Suddenly, there it was. She filled it immediately with the aged, the desitute, and homeless crippled children. "Must I move off?" Mother Cabrini then asked of the man who owned it. "What shall I do with my patients?"

And the man said, "No, no of course not," and thereupon did what Mother Cabrini had hoped and intended he should all the time. He donated the land to the hospital already on it. He could well afford the gift, as Mother Cabrini knew before she turned the first spade.

Her first American convent and school are at West Park, N.Y. That large piece of property along the Hudson came on the market at a very low price because, it was rumored, there was no water. But Mother Cabrini tucked up the skirt of her habit and took a twig in her hand. Then she moved from one border to another in the role of a dowser—one who can find subterranean supplies of water with a divining rod. And, of course, Mother Cabrini found water, and bought West Park.

Immediately thereafter she sailed for Rome, in a season of typhoons, icebergs, and fog, to bring back seven more Sisters to take over this new project. It seemed none of them would venture a voyage across so many miles of ocean unless Mother Cabrini were with them.

Seattle, Wash., was a city which had always challenged her. Its population was not strong in either Italians or Catholics. Mother Cabrini wished to buy a large old hotel there and turn it into—as usual—a hospital for the old and the very young. But she ran into an agreement between the banks and loan companies of the entire area not to lend her any money. It would, said the real estate men and many organizations, bring down property values everywhere if a Catholic orphanage, hospital, school, etc., appeared within the residential section where this hotel was located.

If we do not lend her any money, they agreed, she cannot complete the purchase. So the little nun was turned down everywhere she went.

One day on entering a church she found a beautiful marble reproduction of Saint Anne reading from Scripture to the Blessed Virgin as a child at her knee. Mother Cabrini knelt to pray, and when she rose noted that the pages of the book from which St. Anne was reading were blank. From one of her capacious pockets, Mother Cabrini produced an old fashioned fountain pen—and with careful hand wrote upon the page: $26,462.

"And what does that mean?" said a Sister who was with her.

Gently, almost apologetically, Mother Cabrini said, "I just wanted to be sure she knew how much I need in order to buy that hotel."

Two days later one of the bankers cracked. Looking into the bright blue, pleading eyes of the little nun, he found it impossible to say no.

Often, she managed to get in ahead of big business and real estate operators, as when she gobbled up Chicago's old North Shore Hotel. The cops on the beat, her good friends always, helped her make some exact measurements so that she would come with papers all prepared for the corner she wanted. And by the time anyone else got ready to make an offer she had every bed filled with helpless elderly patients who could not be moved without damage or danger.

Upkeep was, of course, another matter. Mother Cabrini devised other methods for that. When bills came she was known to stamp them PAID and send them back. Everyone accepted this, no one ever complained, and Mother Cabrini explained gently that she knew they really wished to contribute to God's work, which was her work, and she was saving them a lot of time and trouble. So this was a blessing to all.

As we climbed the hill, and walked through the grounds, Mother Cabrini did not suggest that age or ill-health had halted her round of world travels. We talked gaily about the Rose Parade, to come on New Year's Day. And she spoke in a voice warm with love and admiration of some of the Missionary Sisters of her Order who at that exact moment were serving in cold and heat and loneliness. "But I did not send them to the leper colony," she said. "There were too few lepers; a sister would not have enough to keep her busy and that is always wrong."

She became thoughtful for a moment and then said, "Perhaps I am wrong. How many lepers did Christ heal? Ten—I must find out whether there are ten lepers in this colony that they have asked us to undertake." As we talked I became aware that she had herself established all the missions of the Sacred Heart. When a mission, convent, hospital, school, or orphanage was in working operation, a working staff of Sisters would be installed. Then she herself would move on to start a new one somewhere else. And she chose that staff as a great general might choose a staff on the battlefield.

"For example, you will not win a French nun by contradicting her. You must realize that the French character is different from ours and a little more fiery. Soon I will accept a German candidate who is proficient in German, English, and French, but she too will have a diverse character. We must learn to get along with all... otherwise we shall not be able to go to foreign missions. Americans, for example, are very forward. How will we treat them if we have not sufficient virtue to bear with them?"

I did not, as I say, have any idea when I walked up the hill to the chapel with her that she herself was mortally ill. True, she seemed so frail that a good strong Santana wind from the Mojave desert around the corner might blow her away. Later that day walking through the gardens of the Villa Cabrini in Burbank, Mother Cabrini told me she meant to stay there for some time. Where, she said, with her joyous smile, it is so warm and pleasant, and "I can go each day to my chapel to pray."

Very shortly after I saw her there, she made a sudden and seemingly inexplicable move and returned to her beloved Frank Cuneo Hospital in Chicago. Evidently she had had a warning—for there she died quietly and without pain, when she was 65 years old.

I did not realize in 1916 that I was walking up that small perpendicular hill back of Burbank, Calif., with a saint. In 1972 I knew.

We stood in the bright noonday sun, gazing up at the little white chapel atop a small peak in the first range of California foothills. Bonnie McCarthy, now in charge of this beloved shrine, several ladies of the Cabrini Literary Guild, my daughter and I, and a uniformed guard. Though he was most courteous, I did not think Mother Cabrini would approve of him there. She placed her reliance only in heaven. However, the red tape Saint Frances Xavier Cabrini always ignored, now seemed to be trying to separate her from ordinary people. The chapel where she used to pray was padlocked, chained, and bolted! The trail up to it was rough and stony, overgrown with cactus and tumbleweed and matted grass. Twisting and turning sharply, it rose at a stark angle. I suggested we begin the ascent. "No, no," everybody said loudly.

My daughter Elaine who, as usual, was beside me when the going was stark and steep, said No louder than anyone.

Not at your age. They weren't saying this aloud. I could hear it, however, as plain as though they'd shouted it.

But as I started up the hill over all the protests, I was floating without any weight of my body or protest from my bones and muscles. I was floating as Mother Cabrini had always done when she was old, and I now was. I knew she was walking it with me once more.

I felt my daughter beside me in watchful attention. I had a moment of knowing what it means to have a daughter who walks up hills with you when you insist on going—against all sense. I knew then, that second time, about St. Frances Cabrini.   ✧

THE PERFECT ASSIST

Back in the early 1900's, a boy could take his best girl on a date for 50¢. The nickelodeon was 5¢, sundaes were 10¢, and car fare another 5¢ each way, for a total of 50¢ for two.

My older brother Hugh and I often double-dated. Many times on Sunday afternoon we would take a walk to the park or nearby woods. Eventually others joined us until we became a sort of loosely knit club. Anyone could go along just by being at Ninth St. and North Grand Ave. at two o'clock. Sometimes boys came singly, and sometimes a couple of extra girls would be there.

One of the loners was Marty, a very likable chap who seldom dated. He was helping with a large family of younger brothers and sisters and consequently seldom had much spending money. This one balmy summer afternoon one of the girls brought her cousin along. Marty and the new girl seemed to gravitate toward each other. They laughed and talked as they walked side by side.

Then someone suggested we all go to the nickelodeon. Marty didn't seem to want to join in. I was wondering about this when Hugh, more or less the ringleader, called out, "Hey, Marty, catch. Here's the money I owe you."

Marty seemed surprised as he caught the shining half dollar. Hugh always had ample spending money, so that night I asked him why he'd borrowed from Marty who had so little?

"Oh," he answered, "I didn't owe him any money. But I was sure the reason he didn't want to come along at first was because he was broke. I couldn't go up to him and offer him money, so the only thing to do was toss it publicly. I know he'll try to pay it back, and besides, I've already gotten my money's worth."   Shan O'Laughlin.

School Days

The Littlest Atheist

When I entered the boarding school, I didn't
know whether God was a what or a who

By ANNE BOWEN
February 1986

YOU'VE HEARD OF the Lit-
tlest Angel? Well, I was the
Littlest Atheist. Although I lived
in a town with well-attended
churches everywhere, I had no
idea what really happened in
these places. To me, Easter was
a time to dress up and enjoy what a magic rabbit had
brought. I loved Christmas, but
I didn't understand its real
significance. I was fascinated by
religious cards and creches, but
as to the real identity of that
little kid in the manger, I hadn't
a clue.

Daddy was an atheist. My
mother did believe, but she was
"low key" on the subject. I suppose she thought I would even-

tually learn about God through
a sort of spiritual osmosis, and
that it was better for me to know
nothing for the time being, than
to be buffeted by Daddy's sometimes long-winded theological
theories. And so it would have
gone, if I hadn't, at age 5, wanted
my friend Ann Marie to come
out and play on a Saturday
evening. Her mother explained
that my pal couldn't come out.
She was being shampooed and
bathed in preparation for Sunday School the next morning.

"*Sunday* School?" I asked.
"What's that?"

Ann Marie's mother was
shocked. "Sunday School," she
replied, "is where we learn about
God."

Now I was really baffled. I

495

looked up at her and asked *"God?* What's *that?"*

Ann Marie's mother wasted no time in calling my poor Mama and voicing an opinion. It wasn't long before Mama, in turn, broached the subject with my father. "I think we should send Anne to Sunday School with Ann Marie for a while."

It took a moment for this revolutionary thought to sink in, and then Daddy said: *"Sunday* School! You *know* they'll just teach her to cut and paste."

Mama just looked at him. After a minute or two, he hedged with a vague remark about wanting to teach me from the Scriptures himself, sometime, someday. (It was a curious thing about him that, although he professed not to believe in God, he truly loved the Bible, especially the Old Testament. When his King James version came to me many years later, it showed signs of being well used, and favorite passages were underscored.)

But he didn't resist strongly, and I really did attend Sunday School for a while. Daddy was right, though; I didn't gain much from it. I suppose that the teachers made the logical assumption that I had at least some basic understanding of what was going on, but they were wrong. To me, our study was not about God, but rather some crazy people whose names I had never even heard before.

Actually, my mother was the nearest thing to God that I had to believe in. I sensed instinctively that she had been my beginning and that I owed my existence to her. Although other people loved me, she seemed to love me the most. I could take almost any question or problem to her. She was always as much a source of comfort as was humanly possible and, although she might punish me at times, there was nothing I could do that she couldn't ultimately forgive. When I was nine years old, however, she died.

Even the perspective of years cannot make this loss seem less than terrible. It was traumatic for Daddy, too, and he had another problem—how best to care for me. Fortunately for us a neighboring suburb boasted a fine educational complex, with boarding facilities for the students, run by the Sisters of St. Joseph. The sisters at Our Lady of Bethlehem Academy were sharp, sophisticated, and down-to-earth. They took good care of the children entrusted to them, maintained high academic standards, and tried, as much as possible, to love and comfort little, often lonely, kids. With their keen sense of humor and adventure, the Sisters related very well to young people.

And, oh, yes. They *did* believe in God.

After a frantic week of shopping for school and wardrobe supplies, all systems were ready. Every personal possession of mine—uniforms, underwear, socks, brush and comb, even my toothbrush and plastic soap dish—was marked with my identification number, which was 44.

On the appointed Sunday, laden with luggage, extra coats, and my favorite doll, Daddy and I introduced ourselves to Sister Lucy, whose realm included my dormitory. The little woman, nearly a head shorter than I even then, watched us wading up to her and she did not look impressed. In fact, she was regarding my hand—or, more specifically the object therein—as if it were a poisonous reptile.

"Little girl," she said, "is that GLASS? A *glass* glass?"

I looked down and realized that she had made a good assessment of the situation. There, indeed, was a retired peanut butter glass, emblazoned with Goofy.

"Mr. Bowen," she said, looking at poor Daddy sternly, "we specifically asked that you provide a *plastic* tumbler for Anne. Do you know what happens to *glass* glasses when they are dropped?" My father looked thoroughly cowed and almost stammered as he admitted that the plastic tumbler was the one

thing we had forgotten, and he had hoped that, just this one week . . . He finished with an appealing "I'm doing my best" look and Sister Lucy gave in reluctantly.

The other girls were getting ready for Lights Out. I will never smell a combination of Palmolive soap and Colgate toothpaste again without remembering my first night in the dorm.

Monday morning was a sobering experience. I had always hated getting up, even when Mama had been there to help. When our time had come, Sister Lucy ("the guy who got the bugler up") would emerge from her little room miraculously dressed, groomed, and eagle-eyed, as though she already had been up for hours. First, she'd turn on the lights. For those of us who didn't respond to this, she also rang a bell. Not only were we supposed to get ourselves up and dressed, but we also had to kneel in the aisle by our beds and *pray.* The floor was hard, and it would be a long time before I could learn the words that the other children were mumbling. Prayer itself was a new experience for me. I now realized that God was not a *what,* but a *Person,* and Someone highly regarded.

On Tuesday and Thursday mornings, all the little girls pinned on their navy-blue beanies and marched, in double file, off to something called Mass. I went with them but, because the Sisters respected the fact that my father professed no religion for himself or me, they didn't try to indoctrinate me as to the meaning of the ceremony. In fact, no one explained anything. In those days, the Mass was performed in Latin and the priest and altar boys did this with their backs to the . . . er . . . audience. The things that the man in the colorful vestments did seemed furtive and intriguing, like a magic act. While the other girls read from their missals, I watched for the trick.

It was an odd thing about these early morning Masses. It seemed as though the other girls were as sleepy as I, but they never seemed to mind going to Mass and, in some odd way that I couldn't understand, it seemed to strengthen them and improve their day. I wondered if the white wafers they swallowed had some sort of tonic effect.

It was tough slogging, but I survived my first week at school, although on Thursday evening Sister Lucy's dire predictions about my *glass* glass came true. Goofy died a terrible death on the bathroom tiles at the worst possible time . . . Bath Night.

A half hour later, as I left the bathroom, broom in hand and head bowed, Sister Lucy was huffing and puffing behind me. I knew she was angry because she was calling me *Miss* Bowen. As we came into the dormitory she clapped her hands and we all jumped as though we had been shot. "Girls," she said, "We're all exhausted and looking forward to bedtime, but Lights Out will have to be delayed tonight, because of *Miss* Bowen's glass glass."

The other girls looked at me gratefully. No matter how long the day, we were never as tired as Sister Lucy, or looked forward to bedtime as much as she. If the awful moment of Lights Out had been delayed because of my glass, the other kids figured they owed me one.

By my second week at school, I had discovered the rule of survival for all newcomers to the Church:

A. Always try to sit behind someone who seems to know what is going on.

B. Always do what that person does, no matter what.

I genuflected, knelt, stood, and sat on cue, not without a lot of surprised, coltlike clattering and banging. I did anything the person in front of me did, without question. One day the child in front of me apparently felt faint, sat down and put her head between her knees, and I promptly followed suit. We would probably still be sitting there today, if a fluttering nun hadn't rescued both of us.

One day after Mass, something new happened. Sister Francis Therese, our teacher, left, taking some of the girls with her, but most of the class stayed in the chapel, including the girl in front of me. Of course, I stayed too. Everyone seemed to be taking it all very seriously, indeed. We were there a long time, until finally each girl had left, one by one. I followed suit. Mine was not to reason why.

Eventually, I found myself following the girl in front of me to a room across the hall in which were situated what appeared to be phone booths. I assumed that this must be a chance to phone our parents and say "hello." When she emerged from the booth after a while, she held the door open for me. I stepped in, looking around in the murky gloom for the phone. And so it came to pass that I made my first confession.

I wasn't sure what to do, but the space was so small that I had no choice but to kneel. There followed several minutes of silence, as my eyes adjusted to the dark. There was a grille in front of me and through it I could see a man. He looked tired.

"Hi," I said.

He sighed. This was going to be one of *those* days. But he ventured gamely, "Would you like to start your confession now?"

There followed a stricken silence on my part. I didn't know what he was talking about, but was reluctant to ask, "Confession? What's that?" He apparently thought I had forgotten the formula, because he started to coach me: "Bless me, Father, for I have sinned ... "

More silence.

Again, he tried to help. "It has been *how* long since your last confession?"

"I don't think I've ever done this before, Father," I ventured.

"This is your first confession?"

"I guess so," I admitted. "What *is* confession, anyway?"

Now Father was speechless.

"Little girl," he said, as though he had been struck by a staggering thought, "you *are* Catholic, aren't you?"

I managed to resist the temptation to ask, "Catholic? What's that?", but instead answered, "Oh no, Father."

We stayed there, the two of us. He stared into space, without blinking, or even appearing to breathe, as though he had been struck dead between one moment and the next. I knelt there, watching him avidly.

"Well," he said finally, "since you aren't a Catholic, you can't make a confession. But if you *were* Catholic, and you wanted to confess, you would tell me about anything wrong you have done since your last confession, and then you would ask God to forgive you. Now, have you done anything wrong during the last two weeks?"

I struggled to come up with something, but the outlook was bleak. My entry into a boarding school environment had awed me into unusually good behavior. Nevertheless, I was determined to give it a try.

"I forgot my beanie in my downstairs locker last Monday, so I didn't have it in the dorm when it was time for us to go to Mass. Sister Lucy was very upset."

Father was not impressed. "You didn't mean to do that, did you?" he asked kindly. "You didn't want to upset Sister, did you?" I could truthfully answer "No" to all of the above. No one in her right mind would *want* to upset Sister Lucy.

I told him about the broken glass glass, and how upset Sister Lucy had been about that. He started to say: "But, you didn't mean to . . . ", and this sentence ended in a stifled snort. Now that initial shock had worn off, he could appreciate the humor in this bizarre situation.

I suppose he knew I was scared, because he took the time to tell me the joke about the little boy who always confessed that he threw peanuts down the stairs. We both enjoyed a good laugh over the punch line, until Father pulled himself together and resumed a serious tone. He asked me what my name was,

and what grade I was in, and who my teacher was. Then he blessed me, even though this hadn't been a real confession.

When I emerged, blinking, into the daylight again, the next little girl was leaning against the wall, where she had been waiting more than 15 minutes. I graciously held the door for her, while she stared at me with new respect.

It wasn't easy, but I got used to boarding school, and began to form close friendships with the people around me. One of the closest relationships I formed was with a Person I had never seen, and whose existence I hadn't even known about for the first decade of my life. This was slow in happening, but it had actually begun on my first day of class.

My Dad had registered me in the school three weeks after the Fall term had actually begun, so I had some catching up to do. Sister Frances Therese told me I could spend the first day reading by myself the textbook chapters the other children had already finished. I did this, and quickly caught up. I asked her if I could browse through a cabinet full of books in the back of the room. Because the other girls were struggling with their multiplication drills, she readily agreed to this.

The most interesting book

had a cover picture of a man in a pointed hat, and a child kissing his ring. It was the "Baltimore Something-or-Other." I opened it to the first page, and there, in bold type, was the question I had once asked Ann Marie's mother: "Who is God?"

Soon I was fascinated, standing there as though rooted, reading page after page. Sister asked me what I was reading, to which I replied, "I'm not sure." When I showed it to her, she regarded it nervously, in much the same way Sister Lucy had looked at my Goofy glass. "That's a *catechism,*" she said. "Who gave you that?"

I told her I had found it in the bookcase, and tried to reassure her. "It's really *very* interesting," I chirped, but she was not enthusiastic.

"Oh dear," she said, "I don't think your father wanted us to convert you."

It was too late. The idea that Daddy found so hard to accept seemed perfectly logical to me. Just as we all fit into a social order or plan in this world, so also do we belong to a greater order, which we don't fully understand, but which is there just the same.

There is a lot to be said for God, I realized. He is a Person, but more than we; patient when we are not, strong when we are weak. Most of all, God is permanent. He is to the souls of men what the sun is to a single year's crop of clover . . . Someone who was there before us and who will be there when we, and our opinions, are gone. An oddly reassuring thought.

I had learned a lesson when Mama died. Human nature is frail and mortal. No matter how loving or dedicated, a human being can leave you, but God is "in for the count." Madlyn Murray O'Hair would say that this God is a security object, and certainly I needed security, but it doesn't follow from this that He doesn't really exist.

When I told the Sisters one day that I wanted to join the Church, I assumed they would be thrilled. They weren't. They urged me to reconsider and be absolutely sure that this was really my own decision, and that I wasn't being pressured into anything.

I could see what they meant, but no one had actually tried to convert me. Indeed, I had had to work hard to ferret out the information I needed to make the decision. Yet, my situation in itself contained subtle pressures; I was rather lonely, missed my mother, was occasionally homesick, and also now belonged to a group where I was the one who was different. To become a Catholic just to be like the other girls would have been a strong temptation, but the fact remained that I had formed a strong bond with God, that I truly believed in Him, and had also found a viable way to express my faith. Why is it so hard to believe that a child could make a decision like that for herself?

The Sisters suggested that I ask Daddy for his permission first. "Better you than us," was unsaid, and telling Dad about this did give me a qualm or two. But I was in for a surprise. He was not only *not* angry, but seemed enthusiastic, saying several times that he was glad I had "something like that" and, "It will mean a lot to you as you get older." He never seemed to mind that I had become a Catholic and, many years later, he would ask me, almost wistfully, if I still belonged to the Church. It sometimes seemed to me that, like most atheists, he really *wanted* to be convinced, but never could be.

Armed with his consent, I was finally able to shoehorn myself into an instruction course designed for children who were preparing for First Communion. I, of course, was also preparing for Baptism.

We really cut it close, doing "the whole drill" in one week. I was baptized on Sunday, April 8, 1951, at St. Mary's Church in Woodstock, Ill., where my Dad lived. There I was ushered into the Church by Father Egan, a crusty old man who usually spent his Sunday afternoons ferociously gunning down the pigeons who lived on the church roof. I stood between my godparents, Madeline and Jerry, reciting with them the responses that they would have made for me if I had been an infant. We worked our way through the Apostles' Creed (which I had barely learned two weeks before), firmly renounced Satan (Father Egan looked skeptical), and the ceremony moved along quickly. Father seemed to favor total immersion; my blouse became so soaked with holy water that I made the Sign of the Cross over it before I threw it in the laundry at the end of the day. That night, when we were getting ready for Lights Out, the other girls surprised me with a gift—a small rosary of a color that we called "Our Lady's Blue."

On Tuesday, I made my second confession, this time armed with a list of sins whose evil intent no one could deny. Packed away in shiny boxes were a white dress, veil, shoes and stockings, all destined to play their part in my First Communion, which I would receive on April 15 (only a week after my baptism) in the pretty little chapel at school.

On Saturday afternoon, the other First Communicants and I had a light supper, and spent a peaceful evening (without television, radio, or other distraction) thinking and discussing the coming event. The fact that I was a couple of years older (and several inches taller) than the other little girls didn't bother me. Now that I believed in The Man Upstairs, I never felt alone.

We had a snack before we went to bed, something designed to fortify us for the long fast ahead, and, when we went up to the dorm, we found that the Sisters had tied pieces of burlap over the water fountains so that we wouldn't accidentally take a sip after midnight. The others seemed to sleep soundly, but I had a restless night. I remember pacing up and down the tiled floor in the bathroom, sometimes stopping and leaning on a sink, staring down into the drain and thinking about what was going to happen.

For all the preparation, my actual First Communion came as an electrifying surprise, an unforgettable sensation. It was as though Someone had, in a spiritual sense, embraced me. I didn't know then that there was a black spiritual entitled "Jesus, Be a Wall All Around Me," but that's what I hoped He would be, and He came through. From that day on, no matter what happened, I always felt *protected.*

The Sisters had worried that my newfound faith wouldn't

last, but it did. It sustained me for many years. And yet, a few years ago, there did come a time when I had a crisis of faith. I was deeply in debt, trapped in a job I didn't like, and dreadfully tired because of a progressive health problem. Old things in my life came back to haunt me. I was depressed, and angry, too.

The anger even began to come between God and me. Jesus taught us to ask: "Forgive us our trespasses, *as we forgive those who trespass against us.*" I knew that if God really decided to take me up on that, I would be in big trouble.

After a busy week of anger and depression, it was a chore to do virtually anything over the weekend, and I began to miss Mass occasionally. If I did go, it was hard to concentrate. The thing that kept me coming back was the Eucharist. Angry as I was, it still did something important for me. But one day, when the bell rang, and I said to myself, "Oh Lord, I am not worthy . . . ", a horrible thought bubbled up. I knew that I really wasn't worthy, and I wouldn't take Communion again until I was. Confronting that thought was so terrible that I stood up and left church without even genuflecting. It was almost as traumatic as my mother's death.

It would be more than six years before I came back to Church, one of the darkest periods of my life. Sunday mornings were the worst—times of loneliness and apathy. I would slump at home in my pajamas, reading a book, and hear the church bells in Oak Park ringing, but not for me.

Eventually, I got my life back in order, but was afraid to resume attendance at Mass. What was I afraid of? That God would punish me? That something terrible would happen? No, my worst fear was that I would walk into church, kneel down, and *nothing* would happen.

One year I resolved that Ash Wednesday, the beginning of Lent, would be a new beginning for me. When I received my ashes, I promised personal sacrifices to make this Easter a meaningful one, again. Still, I couldn't work up the nerve to go to Mass. I told myself that I would definitely attend church on the evening of Holy Thursday.

When that day came, the people in our office were swamped with the extra work involved in a large conversion of word processing information from one system to another. We had already worked many Saturdays and evenings, and we were tired, and I was hungry. I kept thinking about onion rings. The little restaurant on the street where I live sells the best onion rings in the world and, if I hurried right home, I could get there before they closed. I could

just relax, eat onion rings, and watch television. Then I remembered church. It wasn't an easy thing to do, but I knew that if I didn't make the right decision then, I never would.

When I got to church, it was half an hour before Mass was due to begin. I summoned up my nerve, rushed in, knelt down, and frantically tried to pray, but I was interrupted again and again by the clamor of nervous distraction. The more I tried, the more I failed. Finally, I gave it up.

If I had left then, it would have been all over—but I was tired, the church was peaceful, and there was something to be said for just sitting there, quietly. I was staring down fretfully at the clasp of my purse when suddenly the most amazing thing happened.

Someone embraced me.

It was something almost as tangible as a physical hug or kiss. I looked up—positively stared—at the altar. A wave of love was coming toward me. During the years when I was away from the Church, I had rationalized that God was everywhere, after all, and not just in church. Nevertheless, someone was *very* glad to see me there.

Madlyn Murray O'Hair would doubtlessly feel that this little essay has been an ego trip on my part, and she would be right. It was, after all, something that happened to me, and I've enjoyed telling you about it. But that doesn't detract from the importance of what happened.

When I was small, my mother was like God to me. Now I realize that God is rather like my mother. Whatever my failures, He still loves me and thinks I'm special. And the wonderful thing, the mystery that defies our finite, human understanding, is that He, in his infinite way, has this special, individual regard for every person He has created.

Anyway, that's what I believe and, if that belief gives me a feeling of security, I guess Madlyn Murray O'Hair will just have to learn to live with it. ◇

FATHER AND SON

The youngster was making his first stab at olive-eating. He watched his father eat one, with obvious enjoyment, then he tried one himself. The father took another and smacked his lips over it. The boy tried again. When his dad ate still another olive with pleasure, the youngster burst into tears.

"What's the matter, Son?" asked the father.

"You're getting all the good ones!" Mrs. Nancy Tyler.

*

A commotion in the basement brought Mother down from the kitchen. She found little Johnny crying loudly. "Why are you crying?" she asked.

"Daddy hit his thumb with a hammer."

"But why are you crying about Daddy's thumb?"

"I didn't cry at first," replied Johnny. "I laughed." *Liguorian.*

*

A small boy returned home from school and told his father that he was second in his class. Top place was held by a girl. "Surely, John," said the father, you're not going to be beaten by a mere girl?"

"Well, you see, dad, explained John, "girls are not nearly so mere as they used to be." Henry E. Leabo.

*

A lady went into a bank and announced that she would like to open a joint bank account.

"With whom?" she was asked.

"With whom?" she replied. "With someone who has some money, of course." Henry E. Leabo.

I Was a Fifth-Grade Religious Fanatic

In search of the ultimate holy card

By GREGORY R. WEBB

June 1981

I T BEGAN INNOCENTLY enough the summer before I entered the fifth grade at Holy Ghost School. I had just become a proud owner of my very first missal, a really big deal in those days.

Several factors were involved in a missal owner's prestige. The first factor was size—the bigger, the better. The second was the cover. I opted for a vinyl leather simulation with a cross in the middle. A zippered cover was the height of luxury, but well-beyond my limited financial means. The third factor was the number of ribbons used as page markers. Last, but certainly not least, was the quantity and quality

of the holy cards inserted among the pages.

All in all, I was quite pleased with my Maryknoll missal which tied with the other major competitors in terms of size. My vinyl cover was suitably impressive with the cross on the front distinguishing it from cheaper versions. Ten ribbons dangled from the bottom in a rainbow of colors. I was even satisfied with my small selection of holy cards: a picture of a guardian angel, one of the Holy Ghost, and one of St. Francis of Assisi.

One day I entered the pew where Sister Marie Madeline was sitting. I waved my missal several times in her direction to make sure she noticed it, and she appeared to be suitably impressed. Then she produced

Reprinted with permission of the author.

506

her own well-worn missal, moderate in size, but nicely covered, and opened it to commence her devotions.

As I craned my neck to count her ribbons, I was suddenly struck by a holy card of the Infant of Prague. Encased in plastic, it was the most beautiful thing I had ever seen. As her fingers slipped through well-thumbed pages, I caught glimpses of other cards of assorted sizes and descriptions. My craving for holy cards had been born. I had a mission in life.

My dream quickly became an obsession. When I had exhausted every local source of holy cards—priests, Brothers, Sisters, relatives, religious goods stores, funeral parlors—I found a book in the school library that listed all the Religious Orders in the country. I reaped a bonanza through a series of personalized requests for holy cards. With each request I explained the significance of my collection and enclosed my 25¢ allowance as a donation. I received generous replies and an ever-expanding assortment of cards.

I soon had mementos of more saints than most people knew existed. As word of my collection spread, a small squad of third- and fourth-grade holy card "groupies" started hanging around me in church in hopes of receiving any cast-off duplicates.

Within a few months I had netted 199 cards, and I knew exactly which one I wanted to be number 200: Pope Benedict XV. The addition of this elusive Pontiff, who reigned from 1914–1922, would complete the portion of my collection covering the Popes of the 20th Century.

It was this obsession that led to my choice of a Halloween costume that year. Most other kids my age were witches, goblins, pirates, or Davy Crockett. I was the only kid making the rounds dressed as the Pope.

I had several examples of papal dress from my cards of recent Popes (except you-know-who, of course) and had seen many photos of Pope Pius XII, then in office. I opted for the simple elegance of the white cassock with shoulder cape, a pectoral cross, and white beanie. With some help from my mother, I made the cassock from a white robe my sister had once worn as an angel in a Christmas pageant. The cape had been an old sheet. The beanie was real. I covered my sister's red school beanie with part of the sheet that provided the cape. My pectoral cross was two small pieces of wood covered with tin foil and hung from my neck on a long, white shoestring. As I gazed at myself in the hall mirror, I was filled with a serene dignity. I hoped God was watching me closely, and, suitably impressed, would hasten the delivery of Benedict XV.

I left the house with a regal gait that added to my papal aura. I approached the first door and rang the bell. As the door opened, not knowing the proper Latin term, I reverently said, "Trick or Treat." I'm not sure what I expected from the lady who answered—a piece of candy or a solemn genuflection.

Instead she shouted, "George —this one's really weird!" As I extended my sack to catch the goodies, I was doing my utmost to fix my ten-year-old features into a passable imitation of Pius XII.

George, meanwhile, had ambled over, given me a quick glance, and said, "Aw, Madge, the kid's a ghost!"

A ghost? I was stunned. Hadn't they noticed the cassock? The pectoral cross? The beanie? I was shattered. But George was not the only one who misinterpreted my costume. I was greeted as a "ghost" at nearly every stop that night. The only place I was properly received was the Holy Ghost Convent where, unbeknownst to me, my mother had phoned ahead and warned of my papal charade.

After Halloween, I added a new obsession to my search for Pope Benedict.

On my birthday in early December my mother, while apologetic for not having located a card of Pope Benedict, presented me with a holy water font for my bedroom wall. It brought out my finest religious instincts. As luck would have it, my birthday coincided with a religion class on the nature of sacramentals.

Sister Alameda had a way of telling stories that held us spellbound, as when she described her own devotion to the use of holy water. Each night she would sprinkle a few drops of holy water around her bed to insure she would not be disturbed by the devil.

My ears perked up. No one was more interested in warding off the devil than I was. And I certainly wanted to have nothing to do with him in my bedroom—after dark! After all, for all I knew, he may have been responsible for hoarding all the known holy cards of Pope Benedict XV.

I took her advice and secured some holy water from the large metal font in the church. At first I sprinkled a few drops around my bed at night and promptly fell asleep, secure in the peace of mind it afforded.

Soon, however, my exuberance got out of hand. While I

knew I was safe in bed, I began to worry that the devil might suddenly appear in the corner, in the closet, on my dresser, or at the window. I now gave the entire room a liberal dousing each night. I was getting the protection I needed, but it was becoming harder and harder to conceal my holy water habit.

The small amount of holy water stored in my little font was insufficient to handle the job. The priests were at a loss to explain the sudden surge in holy water demand. I had to sneak into church at odd hours for refills, which I placed in empty Miracle Whip jars. Before I knew it, I was using half a jar of holy water every two days.

Finally my mother demanded an explanation for the water spots that marred everything in my room, and convinced me to curtail my nightly rituals. To this day, though, I can't pass a holy water font without feeling a deep-seated urge to reach for an empty mayonnaise jar.

The close of my holy water period allowed me to renew my search for Pope Benedict with undiminished fury. And by now I had a number of helpers. Anyone who knew me at all was aware of my desperate yearning. There were still a number of Religious Orders yet to be contacted within the U.S., the only limitation being my mea-ger weekly allowance. And I fully intended to take the search overseas should that become necessary.

Sister Alameda, as if to provide other outlets for my fanatical tendencies, continued to regale her religion classes with tales of the supernatural. The "Hello, Jesus" story is but one example.

As she told it, Bobby was just about our age. An all-American boy, he was also extremely pious. (The story struck home immediately.) Every day he would take a few minutes from his recess to visit the chapel. He would kneel in front of the Blessed Sacrament and whisper, "Hello, Jesus — this is Bobby." One afternoon, after leaving the chapel, Bobby was struck by a speeding car and was rushed to the hospital. As he lay mortally injured, the priest arrived. As he held the host in front of Bobby, the host miraculously spoke, saying, "Hello, Bobby — this is Jesus."

We were mesmerized. We could hardly wait for the recess bell to ring. As soon as it did, 30 pairs of little feet raced towards the church door. The normal stillness of the sanctuary was filled with a noisy chorus of youthful voices: "Hello, Jesus, this is Barb"; Hi, Lord, this is Greg"; Howdy, Jesus, this is Judy."

The number of visitors during recess rapidly diminished as the weeks wore on. Only the more reverent managed to keep up the pace. I lasted longer than most.

The school year came to an end without my having found a holy card of Pope Benedict XV. During the summer vacation I devoted less and less time to the search—and to my collection as a whole. In fact, my overall attitude toward religion evolved into a calmer, more normal adolescent devotion. My fanatic days had apparently ended.

For the next three years at Holy Ghost School, my holy card collection gathered dust on my closet shelves. It seemed destined to share the sad fate of most childhood collections.

But my graduation from the eighth grade changed that. Amidst all the parties, ceremonies, and gifts, came an envelope addressed to me from Sister Alameda, who had been transferred to another school the year before. As I opened the envelope, a holy card fell out onto my lap. Even as I reached for it, I knew which one it would be. The search was over.

My holy card collection remains a treasured possession to this day. And, though my fanaticism has long since subsided, every Halloween I secretly hope to find—somewhere in the crowds of goblins and witches— a little ghost wearing a white beanie.　　　　　◇

RUSES OF ADVERSITY

A middle-aged woman, the society dowager type, walked into an exclusive dress shop. Approaching the clerk, she said, "That yellow hat with the purple feathers, would you be kind enough to take it out of the window for me?"

"Certainly, madam," the clerk eagerly replied. "I'd be happy to."

"Thank you," said the woman, walking toward the exit. "That awful thing bothers me every time I pass."　　　　　F. G. Kernan.

*

A candidate for the police force was being verbally examined. "If you were by yourself in a police car and were being pursued by a desperate gang of criminals in another car doing 40 miles an hour along a lonely road, what would you do?"

Hesitating only for a moment, the candidate replied, "Fifty!"

Lucille J. Goodyear.

The Day We Read for the Eighth Graders

And learned poor Wayne Brady's special talent

By DONNA FLAHERTY HART
November 1979, condensed from *Kansas City Star Magazine**

I N THE SPRING, when all the trees begin to blossom, I don't think of lost loves the way I guess you're supposed to. I always think of Wayne Brady.

He was a loser. I was only a first grader and didn't know the term then, but I knew one when I saw one. To begin with, he wore the earflaps on his cap down, even in September, and he wore knickers made out of some funny kind of material that sort of whistled when he walked. But the worst thing was that at St. Brendan's School, in 1936, he was the only pupil whose mother walked him into the class each day and kissed him good-bye in front of everyone. She

always said, "Be good now, Baby," even though he was six years old.

Sister Mary Catherine, our teacher, tried to help him. She was young and dedicated—to God, country, and Palmer penmanship. Wayne was a challenge she accepted cheerfully.

She knew God had given everyone a special talent. She talked about that every day. She said all we had to do was discover our talents and then cultivate them.

My talent was reading. I was already up to the part where Grandmother comes with the cookies when the rest of the class was working on "See Dick run."

Monica Fogarty's talent was coloring. She could finish a

whole picture without getting out of the lines. I'm sure the Fogartys were rich; Monica had the deluxe Crayola assortment, the one with burnt sienna.

Marty Columbo's talent was cleaning blackboard erasers. He just had a knack. Then there was Raymond Wozniak. Arithmetic was his thing. Sometimes, when Sister Mary Catherine flashed the flash cards, Raymond asked not to play so that someone else could win.

One by one we found our talents. All but Wayne. (Rose Ann Eisner didn't actually find a talent, but she didn't need one. She looked exactly like Shirley Temple. She had Shirley Temple curls, dimples, hair bows, and dresses. She even wore patent leather tap shoes, without the taps.)

I don't know how Wayne made out on the playground. It wasn't integrated. Girls played on one side of the building, boys on the other. I do know that when he lined up with the other boys after recess they were never pounding him on the back the way they did kids like "Huge" Brennan or Dominic Fatimo.

That was another thing Wayne couldn't do. Line up and march. We'd make two neat lines in front of the building, boys in one row, girls in another, first grade first, and so forth. Sister Mary Clement sat at the piano in the downstairs hall. When she got the signal, she really hit it and we started to march.

It sounded great, but about three times a week Wayne's shoelace came untied and he tripped going up the steps. Then the boy behind him would trip over him. Sometimes they went on tripping and falling all the way back to the fourth or fifth grade. Sister never missed a beat. When I was older and read about the brave musicians playing while the *Titanic* sank, I thought of her.

I n the spring Wayne suddenly began to do better. He could write on the blackboard without breaking the chalk, he could add a little and—glory be—he could read. Sister Mary Catherine was radiant. "Oh, Wayne," she said, "God loves you so much he has let you blossom in the spring." The whole class was caught up in Wayne's success.

Finally Sister announced that Wayne would go with five other readers (I was one) to read for the eighth grade. To say this was an honor just doesn't get it. It was something to think about at night before you went to sleep. It was something to tell your grandmother. It was BIG.

We practiced all week. Then, on Friday morning we lined up, holding our blue Cathedral readers with the bookmarks in place, and walked quietly through the downstairs hall and up the steps to the eighth grade. Tim Dunn, our leader, knocked on the door. A bored looking girl opened it a crack and said, "Yes?"

"Please," said Tim, trying hard to speak calmly, "tell Sister Rita Rose that the first grade has come to read." The girl shut the door. We could hear people walking around, closing books, putting things away. Finally the door opened again. We followed the girl to the front of the room.

"Sister Rita Rose," she announced, "the first grade has come to read."

We took our places facing the class. Their eyes were on us. Sister Rita Rose moved to the back of the room. Her eyes were everywhere.

I read first. No one else wanted to, so I volunteered. It was my talent. Tim read next. He was nervous because a big boy in the front row was crossing his eyes at him, but he did very well.

Then it was time for Wayne. He swallowed. We waited. He swallowed again. I felt sick.

He opened his mouth. Not a sound. We stood and waited. A couple of eighth-grade girls giggled. The boy was crossing and uncrossing his eyes. Wayne moaned. And then it happened. Wayne threw up. All over his book. All over the floor. All over everything.

Sister Rita Rose calmly sounded a "red alert" or whatever you sounded when you needed the janitor in a hurry; most of the eighth-graders sat spellbound. Then the first grade came unglued. We just stood there and sobbed.

Somehow Tim got us lined up again and we walked quietly, holding our blue readers with the bookmarks in place, down the stairs, through the downstairs hall and back to Sister Mary Catherine and the first grade.

That afternoon Sister Mary Catherine talked about loving and caring. She said some special people, like Wayne, have a talent for making other people care. I didn't know the word *compassion* then, but I knew compassion when I saw it. ◇

INFLATION ADJUSTMENT

Husband to wife: "What do you say we take this money we've been saving toward a new car and blow it on a movie?" Doris Carducci.

Poor Bandaged Children of Eve

God understands all things, even a child's
mispronounced prayer

By SISTER MARY JEAN DORCY, O.P.

November 1953, condensed from *Shepherd's Tartan* *

I am not an ex-nun, nor a fugitive from my Community, and I have no bone to pick. I have been a professed member of an excellent Community for 18 years. My opinions do not necessarily represent the thought of that Community. I write as a private individual, and my opinions, like those of any other American citizen, are my own. My occupation I usually give as "teacher" because it sounds respectable; people are always suspicious of artists. My family consisted of two long-suffering brothers and five pretty and witty sisters, and a set of parents old-fashioned enough to consider such a family quite normal.

OUT OF THE MOUTHS of babes come some heart-warming blunders, without which the lives of teachers would be glum indeed. The pity is that teacher is often allergic to anything like originality in her young pupils. It's a disease she contracted in normal school, and it leaves its mark upon her for life. A child walks blank and unspoiled into her classroom, his mind open, his nerves sound. By every means in her power she strives to complicate his ignorance until he is graduated, a tattered wreck who no longer sees any possibilities in spelling and has lost all curiosity about the least common denominator. Bound by iron-clad rules, he no longer trails clouds of glory, only gnat-like clouds of facts, such as: *i* before *e* except after *c;* 6 x 6 is 36; the Spanish Armada was defeated in 1588. No wonder heaven is for children!

Children alone have the courage to trifle with the rules that generations of unimaginative adults have laid down. "O my God, make Bismarck be the capital of New Hampshire," wrung prayerfully from the heart of a hard-pressed 5th-grader seems no more impossible to a child (perhaps also to God) than some of the more stately petitions He gets from His college-level correspondents.

Consider for one moment the joy of the direct approach. Forget the rules of grammar and syntax and arithmetic with which you have blighted so many young lives. Pretend that you are nine years old. Shuffle off the garment of adult flesh. Return to the state of youthful ignorance, where you thought Pennsylvania was large and pink, and Vermont small and lavender. Shed decimals, fractions, and compound interest, not to mention income tax. Breathe air uncomplicated by politics, philosophy, or afternoon teas. Look up at the world again, instead of down your nose at it. And there, under the spreading chestnut tree, the village smithy stands—of course, you remember: Blessed John the Blacksmith and Blessed Michael the Dark Angel!

The ponderous words in which we clothe ideas in this never-too-graceful language often betray us in our prayers. Here of all places we are dead serious; our poor mischievous mind is on its good behavior. It is no place for joking. Running a close second is the catechism, with its completely sober statement of dogma. And yet, with this unpromising material, countless unsung urchins have developed private and hilarious heresies. The most brilliant heresiarchs in history have had to work much harder for results, and gave far less entertainment for their pains.

Some of the connections our children make are more intelligent than we are willing to admit. One prays earnestly, "Give us this day our day-old bread." Not money, not power, not quail-on-toast, but bread—specific, stale, solid, day-old bread. It is something that we adults, shut from heaven with a dome more vast, would never think of asking heaven to give us. How often we would be telling the truth if we just acknowledged, "O my God, I am partly sorry for having offended Thee—"

You've heard of Gladly—Gladly, the Cross-eyed Bear? It's an old story, but ah—how quickly we forget its lesson! You can visualize it yourself: the stiffly starched little girls, the cleaned-and-pressed little boys shined up almost beyond endurance, the Sunday-school teacher innocently plunking out the accompaniment as her erring lambs bleat, with all the ardor of young hearts, "Gladly, the Cross-eyed Bear!" You can just bet on it that she never thought of such a beast. She seldom thinks of bears, in fact, except bear and forbear, who probably are not cross-eyed. But to her unspoiled little satellites, a cross-eyed bear is just as good a subject for a hymn as a lot of other things people might name.

You learn very early that when a 2nd-grader tiptoes up to your desk and inquires, "Sir, how do you spell *azzitizzin* — you know, Sir, I will be dumb on earth azzitizzin heaven?" it's no sign he has a drop of irreverence in his system. If he asks about the Forty Hours' Commotion, you take it calmly. He will just as fervently proclaim, "I plejja legion to the flag an tooth a repub brick where Richard stands; one ration in the visible with liberty and just as for all."

Dolores Whitney is one of those people who exist only in words, like Richard who stands on the republic, life is Ernest, and sudden Sally. At least one child in every generation will get up the courage to ask who she is, and will hopefully repeat, "Hail Mary fulla grace Dolores Whitney" to see if you can identify her. Nobody means any harm by it, but — words, words, words!

The call on a teacher's vocabulary is tremendous. She has to have in her head a six-column polyglot edition of what are to her the simplest and most obvious truths, because her words and her children's may be centuries apart. You, for instance, give a dramatic rendition of the Flight into Egypt. Your rapt audience pictures St. Joseph phoning United Air lines, Our Lady packing luggage. While you trudge piously beside the Holy Family across the burning plains of "Egypt's desert bleak and wild," your children have left you far behind and are already landing in Cairo.

If you should tell them that the angel told St. Joseph to take our Lady and flee into Egypt, one of your budding naturalists will be sure to bring you the picture from her book and ask you, "If you pleathe, Thither, where ith the flea they're taking?" You can't win.

A classic among the outpourings of uninhibited modern minds is this gem by a 4th-grade boy:

The Flight Into Egypt

Act I: *Bethlehem*
JOSEPH: ZZZZZZZZZZZ
ZZZZZZZZZ ZZZZZZ
ZZZZZZZZZZZ

MARY: Zzzzzzzzzz Zzzzzz
zzzzzz Zzzzzzzzzz
JESUS: zzzzzzzzz

ACT II: *Bethlehem*
ANGEL: Wakest thou, Joseph,
you got to takest the Child
and His Mother and flee-est
into Egypt.
JOSEPH: Wakest thou, Mary, we
got to takest the Child and
flee-est into Egypt.
MARY: Wake up, Jesus.

ACT III: *On the way to Egypt*
JOSEPH: Silent
MARY: Silent
JESUS: Silent

Act IV: *Egypt*
JOSEPH: Look, Mary, those
people are worshiping idols.
Isn't that awful?
MARY: Look, Jesus, those
people are worshiping idols.
Jesus looks.
THE IDOLS: Crash! Boom!
Bang!
(The End)

Although I have seen more
than one play that would have
profited by a 3rd act like that,
you can still see teacher's
problem.

God's world is a never-
ending source of awe to a
child. Fascinated, he watches
it unfold its mysteries: ripples
in the water, baby ducks, a
caterpillar. He is continually
bumping himself against the
world that man has made. Its

furniture is too big for him,
its jokes are not funny to him,
and he is constantly being
rebuked for trying to make
the best of it. It is a bitter sort
of betrayal to find that even
words cannot be trusted.

God can be expected to
understand all things, and it
does not greatly matter that a
child cannot, with his limited
experience, realize the meaning of the words he uses. He
will some day. We who are
old enough to be mildly scandalized when a child takes
undue liberties with an established formula of prayer sometimes forget that there are two
sides to the question. We are
the teachers, and it is our business to see that the words he
uses are the right ones, even
if he does not at the moment
understand all their meaning.

But ours is the humbler
office, after all. We deal only
with the letter. It is they who
teach us with what frank
admission of dependence we
are to plead our case to a
God who can accomplish anything if He will. We tell a child
dutifully that prayer is a lifting
up of the mind and heart to
God. Up is a definite direction to him, and he logically
looks up, higher than himself,
for help. We are older, wiser;
scientists have told us there
isn't any up, and we measure
God's greatness by our little-

ness, and our prayers do not always soar very high. They can't; they are fettered to ourselves and to our limited view of what we, personally, think ought to be done.

A child realizes that he has limitations: his report card is a standing testimony of it. There are lots of things he knows he doesn't know. To him, everyone from the child in the grade above him to the school principal and on up to God is wiser than he. When he needs help, he knows enough to ask somebody for it. How many years has it been since we self-sufficient mortals remembered to do that?

Let us pray with the little English girl, evacuated from London during the blitz. "Dear God, take care of daddy and don't let the bombs get him; take care of mommy and don't let her be scared; and for heaven's sakes, God, take care of Yourself. If anything happens to You, we're sunk!"

May the divine sisters remain always with us, and may the souls of the faithful be parted, through the mercy of God dress in peace. Amen.   ◇

HEARTS ARE TRUMPS

During my freshman year at an all-girls Catholic academy, my mother had to take a leave-of-absence from her factory job to undergo cancer surgery. Finances were tighter than usual, but still Mama managed to let me go on an end-of-the-year outing with my class in early June.

We girls were having such fun in the paddle boat, when accidentally my glasses were knocked out of the boat into the lake. Knowing the extra expense involved in replacing them, I was deeply dismayed to have to burden Mama with the news. As usual, she took the news patiently, but worried about the expense.

Several days later there was a bake sale at school. Preoccupied as I was with Mama's health and our money situation, I only vaguely wondered, "Why a bake sale at this time of year? Why wasn't I asked to contribute something?" I was embarrassed at not having extra money to buy anything, but the sale seemed to be a success.

At the end of the day, Sister called me to the front of the class, and, along with my best friend, presented me with the bake-sale proceeds of $25, exactly what my new glasses would cost! It was the kindest, gentlest act of charity, and 26 years later, I still get misty-eyed recalling it.

Mrs. Brenda Bryant.

Sister Bridget and the Song of St. Patrick

A lesson on "friendship in charity"

By THOMAS BYRNES
March 1985

S ISTER BRIDGET'S statue of St. Patrick stood little more than two-feet high in my third-grade classroom, but the vivid colors of the bishop's vestments gave him a life-size presence in the room. His right hand held a crosier; his left, in a gesture of banishment, commanded a snarl of serpents at his feet to be gone from Ireland forever.

The statue was Sister Bridget's own, a gift, she said, from her parents in honor of what the *Book of Armagh* called "the great friendship of charity" that existed between the Apostle of Ireland and Sister's 5th-century patroness. "Through him and through her," she was fond of telling us, "Christ performed

many miracles." We were willing to believe that through St. Patrick's statue and through Sister Bridget He might one day perform still another miracle. There came a time when many of us were sure that He did.

O n the corner opposite our parish buildings was a small store called Casey's Canteen. Its merchandise was a motley of tobacco, candy, newspapers, a few sporting goods and dry goods, a small soda fountain, and fireworks around the Fourth of July.

The Canteen was also a popular hangout for the older boys. There they would gather before and after classes to socialize, argue, test their lung power, wrestle, expand their street-

519

smart vocabularies, and lose all track of time.

If Johnny was late for school or for dinner at home, it was a safe bet he could be found in the Canteen. Urged on by phone calls and letters to the school from angry parents, Father Scanlon would periodically march to the corner and disperse the boys with a warning not to return until they learned how to behave like gentlemen.

Casey felt this was a serious restraint of trade. "Can't you let them be?" he asked Father Scanlon once. "What harm are they doing?"

"For one thing they're creating a disturbance," Father replied. "For another they're giving bad example to the younger children. It's a businessman's responsibility to keep order in his place of business."

"I'll be glad to keep order," Casey retorted, "if you'll supply the straitjackets."

In a day or two the boys would drift back and the cycle would begin again. This was the uneasy cold war that prevailed until Sister Bridget called on St. Patrick for help.

Terrence Casey, the store-keeper, was a dour and spidery old man who felt that life had dealt him a losing hand. He wore a permanent expression that was as gray and cheerless as his old gray sweater. For the most part he left the handling of the day's business to his nephew, Kevin McBride, a hardworking young man who followed his uncle's policy of "leave bad enough alone." Casey moved about silently in the background like a preoccupied ghost, seldom speaking except to lob an occasional verbal shot at the nuns and clergy across the street.

He had been born in Ireland and had come to America as a young man. A dreary monotony of bad luck and misadventures, partly due no doubt to some gloomy gene in his make-up, had finally turned him away from the faith of his fathers. He had the lapsed believer's talent for blaming all misfortune on the God he was otherwise unsure of. "Who's up there looking after me?" he'd mutter when business was slow.

The nuns knew who was up there. They prayed for him every day.

Casey admitted to but one joy in his life—his only grandson, Denis McKay, who sat next to me in Sister Bridget's third grade. Denis was as sunny and gregarious as his grandfather was bitter and unsociable. The fact that he was the slowest reader in the class seemed to bother him not a whit.

But it bothered Sister Bridget. My classmate's reading disability was to her an intolerable handicap that had to be lifted. Then one day, after praying to St. Patrick, she came to see it as something more—an opportunity to show her love for God in overtime. She offered to tutor Denis after school for an hour every Tuesday and Thursday.

Mrs. McKay was delighted and grateful, even though it meant she would have to pick up her son by car. The family lived on the far outskirts of the parish, and the idea of Denis walking the long distance home alone was not to her liking. And so it was arranged.

Denis was at first rebellious, encouraged in his feelings by his grandfather, who thought the plan was "a lot of nonsense." Being kept after school for whatever reason was to Casey a punishment. "What's the poor kid done?" he'd ask. "So what if he can't read fast? I'm a slow reader myself."

But as a few weeks went by and his progress down the printed page improved from a stumble to a slow walk, Denis began to enjoy these sessions more and more.

They began, as I observed whenever it was my turn to stay and clean the blackboard, with a short prayer to St. Patrick. "Dear St. Patrick," they would both pray, "help us to see the beauty of God's creation as revealed through the printed word. Amen."

The readings were not the passages Denis had labored over during class. With St. Patrick listening, it seemed only fitting that they be Irish stories. And so Sister led her pupil through the misty vales of the fairy folk, through old ballads and the lives of the Irish saints. Denis's self-confidence continued to improve. St. Patrick was doing his work well. But his most difficult challenge was yet to come.

One Tuesday morning Denis announced that he had a new baby sister. His mother would not be free to pick him up for a long time. Instead he would go to the Canteen when his lesson was finished, and his grandfather would drive him home at 5 o'clock.

"My grandpa was mad," Denis said. "He wanted me to forget the lessons and go home with the other kids. But my mother wouldn't listen to him."

"Good for your mother," Sister Bridget managed to answer as her face paled. You could tell what she was thinking— "This innocent little eight-year-old in that awful place for a whole hour!"

"Very well then," she said finally. "You go to your grandfather's tonight. But ask him if he will please come to see me after our lesson on Thursday. Here, I'll write a note."

She tucked the paper in

Denis's shirt pocket and said, "Tell him it's very important." She sent up another prayer to her favorite saint, "Protect this child from all harm."

Casey arrived promptly at 4 o'clock. I slowed down my cleaning of the blackboard to make sure I'd see everything.

Sister greeted her visitor warmly. "Well, well, Mr. Casey, how nice to see you!"

Casey grunted, but continued to stand in the doorway as four-square as Blarney Castle.

"Come in," Sister insisted. "Denis wants you to see his room."

Denis took his grandfather by the hand and Casey moved inside. As he went from one point of interest to another—a display of student art, a group of A-plus arithmetic papers on the bulletin board, and the statue of St. Patrick—Sister added comments on her own, all in praise of Denis's progress in reading. Finally, unable to refrain any longer from asking the question all Irish ask each other when they first meet, she inquired, "What part of Ireland are you from, Mr. Casey?"

"County Wicklow," said Casey, showing just an edge of the old pride that had lain buried so long under the merchandise of his store.

"County Wicklow!" Sister exclaimed. "My parents are from Wicklow, too! One of the most beautiful counties in all of Ireland!"

"*The* most beautiful," said Casey firmly.

"But do you know," Sister skipped on, "Wicklow blood is the most stubborn of all?"

Casey lifted his bushy gray eyebrows to signal that he wanted proof of this.

"Stubborn," Sister repeated. "Why, do you know that when St. Patrick first brought the faith to Ireland, it was on the shores of Wicklow that he landed? But the druids and the people would have none of him! They actually drove him out. And the poor man had to find a more friendly place to begin his mission."

Casey rubbed his chin. "I was never much at history," he admitted.

"But when they finally did embrace the faith—oh, what a glory of saints they produced! Kevin, Columba, Columbanus, and so many more! We have a priceless heritage, Mr. Casey!"

Casey smiled a tiny, reluctant smile.

"Now then, please sit down, Mr. Casey," Sister said, "up there at my desk. Denis wants to show you how well he can read."

When Casey hesitated, she added, "It will only take a minute."

Denis stood at the front of the room, a slender book in his hands, facing his grandfather.

He cleared his throat and began with an introduction Sister had written herself:

"Saint Patrick wrote this song to protect himself and his monks from their enemies."

He cleared his throat again and reached back over 15 centuries for the words Patrick invoked against the old chieftains who tried to stop him on his way to Tara:

I arise today
Through a mighty strength, the invocation of the Trinity . . .

Casey's eyes opened wide at the ease with which Denis handled the word *invocation.* The words rolled on:

I arise today
Through God's strength to pilot me,
God's might to uphold me . . .

Casey's dumbfounded gaze never wavered. All signs of his initial discomfort had slipped away. He was lost in the beauty of the hymn riding on the young eager voice as lightly as a currach on the sea.

When Denis came to the passage,

Christ with me, Christ before me, Christ behind me,
Christ in me, Christ beneath me, Christ above me,

there were tears on the old man's cheeks.

Christ in every eye that sees me, Christ in every ear that hears me.

A few days later Denis told Sister, "Boy, was there a row in the Canteen yesterday afternoon!"

"What about?" Sister gasped.

"Grandpa told a bunch of kids to stop talking like they were, and when they kept right on he threw them out!"

"Thanks be to God!" breathed Sister. But she was looking at St. Patrick when she said it.

Mrs. McKay never had to pick up Denis again after his lesson. His grandfather insisted on doing it, and on dropping in now and then to see how his grandson was getting on.

Occasionally as Casey moved, still wraith-like, in the back shadows of his store, he could be heard singing to himself, "In every eye that sees me . . . in every ear that hears me. . . . "

When Denis played the part of a shepherd in a Christmas pageant, held in the broad sanctuary of the church, Casey was there, his first time inside God's house in years.

He was there to see Denis in a Forty Hours procession.

He was there one Sunday

when Denis sang in the boys' choir.

And one Saturday afternoon before Easter, when Denis was in line before the confessional, Casey was there.

"Friendship in charity," the *Book of Armagh* called it—the friendship between St. Patrick and St. Bridget. Through the two of them, Sister had said, God worked many miracles.

But this one, I feel, came from a friendship in charity that included another Bridget, too.

St. Patrick can correct me if I'm wrong.   ◇

QUESTIONS AND ANSWERS

At dinner one July evening my nine-year-old daughter Alice mentioned that she had seen her former teacher at the playground. I asked her how the teacher was and Alice replied that she didn't know. "Well, didn't you even speak to her?" I asked.

"In the *summer?*" she asked indignantly.   Lois Robin.

SEASONS' REASON

The teacher was explaining to her fourth graders that heat makes objects expand, while cold makes them contract.

Asked to give an example of this phenomenon, young Tommy piped up, "In the summertime the days are long, but in the winter they're short."

Mrs. A. Mayer.

RUSES OF ADVERSITY

The baseball manager was holding skull practice with a group of rookies in spring training.

"Just visualize this," he said to a young pitcher. "We're winning, 1 to 0, with the Yankees at bat in the last of the 9th. They have the bases loaded, with nobody out.

"At this point you're called in as a relief pitcher to face Mickey Mantle. The count on him is three balls and no strikes. What would you do?"

The youth remained in deep thought for a moment. "Only thing I can see to do there," he said at last, "is to pick a fight with the umpire and get kicked out of the game."   *Wall Street Journal* (5 May '61).

The Sun Danced at Fatima

In a cold rain, thousands of believers and skeptics witnessed the miracle that Our Lady had foretold

By JOSEPH A. PELLETIER, A.A.
February 1984, condensed from the book*

OCTOBER 13, 1917. For days people have been trekking the roads and even sailing the sea lanes from the islands toward Fatima, the geographical center—now fast becoming the religious center—of Portugal. And since last evening thousands upon thousands of persons have been praying and singing hymns at the Cova da Iria while an endless stream of visitors has continued to flow in all during the night and morning. The certainty of biting October winds, the threat of chilling rain, terrifying rumors of a bomb that will be exploded near the tree as the children talk to the apparition, these and other hazards have not been able to deter the 70,000 people who have set out to witness the great miracle announced for noon today by the Lady of the carrasqueira tree.

What a crowd this is that waits so heroically beneath umbrellas in the pouring rain for three simple mountain children from the unknown hamlet of Aljustrel! Never has Portugal in all the long centuries of its existence witnessed anything quite like it.

The ever enlarging throng, made up of all professions and classes, and of all shades of opinion, belief and unbelief, is packed so tightly from the entrance of the Cova to the tree of the apparitions that it is practically impossible for the seers to advance. Seeing their desperate plight, a chauffeur picks little Jacinta up in his arms and, pushing vigorously forward, slowly opens a path toward the rustic arch with its cross and lanterns. "Make way for the children who have seen Our Lady," he shouts repeatedly, as he elbows his way forward.

O Senhor Marto follows close in the children's wake but he is less fortunate than they. Seeing him pressed and pushed by the milling crowd, Jacinta becomes worried and shouts, "Don't crush my father!"

Finally the tree of the apparitions is reached without serious incident. The tree, which is now but a branchless trunk, was decorated last night with flowers and silk ribbons by Senhora Maria Carreira, the self-appointed caretaker of this primitive, growing shrine. Having arrived very early this morning, the good woman now stands very close to the carrasqueira tree, where she eagerly awaits the Lady's coming and her long-promised miracle.

On reaching the spot of the apparitions, the chauffeur sets Jacinta down on the muddy ground. The pressure and excitement of the crowd at the sight of the seers is such that the youngster becomes frightened and begins to cry. But she quickly regains her calm and composure when Lucia and Francisco place her between them.

Moved by an inner compulsion, Lucia asks the people to close their umbrellas and to recite the beads with her and her two cousins. This they gladly do, happy at the opportunity to pray with those who have seen Our Lady.

Among the people standing near the hallowed tree of the apparitions are Jacinta and Francisco's father and mother and Lucia's mother. A priest who has spent the night near the rustic arch is also nearby. When the awaited hour of noon finally arrives, and the crowd gradually calms down, the priest engages the seers in conversation.

"When is the Lady supposed to appear?" he asks.

"At noon," Lucia replies.

"Look," the priest declares, as he takes out his watch and glances at it, "it is already noon. Our Lady doesn't tell lies! Something seems wrong here. We shall soon find out."

As time goes by without any sign of the Lady from heaven, the priest becomes impatient. He removes his watch again and looks at it.

"It is well past noon." he cries, whatever faith he had in the apparitions now gone. "This whole affair is an illusion. Let everyone get out of here."

But Lucia refuses to move. Whereupon the priest, firmly convinced that the apparitions are pure fictions, a serious menace to the spiritual welfare of the thousands of expectant souls who stand breathlessly by, tries to push the three children away from the spot where they so confidently stand. Lucia, whose respect for the clergy is very great, is disturbed and saddened by the priest's aggressiveness and determination, but she by no means shares his views, and she quickly voices her protest:

"Whoever wants to go away may do so. But I am not going. This land belongs to my father and I have a right to stay here. Our Lady said that she was coming. She came before and she will come again this time."

Then she glances expectantly toward the east whence the bright light and the beautiful Lady have always come. Instantly a smile of exultation brightens her face, and she and her young cousins simultaneously exclaim: "Ai!"

Raising her head so that her voice will carry farther, Lucia shouts: "Silence! Silence! Our Lady is coming! We have just seen the flash of light!"

It is exactly noon by the sun, though close to one-thirty according to the official government time.

The bright light that Lucia and her two cousins see in the east advances rapidly toward the decorated stump of the carrasqueira tree, where it finally comes to rest.

Once again the lovely Lady of light stands in all her brilliant splendor before the blinking eyes of the enraptured seers. And again they find themselves engulfed in the glowing light that emanates from the Lady and that envelops her person and the mutilated tree upon which she rests her feet.

Slowly but quite visibly the expression on the three children's faces becomes more spiritual as the power and beauty of the vision pervade their bodies and souls.

Lucia and her two companions are completely absorbed in the resplendent Lady, who today is more brilliant than ever. She shines with such fierce intensity that the light emanating from her, though not actually hurting the seers' eyes, does cause them to occasionally blink and lower them. Except for her added brilliance, the Lady is exactly as she was on the other days. She is draped in the same clothes of white light, her hands are again folded with the rosary hanging between them and over the back of the right hand, and her beauty is still such that it fills the children's souls with an indescribable joy, a foretaste of heaven.

As Lucia is so completely lost in blissful contemplation that she does not speak, Jacinta nudges her with her elbows and says:

"Lucia, talk to Our Lady! She is already there waiting."

Thus abruptly recalled, Lucia sighs heavily and then finally addresses the heavenly visitor.

"What do you want of me?" she asks.

"I want a chapel built here in honor of the Lady of the Rosary. Continue without fail to say the beads every day. The war is going to end and the soldiers will soon return to their homes."

Since the Lady has promised to say who she is on this day, Lucia now inquires of her:

"Will you tell me what your name is?"

"I am the Lady of the Rosary," comes the reply.

Recalling the numerous requests that have been confided to her for this occasion, Lucia speaks again.

"I have many favors to ask. Many people seek cures and conversions."

"I will grant some of the requests but not all of them. They must amend their lives and ask forgiveness for their sins," the Lady answers.

Then, with a look of great sadness that deeply moves the children she adds: "People must not offend Our Lord anymore, for He is already greatly offended."

These grave words, which impress the seers far more than anything else the vision has said, are her parting request and mark the end of her visit over the carrasqueira tree.

Though the Lady from heaven has pronounced her last words, the epic of Fatima is not ended. Indeed, its most dramatic episode is about to begin.

As the celestial visitor takes her leave, turning toward the east and gliding slowly upward in that direction, Lucia looks at the sun and, although she is unconscious of the fact, she emits a loud cry: "Look at the sun!"

Though Lucia is as unaware of her shout as she is of the presence of the crowd around her, there is a good reason for her sudden exclamation. For, as the Lady ascends in the direction of the east, she opens her hands and turns her palms upward toward the center of the sky. At this precise moment the rain stops and the heavy gray clouds suddenly burst asunder, dashing to the sides in broken, transparent strips and puffs. From the Lady's upturned palms rays of light are reflected upon the sun, which can be seen without discomfort by the naked eye as a spinning disc of brilliantly glowing silver.

Yet, strangely, it is not the fast spinning plate of brightly shining silver that absorbs the attention of the three seers. Their gaze is riveted on something else. Though they notice the rotating silvery sun, they also observe beside it something else that the other people do not see. They see the Lady of the Rosary. She, who a moment ago was rising with motionless feet toward the east and into the clouds where she finally disappeared, now stands to the right of the sun, whose light is paled by her brilliance. She is still all of light and is clothed in a dress of glowing white, just as she always was over the stubby carrasqueira tree. However, this time she wears a mantle of blue.

And, what is more important, she is not alone. She promised that she would come in October with St. Joseph and the Child Jesus, and that she herself would appear as Our Lady of Sorrows and as Our Lady of Mount Carmel. Now that promise is being fulfilled. In addition to the Lady the children see St. Joseph with the Child Jesus standing at his right side. Both are dressed in red, and both are

blessing the world. All three persons are close to the base of the sun, with Our Lady on its right and the other two on its left.

This apparition of the Holy Family does not last long and is immediately followed by changes of light and a vision of Our Lord and Our Lady which Lucia, alone of the trio, is privileged to enjoy. She sees the bust of Our Blessed Savior, from waist to head, clothed in red and at the right side of the sun. As she gazes lovingly at Him, she notices that He is making signs of the cross with his hand over the people. At the left of the sun, dressed in purple, she sees Our Lady of Sorrows, yet with this particularity: there is no sword piercing her heart.

Then again, while Our Lady remains on the right of the sun, another change of light takes place and she appears to Lucia clothed in strange garments that the child has difficulty identifying. But, as she has twice promised the children to come as Our Lady of Mount Carmel, and, as there is something hanging from her right hand, Lucia supposes that this object is a scapular and that the Lady she is contemplating is Our Lady of Mount Carmel.

While Lucia is absorbed in the apparitions of Our Lord and of the Blessed Virgin as Our Lady of Sorrows and Mount Carmel, her younger cousins are busy contemplating the sun. Together with Lucia they had seen the sun as a whirling mass of flashing silver at the moment when the rays from the departing Lady's upturned palms had first focused their attention upon it. But since last time it has changed in appearance and now as Lucia is lost in contemplation of the solar tableaux, Jacinta and Francisco gaze spellbound at the sun, which they see as a weird disc that turns rapidly on its own axis and casts off beams of colored lights in all directions. Shafts of red light shoot out from the rim of the sun and color the clouds, the earth, the trees, the people; then shafts of violet, of blue, of yellow, and of other colors follow in succession and tint all these objects with the various hues of the rainbow.

But Jacinta and Francisco are not the only ones to whom it is given to witness this fantastic display of heaven-made fireworks. For this grandiose spectacle is part of the great miracle that the Lady from heaven promised she would perform and which she declared would be for all abundant proof of her apparitions.

Seventy thousand amazed and tense faces are raised and pointed at the colorful spinning sun. And they have been this way ever since Lucia unknowingly shouted: "Look at the sun!"

and the clouds suddenly split apart. One of the things that strikes most of the people as they fix their marveling eyes upon the sun is the fact that they can look at it without pain or harm.

How can one describe this stupendous sight? Though the color of the whirling mass resembles the moon, in that it is closer to white or silver than to gold, it is more like a disc or flat plate than a solid ball. Yet there are some who wonder whether its flatness is not simply an impression or an optical illusion attributable to the terrific speed at which it rotates upon itself.

But even in color the spinning disc differs considerably from the moon, for its silvery tone is not in the least dull or lusterless. It glows with an intense and rich brilliancy, and, if this were not enough to convince everyone that it is not the moon, the intense heat that radiates from the rotating object would suffice.

One of the most fascinating things about this whirling silvery disc is the rim of color around it. At first this rim is red and the contrast of the red on the silver is so great that the sun looks like a hoop or crown of fire, empty in the center. But this outer border of flaming red changes color, from red it goes to violet, then to blue, then to yellow, and on down through all the hues of the spectrum. And the spinning sun appears alive with color, for all the constantly changing hues of the border are sent off in great beams of tinted light that transform the clouds, the Cova da Iria, and the surrounding countryside into a veritable fairyland of colored wonder and give to the sun the appearance of a gigantic pinwheel.

When the sun first becomes visible through the rain clouds its motion is one of extreme rapid rotation upon its own axis. It spins and casts off colored rays for two or three minutes. Then it ceases its rotating and play of lights and begins to tremble and roam within the opening in the clouds, occasionally passing behind a transparent strip or puff. Shortly it begins to whirl again painting everything with great shafts of red, violet, blue, yellow, and other colored light. After some three minutes of this it again ceases its whirling and splashing of color to move and wander about anew within the break in the clouds.

And finally now, as Lucia gazes intently at the last of the solar apparitions, that of Our Lady of Mount Carmel, the electrified throng sees the sun begin its exotic dance for a third time. It starts again to turn at terrific speed, casting off the same changing, gorgeously colored rays.

Then it ceases its dizzy spinning and spraying of colored light. And once again it trembles and moves. But this time it does not advance horizontally across the sky. It seems to have shaken itself loose from its moorings by its gyrations and unusual movements and to be falling from the sky. Indeed, it plunges in zigzag fashion toward the earth and the horrified spectators, who stare with faces white as death. Closer and closer it comes in its grotesque, reeling descent. Terror that in many cases borders on panic strikes into most hearts as this soulless monster of scorching heat staggers implacably downward, getting bigger and warmer as it nears the earth. Surely, think those whose minds are not completely paralyzed by fear, this is the end of the world and everyone will be either crushed or burned to death by this hurtling molten mass. Cries of horror and anguish rise from all sides as the majority of the multitude fall to their knees on the wet muddy terrain. Tears of supplication and contrition stream down the cheeks of men and women alike. Public avowals of sins and open professions of belief in the apparitions rend the air. Fervent pleas to the Lady ascend heavenward from all quarters.

"O my God, we are all going to die!"

"O God, forgive us our sins!"

"Mary, save us!"

"I believe! I believe!"

"Miracle! Miracle!"

But just when the suspense reaches its peak and it seems that the careening sun is about to obliterate everyone, it halts in its downward course and speedily reverses its zigzag path. It goes back to the heavens. There is stops moving and begins to shine again with its customary golden glow and its usual unbearable glare.

Blinded now by the sun's normal brilliancy, the people quickly lower their blinking eyes. Indescribable feelings of relief and of joy come over them as they realize that they are now out of danger and that they have just witnessed the great, long-awaited, and much publicized miracle.

It is not long before the spectators at the Cova da Iria, including the atheists, the skeptics, and the liberal newspaper reporters, are excitedly exchanging their profound and reverent impressions. They soon discover that, while the description of detail imparted to one another often varies considerably, they have all witnessed the same miraculous phenomena.

After the dance of the sun, numerous groups assemble at the Cova da Iria. One of the large gatherings is huddled around 47-year-old Maria do Carmo dos Santos, who comes from Arnal, a village forming part of the parish of Maceira. Word has sped through the Cova that this good woman has miraculously been cured of a serious ailment.

Very sick for five years, Maria do Carmo had manifested all the symptoms of tuberculosis. Moreover, since the early part of 1916 she had suffered sharp and continual pain in her whole body and had experienced other discomforts which had seemed to indicate that she was afflicted with a uterine tumor. Things had gone from bad to worse and eventually she had not been able to eat or sleep.

In July, she first heard about the unusual things occurring at the Cova da Iria. Although the Cova was 22 miles from Arnal, she promised to walk the distance barefooted four times in the hope of obtaining her cure from the Blessed Virgin.

When August 13, the date for the first trip arrived, her husband protested. "We are poor and have not enough money to take a carriage," he said, "and your going on foot is out of the question. You would probably die on the road. So you had better resign yourself, I am not going to let you go."

That is what the good man

said and meant, but his determined spouse succeeded in changing his mind and they left together at one o'clock. With his help, she hobbled along as well as she could for several long and agonizing hours. When the two of them reached Fatima, she was one mass of pain from head to foot. But she had been there only a few minutes when she began to feel better. And not only was the return trip home much less exhausting, but she found that her appetite had improved and that she could really begin to take food.

She went again to the Cova on September 13. This time she made the trip with greater ease, and her health continued gradually to get better.

Today proved to be quite a test of her faith in Our Lady. Her husband and she had hardly left home when they ran into heavy rain. It poured all the way and when the poor, sick woman arrived she was soaking wet. But again she felt better, and now her pains, her cough, the swelling of her limbs, and the other symptoms of sickness had disappeared. At this very moment she feels much stronger and also very hungry.

As the people mill around, there is joy and gratitude, as well as astonishment and excitement, on their faces. And some people are just now discovering the sudden and unexpected drying of their clothes. Everyone was wet through and through at the start of the dance of the sun, but now all clothes are dry.

Was it the intense heat of the falling sun that dried soaked clothes in a few brief moments? No one can say, but all are convinced that in one way or another this hitherto unheard-of phenomenon must be attributed to a special intervention of the Almighty. ❀

MODERN TIMES

Two young housewives were discussing the cost of living. Said one: "We're going to go on a budget as soon as Jim starts earning enough to make it work." Dorothea Kent.

*

Genevieve was playing upstairs when her mother called to her, "Genevieve, come down here. I'm afraid you'll get into mischief up there."

The youngster replied, "No, I won't. I don't know where you keep it."

Grit (30 Nov. '69).

The Cures
at Lourdes

More than 5,000 have been recorded, but only
64 have met the rigorous standards of Church
recognition as miracles

By PATRICK MARNHAM
September 1981, condensed from *Lourdes: A Modern Pilgrimage* *

THE DOORS of the Medical Bureau at Lourdes are the ultimate goal of every sick pilgrim. If you are cured at Lourdes you go there to report the event. By doing so you start a process of investigation which can take many years. Nobody knows how many people have experienced cures at Lourdes. But records of one sort or another have been kept since the 12th apparition, and the archives of the Medical Bureau go back to 1878. More than 5,000 cures have been recorded, of which only 64 were eventually proclaimed miracles.

For Marie Kerslake, from

Norton St. Philip in Somerset, England, who experienced her cure in July, 1978, arriving at the Medical Bureau was a rather intimidating experience. She had been increasingly disabled by chronic arthritis for 16 years, her condition was deteriorating, she was in constant pain, and her finger joints, knees, and back were all so badly affected that she was virtually crippled. In July 1978 she joined a pilgrimage. After Mass in the church at Gavarnie, during one of the pilgrimage excursions, she found herself able to leave her chair and her sticks and collar and walk for some distance up a steep hill. She felt no illeffects at all. Ever since then her mobility has enormously improved, she has never needed her equipment again, and she is now able to run, weave tapestry, and lead a fully active life. But she remembers her first entry into the Medical Bureau as a worrying moment.

The Bureau's initial investigation deals with about two reported cures a week, although the number can fluctuate considerably. As in the normal course of events, Mrs. Kerslake saw Dr. Mangiapan, director of the Medical Bureau, who made a preliminary investigation. In Mrs. Kerslake's case her account and his examination were sufficiently interesting for him to discuss her case with the pilgrimage doctor, and to open a dossier. She was then asked to return in 1979, and to bring her medical records and a report from her own doctor at home.

The real work of the Bureau begins with this second visit, when any doctor in Lourdes can attend the examination. When the examination is complete its findings make the second entry in the dossier, and the patient is asked to return again for a third time, a year later. At this stage the initiative moves to the doctor of the pilgrimage and the pilgrim's own doctor. The Bureau cannot normally proceed with the investigation if the pilgrim's own doctor refuses to cooperate.

The director of the Medical Bureau is in a curious position. All his patients come to him because they are feeling better. The better they feel the more concerned he becomes about their condition. If they start to feel worse he must start to lose interest in them. A cure passed by the director of the Bureau has about a 1-in-3 chance of being proclaimed. But a cure reported to the director has only a 1-in-22 chance of even being passed on, and only a 1-in-70 chance of being proclaimed.

In the popular mind, Lourdes means miracles. But miracles are a problem. Dr. Mangiapan tells a story about a newcomer to Lourdes who went to the Medical Bureau and asked, "Please, can you tell me at what time the miracle will occur?" There has never been any trouble in persuading the faithful to believe in miracles. They see them everywhere.

But the medical investigations of Lourdes are a determined attempt to restrict the number of miracles. The first point to be made at Lourdes is that the question of an inexplicable cure and the question of a miracle are separate. The Bureau and the International Committee are solely concerned with the question of an inexplicable cure, for which the following requirements have to be satisfied:

1. *Was the cure* sudden, unexpected, and without convalescence? Complete? Lasting

(a minimum of three or four years)?

2. *Was the disease* serious (through the degree of invalidity or risk to life)? Organic and not functional (based on definite disease)? Objectively proved (proved by tests, X-rays, or biopsies)?

3. *Was the treatment given, if any,* responsible for the cure, wholly or in part?

The actual list of questions which the International Committee asks is more detailed and technical than this, and is itself in process of revision. But the exact conclusion to which the Committee works is that "the cure established constitutes a phenomenon contrary to the observances and expectations of medical knowledge and is scientifically inexplicable." It can be seen that there is a great distance between the cripple who gets up and walks, and the cripple who gets up and walks and is proclaimed to have benefited from a miracle.

Of course the popular phenomenon of a Lourdes miracle has very little to do with this careful process of investigation. There was the "miracle mother of Lourdes," for instance. This turned out to be a woman from Worthing who had been told 11 years earlier that she could never have children. While on holiday in the south of France, she and her husband realized that they were close to Lourdes and made a detour to pray. Three months later she was found to be pregnant. She duly gave birth to twin boys and said that though she was not very religious this was certainly a miracle to her. Whatever its meaning to the person involved, this would never be considered an official cure, let alone a miracle.

As far as the authorities at Lourdes are concerned, such reports are significant only for the continuing public interest they reveal in the possibility of miracles. As an example of a cure which was judged incomplete, there was the case of a woman who was completely paralyzed. She was then cured in the baths, but one hand remained inert. It is quite common for the healed to bear some reminder of their previous state, but it must not, as in this case, be so marked as to compromise the completeness of the cure.

Sometimes the cure is complete but does not last. This happened to one English pilgrim, a woman of about 40 who came to Lourdes with Parkinson's disease. She was a believer and was cured, but her husband, an agnostic, remained unimpressed. After a year she came back for her first examination and seemed to be well, but one of the doctors noticed a very slight tremor in one hand. Her disease had returned and she is now very ill again. But she does not feel bitter about her relapse. She says that she and her husband still had a wonderful year.

Sometimes a cure owes more to human excitement than to anything else. One day when Princess Grace was making a highly publicized visit with the Monaco pilgrimage, one of the sick pilgrims was reported cured. *Life* magazine immediately described the event as a miracle, but the Monaco pilgrimage doctors said that the girl in question had been suffering from an unhealed wound to the leg after a motorcycle accident in which her fiance had been killed. They were delighted that she felt better and that the wound had finally healed, and they expressed the view that if she soon found a new boyfriend they would hear no more of her accident.

For the pilgrim who wants to know about the genuine cures, the best place to apply is the picture gallery outside Dr. Mangiapan's office. Here the walls are lined with the portraits of famous old cases dating back to the 19th century.

The two cases supposedly distorted by the author Emile Zola are both proudly displayed. Marie Lemarchand (Miracle No. 17), whom the novelist called Elise Rouquette, appears as a handsome, middle-aged person surrounded by two sons, two daughters, two twin daughters, and a husband with a splendidly waxed handlebar mustache. She was cured instantaneously in the baths on Aug. 21, 1892, of lupus (T.B.) of the face, and of something vividly and chillingly called "dog's muzzle." Zola describes it as follows: "It was a case of lupus which had preyed upon the unhappy woman's nose and mouth. Ulceration had increased, and was hourly increasing—in short, all the hideous pecularities of this terrible disease were in full process of development, almost obliterating the traces of what once were pleasing womanly lineaments." To look again at her picture is to see the full reward of her cure.

Justin Bouhort (Miracle No. 5) is also pictured—as a man of about 60. He was cured in July, 1858, at the age of 2 of a condition then diagnosed as consumption.

For English pilgrims there is a picture of John Traynor, who is considered one of the greatest of Lourdes cures, and a picture of Sarah MacLoy of Birmingham. The caption says that she was cured of cancer of the cervix on August 8, 1962, and that this was registered as a cure by the Medical Bureau in 1965. (Eight months after the registration of her cure she became ill again of a possibly associated condition.) The only other

English cure to have reached the same level recently, that of Margaret Gresham, whom the Medical Bureau certified in 1963 to be certainly and inexplicably cured, was not passed on to the International Committee on the grounds that she had had a functional condition which could not be related to an organic disease. Her picture is not displayed in the exhibition.

A recurring reason for the elimination of a possibly miraculous cure is "absence of cooperation from the patient's own doctors." Professional hostility to Lourdes was once so fierce that it could bring a brilliant man's career to an end. But today total hostility is the exception rather than the rule. The most it usually amounts to is an aggressive skepticism—doctors demand proof not of the inexplicability of a cure but of the existence of a miracle. However the hostility remains strong enough to persuade many doctors who have the misfortune to treat a patient who is subsequently cured at Lourdes to withhold all cooperation, lest they become guilty by association.

The medical hostility towards Lourdes probably reached its peak with the attack on Alexis Carrel in 1902. Carrel, who was eventually awarded the Nobel Prize for his work on blood-vessels, was then a young doctor attached to the Faculty of Medicine at Lyons University. Mainly out of curiosity, he accompanied a Lourdes pilgrimage. On the train he noticed one case in particular, that of a young woman called Marie Bailly, who presented all the symptoms of tuberculous peritonitis. She was in such a bad condition that Dr. Carrel considered it rather scandalous that the pilgrimage had agreed to take her. She had a family history of tuberculosis. She was spitting blood. Fluid had been drawn from her lungs. She had a pulse of 150 and her face was already turning blue. She presented the familiar symptoms of a case in the last stages of the disease, and Carrel, among others, considered that she was dying. Her sudden and complete cure after the bath and during the Blessed Sacrament procession took place before his eyes and Carrel made a report on the matter, which he accepted as a miracle.

Carrel concluded that these were highly significant events which "prove the reality of certain links, as yet unknown, between psychological and organic processes. They prove the objective value of the spiritual activity which has been almost totally ignored by doctors, teachers, and sociologists. They open up a new world for us."

Few doctors would now disagree with this opinion. But the reaction of his colleagues at the university was so hostile that Carrel had to leave. He went to New York, joined the Rockefeller Institute, and carried out the research which was to win him the Nobel Prize nine years later. As he said in *Journey to Lourdes,* his account of the case of Marie Bailly: "There is no denying that it is distressingly unpleasant to be personally involved in a miracle."

Current skepticism about Lourdes cures was summarized in *The Dictionary of Common Fallacies* (1978), the fallacy in this case being that "there are miraculous cures at Lourdes." The basis of the criticism is firstly that the cures are caused by "the excitement of the journey, the prayers, and the hymns . . . the ever increasing emotion generated by the atmosphere of the shrine . . . the healing breath produced by the unknown force which emanates from crowds during violent demonstrations of faith." That might be considered a fair description of the preparation for any intense religious experience, and therefore a proper preparation for receiving the sign from God which, according to the Church, is what a miracle is. Neither prayers, nor hymns, nor the healing breath, nor the unknown force of faithful crowds forms part of the scientific doctor's vocabulary. They are merely secular ways of describing a religious occasion.

The second criticism mentioned in the *Dictionary of Common Fallacies* concerns the standards of the Medical Bureau, as evaluated in a book entitled *Eleven Lourdes Miracles* by D.J. West. Dr. West's book, published in 1957, was funded by a grant from the Parapsychology Foundation of New York, and Dr. West was at that time the research officer to the Society for Psychical Research. The experience of Marie Kerslake when she returned to Lourdes in July 1979 for her second examination shows something of the investigatory procedures which for various reasons Dr. West found defective.

On the second day of her pilgrimage, Marie Kerslake faced her first full examination at the Medical Bureau. As an English pilgrim she might have expected a smaller panel than a French or Italian patient, but there were 14 doctors, almost all English-speaking, waiting for her. They had her complete medical history, her X-rays from the Royal National Hospital for Rheumatic Diseases, and reports from her own doctor, Dr. J.D. Corcoran, and from the specialist who had treated her, Dr. Cosh. The examination took three hours. At 5:30 that evening she returned for another examination, this time by 25 doctors, which lasted until 7:45. The examinations were very thorough, quite painful, and sometimes quite hostile. The atmosphere was not at all like that of a normal medical consultation, where a sympathetic doctor is trying to heal a patient. These doctors were detached, skeptical, and, in the words of one of them, inspired by the spirit of the devil's advocate. An attack of meningitis, suffered 18 years before, aroused a certain interest. Her eyes and coordination were tested. She was weighed and measured.

If Marie Kerslake's case is considered sufficiently interesting, she will be asked to attend again in 1981 and possibly for further years after that. And, provided that the Medical Bureau eventually obtains enough information about her previous condition and satisfies itself that her cure was genuine, lasting, and complete, her case will be passed on to the International Committee.

The International Committee meets once a year and usually in Paris, for the convenience of its foreign members. The Bishop of Tarbes and Lourdes is present at its meetings, but it has its own president, drawn from among its majority of French doctors. At the moment the president is Professor Henri Barriere. Other members come from nine other countries: Ireland, England, Scotland, Belgium, Italy, Germany, Spain, Holland, and Luxembourg. All the members of the Committee are Catholic.

The procedure, in so far as the cures are concerned, is for Dr. Mangiapan to introduce the dossier, and the Committee then appoints one or more of its number, preferably a specialist in the disease in question, to be *rapporteur*. He would normally see the cured person and talk to his doctors. He also would review all the papers in the case. About three months before the next meeting his report is circulated to the Committee members, so that it can be debated on an informed basis. The Committee frequently delays for some years after a report is presented to see if there are any further developments in the patient's condition. The Committee pronounced on the case of Serge Perrin (Miracle No. 64) four years after it had been put forward by the Medical Bureau; and delayed a similar time in the case of Vittorio Micheli (Miracle No. 63. For a detailed account, see "A Cure at Lourdes," *CD* Sept. 1979, p. 89). The final decision is taken on the basis of a simple majority.

It is clear that by the time a case is approved by the International Committee it has been considered at numerous levels. It has impressed the patient's own doctor and the pilgrimage doctor. It also has been approved by the director of the Medical Bureau over three or four years and it has been considered by several dozen doctors, selected at random from among those who go to Lourdes from all over the world. It has further been carefully reinvestigated by a committee of senior doctors drawn from all the main European countries which send pilgrimages to Lourdes. In other words, there is a convincing medical argument for an inexplicable event. But that does not mean that it is a miracle. All the International Committee can do is pass its decision and its report to the bishop of the diocese in which the pilgrim lives at the time of the cure. All further action, if any, must be at his initiative.

Here is the last obstacle, and no slight one, in the path of those who have been cured at Lourdes and who believe that they have experienced a miracle.

The canonical commission is an antiquated inquisition which is preoccupied with theological criteria, and which is quite capable of introducing an entirely new element into the considerations of the International Committee. For instance, the commission appointed by Bishop Theas in the case of Thea Angele (Miracle No. 53) consisted of a president (the senior diocesan canon), two assessors (who were also diocesan canons), one *rapporteur* (who presented the medical evidence and the story of the cure), one devil's advocate or promoter of the faith (who was the principal of the diocesan seminary and who argued against the miracle), and one medical expert, a doctor from Tarbes. It is hardly surprising that such a singular body, pursuing its canonical investigation in various French or Italian dioceses, should occasionally appear to be a law unto itself.

It is not uncommon for a bishop to make absolutely no response to the report of the International Committee, not even an acknowledgement. This happened with the Archbishop of Liverpool in the case of John Traynor. And there have been other cases, too. Since the war, the Lourdes medical authorities have heard nothing of four cases in which the dioceses of Nantes, Lille (twice), and Milan have either failed to reply to all queries or refused to give any reasons for taking no action.

That the canonical authority should ignore the medical reports is bad enough, but there is another form of negative decision which the International

Committee must find even more frustrating. In the *Bulletin of the International Medical Association of Lourdes* for May 1971, Doctor Olivieri, then medical director, lamented the "unfortunate series of five cures recognized as medically inexplicable by the International Committee but postponed or rejected by the ecclesiastic authority." He was referring to the cures of one Frenchman, one Frenchwoman, one Belgian woman, and two Italian woman dating back to 1952, all of which had been approved by the medical authorities in 1962 and 1964. And in each case the bishop's reason for taking no further action was a medical one. For although the canonical commission is primarily concerned with theological matters, it has to understand the medical report, and this means that it usually appoints its own medical adviser. So here the whole medical question can be reopened, but this time it can be effectively decided by a single doctor. This is what happened in these five cases.

The Archbishop of Antwerp ruled that he was not in a position to pronounce in favor of the miracle relating to the cure of Simone Rams, of cancer of the thyroid, because of the different interpretation of the case history by his medical expert. The Bishop of Dijon reached the same conclusion in the cure of Berthe Bouley of multiple sclerosis. The Bishop of Blois made the same ruling in the cure of Edmond Gaultier, of the after-effects of meningoencephalitis of unknown origin, because of "an insoluble lack of medical proof." The Archbishop of Salerno produced the same reason for refusing to proclaim the miraculous nature of the cure of Anna Santaniello, from mitral stenosis (heart disease). And the Archbishop of Sassari did not even nominate a canonical commission to consider the cure of Marchesa Mura, of axillary adenopathy (glandular disease), due to the rooted objections of her own specialist who lived in the diocese, and who questioned both the cure and the diagnosis made in Lourdes, and even his own patient's mental balance.

At the end of the exhausting process of investigation which supports each proclaimed Lourdes cure, there lingers the doubt about whether it was worth it. It is, after all, a very strange business. The hostile critics of Lourdes say that the doctors are all believers, and that when it comes down to it they have merely to rubber-stamp an unusual event and say that something inexplicable has happened, and that that is not really so much to say.

Certainly the whole purpose of the Bureau and the Committee is to say that medicine has nothing to say, and knows nothing of what happened. For many doctors, that in itself would serve to condemn the good sense of the proceedings. How can so many learned men sit there and solemnly compete to reassure one another about their combined ignorance?

And what, in the final evaluation, does the process of proof add to the miracle? Originally the Lourdes Medical Bureau set out to disprove accusations of fraud, gullibility, and superstition. Then it battled with the suggestion that all the cures were of hysterical illness. Both those battles are long since won. So what is the present purpose of establishing a certainty about a miracle, a sign from God? Naturally, the work of the Bureau will continue. But it is impossible, after all, to prove that the most routine cure is not miraculous.

And suppose one has no doubts? Suppose one sees the hand of God everywhere, as any believing Christian must? If you are such a person then you are one of those whom the shrine is for. Do you yearn for nice distinctions to be made between fact and mystery? Do you strive to reduce mystery to a minimum, and so reduce the incidence of its healing? What is the purpose of certainty about mystery? All that is written about the cures of Lourdes cannot take away the choice which exists from the very beginning of the argument. The critics of Lourdes say that, "Because something is said to have happened which does not fit with natural explanations then clearly it did not happen." The protagonists say, "Because something happened which does not fit with natural explanations there must be a supernatural explanation." In logic both are bad arguments which depend on opposing acts of faith.

And for those without either faith, does it matter? They are left in the end with nothing to be certain of except the undisputed reality of the cure.

• The epileptic boy, aged six, was carried into the baths by his mother 40 years ago. All his life, once a fortnight, this child had had a major fit. Before she bathed him Mme. Armand-Laroche told him to pray to the Virgin for his cure. "No," he replied, "I will pray for the cure of all sickness." Dr. Armand-Laroche has never had a fit since.

• The experience of Rene Scher as he sat among the sick pilgrims for the Blessed Sacrament procession and realized he could see, and looked round at the vast crowd and was afraid.

• The feelings of Marie Bigot (Miracle No. 59), who was cured in successive years (1953 and

1954), first of paralysis and then of total deafness, both times during the Blessed Sacrament procession. She remained, however, totally blind (all as the result of a stroke) until on the train home in 1954, lying awake in the night, listening to the sounds that had returned to her, she thought that she imagined the lights of a terrible storm, and was told that she had just seen the lights of a passing station. Her eyesight too was perfectly restored.

• Serge Perrin (Miracle No. 64), sitting in his chair at the Anointing of the Sick, crippled, almost blind, suffering increasingly violent fits, deteriorating steadily for two years, in a dying condition, and saying suddenly to his wife in his super-precise accountant's diction: "I do not know what has happened to me, but I have the impression that I will not need my sticks much longer, and that I could walk." He was correct to the last decimal point. He could walk, and that afternoon his sight was so good that with one eye he could read the signs across the esplanade.

• Or Evasio Ganora (Miracle No. 54), a farm laborer from Casale, who was found to have Hodgkin's disease. He responded to no treatment, he grew weaker and weaker, he was thought to have only a short time to live until, on being immersed in the water of Lourdes, he felt a great warmth run through his body. He got up, walked back to the hospital, and at once began to work as a stretcher bearer. Years later he was crushed beneath a tractor and was invited, as he lay there, to pray to the Holy Virgin to save his life. He declined, on the grounds that he had had his turn.

• And the husband of Alice Couteault, himself a nonbeliever, waiting on the platform at Poitiers for his wasted, twisted, incoherent, and incapable wife to be carried off the train, dying, as she had been for three years, slowly and before his eyes. And waiting while it stood there, and wondering why no one got off it from one end of the platform to the other—until a door opened in the distance and one small figure climbed down and began to run towards him down the long empty platform: Madame Couteault, instantly and perfectly cured of multiple sclerosis during the Blessed Sacrament procession. By the time Miracle No. 58 reached Monsieur Couteault, he was unconscious on the platform, and it was he who had to be carried home.

• "In that instant," said Gabrielle Clauzel (Miracle No.

46), referring to the moment at Mass on August 15, 1943, her birthday, when her paralysis, pain, racing heartbeat, and inability to eat, all just left her, "In that instant, I was well." ❦

SIGNS OF THE TIMES

From a savings and loan: "Save your money. It may become valuable again." J.S.

*

From a hardware store: "Love thy neighbor. Paint thy house." John Sierzant.

*

In our town square: "No ball playing. No bicycle riding. No pets. Remember, this is your park." Thomas LaMance.

*

On the door of the church's nursery: "Bawling Alley." Richard Uecker.

*

At a bakery: "When Betty Crocker turned 18, she began to sift for herself." Lorene Clark.

PEOPLE ARE LIKE THAT

Hockey is big in Minnesota, even with the little kids. So when our third son was seven years old, he joined the local hockey association's beginner team.

The coaches for kids in this age group need much more than a knowledge of hockey strategy to be effective. Most of the young players are only beginning to learn physical coordination and often spend more time lying on the ice than skating on it. Hockey can easily become a very discouraging activity for these kids.

We were glad our son's coach, Mr. Hanson, had a special gift for working with beginners. No matter what a kid did or how much skating talent he lacked, Mr. Hanson never downgraded him. There were no mistakes under his guidance, only learning experiences.

On the afternoon of the first game, the kids gathered like little chickens around their coach. Mr. Hanson called out the positions for first line as he pointed to his choices: "Tom, center. Rick, right wing. And Steve, you play left wing." Just then he noticed a puzzled look on Steve's face. "You do know which is left, don't you Son?"

Eagerly Steve's hand shot up—his RIGHT hand. The coach responded immediately, "No, I meant your OTHER left." Theresa Cotter.

Sin

Whatever Became of Sin?

Dr. Menninger speaks to disheartened clergymen

By KARL MENNINGER, M.D.

February 1974, condensed from the book*

I N 1967 I LECTURED at the Princeton Theological Seminary. One always learns from teaching, and what came home to me from this highly intelligent and idealistic audience was an anxious and unsettled feeling. The role that these young clergymen had chosen

Dr. Menninger is a psychiatrist, co-founder of the Menninger Clinic in Topeka, chairman of the Menninger Foundation, and author of "The Human Mind," "Man Against Himself," and "The Crime of Punishment."

*Published by Hawthorn Books, Inc., © 1973 by the author. Reprinted with permission.

as a lifework had seemingly diminished in importance and some wondered if they might have chosen the wrong profession. The depressed, discouraged mood of the general population had spread even to them.

A discouraged clergy? Could anything be more paradoxical?

And not because their flocks had fled. Not because they themselves had lost faith or ceased to feel concern for their fellow man.

Why, then? I asked them. Diverse things, they said: inability to communicate, inadequate financial support, lack of interest on the part of parishioners, disengaged youth, apparent irrelevancy of the church in modern life, the competition of yoga, communism, satanism, groupism, and materialism.

Of course I had had some idea of this trend. But it had not really come home to me, in spite of my occasional participation in the seminars for clergymen of all faiths at the Menninger Foundation. So I pursued my inquiries further.

I visited Carlyle Marney, who conducts the remarkably successful Interpreter's House for discouraged pastors. He said, "From some 8,000 laymen and ministers with whom we have conferred, five principal problems emerge: a loss of nerve, a loss of direction, erosion from culture, confusion of thought, exhaustion . . . they have lost heart. But they can be revived."

One distraction of the modern clergy is the multiplication of methods for dealing with troubled people: psychoanalysis and other psychotherapies, Zen and yoga, sensitivity groups, encounter groups. Magic cures for ills of the body, mind, and spirit seem to leave little for the clergyman to do. They seem to have lost a conviction of their importance, their usefulness. They seem uncertain about their purposes.

In addition to the state of mind of these discouraged seminarians, I became increasingly aware of the mood of the general public. People are worried.

There are almost daily reminders of our environmental sins and the impending consequences made probable by them. There is the repeated message that a little stealing and bribing and cheating might as well be overlooked, since it is "being done" everywhere. There is a general depression of spirits which the newspapers profess to be unable to explain.

About this time I came across a quotation from Arnold Toynbee. It fitted into my observations about the young clergymen.

"There has always been a morality gap, like the credibility gap of which some politicians have been accused," Toynbee said. "We could justly accuse the whole human race, since we became human, of a morality gap and this gap has been growing wider as technology has been making cumulative progress while morality has been stagnating. . . .

"Science has never superseded religion, and it is my expectation that it never will supersede it . . . Science has begun to find out how to cure psychic sickness. So far, however, science has shown no signs that it is going to be able to cope with man's most serious problems. It has not been able to do anything to cure man of his sinfulness and his sense of insecurity, or to avert the painfulness of failure and the dread of death. Above all, it has not helped him to break out of the prison of his inborn self-centeredness into communion with some reality that is greater. I am convinced that man's fundamental problem is his human egocentricity."

Egocentricity is one name for it. Selfishness, narcissism, pride, and other terms also have been used. But neither the clergy nor the psychiatrists have made it an issue. The popular leaning is away from notions of guilt and morality. Some politicians, groping for a word, have chanced on the silly misnomer, *permissiveness.* Their thinking is muddy but their meaning is clear. Disease and treatment have been the watchwords of the day and little is said about selfishness or guilt. And certainly no one talks about sin.

I am not attributing any special moral failure to the clergy, nor to my own profession. We all get caught in the waves and currents of popular interests.

But a trumpet call like Toynbee's compels one to reflect. We know that the principal leadership in the morality realm should be the clergy's, but they seem to minimize their great traditional role to preach, to prophesy, to speak out. An ounce of prevention is worth a pound of cure, and there is much prevention to be done for large numbers of people who hunger and thirst after an authoritative direction toward righteousness.

Is this presumptuousness on the part of a psychiatrist? Some will regard my present letter to the clergy as amateur theology. Perhaps it is. Tillich said that anyone who had a degree of ultimate concern was a theologian. One's life is, after all, an expression of all his 'ologies, including his private theology.

Nearly 50 years ago I was associated with a brilliant colleague, Dr. Logan Clendening. We had an office together. We taught at the same medical school. We spent many hours talking together. At about the same time we each wrote a book, *The Human Body* (Clendening) and *The Human Mind* (Menninger).

I proposed one day that together we write a third book, this one to be entitled *The Human Soul.* Clendening was intrigued with the idea. We even sketched some of the chapters. But time passed and our ways separated. We never got that book written.

Maybe I am still trying to write it, a book describing the confluence of the streams of our knowledge about health. Neither theologian nor prophet nor sociologist, I am a doctor, speaking the medical tongue with a psychiatric accent.

For doctors, health is the ultimate good, the ideal state of being. And mental health, some of us believe, includes all the healths: physical, social, cultural, and moral (spiritual). To live, to love, to care, to enjoy, to build on the foundations of our predecessors, to revere the constant miracles of creation and endurance, of "the starry skies above and the moral law within" —these are acts and attitudes which express our mental health.

Yet, how is it, as Socrates wondered, that "men know what is good, but do what is bad"? ❏

HEARTS ARE TRUMPS

On Easter morning, I looked at the cards and potted lilies next to my hospital bed and cried. For months I had planned on flying to spend the holidays with my son's family, but three days before I was scheduled to leave, an old respiratory ailment had flared up. Physically, I was better now, but I was still sick at heart.

Suddenly I heard a noise at my door. It turned out to be a little girl, maybe five years old. One of her arms was in a sling. Under the other, she carried a book almost half as big as she was. She peered into the room uncertainly, then asked, "Lady, can you read?"

Happy for the company, I said, "Yes, I can read. Do you need help?" Carefully she climbed up on the bed next to me, opened her book, a children's collection of Bible stories, and handed it to me. I began reading, and soon we were chatting and laughing, as I tried to answer her questions about the stories.

The morning flew by, and soon a nurse leaned into the room and said, "So, Caroline. Here you are! It's time for lunch." Without a word, the little girl leaned over and kissed me on the cheek, then took her book and disappeared. I was in the hospital for two more days, and each morning Caroline would bring her book.

The day I was packing for home, the nurse came to wish me good-bye. "Thank you," I said, "but I'm going to miss that little Caroline. I don't think I could have made it through the holiday without her."

"I'm sure she'll miss you too," the nurse said. "Her parents finally arrived last night to take her home. She'd been staying with her grandmother while they were away. The grandmother was driving Caroline home from a movie; there was an accident. The grandmother didn't make it to the hospital."

As I packed, I said a silent prayer, thanking God for helping two lonely people find each other when they needed comfort most. R.M.B.

Turtle Morality

Compassion for the sinner does not exclude condemnation of the sin

By WILLIAM J. BAUSCH
February 1975, condensed from *U.S. Catholic* *

THE MEDICAL DIRECTOR at a recent rock festival has urged that "officially sanctioned drug concessions" be allowed at such events. Among his patients had been youths who had been sold hog tranquilizers as drug tablets. "Since the vendors are selling bad drugs and no one's trying to correct this, the best thing to do is to make clean stuff available by the promoter through people with drug-abuse experience."

This statement epitomizes as well as anything the ethical dilemma that now confronts us. Look at what the doctor is saying: kids are on drugs; it is a fact of life, like it or not. Rather than have them zonk out with bad chemistry, let us at least provide them with officially sanctioned "clean"

---

*This article © 1974 by Claretian Publications. Reprinted with permission.

drugs and so control the drug aftermath.

What the doctor is saying is sensible, practical, and humane. But this very common sense is at the bottom of the dilemma.

Drug-taking is such a prevalent part of America's culture that we are rather rapidly losing the ability to look at the root of the problem. Our concern now is how to help drug-users live comfortably, how to help them escape mental guilt and hurt.

There are many other examples. We are quickly approaching the state of affairs when remarriages will outnumber first marriages. Divorce has become so commonplace that elaborate machinery is being worked out to make divorce more simple and more humane. Even the Catholic Church is easing the requirements for annulments and remarriage.

All this is as it should be. But, and this is the point, in all of this charitable and correct effort the original value of a permanent, monogamous marriage is holding up less and less. Some classes in Catholic high schools now spend more time in discussing how to assist the divorced Catholic than in fostering the pristine ideal of Christian marriage.

Or take sex. A director of Planned Parenthood tells parents they must explain birth-control methods to their children. "Denying a girl birth-control information doesn't mean she is going to stop having sex."

If teenagers are increasingly sexually active then pregnancies become a fact, and so abortion, sterilization, and birth-control methods seem a necessity. Why subject a 16-year-old girl to a pregnancy and premature motherhood?

We are rightfully caught up with the humanness of it all. But once more, how much time, effort, money, and energy are being spent on showing the merits of chastity? According to the media (do they reflect or create values?) there is a great deal of teen sex, so be sensible.

We have made the stop-gap measures and empathy so sensible that the original values are fast fading out. There is no strong voice to call a halt, or even to remark on the unseemly haste with which we have slipped into casual drugs, abortions, sex or whatever.

Perhaps it's that word *casual* that is so critical. We have adopted a morality of casualness because we have been propagandized into a mass morality of expediency. There are huge profits in rock festivals, in abortions, and in sex—which not only sells all other products but itself has become so salable.

Technology has made the follow-up solutions so palatable that any prior restraint, self-control, discipline, or moral viewpoint are unnecessary. The after-the-fact concern has become so widespread and so comfortable, the filter mentality is so much a part of our culture (enjoy the smoke but not the cancer, the soda but not the calories, the sex but not the baby) that we have evolved a turtle morality.

You remember the old story of the little boy who found a turtle and made it his pet. One day, all of a sudden, the turtle rolled over on its back and died. The boy was heartbroken and would not be consoled.

Finally, the father said, "Look son, here's what we'll do. We'll have a little funeral ceremony and you can invite your friends (at this point the boy stopped crying). Then we'll put the turtle in my cigarette box (the boy is interested) and then we'll get some ice cream and cookies and have a party afterwards" (the boy is smiling from ear to ear by this time).

No sooner had the father said this than the turtle flipped over on his legs and began to walk away.

"Oh, Daddy," exclaimed the boy, "let's kill it!"

That's turtle morality. The original value is lost in the attraction of the kindly solution. Everyone is so taken up with the helping hand that they elevate the tragedy (as it was once considered) into a virtue. The original incident of the turtle's death is no longer important.

Nowhere is this seen more clearly than in the whole abortion issue. The question of abortion is no longer a question about the facts. Everyone knows by now what modern medicine has determined: the early heart beat, the muscle movements, the early formation of limbs, the measured brainwaves show that this six-week or four-month old "thing"—reacting to light and darkness and sucking its thumb—is a living human being.

So it is not a question of whether this fetus is living or human; it is a question, rather, of value. Do we value this life enough to think it outweighs the mother's inconvenience? Or has turtle morality so conditioned our minds that as we hasten to assist the female caught in a troublesome pregnancy we gloss over the original question, the value of life itself?

In the Sept. '73 *U.S. Catholic,* Valerie Vance Dillon wrote:

"With so many other 'pro-life' educators I have 'proved' the existence of life to thousands of people. We have dazzled them with the *Life* photos showing fetal humanity and awed them with tapes of recorded heartbeat of an unborn baby at three months. But is this enough today? I think not.

" 'Okay,' a fresh-faced blonde girl said to me, 'so it's alive and it's human, but is it person?' Increasingly, that question comes up. Situationist Joseph Fletcher's criteria for what constitutes the truly human have filtered down to the 16-year-olds. The 'quality of life' mentality is flourishing."

The process is complete: what was formerly wrong begins to win our tolerance, then our compassion, until at last we see it as a "right" to be claimed.

You can see the heart-breaking dilemmas for average parents who cling to religious tradition. Parents are aghast at their daughters bringing home college boy friends to share their bedrooms during the holidays. They are distressed at the casual drug-taking of their offspring, and at rapid divorces of their children and friends. Yet if they protest they are made to appear not only "not with it" but, by a final irony of compassionate fervor, "unchristian!"

In a country where opinions, measured by Harris and Gallup, become the standard of right and wrong, the turtle morality reduces all ethics to convention.

In an intriguing article in *Blackfriars,* Stanley Hauerwas warns against too-easy ethics and turtle morality. He argues that ethical issues should not be viewed in modern jargon and in the spirit of the latest pop culture, but in the light of the Gospel. And he points out that ethical standards are not the same as pastoral compassion. For example, a man in an unhappy marriage may develop a friendship with his secretary. Their genuine concern for each other finally leads them to a sexual relationship. Some counselors, in reaction against a former condemnatory position, may go the opposite way and express a compassion that sees positive good in this second relationship.

Richard McCormick commented in *Theological Studies* (June '73), "Hauerwas warns that unless we are clear as to what has gone on here we will not be able to minister to this man at all; we will not be able to raise the painful questions that lead to the deepening of one's moral life. When the ethical is completely identified with pastoral compassion then there is no basis for pastoral concern. Behind this ethic of sentimentality there lurks the distortion that the aim of the moral life is not the good but adjustment. The therapeutic triumphs over the moral."

Or, as we would say, the delights of sympathizing with the man in question, the humane compassion for his plight, leads to a focusing on his adjustment rather than to a discussion of the original moral issue of fidelity and adultery, and whether the Gospel matters.

What we are trying to say is that in reaction to a past condemnatory attitude we have slipped into a false compassion which almost wipes out the demands of the Gospel. We are spending more energy on adjusting to the unfortunate and morally wrong situation than we are on probing the original ethical question and stating the Gospel demands.

This is not to say that there is no good in the new attitude of sympathy and in being less hasty in judging. It is only to say that a certain sentimentality is taking over, and that there is not an equivalent energy (and courage) shown in reaffirming that the Gospel makes radical demands of its own that transcend even human compassion. Whether we are talking about drugs, or divorce, or euthanasia, or premarital sex, or whatever, the Christian must not fall into a benign humanitarianism or into a mass-media sentimentality. We must take a careful look at what the creeping expediency of turtle morality is doing to the Word. ❑

TEAM WORK

The motorist walked across the field to where the farmer was plowing.

"I just ran over your rooster," said the motorist, "and I'm willing to replace him."

"Fine," replied the farmer, "let's hear you crow." Helene Levio

ALL IN PUN

The jungle Olympics were over and a dejected cheetah sat on the sidelines. He had failed to win even one prize. "I can understand losing the other events," he said to another cheetah who had also failed to win anything. "But I thought we're supposed to be so fast that surely we'd win the races. Imagine, being outrun by an elephant! It's disgraceful."

"Well, that's the way it goes," his friend said philosophically. "Cheetahs never win." *Woodmen of the World.*

THIS SPORTING LIFE

Two dishonest boxers were matched for a bout, and each had secretly bet on himself to lose.

The fight went along slowly with hardly a blow struck until one delivered a light thrust which accidently hit his opponent, who promptly fell down. The referee started to count him out.

The other was stumped for a minute, but at the count of nine he rushed over to the prone boxer, kicked him, and was at once disqualified.

Anna Herbert.

*

In filling out an application for work, a former ballplayer was stumped at the section dealing with his reasons for leaving his last job. After a while he wrote: "No curve ball." Richard E. Blake.

Slavery and Abortion

It is a good analogy: both deny basic human rights

By WARREN A. SCHALLER
December 1972, condensed from a press release*

SOME PEOPLE say that slavery never came to an end. Slavery is not just owning humans as property. It is the denial of basic human rights. And people still say, at least implicitly, "The Negro is not as human as I am. The Jew is not as human as I am. The unborn is not as human as I am."

Prejudice requires that there be a distinguishing feature between the subject and object of the prejudice. This must be some obvious characteristic. The subject never wants to run the risk of getting himself mixed up with the objects of prejudice. Therefore, the white man can be prejudiced against the black, knowing that he will never be

black himself. The Aryan can be prejudiced against the Jew with the same safety. And the already born human being never need fear a return to the womb.

There must be a net gain from maintaining the prejudice. Examples are cheap labor in the plantation economy, racial purity, or in the case of abortion, hopes for solutions to personal and social problems.

Attitudes of prejudice are not conscious. If they were conscious, they could be disproved. However, people who are prejudiced are not susceptible to logical thinking. "I can see that he (Negro or Jew or fetus) is human in some ways, but he's not a person and so should not have the same protections or rights that I have." No matter how many of these reasons

*Distributed by Minnesota Citizens Concerned for Life, Inc. Reprinted with permission.

555

you disprove, the opposition still comes back with "yes . . . but. . . ."

Prejudiced argument is not clear and congruent. This is remarkable in otherwise perceptive and logical people. For example, a doctor maintaining that the fetus is a part of the woman's body.

Yet two different blood types are incompatible in the same body. How is it that the mother's blood can differ from the child's in type and factor, if they are both the same body? Or the child's body may be dead and the mother's body alive. How is it that the same body can be both dead and alive at the same time? Obviously they are two separate bodies.

Prejudice is full of arbitrary distinctions and boundaries. A slave owner would have felt that interracial marriage is an evil and that fornication is an evil. It would seem logical that interracial fornication would have been even worse. But no, sexual relations with a slave were perfectly all right.

The abortion phenomenon is likewise full of arbitrary boundaries.

1. A fetus can be aborted legally—that is, "before he becomes human"—at 12 weeks, 18 weeks, 20 weeks, 24 weeks, or 28 weeks, depending upon where the mother lives.

2. In some jurisdictions, the fetus may be aborted (that is, he does not have a right to life) if he is the product of a rape, but not if he is a product of normal intercourse.

3. The fetus has guaranteed rights to inheritance (to sue for damages, etc.) but not to life in some jurisdictions.

Lacking good reasons for his prejudice, the prejudiced person often claims that his opponents lack "compassion," "experience," and are merely Roman Catholic, and "old-fashioned." This is an attempt to bypass lack of logic by creating a red herring.

There once were people who said, "I'd never buy a Negro myself. I don't believe in slavery. But I wouldn't want to force my moral position on someone else. After all, the law isn't designed to enforce ethical values. The law should be neutral. If a person doesn't want to own a Negro, he doesn't have to buy one."

This "I would never buy a Negro myself" argument is often used in the abortion controversy. The argument goes something like this: "I'd never have an abortion myself. I don't believe in it. But, I don't think I should impose my morality on someone else. After all, if you don't believe in abortion, you don't have to have one. But if a woman wants to have an abortion, she should be able to get one under safe medical conditions."

Both arguments assume the rights to alienate what our Declaration of Independence called "unalienable rights." In the case of the Negro, it is the unalienable right of liberty. In the case of abortion, it is the unalienable right to life.

The Declaration of Independence says we have three unalienable rights: life, liberty, pursuit of happiness.

What happens in a conflict of those rights? Supposing a young man mistakenly feels that he would fulfill his happiness by having sexual relations with a young woman—even against her will. The law says the girl's freedom of choice takes precedence over his pursuit of happiness. Suppose the young woman is pregnant and wants an abortion. Even though it conflicts with her liberty, the law prefers to protect the right to life of the unborn.

Both arguments assume that the law can be neutral on the matter of a basic right. What would happen to the Negro if the law withdrew all protection and became neutral? If the law became neutral, it in effect would withdraw protection from an individual.

Both arguments assume that the law cannot legislate morality. However, religion also says, "Thou shalt not kill," "Thou shalt not steal," "Thou shalt not bear false witness against they neighbor." If these principles were dropped from the law just because they have a religious or moral base, our society would be an anarchy.

Cicero said, "There are two kinds of injustice: the first is found in those who do an injury, the second in those who fail to protect another from injury when they can." ❑

HO HO, OH OH

The night before my husband and I were to leave on a trip, I discovered I had cleaned out the refrigerator so thoroughly that there would be no eggs for breakfast. I wrote a note for the milkman, telling him we would resume delivery when we returned. I added another few words, asking him to leave us two eggs, and to be sure there would be no mistake, I wrote, "Not two dozen, just two."

Next morning, when I opened the dairy box I found them. Inscribed on the eggs in bold black letters were: "HIS" and "HERS."   Mrs. Joseph Felice

Things

Do We All Want to Live in K-Mart?

Would all those "things" finally satisfy our longing?

By SONIA GERNES

December 1980, condensed from *Notre Dame Magazine**

MY FRIEND Judy does speech therapy with four- and five-year olds at a community health agency. One day, she asked her children where they would live if they could live in any kind of building in the universe.

One chose a ranch, another a castle, another a space station. One little boy couldn't make up his mind. He vacillated between farms and outer space and firehouses. Finally, when the others had gone on to something else, he stood up and yelled, "I know! I wanna live in K-Mart!"

I cherish that story. I'm amused at the thought of bedding down each night amid discount oil filters and genuine vinyl handbags, or circling forever with a shopping cart among ladies in polyester pants with carts full of malted milk balls and tube socks and "dusters in spring colors."

But the story means more to me than that. There is a greedy five-year-old in me still, and I can see that child's eyes widening at the towers of games and battery toys and racing cars, the bins of Milky Ways and

Snickers, and enough color TVs to tune in every channel at once. It's a greedy vision of paradise, but a real one. It consists of "things."

Things. You can't talk about the good life without them. A week in the Rockies with air that rings clear as crystal, and streams that pulse and plunge at the same speed as your heart, may not be a "thing," but a plane ticket to get there is, and so is a backpack.

What do you do with things? How do you get them and how do you get rid of them, and how many do you need?

My students once told me that you can't live a good life on less than $30,000 a year (about twice my salary). But Wordsworth said, "Getting and spending, we lay waste our powers." And St. Francis advised his followers to own nothing. If you have a book, he said, you need a chair to sit in to read it. And if you have a chair, you need a house to keep it in.

There's validity to that advice, but I doubt that many of us are going to take it literally. My life already includes the books and the chair and the house.

One of those books is an ancient prayer book that my father's cousin gave me recently. She says it belonged to my great-grandfather and was passed on to her by Aunt Nett.

It's full of old, well-worn holy cards.

One is particularly ugly. It's a shiny little-boy Jesus in a short turquoise gown with a nicely planed cross over his shoulder. He's a little walleyed and has dimples in his knees. My father's cousin says it was Aunt Nett's favorite. "She used to call it 'my little chromo,'" she says, and explains that chromolithography was a popular printing process in those days.

I can only guess at what consolation the holy card brought Aunt Nett. Perhaps in some way it encapsulated her childhood. ("Netty Gernes, Wilson, Minnesota" is inked on the back in a young hand.) Perhaps in its day the chromo printing process made possible vivid colors that had a genuine esthetic value for her; perhaps it was simply the only one of its kind she'd seen.

I remember her hardly at all. I'm not even sure whose aunt she was, but we used to visit her once in a while on Sunday afternoons when I was small. I picture her as tall and thin, with a faded voice not quite big enough to fill the dead air of her upstairs room at the old folks' home.

I remember a basket in her room, or I think I do. It was fine brown wicker, with beads and tassels on the cover, and I probably suspected there was candy in it. Aunt Nett was a seamstress all her life, so more likely it held thread.

But that's what's left; a little walleyed chromo, and the memory of a basket that may still survive in some relative's attic. It hardly sounds like "the good life." But who am I to know? At least the little chromo has these things to tell me: there is no ratio between the monetary value of a possession and its emotional worth; and possessions have the power to console. And the well-worn chromo tells me something else: the good life consists of savoring.

When I lived in Seattle, I had few possessions. I lived in furnished rooms and apartments for most of the six years; my typewriter was ancient; I got clothes from rummage sales. Yet, I don't think I pitied my poverty very often. A graduate student expects to be poor, and I did a great deal of savoring.

What I possessed was the Northwest itself. I would ride the bus to school, caught in my own morning grayness. The bus would top a hill, and the whole Cascade mountain range would be mine. Or, I would tire of books and go to the library steps; there, I could almost touch Mount Rainier rising above the Drumheller Fountain. In spring, the litany of flowers in that moist climate could make me forgive the rain.

I no longer live in Seattle.

When February closes around me here in the flatlands of the Midwest, I think I would dump all my hard-earned possessions to live in those mountains again. But I wouldn't dump my job; I wouldn't dump teaching and writing and the study of literature. That's part of the good life, too: making your living doing what you most want to do.

And if I do less savoring of scenery here in Indiana, there are consolations. My friends tease me about being the "auction lady," the scavenger, but there has been a joy for me in rehabilitating old furniture, in bidding on the battered white dresser knowing there is walnut underneath. The warmth of a wood grain emerging has comforted me for the loss of mountains, as Saint Mary's Lake has consoled me for the loss of Puget Sound.

I know something, then, about the consolation of possessions, of a little chromo or a walnut chest. Yet I wouldn't treasure my furniture so much if I hadn't brought out every grain of most of it—if I hadn't caned the rocker strand by strand to clear my head between bouts with final exams. The good life is lived in such moments.

I remember one of the few wise things I did as a child. On my 10th birthday, my cousin gave me a two-pound box of Fanny Farmer chocolates (I had had only dimestore chocolates before.) I dutifully passed it around once, and then hid it in my underwear drawer. Every day thereafter I allowed myself one piece. I nibbled oh so slowly, prolonging every bite of the chocolate mints and the butter creams. I've had nothing so delicious before or since.

I'd like to give that box of chocolates to the boy who wants to live in K-Mart. I'd like to give him the chromo, too, but I don't think he'd understand.

What is so often misunderstood about American materialism is the longing behind it, the sense of promises made to those who trusted in some shining land to bring them "the good life."

We stuff our shopping carts. We pile up box after box, though we suspect they are empty. We try to gather to ourselves something of the promised land, and when that fails, we console ourselves with quantity, the worst of tactics.

There's a kind of naive, misguided optimism about that endeavor that touches me: all that yearning among the shopping carts, all that longing for paradise.

Sometimes, on summer nights, I think that if I were in exile—if I were to live abroad for years and not return for reasons of the heart or head or pocketbook—I would think of America, not as the hills of Seattle, or the upper Mississippi valley of my youth, but as a hot night in Indiana at a shopping center. I would think of the ladies in stretch pants, and the clinging children, of the orange and purple clouds waving the day's last colors above the movie marquee, and of the blacktop prairie pocked with shopping carts. I would remember that the neon lights were just beginning to brighten in the dimming air, and that somewhere in the twilight was a sweetness that could break your heart.   ✳

UNFILTRATION

Victor Borge once felt called upon to explain why the keys of his own piano are yellow. "It's not really because the piano is old," he insisted. "It's just because the elephant smoked too much."

Philadelphia *Inquirer* (28 July '63).

We Used to Be Poor

but got rich just by unstashing things

By RALPH REPPERT
March 1964, condensed from the Baltimore Sunday Sun Magazine*

M Y WIFE Harriet decided last week that we aren't ever going to be rich. She didn't blurt out, "Ralphie boy, I can see now that you're just never going to make it." No, it was more of a gradual thing that sort of took root by itself, grew, and bloomed.

It began with the Madeira table linens which somebody gave us for a wedding present and which Harriet has since kept stashed away in the attic.

I don't know why people squirrel away pretty things like that. Unconsciously, I think, we were saving them for the day when we could buy just the right kind of diningroom furniture, china, silver, and so on. Then, in the event that we had a duchess or a movie star or perhaps a U.S. senator to dinner, we could break out the Madeira linen and show it off in the setting it deserved.

Harriet ran across the linen while looking for something else, and decided on the spur of the moment there wasn't any point saving it any longer. She also brought down a pair of silver candlesticks—another wedding present—to set off the linen.

Dinner that night had a touch of magic. The fine old pattern of the tablecloth caught the candlelight in a way that dressed up the whole dining room, so that even the hamburger looked aristocratic.

A day or two later Harriet trotted out the good china, because the Madeira linen deserved the best we had. Then came the good silver because, as Harriet put it, "it's the *least* we can do for the china."

I broke out the bottle of brandy Harriet bought me three

Christmases ago. (I had been saving the occasion for some deserving guest.)

After two glasses of brandy apiece, Harriet and I came to some conclusions.

1. Undoubtedly we will never be able to buy furniture for what we would consider a perfect dining room—or perfect living room.

2. So let's use the few nice things we have with the furniture we now have and make the most of it. In short, let's reach out right now and take a big bite out of life, while we can still bite with our own teeth.

3. Speaking of deserving guests, who is more deserving (pass the brandy, dear) than we are?

Never has a set of ideas taken over a house so completely.

I am now wearing the only pair of real silk pajamas I own, as if there were no tomorrow. I also slouch around in my good robe, which I've kept in reserve all these years in case I had to go to the hospital.

We decided to take the slip covers off the furniture in the living room. It did so much for the room that I went out and took the cold plastic covers off the car seats. It's a luxurious feeling, sitting on plush.

Harriet took our "company" percolator off the shelf and made an everyday percolator

out of it. She has also pressed into everyday service a stainless-steel carving set that had never tested meat.

I now shake up a cocktail before dinner in my good silver shaker, and I pour into the best crystal we own. I will never drink another martini out of the little jar the cheese spread came in. I hadn't realized it before, but having a cocktail out of the right kind of glass is really half the enjoyment of a drink.

I went through my golf bag, threw out all the dirty, cut-up balls, and broke open a carton of new balls I got two birthdays ago. I also bought a big bag of new tees. I now use one tee per hole, and don't even look for it after driving.

All these years I have been getting a week's mileage out of every razor blade. Toward the end of the week, I'd have to hook my toes under the bathroom water pipes and pull the razor with both hands. Now, for pennies, I use a new blade once each day, then throw it away.

Realizing that you're never going to be rich is a grand discovery. It puts a spring in your step and a gleam in your eye. It gives you a peace of mind and freedom of movement you wouldn't have believed possible. It's wonderful. It's like being rich. ✳

Haggle Your Way to Heaven

The price of salvation is not fixed.
Make an offer

By KENNETH GUENTERT
January 1984, condensed from *Salt* *

I F YOU WANT to buy some-
thing in a Middle Eastern
open-air market, never accept
the seller's asking price. It is
anywhere from three to ten
times the acceptable price.
Haggling, you see, is a way of
life in the Middle East. And you
need to understand the importance of haggling to understand
many stories in the Bible.

Take the passage in Genesis
18 where Abraham negotiates
with God about the destruction
of Sodom. Abraham wants to
know if God will preserve
Sodom if he can find 50 righteous citizens.

God says yes.

Then Abraham asks if God
will preserve the city if 45 righteous can be found.

God says yes.

And the dickering continues
until God agrees not to destroy
the city if ten righteous citizens
can be found.

I thought about this in relation to the story of the rich ruler
who wanted to know what he
must do to gain eternal life (Luke
18). Jesus told him to keep the
commandments. He had, the
ruler said, since childhood. Jesus
then told him he lacked only
one thing. He should sell all
his possessions and give them
to the poor. A high price. Too
high. The ruler accepts the
price at face value and walks
away.

He did not negotiate.

In the Middle Eastern market you don't walk away except
as a ruse (hoping the seller will
lower the price) or unless you
are not a serious buyer. The

rich ruler apparently was not interested in paying any more than he already had.

Some of us are like this rich young man—not because we are rich—but because we refuse to haggle with God. We take the injunction to "sell all that you have and give to the poor" at face value and then dismiss it as outrageous.

If Jesus is the Lord, his words are as negotiable as the God of Abraham's. And so they are— even in this story.

When the man walks away, Jesus tells the disciples that it is easier for a camel to get through the eye of a needle than for a rich man to get to heaven. The disciples groan at the hardness of the message.

"Who can be saved?" they ask.

"All things are possible with God," Jesus says. In a sentence, the rich man is off the hook.

So it is elsewhere. Jesus' words have a hardness about them. No divorce; no, not even lust. Yet when confronted with the sweaty reality of a woman's adultery, He shrugs and forgives. He would do it again. Seven times 70 times. Can He be less forgiving to a young man who keeps the commandments but cannot part with his possessions? No. The young man had only to make an offer.

Zacchaeus, whose story follows that of the rich man in Luke's Gospel, was willing to make an offer. "Behold, Lord, the half of my goods I give to the poor; and if I have defrauded anyone of anything I restore it fourfold."

Jesus did not insist on his original price. He accepted the tax collector's terms, closed the deal, and gave Zacchaeus what he wanted: salvation.

Zacchaeus was a serious buyer. He made an offer out of the generosity of his heart. So what if it was not the asking price? It was enough.

What is asked of Christians is to not walk away. Jesus is selling salvation, and the asking price is to "sell what you have and give to the poor." Terms are negotiable, but from the asking price you can see what is expected: 1. a detachment from possessions and 2. generosity toward the poor. How people live this out, assuming they choose not to walk away, is a matter of prayer and struggle.

People have different ways of confronting the message. Nowhere is there any indication of how little the buyer can get away with. Presumably, the message and the price have something to do with each other. Accept the message, and detaching oneself from possessions comes rather naturally, out of one's heart, as it did for Zacchaeus. Some give away all their possessions, some half, some a tenth. Some open their houses to the stranger and wayfarer. The price one is willing to pay must match the value placed on eternal life. As one becomes more aware of what eternal life means, the simple truth is that the price one is willing to pay gets bigger.

The important thing is: don't walk away.   *

FRINGE BENEFIT

In our suburban neighborhood we sponsored a charity bazaar and I was driving a carload of neighbors to the big event. The subject of husband-wife arguments came up, and each woman related what happened when she and her mate had words.

"My husband doesn't give me a chance to argue," I said. "Whenever we disagree he walks out of the house and starts in sawing or hammering or pouring concrete."

One of the women in the back seat spoke up. "You must have had some dillies, my dear," she laughed. "I've often wondered how you managed to add a bedroom, a bath, and a patio to your home in a year."

Mrs. Thomas April.

SIGNS OF THE TIMES

Outside a Florida fried chicken restaurant: "Our Drums Can't Be Beat."
Hazel M. Odley.

*

At a dairy: "You Can't Beat Our Milk, But You Can Whip Our Cream."
Thomas LaMance.

*

On a hypochondriac's tombstone: "I Told You I Was Sick."
Mary G. Tschida.

*

In a South Bronx, N.Y., pet shop: "Chock Full O'Mutts."   D.L. Getchell.

*

At a bicycle shop: "Peddlers Welcome."   Loretta E. Nelson.

*

On a bookstore going out of business: "Words Failed Us."   Ralph Foral.

Thought Provokers

Picking and Choosing in Religion

It leads to the easy way out

By JAMES HITCHCOCK
September 1974, condensed from *The Critic* *

W E ARE IN danger of turning Christianity into a kind of supermarket—laying out a vast array of doctrines, cults, personalities, art works, disciplines, from all the religions of the world and saying, "Pick what you want." People fill their baskets with almost limitless combinations.

However, buyers who expect new goods all the time soon find a steady diet intolerable. More serious, as far as religion is concerned, the sense of urgency, of life-and-death importance, is lost. Picking and choosing can

become a way of life, but it is not ultimately very satisfying. Finally the fact that to adopt or discard any particular religious belief seems to entail no serious consequence, makes the whole activity stale and rather pointless.

What is being lost in contemporary Christianity is contained in Christ's words, "You have not chosen Me; I have chosen you."

The enlightened Christian now tends to think instead, "I was born a Christian and, having been thus culturally conditioned, I am most likely to find meaning in some version of Christianity. However, this does not preclude my becoming immersed also in as many

567

other traditions as possible, some of which may actually be superior to Christianity in certain important respects. I have in fact an obligation to be critical of my own tradition and to seek to change it whenever this seems appropriate." An attitude farther removed from the spirit of the New Testament would be difficult to imagine.

Religion is specific and concrete or it is nothing. One cannot be religious-in-general, because religion is a way of life, not a philosophical framework for apprehending the universe. As a way of life it also must be demanding. Under certain circumstances it must in fact demand heroism, even martyrdom.

Close to the heart of religion is the sense of submission, the acknowledgement of a power infinitely superior to the individual. One may submit to this power freely, as the mainstream of Catholic theology insists is the case, but there is no sense of the judicious weighing of alternatives, the kind of picking and choosing one might engage in before buying a painting or even marrying a spouse. The individual is free to refuse submission, but such a decision is fraught with the gravest consequences.

We are now in the midst of what amounts to a campaign to rob Christianity of its power, to remove from it any sense of urgency or ultimacy. Instead of submission, the dominant spirit is that of manipulation. Rites, laws, doctrines are picked up, laid down, or altered to suit the "felt needs" of individual Christians at any given moment (thus we are secularists one year, would-be mystics the next). Everything pertaining to religion is made cozy and familiar. Reverberations of strangeness, power, and distance are deliberately muffled.

It seems valid to ask whether this spirit does not mask a fundamental and unacknowledged atheism, a belief that everything that has been thought to pertain to "God" is in reality manmade and hence can be altered by man at will.

Christianity is being short-circuited by many of its adherents. All attempts to make contact with the ultimate are greeted with skepticism, ridicule, annoyance, even hostility. Constantly Christians are recalled to the mundane world. There is a fear lest they linger too long on Mount Tabor. Aspects of Christianity traditionally having to do with "transcendence" (prayer, worship, fundamental dogmas) are reinterpreted to give them a worldly focus. The transcendental dimension is not denied but becomes unnecessary ("Believe in it if you like but don't make too big a thing of it").

The central problem of modern Christianity is not that it is too "rigid" but that for some time it has been sending out weaker and more confused signals concerning its basic identity and the message it wishes to convey to the world. In the process many Christians have become accustomed to the faint hum, and their ears hurt if the volume is turned up. In the words of Dean Kelley of the National Council of Churches, they are comfortable living in a dying Church and they are instinctively averse to any attempt to save Christianity by reaffirming its right to make demands on its members.

In the post-conciliar era we have witnessed the peculiar phenomenon of clergy who believe the laity suffer from an excess of piety and who regard it as one of their principal tasks to reduce this fervor to manageable proportions. Sometimes explicitly from the pulpit, and in countless implicit ways, Catholics have been told in effect, "Be religious, but don't overdo it. There are many more important things than piety. Slow down." Thus the falling off in church attendance and other measurable signs of Catholic decline sometimes represent not a rejection of the Church by laity but their following what they perceive as the current Catholic line.

Some enlightened friends of Christianity wish to see it "reformed" only so that they need no longer worry about possible outbreaks of religious fervor. There are even Religious professionals, clergy, nuns, theologians, educators, who seem to live in equal dread of the same thing. Nothing embarrasses them more than an encounter with serious piety.

Appearing often in a public guise of self-doubt and confusion, often apparently apologetic about its very existence, the Church today contrasts unfavorably with a host of new movements which manifest exactly the confidence, zeal, and determination which the Church lacks. Political groups, various schools of psychotherapy, and the newer religions do not hesitate to make the kinds of demands on their people which the Church no longer makes.

There is now much hostility in the Church to the very idea of orthodoxy, some of which is justified by the fact that orthodoxy has often been, as charged, an exceedingly rigid and unimaginative thing. But the larger point is that it attempts to preserve, in some usable form, the most profound insights of religion at those moments when it is most fully conscious of itself, at the height of its spiritual power.

Recognizing that these moments cannot be expected to last for long, the Church defines dogmas, fixes rituals, and canonizes saints so that some reserve of this power can be handed on to spiritually poorer ages which may be in danger of losing sight of the basic mysteries. The often compulsive rejection of everything from the Church's past is further evidence of the desire of some people to live in an impoverished and undemanding religious environment, in which nothing hinders the total accommodation of Christianity to the present cultural milieu.

It is true that in one important respect reformers have sought to make post-conciliar Catholicism more demanding than traditional faith, the great and complex area known as social justice. For the most part this has been to the good. However, much of this renewed social concern is indistinguishable from a general idealistic humanism; there is little which is specifically Christian or Catholic about it. A viable religion needs its cult and its distinctive moral code as well as its general ethical awareness. Otherwise it simply blends into the landscape and gets lost.   ◆

PEOPLE ARE LIKE THAT

While in the final weeks of Air Force electronics school, my morale and that of my bunkmates sank to an all-time low. We were counting the days until our first leave since basic training. My letters to home undoubtedly reflected the tension we all felt. In one letter, I stated that the unceasing inspections, cleaning, polishing, and marching had pretty well eliminated laughter in our room.

Our families wrote words of encouragement; mothers sent cookies. But the youngest of my three brothers decided to lend his own special assistance. On his own, and in secret, he scoured the neighborhood asking for old magazines and newspapers, until he had collected a small mountain of paper.

Several days later I received a bulging envelope, addressed in my brother's unmistakeable scrawl. Inside were hundreds of clippings of cartoons and jokes. I passed them around to my bunkmates and soon the room was filled with laughter. Before the day's end, everyone in the barracks had a favorite cartoon stuck in his billfold, used as a bookmark, or taped to the inside of a locker door. My little brother's unique thoughtfulness had brightened the day for all of us.   William Scott.

Are We Forgetting How to Think?

"Feelings" alone cannot tell us the difference between right and wrong

By CALVIN D. LINTON
condensed from "How Are You Feeling," published in *Christianity Today*

"HOW ARE YOU FEELING?" the sunburn victim was asked. "Far too much," he replied.

So, it seems, are we all. Today, in practically every aspect of life, including education and religion, emotional intensity and subjective judgment are increasingly valued more highly than facts and logic. One finds evidence not only in the more obvious arenas—among shaven-headed groups hypnotically chanting "Om," or in the "consciousness raising" classes. The cult of feeling also has invaded the groves of academe, and the innermost court of the temple of religion.

In a recent seminar on Shakespeare a teacher repeatedly

asked, "But how do you feel?" about this or that. One student, thus exhorted, said that, for him, subjectively, *King Lear* is a comedy, and the blinding of Gloucester hilarious.

The impediment to this critical judgment—that it is wrong—was not permitted to stanch the flow of gabble. Rather, the student was commended for the "freshness of his personal vision." The implication, of course, is that nothing said about *King Lear* is, objectively, either right or wrong, but only either deeply felt (valid) or merely rationally demonstrable (irrelevant).

For obvious reasons, the cult of sensibility has made few inroads into the teaching of mathematics and the hard sciences. But its form is often

571

unmistakable beneath the technical (or pseudo-technical) language when scientists express social, philosophical, or religious opinions.

Neither *feeling* nor *reason* can be satisfactorily defined, nor can *subjective* and *objective* be precisely separated. But we all have a working understanding of the difference between emotion and intellect, and know that without the interplay of both, man is less than human.

In the Christian view, of course, the will, intellect, and emotions were all marred in the Fall, as was the body. Thus, both reason and emotion are susceptible to error. But there is a clear hierarchical relation between them, and reason must be assigned the higher seat.

Paul probably spent a great deal more time reasoning with his hearers in Ephesus than in feeling with them, and Isaiah issued his call to come and reason, not feel, together. Emotions normally come after thoughts, circumstances, and conditions. We do not "authenticate" God by feeling emotional about Him; rather, we feel the emotion because He exists and has revealed Himself to us. "This is the Lord's doing; it is marvelous in our eyes," the Psalmist says.

We are not sinners because we happen occasionally to feel guilt; nor are we virtuous because we sometimes feel complacent about not being so bad as some we could name. God's existence and our moral condition are objective facts, like the chemical composition of salt.

Man would like to have it otherwise, and to believe that his own consciousness, not God, creates reality. This, of course, is the ultimate rebellion, the essence of pride.

Easily following this rebellion is a belief in man's natural innocence at least, and natural goodness at best. And for some reason, perhaps because it is less burdensome to feel feelings than to think thoughts, it seems natural to imagine the emotions to be the most positively virtuous of man's capabilities.

The dogma of the natural goodness of the emotions has myriad devotees today, and its doxology is usually some variant of Swinburne's "Glory to man in the highest!" Its worship services may be as irrational as Israel's orgy about the golden calf, its emotions as intense. Its noise, thanks to electronic magnification, is even louder. And if old Reason interferes, clout him with drugs and you will soon see him skipping about on his thin shanks with the best of them. "My great religion," wrote D.H. Lawrence, "is a belief in the blood, the flesh, as being wiser than the intellect. We can go wrong in our minds.

But what our blood feels and believes and says is always true. The intellect is only a bit and a bridle."

The cult of sensibility is able to accept as "true" two or more beliefs that, to reason, seem mutually contradictory. To one a portion of Scripture may "feel" like God's word; to another it does not; and both estimates are accepted as true, without the tiring quest for objective realty.

Morality by feel (sometimes called "situational") may at different times call an act either bad or good, depending on one's "vibes." ("Woe unto them that call evil good, and good evil; that put darkness for light, and light for darkness, that put bitter for sweet, and sweet for bitter! "—Isaiah 5:20.) From here it is quick work to declare that any act, whether of supreme beneficence or of abominable atrocity, is equally good if it intensifies one's "isness."

The cult of sensibility also authorizes man to concentrate his attention where he wants to anyway: on himself. Communication, therefore, becomes not a shared search for truth beyond ourselves, but a mere description of our feelings. Each talks about himself, to himself. Some people, for example, require us to listen interminably to how they feel about being saved, not about the objective reality of a cross and an empty tomb. Some even go so far as to assert that unless one has the right feelings (the more intense the better) he is not truly Christian at all, or at least not of the elite class.

I do not mean to depreciate the emotion, chiefly joy, which results from the objective fact of salvation. But the feelings are secondary. John does not say that he wrote in order that we may feel saved, but that we may know that we are (I John 5:13). Emotions are unreliable. They may be falsified, and they may be induced, chemically by drugs or psychologically by self-delusion. They are not themselves evidence of objective reality.

Among the unique glories of the Gospel are its historicity, its objective reality, its revelation of what God has done (not what men feel about what He has done), and its emphasis on the sovereignty of God and the irresistibility of his will. There is doubtless a place in evangelism for a description of one's emotional response to these things. But compared to our duty to give the *reason* for the hope that is in us (I Pet. 3:15), it is a very small one. ♦

Secularism

It pervades our lives, alienates family members, and shapes the future

By JAMES HITCHCOCK
December 1979, condensed from *Columbia**

SECULARISM is a philosophy with many adherents who deny that it even exists. But this fact does not eliminate its existence. It merely makes it more difficult to deal with.

The word *secular* comes from the Latin *saeculum,* meaning "an age" or "a time." Christians contrast *saeculum* with eternity. So a secularist is someone who limits his vision only to this world, who refuses to see things in the light of eternity.

Of course, Christianity is not an escape from time. We all hope for the world which is to come, but we must take this world seriously and do the best we can while we are in it.

There is, however, one very important difference between Christian secularity and mere secularity. Christians believe that *life in the world is itself made possible by the life of God.* All that human beings do is rooted in God, and when people sever those roots they lose the ability even to do what is right in a purely worldly way. Thus time and eternity are not really opposites for Christians; they complement one another. But eternity takes precedence, not only because it lasts forever while time passes, but also because eternity really makes time possible.

There have always been secularists, people whose minds were more on worldly things than on religious things. But about 1700, the real age of secularism began. For the first time in Western history, a significant number of people began to express public doubts about the truth of Christianity. Although the bulk of Westerners remained believers, since the 18th century

Christianity has been on the defensive in most parts of the Western world.

Secularists most often prefer to call themselves "humanists," which also creates problems. For we are all humanists, in that we have a high regard for human beings and accord human beings a special status in the universe. We value everything which makes life more humane—kindness, courtesy, compassion.

In fact, it can be argued that the only true humanists are those who believe in God, because only belief in God gives us an adequate reason for believing in man. That a true sense of human dignity depends finally on belief in God is suggested by several facts:

• Increasingly, only religious believers look forward to the propagation of the human race with optimism. Non-believers are obsessed with the possibility of too many people and the wrong kind of people.

• Only believers fully perceive the threat to human life and dignity in the growing acceptance of abortion and euthanasia.

• Only believers, for the most part, insist on certain minimal standards of dignity and morality for human behavior, especially in the crucial area of human sexuality. Non-believers are increasingly willing to tolerate almost everything.

If both *secularism* and *humanism* are ambiguous terms, by putting them together we can make them clearer. "Secular humanism" means a philosophy in which man insists that he is on his own, with no need for God. This idea was perhaps first proposed by the 19th-century German philosopher Paul Johann von Feuerbach, who argued that man never could be truly free so long as God existed, that God, like a great father, always would cramp man's style.

From the beginning, secular humanism has usurped the vocabulary of freedom. Many sincere Christians have been lulled by this rhetoric into thinking that secularism is an essentially benign movement, one which has good will for all men and all human ideas.

But it is important to recognize that from its beginnings secular humanism has not merely proclaimed its independence from organized religion but also its hostility to it. In democratic countries like the U.S., most secularists do not advocate direct action to suppress religion. However, they want to deny religion any legitimate public expression, any influence over public policy.

The most influential anti-Catholic intellectual in America in the 20th century was Paul Blanshard, a militant secular humanist. Although Blanshard's primary attack was on the Church as the enemy of freedom, he also asked the question, "Why allow Christian salvationism to flourish side by side with scrupulously accurate science as if they were legitimate twins in our culture, when you know that the Christian doctrine of salvation is untrue?"

The secularists' primary area of action has been education, since education—along with family influence—is the principal means by which people's beliefs and values are formed. The earliest secularists, in the 18th century, were convinced that their first task was to destroy the Church's influence over education.

In America, church schools retain the legal right to exist, although in 1925 a legal challenge to their existence went all the way to the Supreme Court. Recently the Internal Revenue Service which grants tax exemptions to these schools and state departments of education has put renewed pressures on religious schools, setting standards of operation which could hamper them severely and eventually force their closing.

However, the most obvious form of discrimination against them has been the continuing and dogmatic refusal to grant them any form of public aid, even though Catholic, Jewish, and Lutheran taxpayers, for example, are thereby forced to pay double for their children's educations.

While the government makes it more and more difficult for churches to maintain their own schools, courts are vigilant against the least sign of religious influence in the public schools—not only prayers but also moments of silence, not only the Bible taught in the classroom but also Bible-study groups meeting outside class time. It is now permissible to expose students to propaganda from Planned Parenthood, for example, but not to anything specifically religious in character.

Here secularism has won a notable victory. Supposedly the schools are required by law to be neutral among the various religions and between belief and unbelief. But true neutrality would mean treating all religions equally. Instead the American public schools are required to snub all religions.

For the most part, teachers in public schools do not openly attack religion although at the college level they frequently do. But for secularism to be the working philosophy of the schools it is not necessary that they be hostile to religion. It merely is required that they ignore it. Students thereby come away with the impression that religion is not important, or, if it is important, that it is a purely private and personal thing. They become used to the secularist idea that all questions, including questions of moral values, are decided independently of any religious considerations.

Young children in particular, for whom teachers can be authority figures almost as powerful as parents, are likely to conclude that if the teacher never speaks of God or Jesus, God and Jesus cannot be very important.

Closely related to education is the authority of the family, which Catholic teaching holds has primary responsibility for the education of children. Many secularists, perhaps most, are themselves family people— husbands, wives, and parents. Nevertheless, the attack on religion and the attack on the family almost always go together.

To understand this it is necessary to understand several assumptions of secularism which are not frequently discussed. The most important of these concern freedom and progress.

It was among the secularist thinkers of the 18th century that the philosophical idea of progress first took its familiar form— the idea that human life will, if the proper conditions are created, continue almost automatically to improve.

Christians can, of course, accept this idea to the extent of thinking that it is possible to improve the world through effort, and throughout history many Christians have endeavored to do so. But the secularist idea of progress rests on the belief that human nature can be perfected. It denies the reality of sin. It comes to be strongly biased in favor of whatever is innovative, seeing in these things the signs of progress, and is consequently biased against whatever is traditional and venerable. The family, as the oldest institution of human society, cannot escape secularist suspicion.

Progress is achieved primarily, in the secularist view, through maximizing human freedom. In general the freer people are from all laws, authority, and tradition, the better off they are and the more society is progressing. While admitting in theory that freedom can be abused, in practice most secularists automatically choose to remove moral and social restraints wherever they exist. The family is thus a doubly suspicious institution, not only because it is very ancient but also because it is the seat of the most powerful and effective kind of human authority.

Many secularists believe that families still exercise altogether too much influence and authority over children. They regard the schools as the vehicle for inculcating in young people a properly progressive outlook in the world, and they regret that parental influence still is likely to be so strong that this indoctrination is not completely successful.

The most sensitive area of this conflict is inevitably sex, because sexual beliefs and behavior are so personal and so deeply held. Although some secularists may hold fairly traditional ideas about sexual behavior, instinctively they tend to support all kinds of sexual freedom, from the reflex assumption that whatever is old is probably wrong and that whenever the acceptable boundaries of human behavior are extended it is a good thing.

It is a dogma of secularism that human actions do not have any supernatural significance and that human beings therefore can do whatever they wish, short of harming others. Even this last restriction gives way when things become really "inconvenient," as in abortion or euthanasia. Free sexual behavior is for secularists an important test case for showing that people do not have to be bound by the authority of a moral law greater than their own desires.

It is also important for "emancipating" people, especially young people, from the influence of Church and family. Individual secular humanists may not themselves be hedonists, but they support hedonistic activities: extramarital sex, homosexuality, pornography, decriminalized drug use, because these activities involve man's assertion of freedom from all restraint.

This secularist philosophy has permeated the public educational system of America for at least the past 50 years. As a result, it has come to dominate much of the thinking of the educated classes in America— the teachers, lawyers, doctors, journalists, and politicians.

For a long time this fact was obscured, because many individual professional people are devout religious believers. But now the major professional associations like the National Education Association have shown themselves eager to support it. The implicit attitude of their leadership is, "Individual doctors, lawyers, or teachers may be religious believers, but their beliefs are purely private and should not influence public policy."

However, the most striking evidence of the triumph of the secularist mentality is in the communications media and the government. It used to be a joke that God and motherhood were two things immune from attack. In the past decade, however, both have become highly vulnerable.

Anti-religious propaganda,

and particularly anti-Catholic propaganda, now saturate television and the press. Religious belief is ridiculed or made to appear unhealthy and deforming, even as skeptics are treated as moral heroes. Belief is treated most often as a sign of insecurity or of being hopelessly out of date, while doubt is presented as a sign of intelligence and courage. Similarly, for several generations of college professors, a student's loss of faith while in school has been taken as a sign that the student at last is really thinking.

The mass media are the most influential educational institutions in modern society. If they propagate, as they do, a combination of anti-religious and hedonistic messages, their influence outweighs much of the good which families and church schools attempt to effect. We now are faced with the very serious situation in which most people, even Church members, possess, without knowing it, an essentially secular way of looking at the world, a way which the media has made seem natural.

The degree to which popular entertainment is saturated with pagan values is something which even devout Christians often cannot bring themselves to recognize. Pop-music, countless films and television programs, and the paper-back industry glo-rify the combination of sex and violence, and preach a totally hedonistic lifestyle. Stars who win public adulation, especially from young people, use that prestige to denigrate marriage and the family and to glorify drug taking. Sexual deviation of all kinds is celebrated and its practitioners treated as courageous prophets.

The same secularism now pervades government. On all levels officials use their authority to promote essentially secular ends. Judges hand down decisions which interpret the idea of freedom in the way secularists want it interpreted—for example, the alleged constitutional "right" to an abortion. Bureaucrats in the educational and health fields move towards a situation in which only thoroughly secularized institutions receive any kind of public support and others virtually are driven out of existence. Government programs of all kinds, but especially in sex education, tend toward the weakening of the family, often quite deliberately. Finally and most ominously, government officials are increasingly committed to the idea of population control concerns which carry with them immense potential for control of human lives.

In the democratic system government is theoretically answerable to the people, and the ranks of elected public officials include a high proportion of people who are church members, some of them quite devout. Their influence, however, is severely limited.

It is limited first by the fact that elected public officials, even the President, in practice find it quite difficult to control government agencies nominally under their jurisdiction. However, their limits stem even more from the fact that so many politicians who are themselves religious believers have swallowed the secularist definition of their role.

Countless politicians in the past decade have said, "Personally I am opposed to abortion, but I cannot impose my views on others." Religious believers have been brainwashed into thinking that they have no right to be guided by those beliefs in the political realm, even as secular humanists are quite willing to "impose" their beliefs on other people, and do so constantly. It is a sad fact that prominent Catholic politicians in America go out of their way to show that they are not guided by religious concerns.

In the end religious believers have largely themselves to blame for this state of affairs. Believers in general, and Catholics in particular, have been complacent, passive, and timid—slow to recognize when their beliefs are threatened and even slower to respond.

The vulnerability of so many believers to secularist propaganda is directly traceable to their simple worldliness. Enjoying the fruits of a prosperous and materialistic society, they have become comfortable and lax, unable to recognize that there is anything seriously wrong with their world.

Attacks on religion, including the possibility of legal restraints on religious freedom, probably will continue to increase in the remaining years of the 20th century. There is still the possibility of countering these attacks, through an effort which must be broadly ecumenical but which is rendered difficult by the degree of secularist influence that already exists in the Churches themselves. Those Churches not heavily secularized will have to show the way.

More important, genuine religious believers will be forced more and more to define precisely what are the big differences between themselves and non-believers. They may well have to accustom themselves to living in ways which the world around them will find strange and which will require almost heroic decisions. The day may be coming once again when, as Christ foretold, those who persecute his followers will think they are doing something virtuous. ♦

Second Thoughts

What Couples Learn after Marriage

And wish they'd known before

BY PHILIP YANCEY

May 1980, condensed from *Campus Life**

WHEN I DECIDED to interview several married couples especially selected for their frankness, I expected to make startling discoveries about married life. If I could get ten couples really to open up and say what marriage was all about, I thought, perhaps I could help a lot of people planning marriage.

I found plenty of surprises. First, that Christian marriages have problems and tensions, just like other marriages. But the big surprise was that practically every couple wanted to talk about what happened *before* they were married.

When I'd bring up a question about sex, instead of telling me about sex tensions in marriage, they told me about how they'd

gotten on the wrong track in high school. When I searched for secrets they had uncovered about each other after marriage, I learned that the signals had all been there before the ceremony—they had just been "too in love" to hear them.

After listening to all these couples' tales of love and woe, I began thinking that maybe what's needed, even more than a book on how to survive marriage, is a good book on how to know what you're getting into. Here are some things I learned, straight out of real people's lives.

"**D**o you really know each other?"

It seems like a strange question for our day. Couples pair off and spend every possible second with each other. They squeeze every moment out of a date. Yet one couple told me, "I think we spent more time picking out our wedding bands than thinking about our compatibility."

Love makes us feel so good, because we're wanted and accepted, that it can blind us to the person who's doing the wanting and accepting. But what is that person really like? Does he or she have qualities which can last through the tensions of raising a family and buying a house and facing illness?

How do you find out about someone? Chances are you can't trust your own judgment completely. Talk to your friends and ask how they think you fit. If you can swallow your pride, talk to your parents. They'll likely be rougher on a date than anyone else, because they have more at stake. They want the best for you.

If you're really serious, there are professional ways you can find out about each other. Many school counselors and pastors give personality profile tests, like the California Test. The tests are fun to take and they make you think about yourself in ways you probably never have. And they don't come up with a "Get married/Don't get married/Neither of the above" answer. They point out similarities and differences between you that you should be sensitive to. They don't make the decision for you.

Another important clue is your taste. Will you get bored with each other after two years? One couple told me, "After two years all the romance had worn off and we realized we were totally bored."

"I like to listen to music on the stereo to relax, while Stephanie insists on watching TV cop shows," the husband said. "I like quiet evenings to unwind from a hard day, just reading or listening to music. She always wants to talk or do something manual. I like a simple life—a couple of huge bean bags for chairs, one set of plastic dishes and glasses. Stephanie insists on china and silver and new clothes and stuff. Neither of us wants to give in. The funny thing is, we knew about our differences before we were married. We just thought it would be different, that love would cover all those things."

Sometimes love in marriage does change people. But the big differences between you now will carry over into your marriage.

One couple I talked with differed from the others because their marriage seemed to work so well. They disagreed and fought like everyone else, but overall they seemed happier and more in love than any others I talked to. I asked them why, and the husband said, "I think it's because we agreed on certain principles about our marriage while we were still engaged. We agreed on how far to go in fights and arguments, and on what threats were off limits. We agreed to encourage each other every day. And we found that every agreement we made before we were married was ten times more important than agreements we made after the wedding. Somehow we respected them more."

L ove, though beautiful, can be dangerous. It can pull you closer to a person than you've ever been, but it also can trap you with that person long after you should have parted. You can see it in any high school or college. Look around at the couples who spend the most time together. Some of them are sullen and unhappy all the time. Yet they hang onto each other. It could be they're in a trap and they don't know how to escape.

This is a sticky one to talk about with couples, because people don't like having someone shake his finger and say, "Now listen, are you sure it's not time to break up?" We naturally rebel against that kind of preachy tone. So I'll just tell you about the traps mentioned by the couples I interviewed.

The Sex Trap. This ranked highest on the list. Almost every couple mentioned it. One was particularly eloquent. "Sex was like glue in our relationship.

Every time something would rip and tear between us, we never dealt with the problem. We covered it over with glue. But when we were married we were left with a marriage made up of tears and rips. And suddenly sex didn't seem so special anymore. It lost its healing powers."

Do you turn to sex to patch over hurts and misunderstandings? Do you blame a lot of frustrations and tensions on your lack of sexual freedom? Do you allow sex to keep you from other people and other situations which might teach you more about each other? Does one of you use sex as a weapon? Does your partner pressure you with the line that sex is proof of your love?

These couples told me sex was the biggest liar of all the traps. Sex shouted at them, "See, we are in love. Our affection proves it," all the while keeping them from the honest, hard questions they should have been asking.

The Lemon-squeezer Trap. Second on the list was the trap that occurs when one partner decides his mission in life is to change the other and squeeze out all the undesirable qualities. Sometimes it's done with the best of intentions.

One guy made it a personal campaign to rebuke his wife every time she was in a bad mood or got angry or criticized someone. He thought he was doing a favor by improving this girl. Actually he was squeezing her until she broke, and she still hasn't recovered from her horrid self-image. Before marriage, she took his rebukes more readily, because she wanted him so badly. After marriage, she had no escape.

One girl nagged at her boy friend about every detail: the muddy shoes he wore, the way he drove the car, his lazy friends, the country church he went to. Now married, he still has all the built-up resentments against her. He sees her as a nagging burden who takes all the fun out of his life. He looks forward to business trips when he can be away.

Each partner has to make certain changes. But if you can't approach those changes in a spirit of love and cooperation, you break up. One man said he had a miserable marriage for 13 years. Then one day he learned to stop saying, "If you love me you will . . . " and to look for ways to say, "Because I love you I will . . . "

A human being is a fragile, delicate thing. Everyone needs support and affirmation. Marriage can be the best environment for support or the worst, depending on how you approach it.

The Pity Trap. Love and pity can be easily confused. One guy I interviewed grew up in a sad home where his mother would shout abuse at him. His girl friend sprang to the rescue and would lovingly soothe him and build him up. That was great. But the whole relationship became based on his girl friend's concern for him. He enjoyed her attention and affection and never saw his own responsibility to try to meet *her* needs. It was a one-sided romance, and the problem still recurs in their marriage.

God can use love to heal broken families. But marriage is give-and-take, and both people must contribute or it will die. If your romance is based on pity, you're walking on thin ice.

"How do you face crises?" This is a hard question to answer for many unmarried couples. If you live at home, you probably haven't run into tough financial decisions. Unless there's been an accident or illness, it's hard to know how you will face a crisis.

But marriage involves crises, and it's good to think how your partner would respond. If one is nervous and insecure under pressure, the other should learn to balance those feelings.

One important question to ask is: Do we turn to each other under pressure or does pressure split us apart? (A related and very important question is: Does pressure turn us toward God, or do we resentfully turn away from Him?)

One couple faced a damaging blow after two years of blissful marriage. The girl came down with Hodgkin's disease, cancer of the lymph glands. Suddenly he had to care for her constantly, postpone college, manage the house, keep money coming in, and be strong emotionally. She had to face the 50-50 chance of death. It was a strain for a young couple.

The girl was cured after two years of painful treatment, and their marriage survived stronger than ever. Why? "I worked as a chaplain's assistant at the hospital," Fred said, "and I saw the way other couples handle crises. If you're in the pattern of turning to each other and supporting each other, you'll do the same thing in a crisis. The pressure and heat will weld your love. If you're in the pattern of pulling apart and feeling sorry for yourself the crisis can open up permanent wounds."

Crises are a good sieve to screen out mushy, weak love. True love flourishes when one partner is in need.

And don't underestimate the value of money. Most surveys report that well over half of the marriages which break up within two years do so because of money disagreements. Make it a point to find out how your partner feels about money, and decide mutually on what kind of life-style you want to lead.

When I asked the couples what qualities were most important to them in their marriage, there was surprising agreement. Everyone admitted communication was very important. You can't clam up in marriage; you've got to be willing to share, even when it hurts. Those who learned to do that in the dating stage had an advantage when marriage came.

Honesty was mentioned next. Marriage destroys your secrets. When you live with a person so intimately, it's hard to hide things. Dishonesty puts a wedge between you.

Words like *tolerant* and *flexible* and *considerate* were used often. Those couples who went into marriage with fixed ideas of what it would be like usually were surprised. You both will change, your relationship will change, and you need to be prepared to adapt.

Love, of course, was most commonly mentioned. Most couples went to great pains, however, to point out that their idea of love changed immensely after marriage. The concept became much less romantic and more practical. For the best description of the love they mentioned, read 1 Corinthians 13 in the Bible. It's not the kind of love you see in movies and on TV, but it's the kind that can make a marriage.

After reading these problems and disagreements and surprises, you may be saying, "I'll never find a relationship that meets all those characteristics." Cheer up. You'll never be fully prepared for marriage. It's bound to spring surprises. The important thing is to know your partner well and to make sure you're in tune with God's will.

Remember, all the couples who shared these problems were still married and most described themselves as happily married. They shared their problems to help you avoid the same pitfalls.　　　　　　𝒶

PERFECTION

A woman wanted her apartment done over while she was out of town. This woman, it seems, was very fussy, and insisted everything in her home be the exact shade she specified. So, to help the painters, she left an ash tray as a sample of the special color she wanted the ceiling painted.

After trying vainly to mix the shade she had indicated, the painters finally painted the ash tray, then the ceiling. Upon her return, the woman was delighted.　　　　　　　　　　　*Our Young People* (Feb. '41).

SHORT AND SWEET

"What is your opinion of my painting?"
　"It isn't worth anything."
　"I know—but I would like to hear it anyway."　　　Lane Olinghouse.
*
"I thought the doctor told you to stop all drinks?"
　"Well, you don't see any getting past me, do you?"　　　Lucille Harper.
*
"Have you read my last book?"
　"I hope so."　　　　　　　　　　　　　　　　　*Ireland's Own.*
*
A workman was on top of a ladder cleaning the clock on city hall when a nosey fellow called up to him, "Is something wrong with the clock?"
　"No," was the reply, "I'm just nearsighted."　　Dane County (Wisc.) *News.*

If I Were Starting My Family Again

A father looks back and finds some lessons
along the way

By JOHN DRESCHER

June 1974, condensed from *The Mennonite**

THE MAN sitting across the desk from me showed all the anguish of any father whose son has gotten out of line. "What should I have done differently?" he demanded. "You're a counselor. If your children could be small again, what would you do?"

This father's words stay with me. Although they were put to me in a blunt way that day, it was not the first time I had heard them, or something like them. They must be in the minds of many parents, if they take parenthood seriously.

What has experience in counseling taught me? Where would I put the emphasis if my children were small again? I have pondered these questions and some things seem clear.

*L*ove his mother. If I were starting my family again, I would feel free to let my children see that I love her. It is too easy for parents to assume love, to take each other for granted, and so to allow a routine which can dampen the deepest love.

After I spoke on family relationships to a large group of fathers and mothers, one father approached me and said, "If I understand you this evening you said the greatest thing I can do for my child is to love his mother. Is that correct?"

"Yes," I answered.

When a child knows his parents love each other, there is a special security, stability, and sacredness about life. A child who knows his parents love each other, and who hears them expressing that love, needs little explanation about God's love or the beauty of sex.

I would try to do little thoughtful things for her. True love is visible. I would show special kindnesses: opening the car door, placing her chair at the table, giving her little gifts now and then, and writing her love letters when I am away from home. I would take her hand as we stroll in the park. And I would whisper loving words about her in the ears of my children. I would praise her in their presence at every opportunity.

Does all this sound sentimental? Many families need more of this kind of sentimentalism. Love, like a plant, needs nurture. We must do the things love dictates or it will die.

L *isten to my child's concerns.* If I were starting my family again, I would do more listening. Most fathers find it hard to listen. We are busy with the burden of work. We are often tired when we arrive home. A child's talk seems like chatter, unimportant. Yet we can learn much more by listening than by talking, especially from our children.

I would listen when my child shares his little hurts and complaints, his joys, what he is excited about. I remember the time my busy father listened to me, as a 1st grader, when I came home frightened about a situation at school. His calmness and concern relieved my fears. I was ready to return the following day full of courage and confidence. Had he simply said my fear was foolish or had he refused to hear me out, my fears would have grown.

I would try to keep from staring into space when my child is talking to me. I would try to understand what my child says because I now believe that the father who listens to his child when he is small will find that he will have a child who cares what his father says later in life. I now believe there is a relationship between listening to a child's concerns when he is small and the extent to which he will share concerns when he is in his teens.

If my child were small again, I would stop reading the newspaper when he wants to talk with me. And I would try to refrain from showing impatience at the interruption. Such times can be the best times.

One evening a small boy tried to show his father a scratch on his finger. Finally, after his repeated attempts to gain attention, the father stopped reading and said impatiently, "Well, I can't do anything about it, can I?" "Yes, Daddy," his son said. "You could have said, 'Oh!' "

I would pay more careful attention to my child's questions. It is said the average child asks about 500,000 questions by the age of 15. What a privilege for every parent: a half million opportunities to share something about the meaning of life!

These early years are the years for teaching. And by the time the child reaches 15, parents have done most of the teaching they will ever accomplish. By then the child knows what the parents believe.

Give a feeling of belonging. If I were starting my family again, I would try to use every opportunity to give my child a feeling of belonging. It is essential for a child's security and feeling of worth. And when he feels he belongs in his family and is of real worth there, it is not a big further step to feel accepted, loved, and of worth to others, including God.

How are feelings of belonging generated? By doing things together. By sharing common concerns and trusting each other with responsibilities. Celebrations of birthdays, when the person rather than the gift is central, create a sense of belonging. A sense of belonging is built into a child when prayers are prayed on his behalf, when his opinions are valued, and when he is included in the serious and comic experiences of the family. He feels he belongs when he is invited to be involved in the work of the family.

Praise my child. If I were starting my family again, I would often express words of appreciation and praise. Children are reprimanded for making mistakes. But many children seldom hear words of commendation and encouragement when they do a job well or exhibit good behavior.

If the youngster blew a horn, I would try to find at least one note that sounded good to my ear, and I would find some sincere praise about it. If a school theme was to my liking, I would say so, hoping that it would get a good grade when it was turned in. If his choice of shirt or tie, of socks or shoes, or any other thing met my liking, I would say so.

Probably nothing more encourages a child to love life, to seek accomplishment, and to gain confidence, than the prospect of sincere praise; not flattery, but honest compliments.

Take more time with my child. If I were starting my family again, I would plan to take time to do more things together. In every father's week there are 168 hours. He probably spends about 40 hours at work. Allow another 15 for driving to and from work, overtime, and lunch. Set aside 56 hours a week for sleep. That leaves him 57 hours a week to spend elsewhere. How many are spent with his family?

A group of 300 8th-grade boys kept accurate records of how much time their fathers actually spent with them over a two-week period. Most saw their fathers only at the dinner table. A number never saw their father for days at a time. The average time father and son were alone together for an entire week was 7½ minutes.

A friend told me, "When I was around 13 and my brother was ten, Father promised to take us to the circus. But at lunch there was a phone call. Some urgent business required his attention downtown. My brother and I braced ourselves for the disappointment. Then we heard him say, 'No, I won't be down. It will have to wait.'

"When he came back to the table, Mother smiled, 'The circus keeps coming back, you know.'

"'I know,' said Father. 'But childhood doesn't.'"

One prominent businessman asked another, "Would you like to know what I am giving my son for Christmas?" He showed a piece of paper on which he had written: "To my son: I give you one hour of each week and two hours of every Sunday to be used as you wish."

Laugh more with my child. If I were starting my family again, I would laugh more with my child. Oscar Wilde wrote, "The best way to make children good is to make them happy." I see now that I was much too serious. My children loved to laugh, yet I often must have conveyed the idea that being a parent was painful.

I remember when I laughed with my children—at the wonderful plays they put on for the family, at the funny stories shared from school, at the times I fell for their tricks and catch questions. I recall the squeals of delight when I laughed with them and shared in their stunts on the lawn or living room floor. And I remember the times they told of these times with joyful expressions, years later. I know when I laughed with my children our love was enlarged, and the door was opened for doing many other things together.

So in answer to the father who sat across the desk, I have jotted down these reflections. Like most important experiences in life, none are great ideas or difficult to remember. But these simple suggestions can make life with children more fun and shape the future of a child more than those great things which demand a great deal of money or exceptional ingenuity. Somehow we manage to handle the big things of life but forget that life is largely made up of little things.   𝕚𝔞

IN OUR PARISH

In our parish, our family was watching the telecast of *The Greatest Story Ever Told,* a movie about the life of Christ. I could tell that my seven-year-old daughter, about to make her First Communion, was greatly moved. As Jesus journeyed to Calvary, tears rolled down her cheeks.

She was absolutely silent until after Jesus had been laid in the tomb. Then, catching my eyes, she suddenly grinned. "Now," she said, "comes the *good* part!"   Judie Flotron.

*

In our parish, our Sunday bulletin is a valuable form of communication. Nevertheless, it does contain an occasional error. One issue had this announcement: "The ladies of the church have cast off clothing of all kinds and may be seen in the church basement."   Joyce Gracia.

THIRD-BEST FRIENDS

After Steve's first four months at kindergarten, he told his mother his current loyalties. "I love you the best. Then comes Daddy. And teacher is last. But in between come a lot of dogs."   Lucille S. Harper.

*

A man wrote to a hotel to ask if his dog would be allowed to stay there. He received the following answer:

"Dear Sir—I have been in the hotel business for over 30 years. Never yet have I had to call in the police to eject a disorderly dog in the small hours of the morning. No dog has ever attempted to pass off a bad check on me. Never has a dog set the bedclothes on fire through smoking. I have never found a hotel towel in a dog's suitcase. Your dog is welcome.

"P.S.—If he will vouch for you, you can come, too."   *Ireland's Own.*

*

Little Terry had just bought a newly-weaned puppy. The woman, who sold it to him, suddenly said, "Oh, dear! Maybe I shouldn't have let him go. I'm not sure he's big enough to eat yet."

A look of utter horror flashed across the boy's face. "Gee, lady," he said solemnly, "I wasn't going to *eat* him. I just want him for a pal."

G. G. Crabtree.

Vatican II, Behind the Scenes

I Caused Vatican II ... and I'm Sorry

By LUCILE HASLEY
May 1968, condensed from "U. S. Catholic"*

M Y INFLUENCE as a lay-woman, singlehandedly molding papal decisions, has been fantastic. I first became aware of my eerie power by accident. No sooner would I write a funny essay about some bit of Catholic legalism than the unchangeable Church would suddenly change the ruling.

For instance, there was that harmless little essay I wrote about my mother, who came into the Church after 47 years as a Presbyterian. Every Christmas eve while she mixed the sausage dressing for the holiday turkey, she would get sore at

Rome. "Abstinence!" she would mutter darkly, "I just wish the Pope had to make this dressing without tasting it!" Shortly thereafter, of course, Pius XII took care of the trouble.

Then there was this piece I wrote about scruples. "There were Catholics, it seemed, whose insides curled up because of the have-I-broken-my-fast phobia: swallowing a gnat, chewing a fingernail, using Vick's nosedrops, having a snow-flake melt on one's lip. Not to mention the drop of water from one's toothbrush."

This essay, as I recall, was very well received—for about six months. Then the Vatican moved in to let us drink water

*This article © 1967 by Claretian Publications. Reprinted with permission.

any time. By then I knew that someone was sneaking my little essays into the Vatican and that I had become a great court favorite.

There was that essay I wrote about fishing: how I hated to bait my own hook and how my husband would no longer do it for me. That is all I said, really, but the Pope must have divined that I had turned against fish at the table, too. Very well, he would make it official.

There are a few things I would like to make clear. When I complained about the Sister-says syndrome in parochial school I never intended that they should just walk out. ("OK. If that's the way Mrs. Hasley feels, we'll just go work in Appalachia. Pooh to the suburbs.")

Sometimes, I do wish that Rome wouldn't try quite so hard to cater to my every whim. I simply cannot bring myself to reread the book I wrote, an ecumenical dialogue with a Unitarian, just as Vatican II went into action. Certain passages are branded on my brain. Like: "I'll be very disappointed if this Council bogs down in red tape and comes up with just piddling changes. Like changing a few psalms in the Easter liturgy or something." I think my expression "piddling changes" ought to go down as a classic.

But here's the paragraph that makes me wake up at night in a cold sweat: "My pastor and I are having great fun deciding on the type of wife he should take to his bosom in case the Council should abolish celibacy for priests. He claims a definite preference for 25-year-old blondes. Just the same, I have promised him a kitchen shower, when and if."

Dear Lord, I didn't mean it. A pots-and-pans shower is the last thing I would dream of arranging for any priest. Having his head examined would have priority.

It seems clear that I should get into another field of writing. I think I will try long-range prophecy. This is the "in" thing today.

Msgr. Ivan Illich, for example, predicts a time when there will be no churches, just small groups of friends, occasionally gathering for Mass in homes.

Well and good. That is a man's prophecy. Now it is my turn. I predict that, after this has come to pass, a housewife in Detroit is going to wake up some fine morning and say to herself, "Listen, why in the world must I clean the house, borrow folding chairs from the neighbors, and serve coffee and cake to this crew? This is the third time that I've been stuck with Mass.

"Why don't we build some sort of shelter, with permanent benches, and hire a janitor to keep it up? In his spare time, he could do a little studying and become our permanent leader. We might even give him a sort of uniform, something simple, like wearing a white bandana around his neck, to set him apart." I predict that this Detroit housewife's idea, though radical, would spread like a forest fire.

I also predict that, in 1997, an ancient scroll called the *Baltimore Catechism* will be found on the shores of Lake Erie. Startled theologians, upon reading that "God is a spirit, God is everywhere, God is love," will be struck dumb at the clarity and simplicity of it all. "Now this," they will murmur, "is truly relevant to our age. How did we ever get so sidetracked with all that Ultimate Reality business that the people could never grasp?"

How sweet it will be: my new career of writing long-range (very long-range) prophecies instead of dangerous fly-by-night essays. ✣

BEDTIME STORIES

When I was growing up, four of us kids slept in one bed. It was pretty crowded when we got older, so my mother made me my own bed by putting a hard board between two chairs.

I always dreamed of the day when I'd be able to afford a mattress. Finally, I got there. I bought myself the biggest, softest mattress I could find. Within a week, I was getting terrible backaches. I went to a doctor, and he told me, "Sleep on a board."   Sam Levenson in *Smiles*.

*

Fred's wife was always complaining about cold sheets, so he bought her an electric blanket. At first she was apprehensive about sleeping under all that wiring, but Fred assured her it was safe, and in no time she was asleep.

Fred didn't know, however, that before turning in she had put a ham in the oven to bake all night at low heat. It was 3 A.M. when he awoke and smelled something cooking. He shook his wife. "Darling!" he cried. "Are you all right?"   *Capper's Weekly*.

*

One night my two grandsons decided to share the same twin bed. When this had gone on for a week, I asked six-year-old Jimmy, the older boy, to explain. "You see," he said, "when Timmy sleeps in his own bed, he gets nightmares, but when he sleeps in my bed, he has cartoons."

Mrs. H. Priday.

The Japanese Bishop and the Italian Photographers

No archimandrite, he

By BERNARD BASSET, S.J.
August 1963, condensed from the *Priest in the Piazza**

I T WAS EASY to order photographs during the 2nd Vatican Council in Rome. You just looked through the thousands of groups of Conciliar Fathers, made up your mind, placed your order, paid your money, and claimed your receipt. I ordered a group of five English bishops in a minute and a half.

Getting your copy, however, took longer, as I discovered on the following day. My receipt, when presented, caused considerable trouble, much whispering and consultation, followed by an unavailing search. It was generally agreed that Enrico would have found it in a moment but Enrico, alas, was now in

Livorno visiting his parents' grave.

I was invited to present myself at the Centro Fotografico, elsewhere in the town. Four eager helpers rattled off the directions; I must cross the Piazza Siso Quinto, cut down the Viale di Pio Decimo, turn into the Via di Papa Onorio Terzo, and then keep straight on. "You can't miss it," they said in cheerful Italian. One had met the same phrase and the same optimism in Spain, England, Germany, and France.

Noting my hesitation, a young man took me to the door of the shop to explain. I was to take the *prima a destra,* then the *seconda a sinistra* and go right ahead. The signpost across the road said "Napoli," but I put my trust in God and took a breath. I owed it to the English bishops and must not fail.

At the *prima a destra,* I fell in with a Japanese bishop, small, friendly, enigmatic, as puzzled by the Roman traffic as I was myself. After three weeks in Rome—and who can blame him—his only word in any European language was "No." Happily he did not need to explain his present mission, for the receipt in his hand was similar to my own. Together and smiling we went, *prima a destra* and *seconda a sinistra,* to end in a cul-de-sac called after a great Renaissance Pope. Our destination was now obvious for the only shop in sight bore the illuminated sign "Centro Fotografico" with a subheading "Fotografia Istantanea" which, at the time, sounded encouraging though I now know that it meant something else.

A small woman in a red jumper stood behind the counter, up to her eyes in episcopal photographs of every sort. Bishops in miters, copes, soutanes, or mufti lay upside down on the counter and on all the shelves behind her back. To the left stood an impressive pile of envelopes.

Gestures come easily in Rome, and to her gesture of welcome and enquiry I made one worthy of a Borgia to indicate that the bishop should go first. He said "No," for he had nothing else to say. She, without

hesitation, grabbed his ticket, slapped it on the counter, studied it for seconds, and then, pulling the envelopes toward herself, began searching through the pile. She talked to herself, and it became clear in a moment that her teeth were first designed for another mouth.

She had covered 200 envelopes when the phone rang. Dropping the pile, she darted behind the scenes. For ten minutes we heard no more than *"Si, si, si,"* an occasional *"Non ho capito,"* with the archangels Michael, Gabriel, and Raphael squashed in between. The Japanese bishop said "No," and slipped into a trance.

When the woman returned, a little flustered, she resumed her counting from the top. She was under pressure now. Other customers had arrived, a fierce-looking man with a camera, who looked American but spoke only German, a German-looking bishop who spoke only American, and three nuns who said nothing but produced a collection box. Three young seminarians peeped in, saw the two bishops, and popped out.

The fierce-looking man announced in broken Italian that the Japanese camera which he had bought from her yesterday simply did not work. To emphasize the point, he slapped the camera with so much vigor that two or three vital parts fell out.

The Japanese bishop came out of his trance to say "No." The red-jumpered lady abandoned the envelopes to stand back, wringing her hands. She announced dramatically that her son had gone to God, her husband to Livorno, her daughter to the dogs—the Italian phrase is more expressive—and that, really, she could not run the shop singlehanded, General Council or not.

This over, she snatched the pile of envelopes and started again from the top. Two unusual men, Eugenio and Demostene, now appeared behind the counter to encourage the search while picking their teeth. Meanwhile an Italian friar sidled up to me and, in perfect English, asked after the Archbishop of Canterbury. When the Japanese bishop said "No" for me, the friar replied "By Jove," and sidled away.

Another ten minutes had passed before, finally, with a good deal of helpful comment from Eugenio and Demostene, the wanted envelope was at last revealed. We stood around cheering, congratulating, praying, as the Japanese bishop opened the flap to produce his prize.

Something had gone wrong. The photograph was of a gloriously appareled archimandrite, kindly, but possibly not even in union with Rome. Demostene roared with harmless laughter while Eugenio tried to persuade the Japanese bishop that the photograph was the living image of himself. The Japanese bishop said "No" twice and very quickly, for once meaning exactly what he said.

At this stage of the crisis entered a cleric whom I took to be a Jesuit—he carried a breviary, an umbrella, and a round, dilapidated hat. Being a Dutchman, he could speak five languages, not one of them Japanese. I guessed that he must be a Jesuit because he made himself all things to all men and took in the situation at a glance. He inspected the broken camera, asked me in perfect English about Coventry cathedral, with special reference to the stained glass. He understood in a flash the tragedy of the archimandrite and took the offending photograph from the Japanese bishop's trembling hand.

The red-jumpered lady answered *"Non ho capito"* when he addressed her in Italian, followed by German, French, and modern Greek. She announced that we would all have to wait until her husband came home from Livorno, where he was rightly visiting his dear parents' grave. Eugenio and Demostene, she said, were only taxi drivers, off duty, and could hardly be expected to recognize all the bishops of the one and holy Catholic Church. She shed a few tears and, to end all discussion, put her hand to her mouth to remove her teeth.

Spontaneously and to lessen the tension we all then kissed the Japanese bishop's ring. The Dutch Jesuit—I am only guessing—was now mending the Japanese camera, whose furious owner was arguing with Eugenio about football, while Demostene, tooth picking over, rummaged through the pile of envelopes in a casual and half-hearted way. Nevertheless, he it was who suddenly produced my photograph of the English bishops from an envelope marked in pencil "Los Angeles." I prayed to St. Gregory the Great.

The red-jumpered lady resumed her teeth to declare that had Enrico returned from Livorno he would have found the photograph in half the time. The Japanese bishop joined Demostene in saying "No."

The Fotografia Istantanea had now taken me 40 minutes and I was prepared to go. The Dutch Jesuit had mended the camera in ten. Only the Japanese bishop was unhappy, and as he could say little or nothing about it, he looked like being thrown to the wolves. He utterly refused, even for the sake of Christian unity, to accept the archimandrite as himself.

The Dutch Jesuit had just drawn a deep breath to try again in Latin when the door of the shop flew open.

Was Enrico back from Livorno at last? No! Framed in the door stood the gloriously appareled archimandrite, obviously furious, and with a photograph of the Japanese bishop in his hand.

After the first moment of shock, I piously hoped that he would denounce us all in white Ruthenian or in some other rich Middle-Eastern tongue. Instead, he banged down the photograph on the counter and declared in a very broad Boston accent, "Say, who do you guys think I am?"

The Japanese bishop relaxed at this—he had not wasted the years of American occupation—and, in a Texan drawl, he said something which sounded like "Hi yah, Babe."

The spirit of reunion now triumphed as West, East, and Farther East fell into each other's arms. ✠